Voices Out of Africa
in Twentieth-Century
Spanish Caribbean Literature

The Bucknell Studies in Latin American Literature and Theory
Series Editor: Aníbal González, Yale University

Dealing with far-reaching questions of history and modernity, language and selfhood, and power and ethics, Latin American literature sheds light on the many-faceted nature of Latin American life, as well as on the human condition as a whole. This series of books provides a forum for some of the best criticism on Latin American literature in a wide range of critical approaches, with an emphasis on works that productively combine scholarship with theory. Acknowledging the historical links and cultural affinities between Latin American and Iberian literatures, the series welcomes a consideration of Spanish and Portuguese texts and topics, while also providing a space of convergence for scholars working in Romance studies, comparative literature, cultural studies, and literary theory.

Titles in Series

http://www.departments.bucknell.edu/univ_press

Voices Out of Africa
in Twentieth-Century
Spanish Caribbean Literature

Julia Cuervo Hewitt

Lewisburg
Bucknell University Press

Associated University Presses
2010 Eastpark Boulevard
Cranbury, NJ 08512

The paper used in this publication meets the requirements of the American National Standard for Permanence of Paper for Printed Library Materials Z39.48-1984.

Library of Congress Cataloging-in-Publication Data

Cuervo Hewitt, Julia, 1946–
  Voices out of Africa in twentieth-century Spanish Caribbean literature / Julia Cuervo Hewitt.
      p. cm. — (The Bucknell studies in Latin American literature and theory)
  Includes bibliographical references and index.
  ISBN 978-0-8387-5729-1 (alk. paper)
  1. Caribbean fiction (Spanish)—20th century—History and criticism. 2. Africa—In literature. 3. Caribbean literature (Spanish)—African influences. 4. Caribbean Area—Civilization—African influences. I. Title. II. Title: Voices out of Africa in 20th-century Spanish Caribbean literature. III. Series.
  PQ7361.C85   2009
  863′.6409729—dc22

                                                                              2009011592

To the memory of my parents:

Julia Swanberg,
Gonzalo Cuervo

To Antonio

Contents

Illustrations

Acknowledgments

I WANT TO EXPRESS MY GRATITUDE TO THE MANY PEOPLE WHO INDIRECTLY and directly helped me write this book, especially to my parents whose life and death were so closely related to this study. I thank those in the United States and in the Caribbean, practitioners, scholars, and writers who unbeknownst to them gave me a helping hand in this project. I am in debt to friends and colleagues for their support, especially Aida Beaupied; Mary Barnard; Laurence Prescott; Aníbal González Pérez for his encouragement, guidance, and suggestions; and to my daughter, Maria Cristina, for reading parts of the manuscript. I am specially grateful to César Leante for the insightful conversations we shared in Madrid in the first stages of this project, and to other writers and scholars, some like Manuel Zapata Olivella no longer living, whose conversations and work informed in different ways my research. My gratitude goes most especially to Antonio Benítez Rojo, for his wisdom, for the knowledge he shared with me through the years, and for his unrelenting encouragement, curiosity, and intellect.

I give special thanks to Josephine Weiss for a Fellowship in the Humanities that allowed me to begin the early stages of my research; to the Pennsylvania State University College of Liberal Arts for a course release; to the Penn State University Africana Research Center for a research travel grant; to the Heritage Collection at the University of Miami, Florida, for allowing me to have access to Lydia Cabrera's papers; and to the Fundação Pierre Verger, in Salvador, Brazil, for allowing me to read the entire Cabrera-Verger correspondence. I would like to express my deep gratitude to my childhood friend, Dolores Triana, for the photos of ceiba trees that she so kindly took in Havana for this book.

Abbreviations

DW	*The Decline of the West: Form and Actuality*
DW 2	*The Decline of the West: Perspectives of World History*
KW	*The Kingdom of This World*
NONA	*La noche oscura del Niño Avilés*
QPN	*Querido primer novio (una historia proscrita de amor y naturaleza)*
RI	*The Repeating Island*
TTrappedT	*Three Trapped Tigers*
TTT	*Tres triste tigres*

Voices Out of Africa
in Twentieth-Century
Spanish Caribbean Literature

Introduction: Passage to the Caribbean

THIS BOOK IS AN EXPLORATION OF THE PERFORMATIVE REPRESENTATION in Spanish Caribbean literature of Africa and of those cultural and religious expressions that we have come to call African in the Caribbean. It is also an in-depth study of the complex codifications and symbolic structures of such representations. My main argument in this study is that the literary representation of Africa and "Africanness," meaning practices, belief systems, music, art, myths, popular knowledge, in Spanish-speaking Caribbean societies, constructs a self-referential discourse in which Africa and African "things" shift to a Caribbean landscape as the site of the (M)Other. In other words, those representations (informed by Afro-Caribbean rituals, local memories, belief systems, and oral traditions) often articulate a "longing," a desire, for a lost body and a lost time often conceived in literary and artistic expressions in a maternal structure of signification. By affirming cultural differences, representations of Africa resist persistent patterns of exclusion, and also question the dominance and authority of Western epistemology. This book explores how the literary representations of Africa, and African expressions in a Caribbean context, imaginatively rescue, and at the same time construct, a Caribbean cultural imaginary conceived as the Other within that associates Africa with a cultural womb. Spanish Caribbean literature represents such concept as the memory and the body of the (M)Other. Such representations address a geographic and metageographic maternal cultural space in the Caribbean imaginary that is, and is not, African. Foundational to this study is Antonio Benítez Rojo's proposition that the Caribbean text opens itself to two different orders of reading. The first order, he claims, is "a secondary type, epistemological, profane, diurnal, and linked to the West—the world outside;" and the second order of reading is "the principal order, teleological, ritual, nocturnal, and referring to the Caribbean itself" (*RI*, 23).[1]

This book proposes a reading of several twentieth-century texts (most of them already classics in Spanish-American literature) from the gaze of that second, but yet primary order of reading. These orders of reading are intertwined and interdependent on each other; one signifying on the other. Thus, a reading of Spanish Caribbean classics from solely a Western gaze renders a Caribbean different from the one constructed by Caribbean writers in a dialogic play of significations. Such interdependence has much to do with the definition of—or an attempt to define—national and cultural "differences" in the Caribbean;[2] and with the "knowledge" that, to be a Caribbean, is to be in some ways always something other. Such notion of being other is further staged by the diasporic movements that have always characterized Caribbean history. In this sense, being Caribbean is being this AND that, one AND another.

In the Spanish Caribbean, where being mulatto (as Nicolás Guillén highlights in his "mulatto poems") is different from being white, black, or Indian;[3] and where shades of color may create differences within races and classes, there is a certain Caribbean logic to the notion of racial and cultural simultaneity as a condition for being Caribbean. In the light of such *mulatez,* definitions of cultural identity further complicate matters because they more often than not negate the African elements of Caribbean Hispanic societies. The hyphen, which expresses simultaneity and hybridity, also expresses a gap, a lack, in the effort to represent the notion of being "other than," as in being Afro-Hispanic, Afro-Caribbean, Afro-Cuban, Afro-Dominican, Afro-Rican. Such hyphenated identity becomes even more complicated by diasporic movements that produce greater plurality: Afro-Cuban-American, or Afro-Puerto Rican-Dominican-American, and others. In these cases, the Afro element often disappears from the hyphened equation. Nonetheless, the hyphen intimates the always already condition of being other, multiple, dual, AND. The Deleuzian logic of the AND is not foreign to a Caribbean way of thinking. In Cuba, for example, the patron saint, the *Virgen de la Caridad del Cobre* (Virgin of Charity), is a manifestation of the Virgin Mary AND the African, Afro-Cuban, deity of love, *Oshun. Shango* is the *Yoruba* deity of thunder AND the Catholic female saint *Santa Barbara,* AND the Cuban-Chinese *San Fakón* or *Sa-Fa-Con.* At the same time, the geographic displacements that characterize Caribbean conditions in the twentieth century problematize cultural, ethnic, and racial definitions extending and enhancing the AND across transcultural lines, diasporic conditions, and transoceanic definitions of plural national and cultural identities. In order to articulate this impasse of Caribbean consciousness, critical thought too often drags behind the rapid movements of cultural exchanges and negotiations in the attempt to reevaluate that site of Knowledge we have come to call Afro-Caribbean.

Africa in the Spanish-speaking Caribbean is an important element in the formation and formulation of its history and society, although such contribution is often negated by myths of *hispanidad.* Thus, Spanish Caribbean writers represent the African experience in the Caribbean as an integral part of the Caribbean experience. These representations often take the form of hermetic codes and oblique references to belief systems, rituals, and popular knowledge; as well as the reenactment of cultural codes and signifying linguistic plays in Caribbean speech, parody, and musical rhythms. Often such literary representations "resist" translation. Words associated with non-Western belief systems like the *Yoruba/Lucumí* words *ashe,*[4] or *aché,* and *egbó, ecobio/ekobio,* which belong to a popular Caribbean ritual language, are rooted in the Caribbean experience (an experience that includes multiple languages, African, Asian, and European), making it difficult to translate popular concepts to writing, to Spanish, or to any Western language. The problem with the theme of translation in this study becomes most acute in Lydia Cabrera's writings and in Cabrera Infante's *Tres tristes tigres,* a novel in which the slippage of language and the inaccessibility to culture through translation is inscribed in the narrative structure and language of the text.[5] The gaps left by language, orality, and writing in Cabrera and Cabrera Infante's writing, and by cultural translations resulting from differences in belief systems in the Caribbean (which are always changing and adapting to new circumstances for political or diasporic reasons), establish a complex space of cultural mediation. That space offers a repetitive and self-referential discourse of mediation by reinventing local memories perceived as African.

The problem of articulating, engaging, and negotiating ideas about Africa and Afro-Caribbeanness in Spanish Caribbean literature is that the written word is limited by language. The history of the Caribbean, as of America, is marked (from the very instant of the first encounter between European and First Nation people) by those limitations. Terms (often untranslatable to Western languages) are objects of empirical Knowledge, subjected to scrutiny, debated and always debatable. Meanings may be fluid, given to misreadings, ambiguous, and of plural significations. In that linguistic entanglement, narrative performances of "Afro-Caribbeanness" awaken memories and historical inquiries on cultural negotiations, hybridity, authority, local knowledges, and power. From those entanglements, however, emerges a coherent discourse that, although fragmented, and diasporic, it reenacts, rearticulates, rethinks, and transforms itself into a discourse on Africa and "Africanness" in Spanish Caribbean literature.

There are several discursive veins running through the chapters of this book: Africa and those cultural characteristics we call African as a sign for a Caribbean space of its own in Caribbean fiction; the representation of the Other, Africa, as mother and as the site of a discourse of resistance that disrupts and questions Master Narratives and official discourses; the notion of writing as transformative and ritualistic. This study argues that in Spanish Caribbean literature representation of the Caribbean landscape often becomes the discursive space of the (M)Other: a maternal structure of significations associated with freedom, a lost space, and a lost body and time. Hence, the repetitive image of *monte* (meaning nature and culture), conceived as (M)Other, becomes a plural sign for a poetic space of knowledge, local memories, and historical longings, as well as an invisible cultural space within. Aware that the Caribbean is a plural and rhizomatic zone that resists any one single order of reading, Caribbean writers like Antonio Benítez Rojo and Edouard Glissant propose the Deleuzian metaphor of the rhizome as a way to approach zones of instability, simultaneity, and plurality in the Caribbean. For Deleuze, the "rhizome", as metaphor, provides an alternate image to the traditional arboreal metaphor of Western Epistemology. It is, he writes: "like the grass roots that intercept each other and spread in different directions having no central point or position, consisting only of multiple entryways and exits and its own lines of flight."[6] Remembering that in a rhizome there are no points or positions, only bifurcating lines, Deleuze's concept of "rhizome" is in agreement with Benítez Rojo's concept of the Caribbean as a meta-archipelago: a place that is "neither a boundary or a center" (RI, 4), where "the spectrum of Caribbean codes is so varied and dense that it holds the region suspended in a soup of signs" (RI, 2).

In the difficulty of representing Afro-Caribbeanness as the entanglements of a rhizome, the Spanish Caribbean "performative narratives" explored in this book articulate a unique conscious self-referentiality that follows a ritualistic search for cultural Caribbean archaics. Benítez Rojo proposes a certain order in what seems to be chaos in the Caribbean experience. On the other hand, Glissant defines such entanglement of relations in the Caribbean as an "enmeshed root system, a network spreading either in the ground or on the air, with no predatory rootstock taking over permanently."[7] The voyage in the following chapters through the literary representation of cultural archaic (codes, symbols, rituals, African belief systems) in Spanish Caribbean literature also follows to some extent the logic of the rhizome as expressed by Glissant and by Benítez Rojo in a Caribbean context.

Stemming from that sense of "rhizome" and from the gap of language in the conceptualization of the Caribbean as an "in-between" zone of movements, entanglements, displacements, simultaneities, and coexistence, the title for this book, "Voices out of Africa," addresses the notion of an Africanness in the Caribbean that comes from Africa, but that no longer is African. It also addresses the effort to articulate a sense of source, a (m)other corpus, of an archaic different from Western codes in the Caribbean, AND, at the same time, an African space (a loci) no longer African but Caribbean. For example, Cuban santeros (Afro-Cuban priests) have traditionally displayed in the front room of their house an altar with Catholic saints and Christian symbols, and, in a back room, another altar of greater importance, hidden from public view, with African objects and religious symbols (clay pots, iron caldrons, gourds, shells, rum, coconuts, eggs), displayed for a given purpose and meaning. An iron kettle, for example, represents (is) *Oggun,* who presides over metals; a gourd, *Osaín;* copper bracelets and sweets, *Oshun;* a double ax, and a double spade, *Shango.* This study is interested in the literary representations of that "back room." Yet, at the same time, it explores the spaces "in-between" the front and the back room: the spaces of entanglements, and the gaps left by "performative narratives" in their representation of that zone of instability, dance, and plurality we call Caribbean culture, Afro-Cuban, Afro-Puerto-Rican, Afro-Dominican, or Afro-Caribbean. That "in-between" zone that Gustavo Pérez-Firmat addresses as *Life on the Hyphen. The Cuban-American Way* (1994), is also a diasporic zone that extends out of the Caribbean, and moves back toward the Caribbean, in an inter-Caribbean exchange.

A case in point of such exchange and entanglement, in the context of the Afro-Cuban, Cuban diaspora, is Willie Chirino's song, "Mr. Don't Touch the Bananas." This is a humorous song about a "party" that is taking place at a home, one would assume in Miami, Florida. A Cuban "guy" takes two of his Anglo friends to what seems to be a traditional "pot luck." One of them notices bananas on a table and, assuming that they are there for the guests, reaches for one. A woman notices the "move," and goes into shock. As other guests try to help her by giving her smelling salts, a voice shouts to the probably-confused transgressor what turns out to be the chorus of the song: "Mister, don't eat the bananas, the bananas are for Changó" (Shango). The song portrays, with irony and humor, a case of cultural misreading based on the codes of Afro-Cuban rituals and religious practices, which are woven into Western Christian cultural codes in the United States. Those that partake of the ritual "knowledge" and codes would have known immediately that the bananas on the table were offerings to the Afro-Cuban deity of thunder, lightning, and the drum, Shango, the ancestral African king of Oyo, in today Nigeria, AND, at the same time, the female Catholic saint Santa Barbara, AND the popular phallic orisha/saint womanizer, drummer, warrior, who is also the Great, but very capricious, Judge, AND for Chinese-Cubans, or Afro-Chinese-Cuban-Americans, San Fakón. One can only imagine the surprise the two guests would experience, their bewilderment, as they asked themselves: Who is Changó? Years before, another Cuban singer, actor, and drummer, Desi Arnaz, (as Ricky Ricardo) introduced, and became famous for his performance at the beat of the *tumbadora* (drum) in "I Love Lucy." He became associated with his song *Babalú,* a song to the Afro-Cuban orisha, *Babalú Ayé.* Most likely, the majority of the viewers in United States had no idea of who or what was Babalú Ayé (the Afro-Cuban orisha of sickness, the Great Divine Healer, whose syncretic image in Cuba is that of Saint Lazarus).

With the Cuban/Caribbean diaspora, before and after 1959, Cuban/Caribbean music crossed geographical and cultural borders. Celia Cruz, known today in Latin America and Latino communities in the United States as "the queen of salsa," took her music, and with it the Afro-Cuban orishas, to places unimaginable when Ricky Ricardo was playing *Babalú,* or even when Cuban rhythms of African roots, often closely tied to the Afro-Cuban ñáñigo rituals, began to influence American jazz. Like Afro-Cuban rhythms, the Afro-Cuban singer, Celia Cruz, made her mark in the world dispersing the Afro-Cuban *monte:* a rhizomatic religious and metaphorical performative space in Spanish Caribbean literature, interlaced with the complex codes of the Caribbean, and, most recently, as in Chirino's song, of the Caribbean diaspora. This is the plural space and the codes that inform Spanish Caribbean writers in the attempt to represent "difference," the "gap," the space "in-between" the front room and the back room. This is the space where Caribbean peoples and cultures dwell: a space charged with the wounds of slavery, colonialism, neocolonialism, prejudice, and repression, but also dance, and ritual. For that reason, the signifying difference Africa represents in Spanish Caribbean fiction, is also charged with a sense of resistance and defiance against social values, political hegemonies, cultural negations, and colonial and neocolonial myths of racial and religious purity. Difference in Spanish Caribbean societies signifies a mark, a Derridian "trace," a gap, left in Spanish societies by the wounds of slavery, and its aftermath. That mark is inscribed in popular speech by the term *la raja,* meaning the cut, crack, split, slice: as Morinigo points out, an Americanism that infers "a person that is not pure white."[8] Such raja, associated with racial difference, is also the great secret: that which is "hidden" in one's African ancestry, what hides in the back room of one's genetic house. This gap/raja is a repetitive theme in Spanish Caribbean literature, revisited most recently by Rosario Ferré in Puerto Rico in her novel, *La casa de la laguna* (1995) [The House by the Lake], and in the melodramatic Cuban film, directed by Luis Lago, *Miel para Ochún* (Honey, or *oñí,* for Oshun). The "performative" exposure of this raja in Spanish Caribbean literary texts defies historical violence, and recognizes the survival of local memories, while, at the same time, affirming the space of that codified, and hidden, back room as the location of Caribbean culture.

Different from the Francophone and Anglophone Caribbean islands, after the triumph of the Haitian Revolution in 1804, the colonial governments of Puerto Rico, the Dominican Republic, and Cuba implemented to different degrees a systematic program to whiten Caribbean Spanish-speaking colonial societies. As early as the seventeenth century, African cultural expressions were popularized in Caribbean societies; and they continued to survive into the twentieth- and twenty-first century under the guise of popular culture. Fernando Ortiz documents in *Historia de una pelea cubana contra los demonios* that in the seventeenth century the Inquisition attempted to repress African expressions to no avail. These were already blended into most religious and popular festivities in Cuba, in what Fernando Ortiz calls *cristianería,*[9] a mixture of Christianity and *santería.* In

Cuba, Fernando Ortiz, and the writers that, with Ortiz as mentor, began the Afro-Cuban movement in the early part of the century, began to explore and expose the cultural raja of Cuban society as a formative element in the formation of culture and the distinctive characteristic of Cuban culture. In its early stages, it was an intellectual and artistic exercise of discovery and recovery that had important and lasting repercussions by the thirties and forties. In Puerto Rico, Luís Palés Matos was the first one to open the door to the exploration of Africa in Puerto Rican culture, disrupting, with his Afro-Puerto Rican poems, the representation of national values based on the myth of a white creole Hispanic *jíbaro* society. His poems in *Tún tún de pasa y grifería* may offend today the sensibility of African Caribbean scholars with the nativist portrayal of Puerto Rican blacks, but in the twenties they carved a space for an Afro-Puerto Rican literary discourse to which contemporary writers would return years later. It was a discourse of affirmation and also of resistance and defiance. Contemporary writers in Puerto Rico, like Luis Rafael Sánchez, Ana Lydia Vega, and Rosario Ferré also defied a complex social and historical racial taboo to express in their work of fiction what José Luis González documented in "El país de cuatro pisos," and Isabelo Zenón, in his *Naciso descubre su trasero* (I, 1974, II, 1975): that Puerto Rican culture was foundationally African,[10] and, as González points out, that the first Puerto Ricans were African and African creoles.

The Dominican Republic had a very different experience. Haiti invaded the Spanish-speaking side of the island, which remained under Haitian rule for two decades. For this historical reason, and due to the memory of fear and rejection by the Spanish-speaking Dominicans of their Haitian rulers, and to a continuous conflictive relationship with Haiti, a nation linguistically different from the Spanish-speaking Dominicans, there developed a complex negative attitude toward the Haitian, and, in that political entanglement, toward anything African. Under Trujillo's dictatorship, the island suffered its worst wave of repression against Haitians, and anything Haitian. Only recently, years after Trujillo's assassination, have Dominican writers been able to express the complexities of such racial historical entanglements in Dominican society. Popular culture, music, and religious rituals survived censorship as they had done in the seventeenth century disguised in various forms, preserving and transforming local memories and popular knowledge. It was a slow process, often imperceptible to the European world, until there emerged in the Caribbean at large what Wilson Harris defines as a "new corpus of sensibility that could translate and accommodate African and other legacies within a new architecture of cultures."[11] The works chosen for this book are texts that represent and articulate in various ways such corpus of sensibility.

The present study does not analyze Fernando Ortiz's work, but it begins with a text written by Ortiz about nineteenth-century "Black Carnival," a popular name given to the festivities that took place in Havana on January 6, or *Día de Reyes*. His work becomes a specter in every chapter of this book, as in most Afro-Spanish-Caribbean studies. Ortiz's work, and the transformations of his perspectives of what he defined as *afrocubanía*, continues to be pivotal in all studies related to Africa in the Caribbean. His concept of "transculturation," for example, a term he coined in 1940, with Bronislaw Malinowski's blessing, was an attempt to explain a process of cultural exchange for which there were no other terms in the anthropological discourse of the time to express the exchanges and cultural negotiations taking place in the Caribbean. The word "syncretism" was used in reference to religious beliefs, and Ortiz was looking for a term that would describe a cultural exchange in the Caribbean between Africa and Europe, between the native and the foreign. However, any term used, even "transculturation," is a limited signifier unable to express or fully signify fluid cultural exchanges in the Caribbean. More recently, Benítez Rojo proposed a return to the term syncretism, away from the solely religious connotation it has had, as the term that best describes the cultural simultaneity and rhizomatic coexistence of multiple cultural elements (including African) in the Caribbean. My argument is that all of these terms explain only partially the complex movements, plurality, and cultural negotiations in the Caribbean; and that neither one comprehends the dynamics of the Caribbean experience.

There are tangible elements such as references to skin color, music, food,[12] and language (colloquial and ritual), as in words of African origins like *ñampear, ñangotear, fuá, chin chin, ashe, egbo,* that are evident African traces, both in their transcultural modalities and syncretic coexistence. Nonetheless, non-Caribbean readers may not easily detect the literary representation of those elements in Caribbean texts. At the same time, in the Spanish Caribbean, elements of African ancestry that form part of a Caribbean daily experience are not always understood as African even within Caribbean popular culture. And even when there is a clear understanding, sometimes meanings are hidden for fear of exclusion and misunderstanding. For example, in a ceremonial gathering outside of Santo Domingo, I made an indiscrete comment to an elderly woman associating Africa to the rituals of possession we were witnessing. Surprised by my comment, and as a response to a reference I made about a doll dressed in blue representing *Yemayá*, she made it clear to me that there was nothing African "there;" that she, and the other participants present, were all "good Christians."

In the Caribbean there are complex differences within differences. This book explores the performative representation of those differences, with the purpose of exploring plays of similarities in cultural exchanges and in the imaginative space of local memories and knowledges, in the imaginative literary construction of identity. The question, in the context of the

Spanish-speaking Caribbean, is: How to define and articulate in the representation of Africa in the Caribbean an internal point of tension in Caribbean discourses about the Caribbean, and its relationship to Africa? What Stuart Hall calls "imaginative rediscovery"[13] takes a complex turn when articulated by Spanish-speaking Caribbean writers who are not of a clear and obvious African ancestry, but who are part of a culturally Afro-Caribbean mind set and consciousness. In fact, in the later part of the twentieth century, one of the most poignant questions Spanish-speaking Caribbean writers must meditate on is: What happens when the racial other "becomes" self?

Mestizaje and hybridity (racial and cultural) in the Caribbean, as in all of Latin America, come in many forms, from skin color to cultural characteristics and memories, political agendas, and social myths. This is the theme in Ana Lydia Vega's short story "Encancaranublado," in which a Haitian, a Dominican, a Cuban, and a Puerto Rican are trying to reach Miami (in the same boat as a metaphor for the same Caribbean experience). The short story addresses, through a play of stereotypes and subtle cultural references, the entanglements of present day diasporic and neocolonial conditions in the Caribbean. It is also the theme of her short story, "Otra maldad de Pateco" (Another One of Pateco's Mischievous Tricks), in which the son of plantation owners, born with a black head and a white body due to Pateco's trick, is raised by a black slave woman because his parents reject him for his difference: they exclude him and want to get rid of their own biological son. At the end, the young man discovers in his reflection on the waters the true color of his head, and asks Oggun to make his body also black; in other words, to be the person he was raised to be, to be like his nurse mother, and like those around him with whom he identifies. At the end, the orisha grants him his wish. In Ana Lydia Vega's allegorical story, Africa is the mark inscribed in the young white man's body, whose belief system, language, and culture came from the black slave that became his mother: the cultural space of the (M)Other to which now he ontologically belonged.

In Spanish-speaking Caribbean societies, the literary imaginary rediscovery and performative representations of Africa, Africanness, and Afro-Caribbeanness is most often associated with ritual; and ritual, with the transformative act of writing. The representation of ritual, whether it is through the structural disposition of the text, the narrative, or the actual representation of a specific Afro-Caribbean ceremony, reminds the reader that ritual connects participants (the reader) to the sources of life—the forces of being, often represented in Afro-Caribbean literature as a (M)Other space that restores memory, a telluric womb associated with a Caribbean landscape. In this sense, ritual is associated with Carnival; Carnival, with representation and performance; and performance with resistance, subversion, and desire. These associations address a historical process in which African expressions and belief systems often survived through Carnival, as Carnival performances. This is why the first chapter of this study begins with Fernando Ortiz's reading and interpretations of a unique carnival on *Día de Reyes* in colonial Cuba that was popularly known as "Black Carnival." It goes on to explore Alejo Carpentier's early Afro-Cuban poems, most of which he wrote to be adapted to the stage as musical performances, many of them thematically related to "Día de Reyes," and to *ñáñigo* ritual representations. The chapter ends with an in-depth reading of Alejo Carpentier's *The Kingdom of this World* (1949). This is a text that marks an end and a beginning in Carpentier's oeuvre, and a text that became a Master Narrative in Caribbean literature.

My argument in the first chapter is that Carpentier's intellectual construction of the Haitian slave in *The Kingdom of this World* also represents the contradictions and internal conflicts that went into the representation of Afro-Caribbeanness by white Spanish Caribbean writers in the early part of the twentieth century. The novel addresses complex problems in the representation of an African archaic as a Caribbean Archaic, and the entanglements created by the representation of self as Other and of the Caribbean landscape as (M)Other. *The Kingdom of this World* offers a new and different historical gaze for the forties and fifties, in which the agency of an African creole consciousness disrupts the hegemony of Western colonial dominance. Carpentier constructs a historical-imaginary Caribbean space as a mytho-poetic loci acting on history, and as the (M)Other space of an Afro-Caribbean consciousness. *The Kingdom of this World* is an imaginary intellectual rediscovery of an archival Africa always already there within Eurocentric colonial cities in the Caribbean. From that imaginary site, also informed by concrete historical experience, Carpentier tells the story of Africa in America, and of the foundational participation of Africa, as a telluric womb of history, myths, and beliefs, in a creole America in the making. In the rhizomatic entanglement of Caribbean historical perspectives, the main character of the novel, Ti Nöel, arrives at an ethical crossroad, having to decide between evasion and engagement. This is a crossroad that still today resonates with other Latin American writers.

Chapter 2 engages Lydia Cabrera's Afro-Cuban short stories and her ethnological studies on Afro-Cuban religions. Her work rescues through fiction and documentation the Afro-Cuban concept of monte. At the same time, her texts articulate a play of signifying double utterances in which a feminine discourse is "entangled" with the Afro-Cuban cultural landscape of her work. This chapter explores this feminine discourse in association with the construction of an Afro-Cuban discourse, in which the writer talks back to a dominant patriarchal official discourse. Lydia Cabrera's textual transgressions celebrating freedom called the attention of Guillermo Cabrera Infante. This chapter also explores the inscription of the concept of monte, as represented by Lydia Cabrera, in Guillermo Cabrera Infante's *Three Trapped Tigers (Tres tristes tigres),* a text in which the writer, in dialogue with Lydia Cabrera's *El monte,* proposes the act of writing as an ecological voyage through the Cuban urban "jungle" of Havana. I argue that in this novel, it is from that cultural back room of life in Havana that Cabrera Infante inscribes ñáñigo myths and rituals into the narrative fabric and structure of the text.

In the urban monte of Havana, the writer finds one of the most foundational myths inscribed in popular culture and in the representations of *afrocubanía* as conceived by Ortiz and Carpentier. This is the Big Cuban Fish Story of the Afro-Cuban ñáñigo, a story as universal as Melville's *Moby-Dick,* and Hemingway's *The Old Man and the Sea.* The ñáñigos, or the Abakuá secret society, of African origins, was a fraternity of mutual help formed and transformed in Cuba into a creole Afro-Cuban fraternity, that had a foundational role in the formation of popular Cuban culture, especially in Havana and its surrounding areas. Cabrera Infante finds in the ñáñigo an autochthonous metaphor for Cuba with which to articulate, from the gaps of language, a Cuban condition of exclusion and repression that resulted from the aftermath of the Cuban Revolution. My argument in this chapter is that such reenactment in Cabrera Infante's novel is a performance of resistance and defiance that follows a repetitive pattern in Caribbean letters in which Africa, and things African, become a counterdiscourse that resists entrapment. Cabrera Infante's *Tres tristes tigres* offers a discourse of resistance that voices a poetics of freedom that speaks from, and about, the long history of *cimarronaje* in the Caribbean.

The third chapter is a genealogical exploration of the repetitive representation in Spanish Caribbean literature of the figure of the runaway slave, beginning in the sixteenth century until today, and of cimarronaje as a metaphor for the Caribbean. This chapter explores how the image of *cimarrón* (runaway slave) has become a signifying sign charged with political and ideological meanings, transformed and reinvented at different times and from different ideological views. An archeology of this historical figure in Spanish Caribbean letters parallels an intricate trajectory shaped by philosophical and political imaginaries at different historical periods that has turned the figure of cimarrón into a metaphor for political power, resistance, and a counter-discourse of freedom. At the same time, in its repetitive reenactment, the silent voice of the historical runaway slave, whose persistent resistance and never-ending rebellion shaped the history of the Caribbean, remains engulfed in a mist of discursive political agendas and strategies.

The last chapter in this study explores the representation of Africa in a Caribbean landscape in two novels by the Puerto Rican writer, Edgardo

Rodríguez Juliá: *La noche oscura del niño Avilés* (1984), and *En el camino de Yyaloide* (1994), the first two novels of an incomplete trilogy, *Crónicas de Nueva Venecia*. It also explores the representation of Africa as mother, as a space no longer African, in the Cuban landscape, in *Querido primer novio* (1999) by the Cuban writer Zoé Valdés. These novels revisit, reenact, and retransform self-referential discourses on race, nation, culture, hybridity, power, resistance, and writing in the Spanish Caribbean, in two very different neocolonial contexts. Both writers propose a voyage, through memory, to a time past, to a lost body: a libidinous *palenque* (community of runaway slaves) of freedom and desire in the Afro-Caribbean monte. In Rodríguez Juliá's novel, the "Beautiful city" prophesized by Towa, "where the Black [the cimarron] could be himself master of his destiny,"[14] is the cimarrón city of New Venice, a city erased from the collective memory. In Valdés's novel, a similar space, not a city, but the remote rural area of La Fe (Faith), is the site of the Afro-Cuban monte: a maternal space of justice that orders and subdues chaos. Valdés subverts Carpentier's master narrative in *The Kingdom of this World* by restoring to the feminine space of the Afro-Cuban (M)Other monte its archaic powers of creation. The novel re-imagines the Afro-Cuban monte as a feminine space of refuge, but also of entanglements, no longer African, but now Cuban, as the space from which the text talks back to modern forms of internal colonialism, new hegemonic patristic discourses, and persistent old/new structures of power and exclusion.

The importance of looking at the Spanish-speaking Caribbean, and its diasporic dissemination, is that this is the area that provided the first European model in the New World (economic, political, social). That model would be adapted and readapted numerous and various times in the following five hundred years. The Caribbean was the first place and moment of historical and cultural entanglement in what became America (the countries of North, Central, and South America). Yet, it continues to be forgotten and often misunderstood. The Spanish colonies in the Caribbean were the first to establish an African condition in the Americas, reinventing Africa and the New World through a transatlantic mode of slavery that also would condition the great events in the Americas. This early Caribbean experience initiated, beginning with Antonio Montesino's sermon in 1511, in Hispaniola, the poignant questions still asked today in America about race and gender, religion, politics, economics, and cultural borders.

1
Cultural Identity in Difference:
Imaginary Dialogues
(From Fernando Ortiz to Alejo Carpentier)

in the midst of hot abundant tears
I felt a world arise and live for me
—Goethe, *Faust*

The History of the world is none other
than the progress of the consciousness of Freedom
—G. W. F. Hegel, *The Philosophy of History*

IN THE NINETEENTH CENTURY, IN CUBA, THE CARNIVAL FESTIVITIES OF "DÍA de Reyes," on January 6, came to be known also as "Carnaval de los negros" (Black Carnival) due to the large participation of African freemen and slaves, and black and mulatto creoles. In 1925, Fernando Ortiz published an essay, "La antigua fiesta afrocubana del 'Día de Reyes'" (The Old Afro-Cuban Festivity of the Day of the Three Magi), about this unique day of Epiphany in nineteenth century Havana. For Ortiz, Black Carnival was: "una amalgama y refundición en Cuba de multitud de escenas y ritos africanos . . . de significación casi desconocida y olvidada" (a mixture and a recasting in Cuba of numerous African scenes and rituals . . . of nearly forgotten meanings).[1] This day, the most festive day of the year, which commemorated the recognition by way of gifts, by the three Magi, of the newborn Jesus as the Messiah, would become imprinted in the cultural fabrics of colonial Cuban society. It was, Ortiz writes: "sin dudas, una de las más pintorescas escenas de la vida colonial, que de antaño interesó el pincel de artistas y la pluma de los escritores" (no doubt one of the most picturesque scenes of colonial life that attracted the interest of painters and of writers in the past).[2] Following pre-Christian Roman traditions, the most significant custom on this "Día de Reyes" was to give slaves their freedom for one day. Restrictions were relaxed, and slaves were allowed to act as if they were free; and more importantly, to think and experience such possibility. Ortiz writes:

29

La esclavitud que fríamente separaba hijos y padres, maridos y mujeres, hermanos y compatriotas, atenuaba aquel día su tiránico poderío y cada negro se reunía en la calle, con los suyos, con los de su tribu, con sus "carabelas," ufanamente trajeado con los atavíos ceremoniales e indumentarias de su país . . . gozando de la ilusión de la libertad.[3]

[Slavery, which coldly separated parents and children, men and wives, brothers and countrymen, softened that day its tyrant grip and blacks reunited on the streets with their own, with those of their tribes, their brothers, joyfully wearing their ceremonial outfits and national dress . . . enjoying the illusion of freedom.]

It was a day of performances in which masters (like the Magi) granted their slaves the gift of a farcical freedom, and money (*aguinaldos*). In this cultural performance of allegorical negotiations and exchanges, of pagan Roman and Christian customs, the slave's desire for freedom was diffused and disseminated in the chaos of Carnival. The figure of the biblical savior, born to redeem humanity, especially the poor and the oppressed, was associated by analogy with the suffering and sacrifice of the slaves who, in the liturgical performance of the day, were the recipients of gifts. In a complex play of imaginary exchanges, Christian Epiphany came to be associated with the very condition of slavery, and with the passion and crucifixion of the Messiah. According to colonial Christian theology, the toils of the slaves on this earth were to be rewarded in the next if their conduct was exemplary: submissive and obedient. The illusion of freedom on that festive day, associated with the birth and recognition of the Christian redeemer, also offered a different type of epiphany through which Afro-Cubans reconstructed, and reenacted, the absent presence of the Messiah (as the bearer of freedom) in their midst. As in the festivities to Saturn in ancient Rome, or *saturnalias,* the slaves in the Spanish colonies elected a carnival king, a queen, and a royal court among themselves.[4]

In Cuba, and in the other Spanish colonies in the greater Caribbean, a sense of freedom, real and farcical, developed in association with Carnival and with Nativity, especially with "Día de Reyes," as a day for expansion and merriment, but also, as a propitious moment to escape, to rebel, and to resist enslavement and colonial power. It is not a simple historical coincidence that the first massive slave revolt that took place in America occurred in Hispaniola during the Christmas festivities of 1522. Fear of slave rebellions during Carnival, and especially the Christmas festivities of "Día de Reyes," became a signature of colonial life. For instance, after the abolition of slavery, Carnival continued to be a propitious and symbolical moment for insurgency and rebellion. Even the third and last insurgency for independence in Cuba was chosen to begin on February 24, 1895, because, as Ada Ferrer notes in *Insurgent Cuba 1868–1898,* that day coincided with the first Sunday of Carnival.[5]

Black Carnival offered one of the most exotic attractions in colonial Havana. This was the performance of *diablito* (little devil) dancers,[6] or *ñáñigo iremes* of the Afro-Cuban Abakuá Secret Society. By the end of the nineteenth century, this Afro-Cuban group was famous for its diablitos dancers, but also for the violent rivalries between chapters or *potencias*. Ortiz quotes from an article published in 1859 by Ontiano Lorcas, "Los diablitos o el día infernal en La Habana" (1859) (The *diablitos* or the infernal day in Havana), as an example of the perception that by the middle of the nineteenth century the white population had of the ñáñigos:

> En los barrios extremos y calles menos concurridas, campaban por sus respetos los *ñáñigos* cubiertos de un capuchón de burdo género, algo parecido al de los sayones del Santo Oficio . . . En el *ñáñigo* se extremó toda la grosera y bárbara imaginación de las tribus africanas . . . Era de ver con qué feroz entusiasmo seguían las masas de la clase más ínfima del pueblo, sin distinción de edades, sexos ni razas, aquel ridículo madero emplumado, símbolo que enarbolaba cada una de aquellas salvajes agrupaciones ahítas de aguardiente y sangre de gallo, y que, según dilataba la voz pública, tenía por juramento una herida mortal en el pecho de cualquier humano.[7]

> [In the peripheral neighborhoods and less crowded streets, the *ñáñigos* went about freely, covered by a gross generic hood, something similar to the cloaks of the Holy Brotherhood . . . The extreme barbaric imagination of African tribes came together in the *ñáñigo* . . . One had to see with what fierce enthusiasm the lower masses, regardless of age, sex, race, followed the ridiculous feather pole, a symbol hoisted by each of those savage groups full of liquor and rooster blood, that, according to popular knowledge, pledged to fatally wound in the chest another human being.]

This image persisted well into the twentieth century until artists, writers, and intellectuals, and especially Lydia Cabrera's study, *La sociedad secreta Abakuá* (1959), gave the ñáñigo a new image based on a different understanding of the culture: one that saw Africa as a cultural-telluric womb in the Caribbean. In the early years of the twentieth century, the ñáñigo had gained a strong presence in Havana, a city impoverished by the crisis of the post war years and the island's difficult economic, social, and political transition to an independent republic. It was during this time that the ñáñigo became associated with urban criminality. This association motivated Fernando Ortiz to study what he called the *hampa negra* (black subworlds), following César Lombroso's Positivist theories on criminality. Ortiz published his research in 1906 with the title *Hampa Afro-Cubana. Los negros brujos (Apuntes para un Estudio de Etnología Criminal)* (Afro-Cuban Underworld. Black Sorcerers [Notes for a Study of Criminal Ethnology]). This was the first of numerous other studies he would conduct on what he called *afrocubanía*.[8] Ironically, this first book, different from Ortiz's future re-

1. "Día de Reyes" in Havana, 1848. Drawing by Federico Miahle, reprinted and published in Pierre Toussaint Fédéric Miahle's *Albumn pintoresco de la Isla de Cuba,* **Havana: B. May y Cia, 1855.**

search, set out to confirm the centuries old image of African "primitive" "cults" and of Afro-Cuban customs in the New World as dangerous, and thus a menace to the ordering principles of Western society. His work seemed to echo in a different context and philosophy the early ideas held by Europeans in the sixteenth century of the New World as the Kingdom of the Devil, in urgent need of redemption.[9] Ortiz's views in 1906 deemed it necessary to eliminate the "black *hampa,*" and it was for this purpose that he tried to "understand" it. Ortiz writes in *Los negros brujos:*

> Fue antaño el negro africano (luego criollo, mulato o blanco) que en el primer tercio del siglo XIX vino del África Occidental, sobre todo de la tierra Efik y de los Calabares, y fundó en Regla (bahía de La Habana) unas sociedades secretas de hombre solos, de carácter defensivo, muy dados a las pendencias entre sus grupos o *juegos,* y practicaban unidos a sus iniciados mediante juramentos de sangre, ceremonias religiosas, sacrificios de animales, cantos, tamboreos, funerales y demás ritos crípticos, cuyas fraternidades o cofradías, conocidas conjuntamente en Cuba por *ñañiguismo* y por *abakuá* entre los *ecobios* o miembros, aún perduran con sus misterios y lenguajes en este país (Cuba) como en África, con más numerosa grey que en el pasado, **constituyendo uno de los**

más curiosos y originales fenómenos de las transculturaciones africanas en toda América.[10]

[Long ago the African black (later creole, mulatto, or white) came in the first third of the nineteenth century from West Africa, especially from the land of *Efik* and the Calabar, and founded in Regla (Havana Bay) secret male fraternities, for the purpose of defense, pugnacious in their groups or *juegos,* and together made their initiations through blood pledges, religious ceremonies, animal sacrifices, songs, drumming, funerals, and other cryptic rituals. Their chapters or fraternities, known collectively in Cuba as *ñañiguismo* and as Abakuá among the *ecobios* or members, still today continue with their mysteries and language in this country (Cuba) as in Africa, in larger numbers than in the past, being one of the most curious and authentic phenomenon of the African transculturations in all of America.]

By 1925, however, Ortiz's views had changed. He had come to understand the important role Africa had in the development of Cuban and Caribbean societies. At the moment that he was writing "La antigua fiesta afrocubana del 'Día de Reyes,'" Ortiz was more interested in finding the universal aspects of Afro-Cuban expressions, and the role of Africa in the development of *cubanía.* Years later, in 1937, already president of the Society of Afro-Cuban Studies, Ortiz would even establish an analogy between slavery and the political situation during the late twenties and the thirties in Cuba. Ortiz suggested that the same struggle for freedom that began during slavery and colonial rule, still continued at the end of the thirties. He suggested that such struggle would not end "as long as social subordination under the pretext of color, ancestry, or caste continues, which adds greatly to economic subjugation, aggravated by false categories of race and because of delusive preconception."[11]

In "La antigua fiesta afrocubana del 'Día de Reyes,'" still following the models offered by studies like James C. Frazer's *The Golden Bough,* Ortiz contrasts the dances performed on Black Carnival to African and European customs. He concludes that the original ritual role of the diablito dances, as performed on "Día de Reyes," was to exorcise spirits, bury the winter, and prepare for a new beginning, a new cycle of life. For Ortiz, ñáñigo dances were not very different from the Christian concepts behind "Carnival" and "Lent," since the commemoration of the crucifixion and resurrection of Christ is a type of universal ritual of end and beginning, of life and death, which has been part of humanity for millenniums. In Cuba, that Christian millenary custom was superimposed to African traditions in a play of often equal symbolic values: cultural exchanges that Ortiz would later call with Bronislaw Malinowski's blessing, "transculturation."[12]

"Black Carnival," that day of performances, of farcical freedom, and cultural dualities characteristic of cultural expressions in the Caribbean,

also came to be known as *fiesta de diablitos* (festivity of little devils), because ñáñigo dancers recalled for Europeans the devil figures[13] "o más-
caras simulando diablos, que antiguamente solían acompañar las procesiones
católicas del *Corpus Christi* en Cuba, como en España y otros países" (or
masks simulating devils, that long ago accompanied the *Corpus Christi*
processions in Cuba, like in Spain, and in other countries).[14] These diablito
dancers, Ortiz points out, were similar to the character that appears in
Miguel de Cervantes's episode, "Cortes de la muerte" in *El ingenioso hidalgo Don Quijote de la Mancha,* PII, XI.[15] Ironically, ignorant of the ritual meanings of the diablito dances, the general comparisons the white
population made between Carnival expressions and European traditions
made diablito dancers and their public performances acceptable by colonial law, even during periods of harsh repression against Afro-Cuban religious expressions.[16]

   Such comparisons made from a Eurocentric view between European traditions and African dancers, and their regalia with horns and masks, often
led to misunderstandings. For example, as Ortiz points out, in Cuba the diablito came to be known as *Culona* because the white population thought
that the word culona ("big buttocks"), used by Africans and Afro-Cubans
in reference to the diablitos, referred to the wide skirt made of vegetable
fibers the dancers wore, which added a grotesque character to the dancers
and their performance. However, the term used was actually *Kulona* or
lonna, a Mandingo word for *sabio* (wise) and *instruido* (learned): a term of
respect given to ñáñigo priests.[17] The Afro-Cuban diablitos, mistaken by
the white population as buffoons and European devil figures, were Afro-
Cuban priests dressed in their ritual garments performing public ancestral
dances. They were *ñañas* of *Iremes:* impersonators of ancestral spirits, appointed to important religious roles in Abakuá societies. According to Isabel and Jorge Castellanos, "theologically speaking," all members of the
Abakuá society would be "considered *íremes,*"[18] but minor officers were
also known as ñañas, from where the term ñáñigo derives, and whose
dances is a body language of gestures with ritual meanings that only the
initiate or *abonekue* understands.[19] In these street performances, as in ritual dances, the Iremes made mute gesticulations that carried specific meanings.[20] This codified language articulated a certain "knowledge" that only
a marginal sector of the population shared. Such "codified" body language
of mimicry and gestures, incomprehensible to the general white colonial
society, in time came to be inscribed in the cultural imaginary and expressions of Cuban creole society.[21] In part due to cultural misunderstandings
like those pertaining to the diablito dancers (misunderstandings common
to cultural interchanges in America), African religious traditions, rituals and
beliefs, survived often masked by Christian symbols, in a signifying play

of double meanings that came to be inscribed in local memories, religious knowledge, and popular cultural expressions.

During and after the abolition of slavery, Carnival served as a masquerade for acts of resistance. An example can be found in the case of Guillermo Moncada, the black Cuban patriot who, in the absence of Antonio Maceo, became the highest-ranking officer in the rebel army in the province of Oriente. Ada Ferrer writes:

> Oral tradition held that long before the start of the first war of independence [1868], Moncada had used whatever opportunity presented it self to express his antipathy to slavery and Spanish rule. During annual carnivals, for example, he participated in a *comparsa* (carnival band or *krewe*) named the *Brujos de Limones*. The *comparsa* was named after a small army organized by a group of runaway slaves earlier in the century [near El Cobre] . . . The celebration of an organized group of runaways slaves who had combated Spanish military power to free other slaves was possible, or course, only within the context of the spectacle of Carnival. Moncada took further advantage of the opportunity: he declined the offer to serve as president of the *comparsa,* choosing instead to act, as the *bastonero* (baton leader). The *bastonero* had customary license to use his baton against whomever he desired—a license Moncada was said to use against Spanish soldiers.[22]

As with the case of the diablito public street dances, and as in Moncada's masked resistance, Carnival performances became a masquerade for the expression of Afro-Cuban religious beliefs and rituals: and, as such, a signifying counterdiscourse to the master's discourse: a secret language with which to talk back to the empire. By the twentieth century, these manifestations of the African experience were deeply imbedded in popular expressions. Carnival came to be perceived as a signifying element in the representation of the Caribbean experience in terms of resistance against slavery, against "acculturation," and against the assimilation of African ways and beliefs to European society. Understanding that Carnival is a "performative" mode of awakening memories and of freeing hope, especially under undesirable and repressive conditions created by the system of slavery in colonial Caribbean societies, Carnival, whether preceding Lent or on "Día de Reyes,' became the commemoration of a collective "longing" for freedom. Carnival offered the conditions for the possibility of change: in the way of hope, running away, or rebellion. At the same time, public performances allowed slaves to articulate, through dance, music, gestures, or dress, those feelings and desires about which they could not speak openly.

In the Caribbean, while the Carnival performers knew that the old order would return once Carnival was over, and that slavery would again follow the day of Epiphany, the magic of a public performance that conjured freedom left open the possibility, as in all rituals, that the old order could be defeated and a new day could bring about a change coherent with the memories of a time and a space lost. In this sense, the Caribbean experience affirmed through Carnival, the local memories of a time and a space across the ocean associated with the Judeo-Christian idea of the coming of a Messiah. Inscribed in those memories was a sense of hope through the possibility of rebellion: a hope always already there in an otherwise European festivity. As Antonio Benítez Rojo observes in *The Repeating Island: The Caribbean and the Postmodern Perspective:* "Of all possible sociocultural practices, the carnival—or any other equivalent festival—is the one that best expresses the strategies that the people of the Caribbean have for speaking at once of themselves and their relation with the world, with history, with tradition, with nature, with God" (*RI,* 294). In the Caribbean, Carnival, as a mode of performing resistance, carries the memory of repression and sacrifice, but also of hope, in a sense of "becoming other." It is a moment in which the memories of another time and space intersect in the cultural imaginary with a will-to-freedom. Such memories, interwoven in complex codified masked representations, like Black Carnival, created equally complex cultural codes in the Caribbean inscribed still today in national cultural expressions, music, dances, religion, and literature.

In the early part of the twentieth century, writers and musician would turn to the performances of Carnaval de los negros, to ñáñigo rituals and to the representation of the diablito dancers as a tangible expression of Africa in the Caribbean: as the testimony of the survival of African beliefs and practices within hispanidad, and as a way to defy political conditions and oppressive neocolonial social values. The dances and gesticulations of the diablitos, for example, became the basic choreographic elements for Amadeo Roldán's work, as well as an important element in Alejo Carpentier's Afro-Cuban ballets,[23] and several of Nicolás Guillén's poems in the thirties. In other words, ñáñigo rituals (Cuba's Supreme Theater), offered Cuban artists and writers a metaphor for cubanía.[24] By the early part of the 1940s, and by the time Alejo Carpentier writes his novel, *El reino de este mundo* (1949), a unique Caribbean discourse had emerged in dialogue with Antillean *Negritude* and with other Latin American inquiries on national and cultural identity.

AFROCUBANÍA AS PERFORMANCE: REPRESENTING THE OTHER/WRITING THE (M)OTHER

With the abolition of slavery came the prohibition of the performance of diablito dances and of Black Carnival. In 1903, the new Republican government of Cuba also banned the practices of the Abakuá secret society, a prohibition that lasted until the twenties. However, ñáñigo music and dances, as well as other Afro-Cuban expressions, made their way into mainstream carnivals, in no way confused or assimilated, but as different beliefs and expressions coexisting at the same time and the same place with European Carnival. In spite of the nonrelenting persecutions suffered by the Abakuá and by other Afro-Cuban groups, Afro-Cuban rituals continued to be performed in the inner sanctum of private homes. It was during this period that the Abakuás also broke the color line that separated them from Euro-Cuban white society, and allowed the formation of white Abakuá chapters.[25] The result was a mode of syncretism in a religious and also cultural context that the term syncretism cannot fully capture, nor can the words "transculturation," "assimilation," or "acculturation" express. Hence, in recent years, a writer from Martinique, Edouard Glissant, has proposed another term, "the Diverse," to explain the realities and intermixing in the Caribbean multiracial, multicultural, and multiethnic societies.[26]

The early years of the twentieth century was also a time when anthropological and ethnological discourses began to "rediscover" Africa, and Fernando Ortiz pioneered the exploration of what he called *afrocubanía*. It was also the period of the Harlem Renaissance in the United States. Ortiz's research and documentation paved the way for other studies on the role of Africa in Caribbean societies and cultures, and in the twenties, Ortiz became the mentor of a group of Cuban intellectuals and artists that called themselves *Grupo minorista* (Minority Group). The group, which came together in 1923, as Frank Janney notes: "was the Cuban version of *avant garde* groups throughout Latin America at this time, and its members were the human conductors for literary ideas from abroad, and the organizers of local manifestations of the modern spirit."[27] The members of the *Minorista* group began to publish in literary supplements, mainly in *Diario de la Marina, Cuba contemporánea* (1913–30), and *Revista de Avance* (1927–30), informing their readers of new aesthetic and philosophical thoughts coming out of Paris. Many of the Minoristas were interested in Afro-Cuban lore, religions, and rituals and several of them attended public ñáñigo ceremonies. Inspired by new ideas on art and society arriving from Europe, there was also a widespread rejection among the Minoristas of conservative, and traditional bourgeoisie values.

The Minoristas were looking for the authentic in the local, and for new ways of expression. Out of this perspective, the movement, and fashion, known as *negrismo*[28] developed in close dialogue with what Ortiz called *afrocubanía*. Negrismo was an intellectual movement different from what years later would be known as *negritude*—a movement by Africans and Afro-Caribbean artists and writers that came together in the thirties in France. The Haitian writer René Depestre would later describe negritude as: "a new consciousness among black people about the historical conditions of black people."[29] The movement's main spokesperson in the Caribbean was Aimé Césaire, who returned to his native Martinique from France in 1940. In Martinique, together with Rene Menil and Suzanne Césaire, Aimé Césaire founded the journal *Tropique* (1941–44), with the purpose of disseminating the ideas of negritude.[30] Different from the Caribbean negritude during the forties, the aesthetic interests of the Minoristas in the twenties and thirties were largely motivated by a philosophy of nationalism and culture in which "blackness" was a literary trope associated with a discourse of resistance, as well as with new forms of expressions associated with cultural authenticity. Speaking with César Leante, Alejo Carpentier recalled those years:

> ignorábamos el surrealismo cuando este [sic] entraba en su mejor fase. Existía, de otra parte, una fuerte corriente nacionalista. El espíritu de Diego Rivera presidía las artes plásticas y todo artista, en general, buscaba "plasmar lo nacional". Fue entonces cuando nació el término *afrocubano,* Caturla y Roldán empezaron a componer música utilizando los elementos negros y aparecieron los primeros trabajos de Fernando Ortiz. Fue, en fin, una toma de conciencia nacional. Con frecuencia asistíamos a los "rompimientos" (ceremonia de iniciación) ñáñigos en Regla. . . . Esta onda nacionalista no era sólo local, era mundial.[31]

> [We were ignorant of Surrealism when it was entering its best phase. There was, on the other hand, a strong nationalist current. Diego Rivera's spirit presided over all plastic arts and every artist, in general, sought to capture that which was national. It was then that the term *afrocubano* was born, Caturla and Roldán began to compose music using black elements and Fernando Ortiz's first texts appeared. It was, at the end, a national awareness. We frequently went to *ñáñigo rompimientos* (initiations) in Regla . . . This nationalist wave was not only regional, it was worldwide.]

In *Historia de la música en Cuba* (1946), Alejo Carpentier recalls the interest of the Minoristas on Afro-Cuban rituals: "se leyeron sus libros [Fernando Ortiz]—el negro se hizo el eje de todas las miradas . . . se iba con unción a los juramentos ñáñigos . . . así nació la tendencia afrocubanista . . . que llevó a lo superficial . . . pero que constituyó un paso necesario" (we read his [Ortiz's] books—blacks became the center of everyone's gaze . . . With unction people went to ñáñigo rituals . . . That is how the Afro-Cuban tendency was born . . . which led to superficiality . . . but it constituted a necessary step).[32] Such interest, related to the birth of avant garde movements in post World War I Europe, was to be embraced in its early stages as a revolutionary movement that questioned, and brought into conflict, traditional Eurocentric values.[33] It also voiced an anti bourgeoisie attitude that followed modernist ideas. The Afro-Cuban movement was not limited to literature. In music, Alejandro García Carturla and Amadeo Roldán, and, in visual art, Mario Carreño, Luís Martínez-Pedro, Víctor Manuel García, were representative of the new expressions. By the forties, the most important representative of Afro-Cuban expression in art was Wifredo Lam, an Afro-Asian-Cuban painter who returned in 1941 to Cuba from Paris,[34] and who Carpentier and Guillén had met and befriended in Madrid in the thirties. The friendship continued in Cuba, where, in 1943, Lam produced his masterpiece, "The Jungle," today at the Metropolitan Museum of Art in New York City.

In the case of Alejo Carpentier, negrismo allowed him to construct a discourse of resistance and, at the same time, to explore his own personal inquiries about cultural differences, through the representation of the "Other" (Afro-Cubans) in Cuban society. Roberto González Echevarría points out that Carpentier's literary trajectory is the trajectory of most Latin American writers, thus, he suggests, "to come to know Carpentier's trajectory is to come to know the problematic of modern Latin American literature."[35] This trajectory is especially poignant in that it represents a certain anxiety of difference at the center of most Afro-Cuban and Afro-Caribbean literary discourses. Such anxiety is one of the elements that makes Carpentier's early works, and especially *The Kingdom of This World,* so important to understand the complexity of ideas and philosophies that came together in the representation of Africa in the Caribbean in the first half of the twentieth century.

The Minoristas, like other Latin American intellectuals of this period, felt a strong attraction for Oswald Spengler's philosophy in *The Decline of the West* (1918). It was this attraction that impulsed in the twenties the development of negrism as a movement. As Jaimes Arnold notes: "G. R. Coulthard traces the beginning of the Afro-Caribbean movement to the Puerto Rican writer Luis Palés Matos," specifically to his 1927 essay, "The Art of the White Race," published in the journal *Paliedro.*[36] In this essay of "strong Spenglerian overtones," written five years after the emergence of the Minorista Group in Cuba, Palés Matos, like José Ortega y Gasset in *La deshumanización del arte* (1925), claimed that European art was no longer in touch with human basic urges.[37] Spengler's ideas on culture and history, and the vitality of primitivism, also informed Palés's writing in the twenties,[38] as it did the Minorista group in Cuba, and Otega y Gasset's writings in *Revista de Occidente.* In "La (sín)tesis de una poesía antillana: Palés y Spengler," Aníbal González Pérez analyzes Palés's *Tún tún de pasa y grifería* and his treatment of Africa in the Antilles, and concludes that Palés's ideas is to found an Antillean poetry created not from preexisting poetic traditions, but one that would be consequent with Antillean realities.[39] Although Spengler's philosophy carries little weight today, in the first decades of the twentieth century it offered revolutionary ideas for

Latin American intellectuals. In *The Decline of the West,* Spengler addresses major world events by answering the questions and paradoxes left by Positivist philosophies.[40] Positivists in Latin America saw the progress of civilization as a "positive" movement, and rejected "primitive" forms and cultures, which they saw as degenerative, and as obstacles to progress. Positivist scientific theories claimed that faith and magic were atavistic vestiges of primitive societies, and that social progress, guided by Science and Reason, had to eliminate such vestiges. For New World Positivist thinkers, Latin America was an underdeveloped area that, in order to progress, had to rid itself of the atavism and fetishism of its indigenous and black populations. In contrast to such dominating theories, Latin American intellectuals found in Spengler's philosophies new venues of thought, and new possibilities to express American realities.[41]

Following Spengler's vision, Fernando Ortiz departed from his early Positivist theories and began to view Cuba's "blackness" in terms of a rich African cultural legacy foundational to the development of *cubanía,* a term that, like *cubanidad,* as Vera Kutzinski notes, by the early part of the twentieth century already was "for all intents and purposes, synonymous to *mestizaje.*"[42] Somewhat Spenglerian in tone were also Leon Frobenius's views on Africa. Frobenius's *Black Decameron* (1910), published in Spanish in Havana in 1925 by *Revista de Occidente,* informed and supported the growing interest on Africa among *afrocubanistas.* Frobenius also published in French, in 1936, *Histoire de la civilization africaine,* a book of greater consequences in that it would offer a growing group of Caribbean intellectuals a different understanding of the African experience in the Caribbean.[43] It was a new understanding outside traditional colonial prejudices toward Africa. Frobenius's idealistic views on Africa, which he associated with primordial nature and genesis, was foundational for the conceptualization of negritude, and promoted the idea, as Jaimes Arnold observes, of Africa in a "symbolic identification of the hero with the sun."[44] Like Spengler, Frobenius also proposed the notion of a cyclical history.

Important for the Minoristas, and especially for Carpentier, was Spengler's idea that European Renaissance and Baroque were the expression of a cultural moment in the history of Western culture in which faith, myth, and history were one. He believed that this period was the most vital and creative cultural moment of Western civilization. Spengler called this moment in Western culture the Faustian moment of culture,[45] a reference to the sixteenth century alchemist, Dr. Faust, as well as to Johann Wolfgang von Goethe's representation of this figure in German folklore in his *Faust* (1790, 1808). For Spengler, who saw the great aesthetic production of the European sixteenth and seventeenth centuries as culturally vigorous, it was not a coincidence that this was the time in which the independent and rebellious thinker Dr. Georg Faust, a contemporary of Martin Luther, lived and died (in 1540). For Spengler, the vigor of this time (which Faust represented for him) continued to live on in German popular imagination: passing to literature first in the 1587 *Faust-Book,* and later in Christophe Marlowe's *The Tragical History of Dr. Faustus.* It was Marlow's version, however, the one that turned Faust into a national German poetic character.[46]

For Latin American writers, and especially for Carpentier, the faith, magic, and primitivism of Afro-Indo-American cultures kept the New World suspended at its Faustian moment of cultural vigor (as in sixteenth- and seventeenth-century Europe), far from the decline Western civilization was experiencing in Europe.[47] In fact, this is what Carpentier recalls his father (a Frenchman) saying (before Spengler's writings), about the reasons why he left Europe in 1902, that he wanted to live in a place new, vigorous, and in the making.[48] For Latin American intellectuals, America was experiencing what Spengler defined as a Faustian desire for infinity (*DW,* 86): thrusting itself to the boundless (*DW,* 220), "longing for liberty." It is out of this Spenglerian view of history that for Carpentier, as he explains in the prologue to *The Kingdom of This World* (1949), "blacks" and "Indians," the historically ignored, oppressed and condemned by an Eurocentric bourgeoisie, constituted America's saving element. For Carpentier, blacks and Indians, precisely for their faith and magic constituted America's Faustian "soul."[49] In the thirties and forties, as González Echeverría points out, Carpentier assumes "the existence of a peculiar Latin American consciousness devoid of self-reflexiveness and inclined to faith; a consciousness that allows Latin America to live immersed in culture and to feel history not as a causal process that can be analyzed rationally and intellectually, but as destiny."[50] Later, Carpentier would embrace other philosophies, like Existentialism and Marxism, but certain elements of his Spenglerian years would remain in his work.

Spengler's philosophy allowed Cuban intellectuals in the twenties to find a national definition that accounted for its many different cultural elements, including "primitive" Afro-Cuban beliefs and rituals. For them, Spengler offered a promising philosophy that justified and praised the atavistic elements of Latin American societies, where faith, myth, and history, in Carpentier's views, were still one, much like Baroque Europe, or Faustian Europe. Based on this Spenglerian notion, Alejo Carpentier later would claim that contemporary Latin America was closer to Baroque Europe than to contemporary Europe. It was an association justified by Spengler's concept of historical "contemporaneity:" the idea that each major civilization goes through the same stages of culture at different times in their historical destiny, so that a moment of culture in one place could be contemporary to another in a different historical time and place. From this perspective, and in spite of the ambiguities perceived today in Spengler's thought, Baroque Europe could be, as Carpentier and other Minoristas conceived it, contemporaneous to twentieth century Latin America. Spengler provided a new theoretical view on nationalism that justified in the twenties and thirties the rejection by Latin American young intellectuals of European values. In an interview for *Casa de las Americas,* Alejo Carpentier claimed that his early interest in Afro-Cuban lore and rituals, and his participation with the Minoristas, was based on a common social and political interest they shared regarding their definitions of cubanía:

> aunque todos los minoristas tuviesen aproximadamente la misma edad (y era yo el más joven de todos ellos), con nosotros se reunía don Fernando Ortiz. A él debimos nuestro interés por el folclor negro de Cuba. Había en ello un afán de recuperación de tradiciones despreciadas por toda una burguesía. Interesarse por lo negro, en aquellos años, equivalía a adoptar una actitud inconformista por tanto revolucionaria. La obra sinfónica de Amadeo Roldán, de Alejandro García Caturla—por su utilización de materiales populares afrocubanos—causaban el escándalo de los puristas.[51]

> [Even though the *Minoristas* were approximately the same age (I was the youngest) Fernando Ortiz met with us. We owed our interest in black folklore to him. There was a desire to rescue the traditions rejected by the bourgeoisie. To be interested in anything related to blacks was equivalent to have an attitude of inconformity, therefore revolutionary. The symphonic work of Amadeo Roldan and Alejandro García Caturla—their utilization of popular Afro-Cuban material—caused scandal among the purists.]

Ortiz's work offered the thematic material the Minoristas needed in order to define and represent cubanía as afrocubanía: a conception different from the Eurocentric models that had negated at an artistic and intellectual level the cultural imprints in Cuban society of its African ancestry. However, while new themes were being adopted, the Minoristas continued to use traditional Spanish forms as literary models, especially those of the Spanish Golden Age. This return to the Spanish Renaissance and to the European Baroque was in itself the recognition of the vigorous (Faustian) creations in Spanish art and literature of which Minorista artists, musicians, and writers in Cuba claimed to be heirs. It also claimed a Faustian moment of cultural vigor in Cuba, not because Cuba was different from Western civilization, but because it was part of that same Western world already declining in Europe, but saved from that decline by Cuba's African legacy: myths, magic, ritual, and faith.

Nicolás Guillén, a Minorista, claimed that his "mulatto poems," like "Llegada" and "Sensemayá," were inspired by Ortiz's research on Afro-Cuba.[52]

At the same time, Guillén introduced Afro-Cuban themes and rhythm in his poems, but utilized Spanish models, like the sonnet, romance, and madrigal.[53] In his mulatto poems (written by a mulatto, but also because they combine African themes and rhythms in Spanish poetic forms), like in Spanish Baroque poetry, Guillén establishes a counterpoint of popular and learned (*cultismo*) voices: the popular being the experience and speech of Cuban blacks, expressed in a learned poetic sensitivity. Guillén turns to an already existing literary discourse in Spanish literature that began in the Spanish Golden Age in the works of Luis de Góngora, Lope de Vega, and Francisco de Quevedo, writers that had represented in their work the speech and images of black Africans in Spanish society. This continuity of Golden Age literature in twentieth century Cuban literature (Spengler's notion of contemporaneity) led Alejo Carpentier to claim that the literary tradition of black poems that started during the Spanish Golden Age, arrived to its most defining form in Nicolás Guillén's Afro-Cuban poetry.[54] In other words, Carpentier's early works, like Guillén's early poems, are related to, and influenced by, Ortiz's research on afrocubanía, but also by Spanish Golden Age writers, who provided Guillén and Carpentier with the organizing and thematic elements of their work.[55] However, these are not the only European models Carpentier used, as Frank Jenney points out. There are also the specters of other European giants in Carpentier's early compositions.

In the twenties and thirties, painters, musicians, and writers interested in afrocubanía found in Pablo Picasso, Igor Stravinsky,[56] and Federico García Lorca,[57] models to follow. Frank Janney suggests that the main direct disciples of these giants in Cuba were, in plastic arts Wifredo Lam, in poetry Nicolás Guillén, and in music Amadeo Roldán.[58] Lam worked on his Afro-Cuban paintings in the forties, and Guillén began to write his early poems in the twenties, at a time when also Roldán was experimenting with Afro-Cuban choreography. Carpentier wrote some of his early Afro-Cuban poems and ballets in the twenties for Amadeo Roldán or Alejando García Caturla to adapt them to the stage as musical performances. In most of these, ñáñigo rituals, dances, and pantomime also informed most of Carpentier's early writings. Janney notes that during this time even though Carpentier participated fully in local movements, he "remained a marginal man," and that Carpentier's primitivism, with strong doses of naturalism, "did not find sympathetic vibrations among Cuban artists,"[59] like Nicolás Guillén and Emilio Bagallas, who were more interested in the flesh and blood Cuban blacks. Carpentier's representation of Afro-Cubans, Janney adds, is that of "an archetypal being, a symbolic force that the author seeks to evoke and achieve."[60] It was, after all, a complex interest entangled with personal pursuits. At this early stage, Carpentier's representations of "blackness" in a Cuban context are literary constructs envisioned as musical performances and entangled with his own ontological search and philosophical ambiguities, as well as with his own identification with Cuba, as Cuban, but also, and at the same time, with Europe.

No other contemporary European writer would have a more profound effect, and lasting impressions in the production of the Minoristas, and in the poetry of negrism, than Federico García Lorca. He traveled to Cuba in 1930 invited by the Society for Hispanic-Cuban Culture.[61] His visit had mutual effects: his influence on Cuban writers and artists, and these on García Lorca's own poetry.[62] His poetic sensibility and his unique use of European avant garde techniques, attracted Cuban artists who then incorporated elements of García Lorca's symbolism and poetic rhythm into their work. This tendency led Ramón Güirao to write in 1938: "nuestra poesía Afrocriolla es un eco de la moda europea; consecuencia más que iniciativa propia" (Our Afro-creole poetry is an echo of European fashion; a consequence more than our own initiative).[63] García Lorca was able to bring together in his *Romancero Gitano* (1927) elements of Primitivism and Expressionism[64] in his symbolic representation of a Spanish cultural life force or "soul," as primitive, sublime, violent, mysterious, and demonic. With this image, informed by, and deeply rooted in southern Spain's popular imaginary and traditions, García Lorca constructed a Spanish poetics of a complex vitality based on his native Andalucía. His work conveyed a commentary on power, authority, and society that appealed to the Minoristas, who saw similar social and political conditions in Cuba. What García Lorca saw in the Andalucian Gypsy,[65] the Minoristas saw in Afro-Cuban rituals and beliefs, especially in the ñáñigos.

Analogous to the symbolism of the Andalucian Gypsy in García Lorca's poetry, the Abakuá was a secret fraternity of African roots unique to Cuba, to its cultural manifestations, and known, not only for their elaborate theatrical rituals, but also for their resistance to authority, and their codified and enigmatic ritual secrets. Nicolás Guillén's poem "Velorio de Papá Montero" (*Songoro Cosongo,* 1931), for example, is a ballad, following García Lorca's model, to a legendary ñáñigo cultural hero. Carpentier's poems "Liturgia," "Manita en el suelo" (the nickname of a ñáñigo cultural hero), "Blue," "Juego santo," are also examples of ñáñigo themes.[66] The choice, at this time, for using the ñáñigo as representative of *afrocubanía,* but in the looking glass of García Lorca's poetry, provides an example of what Güirao would call an "improper mold," a "rhetorical firmament" taken from the "Gypsy neighborhood of Granada." At the same time, the depth and complexity of García Lorca's work provided new models and new ways of expressing the preoccupations of Cuban writers, especially on the question of culture, nation, and aesthetics.

By the thirties, there had emerged a different poetic sensibility that Ramón Güirao now explains from a different perspective: "fraguada en moldes impropios bajo un firmamento retórico de lunas y panderos de cobre repujados por los caldeteros del barrio gitano de Granada, herido de relucientes aceros de Albacete, entraña ya un acercamiento sincero" [constructed with improper molds under a rhetorical sky of moons and copper tambourines from the Gypsy neighborhood of Granada, wounded by shiny daggers from the Albacete, (Cuban negrism poetry) already intimates an honest approximation].[67] However, Guirao would soon also note that, by 1938: "la poesía afronegrista, esto es, de tema negro, es la más genuina manifestación de nuestra sensibilidad insular" [Afro-Cuban poetry, that is, of black themes, is the most genuine manifestation of our insular sensibility].[68] Yet, as Guirao also points out, "estas incursiones a las ricas vetas de la cantera negra no han alterado el destino social del hombre negro" [these incursions into the rich veins of the black quarry, have not altered the social destiny of the black man].[69] Like the Andalucian Gypsy for García Lorca, Afro-Cubans and "blackness" in Cuba became a literary trope for writers like Carpentier, as it was for Palés Matos in Puerto Rico:[70] an artistic construct associated with social and political resistance, with aesthetic expression, a search for the "proper," cultural rhythms, the local, the cultural authentic, as well as a new way of expressing the Caribbean experience as a counterpoint of Africa and Europe. It was also, however, a general desire to account for the Other, the African other, of intrinsic importance in the development of the culture, and yet too often negated in the discourses on nation, in part because, as Benigno Trigo has shown in *Subject in Crisis* in a Puerto Rican context, Caribbean mixed societies were still too often associated with pathological images of sickness.[71] It could be argued that, in response to such negative images inspired by the impingement still in the twentieth century of Positivist ideas, the early explorations and manifestations of negrismo served to raise consciousness among Caribbean intellectuals. It allowed them to encounter the dynamic forces of a "subjugated knowledge" different from colonial prejudice about the African experience in America. This awareness brought into question the still prevalent social and political Eurocentric myth of a white-creole Hispanic Caribbean.

II

For Cuban intellectuals, writers, and artists, afrocubanía became a codified performing act of resistance, as well as a search for a Faustian vigor in the national "soul."[72] Alejo Carpentier's early Afro-Cuban poems and ballets were written as musicals representations, and Nicolás Guillén's ritual poems, like "Sensemayá," reconstructed and readapted the diablito performances of "Día de Reyes" to a new historical context. Ortiz pointed out, in 1935, that Guillén's "mulatto poems" "come from the language of magic, whose semantic quality is assumed only in their performative invocation."[73] In spite of the differences between Carpentier and Guillén, their poems conjure in different degrees a Spenglerian notion of what Ortiz claimed to be representative of mulatto poetry: "the mystery of the jungle," and "a ritual of conjuration."[74] Guillén's "Sensemayá," in *West Indies, Ldt* (1934), captures the same sense of exorcism of evil spirits represented in the dance of killing the snake performed in the streets of colonial Havana, and later documented by Fernando Ortiz in "La antigua fiesta afrocubana de 'Día de Reyes.'"[75] It is also the same dance that Carpentier recreates in *La Rebambaramba* (1927), a text which, according to Carpentier, "me fue sugerido por la contemplación de un grabado de Miathe, representando las comparsas del "Día de Reyes" [came to me while contemplating one of Miathe's engravings representing the Carnival processions of "Día de Reyes"].[76] This is also the same dance Carpentier revisits in *Concierto barroco* (1974) (Baroque Concert): a dance staged during carnival, but in Italy, the origin of the saturnalias that served as model for the festivities of "Día de Reyes."[77] Carpentier's fascination with Black Carnival in colonial Havana can be perceived in different modalities through out his work, specially in its universal archetype of a "cyclical return" inscribed in the annual death and revival of the snake god.[78] For Ortiz, this dance, as it was performed in Cuba, was a form of collective ritual purification: "expulsión de los diablos relacionados aquí con el Día de Reyes [expulsion of devils associated here with "Día de Reyes"].[79] Nicolás Guillén appropriates the same dance in his poem "Sensemayá," in order to represent with a fresh look the same African ancestral ritual as it was performed in colonial Cuba, but translated now to a new reality, in a different historical time (twentieth century Havana), as an artistic exorcism of a new form of "demonic" entity: foreign capitalists in the Caribbean. Carpentier also utilized the same ritual of killing the snake in his Afro-Cuban ballet, *El milagro de Anaquillé,* in which Carpentier explains that he used "sin modificación alguna, el ritual coreográfico de las ceremonias de iniciación afrocubanas" [with no changes, the choreographic ritual of the Afro-Cuban ceremonies of initiation].[80] In Carpentier's text, ñáñigo dancers exorcise the presence (evil spirit), and capitalist intentions of a North American investor: a photographer that sees the possibility of making a profit from the exoticism of Afro-Cuban sugar cane cutters. Carpentier's ñáñigos represent an ancestral African life force in an Afro-Cuban cultural landscape of faith and magic able to defeat and expulse contemporary demons. It is this same poetic exorcism and defiance against North American intruders in the Antilles that Luis Palés Matos incorporates in his poem, written before 1931, "Mulata Antilla" in *Tun tún de pasa y grifería:* "Imperio tuyo / el plátano y el coco, / Que apuntan su dorada artillería / Al barco transeúnte que nos deja/ Su rubio contrabando de turistas" [Your empire / banana and coconut / Your golden artillery takes aim / at the passing ship, that leaves us its contraband of tourists].[81] Here, the dance of the woman Antillean mulatto-island is a *plena,* a popular Puerto Rican dance of African rhythm, and the mulatto-woman-island dancer directs her sensual "weapons" against the tourists that invade the island.

In another one of his early works, *La Rebambaramba* (1927), Carpentier, like Guillén, turns to Spanish Golden Age literary models, this time the "comedia de enredos" (comedy of errors) that came to be associated in Cuba with "teatro buffo." *La Rebambaramba* is performed as an Afro-Cuban ballet, in a collage of Cuban folkloric characters and themes, including the dance of killing the snake, and the ñáñigo diablito dancers of "Día de Reyes." Carpentier's interest in ñáñigo rituals as theatrical performances can be found also in his poem "Liturgia"(Liturgy), also published in 1927, and also adapted for the stage. "Liturgia" represents the secret ñáñigo ritual that takes place in the sacred room, or *Cuarto Fambá.* The action is centered on the figure of the legendary ñáñigo hero, Papá Montero, to whom Guillén also pays homage in his poem "Velorio de Papá Montero" (*Sóngoro Cosongo,* 1931).[82] Carpentier's poem represents, as musical performance, the initiation ritual of ten new fraternity brothers, or *ekobios (ecobios),* to an Afro-Cuban ñáñigo potencia, or Abakuá chapter. The poem begins with the ceremonial drums: the *tumbas:* African-Cuban ritual "drums" known as *tumba* or *tumbadora.*[83] In Carpentier's representation of the ñáñigo ritual, the drums open (*rompen*) the ceremony known as *rompimiento:*

La potencia rompió.	The ritual began
¡Yamba-O!	Yamba-O!
Retumban las tumbas. . . .	The drums drum . . . .
El juego firmó	The ñáñigo ritual signed
-¡Yamba-O!-	-Yamba-O!
con yeso amarillo	with yellow chalk
en el Cuarto Famba.	In the Famba (sacred) room.
. . .	. . .
El gallo murió	The rooster died

The diablitos begin to dance, jumping sideways like crabs (from Regla): "¡Aé, aé!/ Salió el diablito" (The diablito came out).[84] To this dance follows the ritual sacrifice of the goat: "Chivo lo rompe,/ chivo pagó" (Goat breaks it, goat paid for it).[85] The ceremony continues and, at this point, it is the rhythm itself, the beat of the drum, like in the street performances of "Día de Reyes," that becomes the center of the poem, with the suggested implicit presence of the snake, known in Cuba as *majá:* a sacred guardian animal, like the alligator, for the Abakuá: "¡Aé!/ ¡Los muertos llaman!/ ¡'cucha el majá'!/. . ./ timbal de ñangó./ Rumba y tumba" (The dead are

calling!/ hear the snake!/ . . ./ ñáñigo drums./ Rumba and drums).[86] Papá
Montero is playing the marimba and Arencibia the "bongó." Food is offered
to the deities, and, as in Willie Chirino's song, "Mr. Don't Eat the Banana,"
everyone is reminded not to eat the consecrated food:

Papá Montero	Papa Montero
marimbulero,	marimba player
Arencibia	Arencibia
bongosero.	Bongo player
Quien se robe comida	Whoever steals food
palo tendrá. . . .	will be punished

The ceremony comes to an end. The summoned spirits have eaten the sacred food offered to them: "¡Aé, aé!/ Salió el diablito,/ los muertos comieron"
(The diablito left/ the spirits of the dead ate).[87] The ceremony that lasts all
night ends at dawn.[88] The spirits leave, and a rooster, an animal associated
with the Afro-Cuban (Yoruba/Lucumí) orisha, Shango, a solar deity of fire,
thunder, lightning, and drums (also associated with change) announces the
new day. Shango is not in any way related to the Abakuá belief system of
ritual, but, as Lydia Cabrera explains, many Abakuá ecobios are sons of
Shango.[89] In "Liturgia," a rooster announces the beginning of a new day,
which is metaphorically the entrance to a new reality brought about by the
magic of the ritual. At the end, the ten new ecobios are re-born to a new
day, that is, to a new existence; and, through the magic of the ritual, they
cease to be who they were, and they enter the realm of a new reality as consecrated Abakuá *moninas:* "La luna se va . . . / . . ./ El diablito se fue . . . /
¡Aé, aé!/ . . ./ ¡Diez nuevos ecobios/ bendice Eribo!" (The moon is leav-
ing/ . . ./ The diablito left . . . / Aé, aé!/ . . ./ Ten new fraternity brothers/
blesses Eribo).[90] The poems ends: "El gallo cantó" (The rooster sang).[91]

Like other Minoristas, Carpentier's interest in Afro-Cuban rituals was
directly tied to the discovery and articulation of a Cuban cultural ethos best
represented through the aesthetic forms offered by Afro-Cuban rituals and
religious symbols and codes. The ñáñigos offered the ancestral vigor of
primitive faith, together with myths, history, ritual, as well as the mystery
of a sworn brotherhood, violence, blood, initiation, sacrifice, and a complex institutional structure of peculiar social power similar to García Lorca's
poetics. Like the Gypsy in Spain, the ñáñigo in Cuba also was a target of
social prejudice. Popularly disseminated legends told of Abakuá ceremonies of initiation as acts of violent homicides, and of violent quarrels between chapters or *potencias.* This was the popular image of the ñáñigos as
criminals that had led Ortiz to write *Hampa afrocubana. Los negros brujos,* in 1906. It was also the image Carpentier represented in his first novel
¡Ecué-Yamba-O!, a Naturalist novel constructed following the model of

Emil Zola's novels about a young rural Afro-Cuban creole,[92] Menegildo Cué, whose last name establishes a phonetic play with the name of the Abakuá secret drum, *Ekué,* the same drum Carpentier represents in "Liturgia," and in "Juego santo." In "Liturgia," however, perhaps still unsure of the term, Carpentier refers to it as *ecuá* and *acué.* In *¡Ecué-Yamba-O!,* a title taken also from ñáñigo liturgy, Menegildo Cué goes to Havana where he is initiated to one of the Abakuá chapters. Soon after, he is killed during a violent assault by another ñáñigo potencia. His wife, who was expecting his child, is forced to leave the city and goes to her husband's family in the country to have the baby. Following the same notion of a deterministic eternal return in which Zola's characters are caught, the baby is named Menegildo Cué like his father. As Roberto González Echeverría points out, in *¡Ecué-Yamba-O!,* like in Carpentier's short story "Histoire de lunes" (Moon stories), Carpentier "attempts to situate the narrative focus or source within the unreachable African world of beliefs to which his own consciousness has no access."[93] He imitated Zola's naturalism, Carpentier tells Ramón Chao: "Zola gozaba de un prestigio inimaginable en América Latina. Ya sabes cómo trabajaba Zola. . . . Yo seguí en *Ecué-Yamba-O* exactamente el mismo proceso" (Zola enjoyed an unimaginable prestige in Latin America. You already know how Zola worked . . . I followed exactly the same process in *Ecué-Yamba-O.*)[94] And he concludes that *Ecué-Yamba-O:* "es un intento fallido . . . Pero no todo es deplorable en ella. Salvo de la hecatombe los capítulos dedicados al "rompimiento" ñáñigo" (is a failed attempt . . . But, not all is deplorable in the novel. I saved from the hecatomb the chapters dedicated to the rompimiento (initiation) ñáñigo.)[95] At the same time, Carpentier proposes in his novel a cyclical ritual structure of end and beginning that seems to negate historical time in order to represent ritual performance. In *¡Ecué Yamba-O!* Carpentier also experiments with expressionism and primitivism, like García Lorca, and with the same play of allegories and ritual forms he had used in "Liturgia," and "Juego santo." Carpentier claims to have written the novel in jail, and that he later reworked it and published it in Paris in 1933:

Era una época caracterizada por un gran interés hacia el folklore afrocubano, recién descubierto por los intelectuales de mi generación. Los personajes eran negros de la clase rural de entonces. Debo advertir que crecí en el campo de Cuba . . . que más tarde, muy interesado por las prácticas de la santería y del ñañiguismo, asistí a innumerables ceremonias rituales. Pues bien, al cabo de veinte años de investigaciones acerca de las realidades sincréticas de Cuba, me di cuenta de que todo lo hondo, lo verdadero del mundo que había pretendido pintar en mi novela, había permanecido fuera del alcance de mi observación. Por ejemplo, el animismo del negro campesino; las relaciones del negro con el bosque; ciertas prácticas iniciáticas que me habían sido disimuladas por los oficiantes con una desconcertante habilidad.[96]

[It was a period characterized by a strong interest in Afro-Cuban folklore—
recently discovered by the intellectuals of my generation. The characters were
rural blacks of that period. I must note that I grew up in the Cuban country side
. . . and that later, interested in *santería* and *ñáñiguismo,* I went to numerous ritual ceremonies. Well, at the end of twenty years of research on the syncretism
in Cuba, I realized that the depth, the reality of the world I pretended to paint in
my novel, had remained beyond the reach of my observation. For example, the
relationship of the black with the forest, certain practices of initiation that were
concealed from me by priests with a disconcerting skill.]

It is significant to note that for Capentier the only moment worth saving
in *!Ecué Yamba-O!* is the description of the Afro-Cuban ritual that had attracted him and other Minoritas for years. While reworking his manuscript
for publication in Europe, Carpentier wrote on March 13, 1931, from Paris,
to Alejandro García Caturla, then in Havana, asking his friend for details
on a ñáñigo wake that Carpentier wanted to incorporate to the novel he was
going to give the title of *El chivo que rompió un tambor* [The goat that
broke a drum]:

> Hace algún tiempo me contaste que habías asistido a un *velorio de ñáñigos.* Ya
> tengo una versión de esos *velorios,* la que no creo exacta, y necesito *forzosa-
> mente* algunos datos acerca de ello para el capítulo final de mi novela *El chivo
> que rompió un tambor* que se editará dentro de muy poco. No tengo la preten-
> sión, desde luego, de describir una ceremonia que no he visto, pero . . . quisiera
> que en el diálogo hubiera alguna mención de hechos exactos. . . .
>   ya sabes que en La Habana, si bien se ven a menudo fiestas ñáñigas y jura-
> mentos, el *velorio* resulta casi imposible de presenciar.[97]

[A while back you told me that you had gone to a ñáñigo wake. I already have
a version of those wakes, but I don't have the correct details and absolutely need
exact information about them for the last chapter of my novel, The Goat that
Broke the Drum, that will be published soon. I don't pretend, of course, to describe a ceremony I have not seen, but I would like for the dialogue to include
some facts. . . .
     you already know that in Havana ñáñigo celebrations and ceremonies are
common, but wakes are almost impossible to witness.]

Carpentier described the secret ñáñigo initiation known as rompimiento
(break, initiation), the same he represented in "Liturgia," and, although he
later admitted to having failed in his representation of Afro-Cubans because he did not understand the religious bases for the culture, he believed
that his portrayal of an Abakuá initiation was in itself a valuable document:
a testimony of living, vigorous, and magical cultural archives in Cuban society. At the same time, Carpentier's interests in the experimentation of dif-

ferent forms of expression was associated with the articulation of a sociopolitical concern most Minoristas shared: a concern that was especially important to him in his quest to define himself as Cuban. At the same time, Carpentier also voiced the paradoxes created in Latin America by Spengler's philosophy, which offered the illusion of a cultural youth and vigor for American societies, when, in fact, in the Caribbean, the "primitivism" in which blacks lived was the result of years of economic oppression and social marginality. As Frank Janney observes:

> Many of the Afro-Antillean writers vacillate between the ideal of undiluted primitivism and negritude (as in Nicolás Guillén's "Llegada" for example) and the often bitter knowledge of the corruption of that ideal by the forces of poverty and oppression or by the Black's own duplicity (as in Palés' "Preludio en Boricua"). In the case of Palés and Guillén, the conflict is resolved with humor and the creation of semi-comic figures, the best example of which is "El Duque de la Mermelada" of Palés. In Carpentier the conflict is manifested in a tense naturalism, which approaches the grotesque.[98]

Carpentier experimented with Expressionism, a movement that attracted him in the twenties, and that he uses in *El milagro de Anaquillé* (1927). He also experimented with the grotesque and with what the Spanish writer Valle-Inclán defined at the turn of the twentieth century as *esperpentos*.[99] Utilizing these literary techniques, and written to be a musical performance, in *El milagro de Anaquillé* Carpentier represents an allegorical vision of the vigorous spirit and magic faith of Afro-Cubans, especially the ñáñigos, whose faith in magic allows them to resist and expel foreign exploitation. As in Guillén's "Sensemayá," the magic force of an Abakuá ritual dance, whose magic is based on faith, like the magic of the *anaquillé* doll, is the power that stops a North American investor. Ñáñigo magic, like the magic of the anaquillé dolls paraded on the streets on "Día de Reyes," comes to the aid of the sugar cane workers whose ritual dance (a ñáñigo ritual dance like those of 'Día de Reyes'), awakens the anaquillé figure of the *Jimaguas:* the powerful Afro-Cuban twins, or *Ibeyes*.[100] Anaquillé, Ortiz explains:

> era el nombre que recibían los muñecos paseados en La Habana el Día de Reyes. Era un ídolo o figura propia de los ritos africanos, que al extremo de un palo llevaban los negros bailadores en algunas de las danzas ceremoniales o religiosas.
> Parece posible encontrar el origen del anaquillé allá en África en las efigies que los negros del Calabar llevan a la fiesta bienal de la expulsión de los diablos, cuyos muñecos se llaman *Nabikém*. En el Dahomey son llevados a festividades análogas.[101]

[was the name given to dolls taken to the street in Havana on "Día de Reyes." It was an idol or figure proper of African rituals that black dancers carried at the end of a pole in some of the ceremonial and religious dances.

It seems possible to find the origin of the anaquillé in Africa in the effigies Calabar blacks take to the biannual celebrations to expulse the devils, whose dolls are called *Nabikém*. In Dahomey they are taken to similar festivities.]

In *El milagro de Anaquillé,* Carpentier inverts the figure of evil, traditionally envisioned in Western literature in association with blacks and Indians, in order to cast the white North American foreigner as demonic. In other words, in Carpentier's rendition of afrocubanía, what saves Cuba (and the Caribbean), in *El milagro de Anaquillé,* is Cuba's African legacy. In this text, Carpentier envisions the poorest people in Cuba, the black cane cutters, immune to the influences of foreign capitalism.[102] Such immunity for Carpentier is due to a cultural Faustian force (Afro-Cuban magic and faith) that resists foreign domination and exploitation.[103] His most important argument in this text is his praise of a primitive, but dynamic, Afro-Cuba, whose moral principles and ethics are based on faith and on a belief in magic the writer does not share, but which he uses to express his antibourgeoisie project of resistance through cultural difference. At the same time, Carpentier's *El misterio de anaquillé* articulates a clear political platform perhaps informed by his limited understanding at that moment of Spengler's philosophy; an understanding that soon would be intersected by his attraction to Superrealism. In 1928, writing from Havana to Alejandro García Caturla, in Remedios, Cuba, Carpentier explains that attraction in a letter in which he praises Miguel Angel Asturias as a great literary critic and a progressive spirit; and shows his excitement at the arrival in Havana of Robert Desnoes whom he describes as one of the leaders of the New French Superrealist Movement:

Desde el año 20 el *Superrealismo* ha tomado una importancia formidable. En pintura, sobre todo, su influencia se extiende desde España hasta Polonia. No hay actualmente un pintor joven en Europa, que no sea, hasta cierto punto, *superrealista.* (Lee acerca de esto un maravilloso libro de Franz Ron -*Revista de Occidente* lo editó—titulado *Realismo mágico: post-expresionismo).* . . . Desnos . . . profesa un desprecio profundo por todo lo que no sea juvenil, espontáneo, instintivo.[104]

[Since 1920, Superrealism has gained a formidable importance. In painting, especially, its influence goes from Spain to Poland. Presently, there isn't a single painter in Europe that is not, to certain extent, a Superrealist. (About this you can read a marvelous book by Franz Ron—*Revista de Occidente* published it— titled *Magic Realism: Post-Expressionism).* . . . Desnoes . . . professes a profound dislike for everything that is not youthful, spontaneous, instinctive.]

A year later, Desnos helped Carpentier escape from Cuba, giving him his own passport.[105] In Paris, he introduced Carpentier to André Bretón, who immediately invited Carpentier to collaborate in the *Revolution Sur-réaliste.*[106] Carpentier embraced surrealism[107] and made contacts that would be important for his work in the forties, especially in relationship to the work of Aimé Césaire and Wifredo Lam. Carpentier became a strong supporter of Lam and his work.[108] In 1948, in his article "Lo real maravilloso de América" (Marvelous realism in America), published in the Venezuelan paper, *El nacional,* Carpentier evokes the surrealist celebration of the marvelous when he states, as he also does in the prologue to the novel, when comparing the paintings of André Masson and Wifredo Lam, that in Lam's work one finds "the magic of tropical vegetation, the profuse creation of our nature with all its metamorphosis and symbiosis."[109] Surrealism made a profound impact in Caribbean writers. As Lowery Stokes Sims notes: "Lilyan Kestewat has documented the important influence . . . Surrealist journals and tracts on colonization had on individuals from colonized societies studying in Paris in the 1930s such as the Martinique poet Aimé Césaire, the Senegalese poet Leópold Senghor, and the Haitian writer Leon Damas."[110] Other Latin American writers and artists like Carpentier and Lam were no exception. However, Carpentier later became frustrated with surrealism and rejected the movement, perhaps more for reasons of internal politics, coerced by Desnoes, and by the internal fragmentation of the movement.[111] He claimed that surrealism was an artificial and futile exercise, and that he had tried in vain to explain to Breton that the surreal was an every day "reality" in America:

me pareció una tarea vana mi esfuerzo surrealista. . . . Tuve una reacción contraria. Sentí ardientemente el deseo de expresar el mundo americano. Aún no sabía cómo . . . pero el surrealismo sí significó mucho para mí. Me enseñó a ver texturas, aspectos de la vida americana que no había advertido, envueltos como estábamos en la ola de nativismo traída por Guiraldes, Gallegos y José Eustasio Rivera. Comprendí que detrás de ese nativismo había algo más: lo que llamo los contextos: contexto telúrico y contexto épico-político: el que halle la relación entre ambos escribirá la novela americana.[112]

[my efforts on Surrealism seemed to me a worthless task. . . . I had an opposite reaction. I strongly felt the desire to express the American world. I still did not know how . . . but Surrealism did mean a lot for me. It taught me to see textures, aspects of the American life that I had not perceived, involved as we were in the wave of nativism brought by Güiraldes, Gallegos, and José Eustasio Rivera. I understood that behind that nativism there was something else: what I call the contexts: telluric context and epic-political context: whoever finds those contexts will be the one who writes the American novel.]

In spite of Carpentier's open rejection of the artificiality he claimed to have seen in surrealism, a reaction that may have been more rhetorical than factual, as González Echevarría points out,[113] this period was an important moment in the formation of Carpentier's aesthetic concepts and literary style. He tells Ramón Chao:

> Esa experiencia me fue muy útil. En buen cubano popular diría que me encendió la chispa. Vi cómo mucha gente andaba buscando lo maravilloso en lo cotidiano, fabricándolo . . . en tanto que nosotros teníamos lo fortuito, lo insospechado, lo insólito, lo maravilloso latinoamericano en estado bruto, al alcance de la mano, listo para ser usado en arte, en literatura.[114]

> [That experience was very useful. In good popular Cuban I would say that was a sparkle. I saw how many people looked for the marvelous in daily life, constructing it . . . while we had the fortuitous, the unexpected, the impossible, the Latin American marvelous in its primal form, at close reach, ready to be used in art, in literature.]

Carpentier's concept of a 'marvelous reality' with which he would define America, was a formulation informed in part by his encounter with surrealism, with Ron's concept of "Magic Realism" in plastic arts, and with Spengler's philosophy. In *El milagro de anaquillé,* magic, metaphorically at least, has an ideological importance that Carpentier associates with Spengler's notion of a Faustian cultural force. However, it would not be until 1943, when he travels to Haiti accompanying the actor Louis Jauvet, that Carpentier personally encounters the force of magic acting on history that he represented before as artifice. This trip, as he later observed, inspired him to write his second novel, *The Kingdom of This World,*[115] a text that tried to bring together the contexts he considered to be a requirement for the American novel: the telluric context and the historic-epic context. In a characteristic Carpentierian play with history and fiction, he turned his gaze to the documentation he had gathered for *La historia de la música en Cuba* (1946). And, following the same systematic and rigorous documentation he carried out for that project, Carpentier constructed a fictional text made of other texts,[116] in tightly woven symmetries and counterpoints. In *The Kingdom of This World,* Carpentier would construct a baroque composition, as he then understood the term, as an expression of a Faustian America: a text that would bring together in a counterpoint of history and fiction Caribbean political and telluric contexts.[117]

Carpentier's findings for *La historia de la música en Cuba,* observes Roberto González Echeverría, channeled "Carpentier's fiction into a new course," and "furnish[ed] Carpentier with a new working method, which consists of minute historical investigation and creation from within, a tradition that the author remakes himself with the aid of texts of different sorts."[118] During the forties, as González Echeverría also points out, "Capentier's artistic enterprise," "became a search for origins, the recovery of history and tradition, the foundation of an autonomous American consciousness serving as the basis for a literature faithful to the New World."[119] Negritude was taking its course. There was a new and different awareness pertaining Africa largely based on Leon Frobenius's views of the continent and its people. Aimé Césaire began to publish *Tropique* (1941–45), a journal laden with Spenglerian and Frobenian notions of Africa adapted to a Caribbean context; and Carpentier by the fifties concluded that he had missed, in his previous work, "the relationship of the black with the forest,"[120] as well as the meanings of rituals and the complexities of faith. As much informed by Frobenius as by Spengler, in 1944, in an article on Wifredo Lam's work, Carpentier describes Lam's paintings as "a world of primitive myths," that were Cuban myths, and also Antillean; in which Lam makes an attempt (like Aimé Césaire), to distinguish between "authentic and appropriated primitivism."[121] In general, the forties was a very important period for Carpentier, as well as for Cuban literary circles. The journal *Orígenes* (Origins) (1944–56), which took the place of *Revista Avance,* and in which Carpentier would publish some of his works,[122] was founded in 1944 under the direction of José Lezama Lima. The *origenistas,* and especially Lezama Lima, were interested in the exploration of poetry as a space of poetic knowledge at the threshold of cubanía: a sense of poetic "origins" or primordial cultural space. For the origenistas, myth offered such poetic knowledge, as a foundational space; and, like most of the afrocubanistas, they also had a national and cultural agenda.

The thirties had been important years of learning for Carpentier. Before his trip to Haiti, he accompanied Nicolás Guillén and Juan Marinello, in 1937, to a Spain torn by civil war, to attend an antifascist conference in Madrid.[123] His roommate at this time happened to be George Lukács,[124] whose still-embryonic interest on the theory of the novel and his readings on Hegel, and on Social Realism, probably was a topic of conversation between the two young writers. In 1924, Carpentier had been editor of *Carteles,* and a decade later he became editor of the short lived journal *Imán,*[125] an experience that put him in close contact with the French poet Léon Paul Fargue, the literary advisor of *Imán,* who, according to Carpentier, had been his true teacher in matters of style.[126] He also saw the horrors of World War II at a distance, and came in contact with European philosophies both during the years he lived in France, and later in Cuba mainly through *Revista de Occidente,* whose editor, Ortega y Gasset, had being "profoundly influenced by Spengler."[127] Carpentier notes that during this period he systematically read everything he could find about the history of America,[128] because his desire was to "expresar el mundo americano" (express the American world) and to become a "two-way translator of exemplary European techniques and American 'essences.'"[129] For Carpentier, and his self-imposed mission, Fernando Ortiz continued to be an important source of information about the Cuba Carpentier wanted to express. Furthermore, Ortiz's research, now far from Lombroso's Positivism, followed in the steps of José Martí's exhortations in "Nuestra América" [Our America], toward Martí's idea that Americans must learn first about America, because it is more useful than learning only about Europe. Such exhortation coincided with, and perhaps informed, Carpentier's sense of mission as a Latin American writer. José Martí, the great apostle of Cuban independence, exhorted Latin American men of letters to stop imitating Europe and to seek what was authentically American: hence, to learn about the history of pre-Hispanic civilizations and New World myths.[130] In the Caribbean, where such pre-Hispanic inhabitants had been mostly decimated, such authenticity was found in African customs, myths, and the religious beliefs of a creole vernacular culture.

Ortiz's research intimated the concept of afrocubanía as a counterpoint of differences. His notion of afrocubanía also provided for Carpentier the idea of the universal in the local,[131] an important notion for Carpentier's understanding of human beings and their role in the historical process. Carpentier explains: "siempre pensé que el escritor latinoamericano—sin dejar de ser universal por ello—debía de expresar su mundo, mundo tanto más interesante por cuanto es Nuevo, se encuentra poblado de sorpresas, ofrece elementos difíciles de tratar porque aún no han sido explorados por la literatura" [I always thought that the Latin American writer—without having to stop being universal—should express his/her world, a world of greater interest because it is New, full of surprises, that offers elements that are difficult to address because they have not been explored yet by literature].[132] Following Martí's exhortations to Americans, Ortiz would come to claim that: "without blacks, Cuba would not be Cuba."[133] Ortiz's assertion coincided with Carpentier's own findings: that Cuban music was the offspring of Africa and Europe, and that, until the eighteenth century, Cuban music was composed of African rhythm and Spanish melody.[134] Cuban music was a hybrid creation, a mulatto creation like Guillén's poems, and, as Carpentier found out in his research, African cultures were foundational in the development of Cuban vernacular culture and national identity.[135]

Carpentier concluded that the Latin American world, "so full of mysteries,[136] so full of things still without names," had to be approached by a novelist with vast culture and knowledge.[137] He was that novelist, Carpentier thought. In that role, his project took him to the task of naming an America still "not properly named," to "revelar realidades aún inénitas" [reveal realities still unedited],[138] and to bring together, in one symphonic verbal performance, the telluric and epic-historical contexts in America. Embracing Spengler's notion of a Faustian baroque, Carpentier gazed at his present historical moment in Latin America and became convinced that he lived in a cultural moment contemporaneous to Europe's Faustian period of great artistic production. Spengler's notion of a historical cultural compatibility across time justified Carpentier's claim that the baroque was the proper[139] and authentic aesthetic expression of an also Faustian America; and he thus associated himself as well as other artists of his time with the great masters of the European baroque, and entered a dialogue with the Spanish Golden Age.

Following Ortiz's claim in *El huracán su mitología y sus símbolos* (1947) that the baroque is always already present in pre-Columbian America, Carpentier also claimed, like Ortiz, that America, "era barroca mucho antes de la Conquista: todo el arte maya, el arte mixteca o el Templo de Mitla— ejemplo perfecto- son expresión del espíritu barroco" (was Baroque much before the Conquest: the art of the Maya, of the Mixtec or the Temple of Mitla —a perfect example—are expressions of a Baroque spirit).[140] Benítez Rojo suggests that Carpentier's baroque "is unique in that it assumes its own formal marginality while being at the same time a course; it is the textual representation of the labyrinth that surrounds and leads to the fugitive center of his own Caribbean Otherness" (*RI* 183). At the same time, César Leante proposes that Carpentier is the center of an *engaño* (deceit). Such deceit is the result, he says, of "una admiración desorbitada y un deslumbramiento: . . . Desde *El reino de este mundo* el brillante lenguaje que atrae a la novelística latinoamericana ocasiona un impacto inquietante. Se define como barroca" (an exaggerated and dazzling admiration: . . . Since *The Kingdom of This World* the brilliant language that attracts the Latin American novelist causes an unsettling impact. It is defined as Baroque).[141] Leante adds: "A mi entender, Carpentier sucumbe a una tentación al aceptar el sello de barroquismo con que se acuñan sus libros y todavía más al declarar él mismo que la realidad americana es barroca . . . No es éste el sentido que originalmente Carpentier dio al adjetivo. (In my understanding, Carpentier fell to a temptation when he accepted the stamp of baroque coined for his books and even more when he declared that American reality is baroque . . . That is not the meaning Carpentier originally gave to the adjective).[142] Like Leante, but following a strict definition of baroque art, Alejandro Alonso also questions Carpentier's definition of the baroque:

cuando Carpentier utiliza la palabra barroco debemos entender que no se trata del estilo artístico europeo que domino el siglo 17 y fue importado a América por España, sino que, por analogía con algunas de sus características, toma prestado el término para significar otra cosa, una cierta vitalidad, exuberancia, movilidad, dinamismo, que constituía un rasgo común hispanoamericano o latinoamericano."[143]

[when Carpentier uses the word baroque, we must understand that it is not the European artistic style that dominated the seventeenth century and was imported to America by Spain, but, by an analogy with some of its characteristics, he borrows the term to signify something else, a certain vitality, exuberance, mobility, dynamism, that would constitute a common Spanish American or Latin American quality.]

To understand Carpentier's definition of an American baroque it is necessary also to question Carpentier's understanding of Spengler's philosophy. According to Spengler, the best representative artistic form of the Faustian moment in Western culture is the structure of counterpoint, since, as Spengler claims: "contrapuntal music is a twin sister of the Baroque" (*DW*, 422). Antonio Benítez points out that in a counterpoint, "the signifier is never 'one' since what we listen to (we read) is the always incomplete superimposition of voices that continue on ad infinitum" (*RI*, 175). Hence, it becomes significant that, in order to express America, Carpentier chooses the structure of counterpoint, as did Ortiz, as the artistic structural form with which to express a certain Faustian cultural vigor that, for Carpentier, characterizes the Caribbean and its passionate desire for the "Infinite." For Carpentier, this cultural vigor is the expression of a historical, political, and aesthetic "longing for liberty" (free expressions in art), most visible in historical rebellions and the rejection in Latin America of European and North American colonialism. This was an idea Carpentier shared with other Cuban intellectuals. José Lezama Lima would also make the claim that the baroque in America was characterized by a sense of rebelliousness: a rebellious curiosity for knowledge, which he called "afán fáustico" (Faustian desire, motive, toil).[144] Like Carpentier and Lezama Lima's literary characters, for Spengler, to be truly Faustian, the literary character and the writer must feel forsaken (*DW*, 186), "threatened," and "undermined by an alien metaphysics in its midst," (*DW*, 321). They also must speak the "language of the infinite space," which is symbols (*DW*, 427). The writer must desire freedom, to fly to the infinite and the boundless, always with a sense of Destiny; and to feel the "mythopoetic force of the Faustian soul" in "the myth of the world end" (*DW*, 423). That is the expression and symbol of the Faustian soul: a passionate quest for the boundlessness of the cosmos, away from the laws that binds it.

In a Spenglerian sense, Lezama Lima's notion of the Faustian, as the desire to have and possess knowledge, even in opposition to the law, is associated also to an act of transgression that expresses a Faustian life force, in a Spenglerian sense. For Spengler, the best example of a Faustian moment was the closing scene in Goethe's *Faust*, when the ultimate beauty of life, the passion of a world-force, and death are one. Spengler's Faustian "soul" does not agree with "a duality of world power" because "God is All" (*DW*, 187). Thus, writing, for Spengler, "is an entirely new language" (*DW* 2, 145) that "liberates" "from the tyranny of the present" (*DW* 2, 149). It is the "symbol of the Far" (*DW* 2, 150), "above all, duration and future and the will to eternity" (*DW* 2, 150). It is also "an ancient privilege of priesthood" (*DW* 2, 151). To follow Spengler's notion of the Faustian writer, at a Faustian moment of culture in America, but from the perspective of Carpentier's project of expressing America, the writer must also feel "threatened" and "forsaken" by the world out there, and must assume the priestly investiture of the interpreter and translator[145] of a "far-thrusting" (*DW* 2, 233) America. It is possible that Spengler's philosophy offered Carpentier far more than just a justification for the primitivism of an atavistic and fetishist Afro-Indo-America, and the promise of a future in contrast to a declining artificial Europe. It might have offered also a justification for his own internal conflict as a writer torn between Europe and America: trapped between his French father, his Russian mother, and the land of his birth, Cuba, the language he spoke most of his life (French), and Spanish, the language he spoke with an accent, but in which he wrote; and, ultimately, between his reality, his ontological necessities, his desires, and his ideals. This may be why for Carpentier the baroque in America is not a moment of disillusion and decline, as it is traditionally accepted of the European baroque, but of a sort of creative vigor born out of disillusion and rebellion.

Carpentier claimed that the New World, so different from Europe, was still waiting to be expressed in writing: waiting to be named. The act of naming Latin America, an act that also indicates appropriation, could only be done by a novelist who could see historical parallels across time and cultures, like James G. Fraser in *The Golden Bough,* or like Fernando Ortiz in his Afro-Cuban studies; or like Carpentier himself, who, he thought, was able to understand the universal in the local. Thus, "Culture," being that certain "vast" knowledge which, according to Carpentier, the writer needs to express America, was defined by Carpentier as "el acopio de conocimientos que permiten a un hombre establecer relaciones por encima del tiempo y del espacio entre dos realidades semejantes o análogas explicando una en función de sus similitudes con otras que puede[n] haberse producido muchos siglos atrás" (the accumulation of knowledge that allows a man to establish relationships beyond time and space between two different but similar or analogous realities, explaining one in relation to its similarities with another one that may have been produced many centuries before).[146]

Supported by his own research on the history of music in Cuba, Carpentier began to write his second novel, *The Kingdom of This World,* as a baroque composition that was to be a testimony to a complex, vital, and "forsaken" American reality. It was a text in which he would not overlook again, in the same way, the association of the "blacks with the forest," or the importance of magic and faith in the history of the Caribbean. The text was a personal statement.[147] It also was a break with European avant garde movements, with the artificiality of those movements, especially surrealism, as he explains in the prologue to the novel. In this prologue, Carpentier offers his own interpretation of his own novel in the light of his own personal understandings of the differences between an American reality and a European "artificial" search for forms. In that interpretation, the reader is coerced to approach and perceive Carpentier's novel from Carpentier's own exegesis; and to be an accomplice in his rejection of Breton's notion of the "marvelous" (a term he had used and praised numerous times), in order to embrace Carpentier's own definition of "marvelous realism"[148] as a metaphor for an American "reality."[149]

Not too distant in spite of their differences, from Lezama Lima's ideas of an American baroque characterized by an *afán fáustico* (also Ortiz's idea), meaning a curiosity for knowledge and a spirit of rebellion, *The Kingdom of This World* offers an archeology of a will to freedom in the history of the Caribbean, that is also a movement toward knowledge, epiphany, recognition, and rebellion. Evoking Narcissus's self-recognition upon seeing his image reflected on the water, but in a Caribbean context, *The Kingdom of This World* proposes the self-recognition in the Caribbean of the importance of Africa in the process of "becoming" the Caribbean.[150] Carpentier's novel is about historical awareness, and also about a revolutionary search for freedom. Like Carpentier, and Ortiz, Lezama associates the American curiosity and desire for knowledge (that for him characterizes the American baroque) with Faust. This rebellious curiosity (afán fáustico), reaches its height, says Lezama, in the writings of Carlos Sigüenza y Góngora and Sor Juana Inés de la Cruz, in Mexico, in the seventeenth century, with: "el afán del conocimiento físico, de las leyes de la naturaleza, que van más allá de la naturaleza como tentación por dominarla como el Doctor Fausto" (a desire for physical knowledge, to know the laws of nature, going beyond nature to the temptation to control it like Dr. Faust).[151] Like Lezama Lima and like Carpentier, most Latin American intellectuals were well acquainted with Goethe's work. Goethe, for instance, became a repetitive theme in Alfonso Reyes's essays.

For Carpentier, as he often claimed, America always had been baroque, even before Europe, an idea that goes along Ortiz's line of thoughts. Ortiz claimed that: "la profusa ornamentación del arte mexicano" (the profuse ornamentation of Mexican Art) is what influences European baroque.[152] Carpentier's early proposition of an always already baroque America becomes closely associated with his own proposition of an American "marvelous reality" that he articulates in the prologue to *El reino de este mundo:* "¿Pero qué es la historia de América toda sino una crónica de lo real-maravilloso?" (But what is the entire history America is not a chronicle of the marvelous-real?).[153] At the end, Carpentier's notions of the marvelous in America, apart from the association of the term and Carpentier's use of it with surrealism, as well as Carpentier's notion of a baroque America, are tied to his understanding of what he calls "Faustian blacks and Indians" in America. Notwithstanding, Carpentier's notion of the Faustian is informed also by Leon Frobenius's images of Africa,[154] and by Carpentier's own initial understanding at that time of Hegelian philosophy.

Carpentier's prologue to his own novel further complicates the text's contrapuntal dance of history and fiction by proposing the possibility that the novel may be a supplement to the prologue. Thus, the reader must read *The Kingdom of This World* from the gaps left between the novel and the prologue, and from a certain anxiety about writing inscribed in those gaps.[155] Yet, this prologue is, in itself, an important document in contemporary Latin American literary history. In his prologue, Carpentier proposes a break with his own previous work of fiction, as an act of self re-cognition that he indicates with his rejection of surrealism. As part of such rupture he also indicates his arrival to new forms, more authentic, and "proper" to express the Caribbean. At the same time, the text implies the continuation of his previous interests already explored in his earlier works, including styles and forms he rehearsed in short stories he later included in *Guerra del tiempo*.

In these short stories, Carpentier continued in his earlier attempt to represent African slaves and black Caribbean creoles. That interest, however, had shifted from the outer representation of forms to the internal representation of a consciousness: to the silent gaze of that cultural "other American" Carpentier still could not fully comprehend, but with whom he identified. In spite of Carpentier's personal distance from the Afro-Caribbean "world" he wanted to express, *The Kingdom of This World* is the first of his novels to leave a lasting imprint in Latin American literature.[156] In 1950, for instance, the Haitian writer Mario Tonealba Lossí claimed that in *The Kingdom of This World*: "el escritor [Carpentier] no se limita a la descripción superficial del Negro y su psicología, sino que trata de penetrar en su misterio. Es la primera incursión seria que en relación a esta material se lleva a cabo en el continente" (the writer does not limit himself to a superficial description of the Negro and his psychology, but, instead, he tries to penetrate his mystery. It is the first serious incursion that, related to this subject, takes place in the continent).[157] The main characters in this novel, Ti Nöel and Mackandal, live, as in Carpentier comments of Lam's work, in a "world of primitive myths," closely associated with the forest, with magic, "longing for liberty." In spite of Carpentier's strong doses of Spenglerian philosophy in the novel, Carpentier's representation of "blackness," of Africa in the Caribbean, and of a historical African slave consciousness, *The Kingdom of This World* is a groundbreaking text because it offers the first fictional representation of Afro-Caribbean historical agency in Caribbean history. It also offers the possibility for new literary forms of expression, outside colonial prejudice, inside the literary canon.

At the same time, the novel is a unique exercise in craftsmanship; of forms in which the thematic is incorporated into the structure of the text; and in which the represented "Other," Carpentier's Faustian black Caribbean, is also the metaphoric subject that voices the novelist's own anxieties, tensions, and meditations on cultural difference.

III

After his trip to Haiti, Carpentier began to read everything he could find about the island, its history, and its people. Among such readings was W. Seabrook's *The Magic Island* (1929), a personal account of Seabrook's' travels and life in Haiti, in which Seabrook includes descriptions of Voodoo practices and rituals.[158] In this text, Seabrook wonders whether: "African religions, older than Christianity were perhaps taking back transformed symbols and ritual practices which had originally been borrowed from their continent."[159] Seabrook's Spenglerian meditation leads him to see parallelisms between ancient world rituals and universal archetypes and the exotic and mysterious practices of Voodoo. Often mixing the telluric with the political, Seabrook, who is writing about Haiti during the USA intervention of the island (1915–34), refers to, and praises, the indifference of Haitian Voodoo worshippers toward foreign materialism. Such indifference, he claims, is the result of their strong faith and spiritual vitality. In essence, Seabrook's understanding of primitive faith is not very different from Carpentier's representation in *El milagro de anaquillé* (1927) of the ñáñigo sugar cane cutters, their faith, and the magic of the *anaquillé Jimaguas*. Seabrook also sees a dynamic vigor in Haitian primitive faith, which, he claims, is no longer found in institutionalized Western religions. He writes:

> I learned from Louis [his young Haitian servant] that we white strangers in this twentieth century city, with our electric lights and motor cars, bridge games and cocktail parties, were surrounded by another world invisible, a world of marvels, miracles, and wonders. . . . Voodoo in Haiti is a profound and vitally alive religion alive as Christianity was in its beginning and in the early Middle Ages when miracles and mystical illuminations were common everyday occurrences. . . . mortal I, who have stood with bowed head and good intentions in so many of this world's great gilded cathedrals, mosques, and temples, have never felt myself so close to the invisible presence of ultimate mystery as I did later, more than once, beneath straw-thatched roofs in the Haitian mountains.[160]

In *The Kingdom of This World,* Carpentier expresses a similar Spenglerian concept of "contemporaneity" (between cultures across time) that echoes Seabrook's descriptions of Haitian Voodoo. At the same time, while the novel represents the conflict between two antithetical groups (black slaves and white masters), it seems to privilege Afro-Caribbean magic and faith, as Carpentier does in *El milagro de Anaquillé*. He sees in the local the universal, but privileges an atavistic faith he does not share with his characters. Carpentier embraces "primitive" Afro-Caribbean faith as a way of representing a Faustian world-force that gave Haitians the spiritual and ideological strength to win the first successful war of independence in Latin America, even though it was a war against the strongest nation in Europe at the time, Napoleonic France. It was an unthinkable feat, as Seabrook points out, that Haitians slaves and peasants could overturn an entire colonial system. It was a story of epic proportions that inverted the traditional ideas Europe had of America. In Haiti, and in Haitian history, Carpentier finally found: "este marco extraordinario, y con un tema apasionante que es, además, político. Me encuentro con la historia de las tres primeras revoluciones antillanas. . . . Y por eso escribí este libro. (This extraordinary frame, and a passionate theme that is, furthermore, political. I find myself with the history of the first three revolutions in the Antilles. This is why I wrote this book.)"[161] The history of Haiti not only offered Carpentier the "true" story of what he had represented in his Afro-Cuban ballet *El milagro de Anaquillé,* it also provided him with a historical context:

para mí no existe la modernidad en el sentido que se le otorga, el hombre es a veces el mismo en diferentes edades y situarlo en su pasado puede ser también situarlo en su presente . . . Amo los grandes temas, los grandes movimientos colectivos. Ellos dan la más alta riqueza a los personajes y a la trama.[162]

[for me, Modernity in the sense given to it does not exist, man is sometimes the same in different epochs and to place him in the past can be to place him in the present also . . . I love the great themes, the great collective movements. They give the greatest richness to the characters and to the plot.]

The role of magic and faith in *The Kingdom of This World* is even more significant when we remember that Voodoo is a religious syncretic belief system that came together precisely during the time of revolutionary struggle.[163] It was a unique American creation that had given the Haitian rebels the necessary vigor, strength, and faith to win freedom and political independence. Carpentier associates that Faustian moment in European culture with an American cultural landscape where, like sixteenth century Europe, faith and magic were still important elements. In a complex play of analogies, Carpentier understands, as he expresses in his prologue to *The Kingdom of This World,* that Africans, and black creoles, were the cultural life force that saved America from the decadence of civilization. In a political context, "Faustian," a word that, as Donald Shaw points out, Carpentier had learned from Spengler, came to mean for Carpentier, "as he wrote in 1930, 'full of longing for liberty, for the infinite and the mysterious,' as distinct from 'Apollonian,' which implied clinging to form and exactitude."[164] Spengler, for whom Goethe's *Faust* was the best representative of the Faustian moment in Western culture, also understood Faustian to mean, "longing for liberty" as "the infinite" and "the mysterious," a "faith-forms of springtime" (*DW*, 417).[165] Civilization, in Spengler's definition, was the "tyranny of Reason" (*DW*, 424), an idea that Carpentier also rehearses in *The Kingdom of This World*.

Trying to arrive at the essence of Afro-Caribbean atavism through liturgical and ritual forms, in *The Kingdom of This World* Carpentier sees the world through what Spengler calls the "bird's eyes" of the Faustian soul and not the "frog's eyes" of Western civilization. The result is a Carpentierian counterpoint between the "here" and the "there" (traditionally understood as Carpentier's ambivalence between America and Europe) that Spengler defines as the counterpoint between an "inward look" and the "boundless," the "microcosm" and the "macrocosm," the "proper" and the "alien," the "soul and body here" and the "world around us" "there" (*DW*, 291). Carpentier articulates the consciousness of the "other," the Haitian Faustian slave, in counterpoint to the "tyranny" of Reason in a declining Western civilization, which the white slave owners represent. To establish such counterpoint, Carpentier utilizes European and Afro-American archival texts to express antithetical cosmogonies/consciousness. In counterpoint to European epistemology, he tries to approximate a "true" representation of the consciousness of the Haitian slave (as far as the structure of the novel allows it). However, he could only rely on written Western texts. At the same time, in the process of constructing the Other as a Faustian life-force of cultural vigor, Carpentier could not escape what by now he had accepted as a dialectical movement in history: the movement of a dual consciousness. Salvador Bueno notes that Carpentier's work presents a type of Hegelian dialectic in "la repetición de los ciclos históricos, la negación de un acontecimiento por el que le sucede, la interrelación de hechos y hombres de distintos períodos históricos" (the repetition of historical cycles, the negation of a moment by the one that follows it, the interrelation of events and men of different historical periods).[166] As Bueno also notes, Carpentier's repetition of cycles, "aunque parece repetir el ciclo anterior, lo supera" (even thought he seems to be repeating the previous cycle, he transcends it to a higher level).[167]

Carpentier realized that Hegel's metaphysical concept of history contradicts Spengler's historical concept, yet, in *The Kingdom of This World*, Carpentier counterpoints these two incompatible (antithetical) philosophies of history (in a baroque contrast of opposites). In this unique dance of symmetries[168] and counterpoints, the text seems to follow Ortiz's contrapuntal model of the proper and the foreign—the popular, as in Guillén's poetry, being the Caribbean African heritage. Carpentier's representation of the slave consciousness, as an antithesis to Western thought, had to be constructed out of Afro-Caribbean myths, legends, and religious belief systems that Carpentier largely learned from books, as well as from his conversations with Ortiz, and with other Cuban writers and artists, and, as he claimed, from his visits to ñáñigo ceremonies. This "knowledge" allowed him to bring together telluric and epic-historical contexts in a carefully constructed baroque composition of various counterpoints and tightly constructed symmetries in which he intersects contrary principles: Spengler's concept of historical and cultural contemporaneity in counterpoint to a Hegelian dialectical movement of a double consciousness moving through history. Such narrative play in which the text dances with European contrary philosophies is made possible in Carpentier's narrative scheme, through the utilization, from the gaze of Afro-Caribbean beliefs systems, of the mythological entity that presides over crossroads, the mediator between contrary principles, *Legba/Elegua:* a sort of conceptual "hinge" that allows the coexistence in Carpentier's text of opposite concepts and philosophies.

Like in *El milagro de Anaquillé,* the basic action in *The Kingdom of This World* is the clash between two human groups, staged as a dialectical conflict between masters and slaves. The main character of the story, Ti Nöel, is an allegorical figure that personifies in the novel what Carpentier imagines to be a Faustian world-force in the historical context of an Afro-Haitian landscape. Carpentier represents the consciousness of the slave, Ti Nöel, as a slave whose name associates him with Christ's nativity, and, by analogy, with his passion, death, and resurrection.[169] In that role, Ti Nöel moves freely among historical figures across space and time during a life span that exceeds 100 years (like Goethe's *Faust,* who is also 100 years old when he dies). In the construction of that "other" consciousness, Carpentier attempts to break away from his artificial and deterministic depictions of Afro-Cubans in his earlier work by articulating a difference, through religious beliefs, which he represents as the "proper" gaze of Haitian slaves. The Spenglerian notion of an America contemporaneous to baroque Europe allows Carpentier to dialogue with early models of Spanish literature (like Guillén and Ortiz do) at a time when atavistic faith was also central to the cultural vigor of its artistic production: like in the days of Miguel de Cervantes.[170] It also allows him to establish a direct analogy and contrast between his own work and the work and the literary production of Spanish Golden Age writers. Assuming such contemporaneity, Carpentier writes in his prologue to *The Kingdom of This World:*

la sensación de lo maravilloso presupone una fe. Los que no creen en santos no pueden curarse con milagros de santos, ni los que no son Quijotes pueden meterse, en cuerpo, alma y bienes, en el mundo de *Amadís de Gaula* o *Tirante el Blanco.* Prodigiosamente fidedignas resultan ciertas frases de Rutilo en *Los tra-*

bajos de Persiles y Segismunda, acerca de hombres transformados en lobos, porque en tiempos de Cervantes se creía en gentes aquejadas de manía lupina.[171]

[The sensation of the marvelous requires faith. Those who do not believe in saints cannot cure themselves with their miracles, nor those that are not Quixote can go inside in body, soul and things, in the world of *Amadís de Gaula* or *Tirante el Blanco.* Prodigiously faithful are certain phrases in *Los trabajos de Persiles y Segismunda,* about men transformed into wolves, because in Cervantes's times people believed that some suffered from lupine disease.]

Fernando Ortiz's *Contrapunteo cubano del tabaco y el azúcar* (1940) (*Cuban Counterpoint of Tobacco and Sugar,* 1947), offered Carpentier another textual and contextual model for his novel. Ortiz's text is an allegorical history of tobacco (native) and sugar (foreign) in Cuba. In it, Ortiz appropriates as his model the counterpoint of Carnival and Lent used by the Arciprested de Hita in the medieval classic of Spanish Literature, *El libro del buen amor.* Ortiz borrows the narrative structure of counterpoint from Arcipreste the Hita in order to express what Ortiz called "transculturation" in Cuban society: a process of cultural exchange in which each participant, especially the weaker group, is modified in the process.[172] In this allegorical essay, which for Antonio Benítez Rojo is "one of the most revealing books ever written about the dynamics of the Caribbean" (*RI,* 156), Ortiz constructs an allegorical contrapuntal dance between two important players in Cuban socio-economic history: the white foreign sugar, and the dark native tobacco. In the Spanish medieval text, Arcipreste de Hita establishes a counterpoint between Doña Cuaresma (Lent) and Don Carnaval (Carnival) as an allegory for the conflict between the flesh and the spirit. Using this classical literary text as a precursor, Ortiz personifies tobacco and sugar, two of the most important products for exportation and sources of wealth in Cuba, as the two products that best represent the formation (economy, social structure, politics) of Cuban society. Ortiz's contrapuntal dance leads to a resolution (a synthesis) that allegorically explains the development of Cuba's vernacular culture: *cubanía,* the mulatto offspring of the white, foreign sugar, and the dark, native, tobacco.[173]

As Gustavo Pérez Firmat observes, in Ortiz's text "sugar and tobacco are the leading actors in an allegorical drama that plays out the dominant characteristics of Cuban culture,"[174] yet, in Ortiz's text, "the most fundamental counterpoint . . . is the ontological counterpoint between identity and difference."[175] Sugar represents the invasion "by a 'white' exogenous culture" of the island[176] in counterpoint, in Cuban soil, to the native tobacco. For Ortiz, as Pérez Firmat notes, "a counterpoint designates a relation of at least two terms in which the second term answers or 'counters' the first."[177] This is precisely what happens in *El libro del buen amor.* However, Ortiz misreads or ignores the text's battle between spirit and flesh, "spinning his Cuban allegory from only one of the terms in the original counterpoints" "in the name of the flesh," thus creating, in his Cuban counterpoint, a contrast and not a conflict.[178] Ortiz's contrasting counterpoint between tobacco and sugar is more like a courting dance, a rumba, between male (tobacco) and female (sugar) that ends in marriage with an offspring: allegorically, Cuban vernacular culture. Ortiz transforms *El libro del buen amor's* "sacred" allegory into a profane allegory of Cuban vernacular culture. As Pérez Firmat observes, in Ortiz's counterpoint the "Holy Spirit" has been replaced, in a "*Gnostic* structure" that privileges the carnal, by "unholy spirits:" sugar and tobacco, both being delights of the flesh.[179] The result of Ortiz's imagined union, *cubanidad,* according to Benítez Rojo, is an attempt to address "Cuba's supersyncretic archives" (*RI,* 155).

Like Ortiz's model, *The Kingdom of This World* also privileges the carnal in a counterpoint of black/white, indigenous/foreign, master/slave. Yet, differing from Ortiz's text, *The Kingdom of This World* returns to the original counterpoint of conflict in *El libro del buen amor,* in which one of the two contenders is ousted. The structure of the work, however, like Ortiz's text, follows a Gnostic structure of inversions, at times more reminiscent of Hegel's language of inversion[180] than Ortiz's counterpoints. For Hegel, the New World was "unhistorical" because it was still the land of the future; a land that, according to Carpentier, began its own history before the arrival of Columbus, affirmed it during the wars of independence, and was mapping now its own destiny, and its own identity. In a paradoxical sort of way, especially when confronted with Spengler's notion of history, Hegel's philosophy on history was not unlike the history of Latin America, not unlike the development of Cuban music as Carpentier discovered in his research, and not unlike Ortiz's counterpoint of sugar and tobacco. Hegel's concept of Spirit as Knowledge and Freedom (especially when Hegel's Spirit is translated as Mind as Lukács does in *The Young Hegel*),[181] could then be understood as the "unholy" experience of human consciousness moving through spiraling, dialectic, experiences toward a Spirit-Freedom that is Knowledge. One must remember that Hegelian Knowledge for Cuban writers in the forties, like for Carpentier, was associated with transgression and rebellion: a signature of identity in America. Contrasting Knowledge as self-consciousness, with transgression, at the end of *The Kingdom of This World,* Carpentier's Ti Nöel, like Goethe's Faust, reaches a moment of clarity (Freedom/Knowledge). This moment of epiphany, Ti Nöel's arrival to self-Knowledge, also suggests a mode of resistance represented in the novel by the understanding or awareness of the role human beings play in history, and of the "tasks"[182] human beings must set for themselves: "Now he understood that a man never knows for whom he suffers and hopes. That man's greatness consists in the very fact of wanting to be better than he is. In setting tasks as goals for himself. In the Kingdom of Heaven there is no grandeur to be won," (*KW,* 148–49).[183]

Ti Nöel's final awareness of being-in-the-world articulates Carpentier's own ontological conclusions. In other words, as as allegorical personification of the "Faustian," Ti Nöel's historical and ontological understanding of his role in history, addresses Carpentier's own idealization of an American collective "longing for liberty" that resists the tyranny of Reason.[184] As a statement of his personal beliefs, Carpentier confesses his personal beliefs to Ramón Chao by reiterating once more almost verbatum Ti Nöel's conclusion when he arrives to self "knowledge:"

> la grandeza del hombre consiste precisamente en querer mejorar lo que es; en imponerse tareas. . . . Por ello, el hombre sólo puede hallar su grandeza, su máxima medida en el reino de este mundo.[185]

> [Man's greatness consists precisely in wanting to better himself; in imposing tasks for himself. This is why, able to love in the midst of plagues, Man can only find his greatness, his maximum possibility in the kingdom of this world.]

Unlike Spengler, for Hegel, as Lukács writes: "the point of departure is always the individual consciousness, his view of reality, his actions on the basis of that view and the movement of that stage of consciousness implicit in it."[186] Also, like Carpentier's Ti Nöel, for Hegel, the individual is only an allegory of the universal:[187] of self-consciousness moving toward higher levels of awareness, first as Reason, and, then, as Knowledge and Freedom. As if Carpentier's writing had been informed by Hegel's historical scheme, Carpentier's Gnostic structure in *The Kingdom of This World* places the main character, Ti Nöel, at the center of his ontological quest for an understanding of self and of history, in Haiti, and, by analogy, in the Caribbean. Carpentier explains to César Leante, that he carefully chose: "los nombres de los personajes, que responden siempre a una simbólica que me ayuda a verlos" (the name of characters, to respond to a symbolic order that helps me visualize them).[188] Thus, it could be argued, based on Carpentier's ordering of writing, that Ti Nöel is a carefully constructed allegorical figure that represents, through the craft of symmetries and counterpoints, the consciousness of a creole Afro-Caribbean, as conceived then by Carpentier. At the same time, Ti Nöel is an allegorical *figura Christic* whose mission, task, and martyrdom is to move, through historical dialectical movements, toward Knowledge/Freedom. This mission is particularly significant since the Caribbean, especially Hispaniola, and, specifically, the area that is now Haiti, is the region where the entire machinery of the European conquest and colonization of the New World began. In other words, what America is today began precisely in the same area that serves as the stage for *The Kingdom of This World*. This is also the place where the first slave rebellion took place in the New World, in 1522, in *Natividad* (Nativity): the name given to the first fort the Spaniards built in the north coast of what is today Haiti. Furthermore, Haiti is the nation where rebellious African descendants became the first to stage a successful war of independence in Latin America. In a Carpentierian play of symmetries, Carpentier's Ti Nöel seems to recall Nietzsche's concept of an Overman, able to suffer through sacrifice and to overcome.[189] His sacrifice at the end of the novel entertains the possibility of the rebirth of the community, and of humanity. Carpentier finds this sense of rebirth also in Frobenius and Spengler, both of whom shared a cyclical view of history, and a similar sense of an ending of the present order of things.[190]

In the narrative's play of significations, symmetries, and counterpoints, Carpentier's Hegelian Ti Nöel also recalls Spengler's notion of the "body-soul" as "here" in counterpoint to the "world-around-us" as "there," (*DW*, 191), in a double counterpoint to Hegel's notion of the movements of a double consciousness. Such movements Carpentier "translates" to a New World context as a dance of spirals, of turns and returns, in a Time that moves toward what Spengler conceives as Destiny (*DW*, 122, 422) (to culture's final decline), but also in spirals toward what Hegel understands as Knowledge/Freedom.[191] For a Spenglerian Carpentier, tampering with and interested in Hegelian thought, the decadence of Europe, rather visible after two great World Wars that swept the continent, was proof of the decline of European civilization, in Europe, and, as part of Western culture, also in Eurocentric America. Such decadence in Euro-America was seen in the traditional bourgeoisie values the modernists rejected. However, since for Carpentier what saved America from that decline was the cultural Faustian vigor of blacks and Indians, America's rupture from European thought intimated the potential for a new beginning, but within a Faustian moment of culture. New forms of expressing America were needed in order to communicate such experience to Western readers. Those new forms had to articulate American codes; and those codes were related to the "source" of Caribbean local knowledges, memories, beliefs, magic, myths, that were "proper," in the Caribbean: Afro-Caribbean vernacular culture.

Culturally free from Europe, and no longer bound by a declining European bourgeoisie, America's Faustian elements would give New World societies the necessary vigor so that its authentic, once marginal, subjugated cultures would rise to their greatest moment of creativity. At the same time, the road to cultural and political freedom, in America, seemed to find its Destiny in a Hegelian metaphysics of history,[192] or at least in a Latin American version of Karl Marx's reading of Hegel. It is important to remember that when Carpentier wrote *The Kingdom of This World*, he was crossing philosophical borders, and did not claim to hold a political militant position as he did years later. This may explain Carpentier's choice to counterpoint Hegel and Spengler's ideas on history in *The Kingdom of This World:* a paradox that speaks in Carpentier's structural scheme about his philosophical ambivalence, ambiguities, and, even perhaps, his limited understanding of both philosophies, as Gonzalez Echevarría suggests.[193] Such ambiguities, however, are also the ambiguities of the period in which Carpentier lived: the intellectual ambiguities of a Caribbean awakening to its own history and cultures, but not fully understanding them. Textual ambiguities in *The Kingdom of This World* also intimate a structural narrative play that allows the Afro-Caribbean ritual mediator, *Legba/Elegua,* a central role in the text. In fact, this is the same Afro-Cuban/African mediator between times and realities whose role Carpentier already had rehearsed in "Back to the Source."

IV

In order to reconcile such contrary philosophies of history as are Hegel's and Spengler's, Carpentier turns to Afro-Caribbean beliefs systems and rituals where he finds, central to those beliefs, the image of the crossroad. This is the notion that at the point of intersection of contrary principles, it is where humanity stands, and life takes place. The Afro-Caribbean presider of the crossroad is *Elegua/Legba,* Lord of the Word: the divine mediator. It is at this intersection that opposites forces and principles meet, and coexist. Taking into consideration the "proper" of this Afro-Caribbean concept, Carpentier's craftsmanship constructs in *The Kingdom of This World* a textual crossroad of symbols, codes, discourses, and contrary ideas, both European and African. The concept of a crossroad, represented always by *Elegua/Legba,* is the Caribbean hinge that allows Carpentier to play, meet, and contrast, in the allegorical figure of Ti Nöel, opposite theories and philosophies like Hegel's and Spengler's.

Ti Nöel's experiences through more than a hundred years of historical turmoil and reversals allows him to arrive by the end of the novel to a knowledge that could not be obtained through theoretical abstractions. This is a Hegelian concept that Carpentier applies to an otherwise Spenglerian Ti Nöel. At the same time, contrary to Spengler, Hegel's concept of historical Time proposes that consciousness arrives through a series of inverted (dialectical) movements, to self-consciousness. This is the moment in which, for Hegel, consciousness arrives to Absolute Knowledge/Freedom: a moment that "arises from our governing together."[194] Conscious "becomes" self-consciousness only through a process of understanding, of "becoming through experience," always as a return from the "other,"[195] when a new consciousness arises from the old one. For Hegel, Knowledge is Freedom, and Freedom is the essence of Spirit.[196] This process is a difficult phenomenological road that must be lived (experienced), not learned from books. In *The Kingdom of This World* this is the life-road traveled by Ti Nöel before he reaches an understanding of humanity's being-in-the world. In this process, and through a dialectical encounter with the other, Ti Nöel learns that the causes of human bondage are not just racial, but a condition created (as in Marx's reading of Hegel) by economic and political power.

Ti Nöel's final epiphany seems to constitute a synthesis between the individual and the universal. For Hegel, this is the beginning of Reason, a stage prior to the arrival of Spirit/Freedom. In Hegelian dialectics then, when Reason first appears "it is like dawn," but this is not the end of the process, for it needs to travel still further in order to arrive to itself as Spirit.[197] During this phenomenological process (in its first steps), much like Ti Nöel when he returns to his native land (and like Aimé Césaire's *Notebook of a Return to the Native Land,* 1939), Reason is purely "observant" (*beobachtende vernunft*). It limits itself to notice everything that is around and to question its nature. Three moments characterize this stage of observation. The first two moments are the descriptive one, and the moment of "the signs," when Reason becomes aware of the universality of things and the moment of discovery of the laws of nature.[198] The third one is a moment that coincides with the first chapter of the third part of *The Kingdom of This World,* significantly entitled, in Spanish, "Signos" (Signs).[199] Under the heading of signos, Ti Nöel returns to his native land, Haiti, where he observes the changes that occurred in a now-independent nation, where people, once enslaved, are still not free even after gaining political independence. It is then that Ti Nöel begins to become aware of the universality of the natural order of things. Ti Nöel, much like Hegel's Reason, discovers that the organic world has its own laws; that the laws of the natural world can be just as deceiving as the quest for freedom; that political independence, like the one won by the slaves in Haiti, was not the same as liberty. Ti Nöel's awareness occurs after discovering a Hegelian world of similarities (*afines*) in which there is a battle of opposition and conciliation between the external world (the world of appearances) and the internal world whose origin and meaning is Reason.

To reach this Hegelian understanding of history, and of self, Ti Nöel must go through a second stage of self-deceit. For Hegel, deceit occurs when consciousness believes that humankind pursues its own goal when, in reality, human beings follow the goals for survival designed by nature for their own species: Life's universal goal. At this movement, the individual, who for Hegel is always the universal,[200] finds its intimate essence. It is only then that the individual, like Ti Nöel's historical self-consciousness, comes to full possession of self and can fulfill its destiny. Ti Nöel arrives at the crossroad of historical (Hegelian) Destiny, to encounter yet another different road: the moment and space where Spengler's idea of Time-Destiny, as a thrust to Infinity, intersects Hegel's concept of historical destiny. For the reader, this crossroad of philosophies is an aporia, since for Hegel, the moment Reason "perceives," and is aware of its nature and destiny, it ceases to be just Reason[201] and becomes the totality of self-consciousness.[202]

Turning to the concept of the crossroad as a philosophical, but also a ritual concept in *The Kingdom of This World,* the final scene of the novel is an ingenious play of symmetries and counterpoints constructed out of tightly woven baroque figures and symbols associated with images of "dawn," "awareness," self-consciousness, and freedom. In Carpentier's text these allegorical images suggest a Hegelian historical destiny, but also, at the same time, a Spenglerian thrust into the boundlessness of the Faustian soul, like Goethe's Faust. In fact, Ti Nöel arrives at this stage to be thrust into the boundless infinite, only after a historical voyage through a dialectical movement of an antithetical (slave-master) consciousness. It is here that, in spite of their differences, Hegel and Spengler gaze at each other in Carpentier's text, like the two snakes in *Damballah's vever* in Hatian Voodoo, or as the two intersecting lines (horizontal and vertical) that intersect each other in *Legba's vever.* For Hegel, experience (not book knowledge) is vital in the movement of conscious to self-consciousness. Yet, for Spengler, intellect, the tyranny of reason, appears only at the moment of the decline of a civilization.

Carpentier's reading of Hegel's philosophy in *The Kingdom of This World* recalls Karl Marx's reading of Hegel. For Hegel, says Lukács, when Reason arrives at Spirit, the circle is closed and there is a "transformation of substance into subject, and the annulment of objective reality as such."[203] At this point in Hegel's scheme, objective reality is annulled and only myth remains.[204] This is a concept Karl Marx rejected in his *The Holy Family* because, he argued, then: "history exists only in the consciousness, in the opinion and conception of the philosopher i.e. in the speculative imagination."[205] Hegel's historical movement is conceived as the experience of consciousness, which is the authentic development of the spirit: Freedom. Freedom, then, is essential for the constitution of the State as an organic system of very concrete individual laws that express the true nature and the soul of each collective body of peoples or nations. Following Hegel's thoughts, it is possible to read the "new dawn" with which Carpentier's novel ends, in the "spirit" of a new Hegelian State toward which consciousness moves in dialectical spirals, reaching, with each dialectical movement, a higher level of understanding, as in Ti Nöel's "progressive" movement to historical (self)awareness.

Carpentier's parody of Hegel's historical process[206] recalls the fact that there were three major uprisings in Haitian history. These were not the only major revolts, of course, since rebellions in Haiti occurred often. Notwithstanding, Carpentier orders them into the three stages, to fit Hegel's dialectic movement of consciousness in their correct chronological historical sequence as thesis, antithesis, and synthesis. Such trilogy in Hegel's scheme suggests that consciousness has to traverse the same experience three times. "The various aspects of history that are treated" [by Hegel], observes Georg Lukács, "do not occur arbitrarily as has often been thought; in fact, they occur in their correct historical sequence, which, however, is [also] repeated three times in the course of the work [*The Phenomenology*]."[207] Hegel's textual structure simply means, says Lukács, that "Hegel has divided the process in which the individual acquires the historical experience of the species into different stages."[208] Each time, the individual learns and perceives that he/she must traverse the road again, thus recapitulating the past in its entirety, and starting all over again, but at a higher plane of awareness.[209] Like Hegel's movement of consciousness, in *The Kingdom of This World* Ti Nöel also must live and learn by traversing three different, but similar, moments of oppression; each time at a different plane of consciousness than before. First, he learns to see history as a creation of man's actions. Then, he must traverse the same road again to learn to see history in its concrete social totality.[210] Once again, for a third time, he must traverse the same road, but at a higher plane of consciousness. It is only then, at this third stage, that Ti Nöel is able to arrive to a full awareness of history, and be conscious of his role in history. Remembering Hegel's interest in the individual as universal, Ti Nöel becomes, at a given moment of the narrative, an allegory for humanity.

Having arrived at this point of self-awareness in Hegel's scheme, the individual "looks back over the panorama of history" and arrives "at an understanding of the laws *governing the movements of history,* in short of the dialectics of reality;"[211] it does so, says Lukács, by "recapitulating the past in its entirety—as a summary of mankind's efforts to comprehend reality."[212] Like in Hegel's allegorical scheme, Ti Nöel's recapitulation and final understanding at the end of his life, goes from a local to a universal view of life. It includes nature, not in its ideal form as for the Romantics, but in the physical laws of nature, which Ti Nöel experiences, metaphorically, by transforming himself into different animals and insects. It is through this other experience "in nature," "as nature," that Ti Nöel understands (as Hegel proposes) the natural laws of the species. This knowledge allows him to finally understand his humanity, and accept "the kingdom of this earth."[213]

Closer to Marx's reading of Hegel, Carpentier departs at the end of the text (as far as the political agenda of the text seems to propose), from Hegel's final dialectical reconciliation, and from the passivity of consciousness in the historical movement. For Marx, historical human beings are not passive elements of his/her environment, but must act on that environment in order to transform it. In Carpentier's scheme, Ti Nöel's call to war at the end of the novel is also the writer's call for change, a call that, in spite of a disillusion articulated throughout the novel with a cyclical return of "chains," it is a cry for hope crafted as a Faustian passionate cry for freedom.[214] Ti Nöel's voice (wind-sound-thunder) brings about a battle cry for a new order of things: a new day reminiscent of Carpentier's "Liturgia." Remembering that, for Hegel, Spirit's essence is Freedom, Ti Nöel articulates a will-to-freedom ("longing for liberty")[215] that for Carpentier characterizes the history of the Americas (the Caribbean) in its struggles for liberation and independence. The new day heralded at the end of the novel, proposes a new beginning that can "happen" only through a radical historical transformation of society in which the old myths, which have perpetuated the return of the same order of things, are finally eliminated. These old myths, according to Hegel, as in Ti Nöel's early misreading of Mackandal's metamorphosis, delay the arrival of Man to a historical consciousness. It is at this point that in the narrative's crossroad of discourses, the text seems to contradict itself by privileging reason over myth, faith, and magic.

Although ingeniously intertwined in the novel's structure, Carpentier's utilization of Hegelian philosophy in *The Kingdom of This World* must be approached cautiously. When Carpentier returned to Cuba in 1939, he arrived rejecting Europe, disillusioned with the triumph of Fascism in Spain, and fleeing from the turmoil of the pre-War years. Once back in Cuba, in spite of his earlier alleged political involvements against the dictatorship of Gerardo Machado, he actually remained somewhat apolitical. Like many Latin American and European writers of the time, he had associated himself with elementary notions of Socialism, fashionable during this period, but remained deeply marked by Spengler's philosophy, as it was understood in Latin American circles. Later, he converted to Sartrean Existentialism. However, in the forties, the problem for Spenglerian Latin American intellectuals in accepting Hegel's historical metaphysics was that for Hegel America and Africa were "non historical" lands; and his philosophy of history negated the Spenglerian vigor of a baroque America. For Hegel, also Africa was an "Unhistorical, Undeveloped Spirit, still involved in the conditions of mere nature,"[216] a condition Ti Nöel overcomes and surpasses in Carpentier's text. Africa, for Hegel, did not fit one single category, since Egypt: "was adapted to become a mighty center of civilization, and, therefore is as isolated and singular in Africa as Africa itself appears in relation to the other parts of the world."[217] Unlike Frobenius and Spengler, from the gaze of Latin American writers, Hegel seemed to reiterate an old Western discourse: a traditional European attitude toward Africans as inferior.[218] Hegel claimed that: "African character is difficult to comprehend, for the very reason that in reference to it, we must quite give up the principle which naturally accompanies all our ideas—the category of Universality."[219] Hegel also writes: "In Negro life the character-istic point is the fact that consciousness has not yet attained to the realization of any substantial objective existence—as for example, God, or Law—in which the interest of man's volition is involved and in which he realizes his own being."[220] In a counter-discourse to Hegel's philosophy, it can be said that what Ortiz's work on afrocubanía revealed was precisely the "universality" Hegel negated to the New World, and hence the Caribbean.

In light of Hegel's philosophy of history (which became a ruler with which to think history in the West), the historical fact that the "march toward freedom" in America began with the rebellion of black slaves in Haiti would be a significant Hegelian response by Carpentier to Hegel's idea of an unhistorical America. Carpentier constructs his historical epic, in America, taking the black slave (African and Afro-Caribbean creole) as the main actors in this American epic-story of political, social, economic, and racial struggle. It was a struggle that coincided historically with the time in which Hegel was writing, and, therefore, apart from other "prejudgements" about Africa, it was too close in time for the German philosopher to understand as historical. For Hegel, America was a land of the future, not of the past: "a land of desire for all those who are weary of the historical lumber-room of old Europe." Hegel goes further: "It is for America to abandon the ground on which hitherto, the History of the World has developed itself. What has taken place in the New World up to the present time is only an echo of the Old World—the expression of a foreign Life."[221] This is the predicament in which Carpentier places the Haitian king, Henri Christophe, whose court in a land now ruled by the slaves turned masters, is a Hegelian "echo of the Old World," an imitation of the French court and of all of its decadent elements.[222] Since Christophe's monarchy in Carpentier's novel was a mimicry of Europe, and not an autochthonous expression of America, it turned into ruins (*Le Ferriere*), like the ruins of the Roman Empire. The Spenglerian notion of civilization juxtaposes in Carpentier's text a Hegelian dialectic, which, as González Evecharría points out, Carpentier understands in part from Karl Marx's reading of Hegel.[223] Carpentier is searching for an America ontologically different from Europe, whose mixed peoples give birth to an American offspring that is no longer a copy of Europe.[224] It is from this desire of difference as a mode of liberation that Carpentier articulates a counter-discourse addressed not only to Hegel, but also to Golden Age Spanish writers like Lope de Vega. It is an American discourse not distant from the interest of the Minoristas in their search to express cubanía as the marriage of Africa and Europe, as a mulatto cultural landscape, like in Nicolás Guillén's mulatto poems.

Carpentier's dialogue with Hegel (and with Marx's reading of Hegel) and with Spengler, and with Spengler's readings of Goethe's *Faust,* voices a preoccupation that many writers (especially Latin American writers) have embraced at different moments during the twentieth century. Carpentier's dissolution with politics and with bourgeoisie values recalls Goethe and Hegel's preoccupation with the newly developed bourgeoisie one hundred years earlier, during the same historical period portrayed in *The Kingdom of This World.* In *The Kingdom of This World,* the early part of the novel coincides with the Enlightment, a historical moment contemporary to the French Revolution and its aftermath. Mackandal loses his arm and later runs away in 1750,[225] and Christophe becomes king in 1811, and dies in 1820. This is a period that interested Carpentier, and to which he returns in *El siglo de las luces (Explosion in the Cathedral).* Like Carpentier, Hegel thought of the Enlightment as "the symptom of that great crisis which culminated later in the French revolution."[226] It was a precedent for the Haitian revolution, and, as Lukács notes: "a moment when the *dialectic* consciously emerges," as the "product of social consciousness and not just the result of abstract philosophy."[227] Due to the commonality of these preoccupations, although different in their approach and conceptualization, as Lukács suggests, the preparatory stages of Hegel's *Phenomenology,* says Lukács: "provides evidence of a long and detailed preoccupation with Goethe's *Faust.*"[228] In fact, Lukács notes: "Historically, only one figure may be placed on a par with Hegel: Goethe . . . Goethe and Hegel lived at the beginning of the last great tragic period of bourgeois development."[229] Lukács adds: "Both works express a similar aspiration to provide an encyclopedic account of the development of mankind . . . and to portray that development in its immanent movement, in terms of its own laws. It was not for nothing that Pushkin referred to *Faust* as an *Iliad* of the modern world."[230] Like Hegel and Goethe, Carpentier sets out to construct an epic of the history of the Caribbean, in which he inverts classical *Christomorphism* "as the model for the construction of identity,"[231] in the historical character of the Haitian Christophe, to serve as counterpoint to the birth of the European presence in America. This is a birth marked by the arrival of another Christomorphic prototype: Christopher Columbus.

The archetypal image of the dictator might have been taking form at this time in Carpentier's thoughts as the great Latin American epic. Christophe may in fact be Carpentier's prototype for the grotesque figure of a Latin American dictator first portrayed by Valle Inclán in *Tirano Banderas* (1926), a novel highly praised by Carpentier. This archetypal representation of the Latin American dictator which Carpentier elaborates in later novels, is the realization in America of those fables of antiquity that, in David Quint's words: "the ancient poets set before us [in the] examples of lives, characters, exploits, deliberations, events, upon all of which posterity, when it gazes at certain pictures, may easily take counsel for both its public and private affairs."[232] The epic form was, after all, the marriage of history and fiction, and of the telluric and the political contexts that interested Carpentier.[233] It was also Ortiz's notions of the marriage of the proper (tobacco) and the foreign (sugar) in cubanidad that associated Faustian America (Cuba) with a vital cultural moment in Europe. After all, as Ortiz reminds the readers in his allegorical story of Sugar and Tobacco, that perhaps also: "Faust, that discontented philosopher, probably puffed at a pipe, while the gentle, devout Marguerite nibbled at sugar wafers."[234]

Hegel and Goethe, in Lukács words: "created lasting images of the generic experiences of mankind," in "images . . . comprehensive and large in scope, and yet penetrating and true in detail."[235] The same can be said of Carpentier's *The Kingdom of This World*. In his *Faust,* Goethe, like Marlowe had done before him, chose for his work a historical character already inscribed in German literature and lore that had actually lived in Germany in the sixteenth century. Goethe's rewriting of Marlowe's rewriting of the Frankfurt *Faust-Book* of 1587, about a historical alchemist of the period, turns the text into the writer's concern "with the nature of modern man and the special moral and intellectual challenges with which he finds himself confronted."[236] Goethe's Faust is not a rebel "against Christian dogma only, but against any sort of categorized system of values."[237] Similarly, Carpentier's appropriation of the historical legendary Haitian slave Mackandal, and his creation of an allegorical, fictional, Ti Nöel, inscribes in his text a codified fabric of symbols born out of popular memories and lore in the Caribbean (like Faust in Germany). It is a Carpentierian representation of a Caribbean cultural "soul," in terms of "origin:" conceived as a Caribbean way of being, its historical and persistent "longing for liberty," and its unrelenting cultural resistance to foreign domination.

Both novels, *Faust* and *The Kingdom of This World,* are epic proposals of ethical conflicts, related to the views of the writer about his intellectual and historical challenges. Like Ti Nöel, Faust's life is placed, Victor Langue notes, in "a larger ethical context—the tension between the creative energies of the Lord and the destructive forces of Mephistopheles."[238] Goethe's "Faust's earthly remains are at last transformed into pure perception,"[239] much in the same way that Carpentier's Ti Nöel is transmuted into historical self-consciousness and clarity. However, Goethe's structural theology, or even Hegel's theology, are not "proper" theologies to express an America different from Western episteme. As González Echeverría points out, during the thirties and forties, Carpentier searched for a literary theology of history "that will endow the signs of his narrative with new meanings within a continuum. Afro-Cuban religion offers itself as the symbolic plenum within which to inscribe the flow of such a history."[240] In *The Kingdom of This World,* Carpentier interlaces what he knows of Afro-Cuban belief systems and rituals with what he read about Haiti and Haitian Voodoo, to construct a dance of two historical consciousness in dialectical conflicts: and, at the same time, a Caribbean Faustian contrapuntal dance of epic-historical and telluric contexts. The resulting textual dance of opposites is a master-piece of craftsmanship. In it, the other, the Haitian slave whose conscious-ness Carpentier imagines, echoes Carpentier's own voice, his tensions as a Latin American writer, his anxiety about writing, and his personal tensions with his French father. *The Kingdom of This World* marks a new beginning in Carpentier's own literary oeuvre. It also carves out a space from where to articulate local memories and excluded knowledges in the Caribbean: a space from where to construct, write and rewrite, Caribbean archetypal fig-ures born out of Caribbean conditions.

CROSSROADS OF AFRICA AND EUROPE:
EL REINO DE ESTE MUNDO/THE KINGDOM OF THIS WORLD

In the closing scene of *The Kingdom of This World,* Ti Nöel is "thrust to the boundless" in a Faustian moment in which life and death, myth and history are one. This final moment of "dawn" at the end of the novel parallels the early morning hours of the opening scene, and recalls the movements of con-sciousness in Hegel's historical scheme. This is a moment in which, as Georg Lukács observes, "the beginning and the end of the historical process coin-cide, i.e., the end of history is prefigured in the beginning."[241] For Lukács, this is the moment that announces self-annulment: a return to the identical subject-object, when the "externalization" of spirit into time occurs. This is also the moment when the reintegration of history in the absolute subject takes place and time is annulled. As in "Liturgia,"[242] in *The Kingdom of This World* Carpentier proposes a ritual beginning that follows death, at a mo-ment when historical time is annulled, and, like in ñáñigo and Voodoo cer-emonies, the magic of the ritual "becomes" the reality of the world.

The rhythmic counterpoint of death/birth, end/beginning, or Sunday/Monday that, as Roberto González Echevarría observes, orders the novel,[243] is announced in the opening scene of the text in the counterpoint of two different antithetical sets of cultural codes. Such counterpoint suggests the dialectic movement of a double consciousness represented by the white Eu-ropean masters and the black Haitian/African slaves. For a still-Spengler-ian Carpentier, not yet "converted" to Sartre's model of Existentialism,[244] Haiti represented an important space and time in the history of Latin Amer-ica, because it was Haiti's Faustian vigor and agency that set a new course of political freedom for other Latin American regions to follow.[245] From the gaze of Spengler's notions of contemporaneity, fetishist Haitians, and their faith in magic, proposed in America an older face of Western civi-lization, since Europe, as Carpentier states in his prologue, at one time was also atavistic and "primitive." In *The Kingdom of This World,* Carpentier mirrors two contemporaneous[246] cultural moments from the gaze of two different philosophies. The double movement of consciousness in Hegel's scheme seems to confront itself (as two different moments in Western culture), from the gaze of two different belief systems (Christianity and Voodoo), which Carpentier constructs from other texts and documents.[247] Reminiscing Spengler, who defined the baroque as the counterpoint of "fine sensibility" and "popular feelings" (*DW*, 242), Carpentier structures his text in a rhythmic confrontation of opposites, and in a contrapuntal dance between the writer's fine sensibility and popular Caribbean beliefs.

To represent "popular feelings" in Haiti, Carpentier turns to other texts including his own early works.[248] He takes into account the new views and values of negritude in the Caribbean as expressed in *Tropiques,* Lam's paintings, Lydia Cabrera's research and Afro-Cuban short stories, and Ortiz's latest work. In *The Kingdom of This World,* Carpentier also meditates on new inquiries in the literary canon about culture and nation, and he again inscribes ritual in the very structural fabrics of the text. The result is a tight web of symbolical symmetries. In *The Kingdom of This World,* Roberto González Echevarría has observed:

> There are, moreover, networks of "echoes and affinities," . . . that transcends the arithmological system, and a complete system of Biblical and liturgical resonances that begins with the very title of the story and encompass the numerical concordances. The name Ti Nöel suggests that the slave was born on Christmas Day, and if to this is added his having fathered twelve children, he appears as a sort of *figura Christi;* Mackandal appears on Chritsmas Day; M. Lenormand de Mézy's wife dies on Pentecost Sunday; Brelle appears on Ascension Sunday; and Palm Sunday is mentioned near the end of the story. All of the repetitions and Christian rituals are an attempt to make the action fit into a cycle like that of the liturgical year—an attempt, in other words, to fuse the dynamics of the cosmos and writing.[249]

At the center of these structural symmetries, and crossroads, is Ti Nöel. His name recalls the symbolical presence of the Nativity of Christ, basic to European law and religion, but also to Haitian Voodoo. The name also recalls the signifying presence in the history of the Caribbean of Nativity (Christmas) and its historical association with carnival and rebellion. Following the text's play of symmetries and counterpoints, but also coherent with the structure of Christian liturgy and Afro-Caribbean ritual, González Echevarría notes that the novel (twenty-six chapters total) is divided into two major narrative sections (of thirteen chapters each), and each one is divided into two other sections which make up the four sections indicated in the index. González Echevarría observes that each of the two major sections ends with a thirteenth chapter and that both of these represent a moment of carnival, of social chaos, that announces death and beginning.[250] In the first section, narrative time travels forward following the chrono-

logical history of Haiti from the war of independence to the reign of mulatto rulers[251] (a probable reference to the government of Boyer, which
Carpentier places soon after the death of Christophe to fit his structural textual scheme). At midpoint of the text, however, narrative time begins to
travel backward, toward its own annulment, following a narrative technique he had already rehearsed in a short story, "Back to the Source:" a
technique Antonio Benítez Rojo identifies with a musical structure known
as "crab" or *canon cancrizans* (*RI,* 221–39), and with the *orisha Elegua* (*RI,*
227–28). With this narrative inversion (reminiscent also of the language of
inversion in Hegel's philosophy of history), at the midpoint of the novel
Carpentier's text unfolds into its own opposite, as a mirror reflection of his
other, so that, at the end of the novel, the text, like Hegelian history, has
traveled back to its beginning. Following such structure, the first twelve
chapters narrate the story of the Haitian revolution against France; and the
thirteenth chapter, as González Echeverría points out, constructs a carnivallike moment of revolution and chaos[252] in which the Haitian rebels are
defeating the French and colonial order is coming to an end: "All the bourgeois norms had come tumbling down" (*KW,* 62); and "An air of license,
of fantasy, of disorder swept the city" (*KW,* 63). One of those rebels is Ti
Nöel. He is captured by the French, but his master, Lenormand de Mezzy,
rescues him right before he is to be executed, and takes him to Santiago de
Cuba where other plantation owners had taken refuge.

The second section of the two sections of 12 + 1 chapters in which the
text is divided, narrates backward the loss and disappointment of the ac-
complishments gained in the first half. This is the narration of the destruction and failure of the political independence won by the Hatian revolution,
the return of the chains under a Haitian king, Henri Christophe, and a second rebellion that puts an end to Henry Christophe's tyrannical rule. In this
second section, Ti Nöel returns to Haiti, in a voyage back to the source: to
the old plantation of his birth where he had been a slave. However, before
he reaches his birthplace, Ti Nöel experiences slavery once again, as he had
in the first half of the novel. Once back on the plantation, he transforms
himself into insects and animals, like his teacher Mackandal had done in
the first half of the novel. The last chapter of the text (a second thirteenth
chapter) offers, in symmetry to the thirteenth chapter in the middle of the
text, another carnivallike moment of end and beginning related once more
to revolution. Here, Ti Nöel, now a centenary, joins another revolt, this time
a cosmic re-volution brought about by the same natural forces that had been
summoned by Bouckman in the first half of the novel.[253] This last chapter
of cosmic revolution offers other symmetries, in images of carnival and
revolution, with the first chapter of the novel.

In an ingenious dance of counterpoints, the first chapter of the novel begins with an allegorical ritual trip to the marketplace: a point of intersec-

tion where multiple roads meet and intersect. Since the marketplace is a type of crossroad, the meeting point where contrary principles intersect, the marketplace has an important place in Afro-Caribbean belief systems. In Afro-Cuban rituals of initiations to *Regla de Ocha,* for example, the first day of the seven days of the ritual is known as "market day." This is the first day of a week-long process of initiation: the day when the initiate must go to the market at dawn already dressed for the initiation in order to purchase the necessary items for the ritual.[254] Intimating a symmetrical symbolic counterpoint between the Afro-Caribbean week of initiation and the week of creation in the Biblical story, in *The Kingdom of This World,* Lenormand de Mézy, Ti Nöel's master, takes his slave to the market early in the morning to purchase a stallion. De Mézy chose the young slave because he knew that Ti Noel had "a certain gift," or "wisdom," for such matters (*KW,* 3). In Carpentier's ritual structure, this is the moment when Ti Nöel's initiation begins. It is also the moment when the textual order of inversions that structure the novel begins. The first of such inversions is the reversal of the traditional master-slave discourse. Here, it is the slave, Ti Nöel, the one who possesses a certain "knowledge" his master does not have. Ti Nöel's "knowledge" establishes in the opening scene of the text a play of inversions with which the writer heralds the ordering principle of subsequent chapters. For example, on their way to the market, the white Frenchman is riding on a "lighter-limbed sorrel" and his slave, on a female Percheron. Yet, on their way back to the plantation from the market, Ti Nöel is riding the stallion de Mezzy purchased; and both, master and slave, are whistling two very different songs:[255] De Mézy is whistling "a fife march" and "Ti Nöel, in a kind of mental counterpoint, silently hummed a chantey that was very popular among the harbor coopers, heaping ignominy on the King of England" (*KW,* 10). Ti Noel's "knowledge" is associated now in the text, by way of his mental humming, to defiance, subversion, and resistance. The text warns the reader that, in that carnival-like space where different roads meet, the marketplace, a change, an inversion, has taken place in the slave/master order.

As master and slave travel back to the plantation, Lenormand de Mézy stops at a barbershop to shave, and Ti Nöel waits for him outside. While he waits, he notices four wax heads at the front window of the barbershop. Mentally, Ti Nöel contrasts the four heads (the fifth one being, implicitly, his master's head), with another set of decapitated heads displayed next door at a butcher shop. In a silent form of defiance: "It amused Ti Nöel to think that alongside the pale calve heads, heads of white men were served on the same tablecloths" (*KW,* 4). The different sets of "heads" that call Ti Nöel's attention at this moment allow the writer to articulate the double movement of antithetical consciousness (master-slave) through the representation of two opposite cultural codes (African and European).

In the same way that the diablito dancers masked the ritual meaning of their performances on "Día de Reyes," Ti Nöel's thoughts and beliefs, like the song he mentally hums, are hidden from the master's gaze. Carpentier's de Mézy, like other French slave owners, did not understand the slave's mysterious beliefs and practices, until the slave's uprising. Only then did de Mézy understand the significance of the rituals that had been taking place around him. Only then did he remember Father Labat's warnings after his first visit to the island: that "the Negroes were like the Philistines, adoring Dagon inside the Ark." The Governor mentioned a word that Lenormand de Mézy never head before: "Voodoo." He then recalled the findings of Moreau de Saint-Mery about Haitian witch doctors and snake worship in the savanna and in the hills:

> "Now that he remembered this, it filled him with uneasiness, making him realize that, in certain cases, a drum might be more than just a goatskin stretched across a hollow log. The slaves evidently had a secret religion that upheld and united them in their revolts" (KW, 58).

In a play of double utterances reminiscent of the diablito dances on "Día de Reyes," Carpentier's text suggests a second, but primary, order of reading directed, as Benítez Rojo points out, to the Caribbean. For example, Ti Nöel's amusing subversive meditation on the subject of "heads," among which he places by analogy the heads of white masters, recalls the importance "heads" have in the Death Magic Cult of Haitian Voodoo. In Seabrook's description of this Cult: "life-sized images of human heads, sometimes carved of wood, sometimes cast in lead,"[256] are placed on altars. Each head "is named for the man who is to be slain, and remains on the altar under a sort of death sentence until the death occurs, when the leaden head is replaced by the real head if it can be obtained."[257] The strategic placement of the ritual "heads"[258] in this opening scene of the first chapter heralds the future destruction of colonial rule as well as the narrative ordering principle of the text, thus establishing Ti Nöel's own role as an allegorical agent in the actions to come. It is here that Carpentier's text confronts two different sets of archival codes: Ti Nöel's Afro-Haitian Faustian vigor and "knowledge" and de Mezy's dominant Western European "declining" culture. At this moment, then, Ti Nöel notices even more "heads." It seemed that: "The morning was rampant with heads, for next to the tripe-shop the bookseller had hung on a wire with clothespins the latest prints received from Paris. At least four of them displayed the face of the King of France" (KW, 5). And there were even more heads, those of courtiers, soldiers, magistrates, and intellectuals, all of them figures of the French court that reinforced Ti Nöel's view of European society as weak and effeminate.

It is not a mere coincidence that Carpentier's strategic "heads" in this opening scene also establish a dialogue with Faustian European culture in sixteenth century Europe, specifically with the anonymous *Faust-Book* of 1587, and with Christophe Marlow's *Tragical History of Dr. Faustus*,[259] where the opening scene of the novel is also about "heads." Carpentier recalls, in reference to his definition of the American baroque, that "en *La historia del Dr. Fausto*, anónima, de 1587, nos muestra unos brujos que se cortan las cabezas para mandarlas a la barbería y se las vuelven a colocar en su sitio una vez rasuradas y peinadas" (in the anonymous *History of Dr. Faust*, of 1587, shows us male witches that cut their heads off and send them to the barbershop and then put them on again once the heads are shaved and combed).[260] Since faith and magic in the sixteenth century, as represented in the *Faust-Books* of 1587, is for Carpentier a cultural moment contemporaneous to the America he wants to express, Ti Nöel's gaze is determined by similar notions of magic, now African, he learned from Mackandal. At the same time, Mackandal, like Faust, is a rebel against the morality of his times, and, like the alchemist Faust, he also tampers with, and "knows," nature.

On that day of "heads," in an ironical counterpoint of history and art,[261] history and fiction, Africa and Europe, Ti Nöel notices at last a copper engraving representing a black African King welcoming a European explorer. This new and different image brings to Ti Nöel's memory an imaginary Africa as distant for Ti Nöel as the French court. At the same time, the memory of Africa triggers in Ti Nöel the memory of the myths, history, and legends that he learned from the African Mandingue Mackandal about his native land: stories about the great African kingdom of the Popos, Aradas, Nagos, and Fulas, their histories, their battles, legends, and gods. Mackandal spoke of the:

> the great migrations of tribes, of age-long wars, of epic battles in which the animals had been allies of men. He knew the story of Adonhueso, of the King of Angola, of King Da, the incarnation of the Serpent, which is the eternal beginning, never ending, who took his pleasure mystically with a queen who was the Rainbow, patroness of the Waters and of the Bringing Forth. . . . Moreover, those kings rode with lances in hand at the head of their hordes, and they were made invulnerable by the science of the Preparers, and fell wounded only if in some way they had offended the gods of Lighting or of the Forge (*KW*, 6–7).

Privileging Ti Nöel's African knowledge, not without the ethnocentric irony of the writer's own Western Spenglerian perspective, in *The Kingdom of This World*, Africa is the antithesis of Europe, and Europe, a declining "civilization" whose economic fetishes, self-reflections, and skepticism made it effeminate and weak. Ti Nöel, a Caribbean creole, is the vigorous offspring of a land of contrasts and conflicts,[262] whose perspectives seem to articulate Carpentier's views of history rather than the realities of an uneducated Haitian slave. Ti Nöel was born and raised in Lenormand de Mézy's plantation with no access to the world of the French court. Yet he is able to establish a contrast between the strong and powerful "masculine" African heroes and kings of Mackandal's stories, and the weak effeminate French king portrayed in the paintings that were hanging in the front of the bookstore measuring "the beat of a rigadoon, with his effeminate legs" (*KW,* 7). More like the product of a novelist with a "vast knowledge" able to establish relationships across time and space, than the representation of an uneducated slave, Ti Nöel also imagines the symphony of European violins in the French King's court, and "the tittle-tattle of their mistress and the warble of their stringed birds" (*KW,* 14). Carpentier's counterpoint of two different cultural imaginaries constructs a dance between two *allás* (there): Africa and Europe in the "here" ("proper"), which is America, in a Caribbean landscape.

Masking fiction as history and history as fiction, Ti Nöel's reminiscing of the African King *Dá,* the eternal principle, heralds historical change. Thus, when Monsier Lenormand de Mézy buys one of the decapitated pigs' heads and gives it to Ti Nöel to hold: "Ti Noël clasped that white, chill skull under his arm, thinking how much it probably resembled the bald head of his master hidden beneath his wig" (*KW,* 9). His imaginary interpretation is premonitory of a series of metamorphosis his character will suffer throughout the novel: not unlike the changes suffered by the initiate in Afro-Caribbean ceremonies of initiation. These transformations are intimated in the master-slave inversion of the first scene when Ti Nöel exchanges his Percheron for a stallion, indicating his allegorical metaphorical transformation[263] from the possessor of "hidden knowledge" to the phallic authorial symbol of writing and knowledge in the text. Ti Nöel's investiture in this role[264] takes place, significantly, after Mackandal is imprisoned and burnt at the stake. Mackandal's death signals a beginning, and Ti Nöel impregnates a slave woman (in three consecutive coitus). She later gives birth to twin sons. The fact that Ti Nöel conceives twins is important in Carpentier's ritualistic allegorical scheme, since, mythologically, only storm gods like the African Shango conceive twins. More important, however, is the fact that the Afro-Caribbean divine twins, the *Ibeyes,* sons of Shango, the orisha of storms and thunder, are the *Jimaguas,* the same figure Carpentier represents in *El milagro de anaquillé.* Their indirect reappearance again in *The Kingdom of This World* indicates once more the writer's resistance against colonialism, and forecasts the revolutionary wind that brings about the defeat of the French. Carpentier transforms Spengler's notion of a Faustian moment in the historical development of Western's culture into a static revolutionary moment that could stop the advancement of the tyranny of Reason (and the intrusion of foreign capitalism). This resistance recalls the way in which, as Carpentier suggests from his research on the history of music in Cuba, Cuban music (its African rhythm) resists foreign influences.[265] By the end of the first chapter, Ti Nöel has placed the appropriate heads on the altar, and the contrapuntal dance of a double consciousness begins its textual movement of ontological differences.

In *The Kingdom of This World,* narrative time always stands suspended between two poles: Christian liturgical order and Afro-Caribbean ritual order. Both of these poles, like all religious rituals, follow the order of death and rebirth, end and beginning,[266] which is also the same ordering principle of writing. Such structure implies that the text's ordering principle is no other than a universal symbolic rhythm embedded in the deepest folds of the human psychic in its efforts to conceive an orderly cosmos. Liturgy then, in a Carpentierian sense, is man's imaginary writing of that order, a relationship conceived under certain similar patterns across ages and cultures. In Haitian Voodoo, for example, the ordering principle life/death, end/beginning is already implicit in the image of the Mystic Egg often portrayed in *Damballah*'s *vever* (*Dá*), the snake deity that represents eternal time.[267] The egg represents the suspended gestation of life and the uniting force of all opposite principles of life, as represented by the Afro-Cuban Ibeyes or Jimaguas, and by *Legba/Elegua.* In this Carpentierian dance of opposites, life and representation are as one, like Janus's two faces, as in the baroque where king and buffoon, tyrant and martyr, slave and master are inverted figures of one another. In that dance of opposites, the Mystic Egg, America for Carpentier, holds in suspense the life-force of a new day. Thus, through a careful play of symmetries, Carpentier inverts historical orders through the investiture of signifying masks that allow the writer to represent Ti Nöel in the role of the reader and of the writer: the only author-ial voice in this narrative cosmos capable of summoning the natural forces that can bring the text to its final end/beginning. To reach that moment, in which Ti Nöel's last metamorphosis thrusts him "in the expanse of the universe" (*DW,* 279), in a Spenglerian "boundless infinite," Carpentier's allegorical character must suffer other ritual transformations,[268] like Miguel de Cervantes's Don Quixote.

II

Frederick de Armas notes that when Alejo Carpentier was awarded the "Premio Miguel de Cervantes," on April 4, 1978, his acceptance speech at the University of Alcalá de Henares centered on *Don Quixote,*[269] a work he always admired and considered inexhaustible. In fact, direct and indirect comments about Cervantes's work are often found in Carpentier's novels. De Armas proposes that Carpentier's concept of the "marvelous is modeled on a world vision encountered in Cervantes's romance *Los tra-bajos de Persiles y Segismunda,*[270] where, like in Carpentier's *The King-dom of This World,* the marvelous "stems from a character's imaginative faith, which cannot be presented directly since there is tension between the narrator's experience and the personage's vision."[271] As in Cervantes's last novel, in *The Kingdom of This World* Carpentier plays with alternative vi-sions, and with the ambiguities of faith, magic, and metamorphosis. In both texts, "faith permeates the fictional environment and expands the limits of the real in the narrative;" and both writers, "aware that metamorphosis sig-nifies sudden change, use the transformation as a metaphor for revolt."[272] De Armas further suggests that, in Cervantes's case, "viewed from the artist's perspective," Cervantes's representation of metamorphosis "can represent the poet's revolt against Neo-Aristotelian rules."[273] In this sense, "the marvelous can be seen as rebellion against verisimilitude. . . . and it leads to a truth based on *desengaño.*"[274] While Cervantes tends to rejects metamorphosis "on ethical and religious grounds,"[275] Carpentier does not. After all, notes de Armas, "it is *el reino de este mundo* that is emphasized, a demonic land where metamorphosis as a metaphor for revolt becomes a liberating impulse."[276]

In a unique play of symmetries in which Carpentier contrasts opposite versions of reality, illusion and disillusionment, reason and faith, history and myth, the familiar and the marvelous, history and fiction, the learned and the vernacular, as de Armas observes, Carpentier dialogues in *The Kingdom of This World* with Cervantes's *Los trabajos de Persiles y Segis-munda* (a dialogue Carpentier highlights in the prologue to the novel). Car-pentier shares with Cervantes the concept, central to Ti Nöel's historical awareness, of "Tareas" or "trabajos" (tasks/labor/toil): the tasks human be-ings must set for themselves in their struggle to better themselves within the limitations of humanity. Carpentier's homage to Cervantes in *The King-dom of This World,* however, is most evident in the inclusion of a Cervan-tine *entremeses* (short comedy interludes within a larger work), which he interpolates in the middle of the novel as a two-act story, that mirrors (re-flects and inverts) the larger story (which is also divided into two sections). This is a micro-story about Napoleon's sister, Pauline Bonaparte, and her voyage to Haiti during the Haitian revolution, and about her fictitious re-lationship with an equally fictitious black Haitian servant named Solimán, a Voodoo *hougan.* The larger narrative context in which Carpentier inter-polates this micro-story is the story of the Haitian revolution: the armed conflict between blacks and whites, between servants and masters. The in-terpolated story narrates, within the story of the revolution, the "toils" of a white woman and a black man, Pauline and Solimán, who are finally rec-onciled in a libidinal relationship that transforms each one into the other, in a Carpentierian mode of "transculturation." The story of Pauline and

Solimán recalls Cervantes's *Los trabajos de Persiles y Segismunda,* while, at the same time, it follows Ortiz's allegorical contrapuntal dance of sugar and tobacco: foreign/native, black/white, female/male, master/servant, contemporary/ancient, primitive/civilized.

Carpentier's dichotomy in the "toils" of Pauline and Solimán, between Italy (Europe/Rome) and Haiti (Latin America), recalls Cervantes's dichotomy between northern and southern Italy in his *Los trabajos de Persiles y Segismunda.* Northern Italy, for Cervantes, is a mysterious and remote land where Cervantes's Rutilo experiences the marvelous. In Carpentier's novel, Haiti is a distant marvelous island for Pauline; and, for Solimán, Italy is a distant imaginary land where a different marvelous reality awaits him: where, like Persiles, the Haitian servant also is transformed. In Italy, Solimán turns into an *indiano,* a tale-teller:[277] the fictional hero of his own *engaños* (deceit).[278] It is also in Italy that Pauline is transformed into art, into an Apollonian statue of Venus, an inverted Pygmalion, back to the lifeless work of art. In both texts, Cervantes and Carpentier propose an imaginary trek, a pilgrimage toward truth through lies (fiction), in order to find a greater truth. It is not a simple textual coincidence then, that the section of the novel that tells of the night when Solimán encounters a statue in which he recognizes the forms of Pauline, is prologued by a quote from Segismundo, in Calderón de la Barca's *La vida es sueño* (*Life is a Dream*) (1635). Like Solimán, Segismundo is a character caught in the ambiguity of a reality in which fiction is truth and truth is fiction: a situation not very different from the masked festivities of "Día de Reyes" in colonial Havana.

The allegorical dance between Pauline and Solimán allows Carpentier to counterpoint history and fiction in a micro-text that mirrors the larger story. Historically, Pauline did go to Haiti with her husband Leclerc, and, as Madame D'Abrantes recalls in her memoirs, a text Carpentier paraphrases in *The Kingdom of This Word* for his portrayal of Pauline, she did return to France a widow, haggard, and different from her old self. Yet, in *The Kingdom of This World,* Pauline is also an allegorical figure, like Ortiz's sugar: a metaphor for a Spenglerian foreign, white, effeminate civilization. As such, she is transformed by the colonial experience. What remains of her is only an artificial resemblance: a lifeless statue, like Europe for Spengler. In the Caribbean context that Pauline encounters in Haiti, the process of making sugar destroys the living sugar canes, and leaves only the waste pulp of the plant, much like the body of the slaves in the process of sugar production.[279] That waste, Pauline's remnant as a statue, turns to poison for Solimán who then becomes sick after encountering Pauline's art(ificial) semblance. At the same time, Solimán's effect on Pauline is like the substance solimán: a cure and a poison, like Haiti was for France, like Mackandal was for colonial power. It was only after Mackandal lost his arm in the cane press, and his wasted body was tossed aside, no longer useful and profitable, that he began his systematic resistance against the white rulers. Mixed with the same sugar that brought wealth to the colony, Mackandal's wasted arm turned metaphorically to poison: the venom of anger and resentment that eventually led to rebellion.[280] As the result of resentment and hate (the waste product of colonial wealth), Mackandal began to lash back against the colonial system, resisting slavery by poisoning the masters with a venom he learned to make from local plants in the forest. In Carpentier's text, he acquires such knowledge from a Rada Voodoo priestess. Mackandal's production, the venom he concocted from natural plants, "crawled across the Plaine du Nord, invading pastures and stables" and, "to the general horror, it became known that the poison had got into the houses" and the white "owners had been struck down by the poison" (*KW*, 21–22). Mackandal's knowledge is related to Voodoo, a religious system that came together as we know it today in Haiti during this historical period, and whose "knowledge" is associated in *The Kingdom of This World* with poison, and poison with resistance and will-to-freedom.

Contrapuntal to the historical figure of Pauline (sugar: female, carnal, sensuous, foreign, and related to a system based on slavery), Solimán is a fictional character reminiscent of Ortiz's tobacco (male, dark, native, primitive, demonic, sacred, mysterious, and profane), a native plant associated with "demonic powers"[281] with poison,[282] with "certain hidden mysteries" proper of tobacco, and with rites of passage and initiation.[283] Carpentier's Solimán is not only Pauline's *maseur,* and her servant. He is an *hougan,* a Voodoo priest: keeper of the same "certain mysteries" (reminiscent of Ti Nöel's knowledge of the Cult of the Death) associated with metamorphosis. In that role, he is her teacher and guardian. In that association, Carpentier's Solimán recalls the role the mercurial substance "solimán" had in Golden Age theater as a catalyst for transformation: a *pharmako,* that seemed to beautify while, in reality, it poisoned its user. The etymology of the name Solimán exemplifies a plurality that Carpentier appropriates for the character of Solimán in *The Kingdom of This World.* In the first place, the name brings together two images that were commonly used in the Spanish baroque: "sol" (sun), and "imán" (magnet).[284] The word "solimán" is also a derivative of the Turk *sulumen,* meaning sublimated,[285] a mixture of mercury and chlorine used as a type of disinfectant of poisonous effects; it was used also as a cosmetic. This is the role in which the substance solimán appears in Golden Age texts with the meaning of false beauty and deceit, as in Quevedo's satiral poems; and in Lope de Vega's *El caballero de Olmedo,* where solimán appears as a "mortífero"(deadly or lethal) that first made women beautiful and later killed them.[286] Like Carpentier's Solimán, Ortiz represents tobacco in a way similar to the substance solimán: a plant with medicinal properties and, yet, at the same time, addictive and poisonous.[287] Solimán, in his role of catalyst for transformation, and as a deceitful beautifying poison, is also a literary trope in Fernando de Roja's *La Celestina* (1499). Celestina is a procuress go-between who is deceitful in all of her dealings; and, coherent with her role as social venom, she makes and sells solimán.[288] The solimán-like-love that Melibea finds in Calixto, through the deceiving mediation of the mercurial Celestina, brings about, first, the beauty of passion, and later, the death of both lovers, as well as Celestina's own violent end.

Carpentier's Solimán is a type of Celestinesque Caribbean trickster/priest whose magic and faith seems to come closer to Golden Age theater than to Carpentier's representation of Voodoo as an agent for resistance and revolution. At the same time, Carpentier's Solimán is the personification of the native, the seductive and religious mysteries of tobacco, but he is also the allegorical representation of the substance taken to America from Europe in the sixteenth century. In the Caribbean, and especially in Haiti,[289] the substance solimán was used in the same way it was used in Spain, but it soon acquired a significant role as an instrument of resistance against colonial domination. Even as early as 1528, in Hispaniola, a woman slave was condemned to die at the stake for giving her mistress solimán.[290] By 1786, a period which coincides with the events narrated by Carpentier in *The Kingdom of This World,* it was illegal to sell solimán to any black person, slave or free,[291] because it was used, like Mackandal's poison, as a weapon against white rulers. Carpentier's representation of Solimán is in part coherent with the traditional properties of cure and venom, death and illusion, the substance solimán was thought to have in Golden Age texts, as an element of transformation and metamorphosis, and, in colonial America, as a tool of resistance and colonial venom.[292] In this sense, Carpentier's Solimán is an allegorical representation of the same ritual ordering principle of the novel: life/death, end/beginning. In such allegorical role, and in his association with the native Caribbean tobacco, Carpentier's Solimán intimates a Carpentierian quest for the Faustian (m)other telluric womb of America that Carpentier, like the *origenistas,* finds in the "primitive," the indigenous, and, especially in Afro-Caribbean beliefs.

Once in Italy, Solimán's desire for Pauline becomes the death wish of a return to the past: an allegorical moment that dialogues with Carpentier's own ontological conflicts of cultural and ontological identity. This is a conflict without resolution for Solimán, who, like Faust, finds himself trapped in an internal (here), and an external (there). It is a conflict that thrusts him into the boundless, to infinity, "in the midst of tears," like Goethe's Faust: also trapped "between elation and dejection, between hope and despair."[293] In the case of Carpentier's Solimán, however, Pauline is not his redeeming spirit, like Margaret is for Faust. Pauline becomes solimán for Solimán, in the same way that he turns into poison for her. For Solimán, the Haitian *hougan,* Pauline is the foreign substance (sugar) that seduces him and, in the process, alters his condition.

In his allegorical role, Solimán may be read also as the convergence of *sol* (sun, light, tropic, fire), and *imán,* meaning "charm" and a magnet, a black metal whose attracting force over other metals is equivalent to the effect the Haitian *maseur* has on Pauline.[294] His name is also reminiscent of the attraction Afro-Cuban rituals had on Carpentier. *Imán* was also the name of the journal in which Carpentier served as editor: an experience that, according to Carpentier, marked and transformed his style of writing.[295] In his mercurial role in *The Kingdom of This World,* Solimán serves as an icon for the magic island that changes Pauline's life, where she loses her husband, Leclerc, to the "black plague" (disease and rebellion), and where she is transformed, Haitianized, into the image of a native mulatto. Following Spengler's theory of cultural contemporaneity, Pauline's transformation mediated by Solimán allows the narrator to equate Pauline's Haitianized "primitive" image, with her family's Corsican ancestry. In other words, Pauline recognizes her own cultural past, her cultural "origins," in the "primitive" "atavistic" Haitian hougan. Solimán is a catalyst for Pauline's voyage back to her cultural source: a trek reminiscent of Carpentier's short story "Back to the Source" where a black servant is also the mercurial element that makes narrative time travel backward, to the womb.

Pauline and Solimán's metamorphic attraction toward each other seems to be based on their own cultural gaze with which each one sees and reconstructs the other as a projection of their his/her imaginary. Pauline constructs Solimán from her readings. For her, Solimán is a black man, like the hero in Joseph Lavalée's novel *Un negro como hay pocos blancos,*[296] a text she was reading during her voyage to Haiti. At the same time, Solimán perceives Pauline from the religious imaginary of a Haitian hougan. As a mediator and transformer of realities, Soliman's reading of Pauline Bonaparte from the belief system of an hougan, renders her as a human avatar of the Voodoo *loa Metresse Erzulie* (or *Erzilie*). This Haitian *loa* is associated with the Virgin Mary, but her attributes are closer to the Afro-Cuban Oshun, known in Cuba as the *Pachangara,* or Holy Virgin Whore, and, in Dominican Voodoo, as *Anaísa.* These three feminine deities are Afro-Caribbean natural forces of love, comparable, from a Western perspective, to the Roman goddess Venus: all of them water deities. Taking advantage of the historical fact that Pauline, in Haiti, did become a scandal for French colonial society due the uninhibited way in which she behaved, as Duchesse d'Abrante tells in her *Memoires,* and that Pauline came to be known as the French Venus for her beauty and sensuality,[297] Carpentier has her emerge in Haiti from *The Ocean,* the name of the ship (*L'Océan*) in which Pauline sailed to Haiti (*KW,* 68). Thus, like Boticelli's Venus, Pauline emerges from the ocean waters. Such metaphoric emergence from the ocean, seen from the religious imaginary of a Vooduist hougan, establishes an analogous association between the French Venus, Pauline, and the Haitian Erzulie: a mulatto deity, like the Afro-Cuban Oshun: sensuous, seductive, capricious, kind and terrible. Like Oshun, Erzulie is the epitome of feminine charm and voluptuousness, always associated with water. Similar to the many manifestations of the Virgin Mary, Erzuli, like most loas and orishas, also has several avatars. In fact, she is one of the most versatile deities of the Voodoo pantheon. In Rada Voodoo cults, *Erzulie-Freda-Dahomey* is the *Matter Dolorosa,* sweet and pure, but, in Petro cults, *Erzulie-Dantor* can be violent and destructive.[298] Solimán's relationship to Pauline is similar to that of Erzulie's devotees who reserve a special dressing room for her in the temples, or *Hounfors,* where her jewelry, perfumes, cosmetics, dresses, and all of the necessary items associated with feminine care are kept for the goddess. Like Carpentier's Pauline, Erzulie demands extreme body pampering from her devotees; and, analogous to Ortiz's allegorical sugar, Erzulie (like Oshun and like Anaísa) loves sweets. All three of these Afro-Caribbean female deities of love are also associated with sugar. This is the reason why beautifully decorated cakes, often with rich white frosting, are placed in the altars dedicated to them. There is also another analogy in the text that associates Erzulie with Pauline. Different from the other loas who speak creole, Erzulie, like Pauline, is an aristocratic deity who speaks French.[299]

Pauline's transformation in the text into an Afro-Haitian Venus (or Erzulie for Solimán) happened soon after her arrival to the island where the sun (sol) of the tropics soon turned her skin the color "of a splendid mulatto" (*KW,* 74).[300] From then on, her relationship with Solimán is of a ritualistic aquatic nature, much like the ways of Erzulie. Recalling that, as Kutzinski observes, "the economic and cultural relationship between sugar and tobacco . . . is characterized by promiscuity of a very specific kind,"[301] Solimán is a former waiter at a bathhouse, and he bathes Pauline naked at a pool where she, knowing that he was "eternally tormented by desire," "took a perverse pleasure in grazing his flanks with her body under the water" (*KW,* 72). Pauline also accompanies Solimán to the beach when he takes ritual offerings to "Aguasou, Lord of the Sea" (*KW,* 76); and, when Pauline returned to the ocean, traveling back to France with the corpse of her husband, she carried an amulet to Papa *Legba* carved by Solimán, "to open the path to Rome for Pauline" (*KW,* 78). During the rituals of *resguardo* (protection), performed by Solimán for Pauline's safety, she is the center of the ceremonies, both as a devotee and, at the same time, the object of devotion. Pauline is dressed only with a white handkerchief, an essential element in Voodoo ceremonies,[302] and a color representative of the world of the dead (ancestors), the world of the loas, and also the color associated with Erzulie.[303] When Pauline returns to her native land, France, she has been transformed by the island (Solimán) left wasted like the slaves, like sugar canes, consumed by her American experience, poisoned by the same system she represents: the same colonial order that caused the slaves to revolt.

The Haitinization of Carpentier's Pauline counterpoints the Europerization of Solimán in Italy. After Pauline's departure, Solimán suddenly reappears in the novel as a servant of Henry Christophe, and, after Christophe's death, he travels to Italy with the king's family. In Italy, Solimán seems to adapt to a Western cultural context where the primitive vigor of Voodoo, as Seabrook points out, is left only for museums. Now associated with the figure of Christophe, like Ti Nöel at the end of the novel, Solimán, still a mercurial element, finds himself in a different and distant land where he, like Rutilo in Cervantes's *Los trabajos de Persiles y Segismunda,* must experience the ambiguities of fantasy (magic) and of reality from a very different perspective, no longer through faith. In Italy, like Carpentier's Juan de Amberes and Juan el Indiano in his short story "El camino de Santiago" (The Road to Santiago), Solimán is transformed into an indiano whose identity is now borne out of his own fictional narrations, reminiscing the illusions of beauty, followed by death, that result from the use of the substance solimán. His epic fantasy in which he is the hero also recalls that in Cuba's first epic poem, Silvestre de Balboa's *Espejo de paciencia* (1608), the epic hero, Salvador, is African, an Ethiopian.

In his role of a mercurial mediator, one day, at "dusk," inebriated,[304] Solimán enters a restricted hallway at the Pallazo Borghese, in Rome, to encounter several white, cold, marble statues. As if he were a Black Orpheus entering Hades, he finds among the statues the Venus of Canova, in which he recognizes the lifeless forms of Pauline. In the twilight (the fusion of light and darkness, sobriety and intoxication), Solimán tries to bring her body back to life[305] with the magic, ritual, language of the drum. He uses the base of the statue as a drum (*KW,* 156), but his ritual drumming was in vain, for the art(ifice) that was now Pauline was like a Voodoo object in a museum: the empty recipient of a spirit long gone, like European cathedrals for Seabrook. Carpentier's Spenglerian Solimán was transformed in Europe into waste, empty of his Haitian Faustian vigor, like Pauline. He is not only unable to awaken her, but, from this moment on, he is destined to remain in the underworld of civilization, as a defeated Orpheus. When the ambiguity of such twilight of realities (reminiscent of Lope de Vega's *El caballero de Olmedo*) settles in the imagination of the inebriated Solimán, the narrator suggests that Pauline-Venus-Erzulie seems to be offering an apple (*KW,* 155), for she is also the static representation of a primordial Eve intimating the fall of man. At the same time, remembering that Pauline was the one who seduced Solimán in Haiti, in the twilight of the gallery of statues, the light of a lantern is casting a yellow shadow. Yellow is the color of the moon, a symbol still perhaps reminiscent of Federico García Lorca's work, but it is also the color of Erzulie's Afro-Caribbean counterparts: Oshun and Anaísa. Carpentier's ingenious iconographic play of symmetries establishes a parallel between the images of the seductive statue of Pauline and the biblical *Eva* (Eve): the "origin" of sin, as an act of transgression. In a movement of spiraling reversals and re-volutions, the end of the novel (like the end of the entremés) closes with the inverted image of *Eva* (Eve) in the figure of *Ave:* a bird in flight, a vulture. In Afro-Caribbean cosmogony the vulture is a symbol of *Legba-Elegua,* Lord of metamorphosis: who presides over the transforming possibilities of the Word, and, as such, the mercurial bridge between the "there" of Voodoo misteres (like the Afro-Cuban *potencias*) and the "here" of humanity.

As a cryptic message in Carpentier's text that Western discourses alone cannot articulate the experiences and the complexities of Caribbean societies, Solimán dies in Rome from European malaria, but with the symptoms of soliman poisoning. The mercurial agent is left suspended by the novel at a moment before his implicit death, still calling for Papa *Legba* who was far away from the ruins of European civilization, back in Haiti. Solimán dies like a Faustian character, "forsaken," and abandoned, like Ortiz's allegorical tobacco. To smoke a cigar, says Ortiz, "es elevar suspiros de humo a lo ignoto, anhelando un consuelo pasajero o una ilusión aunque huidiza que entretenga la espera" (is to elevate sighs of smoke to the unknown, longing for a passing consolation, or an illusion that, even though just fleeing, may entertain hope).[306] At this moment in Carpentier's play of inversions, and transformations, the hougan Solimán goes into exile, away from Haiti, while Ti Nöel returns to Haiti, his native land, after his long exile in Cuba. His return takes place, in symmetry with the first chapter of the novel, in the first chapter with which the second half of the novel begins, at the moment when narrative time begins to travel backward like Ti Nöel.[307] At this midpoint of the text, like in Afro-Caribbean rituals, Solimán's ritual death is a necessary sacrifice (end) that brings about change and rebirth. In other words, in Carpentier's narrative scheme, his death is now followed by Ti Nöel rebirth, like Cervantes's Quixote, into a new symbolic role: an avatar of Legba, also associated in Haitian Voodoo with Christ, with the cross, and with the sun.

III

Carpentier's allegorical reversal of Eva into Ave parallels other textual inversions. One of them is the one Carpentier proposes in the dialogue with Lope de Vega's *El nuevo mundo descubierto por Colón,* as preface to *The*

Kingdom of This World. In this quote that Carpentier chooses from Lope's play, the Devil calls himself "the King of the West" and gripes about the fact that Providence sent Christopher Columbus to "discover" the lands he rules. Carpentier's dialogue with the great master of Golden Age Theater proposes a counter-discourse to Hegel's historical concept of America, as well as to a European conception of America as demonic and inferior. Like Otiz's tobacco, and like Carpentier's Solimán, America for Europe was seductive and demonic. In Carpentier's Gnostic inversions of traditional European discourses about America, the demonic native seducer (native tobacco) is seduced by the foreign white (sugar). And both are destroyed in the process, like the waste product in the production of sugar. Yet, it is precisely in that waste that the forsaken Haitian slaves ironically find the Faustian life-force necessary to wage an apocalyptic revolution. Carpentier inverts the European discourse in which America appears as a land ruled by the "demonic" (always portrayed as black or Indian), to find in that demonic element the spirit of cultural redemption that makes America different, rebellious, and culturally vigorous (Faustian). Rebellion in America then is perceived here as an act of resistance against the Law of the Father, Europe, and, such resistance, as an act of liberation: as a libidinous desire to be one's own. Such mode of resistance in *The Kingdom of This World* recalls an American condition that José Lezama Lima describes in *La expresión Americana,* as *afán fáustico* (Faustian will, toil, motive for knowledge): an act of transgression that for Lezama Lima is characteristic of the New World, and of American baroque. Such afán fáustico made of the Haitian revolution, in spite of all of the internal failures, like a fallen angel in Christian mythology. Lezama Lima's notion of a Faustian America, and Carpentier's counter-discourse in *The Kingdom of This World,* recall, and dialogue with, Ortiz's allegories on culture and nation. The biblical serpent, Ortiz writes:

> astuta y soberbia, diríase que emplumada con el airón de su altivez, la que determina en Adán su hombría plena, mediante el fiat humanizador de la palabra tentadora en el oído de la hembra parejera. Adán quedará unido a ésta por el pecado, y entonces le pondrá el nombre de Eva, que quiere decir "madre de los vivientes." Y así la sociedad ha nacido. Tras el Verbo de Jehová, el Verbo de la Serpiente. El uno crea el mundo y sus habitantes; pero el otro crea la humanidad, dándole a los seres humanos su definitiva y específica capacitación individual y social. O sea, la inconformidad, la curiosidad, la experiencia, la razón, el reajustamiento y la creatividad.[308]

> [astute and proud, one could say that plummed with an aire of arrogance, (the serpent is who) determines Adam's manhood, through the humanizing blessing of the tempting word in the ear of the flirtatious woman. Adam will be united to her through sin, and then he will name her Eve, that means "mother of the

living." And thus, society is born. From Jehovah's Word, and the Serpent's Word. One creates the world and its people; but the other creates humanity, giving human beings their definitive and specific individual capacity, experience, reason, readjustment, and creativity.]

Following along Ortiz's assertions, Carpentier's interest in Lope de Vega's play, as Frederick de Armas suggests, was Lope's vision of America, of history, of the popular, and of the epic.[309] However, as de Armas also observes, if Lope's play establishes an order restored by the Christian truth of salvation in the land of the devil that was America[310] for the Europeans, in Carpentier's novel, the only devil image is man himself, white, black or mulatto, holding on to an old declining order, in the recurring role of oppressor. In Carpentier's novel, the New World portrayed by Lope de Vega as diabolic becomes a vital Faustian land moving in dialectic, spiraling, reoccurrences (of repressions and rebellions, destructions and reconstructions), toward a higher level of understanding with which to finally change persisting patterns of power. The allegorical representative of this spiraling movement, Ti Nöel, is also a witness to what happens when the slave becomes the master. Ti Nöel's forced exile and disillusioned return to his native land are reminiscent of Carpentier's own experiences, exiled in Europe during the ruthless presidency of Gerardo Machado, after spending a short time in prison, in Havana, in 1929, and returning disillusioned to Cuba in 1939. Ti Nöel's return marks a moment of transformation in the novel as the birth of a new dialectic movement of conscious: the beginning of an opposite, but similar, although different, order of things, that leads him to *desengaño*.[311]

In contrast to the mercurial Mackandal of the first half of the novel, and to Solimán in the two-act Cervantine *entremés*, when Ti Nöel returns to Haiti he appears to have been transmuted into the mercurial image of Papa *Legba*, the divine transformer, Lord of crossroads and the Word. In Haitian Voodoo as in other Afro-Caribbean belief systems, it is common for the loas (and orishas) to "mount" or possess a person. The "mounted" individual then begins to act according to the characteristics of the deity that "mounts." The same occurs in the Afro-Cuban ceremonies with which Carpentier was acquainted. Legba is the great mercurial-mediator between *allá* (heaven) and *acá* (earth), between realities, or levels of existence, and the only one who could mediate the crossroads of Carpentier's narrative. He is the hinge that holds Carpentier's text together, and the element that allows the reader to move from one order of reading to another. Legba seems to be, in Carpentier's text, an Afro-Caribbean version of Hegel's concept of *mitte:* the glue that holds together Hegel's allegorical plays of antithesis. Legba/Elegua is Lord of metamorphosis, and mediator between levels of existence. He is the bridge between the visible and the invisible (similar to

Mercury and Hermes in Roman and Greek mythologies), and the mediator in Carpentier's text between history and fiction. Furthermore, Legba/Elegua is the only one capable of altering time, one's perception of reality, and the only one able to make time (narrative) travel backward. Capentier's new investiture of his main character explains why when Ti Nöel returns to Haiti he is not only knowledgeable of "certain hidden mysteries;" he is also the metaphoric reader, subject, and the witness of historical developments: the mediator, like Legba, between textual realities, and between the text and the reader.

In the second half of the novel, and in contrapuntal contrast with the first chapter of the novel where Ti Nöel is a young slave traveling with his master, Ti Nöel reappears back in Haiti, having returned from exile in Santiago de Cuba, as a free man. He is traveling alone back to the source: to the old plantation of his birth and bondage. He is now an old man, ragged, but strong, limping and walking with the help of a *guayacán* branch, like the image of Papa Legba in one of his avatars: also depicted as a ragged, old, but strong man, traveling the roads with a bundle over his shoulder, limping, and walking with the help of a crutch.[312] Legba's phallic crutch, now associated with Ti Nöel, recalls the earlier association in the text between Ti Nöel and the stallion in the opening scene of the first chapter. In the first chapter, Ti Nöel was able to read into the magic symbols of the ritual "heads" the portentous death, end, of French rule. Now, once again, in the first section of the second half of the novel (in the first chapter of the third section of the novel), Ti Nöel is able to read the portentous "signs" that "reveal" the return of another tyrannical order of things. These are the signs Carpentier places in the chapter entitled "Signos" (Signs).[313] The signs he observes as he walks speak to Ti Nöel of the return of yet another cycle of slavery. Ti Nöel sees signs in the flora. He notices that:

> The few men Ti Nöel encountered did not reply to his greeting, plodding by with their eyes to the ground like their dogs' muzzles. . . . The ground was covered with signs: three stones forming a half-circle, a broken twig in the shape of a pointed arch, like a doorway. Farther on, several black chickens swung head down along a greasy branch. Finally, where the signs ended, a particularly evil tree stood, its trunk bristling with black thorns, surrounded by offerings. Among its roots were twisted, gnarled branches as crutches for Legba, the Lord of the Roads (*KW,* 85).

In a textual play of symmetries between the first and the third sections of the novel (first and second half), Ti Nöel stands at the crossroad of Legba, transformed into the allegorical center of two texts. He not only evokes the nativity of Christ, the Christian redeemer who dies at the cross, and with whom Ti Nöel's name is associated, but, he is also an avatar of Legba, the Afro-Caribbean mediator and Hegelian *mitten* of the textual crossroads. Carpentier's double image of a syncretic Voodoo-Christian union is informed by an existing syncretism in Haitian Voodoo. Christ and Legba are always found together in Voodoo altars, and the cross represents both,[314] as mediators between earth and sky, between the visible and the invisible. Christ-Legba presides at the center of the cosmic crossroad, at the intersection of contrary principles, where humanity stands, like the crucified Christ, like Legba,[315] and like Carpentier's Ti Nöel.

In his representational role of Christ/Legba, Ti Nöel is agent of transformation and metamorphosis; and metamorphosis, in Carpentier's text, as in Golden Age texts, as Frederick de Armas observes, is associated with revolution. In his play of symmetries, Carpentier includes another agent of transformation: *San Trastorno,* or Saint *Bouleversé,*[316] the Haitian loa that oversees Pauline's arrival to Haiti with her husband Leclerc. His death, victim of the "Black Plague," coincides with the carnival-like social chaos that sends the last plantation owners to social chaos (*KW,* 114). This is the narrative moment in which Saint *Bouleversé* (San Trastorno), The Overturner, presides. Saint Bouleversé is an important Haitian loa who brings about change and who presides over the turmoil of social chaos. His worshippers pray to him in order to overturn a situation or (following the same ritual significance of the heads in the Death Magic cult) to destroy or defeat someone or something. Seabrook's version of the prayer to Saint Bouleversé sheds light on Carpentier's last great metamorphosis/revolution with which the novel ends: "Saint Bouleversé, you who have the power to overturn the earth, you are a saint and I am a sinner. I invoke you and take you as my patron saint from this day. I send you now to search out a certain one. Overturn his head, overturn his memory, overturn his thoughts, overturn his house, overturn for me all my enemies, visible and invisible; bring down upon them the lighting and the tempest."[317]

In *The Kingdom of This World,* San Trastorno presides over the defeat of the French and over Ti Nöel's exile to Santiago de Cuba (the middle of the novel and the thirteenth chapter, in the first set of 12 + 1 chapters). Ti Nöel then returns to his native land just as the text's structural narrative begins to travel backwards, paralleling the events of the first half of the text,[318] and he travels back to the old plantation. There, once again, he again travels to the Cap taking the back roads "he had so often traveled in other days, following his master" (*KW,* 100). Then, again, he returns to the plantation of Lenormand de Mezy as he had done in the first chapter of the novel: "vaguely recalling a song that in other days he had sung on his way back from the city. A song that was all insults to a king. That was the important thing: *to a king.* And in this way, unburdening himself of every insult he could think up to Henri Christophe, his crown, and his progeny" (*KW,* 194). Like Mackandal before him, Ti Nöel transforms himself at will into animals and insects. And once again, at the end of the novel, in symmetry with the Great storm that took place the night of the Solemn Pact that marked the beginning of the revolution, a Great revolution in a cosmic storm erases all human remains from earth, turning time backward to a primordial time, back to the source:[319] to a textual "third" beginning that is left suspended in the novel at the moment of sunrise: "dawn."

For narrative time to be able to travel backward, Carpentier places Saint Bouleversé in the beginning of the second half of the text, at the crossroads of historical times, at the moment when the Haitian revolution, aided by the natural powers of the black plague (a larger scale poison than the one caused by Mackandal), defeats French rule. At this moment, the unimaginable occurred: the Haitian peasants and slaves began to win. For a Spenglerian Carpentier, this had been a battle between Faustian faith and the tyranny of Reason. At the same time, for Hegelian Carpentier, this was a dialectic historical battle between masters and slaves: Recalling Carpentier's Spenglerian representation of the cane cutters in *El milagro de anaquillé,* in *The Kingdom of This World,* during the rebellion against the French: "the Great Loas smiled upon the Negroes' arms. Victory went to those who had warrior gods to invoke. Ogoun Badagri guided the cold steel charges against the last redoubts of the Goddess Reason. And, . . . there were men who covered the mouths of the enemy cannon with their bare breasts and men who had the power to deflect leaden bullets from their bodies" (*KW,* 79–80).

The triumph of the Haitian revolution in *The Kingdom of This World* was the result of the vigor of a religious faith Carpentier did not share, but that, in a Spenglerian sense, had carved out a space in the history of the Americas for the agency of creole blacks and Africans, thus proving wrong Hegel's idea of an unhistorical America. The magic stories of Mackandal about the *Gran Allá* (the Great Beyond), Africa, became the stories of a great, equally mythological, *Gran Acá* (Here), which was now an America "proper:" an epic space where Afro-Caribbean loas and human heroes, battling together, defeated the Europeans. Yet, in Carpentier's textual scheme, it is not until the last chapter of the novel that Solimán's prayers to Legba and to The Overturner (suspended in the middle of the text with Solimán's death) are fulfilled. It is not until Ti Nöel raises his clamor to the powers of nature, the forces of the wind, that an apocalyptic storm erases all traces of civilization. In this final moment of the text, Ti Nöel stands at the crossroad where the Words of the *Yahweh* of the Flood and the Great Afro-Caribbean Lords of the Storms, *Shango, Ogoun Badagri,* and *Ogoun Fai* (Marshall of Storms, associated in Cuba with *Santiago Apostol* (Saint James) intersect with humanity. As mediator between faith and action, myth and history, and in his association with the divine forces of the storm, Ti Nöel conjures, and joins in once more, the last revolution in the novel against tyranny. This was the cosmic revolution already heralded in the first chapter with the ritual "placing" of the "heads" on the altar.[320]

Previous to that final apocalyptic moment, Ti Nöel, already settled in the ruins of the abandoned plantation where he was born, takes on the investiture of a King. In this role of an imaginary benevolent ruler, he becomes the antithesis of Christophe, the Haitian king ousted (like the French) by a popular revolt.[321] Ti Nöel's imaginary kingdom is different from Carpentier's rendition of Christophe's mimicry of the French monarchy, yet, equally imaginary, and of similar carnival-like appearance. As if he were a Momo King in *Carnaval de los negros* on "Día de Reyes," Ti Nöel adorns the abandoned plantation ruins with a chaotic mixture of objects stolen from the palace of Sans-Souci during the revolt against Christophe. These anachronous items in Ti Nöel's primitive context, serve to underline Carpentier's anti-bourgeoisie feelings as symbols of the artificiality of European civilization, as fetishes of capitalism, and of decadent European monarchies. From Ti Nöel's Spenglerian gaze, the stolen items lose their "civilized" value when placed in Ti Nöel's primitive space, and acquire a different political significance. Hence, it is important to note that, of those items, Ti Nöel's most cherished possession "was a dress coat that had belonged to Henri Christophe, of green silk, with cuffs of salmon-colored lace, which he wore all the time, his regal air heightened by a braided straw hat that he had folded and crushed into the shape of a bicorne, adding a red flower in lieu of a cockade" (*KW*, 137). Now transformed into a buffoon king, dressed like an Afro-Caribbean Don Quixote turned knight by his own delusions, Ti Nöel: "more majestic than ever in his green coat, presided over the feast, seated between a priest of the Savanna, who represented the native church that had sprung up, and an old veteran" (*KW*, 139–40).

Carpentier's Ti Nöel rules an imaginary world constructed, not from books like Cervantes's Don Quixote's, but from Mackandal's African stories (oral African archives in the Caribbean)[322] which still came to his mind in "blurred recollections" (*KW*, 138). These stories of a far away Africa, like the novels of chivalry read by Cervantes's Alonso Quijano, were also about princes, great kingdoms, and valiant warriors, magic and sorcerers, holy men and divinities. Like Don Quixote, Ti Nöel felt "the conviction that he had a mission to carry out" (*KW*, 138), and "appointed any passer by a minister, any hay-gatherer a general . . . It was thus the Order of the Bitter Broom had come into being, the Order of the Christmas Gift, the Order of the Pacific Ocean, and the Order of the Nightshade" (*KW*, 138). The local farmers had accepted Ti Nöel's new royal status, and, "when the women saw him approaching, they waved bright cloths in sign of reverence, like the palms spread before Jesus on Sunday" (*KW*, 138). In his imaginary messianic role as king:

At a festival of drums, Ti Nöel had been possessed by the spirit of the King of Angola, and had pronounced a long speech filled with riddles and promises.

Then herds had appeared on his lands. . . . Seated in his armchair, . . . Ti Nöel
issued orders to the wind. But they were the edicts of a peaceable government,
inasmuch as no tyranny of whites or Negroes seemed to offer a threat to his liberty (*KW*, 139).

For a Western reader, Ti Nöel's orders to the wind are the result of se-
nility. After all, he is a centenary who has been talking to objects and to
imaginary people. However, from the perspective of the African archive of
Mackandal's teachings, Ti Nöel is associated in the text with deities of
storms: with Legba/Christ, Lords of the Word (the wind-sound of speech),
presider of creation/destruction, and transformation. After all, like Shango,
father of the Ibeyes, Carpentier's Ti Nöel also fathered twin sons. As an
avatar of Legba, the text recalls that in the Caribbean Legba is also represented as a one-legged deity, and that the native Caribbean one-leg entity
of destruction and creation, the pre-Columbian *cemi* Huracán, the great
whirling winds or *remolinos,* is also the space where Legba resides. As a
writer of "vast knowledge," Carpentier's readings of the ethnological
works of the period, including Ortiz's work, must have allowed him to establish an association between the wind, as an archetype of creation, with
the Haitian snake-god *Dá,* and Dá with the pre Columbian Caribbean *cemi,*
Huracán. In *El huracán, su mitología y sus símbolos* [Hurricane, its mythology and symbols], published in 1940, a book Carpentier was familiar with,
Ortiz wrote that this one-legged wind symbol existed before the earth was
created: "todo lo que se mueve sin pies, lo sinuoso, lo dinámico," (everything that moves without legs, everything sinuous or wavy, everything dynamic),[323] "el movimiento, la fuerza, la vida misma" (movement, force,
life itself). In association with the "wind" (remembering that Ti Nöel's
earlier "humming" of a song of resistance was a wind-sound of implicit revolution), Ti Nöel seems to be embodying humanity rising above political
and social blindness, in a role not too distant from Carpentier's own historical and political preoccupations during this period.

In Afro-Caribbean religious thought, it is believed that only those humans who have reached a higher plane of existence can transform themselves into animals and plants. While informed by these beliefs, in *The
Kingdom of This World,* Mackandal and Ti Nöel's transformations to the
animal world are textual plays constructed from the gaze of the Western
writer. Thus, transcendence in Carpentier's novel is not metaphysical, but
ethical and aesthetic. Transcendence, then, in accord with Ti Nöel's inverted transformations "to" the realm of "this world," points out a movement of historical awareness, mediated, in Carpentier's narrative scheme,
by the Afro-Caribbean mercurial Legba, as the symbolic presider of the
Word: the writer. Remembering that the representation of the slave's consciousness is no other than a textual performance, what seems to preoccupy

Carpentier is how to represent the political and telluric contexts in an American cultural landscape where myth and history are one, as in baroque Europe and in African oral archives, but in a different Caribbean political context. This may help explain why when Ti Nöel learns that a new set of tyrants, mulatto rulers (the synthesis of the antithetical struggle between white and blacks, but also the offsprings of the foreign and the native), a new aristocracy, have returned (*KW,* 163), he reflects on his past no longer in mythopoetic terms, but in terms of the epiphany of a historical consciousness to which Ti Nöel suddenly arrives: "Mackandal had not foreseen this matter of forced labor. . . . The ascendancy of the mulattoes was something new that had not occurred to José Antonio Aponte, . . . this spurious aristocracy, this caste of quadroons, which was now taking over the old plantations, with their privileges and rank" (*KW,* 142).

Ti Nöel now perceives himself as being dethroned from his utopian kingdom, as a ruler unable to help his subjects now: "bowed once again beneath the whiplash. The old man began to lose heart at this endless return of chains, this rebirth of shackles, this proliferation of suffering, which the more resigned began to accept as proof of the uselessness of all revolt. Ti Nöel was afraid that he, too, would be ordered to the furrow in spite of his age, and as a result the thought of Macandal took hold of his memory" (*KW,* 143). In a carnival-like act of resistance, Ti Nöel decides to change his human mask: to exchange the costume of a king for that of an animal in order to escape the decadent world of humans, as he thought Mackandal had done. Nonetheless, once in the animal world, he relived the same experiences he had in the human realm. First, he willed himself to become a bird; and, from the Spenglerian perspective of the Faustian "bird's eye," "he watched the Surveyors from the top of a branch" (*KW,* 143); but he soon found out that the natural world was ruled by the same ordering principles of oppression, abuse, and fear that he had already experienced as a man. In a perpetual cycle of externalizations from self, transformed into a stallion Ti Nöel had to escape from the lasso of a surveyor. Then, in the form of a wasp he got tired of their monotonous constructions, and, when he entered the kingdom of the ants, he found himself "carrying heavy loads over interminable paths under the vigilance of big-headed ants who reminded him of Lenormand de Mézy's overseers, Henri Christophe's guards, and the mulattoes of today" (*KW,* 144). Later, embodying a goose, he found the geese clan to be "a community of aristocrats, tightly closed against anyone of a different caste . . . Ti Nöel quickly gathered that even if he persisted in his efforts for years, he would never be admitted in any capacity to the rites and duties of the clan" (*KW,* 147). Ti Nöel, like Carpentier, learned that he could not run away from himself, from his human condition, masking himself as other: "It was then that the old man, resuming his human form, had a supremely lucid moment. He lived, for the space of a heartbeat, the finest moments of his life; he glimpsed once more the heroes who had revealed to him the power and the fullness of his remote African forebears, making him believe in the possible germinations the future held" (*KW*, 148). Then, in a moment of epiphany, he understood that:

> "man's greatness consists in the very fact of wanting to be better than he is. In laying duties upon himself. For this reason, . . . in the midst of his misery, . . . man finds his greatness, his fullest measure, only in the Kingdom of This World" (*KW*, 148–49).

Ti Nöel gains consciousness of historical time, of his past as history. As in Hegel's historical scheme, his arrival to self-consciousness is the return from the other, as other,[324] through a life time of personal experiences. Voicing Carpentier's own (Cervantine) views, Ti Nöel comes to understand, to Know, humanity at the end of his life. He arrives at a self-awareness that allows him to discern between his magic-imaginary evasion of reality and his "real" human condition. Finally, like Alonso Quijano, Ti Nöel's lucid awareness of his being-in-the-world brings about his death: a Spenglerian moment of Destiny, but also a "ritual" moment of life born out of death. Both Quijano and Ti Nöel had constructed imaginary worlds out of mythical and fictional narratives. Both characters lived in an imaginary world constructed out of rhetorical values and social myths, and both came to finally understand the fictional aspects of those ideals at the end of their lives. In both cases, the epiphany of re-cognition was followed by death. However, different from Cervantes's novel, in Carpentier's ritual text, death is followed by life, as in Afro-Caribbean rituals of initiation, as in Carpentier's "Liturgia," as in Nietzsche's concept of rebirth, and as in Frobenius's natural cycles and notion of primordial genesis, and Spengler's ideas of a cyclical history.

Ti Nöel's awareness of his life as historical time, makes him realize that the path he must take in order to affirm his humanity, is not avoidance, but resistance. Understanding now his task in life, in this world, Ti Nöel suffers yet another metamorphosis, for he, at the end of the novel, no longer conceives the world as magical, but as *Trabajo*, toil, "task:" an existential truth (paradoxically mediated by Carpentier's readings of Cervantes) that sets him free through *desengaño*. He is finally able to understand Mackandal's magic world of African heroes and of metamorphosis, not from the metaphysical perspective of magic, but from the Hegelian allegorical perspective of history. It is a new and different understanding of his humanity which, in the context of the text's ritual structure, indicates the initiation of Ti Nöel to a new reality, away from magic, into the new awareness of being a historical being. His one hundred years of life had been a ritual process (like the seven days of initiation that begins with market day) leading to that moment of Knowledge/Freedom, reminiscent of the new reality he enters at night in the Great Void of the final storm. Only then, can Ti Nöel understand that Mackandal's masks, like the kulonas the diablito dancers wore for their public performances on "Día de Reyes," were not forms of evasion, but an act, a Carnival gesture of re-cognition and defiance. Metamorphosis for Mackandal, Ti Nöel now understands, was in fact an act of revolution in the midst of tears, reminiscent of Goethe's Faust.

Consciously aware now of historical time, Ti Nöel, actor, and agent, like Hegelian consciousness in the historical process, not a passive witness, finally understands that rebellion is the only route to the apocalyptic "overturning" of his historical condition. It is a consciousness already intimated in the beginning of the novel and heralded by the onset of the revolution for independence at the midpoint of the novel. As a symbolic storm deity, Ti Nöel now conceives more than twins, he conjures a cosmic Wind that erases all of man's work in a land of repetitive tyrannies. However, in Carpentier's narrative scheme Ti Nöel's action and erasure are not only a philosophical stand; they are a structural strategy. In the last scene of the novel, the symbolic erasure of Man, and his spoils on earth, establishes a magical moment that coincides with the "erasure of the *vever*" in Voodoo, and with the erasure of the magic drawings in ñáñigo, ceremonies. This is the moment when the ritual drawings, whose magical images possess transforming power, are no longer needed because, at the end of the ritual, the magic of the ritual has already become the reality of the world. In Voodoo and ñáñigo rituals, that moment of "becoming" is consecrated by the act of erasing the figures made in the ritual drawings. The act of erasing represents then that the "here" of the ritual is now the "there" of the world. Following this liturgical structure, in which ritual is interwoven to the very fabric of the narrative, at the end of the novel, the magic ritual of writing conjures a new reality in the reader's imagination.

IV

At the end of his life, when the centenarian Ti Nöel arrives to the conclusion that the end of slavery and of political independence do not necessarily result in freedom, he also realizes that history is a spiraling repetition of similar circumstances. In one last act of resistance, still dressed in Christophe's royal coat, disillusioned, and hopeless, Ti Nöel becomes once more the rebel he once was. At that moment, Ti Nöel noticed that "Toward the Cap the sky was dark with the smoke of fires as on the night when all the conch shells of the hills and coast had sung together" (*KW,* 149). Then, in one final regal act: "The old man hurled his declaration of war against the new masters, ordering his subjects to march in battle array against the insolent works of the mulattoes in power" (*KW,* 149). In his new investiture as avatar of Legba (witness and mediator), Ti Nöel presides at the intersection between earth and sky, and thus over the same apocalyptic wind-sound of the revolutionary whirlwind announced by the conch shells that had called the slaves to the uprising led by Bouckman the night of the Great Pact.

In the spiraling winds of the last textual revolution, Ti Nöel's final moment of awareness coincides with the arrival of the overturning winds, the magic of the ritual text, and the final erasure of the ritual drawings (Legba's vever). This moment, which signals a new reality brought about by the magic of the ritual, responds in Carpentier's narrative to the erasure of the dual image of Christ/Legba which Ti Nöel represents. The erasure here of Ti Nöel, however, does not take place until after he has arrived to Knowledge, to the freedom he finds in re-cognition. Only then "a great green wind, blowing from the ocean, swept the Plaine du Nord, spreading through the Dondon valley with a loud roar" (*KW*, 150). The conjured storm returns the land to a primordial moment, back to the source, to a time before the construction of the plantation: "the last ruins of the plantation came tumbling down. The trees bowed low, tops southward, roots wrenched from the earth. And all night long the sea, turned to rain, left trails of salt on the flanks of the mountains" (*KW*, 150). Ti Noël's final declaration to war, and the uprising of cosmic forces, with which the text symbolically brings to fruition the postponed prayers previously made to The Overturner (San Trastorno), ensues a climatological change that recalls the death of the biblical Messiah, with the graying of the sky, in an image that counterpoints the erasure of the figure of Legba's crossroad in Voodoo rituals, and the death of Christ in biblical stories. The "green wind that emerges from the ocean," recalls once more the image of *Dá:* the green snake-god *Damballah,* the eternal principle of death and rebirth, associated in Haitian Voodoo with the ocean and storms. This is the same loa summoned by Bouckman the night of the Great Pact, and by the *Rada* priestess during Mackandal's resistance, and also by Solimán. This is the same King Dá of Mackandal's stories that Ti Nöel recalls in the first chapter of the novel while he is meditating on the signifying ritual "heads" before him.

Like Legba in Haitian Voodoo, the eternal force of Damballah is related "to the world egg (or single cell) from which life sprang, and to the waters of life, and, consequently to the life of the race as a whole, the ancient source of its life line and its eternal continuity."[325] Taking into consideration the symbolic importance, in the Caribbean, of the storm as a symbol for revolution, and of its association with the Afro-Cuban Yoruba divine King, Shango, the Great Judge, Lord of thunder, lightning, and the drum, Carpentier's final scene constructs an allegorical association between Ti Nöel's final image (standing on a table as an altar, wearing Christophe's royal coat, hurling his declaration to war, and becoming one with the storm), with the orisha Shango, and with the Haitian loa of thunder, *Ogoun Bada-grí*. The later is represented in Haitian Voodoo wearing a French officer's coat and a bicorne, just like Ti Nöel's attire in this final scene, dressed in Henry Christophe's coat and "a straw hat he had folded and crushed into the shape of a bicorne" (*KW*, 137). The association here renders yet another textual play of symmetries since Ogoun Badagrí is the terrible divine warrior of thunder and lightning summoned in Carpentier's novel the night of the Great Pact to aid the Haitian rebels in their cause, and his presence was felt the memorable night of a Great Storm that marked the beginning of the Haitian revolution. Conjured by the rebels with the song: *Ogún Bada-grí/ General sanglant/ Saizi z'orange/ Ou scell'orange/ Ou fait Kataoun z'eclai!* (*KW*, 94),[326] in *The Kingdom of This World*, Ogoun Badagrí is who leads the Haitian armies to their triumph against the French, and, at the end of the novel, his presence is felt again in the allegorical figure of Ti Nöel waging a third and last final battle against all tyrants, and wearing, like the loa, a French officer's coat and a bicorne.

In the final great cosmic storm, but recalling now the magic of the *Jimaguas* in *El milagro de Anaquillé,* Carpentier couples the signifying bellowing of the bulls killed in the construction of La Ferraire, with the thunder,[327] storm, and tidal waves of the last scene. With this association, the text brings together the great twins of nature, sky and earth, in one single image of a "bellowing-thunder." Carpentier's image is a reminder that, as Ortiz observes, the Antillean/Quiché *Huracán*, in its association with thunder, is known also as "he who bellows;"[328] and that in pre-Hispanic myths, it was Huracán, the one-leg supreme force who destroyed the first ungrateful beings with a flood, and whose Word (wind) brought creation.[329]

This last call to war, in which Ti Nöel "hurls his declaration of war," conjuring the power of nature, with his Voice-Wind-Words, heralds again another historical apocalyptic revolution much more sweeping and universal in Carpentier's text than the war of independence. In Carpentier's quadripartite narrative structure, this last uprising in the novel parallels a first rebellion (only implicit in the novel) in the history of Hispaniola. In other words, in Carpentier's narrative scheme the last and third cosmic revolutionary storm is also a fourth major revolution that creates symmetry with the implicit first uprising associated with Nativity. Following the quadripartite structure of the novel (two sections, four parts), and the symbolism of number four in Afro-Caribbean belief systems,[330] the text establishes a narrative symmetry between the first historical rebellion, which occurred in the island of Hispaniola in 1522, during Nativity, a moment already implicit in Ti Nöel's name, and a fourth apocalyptic uprising of cosmic proportions at the end of the novel. In *El huracán*, Ortiz highlights the historical significance of that first rebellion when he recalls Fernández de Oviedo observation that the first major slave rebellion in the Caribbean occurred "on the second day of Nativity,"[331] and the fact that Juan de Castellanos refers in his "Elegía V"[332] to that first slave rebellion that took place during Christmas celebration. In *The Kingdom of This World,* that first historical revolution in the Caribbean, represents an initial prophetic moment in the history of the island, that seems to herald the Haitian war of independence against the French. Yet, Carpentier's allegorical narrative needs another major revolution, which Carpentier finds in the popular uprising that dethrones Henry Christophe, the self-appointed Haitian king. In a liturgical play between three and four, Carpentier represents the last and fourth rebellion as an apocalyptic revolution of cosmic proportions that brings the novel to an end. Ti Nöel participates in all of the rebellions: physically in three, and, even though the implicit first one happened in 1522, before his birth, his name places him allegorically in that first uprising, in symmetry with the last cosmic one, in which he becomes, like in José Maria Heredia's poem, "one with the storm."[333]

Carpentier's last cosmic battle recalls the biblical accounts of the flood, and of the destruction of Sodom and Gomorra. And, at the same time, it recalls the stories of creation in Quiche mythology, told in the *Popol Vuh,* where it is said that Huracán spoke the Word and eliminated the first imperfect human beings, to give way to a second set of beings.[334] The pre-Columbian Caribbean god of storms, Huracán, was associated with earthquakes, fire, and the conch shell. Both, Huracán, and the Afro-Haitian Damballah, are serpentlike wind-water deities conceived as the wind-word force of destruction, and creation. The creative/destructive nature of the great wind in pre-Columbian Caribbean, (and, according to Ortiz, in all of the Americas), establishes the Tempest (the one leg deity manifested in the whirling winds, like Damballah), as the great sky serpent Huracán, a single, but plural image, that brings together in a Carpentierian play of symmetries the cosmic powers of earth, ocean, and sky.

In the image of the wind-word-storm that sweeps over the Plaine do Nord, Carpentier counterpoints Afro-Indo-Euro-American deities, and Afro-Cuban rituals in which the simulation of a storm is an important requirement. As Ortiz observes, Cuban Bantu priests or *nganguleros:*[335] "usan constantemente un signo en sigma que para ellos simboliza a la vez la serpiente, el remolino y el espíritu o la fuerza sobrenatural que opera la magia" (constantly use a sign in Sigma that symbolizes for them the serpent, the whirling wind, and the spirit or supernatural force that produces the magic);[336] and, he adds: "en toda operación mágica de los 'nganguleros' es indispensable el simulacro de la tempestad . . . para lograr la presencia y actividad del espíritu o ente sobrenatural" (in the magic work of the *nganguleros,* it is indispensable to simulate a tempest . . . to bring about the presence and acting force of the spirit or supernatural being).[337] Also in ñáñigo ceremonies, a top, or dreidel, often is spun at the beginning of the ceremony to represent the indispensable simulacrum of a storm; and some Afro-Cuban priest some times use small amount of gunpowder for this purpose. As if the writer were a ngangulero and the text a nganga, Carpentier constructs the ritual storm without which the magic of the textual ritual cannot become the reality of the world. In *The Kingdom of This World*, however, the magic of the ritual storm is associated with a phenomenological spirit of "liberty," toward which history moves in twirling spirals; and with the imaginary apocalyptic presence, in the Caribbean, of the terrible cosmological forces of justice[338] whose final "blow" erases tyranny. In fact, Carpentier's final scene in *The Kingdom of This World* evokes José Martí's call for freedom, riding in the wind and the fury of the Great pre-Hispanic *Cemi* (Huracán), and "scattering the seeds of the new America."[339]

For Ortiz, Huracán is the most autochthonous pre-Hispanic Caribbean symbol of creation, and destruction. Hence, it is the best and most "proper" metaphor for revolution in the Caribbean. It is not surprising then that, for Ortiz, as well as for Carpentier, the duality of the Caribbean wind-word, as creator and destructor, recalls the duality of the Afro-Cuban Ibeyes,[340] the Jimaguas whose magic in Carpetier's *El milagro de Anaquillé* "resists" and disarms foreign intervention. Carpentier's ritual narrative, in its symmetrical counterpoints of life-death, end-beginning, evokes the ritual ordering of chaos, giving symbolic coherence to a history that, otherwise, would seem chaotic and disjointed: making writing a form and a manifestation of the symbolical Caribbean wind-word creator. It is important to recall here that for Spengler: "writing is an entirely new kind of language, and implies a complete change in the relations of man's walking-consciousness, in that it liberates it from the tyranny of the present" (*DW*, 149). Furthermore, Spengler adds: "Writing is the grand symbol of the Far, meaning not only extension-distance, but also, and above all, duration and future and the will to eternity" (*DW*, 150); "writing"—Spengler argues—"is an ancient privilege of priesthood" (*DW*, 151). Carpentier's closing scene in *The Kingdom of This World* conjures "such Grand Symbol of the Far" in the most powerful force of nature, in the Caribbean, in the powerful deity of which Maya-Quiche stories of creation refer to as the Word, the creator, who spoke to say that it was time to come to counsel and to unite the Word to Wisdom in order to light together the World. Ortiz explains, recalling the *Popol Vuh*, that: "el nombre de éste es Una voz que muge, hurakán, la voz del trueno, es el primero; y el segundo es el relámpago y el tercero el rayo" (its name is "A voice that bellows," hurakán, the voice of thunder, is the first one, the second one is the lightning, and the third one is the thunderbolt).[341] In Carpentier's text, this native Caribbean deity becomes the syncretic image of Huracán-Shango-Damballah-Ogoun Badagrí-Yahwe-Christ, as a local but also a universal archetype for the revolutionary unification of Word and Wisdom: the great Light (sun rise) that gives life in Antillean-*Quiche* myths of creation.

Carpentier's final image of a Word-Wind-War that sweeps over a Caribbean landscape erasing the last ruins of civilization, and with them the "tyranny of Reason," is an image embedded in the memory of Spanish American writers.[342] Two decades after the publication of *The Kingdom of This World*, Gabriel García Márquez chose for the end of his novel, *One Hundred Years of Solitude*, the same image of a Caribbean Wind that erases the last vestiges of Macondo. In this text, the Afro-Indo Caribbean storm is charged again, like in *The Kingdom of This World*, with the re-volutionary symbolism that Ortiz had envisioned years earlier:

> Si un día hubiese de desatarse en Cuba una revolución que destruyera como un huracán y creara de nuevo como un soplo de génesis, quizás su más genuino y expresivo emblema, sería el que muchas centurias atrás lo fue de los indios cubanos, nacido de su mentalidad y reverenciado en sus ritos.[343]

> [If one day a revolution like a hurricane that destroys and creates like the breath of genesis would be unleashed in Cuba, maybe its most genuine and expressive emblem would be the same as the one that centuries ago Cuban indians imagined and revered in their ceremonies.]

In García Márquez's novel, as in Carpentier's *The Kingdom of This World*, the Caribbean wind force is the political symbol for an imaginary historical revolution envisioned after Fernando Ortiz's allegorical interpretation of Huracán as a symbol for change. This change, imagined by Ortiz and by the Minoristas in the thirties and forties, had been closely associated, as Carpentier explains to Ramón Chao, with the representation of afrocubanía as an act of rebellion. In 1947, in his study on the pre-Columbian cemi, *El huracán*, Fernando Ortiz compares pre-Colombian Antillean beliefs to the universal archetype of Life born out of a combination of sound and wind (Word). Ortiz here points out that for pre-Hispanic Caribbeans, Huracán was a cyclical, spiraling, atmospheric phenomenon, directly associated with its symbolic counterparts: the wind, fire, rising smoke, seismic movements, the ocean, shells, and, in general, the concept of fecundity. Such association created a complex relationship of symbols, like "winds, rain, lightning bolts, snakes, shells, ears, navels, stars, and fecundity, as well as all the derivatives from the first phenomenon that was the whirling of water and wind, represented in the spiral," all of them associated one with the other.[344]

Huracán was related to the creative powers of the spiraling winds, as the givers of the first puff of life, the divine breath: the Word (Verb). Such was the image, Ortiz notes, nature inscribed in the architecture of the conch shells, where the sounds of the wind and the ocean could be heard as one and the same entity.[345] Because of its natural spiraling structure, the seashell must have been indicative of nature's architectural imitation of the whirling winds of hurricanes, and other wind phenomenon, as if the image of the creator/destructor of Antillean and Maya-Quiche cosmogony, "Corazón del Cielo" (Heart of the Heavens) or "Ojo del Cielo" (Heaven's Eye),[346] had been imprinted during creation like a divine signature on nature. It is very possible, says Ortiz, that Huracán, at one point, could have been represented in pre-Hispanic Caribbean by great conch shells (*cobo*), which Antillean natives also mixed with tobacco for their hallucinating effects in visionary rituals.[347] Ortiz also suggests that tobacco smoke was associated with the storm deity for its spiraling and circular convolutions ascending to the sky, which simulated the image of the one-legged deity of storms. Due to such association with the wind and with the image of Huracán, as the great sky serpent, or one-legged deity (the shape of tornados, hurricanes, or any whirling wind phenomenon), large seashells were placed on the (often round) temples to Quetzalcoátl,[348] just like they were placed on top of the *Caneyes* (Arawak round ceremonial houses) in the Caribbean.[349] They also adorned the entrance of Antillean *bohios,* explained the sixteenth-century Spanish chronicler, Pedro Mártir de Anglería;[350] and, in Maya paintings, the Plumed Serpent (*Kukulcán*) was sometimes portrayed as coming out of a seashell.[351] In contrast to the image of Huracán in pre-Columbian iconography, the Afro-Caribbean mediator Legba/Elegua speaks (voice-sound-wind) to humans through seashells, the divining cowries, in the Afro-Cuban oracle known as *Diloggún.* Also Elegua/Legba is represented some times as a one-legged deity, thus evoking Huracán, and the Central American Caribbean plumed serpent Kukulcán.

In its symbolic image, as the house of the gods and the keeper of the sound-word of creation, and because of their spiraling structures, seashells are a symbol of Time in the Caribbean, and, for Carpentier, of narrative time, like music, as Acosta points out in *Música y épica en la novela de Alejo Carpentier* (1981). Shells are also a universal symbol for creation and femininity: motherhood. Neptune's conch, for example, is a Taurocephalous space always associated with femininity and fecundity, according to Hesiodo. It is in this association that Boticelli represents the birth of Venus, as emerging from a seashell. Ortiz further points out that Venus is born out of the twirling waters: a water *remolino.*[352] It is not a mere textual coincidence then that, in Carpentier's novel, Pauline, a textual syncretism of Venus-Erzulie, emerges from the ocean: the vast mysterious space from which life originates.[353] From these Caribbean mythologies still uncharted, as Carpentier points out in his prologue to the novel, Carpentier brings together the ocean waters, in a Caribbean context, with the aquatic-celestial snake deity Damballah, as the "proper" Caribbean deity to sweep over the Plaine do Nord. For a Carpentier attracted to afrocubanía as an aesthetic mode of resistance, and as a mode to represent a Caribbean's Faustian soul, the ocean becomes the geographic and metageographic amniotic fluid through which Europe and Africa meet in America. In Afro-Cuban myths, Yemayá, the ocean, is the mother womb of the Middle Passage. She is also the mother of the orishas, and the mother of Shango.[354]

In Ti Nöel's final wind/word hurling to war, thunder, the bellowing of the bulls, and the apocalyptic call of the conch shells (wind/water/voice) come together in the very concept of dance, in a contrapuntal musical movement[355] of sameness that moves across time and space, meeting, in the text, in spiraling reversals and mirroring reflections. The image of the word-wind, like the sound that emanates from the conch shell, is an image Carpentier reiterates in some of his texts, as a type of *soplo,* or primordial breath of creation created by primitive musical instruments like the conch shell, or cobos, used by the Amerindians as trumpets. The conch shell becomes a Carpentierian counterpart to contemporary musical trumpets, which, in Carpentier's text signifies, like the pre-Columbian cobo, the Apocalyptic call-wind-sound-trumpets of a biblical judgment day. It is in this symbolic role that Carpentier uses the image of the trumpet in his novel *Concierto barroco* (1974). Hence, the trumpet of Louis Armstrong, whose musical sound, jazz, is the mixture of African and European elements (like Cuban music) announces a moment of spiritual freedom and reconciliation,[356] reminiscent of Paul Niger's "words": "The trumpet of Armstrong at judgment day will be the interpreter of the sufferings of man."[357] This apocalyptic wind-sound of judgment finds a correspondence in *The Kingdom of This World* in Ti Nöel's voice-wind-call to war: the moment when Caribbean telluric and political contexts converge to bring about the great whirling wind of a great re(con)volution that takes the reader in an imaginary trek back to the source.

In his interpretation of the pre-Columbian image of the cemi Huracán, as the ancestral revolutionary spirit in Cuban political and social history, Ortiz establishes, through myths, an association between the Caribbean and Egypt, between the spiraling winds, and socio-political transformations. In that role, Ortiz highlights the ancient Egyptian myths that conceived the circular revolution of the artisan wheel as a metaphor for the force that transforms societies. Ortiz writes:

el ícono indocubano fue símbolo del Huracán y, por lo mismo, lo fué de la revolución como fenómeno cósmico. Revolución que destruye y reconstruye . . . esa rueda revolucionaria transforma las sociedades, según la metáfora milenaria de esos mismos pensadores de Egipto.[358]

[The Indo-Cuban icon was a symbol for Huracán, and, in the same way, it symbolized revolution as a cosmic phenomenom. A Revolution that destroys and recreates . . . the revolutionary Wheel that transforms societies, according to the millenary metaphor of those same thinkers in Egypt.]

Remembering Ortiz's allegorical interpretations of the twirling winds, and of the association of the wind-sound with the structure of the conch shell,[359] Leonardo Acosta observes that in Carpentier's entire oeuvre, "el huracán desatado por las fuerzas naturales precede al llamado de las caracolas, al huracán convocado por el hombre en su ascenso por la espiral de la historia" (the hurricane unleashed by natural powers is preceded by the calling of the conch shells, the hurricane summoned by man in his ascendance in the spiral of history).[360] In Carpentier's texts, Acosta observes, these Caribbean mythological images "van por el mismo camino de las reflexiones de don Fernando. ¿Acaso fue tema de conversación entre ambos?" (take the same course as the reflections of don Fernando. Was it perhaps a topic of conversation between them?).[361]

In Carpentier's early works, Huracán and the caracola, or conch shell, were present with similar meanings as those found in *The Kingdom of This World*. In his latter work, however, beginning with *The Kingdom of This World,* the conch shell appears as an omen of apocalyptic significance, of revelation, an idea closely associated with Afro-Cuban rituals. The divinatory ritual known popularly in Cuba as "echar los caracoles" (to cast the seashells) is an oracle of African origins known in Cuba as *Diloggún,* in which the secrets of nature's mysterious forces are revealed to humans through the letters or figures made by the positioning of the cowries when the *Babalawo* casts them on the divining board. In this Afro-Cuban oracle, the divining seashells are believed to be the house wind-sound of the orishas who speak through them in the voice of the divine messenger and mediator: Legba/Elegua. What differentiates this Afro-Cuban rite from the Indo-Caribbean symbols of the wind is that it is not only through the sound-wind of the cowries that Legba/Elegua speaks in the voice of the priest, but also through the symbolic writing (figures or "letters" in a sort of divine writing), created by the position (or letters) the cowries take when they fall on the divining board. The priest ("knowledgeable" in these hidden matters like Ti Nöel), reads, interprets the figures or letters, and communicates their meaning through recitations and stories. The spoken word, at this moment of the ritual, is thought to be the word of the orisha. Thus, if writing for Spengler is related to the role of the priest, in the Afro-Cuban Diloggún (and *Ifa*), the Word, spoken or written, is related to the notion of revelation (light, hidden knowledge) and the creation of a new reality. In relationship to the later, in Afro-Indo-Caribbean codes and symbols, seashells are also associated with fecundity.[362]

For Carpentier, and for Ortiz, Huracán was the most "proper" American symbol to articulate that Faustian sense of an "endless Becoming" that for

Spengler was "comprehended in the idea of *Motherhood*" (*DW,* 267).[363] Reminiscent of Spengler's notion of Time, Destiny, and the mother, Carpentier proposes in the *The Kingdom of This World* that the Faustian life force, and the dynamic vigor of America he wants to express, is related also to the image of the mother, and to the other, as source. In this sense, afrocubanía offered Carpentier a road (an *Odu*), and an imaginary voyage to an American womb.

V

Carpentier's interest in the Faustian "presence" of the black and the Indian in the Americas, takes him to a sort of "safari" of exploration into American mythologies "still not fully recorded." This is an interest he shared with other Latin American intellectuals of his time, including the origenistas, who sought to find in myths and poetic knowledge a primordial source of culture. The marvelous reality Carpentier found in Haiti, as he points out in his prologue to *The Kingdom of This World,* was not a "privilegio único de Haití, sino patrimonio de la América entera, donde todavía no se ha terminado de establecer, por ejemplo, un recuento de cosmogonías" (a unique privilege of Haiti, but a patrimony of the Americas, where an account of its cosmogonies is yet to be completed).[364] In that American patrimony, there is no other symbol more Meso-American, and more Caribbean, says Ortiz, or more deeply rooted in pre-Columbian life and thought, as the *Gran Remolino* (Great Whirlwind): "cuyo soplo creaba todo el cosmos y al mismo Sol lo impulsaba día y noche para que hiciera su camino sidéreo" (whose blowing winds created the entire cosmos, and pushed the Sun day and night so that it could travel in its sidereal course).[365] In contrast to the European philosophies which, for Ortiz, were as foreign to America as imported sugar, Huracán, the Word-Wind of pre-Columbian Central and Caribbean America, is, like tobacco for Ortiz, the most native, and "proper" symbol with which to express the Caribbean; and with which to express a primordial Caribbean before the arrival to it of Western civilization. Following the Hegelian notion that "the individual is the universal,"[366] the Caribbean whirlwind becomes for Carpentier, as it was for Ortiz, a metaphor for the universal. After all, the image of the wind-word of creation, Huracán, also can be found in pre-Columbian Mexico, where the wind god *Quetzalcóatl,* the serpent-bird god or plumed serpent (Quetzal=bird and coátl=serpent), was represented with a spiral on his chest. The Amerindian representation also recalls the inscriptions of *Thoth,* the Egyptian god of writing, who also was represented with a spiral over his head.

The spiral finds a unique importance in Carpentier's texts in association with time (narrative, historical, and musical time), the whirlwind (remolino), and the conch shell. In Afro-Indo-America, the seashell becomes the house-womb of the voice-sounds of creation, a sound-chamber that calls to war, that heralds, and that reveals invisible realities. Furthermore, in its relationship to the ocean, the seashell is also the telluric womb-mother-house of Huracán.[367] The spiraling structure of the conch shell is a natural symbol for the spiral, as in the spiraling winds of creation, associated in Carpentier's text with change: with revolution, an idea Ortiz found in other world mythologies, including Egypt.

In order to express the universality of the local in America, Carpentier turns his gaze to Egyptian mythology. In it he finds a common cultural-poetic womb that brings together Europe and Africa in the Caribbean. Thus, in the last scene of *The Kingdom of This World*, Western and African archival texts come to a final symphonic final accord of symbols in the figure of a vulture, at dawn. The primordial calm that follows the creative/destructive passing of Huracán-Ogun Badagrí-Shango-Damballah, takes the text in spiraling returns to a moment before its beginning when, after Ti Nöel's disappearance, all that is left is the figure of a: "wet vulture who turns every death to his own benefit and who sat with outspread wings, drying himself in the sun, a cross of feathers which finally folded itself up and flew off into the thick shade of Bois Caïman" (*KW,* 150). This vulture is the only possible witness of the events.

Carpentier's allegorical "wet vulture" in the last scene of the novel, at a moment of dawn like the one that opens the novel, but anterior to it, appears waiting for the sun to rise with its wings unfolded,[368] sitting "with outspread wings, drying himself in the sun, a cross of feathers which finally folded itself up and flew off" (*KW,* 150). Carpentier's textual image of a vulture is significant since, although Carpentier uses the figure of vultures in other texts, there are no true vultures in the Caribbean. There is only a variety of this species known as "buzzard" or turkey vulture, in North America, and *gallinazo, zopilote, galembo, zamuro, urubú* in Central and South America. This American buzzard is called *Aura tiñosa* in Cuba, a term popularized in the island in the rhyme: "Aura tiñosa ponte en cruz,/ y cria a tus hijos como tú" (Aura tiñosa pose in the figure of a cross/ and raise your children like you). These verses inscribed in the collective memory of Cuban vernacular culture the image of a feminine aura with its wings spread open in the form of a cross, drying its feathers in the sun. The fact that Carpentier's "vulture" appears in the image of a cross, like the aura of the popular verses, creates a plurality of intertexts related to the vulture as an observant witness, and messenger, and as the writer (the only one who can benefit from the corpses left in Haiti's tragic history at the end of the novel), presiding over the word/world, in a position vultures take as a way of cleansing. In Yoruba creation stories, and in the Afro-Cuban *Pataki,* the Supreme god, *Olodummare, Olofi* in Cuba, sends the vulture to earth to be a witness and to report to him on the condition of the earth after its creation.[369] In Afro-Caribbean lore, the vulture (aura) is the divine mediator, who, like Legba, and as a symbol of Elegua, is witness, messenger, and interpreter of the higher powers, also the only one able to transcend destruction, and witness creation.

As the mercurial mediator between the visible and the invisible, words, time, knowledge, roads, and doors, Legba/Elegua is the only one who can bring the ritual text to an end. He is the last one to speak, and the last one to leave the ceremony. He must be greeted first and last. He is the one who opens and closes the ritual. This is why in Voodoo ceremonies Legba's vever is the last figure/drawing erased. In keeping with this "proper" Caribbean ritual closure, Carpentier's text closes with the erasure of Ti Nöel, and then replaces him with the primordial figure of the vulture/aura in the figure of a cross, waiting for the sun to rise. Then the vulture also leaves the narrative stage. Once the sun rises, the ritual of writing ends, and the vulture flies away toward the horizon. In this last scene of the novel, Carpentier's vulture/aura is also the plural symbol that allows the writer to counterpoint *Eva* (Eve-Pauline) (the "fall" of man), to *Ave,* (bird) (as in the "bird's eyes" of the Faustian writer). The inversion from Eva to Ave offers the writer another symmetry of double utterances, since aura also means, in Spanish: favor, applause, acceptance, as well as "viento suave y apacible" (soft calm wind), "atmósfera inmaterial que rodea a ciertos seres" (inmaterial atmosphere that surrounds certain beings),[370] also "hálito, aliento" (breath).[371]

Inscribed in all storm deities, as in Carpentier's *buitre/aura,* are the concepts of duality, and androgyny. In an ingenious counter position of time, narrative time and historical time, Carpentier intersects two archival texts (Africa and Europe) in the figure of a vulture (aura/buitre), in the image of the cross (waiting for the sun to rise), at "dawn," like in "Liturgia" where another bird, a rooster, indicates with its crow (voice-wind) the arrival of a new day, sunrise: a new ritual reality. Birds are associated traditionally with solar deities. Thus it is not a mere coincidence that in Carpentier's "Liturgia," like in *The Kingdom of this World,* a bird announces the new day. The rooster is a sacred animal in ñáñigo rituals; and it is also consecrated food for Shango, and ritual food for Elegua; and in ñáñigo rituals it is consecrated food for the sacred drum *Ekué.*[372] However, in *The Kingdom of This World,* a different bird (ave), a vulture, announces the new day, this time not with the sound of a (wind) crow, as in "Liturgia," but with the act of flying: an action associated with the "wind" and "primordial breath" (*aliento*) of creation. From this ritual perspective, *The Kingdom of This World* renders the image of a signifying vulture, in the form of a cross, waiting for the sun to rise, as the proper ritual symbol to bring the narrative to a closure immediately after the ritual erasure of Ti Nöel. Notwithstanding, the new day proposed by the text in association with the representation of a vulture is a moment left suspended, analogous to the potential of life symbolized by the Mystic Egg in Damballah's vever. In other words, it is an ambiguous moment of gestation always already there, never hatching, suspended in the eternal expectation of birth: the eternal continuity of life; life always at the liminal moment of its occurrence.

This last moment in Carpentier's novel could be read as the Mirror Stage in Lacan's theory, since Ti Nöel is displaced in the text by a vulture and by primordial dawn, in an allegorical "return to the mother:" to a primordial moment that recalls Carpentier's short story, "Back to the Source." In this short story, as Carpentier confesses to Salvador Arias, Carpentier constructed a textual performance of his "search for the mother or search for the generative element in the intellectual or telluric womb."[373] Benítez Rojo proposes that in Carpentier's search for the mother there is "also the search for the lost paradise of the Mirror Stage, where the Self and the Other compose the same body" (*RI, 272*). Carpentier's symmetry of images, the search for an American telluric womb in the Caribbean (associated always with the other, the Faustian Indians and blacks), finds in the wind forces of Huracán a primordial mytho-poetic space to represent the lost body of the mother in the Caribbean landscape, its cultures, and its uncharted mythologies. As Benítez Rojo also suggests, Carpentier's narratives have "a structural density that obeys his obsession with reaching the roots of Americaness, its 'telluric womb'" (*RI, 273*). In that search for the (m)other, Carpentier enters the jungles of a literary art style that he conceived as the most "proper" art form to represent a Faustian America: the baroque. Its contrapuntal thicket of codes recalls the primordial undifferentiated *monte* in Wifredo Lam's representation of Caribbean nature and myths in "The Jungle." And it is in such American metageographic jungle,[374] "contemporaneous," but different from European baroque, that Carpentier associates Afro-Indo-Caribbean with the myths and magic of a Faustian-feminine/androgynous force of life and creation.

In an ingenious play of symmetries and counterpoints, Carpentier's representation of the Afro-Caribbean image of *Legba,* in the ritual symbol of a vulture, reconciles the Hegelian "dawn" of a new consciousness, Reason, with the Spenglerian "pre-dawn" of civilization, in the image of the great Egyptian divine mother, Isis. This mytho-poetic figure, in which Carpentier finds, like Ortiz, the universal in the local, becomes Carpentier's proposition for a universal cultural (m)other womb in both Western and African thought. European baroque gave great importance to Egyptian mythology. And Latin American writers in the first half of the twentieth century also found in Egyptian and classical mythology a way to express universal truths as a way to express American realities. Ortiz's explications of the "symbols" of Huracán in the Caribbean, had taken him to propose in 1947 that the conflict between evil and good winds in the beliefs of North Amer-

ican Indians, "no es sino una expresión indiana de las experiencias me-
tereológicas, análogas a las que hicieran imaginar las teomaquias de *Osiris*
y de *Set* en el antiguo Egipto" (is no other than a Native American expression of metereological experiences analogous to those that triggered a cosmogony that imagined gods like *Osiris* and *Seth* in ancient Egypt).[375]
Osiris, Ortiz adds, was represented with one leg, like the Antillean Huracán, to represent the fecundity of the wind.[376] According to the Egyptian
myth, Osiris, Isis's husband and brother, was killed, and dismembered by
his brother *Seth*. The act was carried out with the approval of *Thoth,* the
god of writing, a deity represented in Egyptian symbology with a spiral
over his head.[377] Osiris's fourteen fragments were scattered over the earth
by the wind, but Isis was able to find and reassemble all of them, except
for Osiris's penis. Transformed into a vulture, she laid over the corpse of
Osiris, and from that union, *Horus,* Sunrise, was born.[378] The cult of Osiris
spread all over Egypt, and with it, the representation of Osiris in the figure
of an ox with a white circle over his head; and, in that circle, the figure of
a vulture representing Isis, the great divine mother, unfolding its wings. In
Egyptian mythology, the vulture was also the representation of the goddess
Nekhbet and *Mut,* wife of *Ra,* a principal solar deity.[379] The Egyptian
(African and Western) image of an Isis-vulture with unfolded wings, in the
form of a cross, representative also of the Afro-Cuban-Haitian mercurial
messenger, recalls, at the same time, the representation of the Great Goddess Mother Nature,[380] which, in the writing of Lydia Cabrera would be
associated with the Afro-Cuban *monte* [forest, bush, mount, holy place]. In
Carpentier's symmetrical iconography, the divine vulture (Legba/Isis)
poses with unfolded wings over the shattered island, and then flies to the
horizon at sunrise. This new day, "dawn," is a moment ritually equated in
Carpentier's text with the erasure of the allegorical figure of Ti Nöel and
with the birth of a new ritual reality. Also interwoven in Carpentier's thicket
of symmetries,[381] is the memory of Rada Voodoo cults in which Legba is
associated also with the Sun.[382]

Carpentier's representation of Isis, and of the Egyptian myth of Osiris is
not unique to Carpentier. A few years before the publication of *The Kingdom
of This World,* the Mexican writer Alfonso Reyes (1889–1959), on the subject of a fragmented America that needed to be expressed in a single image
that would be comprehensive of its needs and would express its realities, also
turned his gaze to the Egyptian myth of Orisis. Reyes's ideas on America addressed the efforts by Mexican intellectuals to find a coherent image of a
united Mexico in the aftermath of the Mexican Revolution. For Reyes, the
mission of Latin American artists and writers was to bring the many shattered fragments of America into one single unifying image. Hence, he writes
in his essay, "Capricho de América," in *Última Tule* (1942):

... aquí volveremos a la realidad más profunda de los mitos con que he comenzado estas palabras—, hay que concebir la esperanza humana en figura de la antigua fábula de Osiris: nuestra esperanza está destrozada, y anda poco a poco juntando sus *disjecti membra* para reconstruirse algún día. . . . Como en el juego de dados de los niños, cuando cada dado esté en su sitio tendremos la verdadera imagen de América.[383]

[here we shall return to the profound reality of myths with which I started this essay—we must conceive human hope in the figure of the ancient fable of Osiris: our hope has been shattered and is going about gathering its *disfecti membra* in order to reconstituye itself some day . . . Like a child game of dice, whenever all of the dice are in their place, we will have the true image of America.]

With the image of a bird flying (ave: a word that also means "praise" like aura), Carpentier seems to propose in *The Kingdom of This Word* a unifying image, like Reyes suggests, following the "fable of Osiris," as a Faustian thrust to infinity, of a "forsaken" America still young, vigorous, and different from Europe. Carpentier associates the "forsaken" blacks and Indians,[384] the Faustian redeemers of America (still longing to be free from the returning chains of the European Law of the Father), with the telluric womb (m)other he seeks to represent. As an echo of his early works, Carpentier continues to find a primal force in music, languages, and faith that, like Cuban music for Carpentier, resists foreign influences—and whose rhythms in the Caribbean are African. Carpentier's representation of "dawn" in *The Kingdom of This World* suggests a new beginning, like in "Liturgia," but this time associated with revolution. After all, as Speratti-Piñero points out, Carpentier's vulture flies back to Boi Caiman precisely to where the Solemn Pact that marked the beginning of the Haitian revolution had taken place.[385]

For Carpentier, a writer who lived more years in France than in Cuba, whose father was French, and whose mother was Russian, but who chose to be Cuban because he had been born in Cuban soil (and because it was in Cuba that his father abandoned him and his mother), the "here" that was America, was a Spenglerian inner dimension of body-soul: an ontological space that he related to the Other and to the Mother as the source of cultural vigor. Furthermore, that (M)Other which he found in afrocubanía he related to language, and to music.[386] Benítez Rojo notes that, as if it were a gallery of mirrors, Carpentier's mother, a music teacher, "is reflected in music, music in Carpentier, Carpentier in Cuba, Cuba in the Caribbean, and the Caribbean in America" (*RI*, 273). He also notes that in *La historia de la música en Cuba* (1946), Carpentier proposes that the maternal "heartbeat" of Cuban music is African rhythm. He even goes as far as suggesting, incorrectly so, that one of the first *sones* recorded in the development of Cuban music, the *son* of *Ma Teodora,* was the founder of Cuban popular music (*RI,* 273).[387] The important role of music in Carpentier's work, from the primitive call of the conch shell (which for Martí, as Ortiz points out, was a call to war),[388] to Armstrong's trumpet, underline Carpentier's preoccupation with music and with the (M)Other in association with Self, related to his own anxiety of difference, and to Carpentier's self-imposed mission ("task," "toil") to express and translate America to Europe. In Carpentier, as Benítez Rojo observes from a Lacanian perspective, the "surrender of narrative discourse to music's circular flow can be seen as an effort to maneuver the text toward a space outside the Father's control, outside the Law of the Father . . . This effort is hopeless, of course. In fact, it is doubly hopeless. Although the text may be structured by music, it remains a text, a discourse disseminated within the Symbolic order" (*RI,* 271). Such spiral structural configuration in *The Kingdom of This World,* as music's circular flow, in a movement toward the (M)Other, the womb, the "source," is especially significant because the spiral, related to the snake, time, creation, the wind, and to the dynamic forces of life, is related also to dance and to writing.[389]

Carpentier's search for the (M)Other's cultural heartbeat is a futile revolutionary movement away from the Law of the father (Europe), as Benítez Rojo observes, because, after all, the signature of the Father (Europe), the Law, is deeply inscribed in Carpentier's texts. Hence, the writer is trapped at the crossroad of two sources of legitimatization, both unattainable for Carpentier. Benítez Rojo explains: "On the one hand lie nature and the folk tradition—the Mother, the Imaginary, the round's absence of violence, Carpentier's 'telluric womb.' On the other, lie the languages and episteme of Europe—the Name-of-the-Father, the Symbolic, history, modernity, Carpentier's *La France*" (*RI,* 275). In *The Kingdom of This World,* like the vulture's flight[390] to the shade of Boi Caiman, the writer also flies away from the "tyranny of the present" toward the realm of the imaginary, literature and myths, in an attempt perhaps to "become" other through writing.[391]

Ti Nöel's allegorical erasure from the text is significant for Carpentier's future works since, with the exception of Filomeno in *Concierto barroco* (1974), Ti Nöel is the last Afro-Caribbean main character in Carpentier's oeuvre. Perhaps, as Juan Marinello suggests, this is because Carpentier "trabó contacto con lo negro y lo vio desde adentro pero no les llegó a las vísceras" (came in contact with the black condition and perceived it from within, but he did not understand it in depth).[392] Notwithstanding, still impressed and inspired by the survival of African beliefs and cultural rhythms in the Caribbean, but aware of the fact that he could not understand Afro-Cuban belief systems beyond the gesticulations of rituals and forms, in subsequent novels, and after his conversion to Sartrean existentialism, Carpentier's characters are identified more with the writer's own experiences and perspective than with the expression of afrocubanía. However, he retained his early interest in the atavistic and ritual aspects and forms of Afro-Caribbean belief systems and liturgy, and in the role of music in such rituals. He also remained interested in the primitive instruments and origins of American regional music,[393] in the vigor he saw in the unshaken faith of Afro-Caribbean devotees, the role of magic in Caribbean cultures, and the universal elements of the local. In order to arrive at the essence of atavism in his early works, Carpentier had focused "on the liturgical, the ritual, and the supernatural elements that he has discerned in the Caribbean."[394] However, having reached the understanding that the representation of ritual does not preclude the understanding of that ritual, nor of the people being represented, Carpentier came to understand that ritual is a much more universal element that can be articulated by other means and through different forms.

Ti Nöel's disappearance into the void of myth, displaced in the text by the image of a mercurial, maternal vulture, seems to point to another signifying allegorical inscription in Carpentier's own literary voyage: one that takes the writer away from literature, toward literature. Such voyage, it seems, would suggest that the agency of black Caribbeans, like Mackandal and Ti Nöel, also disappeared from his texts, "sublimated," it seems, into historical meditations on culture, history, and power. Nonetheless, although Carpentier no longer represented Afro-Antillean rituals in the textual fabric of future novels, he still continued to express ritual as a meditation on history, and on human acts and conditions. Like Ti Nöel, Carpentier may have arrived to an understanding of self through the process of writing, and to the impossibility of masquerading the writer's voice with the voice of the "other" he could not be: an "other" whose magic and beliefs he praised (ave, aura), but did not share. It would be his contemporary, Lydia Cabrera, who would come to provide a testimonial account of the Afro-Cuban world of beliefs and faith Carpentier confessed he did not understand, especially in "the relationship of Afro-Cubans with the forest."[395]

The cultural (M)Other that Carpentier associates with his own identification with Cuba, as Cuban, seems to be a central point of tension in Carpentier's texts. Like Ti Nöel, he stood at an ontological and cultural crossroad between philosophies, between Europe and America. Carpentier was a writer, in a Caribbean society, whose cultural identity he understood to be based on difference. And it was precisely that sense of difference that constituted a point of tension in Carpentier's writing: a point of tension from which he wrote about the anxiety of being a Cuban writer living most of his life outside Cuba. In spite of the fact that in Carpentier's texts the Other is mostly a textual performance, Carpentier's representation of an Afro-Caribbean condition (faith, history, ritual, struggle against oppression) became an important model in Latin American literature. It proposed a different mode of writing and a different way of constructing a literary representation of the Caribbean as different from Europe. In spite of the distance between the writer and the subject of his writing, Carpentier constructed in *The Kingdom of This World* a literary metageographic space where blacks and mulattoes, Afro-Caribbeans, were no longer a distant exotic "other," but an integral part of the history and landscape of the Caribbean, as well as important agents in the formation of Caribbean societies: their complex cultural imaginaries, necessities, and "longings." *The Kingdom of This World* soon became a master narrative, and Carpentier's notions of the baroque and of an American "marvelous realism," so firmly interconnected to the writer's interpretations of the role of Africa in the Caribbean, acquired a theoretical life of their own.

2

(De)Colonizing the Other: Writing as Resistance (From Lydia Cabrera's Writings to Guillermo Cabrera Infante's *Tres tristes tigres* *[Three Trapped Tigers]*)

> Myths arise from man's attempt to externalize and communicate his inner intuitions.
> —Wole Soyinka, *Myth, Literature and the African World*

> Su obra es un monumento a nuestros dioses tutelares, la ceiba, la palma, la noche y el monte, la música, el refrán, y la leyenda. Tradición, mito, pasado y magia reconstruidos piedra a piedra, palabra palabra.
> —Reinaldo Arenas, "Diosa instalada en el centro del poema"

WITH THE PUBLICATION OF *CUENTOS NEGROS DE CUBA* IN 1936, IN PARIS, Lydia Cabrera launched a voyage of imaginative rediscovery into the local memories, ancestral African myths, rituals, and belief systems that constitute the African legacy of what Ortiz called afrocubanía. From the perspective of the European avant garde that conceived art and literature in terms of new beginnings, Cabrera departed from Ortiz's documentations, and from the poetic expressions of the Minoristas, in order to explore the syncretic traditions associated with Africa that are still today alive in Cuba, and in the Cuban diaspora. In that process, she offered a new and different view of Cuban society from the gaze of a woman. She offered a unique, although at times ambivalent, vision from a space of power and, at the same time, from outside power, outside European prejudice. Her work recontructed and reinvented an Afro-Cuban discourse that disrupted the national hegemonic concept of *hispanidad* by constructing an in-between cultural space from where to rethink *cubanía* in terms of race and gender. Her work on Afro-Cuban religions also carved a space in Cuban canonical literature for African cultural practices and religious beliefs in Cuba. Most importantly, it opened a window to a way of thinking in Cuba different from Western thought. Lydia Cabrera's short stories and research offered the conditions for the possibility of redefining Cuban nationalism and cultural identity. Yet, in spite of the importance of her texts in the field of Afro-Cuban studies, the prevailing silence by critics of her work suggests that it is still cleaved by political and social tensions, by issues of authenticity and authority, by the ambiguities of classifications, and by the ideological diversity of the Afro-Caribbean landscape.

As a woman, with no political agendas, and at the margins of Cuban literary circles, Lydia Cabrera discovered early in life that her main schism with Cuban society was a conflict of gender. She began to write about Afro-Cuban religions from the privileged position of a white upper-class woman, from, rather than "against," dominant power; but she soon discovered that her interest was not considered in Cuba "proper" for a young white woman of her social status. After the publication in Havana of *Cuentos negros de Cuba* (1940), she faced the fact that she was a woman in a literary world of men, writing on a subject (Afro-Cuban belief systems) then feared and misunderstood by the dominant Cuban society. Like for most Latin American women intellectuals in the early part of the twentieth century, Cabrera became aware very early in life that her gender was a social obstacle she would have to learn to overcome. Since her early twenties Cabrera had expressed her desire to study art in France, but her father opposed it. One day, she pointed a gun to her head and threatened to shoot herself if he did not allow her to study in Paris. He promised her that day that the entire family would move to Paris. However, he was not able to fulfill his promise. Lydia's father died on her twenty-third birthday, May 20, 1923. Years later, in 1927, as the result of her own enterpreneurial efforts, she was able to move to Paris, leaving behind what she then saw as the banality and stifling conservatism of bourgeois life in Havana.[1]

It was in France that Lydia Cabrera became interested in Afro-Cuban religions. She then began to gather information from Afro-Cuban practitioners during her trips to Cuba. That research allowed her to rescue, reinvent, and reconstruct, in the voice of her informers, the magic and rituals of a vernacular Cuban culture whose beliefs and ways of life can be traced to different African ancestries. Today, her work points out the differences between the various African belief systems in Cuba, and their unique contribution to Cuban culture. Cabrera's writings access for the reader a codified cultural imaginary that, whether in fictional constructions, translations, adaptations, rewritings or transcriptions, offers a testimonial voice to a religious Afro-Cuban sector of society previously silenced. Her work of fiction and the testimonial voices of her informers reveal the complexities and the depths of Cuba's African heritage. Different from Ortiz's research, Cabrera's work carved a space in Cuban letters for a national mythology informed by her own field work: a diligent research that allowed her to transcribe in her books the testimonial voices of practicioners of different Afro-

Cuban belief systems. Her work offers a cultural mythology that addresses the story of the middle passage from Africa to Cuba, and, today, the story of a second voyage from the island to the Cuban Diaspora. It is no wonder that for Cuban writers like Guillermo Cabrera Infante, Lydia Cabrera's *El monte* (1954) is "the best book ever written in Cuba."[2] He writes from London in a letter to Lydia Cabrera, March 22, 1975: "el libro cubano de este siglo con mayor calidad es *El Monte*" (the Cuban book of highest quality this century is *El monte*).[3] It is not surprising then that Guillermo Cabrera Infante chooses to include Lydia Cabrera as a character for his novel, *Tres tristes tigres* (1965) *(Three Trapped Tigers,* 1967), in the priestly role of an oracle. *El monte* informs the invisible spaces of the Havana he represents, and provides a mythical codified structure for the novel. In *Tres tristes tigres* Afro-Cuban beliefs, especially those of the ñáñigos studied by Lydia Cabrera in *El monte,* and in *La sociedad secreta Abakuá,* find a significant role in that secondary, but "primary," order of reading that, according to Benítez Rojo, characterizes Caribbean texts.

LYDIA CABRERA: WRITING SELF/ WRITING THE OTHER

May 20, 1902, the day Cuba became a free Republic, Lydia Cabrera celebrated her second birthday.[4] Among her recollections of that day, one stands out: the moment when Estrada Palma, the first president of the new republic, a friend of her father, told her that the festivities in Havana on that day were in her honor.[5] The anecdote highlights the fact that Lydia Cabrera's childhood was intertwined with the birth of the Cuban Republic and with the early discourses on cultural identity and nation-building.[6] In other words, her birthday coincides with an important cultural and racial negotiation that also marks the birth of the Cuban Republic. During the wars of independence waged in Cuba beginning in 1868, race had been a point of conflict. By 1895, at the beginning of the last insurgency, as Ada Ferrer points out in *Insurgent Cuba 1868–1898,* with slavery abolished in 1886, and in order to subvert colonial propaganda in which Spain claimed that Cuban insurgency was a racial war,[7] Cuban patriots elaborated "a conception of a raceless nationality that would come to dominate Cuban thinking on race and nationality."[8] These "patriotic claims about racial integration" were a "powerful, if incomplete attack on the ideological foundations of colonial rule."[9] In 1896, however, with a clear vision of an imminent independence near, the race issue resurfaced among white Cuban patriots who began to plan for the Republic as a civilized (under the specter of Positivism) white independent nation. As a showcase of such "civility" with which to disarm Spain's propagandistic claim that the insurgents were black savages, black Cuban officers in the insurgent army were asked to accept demotion and serve under white high-class officers. When the United States government declared war on Spain and intervened in Cuba in 1898, one of the mandates the new rulers imposed on Cuban leaders, as a negotiation for freedom, was the proof of "civility:" a notion equated with whiteness. However, the ideal of a raceless nationality was too deeply integrated into the national struggle for freedom to allow for the implementation in Cuba of a similar Jim Crow segregation act, as in the United States. In spite of the political pressure, Cuba's Constitutional Convention of 1901 proclaimed universal suffrage the law of the land. As Ferrer points out: "American evacuation, then, appeared to require from Cuban nationalists an evation of principles central to the nationalist movement of thirty years."[10] Political independence now came to depend on the rejection of those basic principles. Under such conditions that left black Cuban patriots defranchised of political power, and under the Platt Amendment that gave the United States the right to return whenever it thought it necessary, on May 20, 1902, Cuba became an independent Republic. Lydia Cabrera's father, Raimundo Cabrera, had been a strong supporter for the separation of Cuba from the United States, as he had been against Spain's colonial rule. It was at this historical juncture, at a moment of political and racial entanglements in the construction of the nation, that Lydia Cabrera was born.

When Cabrera was five years old, her sister, Ester, married Fernando Ortiz, whom she met in Europe during a family trip. He was working then on his first book, *Hampa afrocubana: Los negros brujos (apuntes para un estudio de etnología criminal)* (1906) (Afro-Cuban Sub-World: Black Sourceres [Notes For an Ethnological Study on Criminology]). Although Lydia Cabrera always claimed that Ortiz had no influence on her writings,[11] one would assume that the simple presence of Ortiz as a member of her family since early in her childhood made her aware, if not curious, of a complex cultural African ancestry in Cuban society with which Lydia Cabrera was also in direct contact through her Nana and other black house servants. The fact is that she was familiar with Ortiz's work. She knew that Ortiz inspired an intellectual interest on Afro-Cuban lore and that he was a mentor for writers and artists interested in afrocubanía.[12] However, Cabrera claimed that her own interest in Afro-Cuban religions started when she began to read, in France, books about Oriental religions.[13] This was an interest she shared with the Venezuelan writer, Teresa de la Parra, whom she met for the first time in 1924 in Havana,[14] and with her friend the Chilean poet Gabriela Mistral, who also felt attracted then to Buddhism.[15]

In 1936, Lydia Cabrera published in Paris a collection of short stories translated by Francis de Miomandre as *Contes nègres de Cuba* (later published in 1940 in Havana as *Cuentos negros de Cuba)*. These short stories were conceived and written in Europe, according to Lydia Cabrera, from memories of childhood: from bedtime songs and stories told to her by her black Nana, Tata Tula, and other house servants.[16] It is possible that some of these texts were also tales she heard in the black community of Pogolotti, in the outskirts of Havana, a community she began to visit in 1928 during her trips to Cuba.[17] She shared her experiences in that community with Teresa de la Parra, to whom Cabrera dedicated her first book. Cabrera claims that she began to write her first Afro-Cuban stories in 1934 to entertain Teresa, who was convalescing with tuberculosis in an asylum in Leysin, Switzerland. She sent Teresa short stories with her letters; and Teresa always commented on the texts in her letters, urging Cabrera to publish them. As Sylvia Molloy observes from her readings of Teresa's letters to Cabrera, literature was a complicit mode of comunication between both friends, a way of understanding and exploring the world around them and their being-in-that-world.[18] Molloy suggests a complicit relationship between Lydia and Teresa, bonded by the desire for independence in a patriarchal order that excluded women.[19] For Molloy, Teresa's and Lydia's voluntary exile was a "geographic displacement [that] provided a place to write one's difference."[20] Molloy finds that in Teresa's letters to Lydia the terms "without rules" and "independence" are coded words "for a lifestyle, and yes, a sexuality over which 'they'—family, institutions, modern national state—have no authority."[21] Molloy proposes that Teresa's interest in her indigenous *Musuché* ancestry and Lydia's interest in Afro-Cubans was associated in part with their recognition of the marginal and the excluded.[22] For the same reasons, their interest in the colonial past, Molloy suggests: "should indeed be read as more resistant than reactionary. What is being resisted is not so much historical independence per se . . . as processes of modernization and national state formation that in the name of rationalism and modern progress, engage in tendentious classifications."[23] It is possible that this sense of exclusion based on race and gender in issues related to modernity and nationhood led Lydia to an external exile in France and to an internal exile in Afro-Cuban religions and lore. In fact, years later, exiled in Miami, Florida, reminiscing on those years, Cabrera claimed that the only reason she stayed in Cuba after the end of World War II was due to her friendship with her Afro-Cuban friends who "were so nice" to her.[24]

Like María Eugenia, the main character in Teresa de la Parra's novel *Ifigenia* (1924), who wrote letters in order to understand her own condition, Cabrera wrote to Teresa in the complicit language of literature. Literary language allowed Cabrera to express herself as a Cuban woman in a polycultural society where the ideals of nationhood imagined by patriots like Antonio Maceo and José Martí were "transracial," but not "transgender." Writing *Cuentos negros de Cuba,* an act intrinsicaly related to writing Teresa —who, in turn, encouraged Cabrera to published her work[25]—was also an attempt to rescue the socially silent voices of the elder African descendants whose knowledge, Cabrera thought, would dissappear with their death.

These elders represented a cultural womb associated with her own past, with her Nana, Tata Tula, and others like Omí Tomí. A certain analogy could be drawn between the voices being rescued and the absent presence of Teresa de la Parra's body/voice, a mother/sister figure[26] for whom Cabrera says she wrote her first short stories. As José Quiroga suggests, there seems to be a complicit literary relationship of double texts and double utterances, directed to the voice/body of Cabrera's elder informants and Teresa's body/voice.[27] In a codified play with that absent presence, the text articulates, and is articulated by, an "invisible author" who disclaims the authorship of the text she writes, disguised as a "transcriber," but whose authorship is recognized by Teresa. It can be argued then that Cabrera's writing is a codified act of rescuing, through writing, the voice/body of the (m)other: a cultural and historical past revived through the writing of the stories of childhood, the stories Cabrera heard from the people that "were so nice," like her Tata Tula, Omí Tomí, her friends in Pogolotti, but also Teresa.

Writing on a subject that questioned the hispanidad of Cuban society was an act of resistance toward the conservative Cuban bourgeoise and, also, toward a white male dominance whose discourses constructed a hegemonic national voice that, while by now it included Afro-Cubans as objects of study, it excluded (especially since 1898) the agency of Afro-Cubans and of women in the formation of culture and nation. The French négre used in the title of her collection of short stories further supports that sense of cultural resistance. In the France of the thirties, the word négre voiced defiance toward the exclusion in Western epistemology of African cultures and their history. In a 1967 interview, Aimé Césaire explains to Rene Depestre that sense of defiance: "We [blacks] adopted the word négre as a term of defiance . . . We found a violent affirmation in the words négre and négritude . . . that we are black; that we were black and have a history. . . . there have been beautiful and important black civilization. . . . that its values were values that could still make an important contribution to the world."[28] It is not clear to what extent Cabrera was aware of the gathering of Africans, North Americans, Antilleans, Guianans, and Haitians in Paris during the thirties when négre was charged with a significant sense of defiance.[29] Yet, it is a well-known fact that André Breton's surrealist circle became a crossroad of ideas (Césaire was part of Breton's circle of influence, as well as the Afro-Asian-Cuban painter Wifredo Lam), and that Cabrera, a student of art in Paris, was acquainted with these gatherings.[30] There were other crossroads of ideas, like the journal Cashier du Sud, in which Cabrera published three short stories in 1934, translated by Francis de Miomandre.[31] In 1935, Cashier du Sud published two African tales collected by Leon Frobenious, and translated by Emma Cabire.[32] There was also Revenue du monde noir (1931–32), and cultural events like the 1933 exhibit of African artifacts gathered by Leon Frobenius and displayed at the Museé d'Ethno-graphie du Trocodéro.[33]

In 1942, back in Cuba, Lydia Cabrera translated Césaire's *Cashier d'un Retour au Pays Natal* (Paris, 1939) (*Notebook of a Return to the Native Land*), published in Spanish in 1943 as *Retorno al país natal*, with illustrations by Wifredo Lam and an introduction by the French surrealist, Benjamin Péret. Césaire became aware of Cabrera's work first from *Cashier du Sud*, and later from Lam who left France soon after Césaire. During the years that Lam spent in Cuba,[34] Lydia Cabrera inspired him to express in his paintings his cultural roots, and to represent the invisible natural forces of Afro-Cuban religions in a Cuban cultural landscape, as he does in his masterpiece "The Jungle" (1943),[35] and in other paintings of this period.

In Europe, Cabrera had come in contact with numerous writers and artists,[36] among them Miguel Angel Asturias. He, like other Latin American writers of this period, was interested in the indigenous lore of his native Guatemala, an interest that informs *Leyendas de Guatemala* (1930), a text that both Teresa and Lydia read in 1933.[37] Teresa's own interests followed along the same aesthetic currents of the period. She had written two acclaimed novels in France, *Memorias de Mamá Blanca* (1929) (*Mamá Blanca's Memoirs*), a recollection of childhood memoirs in Venezuela, and *Ifigenia (o diario de una señorita que se fastidia)* (1924) (*Iphigenia: Diary of a Young Lady Who Wrote Because She is Bored,* 1993), a novel in which de la Parra criticizes her homeland, Venezuela, which she represents as a conservative male-dominated society whose sacrificial victims were always women.[38] Her main character in *Ifigenia,* María Eugenia Alonso, had been living in France with her father, but after his death she was forced to return to Venezuela to live penniless in a male-dominated world under the care of two spinster aunts.[39] Cabrera (like Teresa), also left a conservative Cuban society in the twenties to go to Paris to study art; and Teresa (like Cabrera) did not want to return to Venezuela for the very same reasons that her novel had been received "with hostility and resentment and was branded as a 'pernicious,' Voltarian influence on young women readers."[40]

The fact that Cabrera's stories in *Cuentos negros de Cuba* were written, as Cabrera claimed, to entertain Teresa de la Parra, suggests that fiction, for Cabrera, was intended as an epistolary exchange of a complicit literary understanding. Furthermore, this epistolary-literary complicit "performance," whose function was to "entertain," but was grounded also in her reality, carry with it the knowledge of a separation/death that Cabrera wanted to postpone, or at least aliviate, through the written word, by rescuing the voice of the (m)other (black Cubans), like Teresa had done in *Memorias de Mamá Blanca.* Postpoment in Cabrera's writing is related here to memory, to digging into her own childhood recollections informed by the diligent research on Afro-Cuban religions she began in the twenties. It may be pertinent to remember that, in Havana, when Cabrera was a young girl, her father took her often to gatherings of men in literary cafés and to the meetings of the prominent "Sociedad Económica de Amigos de País" (Economic Society of Friends of the Nation), which he presided.[41] This was a world to which Cabrera did not belong for being a woman, and a world she caricatures in her short stories and fables, juxtaposing it to an Afro-Cuban creole society that she associates with the imaginary home space of her childhood. That juxtaposition is often staged in her texts in colonial Cuba, a period that attracted Cabrera and about which she wrote numerous articles before leaving for France.[42] In her complicit dialogue with Teresa, Cabrera brings to her writing these two different Cuban cultural realms that appealed to her and to Teresa. She often shares with her her early findings on Afro-Cuban religious practices. For instance, in a letter Lydia sent to Teresa de la Parra in 1930, during one of her visits to Havana, Cabrera describes the experiences of one of her visits to her "black" friend, also named Teresa. An *Asiento* was taking place, and there were many *babalaos* and *alochas:*

> Vino a verme Má Calista [Morales]; lucumí, alocha, (te acuerdas, *Alocha,* bruja, iniciada) la que mejor llama a los Santos, toda vestida de blanco, con pañuelo blanco a la cabeza y collar de perlas rotas, conmovedor—. . . Llegó de visita Leonorcita de Armenteros—84 años—comadrona, que yá no vé bien, con mantilla y abanico. . . ."—Esta negra defiende la Colonia. Cuba Libre ha sido una gran decepción para ella. De España—"Dios la perdone"—no puede hablar mal. . . . Nunca he visto aquí en la Habana, nada que hubiera podido interesarte tanto.[43]

> [Má Calista (Morales) came to see me; *Lucumí, alocha,* (remember, *Alocha,* witch, initiated) the best one to call the Saints, dresses in white, with a white handkership on her head and a necklace of broken pearls, touching . . . Leonorcita de Armenteros—84 years old—came to visit—midwife, partly blind, with shawl and fan. . . . This black woman defends Colonial Cuba. The Cuban Republic has been a great deception for her. Of Spain—"God forgive her"—(she) cannot say anything bad . . . I have never seen anything here in Havana that would have interested you as much.]

When *Contes nègres de Cuba* was published in France (the same year Teresa de la Parra died), Cabrera's short stories were highly acclaimed, ironically, in part, for the same reasons that Miomandre had praised de la Parra's *Ifigenia* in his prologue to the novel. He wrote: "Not for a moment do we believe this to be literature. . . . We only have the sensation of being admitted to the confidence of an intimate diary. We page through it enchanted, emotionally moved, by the side of the one who wrote it."[44] However, when *Cuentos negros de Cuba* was published in Havana, in 1940, prologued by Ortiz, the reception it received from the conservative Cuban society of the time was as negative as the reaction *Ifigenia* had received few years before in Venezuela. Furthermore, Ortiz's praise ironically negated Cabrera's personal authorial creation by suggesting, as Miomandre had done with *Ifigenia,* that Cabrera's texts were not "literature:"

> No hay que olvidar que estos cuentos vienen a las prensas por su colaboración, la del folklore negro con su traductora blanca. Porque también el texto en castellano es en realidad una traducción, y, en rigor sea dicho, una segunda traducción. Del lenguaje africano (yoruba, ewe o bantú) en que las fábulas se imaginaron, éstas fueron vertidas en Cuba al idioma amestizado y dialectal de los negros criollos. . . . La autora ha hecho tarea difícil pero leal y, por lo tanto, muy meritoria, conservando a los cuentos su fuerte carácter exótico de fondo y de forma.[45]

> [One must not forget that these stories are published due to a collaboration of black folklore with its white translator; because the Spanish text is in reality also a translation, and, it may be said, a second translation. From the African language (*Yoruba, Ewe,* or *Bantu*) in which the fables were imagined, in Cuba they entered the mixed dialect of black creoles. . . . The writer has carried out a difficult but faithful task, and, therefore, of great merit, conserving the stories' strong exotic form and content.]

Remembering that at this time the word "literature" had the negative connotation of being "old fashion," insincere, pedantic, artificial, and distant from life, Cabrera also seemed to negate her authorship, and imaginative creativity by masking her craft with Ortiz's claim that her stories were "translations" and "transcriptions." Perhaps it was an effort to distance herself from what she and Teresa rejected as "literature," meaning an intellectual exercise, which they associated with the banality of the bourgeoisie. Ortiz writes:

> Lydia Cabrera fue penetrando el bosque de las leyendas negras de La Habana . . . al fin fue trancribiéndolas (*sic*) y coleccionándolas. . . . varios de estos cuentos de los negros de Cuba son de una fase africana apenas contaminadas por su culturación en el ambiente blanco, aún con los rasgos característicos de su original africanía. . . . Y su colección abre un nuevo capítulo folklórico en la literatura cubana.[46]

> [Lydia Cabrera penetred the jungle of black (Afro-Cuban) legends in Havana . . . finally she began to transcribe them and collect them . . . several of these stories (told) by blacks in Cuba belong to an African phase hardly contaminated by an acculturation to a white enviroment, even with the charateristic elements of this African origin. . . . And her collection opens a new chapter of folklore in Cuban literature.]

Ortiz's words proved to be prophetic. Lydia Cabrera did open a new chapter in Cuban literature, and a new way of expressing afrocubanía. However, one must question why Lydia Cabrera, whose relationship with Teresa de la Parra had been mediated by the language of literary imagination, simply accepted Ortiz's description of her artistic writing strictly as that of a "translator," "collectionist," and "transcriber,"[47] were it not for the fact that at this time the term "translation" was charged with different meanings. Pérez Firmat observes that in the context of Ortiz's work, "Cuban style is translation style,"[48] in which "the indigenous is nothing more than a certain inflection of the foreign."[49] It is possible that, at this time, and different from the notion "literature" had for Lydia Cabrera and Teresa de la Parra, the term "translation" for Cabrera meant the intratranslation of a culture within a culture, thus giving to the act of writing a sense of immediacy and "life" experience.[50] In other words, "translation," in contrast to the artificiality of "literature," offered an association to the concept of cultural exchange proposed by Bronislaw Malinowski, intimating with it the concept that Ortiz would coin in 1940, in the Cuban context, as "transculturation." At the same time, it is important to remember that in the early part of the twentieth century, as Walter Mignolo points out, "translation was the special tool to absorb the colonial difference previously established. 'People without history' were located in time 'before the present.' People with history could write the history of those people without."[51] Yet, writing the Other, for Cabrera, at this early moment of her work, was associated with the rescue of the body, the Other's body, as the space from where to write her own difference.

It would be hard to negate the strong "Africanness"—as Ortiz called it—of Cabrera's short stories.[52] At the same time, Cabrera's work of fiction, especially the tales and fables in *Cuentos negros de Cuba,* are laden with literary tropes in vogue during the thirties in Europe, and with Cabrera's own unique avant-garde style and imagination. As a student at the *Ecole du Louvre* and the *Ecole des Beaux Arts,* in close contact with artistic movements and aesthetic philosophies of the period, she experimented with different avant-garde techniques, like expressionism, surrealism, and cubism. She also played with counterpoints of the classical and the popular,[53] like in Spanish Golden Age texts. Like in Guillén's poetry, Cuban popular culture is Afro-Cuban. In fact, many of Cabrera's short stories represent (like the popular Spanish baroque "Ensaladillas") the multiples sectors of Cuban society, including various and different Afro-Cuban beliefs. Cabrera's experimentations in her short stories and fables in *Cuentos negros de Cuba* with avant garde techniques offers images like: "Los mares desbordaron de los caracoles; los ríos del lagrimar del primer cocodrilo que tuvo" (Oceans flooded out of seashells; rivers out of the first alligator's cry from sorrow).[54] The new literary forms (informed by avant garde techniques) with which she experimented allowed her to articulate the poetics of a mythical world, in Cuba, which she wanted to "transpose" to writing, while also reinventing that world in the process. In "El caballo de Hicotea" (Tortoise's

Horse), for example, Cabrera presents the enslavement of horse, turned by the evil maquinations of the Yoruba-Lucumi trickster *hicotea* (tortoise) into "her" beast of work. In this fable, a meditation on the injustice of slavery, Cabrera transforms Horse's loss of freedom into a poetics of freedom: the nostalgia for a time of liberty, now lost, and the impossibility of living as an object of possession under the domination of another equal being. Unwilling to accept his condition:

> Compadre Caballo Blanco, perdida la razón huía de este mundo.
> Corrió, corrió, corrió, corrió, hasta que se acabó la tierra. . . .
> Y aún huye, muerto, el Caballo Blanco.
> Por soledades de estrellas. Por el sueño despierto de las estrellas.[55]

> [Compadre White Horse, having lost his mind, ran away from this world.
> He ran, ran, ran, ran to the end of the earth. . . .
> And he is still running away, dead, White Horse.
> Through the lonely stars. Through the awakened dreams of the stars.]

Cabrera's appropriation and imaginary reconstruction of African and Afro-Cuban myths and legends in *Cuentos negros de Cuba* are not very different from Abiola Irele's description of *Negritude:* "the whole movement is expressed through a western mould which absorbs African realities. In short, *Negritude* . . . although African in content, is western in its formal expression."[56] Cabrera's texts followed Western literary models, but, like the choice of the word nègre for the title of her text, they were charged with a signifying sense of resistance in vogue in France during the thirties. Benita Parry points out that: "The multivalencies of Cèsaire's *Negritude* pre-empts both closure and fixity, making it available to rearticulations covering other modes of oppression."[57] In a similar sense, Cabrera's use of nègre articulates a resistance related to race, but like in Cèsaire's definition of negritude, also to gender, and to the defying rescue of an African imaginary, informed and expressed through Western concepts of Art. In *Notebook of a Return to the Native Land,* Cèsaire not only sets out on a voyage of what Stuart Hall calls "imaginative rediscovery,"[58] but, in so doing, he evokes Africa as inscribed in the woman's body.[59] Notwithstanding, as Jaimes Arnold points out: "Cèsaire did not dredge up Mother Africa from some atavistic racial memory," he "had at his disposal the same European intellectual tradition as these (European) writers."[60] It was also the same intellectual tradition that was available to Lydia Cabrera during the thirties in Europe.

In Cuba, the *Origenistas* welcomed Cabrera's short stories as the articulation of a "primal" (new) poetic knowledge, as a new expression of cubanía. Cabrera published several of her short stories and notes from her research in *Orígenes* (1944–56). This poetic space of primordial knowledge in Cabrera's writing, for the Origenistas, and especially for José Lezama Lima, was associated with the mother, the feminine, and with poetry.[61] Maria Zambrano, a Spanish writer who excerted an important influence on the Origenistas, and a friend of Cabrera, described Lydia Cabrera as a "poet of metamorphosis." For Zambrano, *Cuentos negros de Cuba* was an "arte divinatorio al par que objetivo" (objective *ars divinatoria*) that "puede juntar el conocimiento a la fantasía y realizar así la poesía en su sentido primero de ser reveladora de un mundo, el agente unificador en que las cosas y los seres se muestran en estado virginal, en éxtasis y danza" (can bring together knowledge and fantasy to create poetry as a primordial revelation of the world, the unifying agent in which things and living beings are seen in their virginal state, in ecstasy and dance).[62] Always faithful to African and Afro-Cuban sources, Cabrera's literary creations followed European aesthetic styles, but, at the same time, they ascribed to a way of thinking chacacteristic of Afro-Cuban oral traditions, especially the mode of narrating in the *Pataki,* an Afro-Cuban archive that Cabrera describes as: "algo muy bonito en el sistema de adivinación yoruba, lucumí. Son los ejemplos, las moralejas, a eso se llama 'pataki'" (something beautiful in the *Yoruba, Lucumí* system of divination. They are examples, moral stories; that is called "*Pataki*").[63]

The last short story of *Cuentos negros de Cuba,* "El sapo guardiero" (The Guardian Toad) represents the stereotypal old witch, reminiscent of European fairy tales, but with an Afro-Cuban twist, for she is *palera* and *conga,* like Afro-Cuban priests of a *Bantu* tradition known in Cuba as *Palo Monte*.[64] The text appropriates European tropes to express a religious African cosmovision characteristic of Afro-Cuban animistic thought, while at the same time it recreates the battle, in Cuba, between Congo (Bantu) and Lucumí (Yoruba) belief systems.[65] In this story, Cabrera privileges the later, the Lucumí world of her Tata Tula and Omí Tomí, by representing a *congo-palera* witch who, in spite of her strong magic, cannot defeat the primordial kindness and love deeply rooted in earth's ancestral telluric wisdom. Cabrera represents such primordial wisdom, associated here with maternal love, in the figure of an old ancestral toad that recalls the image in colonial Cuba of the old *guardieros:* slaves who, no longer useful to work in the plantation, like Mackandal after his accident, were sent to the edge of the plantation to live, and to guard the animals. Cuban literature represents these guardieros as African elders and keepers of archival African knowledge. The ancestral guardiero in Cabrera's fable, an amphibian (a border subject), awakens when tiny twins, lost in the forest (like Hansel and Gretel), begin to cry from fear. The twins, reminescent of the Lucumí magic twins, the Ibeyes, the divine Jimaguas, "eran los mellizos que andaban solos por el mundo . . . Andando, andando por la vida inmensa, los mellizos, hijos de nadie" (were the twins who traveled alone in the world . . . Walking, walking, through the vastness of life, the twins, no one's sons).[66] The *palera* witch, who imposes her power over the forest, wants to trap them by concocting a magic nganga, or congo-palera magic with dirt from a crossroad and bones from a cemetary:[67]

> La vieja de bruces escupía aguardiente, pólvora y pimienta china,
>   en la cazuela bruja.
> Trazaba en el suelo flechas de cenizas, serpientes de humo.
>   Hablaban conchas de mar.[68]

> [Bent over, the old woman would spit moonshine, gunpowder,
>   and Chinese pepper, in the witch pot.]
> She drew arrows with ash on the floor, serpents of smoke.
>   Talking seashells.]

To protect the innocent twins, the ancestral toad swallows them, and carries them to the edge of the forest, to safety. The frog then speaks "la palabra incorruptible, olvidada, perdida, más vieja que la tristeza del mundo, y la palabra se hizo luz de amanecer" (the incorruptable, forgotten, lost word, older than the sadness of the world, and the word became dawn).[69] In a scene reminiscent of Rudyard Kipling's innocent and threatened Mowgli in *The Jungle Books,* also delivered by his jungle friends to the safety of a town, away from the dangers of the "jungle," the evil Kan, Cabrera's mythological twins, saved by the old toad, leave the forest: "cantando y riendo por el camino blanco" (singing and laughing on the white road).[70] The guardiero toad defies the witch's orders, the law of the forest, saves the twins, and then dies fulfilled with love, peace, and tenderness. When the witch came to kill the toad as punishment, "el sapo, traspasado de suavidad, soñaba en su charca de fango con el agua más pura . . . ya él estaba dormido, muerto dulcemente, en aquella agua clara, infinita. Quieta de eternidad" (the toad, darted with softness, dreamed in his mud pond of the purest water . . . . he was already asleep, sweetly dead, in that clear, infinite, water. Calm with eternity).[71]

Cabrera's image of love and transcendence is, significantly, the last image with which she ends the last fable in *Cuentos negros de Cuba.* Remembering that this is a text Cabrera dedicated to, and wrote for, the convalesing Teresa de la Parra, Cabrera's poetics of transcendence, through death, takes the reader to the oneiric realm of myths where African, European, and also Oriental traditions are confused, or, as Zambrano argued, "metamorphosed."

Infused with Afro-Cuban mythical images, we find a story in which love awakens the hidden and forgotten emotions of the ancestral toad, the maternal wisdom of an androgynous forest, *monte,* and allows the old guardiero to die in peace for having loved. In this short story, care is the most powerful element of transmutation that elevates the spirit of the ancestral amphibian out and away from the negative forces of the world, much like the role of literature in the complicit relationship between the writer, the text, and the reader: Teresa. The fable is a ritual of passage, through "knowledge" and poetry,[72] in a text of double utterances about love, life, and death. Cabrera's short story articulates a poetics of caring at a moment of crisis (Teresa's consumption), and affirms the importance fiction had for Teresa de la Parra and for Lydia Cabrera as a codified language they shared.[73] Ironically, reality, at the moment *Cuentos negros de Cuba* is published, compounds death with the beginning of war, and sends Cabrera back to Havana, where for few years she distanced herself from "writing." After Teresa's death, Gabriela Mistral wrote to Cabrera: "No vas a quedarte a lo niña regalona sin publicar más libro que ése, el trabajo aísla del horrible mundo que estamos viviendo y sólo él salva en semejante infierno de humo sin llamas" (You cannot remain a pampered girl and not publish another book, only this one; work distances you from the horrible world we live in, only it can save [us] from such hell of smoke without fire).[74] In part due to Mistral's words, Cabrera continued with her research, and in 1948 she published a second collection of short stories: *¿Por qué? Cuentos negros de Cuba.*

Like other Cuban writers of this period, Cabrera's *Cuentos negros de Cuba* dialogues with García Lorca's system of symbols,[75] his sense of violence, beauty, mystery, and the plasticity of his musical and metaphoric images, with which he expressed the unique magic and cultural vitality of his native Andalucía. During García Lorca's visit to Cuba, Cabrera showed him an Afro-Cuban world whose magic and vitality equaled, in a Caribbean context, the Andalucian "soul" of his texts.[76] From a Spenglerian gaze, Cabrera's Afro-Cuban stories awakened the "forest stirrings" (*DW,* 402) in a Cuban/Caribbean context. They offered a "mythical quality which does not arise out of scientific experimentation," and "a magnetism whose field of force includes a piece of iron . . . and that imagines personifications like "electricity," "temperature," and "radioactivity" (*DW,* 413). They represented a certain cultural knowledge that Hilda Perera explains as: "la verdad ascendiendo hasta lo infinito" (truth ascending to infinity).[77] Cabrera articulated this boundless search for the infinite through myth and magic, as an oneiric and mythical aspect of the life-force of an Afro-Cuban poetics, alive in everyday life in Cuban society. Such "poetics" recreated cubanía for the Origenistas as an oneiric space of knowledge, a liminal space accessible through memory and myths: a space Reinaldo Arenas would later define, in the context of Cabrera's work, as "la voz del monte, el ritmo de la Isla, los mitos que la engrandecen y la sostienen. La magia con que todo un pueblo marginado y esclavizado se ha sabido mantener (flotar), imponer siempre (the voice of the *monte,* the island's rhythm, the myths that makes the island great, and gives it life. The magic with which a people marginalized and enslaved has been able to survive and prevail).[78] In an article for *Carteles,* Alejo Carpentier refered to Cabrera's stories as a "masterpiece:" that is, a literary work that captured the Faustian sense of magic and primitive life-force Carpentier ascribed to blacks and Indians in America. Carpentier also would say in 1937 in reference to Cabrera's publication in Paris of her *Cuentos negros de Cuba,* "los cuentos negros de Lydia Cabrera constituyen una obra única en nuestra literatura" (Lydia Cabrera's black Cuban stories constitute a unique work in our literature), because she succeeds in taking "la mitología antillana en la categoría de los valores universales" (Antillean mythology to the level of universal values).[79] One must wonder to what extent Cabrera's *Cuentos negros de Cuba* (1940), and later, ¿*Por qué? Cuentos negros de Cuba* (1948) (in dialogue with the discourse of Negritude) informed Carpentier reevaluation of his earlier portrayal of Cuban blacks in his work prior to *The Kingdom of This World,* as representations emptied of the faith, magic, and myths he had been trying to capture in form and structure.[80]

In Cabrera's *Cuentos negros de Cuba,* the humor that characterizes her work of fiction is tinted by French humor,[81] but the themes and conflicts she presents in them are similar to those found in ¿*Por qué? Cuentos negros de Cuba* (1948), and, later, *Ayapá. Cuentos de jicotea* (1971). These are: the power play between the weak and the strong, the witty and the dumb, the survival of the weak through wits in a dominant patriarchal colonial society, trickery (cheating and adultery), envy, pride, the corruption of power and desire, and the role of women as a complex life-force in the Afro-Cuban cosmos. In Cabrera's fables the reader encounters *bilongos,* orishas, rituals of purifications or *ebós,* rituals of possessions known in Cuba as *montar,* by which a deity "mounts," takes possession of, his/her human son or daughter; potions, magic, African songs, European fairy tales, in Cuban creole and *bozal* forms of speech. Cabrera's fictional work also constructs a primordial world in the Antilles comparable to a Nietzchean Dyonissian life, which Perera explains as: "la reconciliación del hombre con la naturaleza, el regreso misterioso a la unidad primordial que según Nietzsche es la fuente generadora del arte" (the reconciliation of man with nature, the mysterious return to a primordial unity which, according to Nietzsche, is the regenerating source of Art).[82] Her short stories articulate a sense of magic infused in a Caribbean cosmovision that is neither African nor European, and, yet, it is both and more. Her short stories are representative of a characteristic syncretism in Cuban society; and thus, in them, there are signifying double-utterances through which Cabrera parodies the many levels and rhizomes of a Cuban society: a society deeply maked by conflictive historical experiences, and centuries of slavery.

II

Lydia Cabrera's residence in Paris during the twenties and thirties coincided with a revival of African cultures that was sweeping through Europe, especially France. It was a revival of sorts associated with the search, through scientific "knowledge," of human origins. In Europe, African art provided new techniques with which to express the abstract through new forms. Lydia Cabrera's short stories, following such models, suggested a different poetic space of culture within the hegemony of cubanía, but also a surreal *marvellous* space which, like Breton's *Surrealism,* refered to an attitude toward nature "governed above all by its initial conception of the poetic image."[83] In other words, Cabrera's short stories in *Cuentos negros de Cuba* represented Cuba's "Africanness" as an every day social negotiation, while also expressing what Pierre Reverdy defined as, in reference to *surrealism:* "The image is a pure creation of the mind. It cannot be born from a comparison but from a juxtaposition of two or more or less distant realities. The more the relationship between the two juxtaposed realities is distant and true, the stronger the image will be—the greater its emotional power and poetic reality."[84]

The intellectual interest in Africa, and in its primal forms as "pure creation" that swept over Europe during this period can be understood best when compared to the interest in the West on the Orient (an interest Cabrera shared). Edward Said explores in *Orientalism* (1979) the development of such interest, which he describes as "a closed field, a theatrical stage affixed to Europe."[85] Said writes: "Philosophically, then the kind of language, thought and vision that I have been calling Orientalism very generally a form of radical realism . . . considered to be reality."[86] "The modern Orientalist—Said adds—was, in his view, a hero rescuing the Orient from the obscurity, alienation, and strangeness which he himself had properly distinguished. His research reconstructed the Orient's lost languages, mores, even mentalities."[87] Said analyzes the construction, in the West, in Western epistemology, of a homogeneous "being" known as the Orient, dissected and ultimately invented from the necessities and realities of the West.

Like the Orientalists, also the Africanists developed a particular discourse of knowledge through which Africa and everything African "acquired a precise intellectual and historical dimension with which to buttress the myths of its geographic distance."[88] However, in the case of the Africanist Cuban artists and ethnologists, that space called Africa, rescued at a distance by Europeans, was, in fact, as it was for Cabrera (for Carpentier, Ortiz, Ballagas, Güirao, Guillén, and other Minoristas), Cuba's popular element: a living daily occurrence in the very midst of Cuban vernacular society, in a nation still defining its cultural boundaries and national myths. It was, they proposed, an African way of being-in-the-world alive and dynamic in the midst of Hispanic Cuban society; but also distant from it, imagined out of new and different necessities, by the new republic of Cuba (only slightly over thirty years old then), still reinventing a national identity and mythology. As Carpentier found out while researching the history of Cuban music, Africa had made deep imprints in the national music, language, food, and cultural codes. For Cabrera, a woman with sufficient distance to be objective about the plays of power around her, it must have been easier and safer to justify the authority of her written work either as a legitimate documentation (a translation) or as "curiosity" (a woman's curiosity), as Ortiz called it. Yet, it was from that objective distance as a woman that Cabrera could safely make fun in her short stories of the weak and powerful, of the dominant, the know-it-all and false pretenders, male-ego, intellectuals, bourgeoisie values, and of the social power play she observed as a child in the patristic gatherings she attended accompanying her father. From a woman's gaze, the dominant and the vernacular circles of Cuban society were equally represented in her writings from the point of view of a witty trickster: from the other side of the looking glass, the space of the Afro-Cuban (M)Other.

In Europe, Cabrera found modes of expressing that Afro-Cuban world she had been "discovering," and whose secrets and magic were interrelated to a sense of (M)Otherness. Like Teresa de la Parra's *Memorias de Mamá Blanca,* Cabrera's short stories also represented an intimate portrait of a socio-mythical world: a metageographic space where, as she observed years later in her book *Yemayá y Ochún* (1974), what closely tied to what Cabrera understood, from the naïve idealism of her avant garde years, as the "abnegación de la madre africana" (abnegation of the African mother) who had given her service and trust during the colonial period as "manejadora insustituible" (an irreplaceable Nana).[89] Cabrera explains the importance of the black (m)other as a cultural womb, based on the fact that during slavery very often the children devoted to their Nana would give her her freedom, and she always had a special place in their home.[90] These black Tatas (like her Nana Tula) among white familities, Cabrera adds, produced a mulatto cultural psyche, which, we must assume, defined Cabrera's own desires and longings, following Malinoski idea of cultural exchange and self-fashioned cultural identity. For Cabrera, her Tata, like the Tatas of other white families, was a personal and societal womb-place of vigor and life, of magic and of myths, comfort and nostalgia, connected to a metageographic mythical space that was Africa in the Caribbean. Recalling that in Spengler's philosophy the moment of vigor in the development of Western culture is symbolic of "maternity" and "care," "the root-feeling of future, and all that is motherly" (*DW* I, 267), the sense of maternal care Cabrera perceives in black Tatas, is expressed also by Splengler as "an existence which is led with a deep consciousness and instrospection of the ego, and a resolutely personal culture evidenced in memoirs, reflections, retrospects and prospects and conscious" (*DW I,* 183). A century earlier, Romanticism, which coincided in Latin America with the struggle for political independence, had awakened an interest in the historical past, and in a search for America's cultural origins and realities. Now, in their unique and different ways, Teresa de la Parra, Gabriela Mistral, and Lydia Cabrera's works were marked by various aesthetic visions of "maternal care," associated with the notion of the "womb" and "source" in the Americas. From a unique Caribbean gaze, Cabrera saw Afro-Cuban beliefs and practices, which she associated with Africa and with the Cuban creole black (M)Other, the conditions for the possibility of an ontological introspection on gender and on race in the reevaluation of cultural differences and national identity.

III

The mythical and telluric (M)Other which Afro-Cuba was for Cabrera, had to be translated to the West in a play of double utterances that masked the writer's own differences. She "translates" an African way of thinking in Cuba, inscribed in Cuban vernacular culture to the dominant society, at the same time that she writes to entertain Teresa. The result are texts constructed as a complicit space of codified knowledges on race, nation, and social exclusion. It is important to note that in Cabrera's short stories, different from de la Parra's Maria Eugenia in *Ifigenia* (who, different from Teresa de la Parra, returns to Venezuela), women cease to be victims trapped by patriarcal societies. This is because Cabrera finds independent female figures in African and Afro-Cuban folklore and religions with which to carry out a revisionist portrayal of Cuban society. She utilizes Afro-Cuban feminine deities (orishas) to articulate a counter discourse to the one presented by Teresa de la Parra in *Ifigenia,* as if she were continuing in her short stories an epistolary dialogue with de la Parra, by portraying woman in her "multiple self,"[91] but from the gaze of an Afro-Cuban imaginary that affirms the agency of women. Cabrera laughs at the male-dominated world, and makes fun of the docile submissive woman, in the same way that the orisha Oshun, in Cabrera's fable "El chivo hiede" (Goat stinks), laughs at the epitome of male dominance and power, Ogun, and at the submissiveness of Oba. In "Bregantino, Bregantín," in *Cuentos negros de Cuba,* Cabrera plays with the structure of the traditional fairy tale[92] in the representation of the classical fairy tale king who wants to find a suitor for his most beloved daughter. Cabrera's sarcasm unveils the king's patriarchal secret: the benevolent king-father loves his daughter "por lo poco que molestaba" (because she did not bother him much).[93] The quiet and therefore "good" princess in this story, like the "traditional" woman of European fairy stories, offers a silent pretext for the action to come: the transgression of a non-submissive woman. However, in contrast to the traditional obedient princess, it is a woman laborer who resists the domination of a dictator (bull) who usurped the throne. This woman, in her silent perseverance and daring transgression, and with the help of the natural forces of the African forest (orishas), brings about the downfall of the dictator.

Cabrera finds models of feminine strength in Afro-Cuban Lucumí cosmogony, in: Oyá, the storm and thunderbolt, wife of the thunder king Shango, and the Virgen de la Candelaria (Virgin of Fire); the great mother ocean Yemaya, Virgen de Regla (Virgin of Regla); and the seductress Oshun, Virgen de la Caridad del Cobre (Virgin of Charity), whose daughters or initiates are revered and feared by men.[94] Androgyny is also an important aspect of the Afro-Cuban divine realm. *Obatalá,* the creator of human beings, is a male and female principle: god and goddess. Thus, in an analogous relationship between Cabrera's texts and the mythical oral tradition that informs her texts (and keeping in mind that Afro-Cuban initiates often display the characteristics of their guiding saints), Cabrera's main female characters reenact the characteristics projected upon them by their female author: characteristics the writer finds in Afro-Cuban beliefs, that she imaginatively enhances ascribing them to Cuban society.

Cabrera's imaginative rescue and rediscovery of Afro-Cuban lore from the gaze of a Cuban woman is exemplified in her treatment of the Yoruba trickster, Tortoise, which Cabrera often portrays as a female trickster, thus transposing the traditional African Tortoise to a Cuban context in the figure of a creole land turtle, *jicotea.*[95] In *Cuentos negros de Cuba* (1936), Tortoise appears in "Taita Hicotea y Taita Tigre" (Daddy Tortoise and Daddy Tiger), "Los compadres" (Coparent Buddies), "El caballo de Hicotea" (Tortoise's Horse), and "Osaín de un pie" (One Legged Osain) as hicotea (land turtle). By 1948, however, in *¿Por qué?,* hicotea appears as *jicotea,* as it is pronounced in Cuban vernacular speech. From then on, hicotea, in Cabrera's texts, is always jicotea, as in "Jicotea lleva su casa a cuesta" (Tortoise Carries her Home on her Back), "El Majá se arrastra" (Serpents Crawl), "La lagartija se pega a la pared" (Lizards Stick to the Wall), "El carapacho a heridas de Jicotea" (Tortoise's Conch by her Wounds). It is not surprising that this impish land creature of the Afro-Cuban monte would become Cabrera's favorite character. In 1971 she published her third collection of short stories, *Ayapá. Cuentos de jicotea* (Tortoise stories), which she dedicates entirely to jicotea.

The transformation of the African Tortoise to the vernacular creole feminine Cuban hicotea can be found as early as in her first stories in *Cuentos negros de Cuba,* although the creole jicotea does not appear until the second collection in 1948. Some of the fables about jicotea that Cabrera published in *Ayapá* (1971), Cabrera wrote in the thirties, forties, and fifties. "Jicotea esta noche fresca" (Tortoise, this cool night), for example, appeared first in *Orígenes* in 1946;[96] and "La Jicotea endemoniada" (Demonic tortoise), was published in *Orígenes,* in 1949.[97] Among the sketches Wifredo Lam did in Cuba, in Cabrera's home, figures "Celebration to jicotea" (1943). In these drawings, like in Cabrera's fables, Lam depicts jicotea as the lowest but wittiest creole trickster. In one of these sketches, today at the Lowe Art Museum, jicotea is enjoying the sun and a drink on the back of other larger more powerful animals.[98] Cabrera claims in the introduction to *Ayapá* (tortoise in Lucumí) that jicotea had been a popular character, not only in Lucumí lore, but with all of the descendants of African slaves in Cuba regardless of the African nation from where they originated.[99] In Afro-Cuban oral tradition, jicotea was a genie like entity, like the *chicherekús,* the magic gourds, the *anaquillé* dolls, and even the orishas Eleguá and Osain.[100] Jicotea is like the monte;[101] conflictive and eternal she always manages to cure her wounds and overcome obstacles. Like African, and Afro-Cuban orishas, Cabrera's jicotea represents a collage of social archetypes and of human conditions in Cuban creole society.[102] However, Cabrera claimed that the stories in *Ayapá* were Afro-Cuban stories she had heard in Cuba, and later humorously recontextualized, and staged in prerevolutionary Cuban society.

Masked by religious symbolism and by the authority of an ancestral tradition, Cabrera's fictional work renders an Afro-Cuban world which the writer treats with the same irreverence she consciously nurtured toward all social types (especially the banality of the upper class). Cabrera's work demystifies patriarchal authority and snobbish intellectuality, and it praises the astuteness of the weak. Her jicotea fables speak of an Afro-Cuban monte in which the dichotomy of good and evil does not exist, and in which each deity, each ritual animal, each human character, incarnates both positive and negative forces in a constant play of power and harmony. Cabrera mocks whites, blacks, mulattoes, women, men, rich, and poor alike. In fact, "if there is a didactic subtext in her stories, it is the unspoken condemnation of authority, power, and corruption in a world in which human beings must be alert and astute or else perish."[103] As part of that discourse, Cabrera not only converts the African trickster, Tortoise (hicotea), into the Cuban vernacular jicotea, but, playing with the feminine gender in Spanish of the word jicotea,[104] she creates a new signifying feminine-androgynous creole trickster different from its African counterpart. Cabrera's jicotea often portrays a strong feminine creole character of magical qualities, faithful to the traditional complexities of the Yoruba trickster in Africa, witty and seductive, a victim and a victimizer, powerful, multiple, a magic being of positive and negative forces.

In Cabrera's stories, especially in *Ayapá,* this sometimes female jicotea, also incorporates the already classical image in Hispanic literary tradition of Fernando de Roja's *La Celestina,*[105] transposed by Cabrera to a "hybrid"

Cuba, as a Cuban creole bawd Celestina like doña Jicotea. Cabrera's jicotea is full of trickeries and hidden dishonesty: a female *vivo* turned into a *viva* by Cabrera, like her character Viviana Angola in "The Monkeys Lost the Fruit of Their Labor." Jicotea's gender transformation occurs for the first time in "El caballo de Hicotea" (Hicotea's Horse), in *Cuentos negros de Cuba* (1936), where an ambiguous "she" hicotea (not yet the creole jicotea of later short stories) fools powerful horse into being "her" servant, her horse. Also in "Osaín de un pie," hicotea is a magical paradoxical female telluric character, intrinsically related to the monte: to its natural forces, to its magic, to its cycles and natural rhythms, in a complicit relationship with Osaín, the orisha of vegetation and medicinal plants. However, a full and complete gender transformation, together with a complete creolization of this trickster (which began in *¿Por qué?* (1948), does not occur until *Ayapá. Cuentos de Jicotea* (1971). Here, in "La excelente Doña Jicotea Concha" (The Excellent Madam Jicotea Concha), for example, Jicotea is the cubanized Celestine-like-Tortoise-Afro-Cuban trickster who can easily outwit rich, but dumb and scrooge, doña Chicken, a rice plantation owner with many black slaves. In this fable, however, jicotea does not portray the same complex ritual quality and the same ontological and magical ambiguities she has in *Cuentos negros de Cuba*. She is now an old creole, go-between woman, envious of her rich neighbor and ready to maneuver things in her favor. Like a creole Celestina:

> Para todos tenía Jicotea; . . . Jicotea Concha allí daba un buen consejo, allá santiguaba, más allá recibía, sabía cortar un ombligo, bautizaba, arreglaba y casaba, sin que a nadie se le ocurriese llamarla cose-virgos ni alcahueta.
> Diríase que cada alma le libraba, sin percatarse, sus secretos, . . .
> Protegida por la sólida e invulnerable coraza de una reputación intachable, sabía los secretos de todos, pero nadie conocía los suyos.[106]

> [Jicotea had something for everyone . . . Jicotea Concha gave a good advice here, there she would give her blessing, further on she would give assistance, she knew how to cut an umbilical cord, baptise, mend {the loss of virginity} and to marry, and no one ever thought of calling her a virgin-mender or a bawd.
> It can be said that each soul would deliver to her his/her secrets without realizing it, . . . Protected by the solid armor of an unquestionable reputation, she knew everyone's secrets, but no one knew hers.]

In the play of differences between Cabrera's jicotea and the African Tortoise, there is a voice in Cabrera's texts that speaks in double utterances and that inscribes a feminine signature to Cabrera's work. At the crossroad of those juxtaposed voices, the jicotesque narrator becomes a signifying mediator, a trickster/translator, between Cuban creole society and an ancestral mythological tradition; between a Hispanic patriarchal society and (M)Other

monte; between history, myth, and magic. As Henry Louis Gates, Jr. suggests, "tricksters are primarily mediators, and their mediations are tricks."[107]
Tricksters speak with a double voice, like a translator, thus translating, in-
terpreting, and shifting from one voice, culture, context, to another.[108] In
Afro-American discourse, he observes, the Signifying Monkey is a trickster figure that has "become a trope of literary revision,"[109] a "signifier
who wreaks havoc upon the Signified."[110] In a similar way, in Afro-Cuban
literature, Cabrera's jicotea is a signifying jicotea: a mediator between cultures, race and gender, who "breaks havoc upon the Signified" and whose
mediation is to trick the reader, and to talk back to patriarchal dominance.

IV

When in 1938 Cabrera returned to Cuba to stay, like many other writers and
artists fleeing from a Europe torn by pre-World War II conflicts, she systematically started to gather information on Afro-Cuban religions as she had
being doing during her trips to Cuba.[111] In 1948, she published *¿Por qué?
cuentos negros de Cuba* (Why? Cuban Black Short Stories). In this collection of Afro-Cuban stories, Cabrera's narrative style moves away from the
avant garde techniques she uses in the first collection, and comes closer to
the narrative style of the Afro-Cuban *Patakí:*[112] the anecdotes that emanate
from the *Odus* (roads or letters), in the oracles of *Ifa* and of the *Diloggun.*
Her short story "Obara miente y no miente" (Obara lies and does not lie) in
¿Por qué?, for example, is a stylized rendition of the *Odu,* or road, *Obara
Melle.*[113] There are also anecdotal reworkings of popular sayings informed
by, and interspersed with, references to Afro-Cuban religious beliefs and
ritual "knowledge." The title *¿Por qué?* (Why?), plays with the idea that the
text is a collection of founding myths of creation, the folklore with which
cultures explain why things are the way they are. She includes stories about
"why Frog does not have buttocks," "why Dog lost its freedom," "why the
sun is far from the earth," "why Crab doesn't have a head," "why Goat has
a foul smell." In spite of their "primitivism," these fables depart from the
criollismo and *nativismo* that plagued Latin American literature during the
first half of the twentieth century. Her humorous and witty satire in these
texts, as in most of her work of fiction, articulate what Henry Louis Gates,
Jr. calls a Signifying play "between surface and latent meanings,"[114] as if
the play of significations in the text were directed to a reader who may or
may not understand them. A similar situation occurs when the *Babalawo* re-
cites the sacred anecdotes of *Ifa* (in Cuba, the *Patakí),* and the "client" (listener) must understand, in the anecdotes he/she hears, an analogy to his/her
own situation,[115] and then take the "proper" road of action.

In "El chivo hiede" (the Goat stinks) in *¿Por qué?,* Cabrera intersects the
same anecdote of the domestication of Ogun by Oshun which she included

in "Bregantino Bregantín" in *Cuentos negros de Cuba* (1936; 1940), but now she inserts the anecdote in a humorous poetic elaboration of the image of the goddess Oshun, of her wits, and powers. The rewriting of the same anecdote renders the orisha Ogun, now "preso y manso" (imprisoned and tame) following Oshun to civilization, "a través del laberinto interminable de árboles cuyas raíces Olofi fijó en la eternidad" (through the labyrinth of never-ending trees whose roots *Olofi* fastened to eternity).[116] While Ogun's characteristics have not suffered basic changes from the previous story, or even from the *Patakí,* Cabrera reworks the text to enhance and further highlight the qualities of the powerful divine sedductress, Oshun. The narrator explains that when Oshun-Yeyé-Dari dances, "baila siempre el amor, la vida que triunfa incesantemente de la nada. Las feas se transfiguran; se alindan remedando los gestos, los coqueteos y remeneos de la diosa" (love always dances, life which incessantly triumphs out of nothing. Ugly women are transfigured; they become pretty when they imitate the gestures, flirting manner, and seduction of the goddess).[117] When Oshun Yeyé-Karí sheds her light, a miracle takes place that turns beautiful the most miserable appearance. Oshun punishes goat for his desire to posses her power of seduction, and then Oshun: "riendo convulsiva, con esa risa tan temida que conocen Babalawos e Iyalochas y que presagia los más duros castigos de parte de la Diosa generosa y compasiva, y a ratos tan cruel y rencorosa, Ochún-Yeré-Karí abandonó la fiesta" (laughing convulsively, with that feared laughter *Babalawos* and *Iyalochas* understand so well, *Ochún-Yeré-Karí* left the party).[118] In Cabrera's recontextualization of the orisha, the importance of Oshun in Afro-Cuban lore is heightened by the fact that she is associated in Cuba with the Virgin of Charity (Virgen la Caridad del Cobre), the patron saint of Cuba, a virgin associated historically with resistance and freedom. Because of her importance, men always treat the daughters of *Oshun* (under *Oshun's* protection) well, out of respect and fear. This is also the case with the daughters of *Yemayá* who are considered untouchable by men: "creen, saben por experiencia los 'souteneurs', que maltratarlas les trae desgracia" [the *souteneurs* believe, they know, that if they mistreat them it will bring them misfortune].[119]

In a play of double utterances between surface and latent meanings, Cabrera's short story, "How the Monkey Lost the Fruit of His Labor,"[120] highlights the superiority of a woman whom Cabrera invests with characteristics proper of Oshun and Yemayá. In this fable, monkeys outwit men, but a woman outwits the monkeys. In a moment of crisis, when the men were about to loose their crop to the monkeys (who were picking the harvest faster than the men), one of the men, knowing that his wife "could fix anything,"[121] went to her for advice. "Viviana Angola doesn't lose heart." The next day, when men and monkeys begin to pick the crop, Viviana, "smiling and vivacious" began "to gently sway, swinging her shoulders and back" as she chanted:

Ayelelé tá kundé
Kuna makando munango
endile!

Soon there is a rich, enchanting melody that stirs the curiosity of the industrious monkeys.[122]

... If Viviana Angola would only stay still a moment with her skirt raised! What does Má Viviana have that chimes and shines so?

The Monkeys sheaves have all fallen to the ground;

... And the monkeys ended up without rice. ... and without ever knowing what was hidden, what was so fascinating, what tinkled and twindled under the skirts of Viviana Angola.[123]

In this unique portrayal of a woman wittier than monkeys and men, it is worth noting that beginning with *¿Por qué?* Cabrera published all of her texts under the label "Colección del Chicherekú," and, later, "Colección del Chicherekú en el exilio." *Chicherekú* is the name of an impish devilish entity in Afro-Cuban lore:[124] a magic doll (an artifice endowed with magic) created by Afro-Cuban priests, and utilized as a power object.[125] The Chicherekú, a popular figure in folklore and popular songs, came to be popularly thought of as more mischievous than evil, childlike. Cabrera's choice for this popular image in Cuban folklore, a magic doll constructed by the *mayombero* and sent to perform his magic works, endows Cabrera's text with a figurative double voice of significations masked by documentation and humor. In other words, Cabrera's text are like metaphorical Chicherekús: the writer's magic art(i)(facts) that she sends to her readers.

In Cabrera's fiction, the jicotesque narrator also often ironically personifies feminine characters with the same characteristics Cuban traditional society assigns to women as being weak, curious, chatty, silent, marginal, noisy, and hysterical. In several of her fables, Chicken is often hypersensitive, a social loser, trapped always in the laborious destiny of having to lay eggs. In Cuban colloquial speech, to be called a "chicken" is to be called a coward, so, chicken in Cabrera's fables is always a chicken; and chicken, in this play of significations, is always also an illusive woman, with no will of her own, resigned to her sexual fate of having to obey her husband. In the story "Susudamba no se muestra de día" (Susudamba does not show himself in daylight), in *¿Por qué?*, "chicken land" with its respective overseeing roosters, who eternally dominate the chickens, was suddenly awakened one night by an intruder, an owl (*susudamba*). The chicken-dames soon fell in love with this "galán de noche" (evening gallant suitor). Cabrera's humorous sarcasm invests the gallant owl that enters the roosters' territory uninvited, with the name of an evening flower of strong sweet penetrating perfume called in Cuba "galán de noche." The association between the sweet-smelling flower (*galán de noche*), and the courting owl(s) that penetrate the chicken house (like the smell of the flowers), is one of Cabre-

ra's ironic puns. This fable, she claimed, is a story Cabrera heard from her
Tata Tula about a dance of owls held during the night because owls do not
want to be seen during the day.[126] In Cabrera's fable, however, the picaresque writer intersects the magic of sweet perfumes as an "agente mágico
que despierta la sensualidad" (magic agent that awakens sensuality)[127] in
the emotionally and socially dormant chickens. Cabrera's signifying utilization of the "Galán de noche" (*cestrum nocturnum*) a flower, which, as
we find in Cabrera's *El monte,* is "recommended for widows who want to
marry again,"[128] is not the only element informed by the popular culture
that Cabrera weaves into the anecdote. To the chickens' surprise, oblivious
to the danger of an owl among them, suddenly there were many more owls,
many gallant suitors calling on the chicken dames every evening:

> —¡Más hombres, más hombres, Santísimo Sacramento!
> —¡Cuántos, Virgen María—si hay para todas—Bendita Seas!
> . . . Las amorosas Gallinas se vieron a diario con sus galanes;
> . . . no temían la autoridad de sus maridos; furiosas se levantanban del suelo
> a toda prisa. Los despreciaban, los insultaban, se las entendían con ellos de igual
> a igual, a puros picotazos. Y no ponían.[129]

> [More men, more men, Holy Sacrament!
> How many, Virgin Mary—{there are} enough for all—Bless you!
> . . . The loving chickens saw their beaus daily; . . . [they] did not fear the au-
> thority of their spouses; they, furious, would suddenly take to fly. They despised
> their husbands, insulted them, dealing with them as equals, pecking at them.
> And did not lay eggs!]

However, all good things come to an end, and, one day, the illusive dames
finally saw their ideal lovers at daylight and the spell the owls had on the
chicken dames was broken. Then, their futile defiance also came to an end,
and the chickens: "Resignadas, recomenzaron la tarea interminable de
poner huevos y criar pollos, sumisas al Gallo, al destino" (Resigned, they
resumed the interminable task of laying eggs and raising chicks. Submissive to Rooster, to their destiny).[130] At the end: "Todo se olvida, pero a veces
—siempre—la Luna trae los fantasmas cuyo amor no ha concluido. Vuelven los Lechuzos que no han de volver, y el corazón les duele—de un do-
lor inmemorial—a las Gallinas" (Everything is forgotten, but, sometimes —
always—the Moon brings phantoms of unfulfilled love. The owls that
will not come back, return, and the hearts of the Chickens ache—with inmemorial pain).[131]

In this fable, in which the reader again encounters in Cabrera's poetics
the nostalgia for that which cannot be, owl appears as the mediating element between the African *susudamba* and the Spanish *lechuzo* (owl). At the
same time, owl is the mercurial entity that transforms and seduces chicken,

masked by the oneiric shadows of the night. Following the basic narrative structure of the Afro-Cuban oracle and of ritual fables in the *Pataki,* the story appears to be a mythical explanation of why things are the way they are, were it not for the paradoxical humor with which the signifying voice of the narrator seems to question the destiny and social expectations of the "lady" chickens. In this sense, Cabrera's fable can be read as an allegory for the condition of women, especially married women, and for an ontological "longing for liberty," associated in Cabrera's texts with the voice of the (M)Other. Cabrera's chickens reiterate a similar feminine discourse already present in Gertrudis Gómez de Avellaneda's novel *Sab* (1838; 1841), the first antislavery novel written in Cuba. In *Sab,* the protagonist, Carlota, although in a racially priviledged position as the daughter of a white slave owner, finds out that, like Cabrera's chicken dames, she was seduced by, and later married, a "foreign" suitor under false pretenses. As a married woman, she finds herself enslaved through marriage to a foreign capitalist who, like Cabrera's *susudamba,* pretended to be what he was not. Like Cabrera's chicken, but also unlike them, who rejected the intruder and remained with their roosters (those of their own kind), Carlotta discovers her husband's intentions and true personality too late. At the end of the novel, the writer compares Carlota's situation as a married woman to that of a slave, and concludes, in the voice of the slave, Sab, that the type of slavery in which married women were held was worse than that of black slaves, because a married woman's servitude to her husband could not be broken. Sab writes in a letter to Teresa:

¡Oh, las mujeres! ¡pobres y ciegas víctimas! Como los esclavos, ellas arrastran pacientemente su cadena y bajan la cabeza bajo el yugo de las leyes humanas. Sin otra guía que su corazón ignorante y crédulo eligen un dueño para toda la vida. El esclavo, al menos, puede cambiar de amo, puedes esperar que juntando oro comprará algún día su libertad.[132]

[Oh women! Poor and blind victims! Like slaves, they drag paciently their chains and lower their heads under the yoke of human laws. Without any other guide than their own ignorant and naïve heart, they choose an owner for the rest of their life. Slaves can, at least, change masters, and hope that saving gold one day he/she can buy his/her freedom.]

When Gertrudis Gómez de Avellaneda (nicknamed Tula) wrote her novel in the late 1830s (published in 1841), it was not yet possible to speak freely about freedom and independence for women, but to certain extent it was possible to speak about the abolition of slavery, and to view the slave, from a Romantic perspective, as a noble victim of an unjust human and divine system. At this time, women, like slaves, did not have the right to vote, and married women could not have control over their own inherited capital. Furthermore, it was also "improper" to go against patriarchal traditions. Gómez de Avellaneda resists this social marginalization of women, and makes use of a racial discourse of freedom (with political undertones in nineteenth century Cuba, still a colony of Spain)[133] to criticize the social bondage of married women. She was speaking out of her own condition as a woman about the "other" in which she saw herself projected: Sab, the representation of Carlota's other. They were related by blood, and both of them were controlled by the same patriarchal society. They were like brother and sister were it not for the significant difference that he was a slave. In the early midnineteenth century, while the freedom of slaves was a growing concern among Cuban intellectuals, the freedom negated to married women was of no interest to the political agenda of that period.

Different from her compatriot, Cabrera writes about Afro-Cubans at a time when to speak of African roots, of a mythical Africa in America, was acceptable, and even in vogue in Europe, especially in the anthropological discourse of the time. Artists like Picasso, Braque, Derain, and Apolloinare (who published in 1917 the first album of Black Sculptures) were interested in African art. Like the interest in the Orient, in vogue at this time, there had emerged a similar interest in Africa. And Afrocubanía for Cabrera, in the thirties, was a concept similar to "the larger formation of European attitudes and practices toward the continent" of Africa, as Edward Said observes:

> [there] emerged what late-twentieth-century critics have called Africanism, or Africanist discourse. Conceptions of primitivism are associated with it, as well as concepts deriving a special epistemological privilege from the African provenance, such as tribalism, vitality, originality. We can see these obligingly serviceable concepts at work in Conrad and Isak Dinesen, as well as, later, in the audacious scholarship of Leo Frobenius, the German anthropologist who claimed to have discovered the perfect order of the African system, and Placide Tempels, the Belgian missionary whose book *Bantu Philosophy* proposed an essentialist (and reductive) vitality at the heart of African philosophy. So productive and adaptable was this notion of African identity that it could be used by Western missionaries, then anthropologists, then Marxist historicans, then, antagonistically, even liberation movements.[134]

Abiola Irele writes of such emerging "Africanism:" "African traditional beliefs and in particular, the native forms of religion, received strong emphasis. African animism tended in general to be placed on an equal footing with Christianity."[135] In Latin America, a form of Nativism, *Criollismo,* as a literary model, inscribed the regional in the expression of national identities and national ethos, in order to help reinvent Latin America as a geographical and human space different from Europe.[136] It is arguable that also in Latin America, as Edward Said observes about post-colonial world literatures:

cultural resistance to imperialism has often taken the form of what we can call
nativism used as a private refuge. . . . To fight against the distortions inflicted
on your identity . . . is to return to a pre-imperial period to locate a "pure" native culture. This is quite a different thing from revisionist interpretations, such
as those of Guha or Chomsky, whose purpose is to demystify the interests at
work in establishment scholars who specialize in "backward" cultures, and to
appreciate the complexity of the interpretative process. In a way, the nativist argues that one can get past all interpretation to the pure phenomenon, a literal
fact beeseeching assent and confirmation, rather than debate and investigation.
Something of this passionate intensity is found . . . in Wole Soyinka implying
the existence of a pure native African experience.[137]

In her study on Afro-Cuban religions, Cabrera seems to take the path of
the nativist as a place of refuge, a notion she shared with other writers in
the thirties, and yet, at the same time, as a mode of engagement and resistance. Not unlike the diablitos in *Carnaval de los negros,* the Afro-Cuban
discourse she helps construct serves to question the patriarchal hegemony
of the conservative Cuban capital where she was raised and to which, like
de la Parra's Maria Eugenia in *Ifigenia,* she had to return in 1938 from
France. Hiding behind Afro-Cuban lore, Cabrera's feminine characters, as
in her representation of the orisha Oshun in her fable "El chivo hiede,"[138]
offer a revisionist representation of Cuba's national ethos from the gaze of
a woman writer. After all, the Afro-Cuban Venus, Oshun, in her double image of the African orisha and the Virgin of Charity,[139] was the (M)Other
Patron Saint of Cuba, a symbol of transracial, transcultural resistence, and,
since the eighteenth century, of freedom. She is known also by some of her
adepts as the *Panchákara* (holly whore) who governs the world, and she is
said to preside over fresh waters, love, gold, coral, and amber.[140] Yet, it
would be wrong, says Cabrera, to think of Oshun always as *panchaga*
(prostitute).[141] Ochun can be young and docile, or old and terrible. Oshun
is also sensitive and merciful.[142] In Africa, Cabrera notes, Pierre Verger
documents that *Iyalode* is the name given to the woman in charge of the
community, but in Cuba, she explains, Iyalode is Oshun.[143] While Oshun
is normally very "giving" and kind, adds Cabrera, in her avatar of Oshun
Yeyé, or "Cachita," she is not so saintly or angelic.[144] She can be punitive
and terrible. Descendents of *Egbados* call her *Afaradí Iyá,* or "Puta Madre"
(Mother Whore):

> Estos le atribuían las formas plenas, los rasgos finos de la nariz, la boca carnosa,
> los ojos vivos—oyu fofo—que les habían pintado los viejos como el tipo ideal
> de las mujeres de su tribu.
>   En este parecer irreverente sincretismo, la diosa yesa, originalmente de piel
> oscura, aunque no de un negro tan profundo como el de la piel de Yemayá, ter-
> minó siendo para los criollos una réplica, en el cielo, de la famosa mulata de

rumbo del siglo pasado, cuyos mantones de burato, igual que la cinta que cruzaba el pecho de Afrodita, tenía el poder de alebrestar al más indiferente.[145]

[These [the *Egbados*] attributed her a voluptuous body, a fine nose, thick lips, bright eyes—*oyu fofo*—like the elders had painted for them as the ideal women of their tribe.

In this seemingly irreverent syncretism, the *Yesa* goddess, originally of dark skin, but not as dark as the skin of Yemaya, ended up being for the creoles, a replica, in the sky, of the famous lavish mulatto woman of last century, whose *burato* shawls, like the ribbon over Afrodite's chest, had the power of cowering even the most indifferent man.]

The feminine aporia of the young-old-docile-terrible-mother-virgin-whore represented by Oshun, can be reconciled only in the rhizomes of Afro-Cuban thought.[146] This Afro-Cuban (m)otherness in Cabrera's writings, provided the possibility for Cabrera to translate into fiction, in a Cuban context, the figure of the African mother-virgin-holy-whore with which her texts subvert Western moral codes. The importance of Oshun in Cuban culture not only questions the Manichean dualities of Christian thought; it also rearticulates Western Christianity, dominated by the mythical mother figure as a submissive self-sacrificial virgin-mother in direct opposition to the sinful Eve. Cabrera's interest in this popular deity, and in the powerful feminine mother figures of the Afro-Cuban monte, becomes evident in one of her latest ethnological texts which she dedicates entirely to Yemayá y Ochún (1974), also written, like *El monte* and *La sociedad secreta Abakua,* in the testimonial voices of adepts. Like Oshun,[147] Yemaya,[148] the great mother ocean, and mother of all of the orishas, was associated in Cuba with the Virgin of Regla. Regla is an area surrounding the Havana Harbor where Yemaya became a favorite "saint" for the ñáñigos.[149] Her association with the ocean and the origins of life makes this Great Mother figure of the ocean waters one of the most important deities of the Afro-Cuban monte. Cabrera expressed her special identification with Yemayá in her epistolary exchange with Pierre Fatumbi Verger, by signing her letters with the name of the mother ocean, Yemayá, instead of Lydia.

Yemaya is an important deity in Havana, especially for the ñáñigos,[150] but it is Oshun, in her different avatars, the female figure that finds a special place in Cabrera's creative writings beginning with *Cuentos negros de Cuba* (1936). In the image created by Afro-Cubans of Oshun, there is a certain way of being that characterizes that popular creole culture Cabrera expresses, as she does in "Suandende," in *Cuentos negros de Cuba.* In this short story, in which the anecdotes recalls Miguel de Cervantes's *Entremés, El viejo celoso* (A Jealous Old Man), and the popular theme in Golden Age theater of the "mal casada," (unhappy married woman), a jealous husband takes his wife to live in the forest in order to keep her away from other men.

One day, Suandende, a water carrier, passes by and sees the woman by the river. In a rumbalike controversy, he approaches her and asks her if he can come closer. In a contrapuntal dance of seductive questions and answers, the text intimates the irony of the final illicit "reconciliation." After the adulterous encounter, the witty woman tells her husband that she lost her "cosa dulce" (sweet thing), like Oshun's oñí (honey), in the waters of the river (which metaphorically she did). While her husband, the *vivío*, looks for her lost "sweetness" in the waters, she and Suadende (the *vivos*) elope. Since the woman is running away from an entrapped situation, and Oshun is the goddess of fresh waters, the humorous pun of the story is that the jealous man is a bird trapper, who wants to keep his wife caged in the forest, next to a river. Ironically, it is there, in the waters of Oshun, where he loses her to Suandende, a water carrier.

In "Apopoito Miama," also in *Cuentos negros de Cuba,* Cabrera's mulatto woman is an avatar of the sensous, but terrible, feminine orishas of the Afro-Cuban monte. Cabrera represents in this text the power of a woman as a charming seductress, independent, not entrapped by any man, gods or poets, and before whom all men cower: "una mulata de ojos claros que tenía el pelo lacio; sandunguera—más retrechera que Oyá—(Virgen de la Candelaria), sonsacadora de maridos y siempre soltera" (a mulatto woman with light eyes and straight hair; witty and charming, an enchanter more crafty than Oya (*Virgen de la Candelaria*) [Virgin of Fire], a wheedle of other women's husbands and always single).[151] Cabrera's praise to the divine whore is also a praise to the feminine Antillean *ashé,*[152] a "tierra, mulata" (a female mulatto land) whose power and sensuousness is associated with the life force and cultural agency of the Afro-Cuban monte. This feminine and androgynous monte in Lydia Cabrera's work, speaks of an invisible space of refuge, and freedom, which Cabrera reconstructs through her writing as a thick forest, a sacred high ground, and a clearing. In the imaginative construction of that space, Cabrera inscribes her own feminine signature of difference.

Lydia Cabrera's texts, like jicotea, like Elegua, like her *Chicherekú* texts, are mediators, transmuters of realities, agents of metamorphosis, but, also, tricksters that bring havoc on the Signified. Her short stories and fables are revisionist and myth making texts that signify upon other texts and discourses on nation, patriarcal hegemony, and culture. As Henry Louis Gates, Jr. explains in *The Signifying Monkey,* "The importance of the Monkey tales for the interpretation of literature is that the Monkey dethrones the Lion only because the Lion cannot read the nature of his discourse."[153] The same can be said of Cabrera's jicotesque texts. In them, authority figures, like Tiger, may be powerful and terrifying, but they lose at the end because they cannot understand the double discourses of Cabrera's female jicotea, nor can the monkeys understand Viviana's dance, nor can goat understand

Oshun. Cabrera's texts force the reader to understand the play beween the literal and the figurative in order to grasp the discursive cultural codifications of Cabrera's *Chichereku* texts.

For Cabrera, as for Ortiz, Cuban vernacular culture was an ontological counterpoint of difference and identity. Her creative writing also reiterates what Gustavo Pérez Firmat notes in Ortiz's work, that "the indigenous is nothing more than a certain inflection of the foreign."[154] Yet, her ethnological texts avoid falling in the same pitfalls as Ortiz's by juxtaposing, in a dialogic relationship, the multiple testimonial voices of her Afro-Cuban informants. She, the ethnologist, appears to be only the organizer and translator of the material gathered, a student of Afro-Cuban culture, as she claimed: " Ha sido mi propósito ofrecer a los especialistas, con toda modestia y la mayor fidelidad, un material que no ha pasado por el filtro peligroso de la interpretación" (My purpose has been to offer specialists, in true modesty and honesty, a material that has not gone through the dangerous filter of interpretation).[155] She adds: "No se comprenderá a nuestro pueblo sin conocer al negro . . . No podemos adentrarnos mucho en la vida cubana, sin dejar de encontrarnos con esta presencia africana que no se manifiesta exclusivamente en la coloración de la piel" (We cannot understand our people without understanding black Cubans. . . . We cannot go very deep into the life of the people in Cuba without finding the African presence, which is not manifested exclusively in the coloration of the skin).[156] Her polyphonic documents register the voices of the others being "dis-covered;" and those voices in Cabrera's research reconstruct an African (m)other that is not defined by differences of color, but that seems to follow, to certain extent (from the gaze of a woman), the discourse on nation as a "transracial" bond based on a common experience. In Cabrera's case, that experience that binds her to Afro-Cuba, to her Nana, to her Afro-Cuban friends, is disfranchisement and exclusion. In this sense, Cabrera's texts break away from Ortiz's authorial gaze, in order to carve a different space from which the (m)other can speak, and to propose that that space is always already a loci of cubanía, and a monte, a refuge, for her own writing.

Ortiz's research in the cultural realm of afrocubanía was based, up until the thirties, on books, including studies made in Brazil, which he applied to a Cuban context. Cabrera disrupts the repetition of intellectual self-referentiality and finds the voices of the subjects studied, transcribing them in her texts as the testimonial voices of Afro-Cuban elders that had been excluded from the hegemony of national discourses. It is difficult to speak of an Afro-Cuban discourse in Cabrera's work (fiction and nonfiction), since that discourse which she (re)creates in the many voices of her informants, is constantly being differed to another voice, and to another and different version of the same stories, anecdotes and "revelations." It is a discourse that projects itself as a self-referential voice, repetitive, but also different

from itself, constructed, created, manipulated, and organized from the privileged position of a writer who socially seems to share nothing in common
with the Afro-Cuban voices speaking in her texts. However, at the same
time, Cabrera's short stories articulate a coherent discourse of resistance
that seems to close the gap between the priviledged voice of the writer, the
subjects that speak in her texts, and the (M)Other being written.

V

Central to Cabrera's work is the most acclaimed of all of her books: a
unique manuscript of ethnological research which she entitled: *El monte:
Igbo-finda, ewe orisha, vititi nfinda—Notas sobre las religiones, la magia,
las supersticiones y el folklore de los viejos criollos y del pueblo de Cuba*
(1954) (Mount/Forest/Holy place: *Igbo-finda, ewe orisha, vititi nfinda*—
Notes about the religions, the magic, the superstitions and the folklore of
the old creoles and the people of Cuba). This is a book written in a counterpoint of voices, including the testimonial voices of her informants and
the writer's own explanations and thoughts about those testimonies that
Cabrera sorts and catalogues according to subjects and categories. *El monte*
is a *Summa* of Afro-Cuban beliefs and traditions, in which, very different
from Ortiz's work, Cabrera includes the voices of Afro-Cuban practitioners as agents, and not only as objects of her study. In *El monte,* however,
the voice of the researcher hides behind the voices of the adepts, legit-
imizing once more, in a different context, the sense of "transcription" and
"translation" Ortiz had given to Cabrera's work in 1940. Those voices also
underline the oral nature of the traditions registered by Cabrera. At the
same time, the interspersed continuum of the voices of the adepts in Cabrera's work alerts the reader to the fact that the text is a cultural poetics based
on local memories and knowledge with which Cabrera reconstructs an in-
tra-history of Cuban vernacular society. The information Cabrera gathers
is based on a local oral "knowledge" that disrupts the dominance of writing, and that, at the same time, underlines the tension between orality and
writing already present in *Ifa* (oral): a tension already intimated in the writing of the Afro-Cuban *Pataki.*[157] In ancestral Yoruba traditions, the words
of Ifa cannot be written because writing changes the magic power of the
spoken word.[158] In Cuba, however, due to historical ruptures, and to the
geographical distance from the cultural context in which these ancient traditions emerged, African anecdotes, as well as rituals, magic recipes, and
other forms of ritual knowledge were written down in order to preserve ancestral memory in a new land. Ritual rules were altered and adapted to writing, and, with time, in Cuba, the written word became an agency of knowledge as important as orality. Cuban *santeros* and *babalawos* register such
"knowledge" in handwritten notebooks known as *libretas.* These note-

books form an archival corpus[159] known as *Pataki* or *Patakín,* which Cabrera defines in *Anagó* as: "'relatos, narración de los tiempos antiguos y de los orishas'. De los odú de Ifá y del Dilogún" (tales, narration of ancient times and the orishas. From the *Odu* of Ifa and the *Dilogun*).[160] She also defines the Pataki as: "algo muy bonito en el sistema de adivinación Yoruba, lucumí. Son los ejemplos, las moralejas" (something very pretty in the Yoruba, Lucumí, system of divination. They are the examples, the morals).[161] Cabrera's *El monte* offers itself to the reader as the summa of these libretas, cutting across sects and beliefs to include the religious thoughts of Afro-Cuban lucumís, congos, ñáñigos, paleros, and other African belief systems in Cuba, as well as different variations within each group.

Cabrera's *El monte* signals a departure in the expression of Cuban culture from a monolinguistic hegemonic discourse by inscribing in the title of the text the linguistic trinity of Bantu, Yoruba, and Spanish, as equal participants in cubanía. With this polylingual title, the text offers a mythical complex world of faith and magic in which the secrets of Cuban vernacular culture are rescued in writing for posterity. It also establishes a play of differences within the various African cultural and religious legacies in Cuba. It alerts the reader to the multiple faces and modalities of afrocubanía; thus representing as textual performance the complexity of cultural exchanges and negotiations.

In the role of mediator and "transcriber" of secret knowledge, which *El monte* unveils in the testimonial voices of practitioners, the text invests its writer with the priestly function of mediator of the word, like Elegua, and establishes Cabrera, in the cultural imaginary, especially in the Cuban diaspora, as Reinaldo Arenas notes, as a *diosa* (goddess) and priestess of the cultural (M)Other womb of afrocubanía. In *El monte,* Cabrera initiates a form of ethnological documentation that can be considered testimonial, in that Cabrera, the scribe, is also the commentator and mediator who interprets and glosses what her informants say. Such counterpoint of voices makes it difficult for the reader to wade through the amount of information *El monte* offers, and to know, or to remember, who speaks and when. In Cabrera's research, her authorial voice seems to be a subaltern voice in contrast to the testimonial voices of her informants. Yet, she is the keeper of a knowledge that becomes the signifying voice of a culture, the mediator of secrets, as if she were a female *Babalawo,* through whom *Elegua* and *Orula* speak. In a close association with the Afro-Cuban monte about which Cabrera writes, her text becomes a monte in itself that the reader must decode from the very codes the text provides.[162] In this sense, *El monte* is a text in which writing intersects, and is intersected by, the space that informs it.

Ashcroft, Griffiths, and Tifflin have observed that in postcolonial texts, the use of native, or African words "seems to be keeping faith with the local culture and transporting it into the new medium. Thus the untranslated words, the sound and the texture of the language can be held to have the power and presence of the culture they signify—to be metaphoric in their inference of identity and totality."[163] However, as they also claim, the idea that "language somehow embodies culture" and that the inclusion in English texts of African words "as *obi* (hut), or *kurta* (skirt)," "seem to 'carry' the oppressed culture," is false "because it confuses usage with property in its view of meaning."[164] Yet, they also claim: "such uses of language as untranslated words do have an important function in inscribing difference. They signify a certain cultural experience that they cannot hope to reproduce but whose difference is validated by the new situation. In this sense they are directly metonymic of that cultural difference which is imputed by the linguistic variation."[165] Cabrera's writings fall under both categories. She tries to keep faith with the local culture she transposes to a different medium, but she also transcribes the language of her informant in which the untranslated word, sometimes translated to two or more languages (Yoruba, Bantu, Spanish, Ñáñigo), including variations within the same Afro-Cuban language, indicate the affirmation of the untranslated word as already "creole" and "national." At the same time, Cabrera's inclusion of African terms and African sounding words, even those she makes up, affirms cultural and linguistic *differences* that cannot be expressed in Spanish, either because they cannot convey the same meaning or because they are simply unthinkable in Western thought. Furthermore, remembering that "the signs of identity and of difference are always a matter of invention and construction,"[166] in *El monte,* Cabrera also legitimizes a Cuban "way of thinking," by showing that in Afro-Cuban thought, there is a unique sense of the familiar that borders irreverence underlining the idea that life is a continuous flow between visible and invisible sources, beween the natural and the supernatural. All of the forces of the monte, orishas, the dead, the living, the organic and the inorganic coexist in one and the same dynamic movement. Monte is not a separate distant space, but a natural space, nonwithstanding divine, where different life forces are actively at play with each other.

Cabrera's *El monte* soon came to be considered the most important archive of Afro-Cuban lore in Cuba, a monumental libreta made public to all readers, not just to initiates: an archival collection of religious anecdotes in their multiple variations, ritual languages, practices, liturgies, remedies, symbols, cosmogony, proverbs. In general, the text is a totalizing effort to document Afro-Cuban religions and lore in the island. It is for this reason that in the Cuban diaspora, although *El monte* is not a sacred text, it can be found in popular lists of sacred texts, and it is suggested readings for initiates to Afro-Cuban cults.[167] Yet, in academic circles, *El monte* is a text often mentioned, badly read, and poorly understood by lay readers not only because of the vast amount of knowlege it includes, but also due to the repetitions, variations of the same anecdotes, mixture of Afro-Cuban belief systems, differences within the same sects, syncretic images, and imperceptive changes in themes or in modalities of the same theme, rituals, and cures, which makes *El monte* a literary voyage into a jungle of cultural codes and religious symbols of a Cuban-Antillean imaginary not different from the Caribbean space portrayed by Lam in "The Jungle."[168]

The very title of Cabrera's text, *El monte,* summarizes the symbolic nature of its context, and articulates the multiple meanings of monte in Cuba as a dense wild thicket, a forest, shrubs, a backyard, an empty city block full of weeds, trees, parks, bushland, or anywhere where there are plants and animals, rocks and metal, flower beds, anywhere where nature, the flora, is accessible, like in the country side or "campo," a farm land, or, in general, the wild, and sometimes just a single *ceiba* tree.[169] Different from "jungle," as in Lam's "The Jungle," and from Césaire's concept of the natural as portrayed in *Tropiques,* monte also means "a high holy place," as in a sacred place, a Holy Mount, a natural geographic and also a metageographic zone. Monte is the sacred, high, natural space where all life forces emanate and exist in constant dynamic give and take movements. It is a sacred zone, a vibrant space of life, a timeless space where all principles of the cosmos converge in "Life's stirrings." In the Afro-Cuban monte, explains Cabrera: "residen, viven, la divinidades" (all divinities reside, live),[170] and she adds in the voice of one of her informants: "'somos hijos del Monte porque la vida empezó allí,'" (we are children of the monte because life began there).[171] "Todo se encuentra en el Monte—los fundamentos del cosmos—y todo hay que pedírselo al Monte, que nos lo da todo." (Everything can be found in the *monte.*——the foundations of the cosmos—'and one must ask the monte for everything, it gives us everything).[172] "La vida salió del Monte" (Life came from the monte). Monte "equivale a Tierra en el concepto de Madre universal, fuente de vida. 'Tierra y Monte es lo mismo'" (is equivalent to Earth/Land and to the concept of a universal Mother. 'Earth and Monte are the same").[173] Monte, as represented in *El monte,* is a cultural and geographic space, a (M)Other Womb, from which to write differences. Monte, in its relation to nature and to the feminine, represent, and is conceived as, a telluric, ontological, and teleological womb: the Great (M)Other, as portrayed in Cabrera's 1936 short story, "Taita Jicotea y Taita Tigre," a text that represents a Cabrera-Lam concept in the early forties of the sensuousness of the Cuban visible and invisible tropical landscape. In this short story, the description ascribed to Cuba's countryside recalls Lam's "The Jungle," in the imaging and "presencing" of the feminine, sensuous, maternal forces of the Caribbean flora:

Las naranjas de miel, famosas en toda la comarca; los mangos, en que se bebía tibio, derretido el sol. Y los caimitos de morado suntuoso, del color de los labios de las negras, y los nísperos, cuya áspera corteza encierra un corazón tan dulce, que el recuerdo de su sabor le llenó la boca suavemente. Y los mameyes y las guanábanas perfumadas, que ya en sazón colgaban doblando las ramas con su peso, henchidas y blandas igual que los senos de las mujeres grávidas.[174]

[Oranges sweet as honey, famous in that entire region; the mangos, its juice like the warm liquid sun. And the *caimitos*, of a sensuous purple, the color of black women's lips, and the *nísperos*, that hide behind their coarse peeling a heart so sweet, that the memory of its flavor makes one's mouth lightly salivate. And the *mameyes* and the *guanábanas* with their perfumes, already ripe, suspended, bending the branches that hold them with their weight, swollen and soft, like the breasts of pregnant women.]

In Lam's "The Jungle" Afro-Cuban natural forces or *potencias* are represented also as an androgynous/feminine exuberant sensuous flora. There are feminine silhouettes, the Great Mother Earth's breasts reminiscent of the mother figure, Yemayá, always there in the flower (known in Cuba as "breasts") of bananas plants (of African origin) that grow abundantly in Cuba.[175] Yemayá, the mother, recalls the memory of the Great Cosmic Ocean Mother from whom all orishas are born, and the amniotic element of the Middle Passage. Lam also represents the libidinous presence of a will-to-freedom in the tropical sensuality of Oshun. Other silhouettes in Lam's forest are horses, a metaphor, in the Afro-Cuban context, for the life forces or potencias in the monte,[176] that interact with humans by possessing them, or "riding" the possessed human. During possession, the human possessed becomes the orisha's "horse," thus the appearance of horselike masks signal the presence of the forces of nature. "The Jungle" captures the Afro-Cuban monte as being the same as the Cuban mythical landscape Cabrera represents as a (m)other womb: a Cuban "meta-monte" that carries the signature of the feminine, the mother, fecundity, and creation.

In *El monte* and in Cabrera's work of fiction, Cabrera constructs a linguistic and mythical "meta-monte:" meaning a seductive space where the voice of the (M)Other articulates the invisible space of a Cuban identity constantly being constructed, shifted to other times, other spaces, and other voices, by the same play of ontological differences encapsulated in the concept of monte. In writing the Afro-Cuban (M)Other, Cabrera inscribes herself in her writing, trapped in the "clearing" her texts have created, and masked by the codes of the very concept of monte she helps construct in Cuban literature. Cabrera's representation of monte is also the space of a codified language that creates a signifying space inside the dominant language, Spanish, and that questions the myth of hispanidad, and of European dominance, in traditional discourses on the nation. In her work, African (M)Other tongues, including *bozal,* construct a ritual voice, a sacred language in which the voice of the mysteries of the monte speak. It is important to remember that Afro-Cuban initiates, especially those entering the Lucumí sect known as *Regla de Ocha,* must learn to speak Lucumí, the Yoruba spoken in Cuba, because the African deities prefer it. Thus, Cabrera's utilization of African terms (or the parody of African voices), create a polyphonic language of its own (masked by humor), informed by Africa, with which to express, articulate, and translate afrocubanía, as other than, and different from, Western tradition. In this way, polylinguism in Cabrera's texts disrupts the hegemonic power of colonial European languages and serves as a reminder that Cuban society is not monolingual. In other words, Cabrera's texts point out the instability of the dominant language; that other languages, and other forms of thoughts and linguistic patterns coexist with the dominant language and culture. Interspersed with humor, *choteo,* Cabrera's text, suggest that the dominance of the hegemonic, and of a monolingual language is only a myth.

In the role of transcriber and translator of the (M)Other, Cabrera, the "priestess," as Reinaldo Arenas calls her, becomes the keeper of the secrets of the *menso,*[177] that magic mirror where the invisible is revealed. Like Elegua (the orisha that speaks through the divining figures or letters over the divining table), Cabrera's texts stand at the crossroad of these two different historical stages of culture: as mediators of both. In this sense, she is the translator, as Ortiz claimed, the creator, interpreter, and reinventor of a language of myths, informed by the language of the oracle and by its written corpus, the Patakí:[178] the language spoken by that (M)Other archaic voice whose meaning cannot be registered in Castilian Spanish, and whose codes cannot be fully translated to other languages. At the same time, that language reveals the secrets of a cultural force Cabrera recodes and reconstructs, establishing Cabrera, the writer and the ethnologist, as a cultural *mamalocha:*[179] keeper of the secrets of the Afro-Cuban monte. Her words mediate realities, through "letters" (drawings and signs), like Elegua and Orula in the oracle. Like in the Odus (roads) of the Diloggun and Ifa, Cabrera "becomes" the mediator who, through stories and anecdotes, "reveals" the mysteries of the monte. At the same time, in that process, Cabrera's texts also hide other secrets, other codes, and other discourses masked, like the atire and gestures of diablito dancers, under the Carnival mask of Afro-Cuban exoticism and primitivism.

VI

Soon after its publication, Cabrera's *El monte* became a signifying sign for a mode of thinking in Cuba that indicated cultural resistance to acculturation, and the survival of a way of conceiving the world different from Europe. *El monte* offered a sort of cultural palenque outside Western epistemology, as a space of difference inside hispanidad. For Cuban writers like Guillermo Cabrera Infante, *El monte,* was: "quizás el mejor libro que se ha escrito en Cuba en todos los tiempos" (perhaps the best book ever written in Cuba at all times),[180] because, as Sara Soto points out, "nos introduce a un mundo nuevo, mágico, sobre-natural, donde encontramos la supervivencia de nuestra cultura" (it introduces us to a world, new, magical, supernatural, where we find the survival of our culture).[181] The disruption of logic and language, as well as the gaps and disparities between orality and writing in *El monte,* and the complexities of translating Cuban culture to western readers, were elements that attracted Guillermo Cabrera Infante. Thus, as a homage to Cabrera, he includes her among Cuba's most important contemporary literary voices (together with Martí, Guillén, Carpentier, Piñera, Novás Calvo, Lezama Lima) in *Tres tristes tigres* (*Three Trapped Tigers*), and parodies her writing style in the section of the novel ironically entitled "La muerte de Trosky referida por varios escritores cubanos, años después o antes" ("The Death of Trotsky Narrated by Several Cuban Writers, Years Later or Before). Cabrera Infante's mimicry parodies Cabrera's use of non-Spanish terms and her effort to translate cultural terms and codes to the reader, but now, in a seemingly unrelated context, in the story of Trotsky's death. This version, ficticiously told, supposely, by Lydia Cabrera, appears under the title: "El indisime bebe la moskuba que lo consagra Bolchevikua," ("The Initiate Takes the Cup that Will Make Him a Cupbearer") (*TTrappedT* 248). He introduces the Afro-Cuban drummer Baró as the "*babalosha* de la vieja Cacha (Caridad)" (the Afro-Cuban Lucumí priest of the old woman Cacha [Caridad]) (*TTT,* 235), humorously confusing Abakuá potencias or chapter with *orishas* and *ngangas.* Cabrera Infante translates Afro-Cuban terms as Lydia Cabrera does in her short stories, but this time in translations in which the signifier slips away from the signified in a Cuban nonsensical *relajo.* Thus, we find the terrible sacred caldron as *olla walabo,* the spirit as *wije,* the notion of approval as *tshévere* (chévere) and *sisibuto,* to request as *o f'aboru,* and a photography fan as *fotu-fotu-fan* (*TTT,* 235).[182]

The translation of one culture to another in *TTT,* and of Cabrera Infante's text to English, seems to prove treason (slippage) in the very act of translation. The English translation produces, for example, "blako-sako" for "saco negro," "ghoulo" for spirit, and others, in an effort to approximate Afro-Cuban popular lingo to an Afro-Americal colloquial speech. (*TTrappedT,* 248).[183]

In his parody, Cabrera Infante constructs a verbal jungle of cultural references and voices masked with nonsense and humor,[184] in which the signifying pun is that the Abakuá Cupbearer is also a Bolchevic initiate: meaning that both are members of secret societies in which dissidence and difference is punished with death. In Cabrera Infante's parody, one text signifies upon the other, addressing a given Cuban condition that the text intimates as a secret; a secret that, like in Cabrera Infante's parodic Afro-

Cuban story, the reader must understand as a play of significations.[185] Cabrera Infante's parody addresses the concept of treason always already present in the act of writing, as a play between signifier and signified—as in the transposition of oral traditions to the written word—in a form of codification though writing that covers up as much as it uncovers. However, treason in *TTT* is bound to the reasons for writing the novel; a reason masked by the idea that the word ultimately cannot reveal any truth. Cabrera Infante uses parody to represent Lydia Cabrera's multiple transpositions, translations, and transformations that create a monte of its own: which Cabrera Infante represents as a type of *ajiaco* (a Cuban national dish made with multiple and various local ingredients, mostly vegetables), and a monte of Cuban voices that, in unison, express the simultaneity and diversity of cubanía. The parody also points to the fact that, in a play between fictional creation and ethnological documentation, Lydia Cabrera's work guides the reader through a jungle of rituals and social codes she reconstructs in order to express the polyphony of Cuban vernacular language (as Cabrera Infante does in *Tres tristes tigres*): a jungle of signifiers whose significations ultimately cannot be signified by the restrictive written signs of Western scriptures.

There are other cultural and political codes in Cuban literature that also inform the Afro-Cuban concept of monte echoed by Cabrera Infante in *TTT*. Cabrera's decoding and recoding of such a symbolic and dynamic space of afrocubanía came at a time when, in the fifties, monte became again, as during the wars of independence in the nineteenth century, synonymous of rebelion and resistance. Soon after 1954, when *El monte* was published, the revolutionary troops led by Fidel Castro were nestled in the thick forests of the high mountains of "la Sierra Maestra" in the province of Oriente. By the late fifties, Monte had become interchangeable with "Sierra," since it was in the highlands, and in the "Sierra Maestra" forests, where the rebels that were fighting against Batista's dictatorship were hiding. The semantic synthesis of monte as a place of refuge, freedom, and life forces, gives way to a polysemantic concept of monte in Cuban literature. In an unpublished essay, José Piedra proposes that monte also offers the additional signification of "clearing" for the transmission of marginal myths within a master code that is portrayed as a "forest" of signs.[186] A semantic ambiguity results from the fact that, in Cuba, monte can designate a "forest" or bushland, a "holy place," but also an open field, a clearing, as Piedra notes, thus, adjusting the meaning of this term to Cuba's geography in which savanas are prominent, and, also, charging this word (which designates the sacred), to mean a special zone different from its surroundings. With this meaning, monte is also conceived as a space of survival, not only of resistance and transgression. During slavery, it was in the monte where runaway slaves sought refuge and freedom. It is significant, for example, that Reinaldo Arenas wrote *Before Night Falls* (1993) (*Antes del anochecer,* 1992) while hidding from the Cuban authorities in the monte of Lenin Park, in Havana.[187] In Cuban vernacular language, "irse para el monte" (go into the forest) or "venir del monte" (come out of, or from, the forest) is a polysemantic image that registers multiple simultaneous possibilities that range from ritual magic to a revolutionary act, and from survival to writing, as in Martí's verses: "Mi verso es un ciervo herido/ que busca en el monte amparo" (My verse is a wounded deer/ that seeks refuge in the monte),[188] José Piedra's definition of monte as a "clearing" within the master "forest" of signs,"[189] explains such polysemy: "as a ritual enclosure of Western texts, it [the clearing] obeys a form of ritual order at once conditionally accepted and set apart by Western rhetoric. The site remains physically within the text but rhetorically at the edge of the text. Marginal voices that previously existed in a 'wild,' unrecorded state at the edge of 'civilization,' now can be recorded in a 'semi-civilized' ritual space within mainstream texts. The result is a compromise between marginal myths and mainstream writing."[190]

In this sense, Cabrera's *El monte* is a 'monte' also in the sense of a "clearing" and "high ground" within a rhetorical Western enclosure where female and black voices are trapped (in and by the text). It is also a place of refuge and a space of transgression of boundaries from where to resist entrapment, and "survive." Cabrera's *El monte* constructed a "clearing," a temple and an oracle of revelation for Cuban writers like Cabrera Infante. It was a cultural archive of sacred codes, magic, and rituals of a non-Western space within Cuba's hispanidad that gave testimony to a cultural force authentically Cuban. It became a "clearing" also for Cabrera's own work, a clearing from which to write difference. Cabrera also collected documentation on the Abakuá society, the ñáñigos, the same group that attracted Ortiz and the Minoristas, and whose music and rituals had been important in the definition and interpretation of afrocubanía. While the Lucumí in Cuba had a stronger influence in the formation of Afro-Cuban cosmogony,[191] it was the Abakuá whose rituals and music marked the development of Cuban vernacular culture, especially in Havana. Lydia Cabrera included limited information about the history and rituals of the Abakuá in *El monte,* but, in 1959, four years after publishing *Refranes negros de Cuba* (1955), and *Anagó: Vocabulario lucumí* (1957), she published *La sociedad secreta Abakuá: Narrada por viejos adeptos* (Abakuá Secret Society: Narrated by old adepts). The text was released only days after the triumph of the Cuban revolution, ironically, on "Día de Reyes," January 6, 1959. This book, the most important study on this group up to then, followed the same style she had used in *El monte.* It was another important testimony to the uniqueness of Cuban culture, and a foundational "clearing" in Cuban literature. However, due to the circumstances of the moment, and the subject (the underworld of Havana), it did not receive the same reception as *El monte*.[192]

La sociedad secreta Abakuá provided details on the rites, ceremonies, history, and symbols, of the powerful ñáñigo groups in Cuba, in a diligent study very different from Ortiz's research. In her introduction of the book, Cabrera rejects the Positivists theories on race and criminology used by Ortiz in *Los negros brujos* (1906). She writes:

> Nos hemos acercado a los ñáñigos tan mal alfamados tradicionalmente, que quizá por lo mismo nos habían inspirado siempre una gran curiosidad, sin miedo ni desprecio. Sin preocuparnos la piel, la forma de las orejas, la anómala implantación de unos ojos de mirada estrábica . . . nos interesaba del ñañiguismo no el aspecto criminoso sino el religioso, y aún más el material poético que habíamos sospechado en sus tinieblas.[193]

> [We have approached the ñáñigos, traditionally of such negative fame, may be for the reason they have always inspired in us great curiosity, with no fear or rejection. Not worried about the skin, the shape of the ears, the anomalous implantation of the eyes . . . we were interested in *ñañiguismo,* not for its criminal look, but its religion, and even more, the poetics that we had intuited in its secret mists.]

The text provided a revisionist view of the negative image ñáñigos had since the nineteenth century; and it offered a counter discourse to everything previously written about the ñáñigo, showing thus that although there were black criminals in Havana, criminality was unrelated to being or not being black, or being or not being Abakuá. Interested, like Ortiz and Carpentier, in finding the universal in the local, Cabrera also finds analogies between the religious ideas of the ñáñigos, and the *Eleusinian mysteries* in ancient Greece, thus placing that unique Cuban sect at the level of other world mythologies. Written like *El monte* in a counterpoint of testimonies given by the adepts, and the ethnologist's interpretations of those testimonies, and including a detailed history of the sect in Cuba, Cabrera's "informants" are the ones who tell the secrets of the Afro-Cuban fraternity, thus narrowing the distance between the observer and the object of observation. Cabrera's testimonial voices also distance the writer from being the single voice that reveals the inner codes and rituals of a secret fraternity that did not allow women to become members, because "women cannot keep secrets." As Cabrera Infante points out, Lydia was the first woman allowed to enter the sacred site of the ñáñigo *juegos,* the *Cuarto Fambá,* where only men, the *ecobios,* or *abanekues,* can enter.[194]

In 1959, Cabrera left Cuba never to return. She took with her, by chance, the documents she gathered throughout the years, letters, and unedited short stories. In Cuba, her books soon became unavailable until 1993 when a facsimile of *El monte* was finally published again.[195] *La sociedad sec-*

reta Abakuá, was not reprinted in Cuba, and the text remained relatively unknown until its second publication in 1969, in Miami. With the triumph of the Cuban revolution, the Abakuá came to be perceived by the new socialist regime, again, like for Ortiz in 1906, as an antisocial group dangerous to the new political ideology that pretended to build a new society. Afro-Cuban cults were redefined officially once more as atavistic and fetichist: contrary to the new political ideology. The ñáñigos again were perceived as a group whose select "secrecy" perpetuated difference, and whose religious practices and "rituals" were part of the very same subworld in Havana that needed to be eliminated by "transforming" African "fetishism," and replacing it with a new historical vision with which to overcome "primal" "superstitions."[196] Race became a taboo suject, and racial conflicts were treated as vestiges of class differences during the "decadent" pre-revolutionary years. Racial conflict under the new Marxist ideology could only be explained as part of a class struggle (already won in 1959), and as vestiges of the past. It was a political situation that, as Carlos Moore claims, made "blackness" and "Africanness" in Cuba an international political strategy that continued to avoid, and negate, internal racial issues.[197]

CABRERA INFANTE'S *TRES TRISTES TIGRES* [*THREE TRAPPED TIGERS*] IN THE LOOKING GLASS OF THE (AFRO)CUBAN MONTE

Lydia Cabrera, as José Quiroga observes, was more heard than read.[198] Cabrera Infante recalls that one day when Lydia Cabrera was asked what she would write in her epitaph, she replied: "the Cuban woman more interviewed of all times."[199] First in Havana, and later in Miami, Florida, Cabrera's home became a sort of temple, a place where friends and scholars, believers and nonbelievers, came to meet her and to hear her speak. Lydia Cabrera and her texts became a bridge for non-initiates to the oneiric wonderland of the monte afrocubano. *Cuentos negros de Cuba,* and later *El monte,* proved to Carpentier that the meanings of Afro-Cuban rituals had eluded him, and that he had missed the complex "relationship of the black with the forest."[200] It is in this role of oracle, of cultural priestess and cultural mediator, that Guillermo Cabrera Infante includes Lydia Cabrera as a character in *Tres tristes tigres* (1967) (*Three Trapped Tigers,* 1971),[201] and places her, significantly, in the section of the text entitled "Bachata" (play or game). Here, as if it were an echo of Hamlet speaking to Horacio, Silvestre Isla (a writer)[202] speaks to Arsenio Cué, a radio actor, recalling a conversation the two of them had had with Lydia Cabrera at her home in Havana:

There are many things in this dream, Arsenio Cué, just as there are in that dream Lydia Cabrera told us both. . . . The day you'd gone to her house, in your new car and she gave you a cowrie shell to wear as a good luck charm which you passed on to me later, . . . and Lydia told us that some years back she'd had a dream in which the sun rose on the horizon and the whole of the sky and the earth was bathed in blood and the sun had Batista's face and a few days later the coup of the tenth of March took place (*TTrappedT*, 457).

As in Lewis Carroll's *Alice in Wonderland,* in Cabrera Infante's Havana, in *TTT,* the multiple realms of the oneiric, like myths and other forms of the cultural imaginary, become tools for satire. This text, which Cabrera Infante never considered a novel,[203] but a representation of language, of Cuban voices, is, as Roberto González Echevarría notes: "a bitter social novel, marked very deeply by the Cuban Revolution."[204] Lydia Cabrera's dream in *TTT* is the recollection masked by fiction of a dream she once shared with Guillermo Cabrera Infante before the triumph of the Revolution, in Havana, at her home, Quinta San José, Marianao, on the same day she gave him a cowrie (for protection). Silvestre's recollection in *TTT* offers an ironical play between fiction and reality, since in *TTT* it is Silvestre, the writer, who ends up with the cowrie Lydia had given Cabrera Infante in Havana. In a letter written in Brussels, March 14, 1963, Cabrera Infante reminds Lydia Cabrera of that day.[205] With this recollection, which seems to also become a pivotal moment in the epistolary relation of both writers, Cabrera-Cabrera, *TTT* breaks the strictures of literary genres, of history, autobiography, and fiction, opening the text across literary genres, to multiple orders of readings.[206]

Cabrera Infante claims that there are "few books more apolitical" than *TTT,*[207] yet, as Emir Rodríguez Monegal notes, in *TTT* there is "a text or subtext that runs parallel to the visible text;"[208] Raymond Souza also reads in *TTT* "elements of ideological subversion;"[209] and Enrico Mario Santí reads *TTT* as "a masquerade ball on stage,"[210] and describes it as: "un vasto poema elegíaco desde las ruinas de la historia, a partir de la experiencia de la traición" (a vast epic poem from the ruins of history, out of the experience of treason).[211] *TTT,* Cabrera Infante explains to Perera: "resultaba un libro político por su ausencia de política: las pocas referencias políticas: aludir a la dictadura de Castro de soslayo, llamar a Fidel Castro un fiasco, sólo reflejaban que el libro ocurría argumentalmente en 1958, pero su escritura se hacía en 1965" (it was a political book only because there was an absence of politics in it: the few political references: the oblique reference to Castro's dictatorship, calling Fidel Castro a "fiasco" (failure), only reflected that the action of the book took place in 1958, but the writing of the book was taking place in 1965).[212] Cabrera Infante offered numerous in-

terviews about his work, and, in fact, still today most critics approach *TTT*
informed by, or in dialogue with, Cabrera Infante's own explanations of his
own work, making the writer the most important reader of this text. As Raymond D. Souza observes: "Cabrera Infante is well aware that his work is a
part of a fabricated tradition from which he takes considerable inspiration,"
[to such a point] "that one wonders if he is not parodying a cherished practice of literary criticism. As his readings have become more extensive over
the years, so have his literary antecedents, in good Borgesian fashion."[213]
In the play between writer, critics, and a text that is also an ontological and
epistemological meditation on knowledge and reality, there are elements
of afrocubanía inscribed in the fabric and structure of this novel that have
escaped critics, who simply have acknowledged the presence of certain
vague references to Afro-Cuban magic and codes.

Cabrera Infante seldom mentioned the incorporation of such Afro-Cuban
elements in his text except through passing comments about, for example,
the success of *TTT,* now a Latin American classic: "Siempre pensé que el
libro [*TTT*] no sería entendido más que por un número muy reducido de
personas que vivían en determinado lugar de La Habana, en una época dada
y alrededor mío" (I always thought the book would be understood only by
a small number of persons around me that lived in a given place in Havana
at a given moment).[214] To understand the book, he thought, was not enough
to follow its linguistic plays and more accessible cultural references, but
also the codes of that secondary, yet primary, order of reading which in *TTT*
is associated with the invisible realm related to the cowrie Lydia gave him
in Havana.

Lydia's prophetic dream offers a bridge into the Afro-Cuban monte, always already there in the invisible landscape of cubanía, in the local memories of Havana, and in the entanglements of its cultural psyche. In an interview with Rosa Pereda, Cabrera Infante notes the importance of religious
syncretisms in his own family: his wife's devotion to *Obatalá* (*Virgen de
las Mercedes* [Virgin of Mercy]) and *Babalú Ayé* (*San Lázaro* [Saint
Lazarus]), as well as the performance of certain rituals, about which he simply concludes: "Hay otros misterios, pero revelarlos (como los de Bona
Dea en Roma) es peligroso" (There are other mysteries, but to reveal them
{like those of the *Bona Dea* in Rome} is dangerous).[215] In *TTT,* a text that
articulates an interest in the performance of the popular, which in Cuba is
associated with afrocubanía, Cabrera Infante appropriates Afro-Cuban
myths and rituals (specifically those of the Abakuá secret society) that inform colloquial linguistic patterns and the cultural imaginary of the Havana
TTT reenacts. Reminiscent of Lydia Cabrera's voyage to the Afro-Cuban
monte in the voice of her informants, Cabrera Infante parodies in *TTT* the
echoes of the bygone voices of a Havana revisited through memory. The
textual reenactment of those voices in Cabrera Infante's text, constructs a

"literary monte" as complex as the oral archives in Cuba that tell of the origin, ritual, and religious beliefs, especifically of the Abakuá; whose traditions and "secrets" Cabrera Infante also inscribes in the fabric of the text. Cabrera Infante's appropriation of Abakuá myths and rituals should not be a surprise. The ñáñigos were already a cultural sign for cubanía. Different aspects of ñáñiguismo, but especially myths and rituals, had been represented by poets, musicians, and painters like Mario Carreño and Wifredo Lam.[216] The figure of the *Ireme,* the secret room, or *Cuarto Fambá,* and of the bygone Voice of the ancestors, *Ekoi,* in *Ekué,* which Cabrera Infante reappropriates in *TTT,* were images already inscribed in the cultural imaginary of Cuban society, and in the Spanish-speaking Caribbean since the nineteenth century, but especially from the twenties to the forties.

One of the explanations Cabrera Infante has offered for *TTT* is that the text is a linguistic experimental play with orality: "mi libro partió del concepto de una literatura oral para llegar a la escritura, del habla y de la voz— el habla cubana, informando la narración" (my book began with the concept of an oral literature in order to arrive to writing, with speech and voice —Cuban speech, informing the narration).[217] Sharon Magnarelli reads *TTT* as a "writerly" text,[218] a term meaning, in Roberto Echeverría's words: "not necessarily writing as such, but a representation of language's own constitution as spacing, a constitution whose visual image is writing."[219] In that representation of language, in which alliteration is a sort of liberation,[220] *TTT* constructs a textual rhizome, as if it were a monte of references. Some of those references are easily accessible to the Western reader, but others are not. The text opens itself to an order of reading that is self-referential, nocturnal, hermetic, as Benítez Rojo suggests of the Caribbean text, directed inward, and informed by Afro-Cuban rituals and beliefs, specifically that sector of Cuban society Ortiz called the Cuban *hampa,* of a strong ñáñigo presence. Lydia Cabrera points out in *El monte* and in *La sociedad secreta Abakuá* (1959) that basic to this group is the memory of a Voice: the Great Mystery from the Great Beyond upon which the Abakuá bases its origins and ontological existence. Remembering that parody recovers the text parodied, in *TTT,* Cabrera Infante pays homage to Lydia Cabrera's work, the woman who revealed to non-initiates what could not be revealed: the secrets of the society, the secrets all *ekobios* pledge not to reveal. Cabrera Infante continued to pay homage to the writer of *El monte* when he observes in *Vidas para leerlas* that Lydia Cabrera was the first and only woman to enter the *Cuarto Fambá,* the ritual room in which ñáñigos perform their secret ceremonies.[221] Most importantly, however, is the fact that by paying homage to Lydia Cabrera, *TTT* celebrates that Cuban sector of African ancestry, the ñáñigos, whose beliefs Lydia Cabrera's work inscribes in mainstream writing, and whose beliefs and rituals had attracted Ortiz and the Minoristas. In fact, the ñáñigos had played a vital role in the development of cubanía, and could be considered cultural ancestors. They had participated in the wars of independence against Spain, in the abolitionist struggle, and in the development of Cuban music. Yet, as if it were a cyclical return again to the prohibition of Black Carnival, when Cabrera Infante was writing *TTT,* the Abakuá were persecuted once more and in danger of disappearing.

In order to represent the voices that inform the rhythms of the Havana Cabrera Infante's text recalls, Cabrera Infante inscribes in the fabrics of his text what Ortiz called "El Supremo Teatro" (The Supreme Theater): ñáñigo ceremonies known as *plantes* or *juegos,* rituals of initiation, of consacration (*baróko*), and funeral rites (*enrolló*). In its textual performative plays (*plante* or *juego), TTT* romances, like Abakuá *plantes* or pantomines, the Abakuá secret, and the memory in their rituals of a Voice gone. The Voice remembered in *TTT,* like the Voice rememorated in ñáñigo rituals (the secret), is the collective "Voice" of Cuba's cultural ancestors: the source and "spirit" of cubanía that, like the ñáñigos, was disappearing from a Havana now under siege by a new political ideology. It was, perhaps, as retold in *TTT,* the same story, but in a contemporary Cuban context, of the old conflicts of power between the *Efik* and the *Efor,* the African ancestor of the Abakuá. *TTT* reenacts the archival African-Afro-Cuban myth about tyranny, resistance, and survival, to tell a similar story but in a new context of power struggle, related once more to the issue of the possession of a truth.

After the triumph of the Cuban Revolution in 1959, the survival of the ñáñigos as a belief system, their rituals, and lifestyle, were again in danger of extinction, now as the result of another repression against "primitive" beliefs and superstitions waged by the new revolutionary government.[222] As Carlos Moore points out, Castro's government conveniently tried to eliminate the rituals and belief systems that allowed African traditions to survive in Cuba by defining them as "folklore,"[223] a term that erased any religious significance. At the same time that it negated the religious context of such Cuban "folklore," the government encouraged "cultural projects" that exalted national folk cultures and lore including the study of Afro-Cuban "folklore" as part of Cuba's African heritage. In 1961, Cabrera Infante's brother, Alberto (Sabá) and Orlando Jiménez Leal, using new filming techniques, made a documentary "about nightlife around Prado and Neptuno streets in the old section of the city and on the waterfront across the bay from old Havana, in the predominantly black Regla,"[224] an area of a strong ñáñigo presence. In this film, which they named *P.M.,* Cabrera explains that, experimenting with new film techniques, the camera "se paseaba por los bares de los muelles de La Habana vieja" (moved around the bars in the harbor of Old Havana),[225] exposing a lifestyle that the new political ideology associated with a pre-revolutionary decadent society, now under attack, and at the brink of extinction. *P.M.* documented the noctural world of music, Cuban music, in many of the bars and nightclubs that had been the birthplace of contemporary Cuban music, and the places where famous Cuban black musicians like Beny Moré performed.[226] According to Moore, in 1961, Walterio Carbonell, a long time Marxist, and the only black Cuban in a high post in the Cuban government, published *Crítica. Cómo surgió la cultura nacional,* in which he wrote: "Thanks to the vitality of these religions [Afro-Cuban], black music could survive: the rhythms and music that gave birth to Cuban music, the highest expression of culture. I have said that these religious organizations have played a politically and culturally progressive role in the forging of our nationality . . . the silence of certain revolutionary writers concerning the political and cultural role of these cults of African origin is becoming highly suspect."[227] The book soon was banned and Carbonell was asked to leave the Cuban foreign ministry. A similar situation would happen with *P.M.*

Soon before *P.M.* was to be released to the public, government officials confiscated the film; and when the journal *Lunes de Revolución,* of which Cabrera Infante was editor, criticized the government for the censorship of *P.M.,* government officials reacted by closing down the journal.[228] Bewildered and incensed by a situation that also left him out of work (until 1962), Cabrera Infante began to transpose the world captured by *P.M.* to writing in a text he first called *Vista del amanecer en el trópico* (1964).[229] The prohibition of *P.M.* made Cabrera realize that:

> esas formas de vida a las que PM descubría su poesía, ese mundo del choteo criollo, del relajo cubano, de la pachanga de donde habían surgido todas las formas musicales cubanas, estaba incoeciblemente condenado a la desaparición. Entonces quise hacer PM por otros medios, perpetuar la vida a una especie y a su medio. Quise hacer de la literatura un experimento ecológico, que no es más que perpetrar un acto de nostalgia activa.[230]

> [those ways of life that *P.M.* uncovered, that world of creole *choteo,* of Cuban *relajo,* of the *pachanga,* from which all forms of Cuban music emerged, were condemned to disappear. Then I wanted to (re)make *P.M.* by other means, to perpetuate the life of a specie and its environment. I wanted to make of literature an ecological experiment, which is no other than to perpetuate an act of active longing.]

It was "the end of the world,"[231] Cabrera Infante would recall years later, a world "que estaba desapareciendo" (that was disappearing).[232] He left for Europe in 1962 on a new assignment. When he returned to Cuba in 1965 for his mother's funeral, he found a different Havana: "Cuba ya no era Cuba, era otra cosa—el doble del espejo—su *doppelänger* . . ." (Cuba no longer was Cuba; it was something else—the double in the mirror—its doppelgänger).[233] Overcoming obstacles, he finally managed to return to Europe to stay. Then, after several revisions, *Vista del amanecer en el trópico* (*View of the Dawn in the Tropics*), a text with a clear political edge (which he came to the conclusion later that it had been an act of treason against his own principles), turned, in a sort of escape from its first version, into *Tres tristes tigres* (1965), (*Three Trapped Tigers* {1971}). This was an experimental text in which the writer tries to imagine the *son-idos habaneros* (Havana's sounds, Afro-Cuban rhythms, popular voices, speech, gone), as if the writer were on an ecological exploration, through memory, of Havana's urban monte. As Enrico Mario Santí points out, when Cabrera Infante returned to Havana, the feeling he experienced of a culture near extinction is compounded with his sense of loss for the death of his mother, his "source of language and most profound sense of identity."[234] *TTT* brings together that double sense of loss in an eulogy to a people, a culture, his own mother (associated with culture and language, myths and orality), in a wake for the (m)other as the voice of an era that had been as important in Cabrera's life as it was in the development of cubanía. In the process of recovering, through writing, the essence or that cultural "spirit" left only to memory, Cabrera Infante journeys into the depths of the cultural imaginary, to the oneiric landscape of local memories and knowledges, and of Cuban cultural codes and myths.

In Regla, where ñáñigos were a prominent presence in the nightlife *P.M.* had documented, Cabrera Infante finds the same afrocubanía that attracted the Minorista Group years early: a world by then inscribed in Cuban literature, music, painting, as well as in vernacular speech in Havana. The most magnificent visible legacy of that world was the Abakuá plantes or juegos, whose mode of speech, codes, and rituals had penetrated popular culture, and whose inner sanctum was the secret *Cuarto Fambá* (Famba Room). Abakuá rituals are based on the worship of ancestors whose spirits are believed to be present in the life of the living. Cabrera Infante incorporates to his text a similar sense of cult to the cultural ancestors of cubanía;[235] and reenacts, in the "performance" that is writing, a "writerly" modality of a Cuban monte and, at the same time, Cuba's Supreme Theater (Abakuá ritual). *TTT* romances in its juegos the textual "pantomine" of the ñáñigo drum-urn: the recipient (like the text) of the faint echo of the Voice of the ancestors, the ñáñigo's *Ekoi,* which *Ekué* represents. Cabrera Infante interweaves in the narrative of the text Abakuá rituals, music, their sense of mystery, their hermetic codes of silence, their sense of independence and freedom, their disdain for the submissive, their sense of rivalry and defiance, their complex system of cultural and social power, ritual violence, and their enigmatic language surrounding a "secret," but, above it all, the Abakuá sense, intrinsic to their beliefs, of resistance to any form of domination.

Lydia Cabrera notes that the *chébere monina* or ñáñigo was "guapetón, jactancioso, impulsivo, ególatra, vanidad quisquillosa e infinita" (flashy, boastful, impulsive, self-worshiping, and of endless fastidious vanity),[236] characteristics that, since the nineteenth century, attracted Cuban youths (white, mulatto, or black). It was that attraction that led to the creation of the first *potencia* (or chapter) of white adepts or ekobios: the *Abadanaran Efor,* founded in the late nineteenth century by the creole mulatto, an Abakuá high chief or *Idiobón,* Andrés Facundo Cristo de los Dolores Petit.[237] Cabrera Infante represents this ritualistic world and the seriousness surrounding the Abakuá, in the spirit of another cultural ritual, or social *juego,* in Cuba: Cuban *relajo* and *choteo,* an intrinsic element of cubanía, and a popular social tool of resistance and defiance.[238] For the Abakuá, concealment and treason are closely tied to language, to a way of telling that conceals truth. The Abakuá ekobios have a secret language with which to hide ritual secrets from non-initiates. It is a codified way of speaking related to their most important pledge, which is to never reveal the Secret.

Cabrera Infante found out with the events associated with *P.M.,* what he already knew from personal experience, that, like in Abakuá ritual mythology, telling, speaking, expressing certain knowledge or a truth, could have serious consequences. As a child, Cabrera Infante learned the dangers related to speaking and writing. His father, a chief editor for the Communist journal *Hoy,* was accused of treason, and he and his wife were arrested and imprisoned for a short time. Although both soon were acquitted, as the result of this trauma in which his mother was almost shot by the policeman who arrested her, Cabrera Infante, then seven years old, lost his ability to speak. His father, unable to find other jobs as editor and journalist, was forced to change professions (like Cué and Eribó in *TTT)* and became an accountant. Worried about the future of his son, his father did not want Cabrera Infante to become a writer. However, in spite of his father's opposition, he began to work as editor, translator, and film reviewer. When, later, he began to write his early short stories, he used his mother's last name, Infante.[239] An obscenity written in English, which he included in his short story "Balada de plomo y yerro" (Ballad of Led and Iron), took Cabrera Infante to prison; he was ordered to pay a fine, to stop his studies at the School of Journalism, and to never publish again under his name. In spite of the strict rulings, he continued to write film reviews under the pseudoname of G. Caín, a pen name he created using the first two letters of his father's and of his mother's last names. He also created another mask, an alter ego, in the character of Silvestre, who appears in several of his short stories:[240] a writer like him who is also from the interior of the island (*TTT,* 303). In Havana, being from the interior was the same as being from the countryside or monte (like Silvestre). By 1961, when *Lunes de revolución* was closed down, Cabrera Infante was already well aware of the consequences words could bring: of the dangers of "telling."

Mario Enrico Santí offers the insightful observation that the muteness of the seven-year-old Guillermo coincides with the meaning "of his mother's last name, Infante, from the Latin *infans,* that means "someone who does not speak."[241] The meaning of his maternal name coincides with Cabrera Infante's experiences of "becoming" a writer, and in 1961 with the sacrificial death of an important journal as the punishment for speaking out. In light of these events, Cabrera Infante's inclusion of the ñáñigo in his text recalls that, ironically, the Supreme Theater in Cuba, the Abakuá plante, is about the dangers of speaking; about the act of hiding a certain knowledge through the mask of performance; about the immolation of an outsider, a woman, who speaks when she comes to possess the Great Mystery: when, like *Sikán,* an outsider and a woman, excluded from the inner circles of power, hears and knows the "secret." Cabrera Infante found in the Abakuá a cultural analogy for his own experiences, in the ritual relationship already inscribed in the culture between silence and power. Like the dancers in Black Carnival, Cabrera Infante also knew from experience that resistance against authority can be performed through masks, acting, codified representation, and silent gestures: something the Abakuá had known and practiced since the eighteenth century.

Cabrera Infante describes *TTT* as an "ecological experiment," an exploration of the Cuban "fauna"[242] in the Havana of the fifties, as if *TTT* were a cultural documentation (like *P.M.*), similar to Lydia Cabrera's *El monte,* of the many voices that make up cubanía. The text offers itself to the reader as a verbal expedition into Havana's popular culture before the triumph of the Cuban revolution, because this was the moment rejected by the politics of a social utopia the revolutionary government wanted to present in the sixties.[243] In that literary voyage, the themes of "treason," "tradition," "death," and "sacrifice," basic to the Abakuá, become also central to the polyphony and signifying plays of *TTT.* Such textual plays further underline the idea, as a double entendre, that "treason" (*traición*) is always already inscribed in tradition, as in the Spanish word, *tradición: (tra(d)ición).* The text is a reminder that the translation of a culture, of religious and cultural concepts, as we find in Lydia Cabrera's work, is a testimony, and a form of cultural rescue, but, at the same time, a form of treason toward the same tradition it wants to rescure, for, in the process, translation betrays tradition by deforming it in the process of its reconstruction. In other words, as the translator of major literary works,[244] Cabrera Infante was aware that translation always fails to reproduce the original in the same way that writing fails to reproduce speech, or that a photo fails to reproduce reality. They are acts that pretend to create a double reality, but, in the process, only reconstruct a different reality, something other, new (sort of its "double in the mirror"). Thus, words like freedom, for example, are terms that can be used to mean its opposite. Therefore, in the act of imagining through writing the Havana documented in *P.M, TTT* reconstructs another modality of *P.M.* by creating something new, different; and, in the process, the text also articulates the complex dynamics in Cuba between history, censorship, and writing. Like *Carnaval de los negros, TTT* performs a supreme Cuban pantomime of resistance to authority by questioning structures of power, laws, canons, and the authority of the signifier; and by reenacting, like the *Iremes* on "Día de Reyes," under the mask of fiction, the "freedom of representation" denied to *P.M.*

In a signifying play between language and myth, *TTT* appropriates the basic structures of thought in Abakuá myths of origin (reenacted in their ritual *juego*), in what Lévi-Strauss calls the structuring "mythical language"[245] that gives coherence and unity to the text.[246] Cabrera Infante denies any association in his novel with Lévi-Strauss's work.[247] Nonetheless, whether or not there is an intentional association and dialogue with Lévi-Strauss's ideas on the structured systems of myths and language or not, myths and cultural codes in *TTT* articulate projections of patterns of thoughts, and expressions of a cultural imaginary, that can be found also, for example, in literature and film.[248] Such "mythical language" in *TTT,* recalls Lévi-Strauss's idea, as he states in "Overture" to *The Raw and the Cooked,* that "the unity of the myth is tendentious and projective; it never really reflects a state or a fixed moment of the myth. It is no more than an imaginary phenomenon implicit in the effort of interpretation."[249] Yet, as Niall Lucy observes of Lévi-Strauss: "myth was a very special form of language but for a reason that was the opposite of why literature (exemplified by poetry) is understood as special."[250] Poetry, for Lévi-Strauss: "is a kind of speech which cannot be translated except at the cost of serious distortions; whereas the mythical value of the myth is preserved even through the worst translations."[251] In other words, the translation of a cultural anecdote to another language and culture may alter the nonessencial elements of the anecdote, as it occurs in Lydia Cabrera's work and in *TTT.* Yet, the translation and transposition of ancestral African myths to a Cuban context, in spite of the changes made, does not alter the cultural mythical value of the old in the new version. Much like *El monte,* a text interested in portraying Afro-Cuban knowledges from the gaze and in the voice (patterns of speech and thought) of the believers, in *TTT,* Cabrera Infante is interested in accessing, through memory and fiction, the thoughts and ways of being of *habaneros,* through the very structure of language, and the language of myths that orders those thoughts. *TTT* takes the reader to the space of fiction (the other side of the mirror), in a sort of "anthropoetics," as Cabrera Infante calls Lydia Cabrera's work:[252] to the depths of the cultural imaginary where daily life, history, and the oneiric are interwoven, rewriting the story, in a new context, of an ancestral Afro-Cuban myth about captivity, domination, and exclusion. In it, he retransforms, rewrites, and parodies the secret Abakuá performance (pantomime) that takes place in the inner sanctum of the Cuarto Fambá, juxtaposing it to another great theatrical performance in Cuba, the well-known tropical shows of the famous Havana nightclub Tropicana, a place that became a metaphor in itself for the Havana of the fifties.

The novel opens with the voice of the MC in Tropicana, introducing (while alternating between Spanish and English) the stars in the text, the performers. Yet, as in the double in the mirror, behind the curtains of Tropicana, the text represents another pantomime: the ritual *plante* that takes place in the hidden space of the Abakuá Cuarto Fambá, a private space of culture where tourists do not, and cannot enter. The complicit reader may apprehend that in the alternating voices, and in the alternating performances in the text, there is a gap. This is a void filled in *TTT* by the echo of the sacred Voice of cultural ancestors: foundational voices that include other writers, musicians, and cultural references inscribed in a Havana imaginary. In *TTT,* the shadow of that imaginary space stands in counterpoint to, and interwoven with, the public space: the show of Tropicana. That second, other, performance opens itself to a second, but yet primary order of reading, one that is hermetic, ontological, ritual, nocturnal, romancing a secret Voice trapped in the text-urn: a certain unspoken knowledge about the dangers of speaking, and the fatal consequences of telling. In the ritual reenactment of a Time and a Space gone, *TTT* articulates in its play of performances a subversive opposition to the structures of power that silence writing (as it had silenced *P.M.*), like the structures that tried to silence Cabrera Infante, and that impose a given hegemony that obliterates threatening differences.

II

The Abakuá foundational myth tells a ritual story of the immolation of a woman, whose death assures and perpetuates the hegemony of patriarchal dominance.[253] *Sikán,* or *Sikuaneka,* says Lydia Cabrera, was an *Efor* woman who went to the river to get water. There, the deity fish *Tanze,* incarnation of the Supreme Being, *Abasi,* entered her water gourd. This chosen woman, *Sikán,* was the first person to hear and perhaps see the Great Mystery that emerged from the sacred waters. Water, for the Abakuá, is where life originates, the medium of the spirits.[254] This explains why the Supreme Spirit, Abasi, chose to incarnate as a fish, *Tanze,* in the sacred waters of the *Fodokón,* in the river *Oddan,* in the Calabar, Africa; and why the sacred spirit chose to reveal itself by going inside the water gourd of a woman (metaphor for the womb). In this faint echo of a *Christic* conception, the African/Cuban story of origin tells of the passing of power from a matriarchal system to a patriarchal society. In that play of powers, the fact that Tanze chose Sikán, a woman, made her special, but also dangerous to the secrecy of the brotherhood. Women could not partake of the secret knowledge, and thus the knowledge that Sikán came to possess endangered the political play of power between the dominated Efor, and the dominant Efik.[255] Thus, Sikán, an outsider to the male hegemony, was sentenced to death. Trapped outside of the sacred waters, Tanze also died and its skin was used to cover the drum-urn, Ekué, in which the divine sacred voice was trapped. However, the voice grew faint. In an effort to bring the voice back, Sikán's sacrificial blood was poured over the drum; but it was not until the drum was covered with goatskin that the echo of the Great Mystery could be faintly heard again. This is the sacred roaring bellow (*bramido*) Ekué makes in the *plantes,* inside the Cuarto Famba, when the drum is played in a manner known as *fragayar.*[256] This is the roar of Ekué that Menegildo Cué hears during his initiation in Carpentier's *¡Ecué-Yamba-O!*

Ekué is also known as the *Fundamento* (foundation) because it unites the Spirit of the Great Mystery and the spirit of Sikán, the woman whose blood (sacrifice) made the *Fundamento* possible: the mother figure of the ñáñigos (represented by a gourd), whose spirit must always be present in the plante.[257] It is believed that the initiation of an ecobio to this society saves the initiate's spirit from being lost in the Great Beyond. This is why when a fraternity brother, or ecobio (ekobio), dies, ritual drawings (or *rayas*) are made on the corpse to mark him so that his spirit can be guided to the proper folds in the spirit world. The act of drawing, making ritual marks (codified writing) on the corpse, on the floor, and on objects, is a type of symbolic writing that has the magic property of transforming one thing into another: of creating a reality. With these drawings, Abakuá *obones* recreate the original mythical space remembered: the river, the palm, and the *ceiba.* The Abakuá ritual markings constitute a complex language whose meanings are revealed to the initiate who has pledged to *callar* (not to speak, not to tell or reveal the Great Secret). Lydia Cabrera documented these markings in *Anaforuana. Ritual y símbolos de la iniciación en la sociedad secreta Abakuá* (1975), making them available to non-initiates, and pointing out in this monumental text the complexity of an Afro-Cuban hermetic system of ritual writing.

The violence between *potencias* made headlines in nineteenth century newspapers. Martín Morúa Delgado repeats such descriptions in his novel *La familia Unzúanzu* (1901) as: "asociaciones de origen africano sostenidas por criollos libertos. . . . Excitaban las pasiones e inspiraban los odios selváticos . . . A orgullo tuvo gran número de jóvenes, lo mismo de color que blancos, el pertenecer a una asociación que les daba fama de valientes" (association of African origin supported by free creoles . . . awakened passion and inspired savage hatred . . . A large number of young men, of color just as white, felt proud to belong to such an organization that gave them the fame of being brave).[258] This is the violence among *potencias,* or Abakuá chapters, that Carpentier describes in *¡Ekué-Yamba-O!* (1933), Or-

2. Ekué: Abakuá drum. Photo by Maria Teresa Rojas. Lydia Cabrera, *El monte*.

tiz in *Los negros brujos,* and Nicolás Guillén in "Velorio de Papá Montero" (Wake for Papá Montero), in *Sóngoro cosongo* (1931); and that reenacted, in Havana, the age long conflict that arose between the Efik and the Efor in Africa for the legitimate possession of the secret Voice. According to Enrique Sosa Rodríguez, in his study, *Los ñáñigos* (1982), these religious conflicts had been, in their African context, a political act by the oppresed Efik against the dominant Efor.[259] In Cuba, where these conflicts continued in a new and different social context, the Abakuá rite of initiation continued to reenact in their plantes the immolation of Sikán. The ancient African society, now Cuban, is made present in its Cuban Supreme Theater: in the druming-roar of the Ekué, and in the ritual memory of ancestral African origins, now in a Cuban landscape.

The origins of the Abakuá, explains Enrique Sosa Rodríguez, can be traced to the African socioeconomic fraternity of the Leopard, in the Cameroon.[260] Women were excluded from this secret brotherhood in which the drum called Ekpe was believed to be the sacred recipient of the Great Secret, the Great Mystery.[261] Like the Afro-Cuban ñáñigos, the members of the Ekpe were men "que no aceptaban golpes de ningún ser humano" (that did not take punches from any human beings).[262] The Abakuá is the fifth stage in the development of this ancestral African society transcultur-ated to Cuba,[263] where the ekobios (ecobios) continued to rememorate the Voice trapped in the sacred drum Ekué (Ekpe)[264] in their juegos, or ritual pantomimes, from which women continued to be excluded. For the Abakuá, the roaring sound that Ekué makes when played during an initiation (when the initiate bonds with Ekué, the ancestral spirit), is also the echo of the di-vine origin of existence, and it holds the meaning of ñáñigo or Abakuá cul-tural identity and history.

The African fraternity of the Ekpe, adapted to new conditions in Cuba, left deep imprints in Cuban society, especially in vernacular speech and in Cuban music. Cuban creole words like *tángana* for *riña* (conflict or fight), *plante* for ritual *juego* (game/play),[265] *ñampear* for *matar* (to kill), among others, are ñáñigo words that have become part of Cuban colloquial Span-ish. The Abakuá also have a secret language, which is a complex figurative speech that only the initiate or *abonékue ecobio* understands.[266] Such cod-ified language has ritual purposes due to the secrecy of the society, but it also serves as a protective tool of resistance and survival, especially in times of social and political persecution. A similar language, known as *ñan-galia,*[267] is a nonsensical speech used to deceive non-initiates by provid-ing false information. Lydia Cabrera points out that such language re-sponds to the fact that the most important pledge of the Abakuá ecobio (his *juramento*), is callar (keep silence), never to tell.[268] For a writer like Cabre-ra Infante, it must have seem a signifying coincidence that his father's name, Cabrera, is a word related to *cabra* (goat), the animal whose skin is used to cover the sacred ñáñigo drum-urn, the recipient of the divine voice, of which the ekobio must not speak. It was also Lydia Cabrera's last name. Hence, Teresa de la Parra gave her the nickname *Cabra* (goat) and *Cabrita* (little goat). It must have seemed significant to Cabrera and to Cabrera In-fante that their last name was a derivate of goat, the animal sacrificed that takes the place of Sikán during the ritual reenactment of her immolation. In a play of ironies, as Santí points out, Cabrera Infante's father's last name, Cabrera, is juxtaposed, in the son, to his mother's last name, Infante, from Infants: someone who does not speak.[269] At the time Cabrera Infante wrote *Tres tristes tigres,* he and Lydia Cabrera felt like inmolated cabras, sacrifi-cial goats for the new ideological order of power.

In Cuba the African fraternity of the Ekpe suffered several changes. Among the ritual transformations it suffered in Cuba was the substitution of the leopard for that of a tiger, even though there are no tigers in Cuba. For the Abakuá, the tiger came to represent strength, power, and royalty,[270] however, a goat took the place of the leopard and of the tiger, giving way to the saying among ecobios: "in the hide of the goat, all men can be brothers.'[271] In the logic of ritual transformation, the roar of Ekué (in the hide of a goat) is always a reminder of the force of the monte (the African leopard and tiger). In Havana, "tiger" became a popular expression to refer to men. This expression, not limited to Cuba, established a symbolic dialogic association in *TTT* between the urban space of Havana with monte, jungle, and its people as the jungle/monte's "fauna." At the same time, in Havana, a strong *macho,* an Abakuá *chébere monina,* and a womanizer were also called tigers. The tiger was also an important symbol for the Chinese immigrants to Cuba.[272] Since the nineteenth century, the Chinese became an important sector of Cuban society. The Afro-Cuban orisha Shango, for example, was known among Cuban Chinese as *San-Fan-Cón;*[273] and in Matanzas, there was a Chinese ñáñigo "land" or chapter known as *Fi-Etete-Efí.*[274] Chinese immigrants also introduced in Cuban society a complex lottery system based on the equivalent value of numbers and images known in Cuba as *Charada China* or *Rifa Chifá.* This Cuban Chinese numerical system provided in pre-revolutionary Cuba a complex cultural and linguistic hermeneutics (cultural codes) with which to say something in order to say something else, in a way, in spite of the differences, similar to the Abakuá secret language. The *Charada* constructed, in the popular imaginary, linguistic games that, like baroque linguistic play, would always hide an enigma.[275]

In *TTT,* the main performers, stars or characters, are close friends: three "tigers" who, like Dumas's *The Three Mosqueteers,* are actually four. The three/four sad (*tristes*) tigers of the title of the novel, however, is also a reference to the first three words of a Spanish tongue twister, that also recalls, in their association with the popular "voices" of Havana, a radio novel very popular during the fifties: *Los tres Villalobos* (The Three Villalobos).[276] The play of three and four in *TTT,* like the diamond shapes and triangles in Lam's work, has its own signifying role in the novel's narrative codes and structure. Coinciding with the Christian symbol of the three, as in the concept of a divine Trinity—an archetype for oneness[277]—for the Abakuá, three is a ritual number associated with the spirit of the voice trapped in the Ekué; and number four, with the cardinal points, space, earth, woman: Sikán, the ritual mother. In Abakuá secret societies there are four obones or chiefs,[278] and each one receives one of the legs of the sacrificed goat. There are also four ritual drums. Apart from its mythological significance, Cabrera Infante also confesses his fascination with the asymmetry of the three,[279] a number *TTT* reiterates, and inscribes in the structure of the text, as in, for example, dividing the text into nine setions (3 × 3).[280]

There is also another friend, an absent but implicit fifth tiger.[281] This is Florén (flora) Cassalis, nicknamed Bustrófedon for his mode of speaking in linguistic plays that transform one thing into another: a mode of speaking, like the novel, in which the signifier always defies signification. Bustrófedon's presence in *TTT* takes place only in the memory of the four tigers' recollections of their diseased friend. He is the absent voice echoed by his four friends who reenact in a linguistic performance his way of speaking in which the signifer always escapes, runs away, from the strictures of the signifying. The text is the reenacment of such linguistic juegos as a remembrance and reenacment of the oracle-like speech of the absent, dead, Bustrófedon. The three/four ecobios/tigers are: Silvio[282] Ribot, who Bustrófedon named Eribó, after the name of a sacred drum in the Abakuá society, *Sese Eribó, seseribó,*[283] because he is a bongó player, a mulatto and an Abakuá ecobio; Arsenio Cué (*TTT,* 399), derivative of (E)kué, the name of the Abakuá drum-urn (also an echo of Menegildo Cué in Carpentier's *¡Ecué-Yamba-O!*) whose significant profession in the novel is to impersonate voices as a radio actor. There is also Silvestre Isla, a writer, Cabrera Infante's alter ego, whose name is associated with the image of monte, and a disciple of Bustrófedon (*TTT,* 223) (whose name, Florén, of "flora," is also related to the wild as is Silvestre, a word that means "wild flora"). Cué (the echo) is the one who speaks like Bustrófedon, and who, in keeping with his ritual role in the novel, serves as an echo of the mode of speaking, or the dead being remembered: Bustrófedon's voice.

Cué (Ekué) and Eribó are two different characters in the novel, but, in ñáñigo juegos, and in the novel's signifying games and parodies, they refer to the same Abakuá ritual drum-urn. For the Efik, the most prominent ñáñigo group in the area around the Havana harbor, the sacred drum Ekué was known as *Bongó.*[284] Yet, in *TTT* it is not Cué and Eribó, but Silvestre Isla and Arsenio Cué (orality and writing) who represent, according to Cué, "los Jimaguas ñáñigos de Eribó" (the ñáñigo twins of *Eribó*) (*TTT,* 405), "idénticos, una binidad" (identical, {a divine duet}, a binity) (*TTT,* 419). The mythical association between the three tigers in the text, recalls also the body of the sacred drum-urn that is said to have been covered by the skin of a tiger, and stands on three legs that represent the three founders of the Abakuá religion:[285] the three tribes from which the Abakuá originated: *Usagaré, Eforense,* and *Bakokó.*[286] It is said that the tail of the fish Tanze, from which Ekué was made, was tripartite; and it was over three rocks at the shores of the sacred river, that the gourd, from which the first ritual bongó (sacred drum) was created, was first placed.[287] In Abakuá plantes or ritual "games" (juegos) these three rocks are placed next to the *fundamento* (the drum that holds the echo of the divine Voice), in the Cuarto Famba (the enclosed room where ritual plantes take place). During the ceremony, three marks are made to represent the sacred number. There are also three Abakuá great chiefs or priests: *Iyamba, Mokongo,* and *Issué,*[288] that are actually four *obones,* the fourth one being *Isuenekué,*[289] just like there is a fourth tiger in *TTT:* Códac, a photographer.

Underlining the central theme of treason in the text, Cabrera Infante appropriates, rewrites, and transforms the foundational story of Sikán's immolation as the result of telling, in the spirit of Cuban *relajo,* or *choteo,* as an intrinsic characteristic of cubanía. The Abakuá mythical story appears appropriately in the form of a comical *vinette,* as a heading to the section of the novel entitled "Seseribó" (*TTT,* 89) (the same title of a short story Cabrera Infante published in *Casa de las Américas* no. 32, 43–59, in 1965). Appropriately, this section, like the text, addresses the dangerous consequences of telling. It tells the story of Sikán, who finds the sacred Ekué in the sacred river. She, a fibber, hears Ekué, chases him, captures him, and tells others about him: "This was a sacrilege." Therefore: Sikán paid with her skin for her blasphemy . . . She wears four plumes with the four oldest powers at her four courners. As she is a woman she has to be beautifully adorned, with flowers and necklaces and cowries. But over her drumhead she wears the tongue of a cock as a sign of eternal silence. It is secret and taboo and it is called *seseribó* (*TTrappedT,* 85–86).[290]

In *TTT,* women, like Sikán, are social victims of male juegos and verbal plantes (a word that also means in Cuba "show"), but, at the same time, it is also through woman that the text's secret is put forth. Romancing women, the text plays with the two main precepts of the Abakuá society: never to reveal the Secret, and never to covet the woman of an ecobio. Sikán's story of transgression and death serves as counterpoint to the confession of a woman in the beginning of the text (a woman who tells the story of having told "stories" in order to hide the implicit story with which the novel begins). The text is written as a type of deceitful *ñangalia* that takes the reader in a journey into Cabrera Infante's "ecological," "tropical," cultural "wonderland." Like Lewis Carroll's Alice, the reader travels through an oneiric world in which every thing is always transformed into another, and images and situations are never what they seem to be. In that play of transformations, reminiscent also of the slippage of signifier/signified in language, but also of the linguistic plays of popular speech in the Havana being remembered, the act of telling a story so not to tell the story behind that story is basic to the order of a novel that finds reality to be "folly" and narration an always already "bad" translation of reality. As Emir Rodríguez Monegal notes, in *TTT:*

> Esta reflexión que invierte el sentido de la realidad y hace de la izquierda la derecha y viceversa, es de incalculables consecuencias no sólo políticas; es, ante todo, el fundamento de una visión ambigua que postula que la realidad que vemos, tocamos, oimos, olemos y gustamos es susceptible de ser encarada desde otra perspectiva radicalmente opuesta.[291]

> [This reflection that inverts the meaning of reality and makes left, right, and vice versa, has incalculable consequences, not only political ones; it is, first of all, the foundation of an ambiguous vision that claims that the reality we see, touch,

hear, smell, and taste is susceptible to be faced from a completely opposite perspective.]

Reiterated through the text, the reader finds the Socratic motif of truth and death, knowledge and punishment. Survival in *TTT* is associated with the endless confessions of false stories that hide another story. Masquerading behind Cuban choteo in order to speak of serious matters unnoticed, *TTT*'s performance recalls the street performances of the Abakuá *Iremes,* the diablito dancers, on "Día de Reyes" in colonial Cuba. The text reiterates, through puns, linguistic references, and private cultural codes, imaginary gestures, and pantomime, the association of the "tigers" with their ritual (metaphoric) mythical role. Eribó, like Cué (who wears dark sunglasses even indoors to hide his mysterious eyes), is a playful parody and a metaphoric personification of the sacred Abakuá drum that echoes the faint memory of Tanze. Coherent with his metaphoric role, Eribó feels that drumming is like standing "between heaven and earth" (*TTT,* 111). His ritual role in the text also informs his conversations with Cué about the secret associated with the possession and virginity of a woman. When Cué speaks to Eribó, his words are a play of double utterances, directed toward two orders of readings in a Bustrófedon-like fashion: a written representation of speech that must be read in two different directions. For example, Cué says to Eribó: "A que sé lo que quieres saber." "—Entonces guárdatelo" says Eribó. "—¿Por qué?," (I bet I know what you want to know.—Then keep it to yourself. Why?),—answers Cué. "No soy un juramentado. Ni siquiera un tambor ñáñigo" ("I am not a ñáñigo. I am not even a ñáñigo drum." (*TTT,* 108) Opposite to his statement, on the other side of the mirror, on the reverse side of his words, Eribó is, in fact, an Abakuá initiate, and, as a *bongosero,* a textual metaphor for the sacred ñáñigo drum, the Bongó. In that semantic play of opposites and doubles, the text explains why his relationship with the bongó is ritualistic and mystical for to play the bongó was like being alone: "entre el cielo y la tierra, suspendido, sin dimension" (suspended between heaven and earth, without dimension). When he was drumming, he was: "jugando con la música de aquel cuero de chivo doble clavado a un cubo de madero chivo inmortalizado su berido hecho música" (playing with the music of the goat hide attached with double nails to a wooden cube, immortalized goat, its cry turned into music) (*TTT,* 111–12). Eribó's association with the sacred Abakuá drum-urn also informs his conversations with Cué and with Benny Moré. As a parody of Carpentier's *La historia de la música en Cuba,* and in relationship to Cuban music (a counterpoint of Africa and Europe) Codac recalls that he did not want to go to El Sierra club because he did not want to find there the mulatto Eribó, or Benny, or Cué, nor did he want to hear them talk about music as if it were about race, about the value of black and white notes, or of the ancestral forms of Cuban music: "(esto

lo dice siempre Cué) . . . y de las claves de madera pasan . . . a las cosas en
clave y secretas y empiezan a hablar de brujería, de santería, de ñañiguismo
([Cué is the one who always says this] . . . and from wooden claves (sticks/
keys/codes/clues) they go on to . . . things spoken in secret codes, and begin to talk about witchcraft, santería, ñañiguismo) (*TTT*, 76–77).

This conversation in which the text re-de-codifies its own codes, takes
place only in Códac's imagination, as a situation that he could encounter if
he were to go inside the nightclub El Sierra. The main theme in Códac's
imaginary monologue is the importance of the African legacy in Cuban music; a thought that makes Códac exclaim: "lo negro ha salvado a Cuba"
(blackness has saved Cuba) (*TTT*, 65). The conversation imagined by Códac, between Eribó and Benny (Moré), offers another "clue" to understand
the text's "revelations:" disseminated into the crossroads of different rhizomatic discourses in continuous signifying plays and slippages. For example, Cué's story about his allegorical death after which he ceases to be
a photographer and becomes an actor (a forced change of profession reminiscent of the necessity in *TTT* to become something else, like Cabrera's
father, and like Tanze who died to becomes the echo of its own voice in
Ekué), is immediately followed by Eribó's similar experience with his em-
ployer in a different, but equally symbolic, death that transforms Eribó
from a *dibujante,* or pencil sketcher, into a musician-drummer: a *bongosero.* Following the textual plays (juegos) of transformations and postponed revelations, the end of Cué's story is postponed until the end of the
novel. Cué's confession is interrupted by the next section of the text, now
narrated by Eribó (after Cué's story), a section that begins with a parody of
the story of the Abakuá myth of Sikán, underlying the Socratic theme pertaining the dangers of telling the truth. Following Cabrera Infante's parody
of the origin of "Seseribó," with the immolation of Sikán, Eribó speaks of
Vivian's secret which she has confided in him, and which Eribó promises
never to reveal. Vivian, a wealthy sixteen-year-old woman, for whom Eribó
feels an attraction, confesses to Eribó that she is not a virgin, in a revelation that contradicts Cué's story at the end of the novel.

The virginity in question here, a common preoccupation in the Havana
of the fifties, may be informed also by Lydia Cabrera's documentation of
numerous and contrary versions of Sikán's encounter with Tanze. Some of
these versions center around the issue of whether or not Sikán was a virgin
when she went to the river (a version reminiscent of Lorca's poem "La
casada infiel" (The Unfaithful Married Woman). Others are an effort to justify Sikán's immolation. Others even depict Sikán as a whore, thus explaining why she was at the river when Tanze found her.[292] Others tell that
only virgins could go near the water for it is sacred, and Sikán was not a
virgin, thus offering an explanation for her punishment. There are so many
versions of any one story, says Lydia Cabrera, "that they could betray the

true concept" the informants want to communicate.[293] Some of these versions of the founding myth establish an association between Sikán's virginity and Ekué. In *TTT,* the loss of Vivian Smith-Corona's virginity (writing) to Cué (voice, orality), and his doubt as to whether she was or not a virgin is a pre-text that plays with the concept of truth, and with the concealment and revelation of a secret central to the novel. In keeping with the secret ritual drum that Eribó represents, he promises Vivian that he will be a *tumba* (*TTT,* 119), a word that in Cuba means "tomb" as well as "drum,"[294] and, in the Abakuá context, a reminder that Eribó is in fact the tomb-urn of the Voice, whose echo is the sound of the drum. Eribó's promise establishes, through a play of signifiers that includes the *abonekue's* pledge to remain silent, the complex relationship between the drum *Sese* (an Efor word for the drum Eribó), the text, silence, and writing. It is in this context that Eribó comments: "saqué mi tumba del closet (una tumba en una tumba)" (I took my drum-urn out of the closet (a tomb inside a tomb {closet}) (*TTT,* 90).[295] In his Cuban mythical role, Eribó is associated with woman and with silence. Abakuá mythology associates *Sese Eribó* with "Mother Nature," and with the Holy Chalis; and, like Sikán, Sese Eribó is a silent drum, therefore, it is never played. Different from Ekué, Sese Eribó can be displayed on the altar, it can be seen publicly,[296] and is covered symbolically with the skin of a tiger.[297]

III

In *TTT,* says Cabrera Infante, there are only two or three stories told and retold in different ways throughout the text.[298] All of them romance an absent presence that "speaks" about the imposition of silence, and the gaps between language and imagination, emphasized, in the text, through interruptions and polysemic plays. In "Seseribó," Eribó's monologue about being a tomb-drum (*TTT,* 53) is interrupted by Cué's recollection of his false death; Cué's story then is also interrupted by Códac's first monologue about the magnificent "cosmic phenomenon" (*TTT,* 84) of Cuban music, the mulatto woman singer, La Estrella, whose growing fame takes her to Mexico where she dies.[299] In his monologue, Códac imagines a conversation between Eribó and Cué about music in which the word clave (clue, key and code) refers to a musical key, but also to the idea of a secret associated with music, *melo,* and with a gap between the physical body and the invisible (cultural) spirit. Códac finds in La Estrella's mode of singing "una belleza tan distinta, tan horrible, tan nueva" (a beauty so different, so horrid, so new) (*TTT,* 64) that when she sings Agustín Lara's "Noche de ronda," Códac feels that Lara's song has suddenly been authored by La Estrella (*TTT,* 67). Yet this "phenomenom" of Cuban music dies in Mexico, alone, forgotten, in a death reminiscent of Tanze's death: in a death already inscribed in the codified juegos of the text. In the popular *Charada China* in Cuba, number eight was equivalent to "death." It is not surprising then that there are eight monologues about La Estrella. *TTT* plays with the role of numbers in Cuban society's cultural imaginary, as well as with the writer's own preoccupation with chance *(azar),*[300] and with "misterious ordering."[301] Already in the begining of the novel, in the first monologue of a woman speaking to her psychoanalyst, she "tells" of a short story her husband wrote about a psychoanalyst who used his client's dreams to know which numbers to play in the *Charada China.* She assumes that the reader/psychoanalyst understands the cultural codes: "whenever they tell him a dream, he goes and plays the numbers. If someone tells him he dreamed he saw a turtle in a pond, he goes and calls his bookie and tells him, Pancho, five on number six" (*TTrappedT,* 67–68).

Like in Lydia Cabrera's prophetic dream, the woman's recollections of a story about dreams engages an oneiric world of myths, desire, chance (azar), informed by a "mythical language" that "structures" in *TTT* the *son-idos habaneros,* interspersed and "revealed" through enigmatic codes from Afro-Cuban beliefs, the *Charada China,* Judeo-Christian symbology, the Tarot, and syncretic forms of Spiritism. To understand the woman's dream the reader is expected to know that in the *Charada China* 6 is *jicotea* (turtle), 1 is *caballo* (horse), 16 is *toro* (bull), 30 is *camarones* (shrimp) (*TTT,* 71); and that 9 is elephant, and not mirror as *TTT* suggests. Cué is obsessed with numbers—like Cabrera Infante is with their "mysterious ordering,"[302] and with mirrors. Cué is specially attracted to numbers 8 (death), 88 (double infinite), and to 9 (*TTT,* 328), the palindrome $3 \times 3 = 9$: the number of the sections in which the text is divided. The mirror, which Cabrera Infante equates here with number 9, is an archetypal symbol for the subconscious (as is water), associated with the same properties of an oracle in that it "reveals" the realms of the invisible. For some Afro-Cuban groups, as for the Abakuá, the *Chambuto* is a ritual mirror that reflects the invisible realm of the spirits. The Afro-Cuban *menso* or *mensu* has a mirror placed horizontally on top, for that same purpose. By equating 9 with mirror, *TTT* departs (slips away, escapes) from the strictures of the codes of the *Charada China,* in order to remain consistent with the internal juego of the text, and to remind the reader that such textual ritual performance is related to the avoidance of entrapment: in order to "circle the square" of writing, and to reenact the gaps of language-myth-writing. In *TTT,* the mirror suggests the reflection of another reality. It recalls the double, an 'other,' in the invisible space of the imaginary, the other side of the text, since the mirror, like the echo, is a symbol for "twins."[303] Cué and Silvestre are "like" twins, *una binidad* (*TTT,* 419) (a binity), and, by analogy, the textual double: writer and reader, orality and writing.

In *TTT,* the mysterious ordering of numbers also structures the novel as well as the mythical role of its characters. Arsenio Cué's name has the numerical value of 22 (*TTT,* 312), a number equivalent to the dove in the *Charada China,* and, in the Tarot, the perfect number. There are 22 parts in the section of the novel entitled "Bachata," a term that in Cuba means *juego* (as in game of chance and Abakuá ritual ceremony), with the meaning "juerga, diversión" (binge, spree).[304] Like in Abakuá's plantes, in *TTT*'s juegos, woman is associated with the mysteries of Life and Death, as in the case of La Estrella; and with the idea of silence and of a "secret" related to women; a secret that women should not know and from which they are excluded. This secret in *TTT* is intimated in the conflict between Eribó and Cué in relation to the possession of Vivian Smith-Corona, who does not know Eribó's secret feelings; and between Cué and Silvestre, over Laura Díaz. The romanced "secrets" intimate a gap in the male textual juegos: a secret associated with number 8 (death). Such silenced "secret" intimates, in a Borgean sense, the concept of infinity. It also intimates, on the reverse side of the page, the reflected other, the invisible made visible in the inverted reflection of the mirror (as in the Afro-Cuban *Chambuto),* of which no one can speak.

Coherent with the codified mythical role of the characters in *TTT* in their association with Abakuá rituals, Cué looks in the mirror and sees his metaphoric other, Ekué.[305] At that moment, like a Cuban Narcissus, he recognizes himself as the mysterious echo (faint echo) of a cultural spirit at the brink of death. Revealing his symbolic association with the mirror (the text), Cué tells Silvestre that the day he went to see the ganster Pipi, he looked into a mirror and for a moment he did not recognize himself; he thought he was someone else (*TTT,* 53). It was only after his allegorical death (a false death that transforms him) that Cué was able to see and recognize his other self (or himself as other) in the mirror. Aware of Cué's mythical otherness, Silvestre, the writer, explains that Cué had gone to the mirror "a mirarse en el espejo y a hacerse la raya de nuevo." "Se reconocía" (to see himself in the mirror and to part his hair, make a *raya* or mark on himself. He recognized his own self) (*TTT,* 428). Like the *Chambuto* for the Cuban *mayomberos,* the mirror in which Cué sees himself also reveals another invisible realm[306] in the text. This is the unspoken secret the texturn holds: the secret spoken only through the ritual juegos, plantes, or show, of a mythical language that, like the Abakuá's pantomine, articulates the inarticulable, the great gap between time and space, the visible and the invisible, memory and writing.

After Cué looks into the mirror during a liminal moment of inebriation he confesses to Silvestre, as if it were an echo of Eugene O'Neil: "No me miro para saber si estoy bien o mal, sino solamente para saber si soy. Si sigo ahí. No sea que haya otra persona dentro de mi piel . . . Si soy si sigo aquí. Sigo aquí. ¿Es un eco, un e Cué, Ekué?" (I don't look at myself in the mirror to see if I am okay or not, only to see if I am. If I'm still here. To make sure that no one else is under my skin . . . If I am, if I'm still here. I am still here. Is an echo, an eCué, Ekué) (*TTT,* 349). Later, following the same dialogue that covers the entire section of "Bachata," Silvestre says: "Debía verte el ombligo. Eres un robot de Cué." (You ought to look at your belly button. You are a Cué robot) (*TTT,* 434). Associating Cué now with Caribbean pre-Hispanic concept of death,[307] Silvestre confirms Cué's image on the other side of the mirror. Cué then replies: "Soy mi imagen en el espejo. Eucoinestra. Arsenio Cué en el idioma del espejo" (I am my image in the mirror. Eucoinestra. Arsenio Cué in the language of the mirror) (*TTT,* 400). The reiterated image of the mirror in this dialogue recontextualizes Cué in *TTT* in the realm of dreams and myths: the imaginary of popular Cuban culture. Those cultural symbols which in Lewis Carroll's *Alice in Wonderland* find epochal references in the figure of a rabbit, a walrus, a young girl, a queen of cards, the cat of Cheshire, in *TTT* find cultural codes unique to Cuban society that also represent the cultural depths of the subworlds of Havana *P.M.* documented. In *TTT,* like in the Afro-Cuban *Chambuto,* knowledge and truth are revealed by way of inversions that intimate the other side of the mirror: a nocturnal, codified, self-referential order of reading directed inward, to the Caribbean. In that order of reading, Silvestre, the writer, now echoing Hamlet, speaks of Lydia Cabrera's dream, and Cué follows: "—Hay más cosas entre el cielo y la tierra, mi querido Silvestre" (There are more things between heaven and earth, my dear Silvestre) (*TTT,* 422). Silvestre then recalls: "Dejé de sonreír. Cué estaba lívido, con la piel pegada al cráneo. Un pescado, recordé" (I quit smiling. Cué was livid, his skin clinging to his skull, A dead fish) (*TTT,* 422).

Consistent with his metaphoric role as the echo of the Voice of the mythical fish trapped in the drum-urn, Cué's ritual performance in the text is informed by his association with water. In the section of the novel titled "Bachata" (juego or game), Silvestre and Cué go inside a bar. Soon after, it begins to rain and Cué's car, a convertible, fills with water. During their rumba-like conversation, they notice a *raya* (a sting ray) swimming in a large aquarium. At first, Cué believes that the stingray is an *obispo* and explains that they, the stingray and the obispo, like sharks (and like Tanze) always die in captivity: "nature's absurd, a fish drowned" (*TTrappedT,* 363), says Silvestre. Cué replies that neither the sting ray, nor the obispo are fish. The seemingly nonsensical conversation romances again the idea that truth cannot be held captive. During this signifying conversation of double utterances that seems to last for hours, Cué reveals in a juego (bachata) of double meanings his association with the Afro-Cuban oracle, with the ritual shells or caracoles: "¡Mayito Trinidad! Fui un día a su casa a retratarlo, y me tiró los caracoles en una ceremonia secreta, a oscuras, en su cuarto en penumbras al mediodía con una velita alumbrando los cauris en una versión afrocubana de un ritual órfico y recuerdo los tres consejos que me dió como recuerdo [de] las leyendas, los secretos de la tribu decía él, africanas, cubanas ya, que me contó. Tres" (Mayito Trinidad! One day I went to his house to take a picture of him and he threw the divining cowries for me in a secret ceremony, in the dark, in his dark room at noon, with a candle to light the cowries, in an Afro-Cuban version of an Orphic ritual, and I remember his advice, three, he gave me, the legends, the secrets of the tribes, he said were Africans, already Cuban, he told me. Three) (*TTT,* 339). As if the secrets of the African tribes had been transformed into the secrets of Cuban society (secrets no longer African but now Cuban, pertaining to the realities of contemporary Cuban society), Silvestre and Cué talk about what for Cué is "El Tema" (The Theme) (*TTT,* 339), the hidden Theme of all of his conversations. A significant part of this taboo theme of which Cué speaks only in codes, or, as in "Bachata," during a liminal stage of intoxication, incorporates the dual significance of "El Sierra" in association with the politically charged "la Sierra" that surfaces in the conversation. Someone in the bar indicates to them with a gesture to keep their voices down (to be quiet: *callar*), Cué reacts:

> "—Ya en este país ni hablar se puede.
> —¿No quedamos en que no querías hablar de política?
> —Se sonrió. Se rió. Se puso serio
>
> [One can no longer speak in this country. . . .
> Did we not agree that you did not want to talk about politics?
> He smiled. He laughed. He looked serious] (*TTT,* 346)

Cué tells Silvestre that he is going to The Sierra Maestra and Silvestre understands that he wants to go to the club El Sierra. Cué refers here to the Mountains where Fidel Castro and his forces are fighting: "Me alzo . . . Me voy al monte" (I am taking arms. . . . I am going to the monte) (*TTT,* 347).

Cué's unspoken theme, politics, is associated here (in the political context of 1958) with resistance and defiance, themes of which one could not speak in 1961. Cué, drunk, assumes that the waiter is a spy for the government and signals Silvestre to be quiet: "Sssss. 33-33. ¿Otra Cábala? (responds Silvestre) . . . . . Sssss. 33-33. Un chivato" (Shshsh 33-33. Another one of your Cabalas? . . . Shshsh. 33-33. An Informer) (*TTT,* 348).

Cué then brings up the theme of deceit in politics as well as the need to keep silent: "—33-33. In disguise. They are devilishly clever. Classes with the Gestapo and the Berliner Ensemble. They're masters of duplicity and disguise. It's incredible" (*TTrappedT,* 376–77). Cué's political references

are unreliable due to his excessive drinking, but, at the same time, his inebriation allows him to enter the oneiric landscape of the subconscious, of
myths and mad-ness (liminality and resistance), of which he does not speak
when he is sober. Cué juxtaposes historical periods, establishing a relationship between pre- and post-revolutionary Cuba, when he associates thirty-
three, a number that during the presidency of Machado, and, later, the dictatorship of Fulgencio Batista, meant a *chivato,* a police informer, with the
Gestapo. Cué's temporal displacement establishes persecution as a common
denominator for both, the Cuba of the fifties (when political revolutionaries and Communists were persecuted), and a Stalinist post-revolutionary
Cuba[308] (when once again the same political censorship and persecution
that closed *Lunes de Revolución* became the order of the day). In this textual signifying *bachata* (juego), Silvestre asks Cué, alluding again to Carroll's *Alice in Wonderland* if he is not "tired of growing and growing and
getting smaller, and smaller, and of going up and down and running all over
the place, and whenever you go there are all these rabbits. . . . The rabbits
that talk and consult their watches, and organize everything and run everything. The rabbits of the (c)age we live in (*TTrappedT,* 379).

The reference here to Carroll's text, recontextualized to the rabbits "de
este tiempo" (*TTT,* 350) (of our times), or in Levine's translation, "the
(c)age we live in," establishes a dialogic relationship between the allegorical figure of the rabbit in *Alice in Wonderland* and Cuban politics in the
1958 and also in 1961, as if one moment were the double in the mirror of
the other. This is ultimately the "theme" always already central to Cué and
Silvestre's conversations; a theme always transformed into self-deferring
thematic fugues (*fuga,* as in an ontological and linguistic escape of the signifier always running away, as in the musical composition, a fugue, in
which two different themes chase each other), in Silvestre and Cué's rumba-
like contrapuntal conversations.

With puns, signifying play of words, and codified cultural references,
Silvestre and Cué's conversation leads to literature and to the silent taboo
theme in *TTT:* politics and freedom. In Cuba, says Cué, laughter is the sign
of the island: "Aquí siempre tiene uno que dar a las verdades un aire de
boutade para que sean aceptadas" (Here one always has to turn truths into
jokes for people to accept them) (*TTT,* 342). "Me sonreí. {Silvestre re-
members} La bebida devolvía a Cué a los orígenes. Ahora hablaba en el
dialecto popular de Códac y Eribó y Bustrófedon a veces" (I smiled. The
drinks returned Cué to his *origins.* He was speaking in the popular dialect
of Códac, Eribó, and sometimes Bustrófedon) (*TTT,* 342). When they finally leave the bar, Silvestre remembers: "Salgo y el mar, el estanque, es
otro espejo" (the sea, the water, is another mirror) (*TTT,* 350). There, a fisherman pulls out of the water an enormous ugly fish, "un monstruo marino"
(a marine monster) (*TTT,* 350). When Silvestre asks what kind of fish it is,

Cué answers: "Eso no es un pez. Es un pescado. Los peces como la gente cambian de nombre cuando se mueren" (That is not a fish. It is a fished fish. Fishes, like people, change their names when they die) (*TTT,* 351).

While contemplating the fish (dead or dying), Cué tells Silvestre to play "Sensemayá," Nicolás Guillén's poem in which performance, like the diablito dancer, is related to resistance, to the exorcism of evil forces: a poem inspired by the Afro-Cuban dance of killing the snake performed in Havana during "Día de Reyes." Silvestre describes the moment when Cué begins to carry a beat with his foot on the boards of the pier. A "Cuésnake," says Silvestre, and Cué responds: "¿No crees tú Silvestre, de verdad, que si uno supiera que su destino es ser pez muerto para siempre, toda una eternidad, cambiaría, trataría no de ser perfecto, pero sí de ser de otro modo?" (Don't you believe, Silvestre, really, that if one knew that one's destiny is to be a fish dead forever, for eternity, one would change, one would try to be not perfect, but something different?) (*TTT,* 352).

The playful analogy offered here between "Sensemayá" and Cué as "cuélebra" (*cué*snake), recalls Abakuá mythical anecdotes collected by Lydia Cabrera that describe Ekué as an elongated fish, like a snake. Cué now sees himself in the reflection of the water, as in the sacred *Chambuto* (mirror): in the oneiric-mythical underworld of culture. It is important to recall here that, for the Abakuá, water is the amniotic medium of its origin and existence, the space of the spirit in which its identity is based. For the secret fraternity of the Ekpe, in Africa, the fish was a symbol of prosperity and life, honor and power.[309] According to Efor legends, the Efik, and the Efor (the first to possess the great secret), were fishing villages; and the Ekoi, meaning "those belonging to the fish," were the Patriarchs of the Abakuá.[310]

Surrounded by water, and due to its geographic shape and position in the Caribbean, Cuba has been compared to a crocodile, a sacred ritual animal that Abakuá *Briches* and Efik place in the potencias and whose ñáñigo name is *Mokómbe,*[311] the guardian of the "secret."[312] Swimming, like the island, in the Caribbean ocean, the image of the Abakuá guardian is charged with a sense of political defiance. This is the image of an island-cocodrile that informs Nicolás Guillén's poem "El Caribe." In this association with water, the ocean that surrounds the island of Cuba, and the Antilles, is Yemayá, Virgin of Regla, a deity worshipped by the Abakuá Efik of Havana as Okande, their patron saint.[313] For the Abakuá, water is the space where life originates, the mother. "Nacemos del agua y al agua volvemos" (we are born from the water and we return to the water)[314] an informant explained to Lydia Cabrera. Since for the Abakuá the element of the spirit world is water,[315] it is believed that the spirit of the dead ecobio returns to the *Fokondó,* the sacred place in the mythical river *Oddan,* the mythical space of the Abakua Ekois, to be reunited with Tanze and

Sikán.[316] In a complex explanation that encompasses the relationship of the sacred drum to water as mother, the Sese Eribó (sometimes syncretized as the *chalis* in the Catholic Mass),[317] is conceived as Mother Nature,[318] and, in Cuba, it is associated with the Afro-Cuban Monte. Abakuá offerings, says Cabrera, are taken to the monte, and to the river,[319] for it is in this combination of earth and water that the forces (voice) of the Great Mystery are incarnated in the fish Tanze and is found by the woman mother Sikán (earth). Symbolically, the Great Mystery, as conceived by the Abakuá, finds a metaphor in Cuba in the national drink, the *mojito*, says Silvestre: "metáfora de Cuba. Agua, vegetación, azúcar (prieta), ron y frío artificial" (a metaphor for Cuba. Water, vegetation, [dark] sugar, rum, and artificial cold) (*TTT*, 321).

In *TTT*, water is associated also with music (remembering that the *Sese Eribó*, the sacred drum, "is" Mother Nature), and music, as in all plantes or ritual pantomine, is associated with the theatrical representation of a spiritual reality, the liminal invisible space of the Secret Voice. This association in *TTT* renders Tropicana: the famous Cuban nightclub in Havana that opens the novel as "performance," a show, a public textual plante, and in which culture and language are the main "stars" of the textual spectacle. The codified signifying role of Tropicana in *TTT*'s play of inversions, surfaces again in the text when Livia speaks on the phone with a friend, Bebe, and the later misunderstands Livia, and thinks that Livia said Tropicama instead of Tropicana (*TTT*, 43). With this humorous misunderstanding, the text intimates, with the slippage of the signifier, the sensuality and sexuality of the world depicted in *TTT* (already implicit in the encounter of the elongated fish, Tanze, with Sikán, at the river). However, such "mishearing" also reiterates the signifying play of the text in which one thing always means another. In this case, the slippage is a reminder that in the secret language of the ñáñigos, the word Kamá means "to speak,"[320] as in *Kamá ribot*, a term that would mean the spirit speaks. Silvestre's play of words when he calls Cué "Kamacué" (*TTT*, 367) is not an incoherent play of sounds/phonemes. It is another textual "clue" (*clave*) to Cué's ritual role in the text's juegos, that would render the meaning: "[E]Cué speaks." At the same time, the humorous misunderstanding of a phoneme that produces Tropicama, a made up word semantically fitting to the sexual connotations of the novel, renders "tropic(k)ama," or "Tropic *kamá*." Thus, the implied meaning, the "tropic speaks" (of serious matters masked as silence, and nonsense), indirectly establishes a dialogue between the novel and the Caribbean discourse of resistance and of the affirmation of Africa as "source." The hidden term (Tropic *kamá*) intimates the codified revelation of a secret the texts holds in the textual gaps of its own ritual/linguistic representations, between the real and the oneiric, orality and writing, entrapment and freedom.

IV

In its juegos, *TTT* establishes an association between Cuban[321] popular culture, water (the sacred environment of the spirit),[322] and music. With this trilogy, the text represents the amniotic element of the Cuban *Ekoi:* the voice remembered in the urn-text. It is in this amniotic, nocturnal, private underworld of the Havana's nightclubs where contemporary Cuban popular music emerged. Códac, the "tiger" photographer, feels that when he enters the nightclub El Sierra, he enters a giant aquarium, and they are all fishes "me zambullo en la música" (*TTT,* 273) (I dive in the music (*TTT,* 278). El Sierra for Codac is a microcosmic fishbowl, a contained ocean, in which La Estrella, a textual avatar of the Abakuá Okande, is the monstrous black whale of the deep tropical waters, a Cuban Moby-Dick. Like Melville's Captain Ahab's obsession with the white whale, so is Códac obsessed with La Estrella, with the mystical attraction of her voice, and with the ontological inquiries surrounding her existence.

In that aquatic underworld of Cuban popular music, the mulatto Eribó "discovers" Cuba (*TTT,* 91), a mulatto woman whose name was really Gloria Pérez, but to whom Eribó gives the stage name of Cuba Venegas. Different from La Estrella, whose sublime beauty is the magic of her voice, and of her freedom to improvise, Cuba, or "Cubita la bella," as her fans call her, offers only the physical appearance of a beautiful body. Códac explains in a comment of double utterances: "quien ve a Cuba la ama, pero quien la oye, y la conoce, nunca puede amarla" (anyone who sees Cuba falls in love with her, but anyone who hears and listens to her can never love her again) (*TTT,* 299). In his signifying play of references Códac articulates the cultural gap between the cultural soul (Afro-Cuban voice-music) and the visual body or landscape (her staged outer appearance) of a mulatto Cuba. It also articulates the gap between Cuba's African rhythms and farsical discourses on the nation. La Estrella's voice is the soul of the island, like Tanze for the Abakuá, a "metaphysical monster" (*TTT,* 281), a "cosmic phenomenon" (*TTT,* 84), swimming free at night, in the sacred, ancestral, aquatic subworlds of Havana's amniotic musical underworld, but a poor maid during the day. In that aquatic oneiric realm, Códac finds the same free spirit of La Estrella in Eribó's bongos: Cuba's "sacred scriptures" (*TTT,* 281). In *TTT,* as for the Abakuá, water must find its balance in earth; thus, the writer, Silvestre (a name that means wild flora or monte), whose last name is also, significantly, Isla (island), provides the earthly element of the ritual duality water-earth so important for Abakuá rituals. The writer in *TTT* is associated also with woman: the mother, the island-monte, Sikán, Laura (and all of them, like the writer, are associated with the dangerous act of telling).

Through La Estrella, the musical phenomenon of Havana nightclubs, the text reenacts the story of the mythical Abakuá fish inscribed in Cuban popular culture. This is the great Cuban fish-story of Abakuá myths, the story reenacted in the Cuban Supreme Theater with each initiation. Such Cuban fish story dialogues in *TTT* with two other great literary giant fish stories told by two other giants of world literature: Melville's *Moby-Dick* and Ernest Hemingway's *The Old Man and The Sea*. The later is a novel that takes place in a coastal fishing village near Havana. It is the story of an old Cuban fisherman who, after many weeks of "bad luck," goes deep into the ocean alone and catches a gigantic fish, but sharks devour it before the old man reaches the shore.[323] Only the skeleton of the fish remained to support his story. Like Hemingway's mythopoetic fish, and like the Cuban mythopoeia Tanze, La Estrella's voice is left only to memory: after her body metaphorically is eaten by sharks. All that remains of this Cuban "fenómeno cósmico" (cosmic phenomenon) (*TTT*, 84), is the echo of a bad recording of her voice. Her death leaves only "el sonido de la tumba," (the sound of the tomb) (*TTT*, 115), in the memory of Cuba's magnificent "black whale." Like the Havana the text "imagines," La Estrella takes with her, to her death, the uncanny mystery of her Cuban voice. Just like Tanze, who dies in captivity when removed from the sacred waters, La Estrella also dies when she leaves the aquatic subworld of her musical element.

In counterpoint to La Estrella (who leaves), Cuba Venega, metaphorically "Cubita la bella" (Cuba the beautiful) chooses as the repetitive theme for her songs, "me voy" (I am leaving), also Cué's obsessive theme. As a textual metaphorical echo of Ekué, Cué fears death and is obsessed with the thought of "leaving." Silvestre explains that Cué is always critical of the climate, of the tropics (*TTT*, 100). In this "sad" tropical island, Cué feels trapped, like the captive voice of Ekué in the drum-urn.

Códac, on the other hand, finds Cuba's saving grace in its "blackness." For Códac, the African Cuban spirit of its African legacy is embodied in the "cosmic" "black whale" (*TTT*, 64) of La Estrella, in her African, now Cuban, rhythm and freedom of expression. He gives thanks to Father Las Casas for bringing Africans to Cuba, because in so doing he saved Cuba: Africans had saved Cuba. "You saved this country" (*TTT*, 65). Yet, what Códac sees in La Estrella is not only the legacy of an African rhythm, but her defiance toward imposed structures, like the defiance of the Abakuá, and of other Afro-Cuban groups, to acculturation, and to extinction. What Códac praises in La Estrella is her resistance to the imposition of any musical structures. She never sang accompanied by musical instruments because they would limit her ability to break away from musical norms in order to create something new and different out of something old.[324] This is the same type of free expression Eribó finds in Beny Moré's playful resistance to musical strictures. Beny, Eribó explains, "hace un círculo de música feliz en la cuadratura rígida del ritmo cubano" (makes a circle of joyful music out of the rigid square of Cuban rhythm) (*TTT*, 92). Beny, in his *sones,* "con su voz, se burlaba de la prisión cuadrada, planeando la melodía por sobre el ritmo . . ." (with his voice {songs}, he made fun of the prison of the square, making the melody glide over the rhythm) (*TTT,* 92). Like La Estrella and Beny Moré, and like Bustrofedon's unrestricted mode of speaking, *TTT* is a text that breaks away from the strictures of writing, literary genders, and the canon, "circling" the square of writing, resisting the strictures of censorship imposed on the text, as on *P.M.* and Afro-Cuban beliefs; taking the old and making something new out of it, like Cabrera Infante does with *P.M.*

With this same sense of experimental freedom, of running away from strictures, from captivity, textual reality in *TTT* is fluid, misleading, like a deceitful ñangalia, always already intimating ontological and epistemological questions about rhizomatic complexities pertaining knowledge and freedom. An example of such fluidity is the story of Mr. Campbell and his walking cane. In this anecdote, in which the text plays also with the wisdom of the Afro-Cuban Patakí, Mr Campbell, a North American tourist in Havana, buys a cane from a street vendor. Later, he sees a poor man carrying what he perceives to be "his" cane. After accusing the man of stealing it, and taking it away from him with the help of a policeman, he returns to the hotel to find out that he had forgotten his cane in his room. The carvings in the walking cane are, not surprisingly in a Cuban context, those of Elegua, owner of the crossroads, the orisha who speaks backwards, the one who inverts reality, the Supreme divine Trickster. This story of self-deceit and false certainty offers an allegory of the juegos of the novel, of its signifying riddles, and of its revelatory ritual codes. In this sense, *TTT* articulates through codified narrative juegos, the *Bustromorfosis* (Bustromorphosis) of reality (*TTT,* 220), in which serious matters are spoken as jokes (*TTT,* 342). Like Elegua, in the anecdote about Mr. Campbell, the central voice absently present in *TTT,* the voice that causes havoc on the signified, is the voice of Bustrófedon.

The anecdote about Mr. Campbell and his misplaced cane is a reminder that the text is a ritual "performance," a juego that begins with, and as a "show" in the famous Cuban nightclub, Tropicana, where cubanía is placed on the stage as "performance." The secret textual performance, however, takes place at another space, in a second, but primary order of reading. Like in the Abakuá secret Cuarto Fambá, *TTT* offers in the space of its pages another "show" or plante that takes place in the invisible, silent realms of the cultural imaginary, where the writer finds a national mythology once African, now Cuban. The same reader, invited to participate complicitly in the textual juegos by the MC in Tropicana, also is taken, unaware, to another secret performance that takes place in the inner sanctum of the text, where the text's secret juegos take place. In the maskarade performance on the stage in Tropicana, the MC functions like the Abakuá diablito dancer of colonial "Día de Reyes," whose gestures and movements are signifying signs informing of another order of reading. In this sense, the bilingualism with which the MC speaks to the audience announces that, performance, in *TTT,* is a double performance in which the public "show" also "reenacts," behind doors, in the back room, an *isaroko:*[325] a codified ritual, nocturnal, secret, Abakuá *enrolló,* a ñáñigo wake for the departed.

In that performance that takes place in the inner sanctum of the text, after Bustrofedon's death, his friends find the recording of nine versions of the death of Trotsky, narrated by nine different Cuban writers, or Ekoi of Cuban literature; among them, Lydia Cabrera and Alejo Carpentier.[326] The recordings, however, are actually Bustrófedon's parody of these writers. The last one is a parody of Nicolás Guillén's poetic style and theme, with the title "Elegía por Jacques Mornard (en el cielo de Lecumberri)," a reference also (in the context of the double) to Jorge Luis Borges's "Pierre Menard." Bustrófedon's textual parody of Guillén ends: "Stalin!/ Great Captain!/ May Shango protect you/ and Jemaja watch over you." (*TTrappedT,* 277). Abakuá funeral rites known as *enlloró, rolló, enyoró,* or *ñampe* inform this parody, in the same way that they inform Guillén's poem "Velorio de Papá Montero:" a eulogy and wake for an Abakuá cultural hero, Papá Montero. In the Abakuá enrolló, the ritual is performed backward, thus every performance, every drawing, or marking, and liturgy is done in the reverse order of the initiation, since the object of the ritual is to release the bond created during the ecobio's initiation with Ekué.[327] This ritual inversion for the dead recalls Bustrofedon's drawing of inverted praying hands. Remembering the political conditions at the time in which Cabrera Infante is writing the novel, the text's parody of the death of Trotsky is another eulogy for the dead spirit of cubanía.

Guillén's style in *TTT* is a homage to Guillén as a Cuban Ekoi, a literary ecobio, but, at the same time, it establishes an association between Papá Montero and the Russian leader, Trotsky, another Marxist ecobio, murdered by his rival, Stalin. Such association is a reminder that also Papá Montero had been assassinated, in a Cuban context, by a rival Abakuá *potencia* in the same way that Trotsky had been assassinated by a brother of the same Marxist order (ecobio), for being an ideological rival (not much different than the story of the conflict between Efik and Efor about the possession of a greater truth). The significance in this story of treason may be that Trotsky's assassination is the model of power that makes Stalin a "Great Captain," and that Guillén's work was at the service of the same revolutionary government that censored *P.M.* and that closed down *Lunes de Revolución.* Furthermore, Trotsky's death is a story of dissidence, persecution, and death as punishment. As a bridge between the present and the past (the political system under which Cabrera Infante writes, and the vernacular culture he imagines in the text), it is quite fitting in *TTT*'s *Brus-*

trofloresta (monte-oracle), to stage a political enlloró for the Marxist ecobio assasinated for being a dissident: since the reasons for his assassination
are related to the same reasons *P.M.* and *Lunes de Revolución* were assassinated. If Bustrófedon, as his name suggest, is a way of reading an oracle
in two different and opposite directions, the enigma of the story of the death
of Trotsky, masked in the voice of Cuban writers, tells in one order of reading, what the other order of reading conceals. In this play of doubles and
mirrors, Guillén would have had to praise Stalin, since he was an official
voice for the Revolution. Yet, the text is not Guillén's writing; it is Bustrófedon's parody of Guillén. For this reason, this text, like Bustrófedon's
name suggests, must be read in its reverse, on the other side of the mirror.
Thus, at the end of Bustrófedon's recording, the echo of his voice disappears, and the voice of others can be heard: the voice of Silvestre, Rine
Leal, popular songs, drumming, Cué and Silvestre's discussions, as well as
recitals and parts of Radio Soap Operas (*TTT,* 257–58).

The fact that the recorded voice is overlapped by many other voices including popular songs, bongós, radio soap operas, and other sounds of popular culture, alerts the reader to the collective nature of the dead friend's
voice as the artificial echo of a culture and a time trapped in the recording.
However, Bustrófedon's voice, like La Estrella's voice, like Tanze's voice,
cannot be trapped, recorded, or written. Both, Bustrófedon and La Estrella,
like the sacred voice of Tanze, are the uncanny "phenomenoms" of the
tropic monte of Havana. Like Tanze and Sikán, they both die to leave the
echo of their voices in the memory of characters who, like the Abakuá ecobios, are the keepers of the knowledge of their existence: a cultural secret
closely tied to the text's play of language and codes.[328] *TTT* is a text in
which, as Roberto González Echeverría points out, "language is written on
the brink of its own extinction, and the past is an evocation that gains reality only as support for the present."[329]

V

In the Abakuá plante, the Great Mystery, the "secret," reveals itself at a certain given moment of the juego in the Cuarto Fambá, when Ekué is played
(*fragayado*). Likewise, in *TTT,* there is a given moment, in "Bachata"
(juego), when Cué (until then also a tumba like Eribó), reveals his "secret"
to Silvestre: that he was the first to "possess" Vivian, a confession that casts
a shadow on Vivian's earlier confession to Eribó. In the same conversation,
Silvestre also reveals his secret to Cué: that he is going to marry the only
woman Cué really desired, Laura Díaz. The confession (possession of a
woman) brings about a schism between the rival twins as it did between
the Efor and the Efik. In the context of Abakuá brotherhood, Silvestre has
broken the sacred pledge of never taking a fraternity brother's woman, and,

at the same time, he has obtained Cue's secret, highlighting the role of the writer as the keeper of the secret knowledge trapped in the text-urn.

Silvestre Isla's ritual role in the novel as "twin" of Cué, the *contrario* [contrary, opposite], echoes the way Cabrera Infante refered to Virgilio Piñera as "a true contrary," "a master and a nobody."[330] It also recalls the role of the *Mpegó* in Abakuá societies[331] as the secretary or writer of the group, the one who makes the magic drawings or markings (rayas), and the one who keeps the sacred texts. Without the Mpegó's drawings, the plante could not take place. Lydia Cabrera points out that the Mpegó is the most important position in the potencia, and he is considered to be the most serious ecobio of the society.[332] The job of the Mpegó is to know and to hold the secret, to keep silence, a role that establishes a symbolic association between the sacred drum and writing (Mpegó is also the name of one of the Abakuá drums). For the Abakuá, ritual writing is the key to the magic of the ceremony, as Isabel and Jorge Castellanos explain: "todo debe ser *rayado* con la tiza amarilla de la vida (o la blanca de muerte, según los casos) . . . Todo ha de estar mágicamente vitalizado de sobrenaturalidad. Sin esas rayas mágicas no habría sacropotencia, todo seguiría pasivo e indiferente . . . El Ekué no se manifestaría y la liturgia sería vana" (Every thing must be marked with the yellow chalk of life {or the white of death, accordingly} . . . Every thing must be magically revitalized with the supernatural. Without the magic markings there would not be sacred power, every thing would continue to be passive and indifferent . . . *Ekué* would not manifest itself and the ritual would be in vain).[333] The Mpegó's drawings, or *anaforuanas,* create the link between the ecobios and the Great Mystery, the Great Beyond. He is the priest of symbols and rubrics.[334] In that role, like Eribó, whose music transports him to the unspeakable in the solitude of his drums, Silvestre Isla, the writer, once in his apartment at the end of the novel, alone in the solitude of his memories, recalls a time and a life that ended with the revelation of a secret, and, subsequently, with Cué's departure (*fuga*), not unlike the departure of Ekué at the end of the plante. At the end of the ceremony, the echo of the voice in the drum goes back to the monte from where it is summoned again at the beginning of the next ceremony (in *TTT,* the next reading).

The bond between Cué and Silvestre (voice and writing) ends with Silvestre's revelation (as the end of their verbal performance). Such revelatory act coincides with the moment in which the pantomime (ritual and text) comes to an end, just as the day and the text are waning. At this final "fading" moment, Silvestre's last thoughts become a meditation on death, a wake for a time past, and a litany for that which is gone, that which in a way Cué has taken with him in his *auto* (car) *fuga* (fugue/escape). All that is left for the writer, Silvestre, when the textual plante is over and Cué leaves, is the oneiric remembrance of something that was, and no longer is (like an echo, Ekué). Such oneiric presence continues to be relived, as if in a ritual, in the reenactment of the juego, in the collective memory of the writer, and in the imaginary act of reading/writing. Like the narrative in *TTT,* Abakuá plantes of initiation, are a staged drama[335] in which the voice gone is remembered through its "performance." The plante begins at night (as does *TTT* in Tropicana), and ends the next day at dusk.[336] As if he were an *abanekue,* at the end of the textual juego, Silvestre enters the gap of night, at dusk, alone in his own apartment, alone with his thoughts, like the initiate who enters the realm of the invisible Great Beyond at the end of the plante.

Informed by Abakuá plantes, in which the act of remembrance through ritual makes present in the collective memory a secret that cannot be revealed to anyone outside of the group, *TTT* intimates an unspoken secret whose revelation can bring about daring consequences. In *TTT,* as in Abakuá juegos, death is the ultimate form of callar (keep silence). Thus, at the end of the textual performance, at dusk, Silvestre, alone, and in silence, looks out the balcony of his apartment, and sees the illuminated sign of a funeral home, Funeraria Caballeros. At the end of his litany on silence, Silvestre evokes the Great Beyond (*TTT,* 444).

Death, in *TTT,* as in Silvestre's final meditations, is a form of leaving (fuga/escape), as heralded in Cuba Venega's theme, "me voy," La Estrella's exile and death, Bustrófedon's death, and Cué's theme and final fuga (both a fugue and the act of running away). Death is also a trope for a secret voice whose performance is associated with woman, mother, sacrifice, and with the trappings of ideology and power. For the brothers of the leopard society in Africa, and for the ñáñigo ecobios in Cuba, the great mystery appears first to a woman. Such unspeakable knowledge, outside of the hegemony of the secret brotherhood, makes woman dangerous, but, at the same time, associates woman with a space of origin, the source of being, and with the divine space of the Ekoi. In other words, it is through woman that the great beyond speaks. Woman, Sikán (possessor of certain hidden divine knowledge), and the great mystery are bonded together. While the act of telling, or confessing, in a woman is dangerous to male hegemony, it is only woman who can bring back the Voice, and it is through woman that invisible truths are revealed. Before each Abakuá plante begins, the voice of Tanze and Sikán must be brought back from the monte, to the drum, to the Cuarto Fambá. This is a role assigned in the ritual pantomime to the executioner, the Ekueñon.[337] Without the spirit/voice of Sikán, Ekué does not speak.

In *TTT,* the voice of woman, rejected and scorned, appears intermittently throughout the text in association with madness and deceit; always excluded from male juegos. Recalling that in the ritual reenactment of the immolation of Sikán, a goat takes her place, Cué expresses his opinion of women as liers: "Vacas, chivas, animales sin alma. Una especie inferior" (Cows, goats, animals without souls. An inferior specie) (*TTT,* 432). Significantly, it is Silveltre, the writer (like the Mpegó, who controls the pantomine reality with drawings, the language of signs), who questions Cué's claim: "Not all of them. Your mother isn't a cow" (*TTrappedT,* 468). The intimated suggestion here is that the secret, which the text-urn holds, and of which it speaks through codes, is associated with woman, mother, and with liminal spaces of knowledge, silence, and mad-ness. In *TTT,* "motherland," sacrificed like Sikán,[338] is the victim accused of "treason" for being dangerous to the patriarchal hegemony. It is not gratuitous then that a text about treason, silence, and death would begin and end with the voice of an anonymous woman.

The novel begins with the voice of a woman who, in a signifying play between confession and deceit, reveals a secret of which the text only speaks in Bustrófedon-like riddles. Her monologues, seemingly directed to a psychoanalyst, intermittently appear in the novel, suggesting, at the end, that this is the voice of Laura: the woman Silvestre tells Cué he is going to marry, and the same Laura whose name comes to him when he is alone in his room, at the end of the novel, and has enigmatic oneiric memories of a girl child named Laura, and sea lions, "morsa: morcillas: sea-morsels. Tradittori":[339] (morsels, *morcillas,* sea-morsels. *Tradittori*) (*TTT,* 445). Remembering that Lydia Cabrera's prophetic dream was also about a rising sun, dawn (*alba*), the self-referencial play of the text in Silvestre's imagination, in which the writer's dream is the text itself, the signifying "clave del alba" (clue/key of dawn) recalls Laura, a name associated with dawn (alba) and with 'glow' or spirit (aura): (*l(au(ro)ra*) (dawn).[340] After all, like the adventures of Carroll's Alice, the complex inter-self-referenciality of the textual pantomine happens only in the writer's dream world, the imaginary world of fiction, the inverted side of the mirror. It is not a textual coincidence then that when Silvestre drifts into the oneiric world of his thoughts, his reflections are immediately followed, in the chronology of the text, by the psychoanalytic monologue of a woman's thoughts about the ambiguity of reality, highlighting, as Suzanne Jill Levine points out, that in *TTT* "there are no originals, only translations. Memory is a text translated into another text."[341]

Critics have failed to note that the notion of treason, in translations, is also an echo in *TTT* of Jules Michelet's *Histoire de la Révolution française.* This textual reference seems to be a reminder for the reader of the political context in which *Tres tristes tigres* is written: a historical moment that mirrors the conflicts, and dialectic inversions (treason of ideals) of the French Revolution.[342] Such act of mirroring a similar political context, in which freedom is always sacrified to a greater dominant truth, is once again spoken (told) in the codes of a secret language, irrationally metaphorical, in the voice of a woman. Hence, the novel ends with the voice of yet another annonymous, demented, woman. In the textual play of mirrors, where things are themselves and also the opposite of what they seem to be (like Silvestre and Cué), *contrarios* (contraries), this insane monologue at the end of the novel appears to be the same one Silvestre transcribed years before at a park. Silvestre tells Cué that it was like a meeting of just one person, Hyde Park style. He thought that her repetitive monologue was full of symbolisms, and the third time he heard it, he copied what she was saying (*TTT,* 299–300).

The signifying voice of madness, articulated by a woman's voice, brings the novel to a closure, intimating in the trappings of the irrational, the echo of another secret voice in *TTT*'s *Bustrofloresta.* Recalling the role of the Mpegó in Abakuá potencias, as the secretary and keeper of the secret, Silvestre is the writer, like the Mpegó, who transcribes (then loses, and finds again) the repetitive words of the insane woman (words that were so meaningful to him): protesting against persecution, against monkeys that persecute her, against the imposition of unjust laws, against those in power and their savagery (*TTT,* 451). The madwoman repeats **"ya no puedo más"** (I cannot stand it any longer), and ends her monologue: "me saca las tripas el mondongo para ver qué color tiene ya no se puede más" (He [the monkey] is taking my inners out to see what color they are no one can take this any longer) (*TTT,* 451).

The woman's repetitive discourse speaks of an unspeakable secret: a certain incoherent truth masked by the performance of in-sanity. Allegorically sacrificed like Sikán, the woman takes refuge in a park (where she no longer feels without air), outside a situation of entrappment she rejects. With the act of "telling," she resists a situation that wants to entrap her, however, she knows that such act may have dire consequences. The seemingly incoherent words of this mad woman, whose revelations are "symbolic" for Silvestre, can only be heard, like the many voices of the text, in the silence of memory, of words the writer transcribes (after listening to her words three times). The woman's voice communicates the notion of a situation in which she feels coerced and betrayed by anonymous "others" she describes as *monos* (monkeys or mindless imitators).[343] Those monos want to impose their beliefs and laws on her. She wants to get away from them, as in another variation of Cuba's theme: "I am leaving." The significance of her words for Silvestre is that she creates a discourse of resistance and rebellion, through riddles and euphemisms, in which a monstrous reality created by reason seems to be the cause for her mad-ness. Yet, in *TTT*'s *Bustrofloresta* (monte), where the written word must be read in opposite directions, from the other side of the mirror, madness then must be the voice of reason, of sanity: her (in)sanity.

The mad woman in the park says that she is running away from an oppressive, stagnating, *locus (non)amenus* (like a cimarrón) toward the "aire puro" (fresh air) of the freedom she seeks in the open air of a city park. She finds freedom outdoors, in a park that ironically is in ruins, where the monos[344] (monkeys) cannot impose on her what she cannot accept. Significantly, the woman's last words are also the last words (the act of telling as a mode of resistance against injustice and domination) with which the novel ends: "ya no se puede más" (cannot stand it any longer). The phrase was a popular expression of political dissatisfaction in Cuba during the Machado regime, and, later, during Batista's dictatorship, to express a desperate political condition. In her in-sanity, the mad (angry) woman intimates that the monos are confusing one thing with another, unable to understand the differences in which cultural identity is based. Thus they must repress (sacrifice) what they consider dysfuntional in order to create and mantain the hegemony of power. Perhaps, like Sikán, the mad/in-sane woman knows a truth for which she must be excluded. Read from this inverted perspective, as the "symbolic" monologue of mad-ness voiced by a woman "in-sane," she reveals a situation similar to the one that led to the confiscation of *P.M.* and the closing of *Lunes de Revolución.* In this sense, *TTT*'s dialogic relationship with the *Satyricon,* as Cabrera Infante "reveals,"[345] can be found not only in the structure of the novel, but also in its criticism of a sociopolitical condition in Rome during Nero's reign, recontextualized to fit the writer's own experiences in pre- and also post-revolutionary Cuba.

If political domination and injustice is the hidden secret in *TTT,* madness and in-sanity in the mad woman's monologue reveals that politics, a "taboo theme" for Cué, according to Silvestre, is also a hidden discourse in Bustrófedon's juegos. Among the recordings he left of distorted and incomplete parodies, a nonsensical song in "tropical rhythm" (like *TTT*) stands out, in which he transforms José Martí's poem "Los zapaticos de rosa" (Small pink shoes) into "Los hachacitos de rosa" (small pink ax blows). Martí's text is about the kindness of a rich girl who goes for a walk on the beach, she sees a poor sick girl who is barefoot, and gives her her new pink shoes. Bustrófedon's nonsensical transformations of Martí's poem renders: "Váyala fiña di Viña/ deifel Fader fidel fiasco/ falla mimú psicocastro/ alfú mar sefú más phinas" (*TTT,* 210), which, when read aloud renders: "Fader Fidel fiasco/ falla mi músico Castro/ al fumar se fuma [e]spinas)" (Father Fidel fiasco/ my musician Fidel errs; with the possible reading of also "my psychocastro errs"/when he smokes, he smokes thorns).[346] Códac, who is the narrator in this section, explains that the game of singing all the possible variations of the names of the people they knew, was a "juego secreto" (secret game) that Bustrófedon further re-represents with the inverted gesture of two hands together in prayer exposing the palms of the hands outward. It is through these ritual juegos of inverted meanings, and signifying transformations, numbers, and palindromes, that the text reconstructs and reiterates the absent presence of Bustrófedon, the voice oracle whose memories and echoes construct the text's silence, its defiance, fear of entrapment, and its "mad" cry for freedom. Bustrofedon's last revelatory juegos take place during the Last Supper which the "tigers" share with their Lord of the Word, Bustrófedon, a Cristic-Legbá of the crosswords, who can alter reality with the magic of a word, inverts reality, and makes time travel backward: the transformer, the mediator, and, like Eleguá, the voice that speaks in the oracle: the text. Bustrófedon, as center of the *Bustrofloresta* that is *TTT* (the sign of higher ground/monte Golgotta: *TTT*), suggests a Christic cruxifiction, or as William Siemens notes: a "human being who became the word," who "died as signified" to be "reborn as signifier."[347] From the perspective of Cuban popular mythology, Boustrófedon proposes a metaphor for the writer, and for the voice of the cultural ancestors, like the Ekoi, Sikán, Tanze (like Virgilio Piñera in Cuba), destined to die due to plays of power and ideology, and to remain as faint echoes in Cuba literature, trapped in the texts, like Sese Eribó, or Ekué.

It is only after Bustrófedon's death that Cué, Códac, and Silvestre find out that Bustrófedon's way of speaking in puns and in a constant transformation of the language (a mode of speaking already inscribed in their own voices) was a pathological dysfunction. His illness, however, made Bustrófedon's language similar to the language of the Afro-Cuban oracles. His speech in *TTT* seems to be only a memory in the space of the imaginary, like Ekué's echo-memory of Tanze. Bustrófedon is orality and oracle. Hence, he did not leave anything written, and the only echo of his recorded voice blended into other voices and sounds. Even his personal confessions were blank, empty pages.[348] Like Tanze, Bustrófedon's unique and mysterious language dies of a physical cause that, ultimately, the doctor's explanation cannot fully explain. In fact, the doctor's reasons for operating further confuses the uncanny mystery of Bustrófedon's way of speaking, in the same way that the reality entrapped in the mirror, the *Chambuto,* cannot be explained through reason or science. The reader may conclude that, if for Bustrófedon the final and ultimate dysfunction was death, a death to which he was destined as soon as the doctor offered to fix his problem, it is because the text's own juego, own play of transformations, is centered around the dysfunction of the structures of political power. His death is the result of a tyranny of reason that refuses to accept differences.

The surgeon opened Bustrófedon's skull to understand his anomaly, and to eliminate his dysfunction in order to "normalize him," but he killed him in the process. Bustrófedon's problem, the doctor explained, was "an anomaly produced by a specific pathology, which in its last stages dissociated the cerebral function from the symbolism of thinking by means of speech" (*TTrappedT,* 232). However, remembering that Bustrofedon's dysfunction is related to speech, and speech in *TTT* voices the echoes of the departed voices of cubanía, it can be argued that in *TTT* the voices of pre-revolutionary Cuba, seen from the ideology of the revolutionary government, are social dysfunctions that must be eradicated, an idea Zoé Valdés reiterates in her novel *Querido primer novio* (1999). From this perspective, the scientific medical operation of Bustrófedon's brain suggests an exegesis of language, a scientific intervention into the unspeakable: the uncanny of oracles, myths, and dreams in the cultural imaginary, a cultural poetics that cannot be understood through science and reason. Bustrófedon's speech and death suggest that the invisible cannot be trapped, in the same way that truth and knowledge cannot be confined. Tanze dies in captivity, Christ at the cross, and Bustrófedon dies on the operating table, and yet, the echo of their voices continues to affect friends and believers. Following *TTT*'s juegos, from the inverse side of the mirror, the text offers the reader another and different justification for Bustrófedon's death. From the perspective of the tigers, the doctor's pathological justification was: "el diganóstico encubridor del crimen perfecto, . . . la coartada médica," (the diagnosis to cover up the perfect crime, . . . a medical excuse) (*TTT,* 223), because what he wanted to do was to find out the reason for "aquellas transformaciones maravillosas" (the marvelous transformations (*TTT,* 223) in Bustrófedon's playful speech.

TTT is a textual Rhapsody[349] as Cabrera Infante claimed, but it is a Rhapsody whose melodies are superimposed to the rhythm of the island, to its Afro-Cuban rhythms: ñáñigo drums, as well as the popular cultural rhythm of local memories and ritual codes. González Echeverría points out that *TTT* "is a wake"[350] for a bygone era. And, in fact, the text is an Abakuá wake, or *enlloró* for the cultural Ekoi, represented in the text through the performance of writing, and of reading. In the Abakuá *enlloró* for a dead ecobio, Lydia Cabrera explains, the adepts sing: "Eribó ribó ribó ribó Yuánsa ribó ¡aé! Eribó consagra al consagrado con lo Divino" (Eribó consacrate the Divine),[351] and the dead is always properly marked (*rayado*) with magic signs (*rayas*) that can guide him to the great beyond, from where it can also return to partake of the ceremonies of the living. The corpse must be taken backward (reading in an opposite direction), since the dead no longer can travel forward.[352] However, in *TTT*'s play of inversions, such a wake also recalls the pantomime of initiation, or *rompimiento* (rupture/break). In other words, on the inverted side of the mirror, *TTT*'s enlloró also proposes its opposite, a pantomime of initiation to another reality that is the secret other side of the mirror, to a truth that cannot be spoken of, a truth that the text intimates for those who understand its codified language. For such initiatory transformation, a ritual death is also required; the reader, like the rayado, breaks with the past and is transported to an alter reality (a different identity), through the revelation of a certain codified secret expressed by magic signs, hermetic language, and symbolic drawings, which the Mpegó, the writer, makes. Initiation, the moment when the simulacrum of Sikán's sacrifice is performed, in the secret enclosed space of the Cuarto Famba, and the roaring of the great mystery is heard, presupposes for the initiate a death that allows the entrance to a different reality. Only then, can the initiate (reader) be a complicit participant "in the secret," after having heard, during the process of initiation, the echo of the Voice. Like Abakuá plantes, *TTT* ends at dusk,[353] when the initiated reader enters that great Gap that language cannot represent.

Fiction, in *TTT,* represents the oneiric landscape of the Afro-Cuban monte, as the metaphoric time-space of the palenque: a space of refuge and freedom, away from slavery, from the *monos* "de estos tiempos" (monkeys of these times). The transformative act of writing in *TTT* suggests an oneiric vogage into a Cuban monte of myths, through a ritual juego of writing that (like all rituals) seeks "infinity in space."[354] *TTT* proposes a textual safari, through memory, into the cultural thresholds of cubanía: into the inner sanctum of the Afro-Cuban monte. In *TTT,* reminiscing the ritual dances of the diablitos on "Día de Reyes," the transformative act of writing articulates a ritual juego that resists entrapment. In that play, or juego, from the other side of the textual mirror, *TTT* "tells" by reenacting, and performing, the constant fuga of the signifier, the memory of the repetitive history of cimarronaje in the Caribbean. In other words, the slippage of the signifier, the fuga, and the theme of leaving, tell a secret story of exile, entrapment, sacrifice, and death. This is the same story of persistence, resistance, and unrelenting will-to-freedom associated with the African experience in America: a story entangled in Caribbean memories and expressions.

3

Cimarrón: The Runaway Slave as *Arch*-Text

> In time I think it will be understood the codes of the Caribbean *there* have much to do with the maroon and the palenque . . . to the extremely complex and difficult architexture of secret routes, trenches, traps, caves, breathing holes, and underground rivers that constitute the *rhizome* of the Caribbean psyche.
>
> —Antonio Benítez Rojo, *The Repeating Island*

IN ANTONIO BENÍTEZ ROJO'S SHORT STORY, "INCIDENTE EN LA CORDILLERA," in *Pasos de los vientos* (1999) ("Incident in a Mountain Pass," *A View from the Mangrove,* 1998), a caravan taking goods across a mountain path is suddenly ravaged by an earthquake. The few survivors run away from the scene except for a black slave and a wounded Tamene (an indian carrier). The Tamene does not want to return to his village because he lost the use of his arm in the accident, and he would be a burden to his family. The slave, an outsider, is not familiar with the area, and he cannot speak. A scar in his throat marks the place where his vocal cords were cut, probably after an attempt to escape. The Tamene offers to take the slave to a maroon camp in the forest, but during the journey they are overtaken by swarms of carnivorous ants whose nests were stirred up by the same earthquake. The Tamene gives the slave directions to the maroon camp, and begs the slave to kill him before the ants devour him. The slave raises the knife to stab the Tamene, hesitates, and then picks him up, puts him over his shoulder, and begins to run. Sitting on top of a mountain, looking at the men below, an old Indian meditates on the futility of the slave's heroic action. As if the text had been written from the old man's point of view, Benítez Rojo offers in this short story an ontological meditation on Caribbean history and on the perilous journeys Caribbeans have taken, and still take today, to reach other imaginary shores in search of freedom, only then, from there, to dream of returning home.[1]

Slavery shaped the history and collective psyche of Caribbean societies. Still today, as Benítez Rojo writes, Caribbean cultural codes "have much to do with the maroon and the palenque. . . . [Not] only to the instinct toward flight to 'freedom' . . . but also to defensive codes, to the extremely complex and difficult architecture of secrets routes, trenches, traps, caves, breathing holes, and underground rivers that constitute the rhizome of the Caribbean psyche" (*RI,* 255). In the Caribbean, the desire for freedom has taken many modalities: from different forms of passive resistance, to open rebellions and revolutions. Freedom often has been conceived as a space, real or imaginary, constructed out of illusions, desires, hopes, and fears, as a space of liberty and dignity. The first reaction of the native Caribbeans upon the arrival of the Spaniards to their shores was to run away. This was an act that sometimes took the form of group suicides (for the Arawaks). With time, running away became more complex, more imaginative, more aggressive, and more repetitive. For centuries, the figure of the runaway slave in the Spanish Caribbean followed a complex trajectory shaped by different philosophies and politics. Although the runaway slave is no longer a historical presence as such, his image has become a Caribbean signature: a shifting and fluid sign of resistance as well as of justification for political power.

The earliest representation of the figure of the runaway slave in the Spanish Caribbean is a drawing by the Spanish painter Víctor Patricio Landaluze (1889), of a slave in the forest (monte), with his clothes torn, defenseless, cornered by two tracking hounds trained to go after fugitive slaves. Landazule's drawing portrays colonial life in the Caribbean in an encapsulated moment. This drawing became emblematic of Cuban history at a time when slavery had just been abolished (1886), and the independence of Cuba from Spain was a political point of conflict. Half a century later, Landaluze's drawing inspired Alejo Carpentier to write a short fable, "Los fugitivos" (1946), in which he portrays a runaway slave, Cimarrón, cornered by hounds in the forest. Carpentier's fable depicts a dog that also runs away from the plantation and becomes Cimarrón's companion in the woods until Cimarrón is caught once again during one of his incursions to the Plantation. Again he escapes. Yet, when Cimarrón and Dog encounter each other once more, Cimarrón remembes his previous companion, but Dog no longer recognizes Cimarrón. Cimarrón extends his hand to pet him, but: "Perro lanzó un extraño grito, mezcla de ladrido sordo y de aullido, y saltó al cuello del negro. Había reconocido, de súbito, una vieja consigna dada por el mayoral del ingenio el día que un esclavo huía al monte" (Perro gave a strange cry, a mixture between a deaf bark and a howl, and jumped to the negro's neck. He had suddenly recognized an old signal given by the foreman of the Plantation one day when a slave ran away to the forest).[2] While in Landaluze's drawing the fatal outcome is left to the reader's imagination, Carpentier's fable articulates the writer's ontological preoccupation with history. From a Spenglerian gaze, Carpentier represents European civilization as having left a devastating imprint in both Cimarrón and Dog. Like Mackandal in *The Kingdom of This World,* Cimarrón knows the dangers he would face if he goes back to the Plantation, and yet he returns to it, drawned to it by lust and desire. Dog and Cimarrón are transformed by a Plantation system whose codes are inscribed in their memory. In that conflictive play of running to and away from the Plantation, and of running to and away from the monte, Capentier's Cimarrón, like the slave in Benítez Rojo's short story, find in the monte both freedom and death.

Mapping *Cimarrón:* Epistemology and History

Running away from captivity and punishment became a way of life in the Caribbean. The early Spanish colonizers called the slaves and the domestic animals that ran away to the forest *cimarrón.* This is a word of dubious origin that equated human beings with wild animals and plants. The term, as it was used in the Caribbean, recalls the meaning of the term "barbarian," which Romans utilized to designate those who stood outside of Roman civilization. Like the "barbarians" for the Romans, in the Caribbean, cimarrones were considered a dangerous threat to the stability of the "civilized" world. The semantics of the word cimarrón as well as the definition of what constituted a cimarrón suffered numerous transformations through the centuries. By the twentieth century, the image of cimarrón was used as fluid signs of nationality, as a mytho-poetic image with which to define the Caribbean, and, often, as a pre-text for the complex elaboration of double discourses of power, resistance, and domination. Notwithstanding, that important historical figure whose continuous resistance, and never ending rebellion shaped the history of the Caribbean, left a disturbing silence in Latin American literature. The runaway slave acquired a voice of his/her own, in Cuba, in Francisco Manzano's *Autobiography,*[3] and, later, intertwined with the writer's voice, in Esteban Montejo's voice, with Miguel Barnet's *Biografía de un Cimarrón* (1966) (*Autobiography of a Runaway Slave*). However, even in those texts the voice of cimarrón has been muzzled by historical silence, by the many writers that reconstruct the image of cimarrón as a political icon, and by different, and often contradictory, political agendas.

Analogous to the representational complexity surrounding the historical figure of the runaway slave, the term cimarrón is also charged with etymological ambiguities. Joan Corominas, in his *Dictionario etimológico de la lengua castellana,* defines "cimarrón" as an Americanism which means *alzado* (a dissident rebel and runaway), *Montaraz* (of the forests and highlands), "aplicado a los indios, negros y animales huídos, 'salvajes'; probablemente derivado de *cima,* por los montes donde huían los *cimarrones*" (given to Indians, blacks, and animals who ran away to the wilderness, "wild;" probably derived of the Spanish *cima* [mountain tops] due to the mountainous forests where *cimarrones* would run to seek refuge).[4] He offers 1535 as the year when the word was first registered in a written text.[5] Marcos Morínigo in his *Diccionario de americanismos* repeats the same definition and gives the same date. By 1914, however, Alfredo Zayas in his *Lexicografía Antillana* suggests, like Father Mir before him, that the word cimarrón has a native pre-Columbian origin.[6] José Arrom accepts and supports this conclusion. Fernando Ortiz also adds his own definition to this etymological debate:

> "Cimarrón:" Zayas se empeña en que sea voz tomada de los moradores del Nuevo Mundo y trae numerosas citas. El padre Mir le precede, y la supone antillana. Ciertamente que esta palabreja, pasada a las Antillas francesas e inglesas, ha dado motivo a malabarismos etimológicos. Y la docta Academia resuelve el problema de un modo sencillo y convincente, de *cima,* que era el lugar que habitaban los *cimarones.* ¡Ni el huevo de Colón![7]

> ["Cimarrón:" Zayas insists that it is a voice taken from the New World's inhabitants and provides numerous references. Father Mir precedes him and assumes it Antillean. The truth is that this strange word, which passes on to the French and English Antilles, has produced etymological malabarisms. And the Scholarly Academy (of the Spanish Language) solves the problem in a very simple and convincing way (saying that it derives) from *cima,* which was the place *cimarrones* lived. Not even (a bigger fib than) Columbus's egg!]

José Arrom observes that both Corominas and Morínigo base themselves in the first edition of Gonzalo Fernández de Oviedo's *Historia general y natural de las Indias* (1535), and that the definition they both take from Oviedo is not found in the first edition but in the second one of 1543, which reads:

> los campos están llenos de salvajina, así de vacas e puercos monteses como de muchos perros salvajes que se han ido al monte e son peores que lobos, e más daño hacen, E asimismo, muchos gatos de los domésticos, que se trujeron de Castilla para las casas de morada, se han ido al campo e son innumerables los que hay bravos o *cimarrones,* que quiere decir, en lengua de esta isla, fugitivos.[8]

> [. . . the fields are full of wild animals, of wild cows and pigs as well as many wild dogs that ran away to the (*monte*) wilderness and are worse than wolves and cause more damage. Also many domestic cats brought from Castille to individual homes, have gone to the countryside and there are many of them now wild or *cimarrones,* which means in the language of this island, fugitives.]

Arrom also consults other references and comes to the conclusion that cimarrón, sometimes written with an "s" (simarrón), is related to the Arawak word:

"símarabo" o "símarahabo" "arco de flecha", y oni símalabo "arco iris" (literalmente 'arco de agua') . . . pudiera traducirse por flecha despedida del arco, escapada del dominio del hombre o, como dice Oviedo, "fugitiva". Y de ahí que símaran equivalga a "silvestre", "selvático" o salvaje . . . a "huído", "alzado" o "bravo" aplicado a los animales domésticos que se tornaban montaraces, y también a los hombres, indios primero y negros después, que se alzaban y en desesperada fuga buscaban libertad lejos del dominio del amo.[9]

[*"simarabo"* or *"símarababo"* "the bow for an arrow," and *"oni símalabo"* "rainbow" (literally "a bow of water") . . . could be translated as an arrow thrown from a bow, escaping (or running away) from man's dominion or as Oviedo says, of the forest, or "wild." From this (it can be deduced) that *"símaran"* is equal to "wild," of the forest or salvaje . . . "a runaway," rebel or brave applied to domestic animals that turned wild (running free in the forest) and also to men, Indians at first and blacks later, that rebelled and sought freedom by desperately escaping far away from their master's domination.]

If Arrom's deductions (together with Zayas and Mir) are correct, the word cimarrón (in its transformations from the Arawak "fugitive" to the Spanish *cima,* with the ending *arrón)* is symbolic of the transformations suffered by the images constructed around the figure of the runaway slave in the Spanish Caribbean. When Oviedo recorded the already common usage of this word, its definition, whenever applied to a human being, was ambiguous and vague, always used to define animals, mostly domestic animals that had turned wild. Trans-Atlantic slavery was still in its early stages, and the reasons for considering a slave a cimarrón (turned wild, fugitive) were vague. Numerous documents were written with the sole purpose of clarifying and defining the number of days a slave could be absent from work before he/she could be accused of being a "fugitive," and punished. In the early part of the sixteenth century a slave could be absent for up to four months before he could legally be considered a cimarrón. Yet, by 1845, in Cuba, the law had already reached its strictest definition and "se consideró cimarrón quien pernotara fuera de su casa sin licencia de su amo" [any (slave) who spent the night away from home without his/her master's permission was considered a cimarrón].[10] Punishments also varied according to the times, as well as the many orders and counterorders given by the Spanish Crown with the objective of solving the runaway problem. In time, as the indigenous population decreased and the number of African slaves increased, the word cimarrón came to mean (just like Oviedo had defined it), "rebel," *alzado, bravo,* and, above all, barbaric and criminal: someone outside of the law.

These individuals that "turned wild," living at the margins of "civilized" society, of Spanish Law, became a serious threat to the stability of colonial towns. The word cimarrón soon became a metaphor for chaos, economic, political, and civil disorder. In the Inquisitor's mind, runaways were heretics threatening the divine and natural order of things. Thus, an equivalency was soon drawn between the rebellious slave and the devil, an association supported by the fact that many of the early African slaves taken to the Indies, and most of the rebellious ones in the Indies, were of Islamic nations like the Gelotes, Mandigues, and Carabalies. The word *Mandigo* (Mandingue), became a synonym for devil or demonic[11] in several areas of Spanish America. The fact that slavery, in its New World modality, began largely with Muslin African slaves only few years after the Reconquest of Spain from the Moors, helped consolidate the semantic relationship between the Africans as "heretics" and the image of the rebellious slave, or *alzado,* as evil, dangerous to the Crown and the Church. Resistance and rebellion had been a constant way of life in the Caribbean since Columbus's first voyage in 1492, therefore, the type of slaves brought to the Indies also became a debated issue. It was thought at first that only African "ladinos" (already in Spain) should be taken to Hispanola.[12] Soon, however, "ladino" slaves[13] were "undesirable" because, as the Spanish Emperor Carlos V stated in a letter of May 1526, they had been corrupted in Spain and arrived the the New World with "bad habits." In Hispaniola, such slaves, the king claimed: "ymponen e aconsejan a los otros negros mansos que estan en la dicha isla pacíficos y obedientes al servicio de sus amos han intentado y provado muchas veces de alçar e an alçado et ydose a los montes y hecho otros delitos" (advise and exort the other docile negroes that are in such island in peace and obedience to their masters, [and] they have attempted and tried many times to rebel, and have rebelled and ran away to the forest and committed other crimes).[14] In order to solve this problem it was decided that only *bozales* (slaves taken to the New World directly from Africa, not from Spain) should be taken to the New World, because they are more docile and less rebellious.[15] Such idea was soon to be proven wrong when the first mass slave revolt (all of them bozales) in the New World occurred in Hispanola, in 1522, in the hacienda of the then-governor of the island, Diego de Colón, only four years after the arrival of the largest shipment of African bozales up to that date.

Nicolás de Ovando, the governor of Hispanola from 1502 to 1508, warned the Crown against laws allowing large numbers of African slaves to enter the island, in part because "all" of the African slaves sent to Hispanola before 1503 had escaped to the monte and were very difficult to capture.[16] In spite of these warnings, African slaves continued to be purchased in large quantities due to the economic advantages of the trade and the decreasing native population. Before 1522, other rebellions had taken place throughout the Caribbean, one of them, as early as 1514, in Puerto Rico,[17] and in 1519 the cacique Enriquillo took to the mountains of Barouco where he resisted for fifteen years. Rebellions and cimarronaje became so common in the early part of the sixteenth century that in 1526 the borough of San Germán, Puerto Rico, asked the King to construct a fort against the threat of Indians and black *cimarrones*.[18] Uprisings (first by native people, and later, African slaves) became such a constant state of affairs in the colonies that it could be said that, during most of the colonial rule, from 1492 to the end of the nineteenth century, Caribbean life revolved around the issues and complexities of the slave system and the enslaved's obstinate resistance to accept enslavement. Since the economy and the survival of the colonies depended on the labor of slaves, a great deal of human energy and financial resources were spent to avoid and to control rebellions, to keep slaves from running away, and to punish those who did. Strict laws were implemented to avoid what was unavoidable: the will to freedom.

The constant occurrence of rebellions, individual and group escapes, and, in general, slave resistance, threatened colonial economy, and was seen as a menace for the security of Spanish colonial life. Since runaway slaves were considered criminals, bandits, and outlaws, numerous documents were written by the Spanish Crown to solve and define the problem. Many of these laws only added to the already-existing lawlessness by justifying punitive measurements sometimes not only toward the runaways but also the masters. These laws, however, were often manipulated and utilized by the Crown and/or other authorities in the island as a justification to confiscate land and property (slaves) for economic or political advantages.[19] As early as the first half of the sixteenth century heavy fines were levied against any white or free black who helped a slave run away, even if only through negligence.[20] The inconsistencies of this law can easily be imagined. Its simple existence implied not only a serious laxity and a lack of ideological coherence in the system, but also a conscious effort (whether for political, economic, or social reasons) by free blacks and members of the white population to help slaves escape from their masters. In spite of the harsh punishments and other coercive methods to force slaves to be docile (as, for example, offering the slave the possibility to marry in order to, years later, receive his/her freedom), slaves constantly tried to escape, resist and/or rebel. In fact, by 1519, in Hispanola, a large number of runaways had already joined the forces of Enriquillo, hidden in the mountains of Barahouco,[21] an area that continued to serve as a refuge to cimarrones until as late as the latter part of the nineteenth century. It was during the period of Enriquillo's resistance that, according to Arrom, the word cimarrón came to mean not just "fugitive" but also alzado in the sense of a "rebel:" a threat to the Crown and to "civilization."

Communities of cimarrones emerged at different times and in different places in the Caribbean, hidden in remote, mostly mountainous, and inaccessible areas. Some of these communities remained unknown for many years. Others, although their existence was known, remained unconquered for decades (sometimes a century), as was the case of the Gran Maniel in Hispanola, which resisted for one hundred years. Little is known about these communities, mostly because their existence depended precisely on the secrecy of their location, and/or because access to them was restricted to a selected few. Much of the documentation available today is based on administrative reports and letters, some made by visitors, priests, army officers in negotiating treaties, pirates dealing in contrabands, and the testimonies of slaves, transcribed into legal language by official scribes. It is certain, however, that these runaway communities, known in Cuba and Colombia as *palenques,* in Venezuela as *cumbés,* and in Brazil as *mocambo* or *quilombo,* proliferated all over the Caribbean and throughout the New World. It is known that many of the runaway communities had a strict government of elders and a main chief or leader. Many of them developed an intense agricultural operation and many traded their products with local merchants, often exchanging honey and wax for other necessities. Some smaller groups (and/or single individuals) depended on theft to survive, raiding nearby villages, houses, mines, and sugar mills searching for tools, women, and slaves to enhance their forces. Since most landowners feared the cimarrones, strict punitive laws were created. According to such laws, the runaway slaves who turned themselves in, especially if they provided valuable information about other runaway slaves and maroon communities, or offered to capture other runaway slaves, were usually pardoned, received a light punishment, or even occasionally were granted freedom.[22]

In *Los guerrilleros negros,* a detailed historical study about cimarrones in the island of Hispanola, Carlos Esteban Deive concludes that, until the nineteenth century in what is today the Dominican Republic, the act of running away to escape slavery happened mostly at the margins of any political consciousness,[23] and never, in itself, created collective political awareness.[24] Since one of the main dividing factors among runaway slaves (many of those forced to be together may not have been from the same region in Africa, or may have belonged to enemy tribes), was personal gain and survival, and since the runaway slave could gain his/her freedom by accepting to track and capture other cimarrones, this divisive incentive was utilized by the administration in all Caribbean colonies to destroy maroon communities and abort slave rebellions. As Mavis Campbell points out in *The Maroons of Jamaica,* a great deal of resentment and/or envy from the slaved population ensued from this tactic, thus destroying the possibilities, at least before the nineteenth century, of any solidarity in the effort to create a united resistance. In Jamaica, observes Campbell, the existence of a marginal yet officially accepted society of maroons as para-social units, different from the general slave population, created a complex relationship that later would affect Jamaican's issues on nationality and identity.[25]

Due to the vagueness of the official definitions pertaining runaway

slaves, Deive points out that very often slaves were accused wrongly of being cimarrones when they had simply left work for a few days in search of
women, alcohol,[26] or to steal in order to obtain goods they otherwise could
not have.[27] As Deive also points out, in Hispanola, by the middle of the
sixteenth century, Africans and their descendants outnumbered the dominant white population, which was estimated to be around six thousand, and,
according to the documentation reported during this period by the Arcedi-
ano of Santo Domingo, Alvaro de Castro, of that total sum, three thousand
were cimarrones.[28] Deive also notes that "Alvaro de Castro denunciaba los
excesivos robos cometidos por los esclavos de los ingenios y haciendas . . .
[en] complicidad de las negras ganaderas que recorrían la isla. Los robos
se hacían, según Castro: 'Unos para pagar el jornal que dan un tomín cada
día a sus amos por avenencias, otros para lo dar a negras, otros para vestir
y calzar . . .'" (Alvaro de Castro denounced the excessive theft carried out
by slaves from sugar mills and farms . . . [in] complicity with black women
herders that traveled through the island. These thefts were done, according
to Castro: "Some to pay the daily wage of a tomín they give to their master for their commitments, others to give to their women, others to buy
clothes and shoes . . .").[29] According to Castro, due to this excessive theft
and social laxity, black slaves in Santo Domingo dressed presumptuously
and wore expensive gold jewelry.[30] Deive argues that such ostentations
must have given the appearance to Castro that the black population in general (free and slaves) was freer than the white population. This social incongruity was the result of the economic and social values and structures
of colonial society, and, in part, of the negotiations of African customs in
Western society. It also points out the early complexities of colonial life in
the Caribbean. In these paradoxically restrictive, yet relaxed structures
born out of a counterpoint between the desire to possess goods denied to
slaves and the denial of a person's own will and destiny as property of others, the concept of property (things, money, and life) was a fluid matter, always vulnerable to higher powers or events. It must be remembered that
also a white man could suddenly lose everything to the Crown if accused
of treason or heresy.

Hysteria and paranoia, resulting from fear and insecurity, was a central
psychological element of colonial life, and thus they played an important
role in dealing with runaway slaves, as with other social, economic, religious, and political transgressions. In 1544, Alonso López de Cerrato,
named by the Crown resident judge (oidor and juez de residencia) of Santo
Domingo, explained in a letter to the King that the reason why so many
slaves were running away was due to the mistreatment and abuse they suffered, but that, at the same time, he said: "la gente de esta isla es tan bulli-
ciosa y alharaquienta que un negro que se vaya dicen que andan ya capi-

tanías, . . . y sobre esto dicen y levantan tantas cosas y tantos rebatos como en el reino de Granada se suelen hacer" (people in this island are so boisterous and given to make a fuss about everything that if a black man runs away it is said that there are hordes of them [cimarrones] around, . . . and over this matter there are so many tales told and so much fuss raised just like in the kingdom of Granada).[31] Such exaggerations and excitement over cimarrones, an attitude which according to López de Cerrato seemed to have been a characteristic of the "boisterous" people of Hispaniola, perhaps was supported also by the fact that many slaves did run away and many of them were in fact forced to steal in order to survive, adding havoc, with their actions, to the already precariousness of colonial rule. Many of the runaway communities lived in peace with surrounding villages and farmers—especially those in the northern sectors of Hispaniola, an area that became a heaven for runaways since this area had remained depopulated after the Crown expelled its flourishing population as a punishment for trading illegally with buccaneers and pirates (*RI,* 47–48). At the same time, several cimarrón leaders became famous for their "criminal acts," boldness, and strength, not just in Hispaniola but in the entire area of the Caribbean. By the middle of the sixteenth century, in Hispaniola, the cimarrón Juan Criollo was the feared leader of the Gran Maniel; in Managua was Diego de Guzmán;[32] in La Vega, Diego de Ocampo;[33] and Lemba was devastating the countryside in San Juan and Azua, kidnapping women slaves from nearby sugar mills and farms.[34] Deive suggests that it was probably Lemba the heroe/criminal to whom the Spanish poet Juan de Castellanos referred to in his poem: "de perversos pensamientos,/atrevido, sagaz, fuerte, valiente," (of perverse thoughts,/ bold, shrewd, strong, brave),[35] summarizing in few words the contradictory image of the cimarrón that was in the process of being constructed in the literary imagination of a gestating Caribbean discourse as a paradoxical being, construed as a brave hero seeking his freedom, unwilling to submit to oppression, but, at the same time, a terrible criminal and social outcast.

The resulting chaos in the sixteenth century that resulted from the on-going slave rebellions and escapees can be read between the lines in Fray Bartolomé de las Casas's *Historia de las Indias,* in an interpolated text in which las Casas tells the story of a fantastic plague of ants that, attracted by the sweet juice of the *cañafístola,* devastated the island of Hispanola:

> Formerly, when there were no sugar mills, our opinion on these islands was that if the Negro did not happen to be hanged he would never die, because we had never seen a Negro dead from a desease. . . . But after they were put into the sugar mills . . . they found their death and their sickness, and thus many of them die every day, and for that reason bands of them run away whenever they can,

and they rise up and inflict death and cruelty upon the Spaniards, in order to get out of their captivity, as often as opportunity permits, and so the little towns of this island do not live very securely, for another plague has come over them.[36]

What las Casas proposes here is that the cruelty with which the Spaniards treated their slaves justified their flight to freedom and their rebellion. Nonwithstanding, at the same time, however justified it may have been, the runaway slaves wandering lawlessly in the countryside turned the needed working hands, that were purchased for profit, into a divine curse for the island. Las Casas saw a historical and theological analogy between the biblical plagues that fell upon Egypt and the cimarrón plague that fell upon Hispaniola.

In las Casas's text, the hidden discourse is no other than Father Antonio Montesino's daring sermon, which he delivered at the Advent Sunday Mass in 1511, prophesizing the sure punishment of God against all Spaniards for the inhumane treatment of other human beings.[37] In essence, Montesino claimed that since the Spaniards in the island, as well as the Crown, had not mended their ways and followed God's commands in the Holy Scriptures, the general insecurity felt in the island, due to the rising number of crimes committed by the runaways and the economic devastation brought about by the large population of cimarrones pillaging the countryside, was a warning by God against the transgressors and sinners: the Spaniards and, by analogy, las Casas himself. Antonio Benítez Rojo points out that las Casas's biblical interpretation of a plague of ants, followed by an ongoing plague of runaway slaves, articulates a personal discourse of confession, guilt, and repentance (*RI*, 88–90). It is also a portrait of the complexities of colonial life at this period and the hardships the system of slavery brought about not only for the ones who suffered the consequences of the system in their flesh, but also for the entire colonial population. The hunters and pursuers of slaves were, in las Casas's argument, suddenly the pursued, the prey; and the slave, the hunter. In other words, Christian Spaniards had been transformed, by their own transgressions against the mandates of God, into the victims of a system they themselves had created. This argument suggested that if in the beginning the African slave was brought to Hispaniola to fill a void left by Columbus's promises of gold and richness in the Indies, the Spaniards strayed away from the path of God; and, like the Egyptians, they were now punished by God with plagues. Like the "ants" in las Casas's fable, which arrived in the island attracted by the sweetness of the *cañafístola* and later destroyed everything in their path, las Casas suggests that also the black African slaves, brought to the Caribbean by great numbers to process sugar (wealth), were now destroying the island: turning sugar into poison. In this sense, the central symbol of this wealth/destruction paradox was the figure of the rebellious slave, the cimarrón, who threatened the stability and order of colonial power. The ambiguities and contradictions in las Casas's analogy signal the discursive play between guilt and prejudice that Benítez Rojo reads in las Casas's discourse, as well as, years later, in José Antonio Saco and Fernando Ortiz's work.[38] Benítez Rojo is referring here to a discourse that characterized the colonial mentality of the period: of the white creole caught between the politics of an intense mercantilism and a religious piety reminiscent of las Casas's argument against the mistreatment of enslaved Indians—but not against the system of slavery itself. Slavery and its consequences became the dominant center of colonial life, its cure and venom, and, ultimately, in the nineteenth century, its destruction. Even after the end of colonial rule, slavery and the complex system that justified it left deeply rooted vestiges in modern Caribbean societies and institutions.

Starting in the sixteenth century, the Church's attitude toward the runaway slave was also contradictory. Deive observes that in 1532 the free population of Hispaniola complained that runaways often took refuge in convents and monasteries under the protection of the monks.[39] Yet, only half a century later, by 1574, the same religious institutions that once protected runaway slaves and indigenous *naboríes,* now chastised and harshly punished their "transgressions."[40] For the Church, and even for las Casas, the simple presence of communities of runaway slaves in the Indies, no matter how peaceful they were, threatened the political and religious order of things. To accept these communities as free and independent entities meant having to accept the existence of communities outside the Crown's jurisdiction, but also outside the jurisdiction of the Church. Therefore, from the official perspective of the Church, these communities stood as a threat to the philosophical and theological order of things upon which society, the monarchy, and the Church were founded. At the same time, it was then common for individual priests to serve and or even live in maroon communities. In this complex play of exchanges and negotiations, the inevitable existence of established communities of runaway slaves became also a source of profit for some individuals and a pretext for others to justify their actions before the law. A clandestine commerce developed very early in the sixteenth century between runaway slaves and local merchants. This commerce continued through centuries in spite of the punishments imposed by the Crown against anyone who traded with fugitive slaves. The punishment, in the case of a Spaniard, meant deportation for life from all of the Indies.[41]

Since under Spanish law a slave could purchase his/her freedom, or the freedom of a friend or relative, eventually there developed a large population of ex-slaves, free men and women, in urban and rural settings. By the eighteenth and the nineteenth centuries the growing number of free blacks and mulattos, many of them urban artisans or poor farmers in the countryside, made it easy for fugitive slaves to pose as free country men and trade goods in local markets. However, due to the constant and increasing number of rebellions and escapes, landowners began to rely on *rancheadores,* or bounty hunters, to return runaway slaves to their masters, and "keep order." Invested with the power of the law, these independent rancheadores began to add to the destruction of the countryside by assaulting and stealing from free black and mulatto farmers. Once more, the same law created to "restore order" and economic stability, began to destabilize the system and to add further damages to the pillaging and destruction blamed on cimarrones. These unlawful practices, carried out in the name of the law, became so common and alarming that, in July of 1623, King Phillip IV sent a royal order to governors condemning these activities:

Los rancheadores nombrados por las Justicias para ranchear negros cimarrones entran con este título en las casas de los morenos horros de la isla de Cuba y otras partes, así en ciudades como en estancias, donde hacen sus labranzas quietos y pacíficos, y sin poderlos resistir les hacen muchas extorsiones y molestias con grande libertad, de día y de noche, llevándose los caballos, bestias de servicios y otras cosas necesarias de labranza. Mandamos a los Gobernadores, que provean de remedio conveniente a los daños referidos y hagan justicia a los morenos, para que no reciban ninguna molestia ni vejación de los rancheadores.[42]

[The "rancheadores," appointed by the Law to track and return black runaway slaves, enter under this title in the home of free color people in the island of Cuba and in other places, in cities as well as in farms, where they do their work peacefully and quietly, and, unable to resist them, cause them many extortions and harm with great freedom {of conduct}, by day and by night, taking their horses, and farm work animals and other necessary things for their labor. We order Governors to provide convenient aid against the said damages and do justice to the color people so that they no longer receive any more harm or humiliation by the "rancheadores."]

From the very beginning of the slave trade every measure and practice created to control rebellious slaves from escaping also created other problems. The law often was not obeyed; it was used to benefit a select few, or it was simply ignored. Partly for this reason, or perhaps because there were always gaps in the law, each official legal order necessitated another counter order to amend the previous ones. As if this play between freedom and oppression had been a prescribed modality of a sugar-based economy, the rewards offered to any person, black, mulatto, or white, free or slave, who apprehended a runaway, brought about other problems and abuses. In 1574, a Royal Edict stipulated that:

Si algún mulato, mulata, negro o negra, persuadiere y aconsejare a esclavo o esclava, que se esconda, y lo tuviere oculto los cuatro meses para efecto de manifestarlo después, y haberlo por suyo, en tal caso los unos y los otros incurrirán en pena de muerte natural; y si los ocultadores fueren españoles, sean desterrados de todas las Indias . . . y si menos de cuatro meses estuvieren ocultos, se les dé la pena conforme a la calidad del delito.[43]

[If a mulatto man or woman, or a black man or woman, were to persuade and advise a slave man or woman, to hide, and keeps him/her hidden during the given four months plotting to denounce him/her later, and take him/her as his own, in such case each one involved will be condemned to natural death; and if the one who hides the slave is a Spaniard, he/she will be deported from all of the Indies. . . . and if the slaves are in hiding for less than four months, they are to be punished according to the nature of the crime.]

The attention given by the Crown to these incidents and the harsh punishments directed to such persons aiding or stealing slaves, and/or plotting a false escape to claim a reward, are indicative of how common such practices had become. The slave's will to freedom threatened to turn, as it did, into a paradoxical play of gains and losses for freemen, as well as slaves, in a complex system of hierarchical powers. Theoretically at least, the master was punishable by the law for punishing the slave. The slave, on the other hand, became a desired good that promoted illicit trades outside of, and at the margins of, the dictates of the law. Following the idea that the desire for freedom, for the slaves, was always an act outside of the law, many of the runaway slaves became buccaneers and pirates; and many of the coastal palenques dealt, helped, and/or traded with foreigners and outlaws. These affinities made maroon communities real tangible threats for the Crown, at first because large numbers of runaway slaves became allies of foreign powers, pirates and buccaneers,[44] and later, because in the nineteenth century, especially in Cuba during the wars of independence, runaway slaves and sometimes entire palenques joined the Cuban insurgent army.[45]

In such a paradoxical order of things, the same system that punished the slaves for running away and for rebelling, also encouraged the breakdown of its own punitive laws by either aiding, or often falsely pretending to aid runaways in order "to take him as his own." Quite often, resistance against, and from inside the law, was so prevalent that it became necessary, though futile, to constantly amend previous amendments to the law. This problem pointed out that from the very beginning of the colonial slave system, the law always served a dual purpose and it was always adjusting to newly constructed needs. It was a sort of legal cimarronaje of the law, in which written documents cancelled out other documents, thus producing a sort of lawlessness produced by the same mandates of the law.

As part of this complex play of power and of invented legality in the discourse of domination, slavery became a space of resistance and, at the same time, of bondage, both for masters and slaves: a space born out of a play

between the will for freedom and the desire for the economic gains provided by the system of slavery. It was this play that made slave economy
vulnerable to its own laws: to a system that in the Caribbean seemed to resist and undermine itself, leaving it always at the edge of collapse. In the
areas where communities of runaway slaves were present, private as well
as public funds were often depleted, since it was almost always the community itself in charge of paying bounty hunters and other troops (sometimes black militias) responsible for capturing and bringing back the runaway slaves, and reestablishing order. Carlos Esteban Deive writes:

> los *cimarrones* y sus manieles constituyeron la antítesis de todo lo que fue y
> representó la institución de la esclavitud, pero al mismo tiempo es innegable
> que formaron parte del sistema, si bien anómala y repudiable por quienes lo sos-
> tuvieron. Si las formaciones sociales esclavistas implicaban, por su propia nat-
> uraleza, violencia y represión, ellas mismas posibilitaron las fugas y alzamien-
> tos, así como la existencia de comunidades *cimarronas* organizadas con el
> objeto de burlar las estructuras de dominacón político-social en que aquellas se
> sustentaban.[46]

> [*cimarrones* and their communities constituted the antithesis of everything that
> was and represented the institution of slavery, but at the same time undoubtly
> they were also part of the system, as anomalous and repudiated as those who
> supported it. If the slave social formations (institutions) implied, by their own
> nature, violence and repression, they themselves facilitated escapes and upris-
> ings, as well as the existence of Maroon communities organized with the ob-
> jective of undermining the sociopolitical structures that supported them.]

By the eighteenth century, the slave system was institutionalized in full
with all of its complexities, and the economy of all the Spanish Caribbean
colonies came to depend more than ever on the Plantation economy. Perhaps it is Cuba the colonial society that best illustrates the contradictions
of that system. In the early nineteenth century, the rising creole bourgeoisie,
who was at the same time the slave owners, defended both a new market
economy and an old feudal system of slavery. This contradiction, according to Manuel Moreno Fraginals, brought the demise of the new creole capitalist, already economically independent (although not politically) from
Spain, and gave way to a new cycle of colonial economic domination.[47] It
was for this reason that the same bourgeoisie that helped finance Spain's
wars against the creole insurgency in Spanish America in the early part of
the century,[48] later became the patriots and the abolitionists of the second
part of the century.[49] During this same period, new philosophies were
slowly reaching America, those of the Enlightenment, and, later, the revolutionary thoughts of freedom and equality of French Romanticism. These new
thoughts began to make an imprint in the sociopolitical views of Caribbean

intellectuals. However, in the case of Cuba, as Moreno Fraginals explains, these new ideas of freedom did not penetrate the creole mentality until the first half of the nineteenth century, when the powerful Cuban bourgeoisie fell again under the economic and political domination of Spain. In other words, the idea of abolition among the bourgeoisie did not emerge until its own paradoxical insistence in retaining the system of slavery brought about its own economic fall.[50] By then, a clear class-consciousness was developing not only among white creoles, but also within the free black and mulatto population. A sense of political equality (the idea that all Cubans were equally enslaved by a colonial master) became prominent among creole intellectual circles. Cimarronaje, however, continued with the same intensity as before, only that by now the free population of blacks and mulattos, larger than ever before, shared a new collective sense of individual freedom, which seemed to be permeating also the runaway communities, especially after the independence of Haiti in 1804. The ideal of freedom became more and more a political act directed toward colonial rule.

Precedence in this struggle for freedom, in Cuba, was the success of a massive uprising in 1731 by the slaves who worked the copper mines of Santiago del Prado, near Santiago de Cuba. They declared themselves "again" free just like their fathers had done in 1677.[51] Their success was in part largely due to the support and protection of maroon communities in the area; many of the rebels were able to hide in palenques and resist for many years until the government granted them freedom and land in 1800. Afraid that this long rebellion would turn into a war similar to the one being waged in Haiti, at the same time that the Cuban miners were revolting, all one thousand and seventy-five descendants of the African slaves taken to the mines of Santiago del Prado (El Cobre) in the seventeenth century were declared free by the Crown,[52] in an unprecedented act that would have political repercussions. These rebels had developed a clear political consciousness, and, although local in nature, their triumph preceded the independence of Haiti. The resistance and success of the miners in El Cobre was not to be forgotten by maroon communities in this area of Cuba, and, years later, when the first major war of independence erupted in 1868, also in the eastern province of the island, entire cimarrón communities joined the insurgent troops. In fact, by the end of the Ten Year War and with the fiasco of the short war of 1879, rebellion and insurgency were seen as a road to personal freedom because, in order to avoid discontent among slaves, Spain granted freedom to the slaves who had joined the Cuban revolutionary troops (16,000 in all).[53]

Other rebellions in the larger Caribbean also paved the way to political consciousness. In 1812, Africans and Afro-Puerto Ricans were the ones who plotted the first revolution in the twentieth century in Puerto Rico. Although discovered and aborted,[54] it was followed only few years later, in

1825 and 1826, by other rebellions in Ponce and Vega Baja.[55] The possibility of a rebellion of slaves joined by the uprising of the African and Afro-
creole population became such a feared threat that in 1826, all blacks (free
or slave) were prohibited from having and/or carrying agricultural tools
outside the working areas,[56] and new laws were created to restrict free
blacks. Colonial authority believed that they were the ones who instigated
the slaves to rebel[57] as it happened in 1812 when, in Cuba, and in other
Caribbean islands:

> estallaron levantamientos [de esclavos] en los ingenios de Puerto Príncipe, Hol-
> guín, Bayamo, Trinidad y hasta en la misma Habana, revelando la insurrección
> capitaneada por el negro libre José Antonio Aponte, que tendía a conseguir en
> Cuba lo que Toussaint Louverture en Santo Domingo.[58]

> [there were [slave] uprisings in the (sugar) mills of Puerto Príncipe, Holguín,
> Bayamo, Trinidad and even in Havana itself, revealing an insurrection headed
> by the free black José Antonio Aponte, who wanted to do in Cuba the same as
> Toussaint Louverture (had done) in Santo Domingo.]

In the nineteenth century, a cimarrón was no longer just a "fugitive" outlaw,
or rebellious bandit, but a political rebel, a true alzado against Spain: a political insurgent. However, with the triumph of the Haitian revolution, Spanish authorities began to represent the colonial struggle against cimarrón
communities as a war of races, and the insurgents, as savage cimarrones.
Slave rebellions became more common than ever before, but now a growing population of free blacks and mulattos supported them; and, for the first
time, Cuban patriots accepted the rebellion of slaves as part of the same
struggle for freedom waged by white creoles, many of them plantation owners. Black and white insurgents identified political independence with individual freedom, the abolition of slavery, and, even if only in theory, with the
promise of freedom and equality. In Cuba, many black and mulatto insurgents became high-ranking officers in the rebel army. Among them were
Antonio Maceo, the "Titán de bronce" (Bronze Titan),[59] Guillermo Moncada, and Quintín Banderas. In fact, the rebel troops were largely composed
of free blacks, free mulattoes, and runaway slaves.[60] In 1869, Ferrer writes:
"less that eight percent of the soldiers under the command of Antonio Maceo
were white."[61] It is historically significant that the word *mambí*, which came
to designate a Cuban creole patriot, a word still used today for all Cubans
who fought against Spanish colonial rule, is of African origin: from the
Bantu word *mbi*, meaning evil, wild, cruel, or savage.[62] The word *m(a)mbí*
was used first by the Spaniards with a similar meaning of alzado, rebel,
much like the meaning of cimarrón during Enriquillo's armed resistance in
the sixteenth century, but became a synonym in Cuba for patriots.

Due to the fact that "many fugitive slaves and entire palenques were incorporated into the army of liberation," Antonio Benítez Rojo questions the official story of a white creole movement: "There must have been a great number of runaway slaves among those fighting against Spain for this to have happened"—for the Cuban army of liberation to have been called "*mambí,* an African word synonymous of palenque, *cimarrón* and "savage.'" In fact, Benítez Rojo writes, "when global investigations of this theme are undertaken, the Caribbean itself will astonish everyone by how close it came to being a confederation of fugitives, of outlaws . . . One might think that there was a huge conspiracy, of which the Haitian Revolution was only a part, the part that triumphed visibly." (*RI* 254). Even José Martí, who had sincerely claimed in his "Nuestra América" (Our America) that the hatred of races could not exist because "there are no races," had a political agenda. To offset and subvert the official propaganda that the insurgency was a race war of savage Africans, this evolution of cimarrón into mambí made it easier in the twentieth century to associate the figure of cimarrón with an ongoing struggle of national identity and resistance against Spanish colonialism. Ferrer observes that after the abolition of slavery in 1886, and once Cuba finally became independent from Spain and, once again, in 1902 from the United States, during the reconstruction period that followed: "the blacks' insurgent's desirability within the national project depended on the erasure of any hint of his own desire."[63] In other words, ironically, Cuba's political freedom from the United States of America depended on the erasure of individual freedom and equality for black and mulatto patriots.

II

Cuba was the only Spanish Caribbean nation in which there emerged in the nineteenth century an important literary movement against slavery. It was a movement closely associated with Domingo del Monte's group.[64] Del Monte was a Venezuelan intellectual who brought together Cuban antislavery intellectuals and writers who voiced a political resistance against Spain based on the inalienable right of individuals and individual nations to rule themselves. The antislavery novel of this period[65] constructed an analogy between the slavery suffered by a colonized nation, oppressed and controlled by another nation, and the slavery of human beings owned and controlled by other human beings. It articulated the national ideals of intellectual white creole writers toward the colonial system and the system of slavery, and utilized the latter as a metaphor for colonial domination. These writers did not endorse an open rebellion of slaves as in Haiti. In fact, the figure of cimarrón as an image of rebellion against the system of slavery was surprisingly absent from these novels, although cimarronaje in general was more common during this period than ever before. The Cuban antislavery novel constructed a discourse of resistance, and, at the same time, a contradictory discursive play of historical avoidance. As William Luis points out, in the antislavery novel the main character, whether black or mulatto is always a "good" slave, docile, kind, and a model of Christian virtues.[66] Such docility becomes evident even in the only existing autobiography written by a slave during this period; written most likely by the request of Domingo del Monte who wanted to use Manzano's biography as proof of the inhumanity brought about by the system. In his *Autobiography of a Slave* (1835, 1840) Francisco Manzano portrays himself, in a discourse reminiscent of Las Casas's defense of the Indian, as a noble "good slave" who only dared to run away from his mistress because of her excessive abuse. Luis notes that, in trying to write about the sufferings under slavery, Manzano "Also uses the manuscript to influence his readers and prove his innocence against all accusations by his masters. Anyone reading the manuscript, whether a member of the Del Monte group or a government official, could understand how a good slave who loved and was loved by his masters had no other alternative but to escape from the cruel marquesa de Prado Ameno."[67] On paper, at least, the law protected the slaves from extreme abuse. That meant that running away could only be acceptable if the slave appealed to the law for protection. Through those proper channels provided by the law (as in the case of Manzano), the accused master could be reprimanded or fined if punishment was proven to be extreme. Under such provisions "certain" escapes were justifiable only for the purpose of seeking protection from the law; thus, theoretically, the law offered a simple way to channel disagreements while still leaving intact the system of human bondage. Under a law that was residual of Roman law, a "good slave" was "good" only if he/she obeyed the master, the authorities, the Crown, and only complained to legal authorities about excess injustice, never about bondage itself. This idea of docility as nobel, was juxtaposed, after the abolition of slavery, to the image of the black rebel patriot who for the sake of country was asked in the late nineteenth century to accept demotion and fight under an inexperienced white officer in order to give to the United States and to Europe the accepted image of a white Cuban creole government.[68]

Just like the colonial government could not condone the defiant and aggressive behavior of a cimarrón, the creole political discourse on independence avoided the image of a cimarrón (meaning a "rebel") as a protagonist in the antislavery novel. The reasons were rather practical: First, because the rebellion of slaves in the nineteenth century was already a reminder of the recent independence of Haiti, now governed by blacks, a situation that, according to Spanish propaganda, threatened to repeat itself in Cuba if the insurgency won. Second, because it was not the savage cimarrón, but the noble suffering slave, whose "justified" escape from "injustice" became a metaphor for the feelings of white creoles, toward the restrictions and estrangement of colonial authority.[69] The rebellion of slaves before 1886 could be acceptable only within the ideals of national freedom and independence. As Ada Ferrer points out, in that struggle, there emerged the ideal of a raceless nationality. However, after 1898, with the intervention of the United States, such ideal, which once inspired insurgency and unity, now, in order to assure the departure of the Americans, "appeared to require from Cuban nationalists an evasion of principles."[70] Independence "had always been a battle of representation,"[71] and now white patriots had to convince the segregated ruling nation that Cuba would not be governed by black insurgents. Black Cuban patriots suffered the betrayal[72] of the nationalist antiracial principles for which they fought. As part of that "betrayal," reminiscent of Cabrera Infante's notion of "treason" in *Tres tristes tigres,* with the advent of political independence in the name of freedom, political power went exclusively to white creoles, and the word *mambí* (at first equivalent to cimarrón) was displaced from its African roots to describe a white Cuban creole patriot.

During the nineteenth century, repression informed the representations by Cuban writers of history and society. While abolition was a controversial but acceptable issue, political criticism could only bring serious consequences. In Puerto Rico, in 1854, the "dark" poet Daniel Rivera intimated an indirect expression in favor of independence in his poem "Agüeybana el Bravo." He was persecuted, and had to leave the island.[73] In Cuba, those involved in the Del Monte group faced serious charges; they were accused of participating in 1844 in the *Conspiración de la Escalera* (The Ladder Conspiracy).[74] Domingo del Monte went into exile, Francisco Manzano went to jail, and the mulatto poet Gabriel de la Concepción Valdés (Plácido) faced the firing squad. For the dominant discourse of the period, cimarrón and mambí, with the meaning of rebel, dissident, and an African savage, could be applied interchangeably to also designate free blacks that were members of a growing *petite* black bourgeoisie. For the most part, with few exceptions, white creole's identification with the "other," the black slave, was a tropological construct. Eventually, in Cuba, the latent racial differences that had deepened at the turn of the century during the American intervention (1898–1902), surfaced again in 1912 in what came to be known as *La guerrita de los negros* (Black's little war).[75] In the twentieth century, cimarrón also became the signifying sign for a nation in bondage: social and political bondage created by internal powers, neocolonial conditions, and the political and economic coercion of foreign powers.

ROMANCING *CIMARRÓN:* A CARIBBEAN LITERARY DISCOURSE

With the end of slavery, the literary figure of the runaway slave began to be defined as an important and complex historical figure. In Puerto Rico, Cayetano Toll y Toste (1850–1930) includes in his *Leyendas Puertor-riqueñas* (1924) (Puerto Rican Legends) a legend, staged a century earlier around 1830, about a runaway slave in a Puerto Rican colonial plantation. "Carabalí"[76] is the story of a slave, Carabalí, who runs away from a plantation, hides in a cave, and there, with a stolen machete, tries to defend himself from the tracking hounds that attack him. During the struggle, Carabalí slips and falls down a cliff into the waters of a hidden creek at the bottom of the cave. The rancheadores leave the site thinking he is dead, and Carabalí is able to live a life of freedom hiding in the monte for the rest of his life. Behind the mask of this nineteenth-century legend that seems to explain the origin of the name "Cueva de los muertos" (Cave of the Dead), there is also an implicit political subtext. According to Toll y Toste's legend: "Carabalí y su cuadrilla llegaron a infundir pavor y espantoso pánico entre los capataces y mayordomos de la hacienda San Blas porque algunos de sus empleados más adictos se habían encontrado asesinados en las cañadas" (Carabalí and his followers brought panic and terror to the foremen and overseers of the hacienda San Blass ever since some of the best servants had been found murdered in the ravines).[77] Toll y Toste writes:

> De las ruinas de este ingenio no resta ya más que un montón de pedruscos de su gigantesca chimenea y el recuerdo de las terribles venganzas de Carabalí, el negro desertor, cuya cuadrilla de salteadores fue por mucho tiempo, el espanto y quita-sueño de mayordomos y capataces.[78]

> [Of the ruins of the Mills there is nothing left but the stones of the hacienda's enormous chimney and the memories of the most terrible of Carabalí's vengeance, the black deserter, whose troop of thieves was, for a long time, the terror and the cause of the insomnia suffered by foremen and overseers.]

Intertwining one discourse with another, Toll y Toste's narration turns suddenly from the dis-order that the runaway slave brought to that region, to a more didactic discourse of protest and resistance directed toward colonial rule: "Aquello era monstruoso por lo inicuo. Una multitud de canas, guiados por pérfidos hombres, husmeaban y perseguían a otro hombre, que se resistía a ser bestia de carga, y lo rastreaban y acorralaban como a un jabalí" (Its iniquity made it monstrous. A multitude of canines, guided by treacherous men, pried and hunted another man, who resisted being a working beast, and they tracked and surrounded him like a wild boar).[79]

A writer such as Toll y Toste could not overlook the phonetic concordance between "j-abalí" and "car-abalí". Echoing the word *marrón* with its sixteenth-century meaning of *marrano:* (pig/heretic) or *ci(ma)marrón,* however now with the purpose of beastializing the slave in order to judge the master and their loyal slaves (accomplices in the persecution and hunt of other slaves who ran away), the narrator judges them to be ". . . seres desnaturalizados más perversos los hombres que los canes, que iban a perseguir despiadadamente a su infortunado paisano" (unnatural beings more perverse than the hounds, who were going to mercilessly persecute an unfortunate fellow countryman).[80] Toll y Toste's choice of words, his use of *paisano* (fellow countryman) to refer to the runaway slave, can only be explained by the anachronistic play of differences between his own experience as a patriot in Puerto Rico and the experiences of the characters in his story. Should the reader assume, as Toll y Toste does, that the slave-master considered his slave a "fellow" countryman? Is there then a hidden discourse inferred in that relationship? Although not clarified by the writer, one may assume that in Toll y Toste's legend there is a sameness between the hunter and the hunted that makes the hunter an "unnatural" and "perverse individual" because he persecutes his own compatriot.

The runaway slaves in Toll y Toste's legend are "unfortunate" victims of the slave system; victims he describes as "fugitivos siervos" (fugitive servants),[81] creating a phonetic echo between the colonial slaves (whites and blacks) and José Martí's image in his "Versos sencillos" of a "ciervo herido que busca en el monte amparo" (wounded deer who seeks refuge in the forest).[82] In Toll y Toste's "Carabalí," the runaway slave is not a passive and docile character like the protagonists of the antislavery novels. His crime, as a "deserter" of the established (and imposed) order, and, thus, a fugitive of the Law, is a problem embedded, according to the narrator, in the master's discourse and his "unnatural" expectations, and not in the nature of the slave. It shows that the criminal is not the slave, but the master. If we keep in mind that at the time Toll y Toste was writing this legend (and even at the moment of his death in 1930) Puerto Rico was a colony, a territory, of the United States, the narrative could be read as an allegory of the political conditions lived by the writer as a *siervo/ciervo* (servant/deer) hiding in the forest of his own writings. The allegorical significance of the legend is intimated at the end of the narrative when Carabalí falls into an abyss and survives. His hunters think he is dead and Carabalí is able to elude them, hidden by their false assumption, and protected by the geographic monte where he hides for the rest of his days. What allows him to go undetected is an imaginary construct: fiction. At the end of Toll y Toste's story, Carabalí disappears into the imaginary space of the legend, in the fictional monte of an invented story that a slave, the astute Monga, created in order to protect him: "de que el alma en pena del infeliz Carabalí era la que salía de noche con su falange de espíritus malignos a asesinar capataces y a robar ganados y aves de la hacienda para ofrendárselos a Satanás, y que no había tales bandoleros" (that it was the damned soul of the unfortunate Carabalí who roamed in penance through the fields at night followed by a "phalange" of evil spirits killing foremen and stealing cattle).[83] Like Mackandal in *The Kingdom of This World,* Carabalí's story shifts from history to myth. Due to that fictional space constructed by another slave, the "spirit" of the rebellious freedom-seeking Carabalí survives in the collective memory of a colonial plantation, much like Mackandal survives in Ti Nöel's imagination, and both of them survive in the imagination of the reader. Similarly, the figure of cimarrón also survives in the collective memory of the Caribbean, as a significant metaphor for colonial resistance. It is important to note that in Toll y Toste's legend, the space of refuge for the fugitive is the space of the imagination, fantasy. Fiction here is like a magical forest (monte) where cimarrón can hide and survive—a magical forest created for the specific purpose of camouflaging reality. In Toll y Toste's legend the imaginary discourse created by an old slave woman displaces the historical discourse of the master, canceling and overpowering, the dominant discourse of the colonizer.

Analogous to the legend of Toll y Toste, at the beginning of the twentieth century the figure of the runaway slave fell into a similar literary silence. It seemed that the abolition of slavery had also abolished the possible historic significance of the runaway as a discursive figure. However, much like Carabalí, the image of the runaway slave survived in the imagination of writers as a symbol of freedom and as a sign of resistance: as an icon to be recontextualized in different contexts to fit the writer's needs and the realities of new historical conditions. In 1936 the Cuban writer Antonio Ramos published *Caniquí,* a late antislavery novel staged in the nineteenth-century Cuba, whose protagonist is again a cimarrón: a fugitive slave who, like in the previous antislavery novels, is not a criminal alzado, but a loyal noble slave persecuted and finally unjustly killed by his white paisano hunters. As in Carpentier's "Los fugitivos," but different from Toll y Toste's "Carabalí," Ramos's representation of the cimarrón Caniquí is that of a runaway servant (siervo), who, like a persecuted deer (ciervo) hides in the forest where he is killed in the waters of a lagoon; where he dies embraced by the orisha Olokun, the mother-father Olokun-Yemayá. The innovative aspect of this novel is that, in 1936, Ramos follows a literary discourse in which, as González Echeverría points out, the runway slave is inscribed "within a textual memory, both African and Cuban."[84] The allegorical runaway echoes once more José Martí's image of a c[s]iervo herido (a wounded deer), but, now, under the influence of Cuban negrismo and Afro-Cuban mythology, Caniquí dies in the arms of the Afro-Cuban orisha. Ramos's novel continues a counterdiscourse of colonial resistance, now in the political context of a post-colonial period, and establishes a dichotomy between the nurturing African deities of the Afro-Cuban monte, and the Christian hunters who, like in "Caniquí" are his compatriots. In Ramos's novel, extreme Christian devotion seems to be more the result of guilt turned fanaticism, rather than of faith. Hence, in *Caniquí,* as William Luis observes, slavery as a theme is not a discourse about a period already past, but an allegory for the political/historical moment the writer is living:

> Like the antislavery and post-antislavery works, the novels written in the repub-
> lic continued a counter-discourse of social and political protest, not only for
> black characters but for whites as well. This idea is best exemplified by Ramos's
> Caniquí, which used the theme of slavery to set forth other contemporary con-
> cerns. Although its plot unfolds in the historical Trinidad (Cuba) of the 1830s, it
> alludes transparently to the existing political conditions one century later, dur-
> ing the time in which the novel was written and published—the Machado and
> post Machado eras of the 1920s and 1930s. Ramos used the slavery period as an
> allegory of his own times and thereby transcended the issue of race. What is im-
> plicit in the novel is explicit in the prologue, where Ramos explains his inten-
> tions, knowing that his work, as Suárez y Romero and others realized during the
> early nineteenth century would only be completely understood in the future.[85]

In *Caniquí,* the image of a slave who flees from oppression, and from un-just punishment, sends the reader to a moment in the historical past when human beings were stripped of their inalienable rights to freedom. Medi-ating between a historical past and a present, the novel offers an allegory of the writer's present, of the oppressive political conditions of his times during and after Machado's regime in Cuba,[86] which Ramos compares to the conditions in which Afro-Cubans lived under slavery. It is also a dis-course that repeats itself in Cuban literature transformed by the political conditions of the writer. Reinaldo Arenas, for example, utilizes the same analogy in his poem "El Central" (1984), staged in a very different con-temporary setting: post-revolutionary Cuba.

During the first half of the twentieth century writers became less preoc-cupied with the historical figure of the runaway slave than with contem-porary social and economic conditions pertaining African descendants. Still influenced by the then in-vogue Positivist philosophies for which "black" subcultures, especially in urban centers, were perceived as crimi-nals, the new anthropological and ethnological discourses of the period opened new aesthetic venues in literature. Afro-Hispanic America was per-ceived now as a national phenomenon related and equivalent to a Speng-lerian notion of primitivism, and to cultural exoticism. However, rebellious black servants and slaves, especially those who embraced African beliefs, continued to be kept at the margin of society, still considered criminals in need of redemption, but, at the same time, victims of a given social order from which they could not escape alone. In 1906, in his "Advertencia Pre-liminar" to *Los negros brujos,* Fernando Ortiz explains that the main objective of his study was to eliminate Afro-Cuban sub-worlds (*hampa*), perceived by Ortiz as a "den of vice" and criminality. Such task could only be accomplished through the "positivist" knowledge of these marginal communities, because they, in Ortiz's own words, threatened the social order of urban centers.[87] For the father of afrocubanismo, the object of observation and preoccupation was, and continued to be, the same "black" plague brought by the system of slavery with a sugar-based economy. It was the same plague that preoccupied Bartolomé de las Casas in the sixteenth century, and later, José Antonio Saco in the nineteenth century. Ortiz explains his "estudio metódico y positivista de la poliétnica delincuencia cubana" (methodological and Positivist study of the polyethnicity of Cuban delinquents),[88] in *Los negros brujos:*

> La observación positivista de las clases desheredadas . . . y de los factores que les impiden un más rápido escalamiento de los estratos superiores, forzosamente ha de producir el efecto benéfico de apresurar su redención social . . . todo esfuerzo intelectual en pro del conocimiento científico, del hampa afro-cubana no será sino una colaboración, consciente o no, a la higienización de sus antros, a la regeneración de sus parásitos, al progreso moral de nuestra sociedad.[89]

> [The Positivist observation of the disinherited classes . . . and of the factors that keep them from attaining a more speedy climb to higher levels, will necessarily produce the beneficial effect of a fast social redemption . . . every intellectual effort in favor of scientific knowledge, of the Cuban {black} underworld, will be no other than a collaboration, conscious or not, in the cleansing of its dens of vice, toward the regeneration of its {social} parasites, for the moral progress of our society.]

During this period, much like previous times, to speak of an African past as an integral part of the social identity of each of the Spanish Caribbean nations was to undermine the complex structures of Western ("civilized") economic power. It would have been also threatening to the official discourses on national identity, which sought out to find its roots in its Hispanic heritage. Anyone who dared challenge such official complicity would have found bitter resistance and criticism. This is what Ortiz eventually realized in the process of his investigations. José Luciano Franco observed in his prologue to *Los negros esclavos* (ed. of 1975), that after thirty-eight years of research Ortiz reached a very different conclusion. By then, Ortiz would claim that:

> Sin el negro Cuba no sería Cuba. No podía, pues, ser ignorado. Era preciso estudiar ese factor integrante de Cuba; pero nadie lo había estudiado y hasta parecía como si nadie lo quisiera estudiar. Para unos ello no merecía la pena; para otros era muy propenso a conflictos y disgustos; para otros era evocar cul-

pas inconfesadas y castigar la conciencia; cuando menos el estudio del negro era tarea harto trabajosa, propicia a las burlas y no daba dinero. Había literatura abundante acerca de la esclavitud y de su abolición y mucha polémica en torno de ese trágico tema, pero embebida de odios, mitos, políticas, cálculos y romanticismo; había también algunos escritos de economía acerca de Aponte, de Manzano, de Plácido, de Maceo y de otros . . . pero el negro como ser humano, de su espíritu, de su historia, de sus antepasados, de sus lenguajes, de sus artes, de sus valores positivos y de sus posibilidades sociales . . . nada. Comencé a investigar, pero a poco comprendí que, como todos los cubanos, yo estaba confundido.[90]

[Without the blacks, Cuba would not be Cuba. This fact {their importance} could not, then, be ignored. It was necessary to study this integral element of Cuba; but no one had studied it and it even seemed that no one was interested in studying it. For some, it was not worth it; for others it was prone to conflicts and bad feelings; for others it was to evoke unconfessed guilts and to punish their conscience; to say the least the study of the Afro-Cubans was a difficult task, favorable to jokes, and it brought no money. There was enough literature about slavery and its abolition and many polemics surrounding this tragic subject, but full of hate, myths, politics, calculations, and romanticism; there were also some writings on Economy about Aponte, Manzano, Plácido, Maceo and other men of color . . . but the Afro-Cuban as a human being, of his/her spirit, history, ancestors, languages, arts, positive values, and social possibilities . . . nothing {was written} . . . I began to research, but soon I understood that, like all Cubans, I also was confused.]

It is not until 1949, that the figure of the runaway slave emerges in Caribbean Spanish literature, in *The Kingdom of This World,* as a symbol of rebellion and resistance, as an archetype for the Caribbean, and as a historic-literary sign for revolution. Reenacting the idea inferred by Las Casas of a black plague brought about by the same system of wealth and labor created by the colonial production of sugar, Carpentier's Mackandal loses his arm in a cane press. His master cuts Mackandal's wasted arm with a machete (as if the slave's arm and the cane the slave was there to process were the same), establishing in the novel, from this moment on, an association between the slave who produces sugar, wasted in the production, and a wealth produced at the expense of the slave's body and blood. Mackandal's dead arm, mixed within the sugar under production, is a reminder of the close relationship between the body of the slave and the cane destroyed to produce sugar: the poison of the sugar (slavery) and the venom Mackandal creates as revenge. As Méndez Rodenas y Guizar Alvarez point out in reference to Luís Palés Matos's poetry, the production of sugar is simultaneously the production of *bagazo* or waste cane fiber.[91] Metaphorically, then, the counterpoint to the abundance that sugar represents for the colonial ruling class is the emergence of resistance, cimarronaje, insurgency, and revolution. In Mackandal's case, he 'becomes' the very venom he produces in the *monte* and introduces into the master's house to be ingested, like his blood mixed in sugar, by those who had maimed him. In his role of venom for the dominant class, Mackandal, a *cimarrón,* is the antithesis of the very same system that created him.

II

Two decades later, and more than a century after Francisco Manzano's autobiography, Miguel Barnet publishes *Biografía de un cimarrón* (1966), the first testimonial account of an ex-slave who had been a cimarrón and also a mambí. Establishing an ambiguous play between ethnology and fiction, Barnet's testimonial text proposes the justification of the writer's historical present by way of a historical past narrated in the voice of Esteban Montejo, a 105-year-old black Cuban creole.[92] Barnet, author and character of Montejo, reconstructed the voice of the silent "other," the runaway slave, whose history had been so important for the development of Caribbean societies in general, and yet, whose voice had been paradoxically silenced by discourses on nation and freedom. Barnet allows the "otherness" of that voice to remain unaltered, while, at the same time, rearranging it to suit the agenda of the text in the context of given ideological expectations. As Roberto González Echeverría points out, the text's importance in this respect is to force literature "to stake out its own domain anew, its own *palenque,*" a task not given to a revolutionary literature but "to a literature that in searing and uncompromising language seeks to rewrite the foundations of a culture."[93] In this sense, Barnet's text differs from Manzano's autobiography. William Luis writes: "from the moment Manzano wrote his authobiography, he passed from slave to author, from the black world into the white, from obscurity into history. Slave rebellions and the killing of whites represent a rejection of white values, but the process of writing is an acceptance of and a communion with Western culture and history. As author, Manzano has distanced himself from African and slave traditions and has erased his past as origin."[94]

Different from Manzano, Montejo subverts traditional stereotypes, and allows the writer, Barnet, to become a cimarrón. Montejo is a man whose criticism of the behavior of others sets him apart from the other slaves for whom he shows a particular lack of solidarity. In Montejo's auto-bio-story, as interpreted by Barnet's own bio-*graphia* through which he re-orders Montejo's story, the rebellious and anti-social slave which Montejo says he was (or Barnet says Montejo was), escapes from the Plantation to be free, to be his own master, and to live alone, in the refuge of the forest, the monte. Montejo, different from Mackandal and Cimarrón, understands the risks of adventuring back to the Plantation and he stays away from it. He mistrusts everyone and is cautious of that space "there" from where he fled. His association with the monte where he finds refuge—inscribed in his own name Monte-jo (of the monte)—makes him, as González Echeverría proposes: "the one who has been to the mountain and returned. He lives on the far side of all change, of all upheavals, because he has already endured the most difficult trials and is in possession of the special Knowledge that such journey confers on him."[95] For González Echevarría, Lydia Cabrera's *El monte* is an antededent of Barnet's text, and in that association, Montejo offers "a textual memory, both African and Cuban. He can incarnate the child, the Messiah, and the old man-prophet: Jesus and Moses at once."[96] Furthermore, González Echevarría notes, Montejo is his mother's name, a descendant of Haitian slaves. Montejo's story and his link to the past matrilineal,[97] further associates Esteban Monejo to the feminine space of the monte as mother. Roberto González Echeverría also notes that Barnet's Esteban Montejo "was born on 26 December, the feast of Saint Stephen [Esteban], the Protomartyr," and that "Esteban bears the name of two important literary protagonists: Joyce's Stephen Dedalus and Carpentier's Esteban in *Explosion in a Cathedral.* He shares more with them: their epic-like wanderings, their authorial propensities, their more or less obvious association with Christ (once removed, since they hark back to Saint Stephen, born the day after Christ's birthday; the first martyr after Him)."[98]

Different from the docile slave of the Cuban abolitionist Romantic novels, Montejo defies authority and has an adamant attitude toward others. He chooses the uncomfortable life of a loner in the forest rather than the life of obedience in the Plantation. He criticizes slavery, as well as his fellow slaves and "their" ways, often describing "them" from the privileged view of an anthropologist. Esteban Montejo's testimonial accounts, in Barnet's text, fill the gaps and silences left by history,[99] yet, in that recaptured voice, Barnet's *graphia* commemorates the past in order to establish a dialogue with Barnet's own historical present.[100]

These associations propose that Barnet's testimonial account of Esteban Montejo's life articulates another type of cimarronaje in which the text becomes an accomplice of the writer who fills with his own voice the gaps and silences left by the testimonial other; becoming, through writing, the same as the other he writes. Barnet's Esteban Montejo is an ex-slave, a cimarrón, a witness, a protagonist, and a narrator, but, like Carpentier's Ti Nöel, Montejo is also an allegory of Barnet's own condition. Montejo's voice and history serves as a protective Monte(jo), or refuge, to the writer who, once in it, much like Toll y Toste's Carabalí, may survive protected by the imaginary space of a testimonial fiction, hiding in the voice of the other, as the other, in the pantomime of that voice that (not very different from Toll y Toste's discursive context) the writer rescues from silence. In turn, that same rescued voice helps legitimize the writer as an integral part

of a new discourse on freedom institutionalized in Cuba in the sixties: a
discourse that, as Carlos Moore points out, turns "racial politics" into "a
foreign policy weapon."[101] Barnet's writing in the voice of the Other, is a
movement in which fiction and history exchange places under similar psychological constructs, escaping into the space of the monte Montejo represents for Barnet. In this complex historical dictate, the writer, by trapping
the runaway in his writing, receives as a reward (like in the sixteenth century), personal freedom and official recognition. At a difficult time when
other writers like Reinaldo Arenas, Lydia Cabrera, and Cabrera Infante,
were marginalized by a dominant discourse that praised dissidence only
when it was staged before the revolution, Barnet finds refuge and redemption in the magic of the monte afrocubano, in the figure of a cimarrón. However, while Barnet's testimonial text fills the gaps and silences left by history, the text opens other gaps, proposes other inquiries, and constructs
other historical silences. William Luis observes:

> If history repeats itself in the "present" does Montejo again feel he has to be
> silent? Is Montejo a silent witness of the Cuban Revolution? And does Mon-
> tejo's willingness to reject modern weapons and take up his *machete,* a symbol
> of past struggles, imply that for blacks nothing has really changed? Or is the
> silence a reference to Barnet's own signature; that is, to one of the changes he
> inserted in the narration, as he indicated in the English introduction? If this is
> so, the silence is a reference not to Montejo but to Barnet's own condition as a
> writer [in Cuba].[102]

During the period following the triumph of the Cuban Revolution, the
antislavery discourse suddenly became the center of a dominant discourse
for political legitimacy. The runaway slave became the symbol of a historical struggle for freedom which, after cycles of rebellions and revolutions,
finally culminated in the Cuban Revolution, a revolution that claimed to
bring to fruition the war of independence left suspended, incomplete, by
the American intervention. Once again, as in the nineteenth century (when
the rebelliousness of a slave could only be accepted by the creole discourse
in the ideological context of political independence), the cimarrón, as a
rebel and a dissident, could be accepted only as a sign for a political struggle "in the past," never within the Revolution, never as anything other than
to justify the present. Barnet's rendition of Esteban Montejo makes of the
ex-slave an Elegua: a mediator between two centuries and two different
discourses. Montejo's lonely and distant nature, his flights to the forest, his
critical views of other slaves, and his peculiar apathy regarding any type of
social, or cultural affinity, or even intimacy, with "his own people," dissappear when he joins the Cuban liberating army, and act that converts him,
a cimarrón, into a mambí. It is at this moment that the narrator's "I" waivers

between a "we" (us) and a "they" (them): "Nosotros, los libertadores, en-
contrábamos las cosas raras y nuevas"[103] (We [the liberators] found everything in the city strange and new),[104] in contrast to "they" "los libertadores
negros"[105] ([they] the black liberators).[106] The racial tension which Montejo did not feel as a mambí surfaces when he encounters the North American troops that invaded Cuba in 1898, the new colonialists of the twentieth century whose actions seem to inform Montejo's view of Cuban history)
from that moment on until 1959: "con los negros no se metían mucho.
Les[107] decían: 'Nigre, nigre.' Y entonces se echaban a reir"[108] (They did
not bother the blacks very much. They called them 'nigger, nigger.' And
then they would start to laugh);[109] "Hoy las cosas se me han revuelto de-
masiado. A pesar de que todo lo principal no se me olvida . . . A decir verdad, yo prefiero al español que al americano; pero al español en su tierra."
("But my head's too much of a muddle these days. Even so, I remember
the most important things."[110] "Frankly, I prefer the Spaniards to the Americans, the Spaniards in Spain, that is.")[111] Then he adds, "Ahora, al americano no lo quiero ni en la suya . . . la partida de degenerados esos que
hundieron este país."[112] ("I don't like the Americans even in their own
country . . . the whole pack of degenerates who ruined this country").[113]
Montejo's politically correct speech in the sixties is closely related to Barnet's needs, and to his conceptualization of the documentary novel. For
Barnet, the language of the documentary novel, as Barnet himself explains,
"must be a recreated spoken language, not a mere reproduction of what was
on tape."[114] He adds: "We must give the readers a consciousness of their
tradition, give them a useful myth or model with which to judge things,"[115]
"I wanted them [the characters] to give a true, more complex and more
combative image of the people."[116] Barnet's explications open the text to
other inquiries as, for example: Who then is "they" for Montejo, and who
is "we" for Barnet?

The unity of Montejo's discourse may be found perhaps in its own contradictions and omissions. For example, in spite of the fact that Montejo
was a centenary who had been living in a nursing home when Barnet found
him, he states with conviction: "Lo que más me ha salvado es que me he
callado, porque no se puede confiar. El que confía se hunde solo"[117] ("What
has saved me is that I keep my mouth shut. You can't trust people. If you
trust people too much you're finished").[118] He then adds: "Lo bueno que
tiene esto (the Socialist Revolutionary government) es que hoy se puede
hablar de todo"[119] [The good thing about "this" is that today one can talk
about anything), and he adds: "la verdad no se puede callar"[120] ("Truth cannot be silenced").[121] Is Montejo an ex-cimarrón whose success has been in
not trusting anyone, yet he contradicts his own character by trusting the
Revolutionary government? Is he (or Barnet) saying what he thinks he is
expected to say? When Montejo speaks of the Revolution, he is not refer-

ring to the War of Independence of 1895 in which Montejo was an active participant. He refers to the Revolution of 1959, of which Montejo was a distant witness in a nursing home. He also often refers to the post-revolutionary years, after 1959, with a codified *ahora* (now) or *esto* (this)—terms still utilized today in Cuba, among other euphemisms, to speak of present situations in Cuba. The term *esto* (this), in Montejo's auto-bio-story, seems to be related in his discourse of rebellion, resistance, and distrust, to his affirmation of the government's policies, understood through distant analogies rather than through personal experience.

The logic in Montejo's movement from resistance and distrust of authority to an affirmation of the historical present lived by Barnet, in which he writes, coincides with a discursive construct contemporary to Barnet's immediate needs, and to a political hegemony that disapproved of any social order previous to 1959. In writing Montejo, let us recall that Barnet is trying "to give a true, more complex and more combative image of the people." Hence, Montejo's biography is a discursive construct that assumes that the Revolution of 1959 is the logical historical resolution to a struggle for freedom that began with the runaway slaves in the sixteen century: a struggle that began with the regional establishment of palenques, turned political during the Wars of Independence (in 1868 and 1895), and that ended in 1959. The historical omissions in Montejo's reconstructed story create a play of similarities and differences: the structure of Montejo's (his)story as an allegory for Cuba's history, and the structure of the writer's own (his)story. Julia Kristeva, in an analysis of Mikail Bakhtin's work, observes that in Bakhtin's models "literary structure does not simply *exist,* but is generated in relation to *another* structure" and that the "'literary word' is an *intersection of textual surfaces* rather than a point (a fixed meaning), as a dialogue among several writings."[122] Like Bakhtin's texts, Barnet also "situates the text within history and society, which are seen as texts read by the writer, and into which he inserts himself by rewriting them."[123] Barnet's *Biografía de un cimarrón* recalls Bakhtin's models in that "Diachrony is transformed into synchrony, and in light of this transformation, *linear* history appears as abstraction. The only way a writer can participate in history is by transgressing this abstraction through a process of reading-writing; that is, through the practice of a signifying structure in relation or opposition to another structure."[124]

Rescued and protected by the monte of fiction, in the space of the imaginary, in a text that through "translation" takes the biography of an ex-slave and superimposes it to the historical context of the writer, a new image of cimarrón emerges in the figure of Esteban Montejo, in a dialogic relationship between writer and narrator. In that mutual relationship, the moment of writing, and the past recalled in that writing, come together as one and the same. In such dialogue, the text displaces afrocubanismo from its religious context and takes it to a political image of past insurgency and present docility coherent with the new ideology. Perhaps this is why Esteban Montejo, who is always cautiously a loner, critical of everything and everyone, a rebel, antisocial even toward his own fellow slaves, suddenly conforms to a historical present: Barnet's present, with which he seems to always already have been an accomplice.[125] For González Echevarría: "Esteban Montejo's ironic wisdom ultimately betrays Miguel Barnet. The true symbiosis of Barnet and Montejo occurs not when one becomes the other, but when both turn out to have been the same all along."[126] In Barnet's text, writing creates the illusion that a sector of society historically powerless has acquired a voice in Montejo, and that that voice placed at the center of a new order of things seeks legitimacy in a dominant discourse that pretends to speak from the margins. In this play of authorial voices, Barnet rescues Montejo who, in turn, rescues Barnet.

III

In *Los guerrilleros negros* (1976), a novel also published in 1982 in Spain as *Capitán de cimarrones,* César Leante romances the life of another historical cimarrón leader in Cuba. Like Carpentier in *The Kingdom of This World,* Leante utilizes multiple documents and literary texts[127] to reconstruct the life of Ventura Sánchez. Coba, as he was known, was a runaway slave who in the early nineteenth century became a well-known maroon leader of the palenque El Frijol, in the eastern province of Oriente. Leante's romanced life of Ventura Sánchez exalts the heroic deeds of a cimarrón whose life is represented in the novel as an allegory of Cuba's fight for freedom up until the triumph of the Revolution in 1959 (an idea the writer no longer holds). This struggle, as Leante's novel proposes, began with the first palenques and with the cimarrón's "irrevocable decisión de permanecer libres" (irrevocable decision to remain free).[128] William Luis argues that:

> Like other recent works, Leante's novel partakes of a tradition directly associated with the revolution . . . Leante, like the present Cuban government, will analyse the past from a specific, revolutionary present. Just as the political leaders and historians have reevaluated history and now view the 1959 takeover as part of a process that began with Carlos Manuel de Céspedes uprisings in 1868, a theme reiterated in Barnet's documentary novel, Leante rewrites that origin by introducing the slave rebellion into literature as the beginning of modern Cuban history.[129]

While in Puerto Rico and the Dominican Republic the figure of cimarrón continued to be relegated in literary narratives to the silence of few legends, in Cuba, the runaway slave came to serve as the politically-correct sign for the writer's re-present-ation of his own historical moment, as an always already-integral part of the new political discourse. As in Barnet and Leante's representation of cimarrón in the context of the Cuban Revolution, the will to freedom of the runaway slave became a pivotal symbol for the discourse of a new center, an official discourse which Roberto Fernandez Retamar summarizes in his essay "Calibán": "nosotros reclamanos como un timbre de gloria el honor de considerarnos descendientes de 'mambí', desdendientes de negro alzado, cimarrón, independentista y 'nunca' descendientes de esclavistas" (We claim as a stamp of glory the honor of considering ourselves descendants of "mambí," descendants of black rebels, maroon, patriots and "never" descendants of slave owners).[130] Conceiving history from the gaze of the other, the oppressed, but articulating that gaze in the voice of the intelligentzia in power, Fernández Retamar takes Caliban to be the cultural and political symbol for a political center that pretends to speak from the margins. Its objective is to embrace—in a stylized act of symbolic brotherhood, following the model Ferrer observes of a "raceless" nationality held by Cuban patriots during the struggle for independence[131]—all Caribbean nations (Hispanic and non-Hispanic nations) whose cultural or racial roots can be traced to Africa: societies who have as a common bond the experience of colonialism and slavery.

Retamar makes a statement of solidarity via that common denominator that unites all post-colonial and neo-colonial nations in the Caribbean: the struggle for political, economic, and cultural independence. This metaphorical brotherhood is inscribed in the Caribbean collective consciousness through the inscription of a common cultural and racial mixture: "Nuestro símbolo no es Ariel, como pensó Rodó, sino Calibán. Esto es algo que vemos con particular nitidez los mestizos que habitamos estas mismas islas donde vivió Calibán."[132] (Our symbol is not Ariel, as Rodó thought, but Caliban. This is something we see with special clarity, we mestizos that live in these same islands where Caliban lived). Fernández Retamar's historical claim is the modified continuation of a nineteenth-century discourse that Ada Ferrer describes as the "transcendence of race and the birth of the nation" not by mestizaje, but rather "forged in manly union during war," "less the product of miscegenation than of masculine heroism and will."[133] In other words, Fernández Retamar's discourse is more political than racial. Although legitimate as the "voice" of the island's cultural/racial "hybridity," Fernandez Retamar's comments border on usurpation, in the sense that he proposes an imaginary cimarrón black-mulatto in the position of political dominance: Fernández Retamar. As Marilyn Grace Miller suggests: "Fernández Retamar seems to again equate "race"—or at least ethnicity—with culture."[134] Vera Kutzinski notes that in this "new Revolutionary" discourse of equality (of rhizomatic entanglements in Cuban history), Fernández Retamar further reiterates what Kutzinski describes in Cuban letters as: a "cross-racial male lineage."[135]

In Fernandez Retamar's representation of Caliban as a metaphor for the Caribbean, as in Montejo/Barnet's bio-*graphia,* rebelliousness is not possible outside its metaphorical ideological significance. From the gaze of the Revolutionary political hegemony, rebellion and resistance in post-revolutionary Cuba can only be a tropological representation. For Fernández Retamar the sign cimarrón cannot signify dissent or a discourse on freedom different from the one approved by the official discourse that chooses it as a symbol for legitimacy. Dissidence, then, is only valid when articulated within the new codes set by the official ideology. And, it can be a patriotic act only when staged prior to 1959. When a counter-discourse of resistance emerges within the hegemony of authorial power, the will to freedom (to resist injustice and oppression) suddenly loses its symbolic historical significance as metaphor, and the dissident writer becomes, just like the runnaway slave during Enriquillo's uprising, an alzado, a savage, a "barbaric runaway turned wild," dangerous, outside of the law.

The utilization of the character of Caliban in William Shakeaspeare's *The Tempest,* as a symbol for the Caribbean, establishes a direct dialogue with José Rodó's "Ariel" (1900).[136] Both literary figures, in their Latin American representations, are a response, from very diferent historical and political perspectives, to the question of how "a culture seeking to become independent of imperialism imagines its own past."[137] One way, suggests Edward Said in *Culture and Imperialism,* is Rodó's reading of Ariel as "a willing servant of Prospero" who, "when he gains his freedom, he returns to his native element, a sort of bourgeois native untroubled by his collaboration with Prospero."[138] Another way, Said adds, "is to do it like Calibán, aware of and accepting his mongrel past but not disabled for future development. A third choice is to be a Calibán who sheds his current servitude and physical disfigurement in the process of discovering his essencial, pre-colonial self. This Calibán is behind the nativist and radical nationalisms that produced concepts of *négritude,* Islamic fundamentalism, Arabism, and the like."[139] The different modalities in which Shakespeare's Caliban has been rewritten as a metaphor for the Caribbean, address different historical and political views in the process of "imagining" one's own national past in one's own "imagined communities." "Each new American reinscription of *The Tempest* is therefore a local version of the old grand story, invigorated and inflicted by the pressures of an unfolding political and cultural history."[140] In the Caribbean, a revisionist view of *Nativism* in Aimé Césaire's *Une Tempête* already identified Caliban's rebelliouness against his colonizer, Prospero, as a symbol closer to the historical experience of the Caribbean. Césaire identifies Caliban as a symbol for a counter-discourse of resistance, as a rightful appropriation by Caribbean writers to represent the Caribbean from a Caribbean historical gaze.[141] It was not until 1969, explains Fernández Retamar, that Caliban was:

asumido con orgullo como nuestro símbolo por tres escritores antillanos, cada uno de los cuales se expresa en una de las grandes lenguas coloniales del Caribe . . . el martiniqueño Aimé Césaire su obra de teatro, en francés, *Una tempestad. Adaptación de* La tempestad *de Shakespeare para un teatro negro;* el barbadiense Edward Brathwaite, su libro de poemas en inglés *Islas,* entre los cuales hay uno dedicado a "Calibán"; y el autor de estas líneas, su ensayo en español "Cuba hasta Fidel", en que se habla de nuestra identificación con Calibán.[142]

[taken with pride as our symbol by three Antillian writers, each one expressing it in one of the main colonial languages of the Caribbean . . . the Martinique writer Aimé Césaire, his play, in French, *Una tempestad. Adaptación de* La Tempestad *de Shakespeare para un teatro negro;* the writer from Barbados Edward Brathwaite, his book of poems in English, *Islas,* in which there is one dedicated to "Calibán;" and the writer of these lines, his essay in Spanish, "Cuba hasta Fidel," which speaks of our identification with Caliban.]

The difference between Fernando Retamar's Caliban and other literary appropriations of Caliban in the Caribbean is that Fernández Retamar is using a symbol already inscribed in the national official discourse of the Revolutionary government, as a sign of political legitimacy for an institutionalized government; and, at the same time, he uses it as a discourse of resistance against neocolonialism. Fernández Retamar is speaking from the center of power, from the voice of author(ity), in the name of the margin, as if it were a counter-discourse to the very authorial power from which he speaks. In this complex play of sub-versions, one must ask who is "we" for Fernández Retamar when he says: "los mestizos que habitamos estas mismas islas?" (we the mestizos who inhabit these islands). Once again, like in nineteenth century, as Carlos Moore claims of Revolutionary Cuba, Fernández Retamar dissipates racial differences for political advantages.[143] The irony in the various re-readings and symbolic recontextualization of Caliban in the Caribbean is that, while the runaway slave is an important historical figure in the Caribbean (a presence that left deep imprints in the socioeconomic systems of the colonies), the integration by Fernández Retamar of this literary persona to an official political discourse is done through a fictional character, displacing history, again, to the oneiric realm of (English) literature. Yet, Fernández Retamar's Caliban, as Said observes, also "signals a profoundly important ideological debate at the heart of the cultural effort to decolonize, an effort at the restoration of community and repossession of a culture that goes on long after the political establishment of independent nation-states."[144] Such discourse also perpetuates, ironically, a complex relationship in the Caribbean between fiction and history, the proper and the foreign, imagination, and national identity. This is a relationship that does not escape Fernandez Retamar, who keenly observes that: "Al proponer a Calibán como nuestro símbolo, me doy cuenta de que tampoco es enteramente nuestro, también es una elaboración extraña, aunque esta vez lo sea a partir de nuestras concretas realidades" (By proposing Calibán as our symbol, I realize that he is also not entirely ours, that he is also a strange elaboration, even though this time it is coming from our concrete realities).[145] The image of Caliban as metaphor for the Caribbean, and of cimarronaje as Caribbeanness, brings up questions about the relationship between identification and identity and recalls Homi Bhabha's notion that: "the question of identification is never the affirmation of a pre-given identity, never a *self*-fulfilling prophecy—it is always the production of an image of identity and the transformation of the subject in assuming that image."[146]

IV

Following a well-known practice in maroon communities in Cuba, in Leante's *Los guerrilleros negros* the young cimarrón, Coba, goes to Santiago de Cuba posing as a free creole to sell the products raised and gathered in the palenque. Listening to conversations in the city between free black men, he learns that:

> los negros habían llegado a Cuba y a esta ciudad a la par que los conquistadores españoles, que habían ayudado a fundarla, que habían laborado en la edificación de sus fuertes y viviendas, cargando, como era de suponer, con el trabajo más rudo, y por lo tanto podían considerarse tan cubanos como los blancos, si no más. Esta era su tierra, su suelo, su país y tenían derecho como el que más a vivir aquí en igualdad de situación con el blanco. Los negros no debían pensar en volver al África—como los blancos no pensaban en regresar a España—sino en ser hombre libres y respetados en Cuba.[147]

> [Blacks had arrived to Cuba and to this city together with the Spanish conquerors, and together with them they helped found it, they labored in the construction of forts and residences, did the hardest jobs, and therefore, considered themselves to be just as Cuban, if not more than the white man. This was their land, their soil, their country, and they had the right, as anyone else, to live here in equal status to the white. Blacks should not think about returning to Africa—just like the whites were not thinking about returning to Europe—but to be free and respected men in Cuba.]

Coba's notions of political and racial ideologies are the same as José Antonio Aponte's, the free mulatto executed by the colonial government only two years earlier, in 1812, for instigating a mass rebellion in Cuba following the revolutionary model of Haiti.[148] Leante's Coba embraces Aponte's political thoughts, thus uniting him, allegorically, to Aponte's revolutionary efforts, and making Coba, in Leante's text, Aponte's disciple. From this moment on, the life of Leante's Coba parallels Aponte's life. As it happens also with Aponte, government troops assassinate Coba and display his de-capitated head as a warning.[149] The historical similarities in the events sur-rounding the deaths of Coba and Aponte allows Leante to represent them as martyrs of a continuing apocalyptic Revolution that their deaths herald. Thus, in Leante's rendition of the historical maroon leader: "Desde sus muertes iguales Coba y José Antonio Aponte se abrazaban" (In the same-ness of their deaths Coba and José Antonio Aponte embraced each other).[150]

In *Los guerrilleros negros,* historical events are faithfully documented, but they are also reconstructed to best fit the writer's historical present as well as the symbolic codified order of the narration. The imaginative re-construction of those events often leaves discrepancies between the ro-manced history and the historical documents.[151] For example, when Leante's Coba is ambushed by government troops, he jumps over a cliff to avoid captivity. Although the novel is consistent with the history of cimar-rón communities and with José Franco's accounts of Ventura Sánchez's death (in "Palenques del Frijol, Bumba y Maluala"), William Luis notes that in Danger Roll's historical accounts pertaining the palenque El Frijol, it is not Ventura Sánchez (Coba), but Manuel Griñán (Gallo), Coba's blood brother and friend, who was taken by surprise by Felipe Fromesta's troops and the one who chose to jump to his death.[152]

Leante and Franco's accounts associate the maroon community of El Fri-jol, in its struggle for survival, with the successful resistance of the miners of El Cobre who after over one hundred years of resistance, finally won land and freedom in 1800. Both writers associate that struggle with the patriots of the Haitian revolution, with Aponte's rebellion, with the wars for inde-pendence in Cuba (1868, 1879, 1895) and, ultimately, with the Cuban Rev-olution of 1959. In Leante's text, fiction and history embrace each other much like Aponte and Coba. It is an ideological embrace made possible in the novel through the omissions and gaps left by history. Nonwithstanding, although Leante seems to base his (his)story on Franco's version,[153] Franco points out that the entire maroon group: "confiados en las promesas solem-nes del gobernador y del arzobispo bajaron la guardia y fueron sorprendi-dos . . . Manuel Griñan (Gallo), el otro gran líder de los rebeldes, recibió a tiempo el aviso de las siniestras maquinaciones del gobernador y del arzo-bispo, y se puso en guardia" (trusting the promises of the governor and the archbishop, they relaxed their guard and were taken by surprise . . . Manuel Griñan (Gallo), the other one of the great rebel leader, received in time word about the sinister machinations of the governor and the archbishop, and he stood on guard).[154] The figure of the cimarrón, in Franco and Leante's accounts, also implicitly recalls the long and successful struggle of the miners of El Cobre, whose freedom preceded both the triumph of the Haitian revolution, and José Antonio Aponte's frustrated rebellion.

Leante's Coba is a martyr in the earlier stages of the struggle for independence/freedom in Cuba. He chooses death (freedom) over a life of bondage,[155] and, in his honor, Griñán, his partner and ideological blood brother, orders all of the palenques of the northern region of Oriente to beat the drums all night long, on Christmas Eve. As in a rite of resurrection, the allegorical rebirth of Coba's revolutionary spirit in the drumming announces the continuation of the struggle, and its future victory. Coba's death offers the messianic prophecy of a new day of judgment. As in Ti Nöel's call to the wind that brings about his erasure, Coba's decision to jump from a cliff to his death makes him a recontextualized Faustian-Romantic hero who, in his fall, reaches for infinity in a "longing" for the ultimate "liberty," in the mystery of "an ineffable sense of forsakenness" (*DW,* 186). Coba emerges "from the interior into the boundless" (*DW,* 199), in an act of "becoming the World-Force" whose destiny will be heard in the wind-force-sound of the drums and the thunder. The association here between drumming, the storm, thunder, and the spirit of freedom, recalls the wind-bellowing of Huracán-Shango-Oggún Badragrí in *The Kingdom of This World.* In *Los guerrilleros negros* the spirit of rebelliousness coincides again with Nativity:

> justamente la noche del 24 de diciembre, la noche del Señor, la golosa noche de Nochebuena, los bulá, premir, catá, rompieron a azotar la fingida noche de la cristiandad. Desplegaron su grito, de dolor e ira, desde Toa, Bumba, Maluala, El Frijol, Todos Tenemos, Caujerí, Vengan Sábalos, La Palma; fundieron sus gritos los tambores en uno solo que cabalgó por las montañas durante toda la noche y se anudó al alba y al sol de la natividad. Renacía Coba en él, y en el canto del cuero iba su voz irredenta. Viajando en el viento vertiginoso de la sierra su eco se desparramó por picos y hondonadas, por firmes y barranco, por valles y cañadas.[156]

> [precisely the night of the 24th of December, the night of the Lord, the sweet night of Christmas Eve, the bulá, premir, and catá drums, began to beat Christianity's feigned night. They unfolded their cry of pain and anger, from Toa, Bumba, Maluala, El Frijol, Todos Tenemos, Caumerí, Vengan Sábalos, La Palma; joined together in one single cry, all the drums as one, galloping through mountains throughout the night becoming one with the dawn and with the sun of the day of Nativity. Coba was reborn in it, and his unredeemed voice traveled in the songs of the hides. Together with the strong winds of the Sierras it swept through peaks and hollows, highlands and gullies, valleys and streams.]

As in Carpentier's *The Kingdom of This World,* the Antillean *cemi* Huracán, joins the African orisha of thunder and the drum, Shango. And, once more in Caribbean literature, drum and thunder, cemi and orisha, voice in unison the same will-to-freedom that defines history in the Caribbean landscape. The incessant sound of the drumming in the high mountains (monte), (con)fused with the thunders of a storm that pounds the region as a divine warning, heralds a final judgment day. The conjoined earth-sky (cosmic twin) drums and thunders made the brigadier feel that the: "estampidos de los truenos . . . encadenándose, remedaban un cañoneo sordo sobre la ciudad" (the harsh explosives of the thunders . . . so close together, sounded like cannon balls falling on the city).[157] It also gave the governor of Cuba, Escudero, the sensation that "un tambor imposible estaba batiendo . . ." (an impossible drum was beating), that "los tambores crecían, se multiplicaban . . ." (the drums were getting louder, were multiplying in number)[158] and, as if nature itself had joined in the rage and mourning of the cimarrones, "un azote de viento lanzó de par en par hacia dentro las dos pesadas hojas. Y esa misma racha apagó la única luz del despacho dejándolo totalmente a oscuras" (a gust of wind blew in, and opened wide both heavy doors. The same gust blew out the only light in the office leaving him in total darkness).[159] That night, and the next day, symbolically December 25th, "atronó el mundo" (the world was deaf with thunder) until sunset when: "el sol rojo y ardiente de Coba" (the red and burning sun of Coba)[160] could be seen in the sky.

Coba's death speaks of the writer's present as an immediate past seen through the looking-glass of a new discourse: a historical moment which, in a retrospective re-reading of history, has found in the figure of cimarrón its legitimate ancestor.[161] Much like Toll y Toste's "Carabalí," Coba's life and death, had fallen into the abyss of a historical silence, to be rescued by the imaginary space of a novel where his spirit now survives as myth, metaphorically camouflaged by the magic *monte* of fiction. In the context of new symbolic codes in the political discourse that began in 1959, the present of the writer articulates the end of Coba and Aponte"s struggle, as a new historical moment mediated by the desire of history: a passion for history that makes the Caribbean writer turn inward, to a Caribbean time and space, and to Caribbean codes and symbols. Lisandro Otero recalled on the occasion of Ortiz"s death, that Ortiz had prophetically spoken at the Capitol, in Havana, during Nativity, only six months before the attack by the revolutionaries of the Moncada army barrack (1953): "Hoy venimos a celebrar como un rito de solsticio invernal, el de la natividad de un nuevo sol, cuando de la noche más larga y oscura del año nace el luminar de los cielos" (today we come together to celebrate, as in a rite of winter solstice, the nativity of a new sun, when from the longest and darkest night of the year, the heavenly light is born).[162] Leante's *Los guerrilleros negros* honors Ortiz's memory and celebrates the allegorical death and spiritual rebirth of the historical cimarrón Coba, placing his historical death at a winter solstice, at the nativity of a new sun.

V

Like Fernández Retamar's Calibán, Leante's Coba personifies the underlying myth in Latin America of the guerrillero: a myth that in the Caribbean has been politically associated with the figure of the runaway slave as a symbol of a continuous spirit of resitance.[163] Leante's account of Coba's death, Barnet's reconstruction of Esteban Montejo's story into a "more combative image of the people," and the rereading of Shakespeare's Caliban by Fernández Retamar are representative of the historical model Fredic Jameson proposes in *The Political Unconscious:* "Only Marxism can give us an adequate account of the essential mystery of the cultural past . . . This mystery can be reenacted only if the human adventure is one . . . These matters can recover their original urgency for us only if they are retold within the unity of a single great collective story; only if, in however disguised and symbolic a form, they are seen as sharing a single fundamental theme."[164]

As if history were an orderly sequence of events, Leante, like Retamar, and like Jameson, suggests a political unconsciousness that, like a unifying thread, weaves the past with the present. For this ideologeme to function in the novel, Coba must gain, progressively, a political awareness that allows him to transcend his personal individual will-to-freedom and become, at his death, the phenomenology of a collective Hegelian spirit of Knowledge/Freedom in the process of Becoming. This process, in Leante's Coba, has several stages. It begins with the stories, legends, and myths of an African past that Taita Quiala narrates to him during his childhood. It continues with Coba's encounter of the political views held by the freemen in Santiago de Cuba of Aponte's ideals, which Coba now embraces, and the ideas he heard from both, Santiago, the maroon chief of the Great Palenque, and from Father Antonio, the palenque's white priest. It is not a mere coincidence then that Coba is instructed in Aponte's revolutionary ideals by another cimarrón named Santiago (reminiscing Santiago de Cuba, and *Santiago Apostol* or Saint James: Ogoun Fai, the warrior loa of revolutions conjured by Bouckman and Ti Noël in *The Kingdom of This World*). Coba comes in contact with Aponte's ideals in Santiago de Cuba, the same place where Ti Noël learned of the triumph of the Haitian revolution. Coba hears about Haiti's triumph against French colonialism and slavery from Haitian sailors who tell him stories of the Haitian triumph, of their struggle for independence, and of Mackandal's fabulous feats, deeds, and magic powers. The mytho-historical figure of Mackandal becomes a model to follow for Coba as it was for Carpentier's Ti Nöel. Like in the case of Ti Nöel, it is also through narration (history, myths, and fantasy) that Coba's ideals and character are formed; and it is through narration that the text reorders, retrospectively, the laws that rule history into one uninterrupted story. In the context of this progressive sequence of events, Coba, and his comrades in arms: "demonstraban un conocimiento preciso y un uso adecuado de las tácticas guerrilleras. . . . Destrezas a las que había que añadir una valentía extraordinaria, que era como un reto abierto a las fuerzas gubernamentales" (demonstrated a precise knowledge and the proper use of guerrilla tactics . . . Skills to which they added an extraordinary bravery, which was as an open challenge to the forces of the government).[165]

The use of the words guerrillero and guerrilla in Leante's novel, identifies the tactics used by maroon leaders in the early part of the nineteenth century, however, such terms recontextualize the historical events of that period to fit a given political ideology in the writer's historical context. Hence, few years later, Leante changed the title of his novel to *Capitán de cimarrones* (Maroon Captain), for the 1982 edition, thus changing the meaning of the events narrated in the novel to their nineteenth-century historical context; to a time when the term mambí was used for insurgents against Spain, and the term guerrillero was the name given to creoles, black or white, who fought on the side of Spaniards against Cuban patriots. A guerrillero then was a Cuban mercenary. As William Luis points out: "The term guerrilla, used in Leante's title, is not of recent usage. But there is no contemporary meaning. Esteban Montejo uses the term in its historical and derogatory context."[166] According to Montejo:

> Los verdaderos guerrilleros eran hombres de monte y estúpidos. A mí no se me puede venir con el cuento de que un hombre de letras se hacía guerrillero. Guerrillero había igual blancos que negros, ésa era la verdad . . .
>   La táctica de los guerrilleros era distinta a la de las tropas libertadoras. A ellos les salía fuego por los ojos. Y eran hombres llenos de veneno, de entrañas podridas. Cuando veían un grupito de mambieses les caían arriba a cogerlos; si los cogían, los mataban sin más. Los españoles peleaban de frente, no mataban así, a sangre fría. Tenían otro concepto. . . .
>   Nunca yo vide gente más odiosa. Todavía, a estas alturas, quedan algunos en esta isla.[167]

> [The real guerrillas were stupid countrymen. Don't anyone try to tell me a man of letters would become a guerrilla. There were white guerrillas as well as black ones.
>   The guerrilla tactics were different from those of the liberating army. Fire blazed from their eyes, they were men full of poison, rotten to the core. When they saw a group of *Mambises* they used to fall on them, and if they captured them they killed them all outright. I never met worse people in my life. Even now, all this time later, there are a few of them left on this island.][168]

By 1976 when Leante published *Los guerrilleros negros,* the words guerrillero and guerrilla had a different political meaning in the context of the Cuban Revolution, as it had been defined by Che Guevara in *Guerrilla Warfare* (1960). Under the codes of the new revolutionary discourse, in which oppression and capitalism are synonyms, the political and philosophical image of cimarrón in Leante's novel had to concur with the meaning given to the word guerrillero in the middle of the twentieth century, not only for reasons of political correctness, but to give an image of progression and sameness to the historical process. In contrast with Leante's choice of guerrillero for the 1976 edition, later changed in 1982 to cimarrón in *Capitán de cimarrones* (Captain of cimarrones), Carlos Esteban Deive ironically chose the same title, *Los guerrilleros negros,* for his 1989 historical study of runaway slaves in Hispanola (today the Dominican Republic and Haiti). Deive's choice of words recontextualizes the image of cimarrón, to a different contemporary meaning. Leante changed the history of Coba's life in 1982, to the gaze of a very different dialogical space, simply by changing the title to fit the changes in the writer's political perspective.[169] In Leante's *Capitán de cimarrones* (a text now different from itself), again like in the sixteeenth and nineteenth centuries, the sign cimarrón suffered a transformation that established it as an icon for an-other sociopolitical discourse, no longer in favor of Cuba's ideology, but of freedom. In Deive's study, however, the already politically charged guerrillero in the twentieth century continues to be applied retrospectively to nineteenth-century Santo Domingo, simply by equating cimarrón with guerrillero. The irony here is that, in Deive's own historical observations, in Santo Domingo until the end of the eighteenth century running away was not related to a collective political awareness:

La convicción, expresada por ciertos autores, de que el *cimarron*aje en grupo puede conducir, y de hecho condujo, a una toma de conciencia política, revolucionaria y nacionalista no es aceptable. Esa convicción, que comparten por ejemplo, Manigat y Fouchard se basa exclusivamente en los acontecimientos de la colonia de Saint-Domingue iniciados a partir de 1789 con la Revolución Francesa y que culminaron, como es sabido, con la fundación del Estado haitiano.[170]

[The conviction of certain authors that running away in groups could lead, and in fact it led, to a revolutionary and national political consciousness, is not acceptable. That conviction, shared by, for example, Manigat and Fouchard, is based exclusively in the events that took place in the colony of Saint-Domingue after 1789 with the French Revolution, and that ended, as it is known, with the formation of the Haitian State.]

Different from Deive's conclusions about the maroon slaves of Santo Domingo, in Cuba in the first decades of the nineteenth century, as the result of the Haitian experience, and of the triumph of the miners of El Cobre in Oriente, there emerged a political awareness among all slaves that established cimarronaje, far beyond the desire for personal freedom, as a conscious act of political resistance.

VI

From the gaze of an ideological discourse that makes cimarrón synonymous of guerrillero, Leante's Coba represents a codified discourse of difficult access whose possibility for encoding must be sought once more in the polysemantic, and self-referential, Cuban monte. Leante's guerrillero/ cimarrón can be read as a historical-literary figure codified by the new discourse it represents, but also, as a literary construct that resists and subverts the same ideology from which it speaks. Reading Coba as a text within a larger text, we find that Coba, like Montejo, and unlike Ti Nöel, is different and distant from the other slaves. In fact, Coba was torn between the strong atavistic feelings he experienced whenever he heard "el golpear de los cueros que repercutían en su sangre con ecos ancestrales" (the beat of the hides that reverberated in his blood as ancestral echoes),[171] and his rejection of the slave's "African ways," of the singing and dancing that he saw as a symbol of bondage. Coba's dissidence recalls Montejo's distance and rejection of his own fellow slaves.[172] Seduced by and yet distant from the slaves' "African ways," Coba embraces his African legacy only through Quiala's narratives of African myths similar to those Ti Nöel learned from Mackandal.

The use of parody and textual references Leante weaves into his text establishes a dialogue with other texts of fiction, reminding the reader that, while Ventura Sánchez was a historical cimarrón, Leante's Coba is a codified text within another text: a literary self-referential construct informed by Leante's historical present. It is in this sense that Leante's Coba may be read as an icon for the gaps and complexities of the Caribbean experience. Coba's historicity and mythology recall Ortiz's counterpoint of tobacco and sugar and Ortiz's struggle in that text to create a national identity based on an ontological counterpoint of Africa and Europe, in a landscape that, as Glissant proposes, "is duration."[173] Similar to Montejo, but different from Ti Nöel, when Quiala dies, young Ventura loses the freedom he had found in Quiala's African imaginary: a mytho-poetic freedom constructed in, and out of, the same space Mackandal constructed a magical world for Ti Nöel. Quiala's mythical stories, like Mackandal's stories, became a liberating force that allowed Coba, like Ti Nöel before him, to find freedom from the tyranny of their present reality. Those stories created an imaginary monte far away from the realities of the Plantation. Hence, after Quiala's death, Coba sought the freedom Quiala's mythical Africa offered him by running away from the plantation to a palenque. It is there, in the refuge of the monte, that he becomes a man, sees the ocean (*mar*) for the first time, acquires political "knowledge" and a given ideology, falls in love with the young cimarrón, Mariana, becomes a maroon leader, and finally meets his death.

It is also in the remote refuge of the monte that Coba and Mariana unite in marital bonds, symbolically by a pond. As already inscribed in her name, Mar(i)ana's[174] presence in Coba's life brings together an African and European imaginary: the image of the Greco-Roman goddess of the forest, Diana, the Afro-Cuban avatar of the Virgin Mary, Oshun (Virgen de la Caridad del Cobre, Patron Saint of Cuba), and Yemayá. After Mariana dies, killed by hounds during a government raid, Coba, transformed now by his lost and by anger, becomes a feared leader. As in Abakuá mythopoetics, once again the sacrificial death of a woman brings about a new reality for a male hegemony associated with rebelliousness, resistance, and nation.[175] From then on, Coba's struggle is a struggle for survival, but it is also an ethical struggle for freedom, land, and dignity.

At the end of the novel, the final thunder-druming of both, nature (storm) and cimarrones, reenacts the discursive presence in the Caribbean imaginary of Huracán-Shango. In Cuba, Shango is a trope for revolution, readapted by Pepe Carril, in his play *Shango de Ima* (1969), in the image of a Cuban Orpheus, owner of the Fire and the Sun, and a symbol of the new day. In *Los guerilleros negros,* Coba, like Carril's *Shango,* is transformed through "el canto del cuero" (the song of the hide),[176] into the apocalyptic image of a new day heralded by a "red" sunset. As in náñigo initiations, Coba's transcendence by death to a different spiritual reality transforms him into the sun hero of a Caribbean landscape: "el sol rojo y ardiente de Coba" (the red and burning sun of Coba).[177] The symbolic relationship in Leante's novel between the Cuban maroon warrior, Coba, and the divine judge, Shango, the spirit of divine justice and rebellion, the great African hero-king-deity warrior, who also felt neglected and rejected by his subjects (and is as capricious as Coba), further (con)fuses Coba with José Antonio Aponte. Aponte was not just a soldier, an artist, an *ebanista,* a rebel, and a conspirator. He also presided over the *cabildo Shango-Tedum,* and was an *ogboni* in one of the most powerful secret orders of Nigeria in Cuba. In Cuba, this *cabildo* was related to the Afro-Cuban Shango. Its members followed in spirit the great African orisha. Being an ogboni was a hereditary position that the ogboni took from the orisha of thunder and lighting as its direct ancestor, and spiritual patriarch. Aponte had reached in the *Lucumí Shango-Tedum* the high priestly rank of an *Oni-Shango.*[178] As part of Leante's romanced trilogy Aponte-Coba-Shango, it is significant that the mytho-historical king, Shango, like Coba, chooses death and commits suicide. It is in the act of choosing his own death that this powerful king becomes and ori-sha, a deity cultural hero-king of his people, and the terrible storm god of judgement and justice. Also, like Shango, the great warrior maroon chief, Coba, is transformed in his death into an *ori* (sha) (meaning guiding intelligence, and spiritual "head") of cimarrones, in their struggle for freedom.

The Colombian writer, Manuel Zapata Olivella, has observed that Shango was the orisha whose omniscient presence was most intensely felt by African slaves, in the drums, tropical storms, and hurricanes.[179] Furthermore, says Zapata: "América se negreó con los africanos, no por su piel sino su rebeldía, sus luchas antiesclavistas" (America was blackened by Africans not for the color of their skin, but for their rebelliousness, and their anti-slavery struggles).[180] Hence, he claims, Shango is the best representative of the idiosyncrasies of the African saga in America.[181] The orisha of fire, thunder, lightning, and the drum is also the one that best represents the conflicts and paradoxes the slave system left imprinted in the collective subconscious of Caribbean societies. This makes Shango, still today, one of the most popular orishas in the Caribbean.[182]

In Leante's novel, like Shango, and like Aponte, Leante's Coba is a historical figure whose death turns him into a mytho-poetic spirit: the spirit of justice and rebellion, and a guiding model for the very own people who betrayed him. Like Shango, Coba was abandoned by his people due to his own self-delusions of power; and like Coba, Aponte was betrayed by Esteban Sánchez, "pardo libre, platero, natural de Matanzas, Gastador del Batallón de Pardos libres de La Habana" (free mulatto, silversmith, from Matanzas, Pioneer of Havana's Batallion of Free Mulattos) and the betrayal was ratified by Mauricio Gutiérrez, "negro libre, carpintero" (free black man, carpenter).[183] Like Leante's Coba, Shango represents the dualities of humanity and of the cosmos. A Yoruba legend tells that Shango was negligent of his magical powers, and carelessly destroyed his own palace and his people with his thunderbolt.[184] Oyin Ogunba's account offers a different account:

> The story of Sango [*Shango*], the legenday fourth king of Oyo, is that he was a powerful, firm, and tyrannical ruler who had a passion for war and empire-building. But his generals later became tired of war and the unlimited sufferings of the citizens and counseled an end to such adventures. Sango would not yield and so his generals revolted and rose against him. Faced with inminent defeat and the prospect of an ignominious capture, Sango committeed suicide, hanging himself on an *ayan*-tree. It appears that Sango's sterling qualities came to be appreciated post-humously and so, he was subsequently deified. He was appreciated as the spirit of adventure, tension, and unrest. In spite of his recklessness, he became in the mind of the people the personification of the principles of state-building and heroic exploits.[185]

Under the dual sign of justice and transgression, power and betrayal, Coba's earlier differences and distance from other slaves can be understood in the light of Shango's duality.

In spite of the solidarity that existed between maroons, free men and slaves (a fact faithfully documented in Leate's novel), Coba only loved the brave, those who had the courage to confront their masters. Hence, he felt a sense of solidarity only toward those slaves that rebelled.[186] For Coba: "un esclavo que no había tenido valor para alzarse, para escapar, para internarse en el monte, y hacer vida de *cimarrón,* no merecía ser libre . . . la libertad era un derecho que se ganaba peleando" (a slave that did not have the courage to rebel, to escape, to go deep in the forest, and live the life of a cimarrón, did not deserve to be free . . . freedom was a right one had to earn).[187] From Tomás, an earlier chief of the Great Palenque, Coba learned to appreciate "en toda su estatura, la dignidad del hombre negro" (to its highest degree, the dignity of the black man).[188] However, for Coba, it was not the color of the skin that united him in brotherhood to other cimarrones and slaves, it was the slave's spirit of rebelliousness: "siempre había creído que quien toleraba la esclavitud sin hacer nada por sacudírsela, no merecía otra suerte" (he had always believed that those who tolerated slavery without doing anything to rid themselves of it, deserved to be slaves).[189] As colonial governments had done in so many other occasions with other cimarrones, Coba and the other maroon leaders were offered their freedom if they signed a treaty agreeing to hunt down other runaway slaves. In other words, they could be free only if they became rancheadores (bounty hunters).

Different from historical Coba, Leante's Coba's distrust of authority and his profound sense of justice kept him from taking advantage of such a contract, as Enriquillo had done in Santo Domingo, Cudjoe in Jamaica, Yanga in Mexico, and other maroon leaders in the greater Caribbean. For Leante's Coba, the written word was a tool that belonged to the white man's world and could not be trusted. It was the Law of the Master, the law he had resisted since the moment he arrived to the Great Palenque. When he arrived at the famous maroon community, he was surprised to find Father Antonio, a white priest, acting as the secret-ary of the community. He wrote down everyone's name in a large book (the palenque's registry). To Coba's dismay, even in that remote space of freedom, "writing" continued to be the organizing factor of civilization. For Coba, writing was related to domination,[190] control, and treason, and yet it had become a necessary tool for the survival of the community of runaway slaves. Ironically, it seemed to Coba that a complete escape from the white man's world was impossible: "tenían que aprender de ellos" (they [the *cimarrones*] had to learn from them [the whites]).[191] Father Antonio's presence in the palenque was a painful reminder that the white world was always already dangerously inserted in that world of freedom founded by cimarrones.[192]

Coba's "reading" of Father Antonio (as a text within the text) intuitively foresees the paradoxes of writing: the complex relationship between the Word of God in the Bible, the Law of the white master, and the Great Registry of the Great Palenque. The latter seemed to be for Coba just like the registry of the Plantation. For those outside of the Law, survival depended on that same Law from which they tried to escape, and on the degree of their assimilation to that Western civilization whose dominating "mark" was writing. Remembering that Leante's Coba differs from historical Coba, José Luciano Franco offers another version of the events. In a letter Franco finds written by Father Manfugás to Governor Escudero on July 31, 1819, Manfugás states that Coba requested to have a white man with his group "que supiese leer y escribir para por su medio avisar a V.S. de todas las ocurrencias, remisión de presos . . . y proponían a un individuo que residía en aquel Partido nombrado Rivero, natural de Canarias . . ." (that knew how to read and write so that through him they could give word to V.S. of all happenings, remission of prisoners . . . and proposed an individual who lived near that region named River, from the Canary Islands.)[193] Manfugás's agenda may not have differed much from Escudero's agenda in Leante's novel. Escudero wanted to disarm the cimarrones in order to catch them by surprise and exterminate them: an act of treason, which Leante's Coba foresees and uses to his advantage. In light of the historical documents available, the reader must question whether the historical Coba actually made such request from Father Manfugás, as José Franco documents, or whether it is Leante, in the voice of his character, whose skepticism about writing leads him to question the ethics of the written word in the struggle for justice and freedom. This is a skepticism characteristic of twentieth-century Latin American writers,[194] who have collectively articulated a certain caution, awe, fear, and contempt toward the written word, especially a suspicion of the word of others in power. Following Coba's misgivings about writing, it is even more significant that, in *Los guerrilleros negros,* the possessor of the "secrets" of writing in the Gran Palenque is a Catholic priest.

Father Antonio problematizes his presence even further in Leante's novel by using his words, and the author-ity vested in him, to lie to the slaves, telling them that the Spanish Courts had already declared them free men and that their rebellion was a way to claim what was already theirs.[195] However, Leantes's Coba did not trust the words spoken by a white man:

aunque les hablase de libertad, la palabra de un blanco podía ocultar engaño. Y el padre Antonio sabía que los estaba engañando, que no era cierto . . . pero necesitaba divulgar aquella mentira entre la masa de esclavos como una verdad. . . . Después de todo, no hacía sino adelantar en el tiempo lo que tarde o temprano ocurriría . . . [los amos] no podrían detener el rumbo de la historia."[196]

[even when he spoke to them of freedom, the word of a white man could hide trickery. And Father Antonio knew that he was lying to them, that it was not true (81) (. . . but) he needed to spread that lie among the slaves as a truth . . . After all, it only would bring sooner what had to occur sooner or later . . . (the master) could not stop the path of history.]

Father Antonio's notion that the end justifies the means, and his desire to speed up the revolution of the masses,[197] construes a complex ambiguity in his dis-course of freedom especially when, in his desire to attain the end of slavery, Father Antonio adopts a traditional condescending attitude in which freedom does not correspond to equality. By perceiving the other, the cimarrón, as an innocent yet inferior being in need of his super-vision, Father Antonio intimates the continuation of an unequal hierarchical system of power that would persevere even after the abolition of slavery. In the midst of these ambiguities, Leante's Coba is the construct of yet another text made up of gaps and silences, enigmatic and impenetrable, in contrast to the legal rhetorical text of the treaty the maroon leaders were asked to sign. As Leante's Coba hears the reading of a text he cannot read, his facial expressions turn him into another enigmatic text that the white man cannot read. Coba's face was like: "la máscara de un ídolo" (the mask of an idol),[198] inexpressive, and impenetrable. Coba's body is at this moment a trope for the very text that the narrator is proposing as the codified ideogram of another ideology. This is one text that cannot be read from the gaze of power: a language of symbols, amulets, beads of different colors, and signifying emblems, signs as impenetrable and complex as the monte where Leante's Coba seeks refuge and protection. At the same time, however, the silent abysm with which Leante's Coba resists treason, also brings about his downfall.

As a classic tragic hero, like Shango, Coba's own blindness and arrogance brings about his death. His negligence toward his maroon friends and comrades, and his lack of solidarity, construct, following the novel's ideological framework, the conditions for his death. Yet, Coba's transgression in Leante's novel is not in the act of signing the treaty that the historical Coba did sign. He signed the treaty only to borrow time and temporarily stop the government's intensifying persecution. He never meant to comply with the white man's terms. His tragic flaw was his arrogance, his contempt toward others, his lack of solidarity with his own people; and, in a peculiar way, it was his stepping "fuera del juego" (outside of the game), which made many of his followers abandon him and leave him vulnerable to an attack. At the same time, the emigmatic solitude he sought in the imaginary of African magical powers recalls Ti Nöel's transmutations into the animal kingdom as a way to escape from his humanity. Like Ti Nöel, Coba began to see himself as the Mackandal of the legends, and began to think of himself as immortal: as a semi-deity chosen by the loas. He was convinced that "los blancos no podían darle muerte porque lo protegían los loas de Africa" (whites could not kill him because he had the protection of the African loas).[199] His followers: "Le oyeron decir, también, que él libertaría a todos los esclavos, que los orishas lo habían elegido para echar a los blancos de Cuba e instaurar en la Isla un reino negro. El vengaría a su raza de todas las infamias a que la habían sometido" (They heard him say that it was he who was going to free all the slaves, that the orishas had chosen him to expel the white man out of Cuba and to create in the Island a black kingdom. He would avenge his race of all infamies to which they had been subjected).[200]

As a faint echo of Ti Nöel's imaginary kingdom, Coba's self-delusions of grandeur and magical powers were linked to a temporary absence of historical consciousness, of which he soon became aware, and soon tried to amend, however, too late. Coba's death, at the moment of his repentance (reminiscent of Ti Nöel's erasure at the moment of self-awareness), sets the stage for a sacrificial rite which brings coherence to the divided group, strength in unity, and the vision of a new order in the rebirth of his spirit as a collective symbol. Like Mackandal and Ti Nöel in *The Kingdom of This World,* Coba is also a victim of his mytho-poetic imagination. His actions are another remembrance that in Hegel's dialectic progress toward Spirit, "deceit" always delays the moment of historical reconciliation.[201] An obstacle to the outcome of history is the leader's self-delusions of power that set Leante's Coba apart from other maroon leaders, destroying the group's solidarity. At the same time, Leante's Coba is another trope for a way of being in the Caribbean experience: what Glissant calls, in reference to Martinique as an example of the Caribbean, a consciousness "always tormented by contradictory possibilities."[202]

Under the dictates of the new revolutionary discourse that serves as the political context to Leante's *Los guerrileros negros,* history is not seen as moving by the dictates of divine beings, or magic, but by its own historical laws, and through awareness and commitment to the historical process. In the context of Leante's representation of that process, Coba's recognizes and repents of his arrogance and negligence (as does Shango). Yet, paradoxically, his re-cognition and "self-awareness" places him outside of the magical forest of African lore and myths that he embraced through Quiala's stories. Leante and Carpentier's heroes are brought to a full consciousness of their historical condition as fugitives of oppression. And, at that moment, they reject the magic and cultural imaginary of their ancestors in order to embrace their role in history as historical beings.[203] However, that magical world of myths, which both novels ultimately reject, is also the Faustian "spirit" that for Carpentier gives identity, dignity, and collective power to Mackandal: the spirit that made possible the triumph of Haitian slaves and peasants over French troops in Carpentier's text. Hence, both novels embrace, in order to reject, the magic realm that allowed Africans and their descendants, to survive acculturation in the Caribbean. Leante and Carpentier articulate the same conflict in the Caribbean between the need to embrace an African past, African mythologies and belief systems, and the need to reject such beliefs, understood as "atavisms" and primitive fetishism, in order to arrive dialectically to historical self-consciousness, as demanded by the political ideology in force in Cuba in 1976 when Leante was writing this novel.

Like Ti Nöel's textual erasure, Coba's suicide/assassination addresses another disturbing silence in Cuban literature: Coba's imaginary rescue of his "Africanness" (the belief in loas and orishas, of power objets, amulets and beads), his cultural origins, is what creates the conditions for his death. Yet, it was that same reconstructed "Africanness" that gave him power and charisma. Even his followers saw Coba through the prism of Coba's own delusion. Such imaginary Coba in Leante's novel (for Coba and his followers), responds to the descriptions and feats of the heroes in the African myths and legends he had heard from Quiala, his African model, and what he had heard about the legenday Mackandal. In order to become his imaginary African "other," Coba:

> se había hecho sajar las mejillas y las finas estrías clareaban como leves surcos el hisurto caracolillo de su barba. Aquellas cicatrices le prestaban la distinción de un cacique africano, lo que contribuía a aumentar su rango y el dominio que ejercía sobre los suyos. Para la mayoría de los hombre Coba no era criollo sino un rey africano que había sido vencido por una tribu rival y vendido como esclavo a los tratantes negreros.[204]

> [he had his cheeks lanced, and the small rows of thin scars whitened the small rows the brisk curls of his beard. Those scars gave him the prestige of an African chief, which contributed to increase his status and the power he had over his people. For the majority of his men, Coba was not a creole but an African king conquered by a rival tribe and sold as a slave to slave merchants.]

Recalling here the complexities of representing the Caribbean from the gaze of the Caribbean writer, Leante's Coba runs away to an African mythical realm, in a voyage back to the source, to the monte of Quiala's narrations. However, he must also run away from the loneliness of that mythical world of differences that his followers construct around him, back to the comforting human solidarity of his fellow cimarrones. Difference is a lonely road that the cimarrón understood well. And it was the loneliness of that condition of difference that lured Carpentier's Cimarrón and Mackandal to return to the Plantation where both characters are captured again. It was that same condition of difference that lured Enriquillo, after fifteen years of resistance, to sign a treaty that allowed him to return to the same world he had fought against, only to die unexpectedly two years later (*RI*, 290). Like Ti Noel, Coba finds himself trapped between an ontological "here" and "there" from where he escapes through death; and it is through that death that, in Leante's novel, he becomes the spirit guide of a people's struggle for freedom (like the orisha Shango). Mavis Campbell observes that in the case of Jamaica, one of the most important sources of strength for the maroon leaders was their African magic. However, for Carpentier and for Leante, that religious landscape of magic becomes a point of ethical tension with which the text articulates an ambiguous, and rather complex, entanglement of guilt and desire in the art-i(o)ficial construction of nationality.

The mytho-poetic monte in Caribbean literature with which the writer reconstructs the silent voices of an African ancestry, offers a dis-cursive space of refuge for the writer who, like José Martí's *Versos sencillos,* seeks a space of refuge in the monte of literature.[205] In the cultural imaginary of the Caribbean writer, monte and palenque become signifiers for a (m)other space of refuge and difference, a space from where to summon the Wind-Storm force of the Word; from where to reiterate an ideological and cultural cimarronaje always already in the archival memories of the Caribbean. Caribbean writes continue to re-think the discursive foundations of a palenque-city of freedom, whose historical leaders still live on in Caribbean local mythologies. Such is the case of Benkos Biojo, the maroon leader of the Great Palenque, near Cartagena de India, Colombia, whose life Manuel Zapata celebrates in his monumental novel, *Changó, el gran Putas* (1983). As if Zapata's hero were an echo of Frobenius's association of the African hero with the sun, and Leante's image of the red sun and Coba's spirit, Zapata makes his cimarrón hero, Benkos, a great American ori-Shango, the protected son and heir of the Afro-American orisha of fire, lightning, and thunder, Shango.

VII

In Manuel Zapata Olivella's *Changó, el gran Putas,* the prophetic voice of the storm in César Leante's *Los guerrilleros negros* returns once more but now in the apocalyptic wind-words of the orisha Shango. In Zapata's epic saga, betrayal is also an underlying theme. Different from Leante's *Los guerrilleros negros,* and Carpentier's *The Kingdom of This World,* Zapata Olivella's text crosses racial, ethnic, national, and genre lines to retell the story of the African experience in the New World from the gaze of a tri-ethnic writer. Also different from Leante and Carpentier's novels, Zapata embraces African beliefs and makes the African orisha, Shango, the center of American history, in an epic narrative in which the writer imagines an African mythical primordial time that leads to, and affects, the present.

Zapata imaginatively reenacts the history of a people out of Africa, but different from the people of Africa,[206] in an epic story that follows along the lines of Fanon's liberation model, while, at the same time, addressing Glissant's call for the reconstruction of the past as "an imaginative reworking of the process of *méstisage* or an infinite wandering across cultures including those of Africa."[207] Dialoguing with Afro-Caribbean discourses, Zapata's text also articulates a discursive mediation between the ideas of "Black is Beautiful" that emerged with the Harlem Renaissance, and Negritude's notions of an "African origin," and of a "black consciousness" proposed by Leon Damas, Leopold Senghor, and Aimé Césaire. In so doing, the writer weaves into the text these and other discourses on nation, race, cultural identity, and mestizaje in Latin America, while privileging the ideas of José Martí and Langston Hughes. In dialogue with Martí's ideals of union and freedom,[208] and with Carpentier's liturgical narrative structure in *The Kingdom of This World,* Zapata also takes the Afro-Caribbean notion of the crossroad, and places Legba as the mediating voice between Shango and Afro-Indo-Americans. Shango's words, in the voice of Legba, addresses from a Modern and a Postmodern view a Caribbean search in the thirties and forties for what Aimé Césaire called, in Jaime Arnold's words: "Africa of the Heart."[209]

Zapata's construction of the African saga, and his choice of Shango, as an African-New World Providence, articulates a response to Glissant's preoccupation with *maroonage* (escape) or "Ex-stasis" as an experience "central to the imaginative discourse of the Caribbean;[210] and to the Haitian writer Rene Depestre's notion of "an ideological *cimarronaje* as the means for Caribbeans to resist depersonalization."[211] Rene Depestre claims, as Benita Parry notes, that rebellion "has manifested itself in religion, in folklore, in art and singularly in Caribbean literatures."[212] In Zapata's saga, Shango functions as a trope for an Indo-African spirit of resistance always already in the collective subconscious of the conquered in America.[213] This explains why the main narrator in Zapata's text is Zaka, a character of Indo-African descent (like the writer), and a cimarrón.

Recalling Homi Bhabha's proposition that "the boundary becomes the place from which *something begins its presencing,*"[214] in *Changó, el gran Putas,* it is from such boundaries that the novel "elaborate[s] strategies of selfhood . . . that initiate new signs of identity."[215] One of such new signs is the image of the palenque conceived by Zapata as a metaphorical city reminiscent of Césaire's idea of a "Beautiful City' where the "Black" could be "master of his destiny."[216] Zapata's version of such space of freedom is a city-nation founded inside the urban colonial space, in which Benkos Biojo is king, recognized as such, and crowned by his people during Carnival. Benkos is a child messiah destined to die for his people, and whose sacrificial Christic death by fire (Shango) brings about the possibility of freedom.[217] Like the mytho-historical king-orisha Shango, Benkos's birth, his life, and his death are characterized by the duality of his origins. Coherent also with such duality, Zapata offers two versions of his birth, romancing a mythical birth, and also the life of the historical Benkos, king of the Great Palenque.[218] Zapata's mythical Benkos is born of an African mother, Sosa Illamba, in the ocean waters of the Great Mother Yemayá where "Yemayá y Changó, lo reciben" (Yemayá and Shango receive him).[219] He is the son of a violent act: the rape by his white father, a slave trader, of his mother, an African slave, during the Middle Passage to Cartagena de Indias. His birth takes place during a powerful storm that destroys the ship, and that allows the newly-born orphan, guided by the orishas, to float over the ocean waters of Yemayá to American shores. In a parody of the biblical Moises, Native American women find him on the waters, and become his adoptive mothers.[220] At the same time, in another parallel version of Benkos's birth and death, he is Domingo Biojo, son of Potenciana Biojo, born in bondage, and destined to be a rebel-king-martyr, a maroon leader, like Aponte, the first initiate (born) to Shango's lineage in the New World. In this human avatar, Domingo/Benkos was born on the seventh day, his mother was assisted by seven African midwives, and he was adopted and raised by a priest, Father (Frei) Claver,[221] whose beliefs and teachings he eventually rejects.[222] Domingo/Benkos was marked with the sign of the orishas at birth, with the two snakes of Legba on one shoulder,[223] but, he was also marked by the teachings of Father Clever, and, thus, with the sign of the cross on the other shoulder.[224] Both marks represent the plural signatures of the syncretism and non-reconciled dualities that characterizes a mulatto and mestizo America. They also recall the ritual dual sign of Christ/Legba in Haitian Voodoo, of Tanze/Christ for the Abakuá, and of orishas and loas and their Christian double (Catholic saints) in the Caribbean.

In Zapata's narrative epic, American history is the result of Shango's Providencial will. Colonial rule, slavery, the intervention of Europeans in African affairs, the Middle Passage, and the history of the African Diaspora in the Americas are Shango's providential curse and plan for his lineage: his heirs in the New World. By reconstructing Shango as Providence, and by shifting the historical gaze from Europe to Africa, Zapata also shifts to Africa[225] the legitimacy and authority of the traditional Eurocentric view of American history. In this process of decentralizing and re(de)familiarizing American history, Zapata constructs a narrative space where freedom is conceived as an African Spirit that offers and demands the end of cultural and psychological bondage, through recognition and self-awareness. In this sense, Zapata dialogues with Glissant's proposition that "the notion of Caribbean unity is a form of cultural self-discovery."[226]

Zapata Olivella constructs a mytho-historical past necessary for the establishment in the novel of a collective identity based on a common bondage with which to replace traditional national myths of difference and exclusion. In *Changó, el gran Putas,* Zapata follows the "thrust of negritude among Caribbean intellectuals," as Glissant observes, in "response perhaps to the need, by relating to a common origin, to discover unity (equilibrium) beyond dispersion."[227] Hence, by proposing Shango as the center of that common African origin, Zapata questions Romantic ideas of national origins and replaces them with a phenomenological measurement of sameness which is no longer based on language or geography, but on a mythical space where Africa is not only a given space of historical hegemony with America, but the phenomenological center of History.

In order to intimate in the text the notion of a bond based on African origins, Zapata Olivella borrows the Afro-Cuban concept of brotherhood and of ritual bonding through initiation characteristic of Abakuá secret societies. He appropriates the Abakuá term *ekovio* (ekobio or ecobio); and he uses it with the meaning ñáñigos give to the term to refer to those who have been initiated as "cofrade de una misma hermandad" (society member of one same brotherhood). However, Zapata reinvents the meaning of ekobio, instead of using terms like "black" and "Negro,"[228] because these are words historically charged with exclusionary connotations. In an attempt to rename, and to redefine, the arrival to Knowledge/Freedom, outside colonial prejudice, Zapata takes the ñáñigo term ekobio across racial and gender lines to include women, as well as those persons, regardless of their background, who share in the same "spirit." For Zapata, ekovios are the members of the same family unified under the same experience, or a higher knowledge: ori.

Changó, el gran Putas is a cimarrón text that runs away from traditional historical discourses on America in order to reconstruct Africa as a mythical space that no longer needs to be staged in the African continent. This is because Africa, for Zapata, is a "real" place, as well as a meta-historical and timeless space always already inscribed in America's history, cultures, and popular imagination. Thus, informed by American-African oral archives, Zapata retells a story of treason, brotherhood, and the revelation of a knowledge told in the voice of the *Ekoi,* or ancestors, whose narrations in the novel reenact (like in ñáñigo plantes), a mythical ori-gin that is both African and New World. In this sense, *Changó, el gran Putas* can be read as the ritual performative representation and reenactment of the African experience in America, as Americans, retold as a mythical-historical epic narrated in the voice of its actors: orishas, loas, cultural heroes, patriots of the different wars of independence in the Americas, and North American Civil Right activists. These are the Ekoi, or ancestors, that narrate the saga of the African experience in America: the violence of the Middle Passage, the Portuguese voyages of discovery to Africa, Spanish colonization (in Colombia), slavery, cimarronaje, the Haitian revolution, American wars of independence, and, shifting the historical gaze from Latin America to North

America, the novel concludes with the struggle for Civil Rights in the United States. Zapata's epic novel offers a warning against the loss of memory, and places Afro-American self-consciousness (North, South, and the Caribbean) at the crossroads of Ifa[229] (the iré road of life, and the sorbo road that leads away from life):[230] where Eleguá/Legba presides, and through whom Zapata-Shango speaks.

In Zapata's epic novel, Shango and Legba share the center stage of the African experience in the New World with the orisha Yemayá, mother ocean, and Shango's mother. Zapata's rendering of the African cosmic mother, makes Yemayá an American womb: always already present in the image of the amniotic ocean waters of the Middle Passage from which Shango's lineage in the New World is born. As as Ode to the African Mother in the New World, the novel ends with the figure of a woman, Agne Brown, as the last heir of Shango's spirit (Freedom/Knowledge), and spiritual lineage in America. The fact that the last Ekoi in Zapata's epic novel is a woman is especially significant because she is the first, and the main listener of the story (the novel) the cimarrón Zaka narrates. She is the one for whose benefit the story of Shango's spirit in the New World is told. Zaka's words change Agne's historical awareness and "convert" her from a passive listener to a committed agent of history. In other words, Agne is the last ekovia to be initiated to an archival Knowledge through Zapata/ Zaka's story. Hence, in that role, she contrasts and complements Benkos's role in the novel, at a different and yet similar historical moment. As a textual twin (Ibeye) to Benkos (his other), she is also an orphan: her father was the victim of the common practice of lynching black men in the South. She, like Benkos, has a black mother, an African womb as origin; and she, like Benkos, rejects the teachings of her white adoptive minister-father. Also like Benkos, Agne recognizes the spirit of her (their) "Africanness," and embraces the mission destined for her by Shango. Like the Ibeyes, sons of Shango, Agne and Benkos embody the spirit of their lineage: a non-Western Logos that did not have to "become flesh" because it had always been a human, and a mytho-historical being. Zapata's allegory recalls Ti Nöel's final moment of self-awareness in The Kingdom of This World, but it also echoes a recurring discourse in the Caribbean that privileges and reconstructs the African heritage as the semiotic space of a maternal language-womb, as found in Ana Lydia Vega's short story "Otra maldad de Pateco."[231]

The fact that Zapata chooses a woman to be the last heir, in the New World, of Shango's spirit, suggests another signifying element in the ritual structure of the text. Agne Brown serves as a reminder to the reader of the special place that the African mother has in Zapata's epic, in the Caribbean cultural imaginary, and in the historical development of American societies. Agne, a woman, and the textual twin of Benkos, his feminine other, and an avatar of the great mother, the Caribbean (M)Other, becomes the condition for the possibility of restoring Benkos's kingdom on earth: a great palenque that brings to fruition the *iré* road to Shango's spirit. Such Great Palenque would bring the new day of a different historical awareness. Yet, that moment does not take place in Zapata's epic because it is a story still happening, reengaged each time with each reading. This iré road is left only as a possibility at the end of the novel: a road forever postponed, left suspended at the crossroads of Ifa, where Zapata's text leaves the reader standing at the intersection between liberation and oblivion. This is also the iré road of Ifa that the Cuban novelist, Zoé Valdés, represents in her novel, *Querido primer novio,* in the feminine signature of the Afro-Cuban mother *monte.*

4

Ilé-Iyá-Ewelabá: Home, Mother, *Monte*. Rewriting the (M)Other, Postmodernity, and the Ethics of Writing (Eduardo Rodríguez Juliá's *Crónicas de Nueva Venecia* and Zoé Valdés's *Querido primer novio*)

> America is a literary and fictional place, a new beginning that is already a repetition.
> —Roberto González Echerravía, *The Pilgrim at Home*

> and the language of my landscape is primarily that of the forest, which unceasingly bursts with life.
> —Edouard Glissant, Caribbean Discourse

As the reader has gathered by now, monte is a liminal and libidinal space in the collective memory of the Spanish Caribbean, as well as a signifying sign for a space of refuge, freedom, and resistance outside the dominant structures of power. It is also a fluid signifier for what Fanon calls, as Homi Bhabha points out, "the zone of occult instability where the people dwell:"[1] a space crossed by differences, relations, and the archaic. Caribbean literature offers multiple revisions and rewritings of the concept of monte. These range from national and political ideology to a poetics of national affirmation, power, cultural subject formation, and resistance. Two works exemplify such re-visions. The first one is *Crónica de Nueva Venecia* (Chronicles of New Venice), by the Puerto Rican writer Eduardo Rodriguez Juliá: a trilogy of which only the first two novels have been published. The first one of these texts, *La noche oscura del Niño Avilés* (The Dark Night of Child Avilés), is a neo-baroque novel that narrates the fictitious events of an African and black creole slave rebellion in eighteenth-century Puerto Rico: a rebellion that never took place in the island. Rodríguez Juliá's fictitious story about such rebellion and about the foundation of an African kingdom, and of its destruction as the result of such rebellion, centers on the figure of the enigmatic figure of Child Avilés. The second novel of the trilogy, *En el camino de Iyaloide* (1994) (In Yyaloide's Road), narrates the life of Child Avilés as a young man. The other text is *Querido primer novio* (1999) (Dear First Boy Friend), written in France by the young Cuban writer Zoé Valdés: a novel about nature, love, and a woman's quest for love and freedom. Rodríguez Juliá and Valdés's texts represent the Caribbean as a fragmented space and time, reenacted by both writers as an allegorical space from which to wrestle with the instabilities of the present lived by the writers. In their novels, writing is an epistemological exercise similar to what Edouard Glissant calls, in the context of the Caribbean experience, the "Diverse,"[2] meaning performance, (re)signification, and reversion: "not a return to the longing for origins, to some immutable state of Being, but a return to the point of entanglement, from which we were forcefully turned away."[3] Rodríguez Juliá and Valdés take a look, through mimicry, parody, and carnivalesque re-enactments of neobaroque sensibility, to that moment of "entanglement" of which Glissant speaks. They find the lost space of an absent hybrid Caribbean body intuited in a mythical Caribbean palenque, lost and forgotten in the process of creolization and de/neo/colonization. The very act of writing in these two novels questions historical constructs of power, and imaginatively rescues and constructs an occult space of African ancestry in the Caribbean.

New Venice: The Broken Memory/The Lost Body

The third text of the trilogy has not been published, however, the prologue to *La noche oscura del Niño Avilés* (1984) already announces the end of Rodríguez Juliá's imaginary saga: the fictitious founding and the destruction of New Venice, a utopian city of freedom founded by Child Avilés in the marshes that surround the city of San Juan, Puerto Rico. Rodríguez Juliá's New Venice is a city-palenque founded by and for cimarrones, workers, and other marginal sectors of colonial society.

In the opening scene of *La noche oscura del Niño Avilés,* Child Avilés, the sole survivor of a shipwreck, like Benkos in *Changó, el gran Putas,* is washed to the shores of Piñones, a black Puerto Rican community. Juan Avilés, a local European settler, discovers the child, and, ironically from then on, the infant of unknown parents is known by the name of his European discoverer: Avilés. Reminiscent of the act of naming the New World as an act of possession, the allegorical act of naming the child after his "discoverer" robs the infant of his own identity. In a biblical parody, that equates Child Avilés to Moses, as the destined leader who would lead his people to a promised land, the creole infant is found floating in a *moisés.*[4] Like Benkos in *Changó, el gran Putas,* Child Avilés is marked by those that believe in his messianic destiny of leading his people to a promised land, and, as Benítez Rojo observes, to "found, in the swamps and streams that ring San Juan, the incredible city of Nueva Venecia" (*RI,* 245): "the sum of cities that transgress" (*RI,* 248). Furthermore, he adds: "the sociocultural codes of *La noche oscura del Niño Avilés* refers, above all, to the community of maroons, the palenque . . . the most representative, and also the most dangerous" (*RI,* 249). Like Benkos, Child Avilés represents the personification of the colonial wound: a construct and a victim of colonialism.

In Rodríguez Juliá's novel, the popular imagination of local Africans and creoles concluded that the orphan survived the shipwreck only because he had demonic powers. Thus, taking advantage of such popular myths that invested the enigmatic infant with supernatural powers, the Bishop of Puerto Rico, Larra, takes the baby as a personal talismanic object. He believes that Child Avilés will enhance his authority over the rebellious Africans and mulattos of Piñones; and, as part of his plan for control, he orders the construction of a room next to the Palace shaped like a human ear. In Rodríguez Juliá's allegorical dialogue with, and parody of Caribbean discourses, the reader cannot forget that for Carpentier and for Ortiz, as Acosta reminds us, the conch shell, associated in pre-Hispanic Caribbean with Huracán and the ear, symbolizes the coming together of culture and nature in an "evanescent and geometric," and "arbitrary and logic" natural architecture.[5] The *caracola* or conch shell, in its relationship to Huracán and storm forces, indicates the notion of "solar beings," and is associated with *lambi,* the large conch shell related to *Agué,* Lord of ocean waters (to whom Solimán prays in *The Kingdom of This World*), and a Haitian term for "ear."[6] Significantly, Larra places the infant in the middle of that ear-shape echo chamber:

"Lloraba el niño y el furioso eco retumbaba en aquella caja de resonancia, hasta encontrar salida por los recovecos esculpidos en las paredes, siempre amplificándose enormemente, como huyendo de su propia monstruosidad" (*NONA,* 25).[7]

La orejuda aterró al pueblo. Lentamente se fue gestando la leyenda del infante poseso que crecía en el Palacio Obispal. Larra sazonó aquellas supersticiones con el rumor que convertía al demoníaco Avilés en protector de su poder (*NONA,* 27).

[The child cried and the furious echo resounded in that sound box until it would find its way out through the crevices in the carvings of the wall, getting louder and louder as if fleeing from its own monstrosity.

The ear-shape construction terrified the town. A legend began to take shape about the possessed child growing up in the Bishop's Palace. Larra spiced such superstitions with a rumor that made the demonic Avilés the protector of his power.]

The daunting presence of the monstrous infant[8] soon produced contrary interpretations about his origins. Some believed that the Child was a messiah, others, that he was demonic. Bishop Larra hired a man of Sephardic origins, Juan Pires, to play the role of an exorcist, but when Pires began to prophesize that he had the power to rid the town of Child Avilés's demons, he began to believe in his own farce. He then proclaimed himself a prophet, and announced that Child Avilés was the Messiah destined to build the New Jerusalem[9] in the marshes surrounding San Juan (*NONA*, 28–29). The emerging different ideas about the identity of the infant intensified racial tension, which Bishop Larra averted with his personal guards, his *guardia brava* (brave guards). This was a group of free blacks whose members dressed in African garments, and were known for their strength and savagery (*NONA*, 21). Colonial authority became divided and Larra's power was challenged. However, before he was deposed, the terror he imposed created chaos and a mass exodus. While the Bishop constructed his "invisible torre de la locura" (invisible tower of madness):

> allá, en los mogotes de la Vega Baja, se fundaron campamentos de exiliados que añoraban el sueño, aquella tierra lejana y prometida. El exilio, el cansancio, la búsqueda persistente del sosiego llevaron a muchos al suicidio, la idiotez o la locura. Larra fundaba así la ciudad maldita, el Pandemónium incesante . . . "Todos los días despedimos caravanas de muy entristecidos ciudadanos que dejan atrás, en el recuerdo, la apacible morada. Comienzan así la azarosa búsqueda del sueño" (*NONA*, 36).

> [And far away, in the hills of Vega Baja, emerged camps of exiles that longed for sleep, the dream of a far away promised land. Exile, fatigue, the persistent search for tranquility led many persons to suicide, to stupidity, to madness. In this way, Larra founded the cursed city, incessant Pandemonium . . . "Everyday we see off caravans of sad citizens who leave behind, in their memory, their calm homes. This is how the random quest for the dream begins."]

With Larra's reign of terror, entire communities of exiles (which the writer significantly calls palenques (*NONA*, 37) sprang up toward the southern areas of San Juan: "Cada uno de estos poblados se consideraban independientes y en guerra con los otros. Las miradas no tardaron en llenarse de violencia y desconfianza" (Each one of these towns considered itself independent from others and at war with the others. They soon began to look at each other with violence and mistrust) (*NONA*, 37). The neo-African guards that protected Larra turned against him. Then, his "tower of desire," "esa infinita torre que ha sido pesadilla de los soberbios y sueño de los dioses" (that infinite tower that has been the nightmare of the arrogant and the dream of the gods) (*NONA*, 42–43), became his tomb. One of the leaders of the rebellion, Obatal, previously one of Larra's guards, broke into Bishop Larra's quarters, killed him, and took Child Avilés, believing that he had acquired a talismanic object of power that could secure his authority. Obatal took over the main Plaza of the city of San Juan, and established in the tower fortress of El Morro, a utopian city of unregimented and licentious freedom. The description of such tower suggests a fantastic place reminiscent of the Tower of Babel, as well as a Caribbean spiral construction reminiscent of a *teocali*[10] (related in a Caribbean discoursive context to the wind-sound of Shango-Huracán), in the very midst of the colonial city of San Juan.[11] Meanwhile, Bishop Trespalacios, who arrived by sea to bombard the city, and to reclaim it in the name of the Spanish king, Carlos III, decides to wait patiently at sea for the neo-African forces to defeat each other. In the midst of this phantasmagoric battle between a neo-African kingdom and the European authorities in Piñones, Child Avilés turns into a power object desired by both contenders. He is the creole "other:" a monstrous hybrid being that becomes, unknowingly, the center of power and desire in colonial society.

Most of the action in *La noche oscura del Niño Avilés* is the chronicle of Obatal's utopian neo African kingdom, its licentious freedom, Mitume's rebellion against Obatal, and the struggle for the possession of the talismanic Child Avilés, who finally ends up under the supervision of Bishop Trespalacios. The text offers the allegorical slave/master struggle between the colonized and the colonizers, the conquered and the conqueror, but, also, the inner struggle within the neo-African forces, and the also fragmented European power. Such divisions highlight the textual contemplations on the founding of invisible cities and on the construction of fragile forms of freedom in Puerto Rican history (*NONA*, 173). As if it were the reenactment of such fragmentations, but from different perspectives, different fictitious chroniclers narrate the novel: Gracián, El Renegado, and Trespalacios, in his "secret" diary. At the end of this first novel, Obatal and Mitume destroy each other, and Bishop Trespalacios becomes the sole possessor, spiritual guide, and adoptive father of the creole Child Avilés, like Father Clever was for Benkos. Unsure of the divinity of the infant, Trespalacios performs a mock exorcism to appease those who believe in the demonic powers of Child Avilés, and declares him divine, the carrier, like Moses, of a messianic destiny for the people. From this time on, Trespalacios makes sure that the creole child adheres to the laws and traditional imaginary of the European State and Church.

The second novel of the trilogy, *En el camino de Yyaloide,* narrates the events in the life of Child Avilés, the motives for his resentment toward Trespalacios, and his transgression against colonial laws and values. In both novels, Rodríguez Juliá reengages historical representation as a heterogeneous interpretative exegesis of events, and as an opposition to a homogeneous view of those accounts: an unchallenged view that serves to configure the past from one single perspective. Trespalacios correlates Child Avilés's transgressive desire for freedom (a desire that leads him to break away from the structures of power that give him his false identity) with madness. The representation of the creole subject as an infant in *La noche oscura del Niño Avilés,* shifts in the second novel, and Avilés's new view of himself and of his historical context engages the detriment results of colonial "fixity:" the fixed and essentialist colonial representation of the creole subject.

The first novel of *Crónica de Nueva Venecia* ends with Trespalacios's delirious reflections on the differences between Utopian and Arcadian cities. He envisions the Utopian city as the creation of Leviathan: "el engendro más monstruoso creado por el humano intelecto . . . verdadero paroxismo de la voluntad" (the most monstrous conception created by human intellect . . . true paroxysm of will) (*NONA,* 316), "hija de la soberbia, oscura pretensión de los que anhelan abolir el tiempo" (daughter of arrogance, dark pretence of those who wish to abolish time) (*NONA,* 316).[12] The Arcadian city, on the other hand (reminiscent of the name of the founder of Macondo in Gabriel García Márquez's novel *One Hundred Years of Solitude,* José Arcadio Buendía), is a creole imaginary city whose instigator in Rodríguez Juliá's novel is Pepe Díaz (*NONA,* 316), a character from Puerto Rican folklore said to have been one of the defenders of the island against an attack by the English.[13] Rodríguez Juliá's allegorical sarcasm constructs, in the delirious mind of Trespalacios, the image of the Arcadian city as a creole construct, different from the foreign English Utopian city in Thomas Moore's *Utopia.*[14]

Like Augusto Roa Bastos's novel *Yo, el Supremo* (1974) (I, the Supreme), Rodríguez Juliá's *Crónicas de Nueva Venecia* offers an allegorical reflection on the many discourses on origin and national identity in Puerto Rico before and after the invasion of the United States in 1898: a moment that still today constitutes a wound in the island's cultural history.[15] The first novel of the trilogy, writes Aníbal González Pérez, "nos ofrece una especie de catálogo alegórico de estas distintas concepciones de la cultura insular, y más aún, las hace chocar entre sí, enfrascándolas en una polémica que el texto representa como una suerte de épica burlesca" (offers us a type of allegorical catalogue of the different types of thoughts on insular culture, and, even more, makes them clash in a polemic the text represents as a type of burlesque epic).[16] Rodríguez Juliá's discourse on the role of utopia in Puerto Rican history and on the discourses pertaining nationhood is not limited to Puerto Rico. As Octavio Paz points out in *Puertas al campo* (1966), "No se nos puede entender si se olvida que somos un capítulo de la historia de las utopias europeas" (We cannot be understood if one forgets that we are a chapter in the history of European utopias).[17]

En el camino de Yyaloide, Trespalacios baptizes the Child in his new role of Messiah during Nativity: "en la misa de gallo de aquel nefasto año de 1773" (in the midnight mass of that ill-fated year of 1773),[18] and sets out to raise him for such destiny. With the baptism of the creole infant, says the narrator: "el Avilés había conseguido, por ser bautizado justo cuando Jesús nacía, lo que llamaban *'la oscura comunión'* con la sangre del redentor." (Avilés obtained, by being baptized just when Jesus was born, what is called *dark communion* with the blood of the redeemer).[19] Child Avilés grows up believing that he is like the heroes in Trespalacios's European imaginary: in the legends and fantasy that formed his upbringing. Under the Inquisitor's guidance, and as a mode of initiation into manhood, Trespalacios sends young Avilés to a Quixote-like quest of exploration into the remote and uncharted marshes near San Juan. Child Avilés's entrance for the first time into the inner, telluric, world of this Puerto Rican monte, a space "favored by the African gods"[20] brings him to the initial point of historical conflict. The novel narrates the libidinous temptations he experiences in the land of Yyaloide; his passion for a creole woman, an *indiana* who lives with her father, Arcadio, in the coastal hinterlands; his return home precipitated by Trespalacios in order to take him away from the "inferior" creole woman; and his initial resistance and dissent against the Law of the Father, Trespalacios. As a parody of the motives that led the Spanish conquerors to the marshes and jungles of the New World looking for El Dorado and the Seven Cities of Cíbola, this creole Puerto Rican Quixote sets out to explore the marshes around San Juan in a novel cleaved by different visions: Avilés's own fantasies (like Quixote) created by his upbringings, the mundane perception of his companion and chronicler, Gracián, a chronicler also in the first novel, and Trespalacios's demented religious and ethnocentric imagination.

Child Avilés finds himself entrapped as a border subject "in-between" the ideals and teachings of Trespalacios, and Avilés's own carnal desire (flesh): his lust for the indiana he meets in the land of Yyaloide. Counterpointing classical and local literatures, philosophy and visual art,[21] Rodríguez Juliá constructs the figure of Child Avilés, in a neo-baroque style, as the space, in the creole body, of what Glissant calls "the point of entanglement"[22] in the Caribbean historical landscape. Child Avilés is the construct of different cultural imaginations: of the African slaves, mulattoes, and creoles of Piñones, and of Larra and Trespalacios's demented theology of domination. As the creole "son of the People,"[23] Child Avilés personifies vernacular culture in a creole society that struggles at the crossroad of a Carpentierian *there* and *here,* but now with new meanings and locations. Such dichotomy in Rodríguez Juliá's novel also articulates what Glissant describes as a characteristic of Caribbean writers, "the tortured relationship between writing and orality."[24] In the cultural history of Puerto Rico, Child Avilés's tribulations speak of a continuous "border" zone that is characteristic of Caribbean societies but, in the context of Puerto Rico, that zone is also further complicated by the border condition of Puerto Rico today as a commonwealth territory of the United States of America. Significantly, at the end, what takes Child Avilés away from the European construct created for him by Trespalacios is lust,[25] the libidinous desire "to be his own," a "longing for liberty" awakened by Faustian passion as lust, longing, despair, and "knowledge." It is significant then that such awakening takes place in the invisible land of myths associated in the Caribbean with Africa. Such space suggests that in the mythical image of the garden of Yyaloide (v.s. the garden of Eden), in Rodríguez Juliá's novel there is an African creole Caribbean space, always negated, but always there, as the condition for the possibility of dissidence inside patriarchal colonial law.

The absence of the third text of the trilogy that narrates the founding of the cimarrón city of New Venice, as a place of hope for slaves and cimarrones (*NONA*, 12), further complicates the reading of the first two novels by suggesting an allegorical temporal present still in the making: a city of freedom already destroyed a century ago that has not been founded yet in the sequel of the trilogy's story. The second novel prophesizes the third, since the seed of Child Avilés's rebellion appears at the end of the second novel after the forced return of Child Avilés to San Juan, once Trespalacios refuses to allow his creole protégé to marry the creole woman he desires.

During the celebrations for the return of the (anti)hero explorer, Avilés and Trespalacios play a card game performed publicly before the local population on a stage with real persons dressed as tarot figures. Avilés challenges Trespalacios's authority through the metaphorical explanation of the figures he chooses to move, almost causing a revolution with the card game.[26] He won the praise of the people when he explained the significance of the tarot image of Justice, by saying that justice: "prevalecerá a final de los tiempos sobre la fuerza, destinando así el gobierno del emperador Caín" (will prevail at the end of time over force, creating in this way the destiny of emperor Cain's government).[27] However, Trespalacios reacted with the virulent repression of the exaltation of the people who cheered Child Avilés's words and carried him on their shoulders;[28] he punished the rebels, and gave Child Avilés a beating for his transgression.[29] The novel leaves Child Avilés preparing to leave by orders of Trespalacios to Havana, Cuba, to the imposed exile of a Jesuit School.[30] Right before his departure, the text leaves Child Avilés in a moment of suspense, as he contemplates a miniature city Trespalacios had given him as a gift. Avilés seems here to be meditating on the possibilities of the existence of such city.[31] At this moment, implicit in his gaze, two cultural ideals and sets of values come into conflict (in a second reenactment of the earlier conflict between Obatal's neo-African kingdom and colonial power): the possibility of a libidinal cimarrón city, a city-palenque constructed in and by Avilés's creole imagination, and the patristic law imposed on him by colonial prejudice and restrictive "supervision." Child Avilés's transgressive performance against Trespalacios, the law, the colonial Father, questions the construct of the Inquisitor's foreign power, and the legitimacy of his authority.

II

The source of Child Avilés's rebelliousness, the point of entanglement for the creole child, becomes Trespalacios's nemesis: a giant (a type of genie of the shores, like Adamastor in Africa)[32] who seems to rise from the ocean water, as an obstacle in the destiny he envisions for Child Avilés. Trespalacios writes in his secret diary: "He visto alzarse al gigante ahí, justo en medio de la bahía, desde el fondo emerge con los ojos oscuros de sargazos, su espalda, tan ancha como el mundo, cobija incesantemente la ciudad dándole esa sombra que huele a hembra" (I have seen the giant emerge there, in the middle of the bay, he emerges from the depth with eyes dark with seaweed, his back, wide as the world, incessantly shelters the city, casting over it that shadow that smells like female).[33] In Rodríguez Juliá's text, that giant awakening in the creole imaginary is associated with rebellion, desire, but also, paradoxically, with a collective loss of memory.

Aníbal González Pérez suggests that *La noche oscura del Niño Avilés* (and by analogy the trilogy) is an allegory about the cultural history of Puerto Rico: "Si por "alegoría" entendemos, como se le define comúnmente, la representación concreta de ideas abstractas o, en un sentido etimológico, *allosagoreuo,* 'hablar de lo otro', no cabe duda, de que *La noche oscura del Niño Avilés* es una vasta alegoría acerca de la historia cultural de Puerto Rico" (If by allegory we understand, as commonly defined, the concrete representation of abstract ideas, or, in an etymological sense, *allosagoreuo,* "to speak of something else," there is no doubt that *La noche oscura del Niño Avilés* is a vast allegory of the cultural history of Puerto Rico).[34] As part of that "vast allegory," the text constructs a neo-baroque play of counterpoints between present and past, the linguistic performance of present day colloquial speech, and the rhetoric utilized by colonial chroniclers, fictitious characters, and historical and folkloric figures. The text is a forest of entangled historical, literary, and cultural references, and of orality and writing[35] in Puerto Rico's cultural history. The story is told through a fluid and timeless sequence of events, in an epic saga that reenacts through parody eighteenth-, nineteenth-, and twentieth-century events and official and popular discourses. In that saga, the forgotten cimarrón city of New Venice emerges as the archival space of those discourses, in which local memories, repressed and forgotten, are recovered through fiction in Rodríguez Juliá's novel.

The irony of Rodríguez Juliá's allegorical epic battles between African/creoles and Spanish colonial law, between Europeans priests (Larra and Trespalacios), and the neo-African armies of Obatal and Mitume, is a reminder that in Puerto Rico there was never a slave revolt of such magnitude, nor the founding of a neo-African kingdom. Yet, as Guillermo A. Baralt documents in *Esclavos rebeldes* (1981) and Benjamin Nistal Moret in *Esclavos prófugos y cimarrones (1770–1879)* (1984), there were numerous revolts and continuous cimarronaje in Puerto Rico during the eighteenth and nineteenth centuries. All of them, however, were soon crushed or aborted by the authorities. Notwithstanding, the intent was there, and that intent, as well as the frustrated hopes of those crushed rebellions, is the untold story that Rodríguez Juliá reenacts, and rescues from oblivion in *La noche oscura del Niño Avilés.* The defiance and demented style of the novel's narrators, the insolent eroticism of the text, the sense of "primitive chaos," and a sense of hopelessness in finding the lost space of Paradise portrayed by the text's neo-baroque style,[36] articulate a sense of frustrated hope for a space other than and different from the colonial city. This is a space, like New Venice, constructed by a creole cultural imaginary, invisible, but always there, in the deep folds of the nation's collective dreams.

Rodríguez Juliá's unfinished trilogy, *Crónicas de Nueva Venecia,* speaks of the fictional founding, destruction, and rediscovery of a city of freedom, a "Beautiful Creole City," founded outside the jurisdiction of colonial law, but whose mere existence was erased from the collective memory. This erasure is what surprises the fictitious writer of the prologue to *La noche oscura del Niño Avilés,* Alejandro Cadalso:

Nueva Venecia desaparece de la historiografía por decisión de las autoridades coloniales del siglo pasado. La presencia de aquella ciudad libertaria y utópica en la memoria colectiva, debió resultar inquietante para un régimen español amenazado por el esfuerzo libertador de Bolívar. Pero lo que resulta verdaderamente extraño es que el pueblo haya olvidado aquel recinto donde el Avilés pretendió fundar la libertad (*NONA,* 11).

[New Venice disappears from historiography by the decision of the colonial authorities of the past century. The presence of that libertarian and utopian city in the collective memory, must have been unsettling for the Spanish rule already threatened by Bolívar's struggle for independence. However, what seems to be truly strange is that the people forgot the existence of that place where Avilés pretended to found freedom.]

This collective loss of memory recalls Legba's warnings in *Changó, el gran Putas.* Like in Zapata's novel, it addresses a preoccupation in twenty-century Caribbean literary discourses with collective memory and amnesia. In this sense, Rodríguez Juliá's novel recalls Derek Walcott's claim in "The Muse of History" that "Amnesia is the history of the New World. That is our inheritance."[37] In the context of Puerto Rican literary discourses, Arcadio Díaz Quiñones reflects on such losses in *La memoria rota (1993)*

(The Broken Memory), and on the colonial mutilation of Puerto Rican social consciousness. Following the same line of thought presented by Díaz
Quiñones, the detailed accounts in Rodríguez Juliá's novel of a racial war
that never took place in Puerto Rico, may be a reticent reminder that while
the revolution in Haiti led to political independence, the loss of memory
and complacency in Puerto Rico created a nation that, for Rodríguez Juliá,
still lives under the illusion of freedom. This is not a new theme in Rodríguez Juliá's work. An earlier novel, *La renuncia del héroe Baltazar,*
staged also in the eighteenth century, tells the fictitious story of a black creole Puerto Rican, Baltazar Montañez, the son of a heroic black leader in
the slave rebellions of 1734, who agreed to marry the white Spanish daughter of the Spanish viceroy. Such an unusual wedding for this historical
period as proposed in this novel by Bishop Larra, was meant to give the rebellious black and mulatto population the illusion of having accomplished
racial equality and having gained historical agency. Rodríguez Juliá's
Baltazar, the son of a cimarrón who fought for the freedom of his people,
was known among Puerto Rican blacks as *Niño Malumbi.* The fictitious
archival scholar who narrates the story explains in a footnote to the text that
"en la santería de Cuba y de Puerto Rico, Malumbi es un travieso dios
menor que rebelándose contra Changó, liberó a la cautiva Eneayá, que es
la diosa de la fantasía, el baile y el olvido" (In Cuban and Puerto Rican *santería, Malumbi* is a mischievous minor god who, rebelling against Shango,
liberated the captive *Eneayá,* who is the goddess of fantasy, dance and for-
getfulness).[38] This fictitious association between fantasy, the loss of memory, and Baltazar, is an ironical reminder that Baltazar's power, as the
viceroy's son-in-law, is a premeditated strategy created by colonial authorities to erase the memory of his own black insurgent father and of the
historical struggles for freedom waged by his people.[39]

In Rodríguez Julia's novel, Malumbi (like Baltazar) rebels against the
great African Judge and King Shango, bringing about a false illusion of
freedom, and, with such illusion, a collective loss of memory. In *La noche
oscura del Niño Avilés,* illusion, imagination, and the loss of historical
memory are also poignant events in the writer's vision of Puerto Rico's cultural history. Yet, the inconsistencies between the events narrated in the
novel (a fictitious slave rebellion that leads to the creation of a neo-African
kingdom) and the documented history of slave revolts in Puerto Rico, suggest a textual meditation on the relationship between desire and the frustrated revolts against colonial domination in Puerto Rico. It also suggests
a meditation on the complexities of the idea of freedom in the cultural history of the island. Concurring with González Pérez and Rubén Ríos Avila,
Erik Camayd-Freixas suggests that: "the novel's true preferentiality is the
twentieth century."[40] Camayd-Freixas goes on to point out striking paral-

lels between Rodríguez Juliá's novel and events contemporary to the writer's own historical times:

> A central marker in the novel's uchronian geography is the transposition of modern Piñones to the eighteen century. Piñones is a lower class, black, beach-front village adjacent to Boca de Cangrejos, where Avilés was rescued from the shipwreck. Modernly, Piñones is famous as a sex haven, with its secluded shacks and *cabarets* . . . where city folk can go for an escapade without being seen by the prudish society of parochial gossipmongers, for whom frequenting the place is already proof of guilt. . . . Piñones is the hidden San Juan, Asmodeo's kingdom, a lascivious space cast outside the city limits, but it is also the bridge between San Juan and Loiza Aldea, the most culturally pure neo-African community left in Puerto Rico. Significantly, Obatal's African kingdom in El Morro was fed by a "supply line" from Piñones that Trespalacios bombarded, a libidinal chord the bishop had to sever in order to found the State.[41]

Piñones is the area where Child Avilés is found floating in a basket, and where the chronicler El Renegado encounters the libidinous garden of Yyaloide in *La noche oscura del Niño Avilés:* references to black communities in this area like Loisa Aldea. Furthermore, *Yyalode* is a name given in Cuba, and more recently in Puerto Rico, to Oshun, the African orisha of love, and the divine seductress.[42] It is thus in the allegorical land of Yyaloide that, in *En el camino de Yyaloide,* young Avilés is side tracked by lust, desire, and passion (the temptress Oshun) from his messianic destiny in his voyage of exploration into the remote territory of the Puerto Rican cultural landscape. In *La noche oscura del Niño Avilés,* and in *En el camino de Yyaloide,* lust is a type of soporific that, infused with the desire for freedom, induces memory loss; but it can instigate also resistance to domination, as it happens with Child Avilés. Pleasure and desire awaken Child Avilés to his most innate need to be his own, to follow a destiny different from what Trespalacios wants for him. After his temptations in the land of Yyaloide, the creole offspring of Africa and Europe in America, "becomes" something other than what, in his own twisted mind, Trespalacios had imagined. The voyage suggested by Trespalacios is an initiation into manhood for Child Avilés: in other words, an obedient entrance into the order of colonial law, not a voyage of self-discovery, as it ends up being, in which the creole child enters the forgotten monte of his own Afro-Rican past, forgotten, and negated. In his voyage of self-discovery, Child Avilés enters a space inhabited by the downtrodden, a creole woman, and by syncretic Afro-Caribbean mythical forces. And, in a parody of Christopher Columbus, who thought he had found the Garden of Eden inland from the mouth of the Orinoco river, Child Avilés also believes that the land of Yyaloide is the Garden of Eden.[43] As a biblical parody, yet different from the biblical story, the creole figura christi of Avilés does not go to the dessert to face temptations, but to the exuberant feminine monte of the island's coastal area, its marshes, where libidinous temptations spark the desire to fulfill his own longings: the freedom to choose his own fate. The creole anti-hero not only falls into temptation, but he embraces it, like Quixote, and sublimates it into an anachronistic courtly love in which the indiana of the marshes becomes a damsel in distress, and Child Avilés, a Quixote-like explorer is destined to become the founder of a utopian palenque-city.

Avilés's voyage into the marshes, to the remote and forgotten mythical land of Yyaloide, is also a voyage into an invisible other space of the cultural imaginary in the Caribbean: that Fanonian "occult space" where Caribbeans dwell. As if it were a continuous dialogue with Caribbean mulatto creole artists and "their" self-representation of a Caribbean experience, Rodríguez Juliá's mythical land of Yyaloide is also reminiscent of Wifredo Lam's recollections of the folklore of his native Sagua la Grande, Cuba. In reference to Lam's imagery, Lowery Stokes Sims writes: "Desnoes also suggested a source for Lam's imagery that has not been offered by other writers: fantastic characters found in folktales that are particular to Sagua le [sic] Grande, Lam's hometown. He cites such lore as the source of Lam's hybrid monsters: 'a serpent of gigantic proportions' emerging from a 'dark cloud' and a 'large mermaid' who 'devours everyone in her path.'"[44] It is in this magical feminine landscape of Caribbean African forces for some, and of primitivism and superstition for others, that Avilés learns that the mythical history of the land of Yyaloide was also the site of another utopian city founded by an African rebel, Mitumo, whose tragic fault also had been lust. According to Marcos, one of Child Avilés's black companions:

> La tierra de Yyaloide había sido muy favorecida por los dioses africanos, . . . en las costas de sus vegas Mitumo había fundado aquella ciudad de agua y aire. Cuando la celosa serpiente la destrozó de tres coletazos quedó ella muy distante de la curiosidad y el comercio de los hombres. El viento borró las últimas señas de aquel edificio donde Mitumo quiso fundar dulce habitación para su pueblo; el miedo y el olvido conservaron la tierra en estado muy idílico.[45]

> [The land of Yyaloide has been greatly blessed by the African gods . . . in the shores of its fertile fields Mitumo founded that city of water and air. When the jealous serpent destroyed it with three flicks of the tail, the city remained distant from man's curiosity and commerce. The wind erased the last traces of that building where Mitumo tried to found a gentle life for his people; fear and forgetfulness kept the land in an idyllic state.]

Mitumo's passion for the deity queen of that hidden land of streams and waterways, the land of an African mermaid zealously guarded by a gigantic serpent, Mato,[46] and whose companion was a manatee (a distinctively

Caribbean water mammal) was the cause for the destruction of the utopian cimarrón city. Driven by the desire to possess the mythical Afro-Caribbean queen, Mitumo captured the mermaid.[47] The serpent, Mato (a manatee in *La noche oscura*), who guarded the African mythical queen, in desperation destroyed the utopian neo-African city. This remote monte is implicitly the same garden of Yyaloide where the "double agent," El Renegado, in *La noche oscura del Niño Avilés,* also deviates from his duties, seduced by the African queen, Johari, while serving as a spy during the war between Obatal and Mitume.[48] It is also in this allegorical garden of Yyaloide, where El Renegado loses tract of time, of his duties, and of the realities of the war. This is also the land described in "an apocryphal manuscript" written by El Renegado, and found in a secret chamber in the ruins of New Venice, that supposedly reads:

> toda esta ciudad de muerte ha sido desatada por mis infames desvaríos en la tierra de Yyaloide . . . Alguien me dice al oído que la ciudad ha vuelto a ser habitada. ¡Han llegado los profetas! . . . Quise visitar la ciudad del olvido, y ahora descubro que todo es imposible, menos ese torturante recuerdo de ella . . . mi dolida memoria añorando las fugaces visiones de su piel olorosa a clavo y canela (*NONA*, 238–39).

> [this city of death has been unleashed by my infamous deliriums in the land of Yyaloide . . . Someone whispers in my ear that the city is inhabited again. The Prophets have arrived again! . . . I wanted to visit the forgotten city, and now I discover that everything is impossible, except for that torturing memory of it . . . my painful memory misses the fleeting vision of its skin that smells of clover and cinnamon.]

This Utopian city, associated with a woman and with the smell of cloves and cinnamon (like Jorge Amado's sensous Gabriela, in *Gabriela, Clove and Cinnamon*), of libidinous desires, left only to memory,[49] is the space where Child Avilés founds New Venice, that palenque city Benítez Rojo describes as "the summary of cities that transgress."

III

To understand Avilés's cimarrón New Venice as a palenque-city of refuge, desire, and freedom erased from the collective memory of Puerto Rico, Camayd-Freixas claims that "one must arrive at the San Juan of Rodríguez Juliá's youth," a time when "The novel's mythical city was located in a stretch of marshlands southeast of Old San Juan, passing the row of brothels that once flanked the bay's port and fed on the cruise ships' mariners and tourists."[50] For the youth of San Juan, Caymad-Freixas observes, the brothels of this area became "a rite of passage into adulthood."[51] The marshlands that Child Avilés explores, an area today "partly filled by a new expressway" that :

> extended from the inner bay to the modern Plaza de Las Americas shopping mall, along the famous Caño Martín Peña. Significantly, what was most recently located in that infectious network of mangrove canals was San Juan's most notorious slum, El Fanguito (The Little Mud Hole), a squatter community of zinc-roofed wooden shacks on stilts over the fetid water . . . Out of sight for decades, the vast slum became visible in all its squalor from the new, adjacent Las Americas Expressway. . . . the picturesque slum, romantically depicted as a "water-color of poverty" in hundreds of stories, paintings, poems, and popular songs, became a central embarrassment for the tourism-driven city, and a negation of the progressivist enterprise proclaimed by the *muñocista* U.S. Commonwealth.[52]

In a "process that mirrors" the destruction "of the accursed mythical city," the slum was cleared and its residents "relocated to housing projects or ferried across the bay to Cataño (like the Avilensians)," and at the end, notes Camayd-Freixas, "El Fanguito was leveled by bulldozers, and the squalor driven underground."[53] El Fanguito, with its muddy water-street, and houses built on stilts, was San Juan's "reverse" and "obscure" side, the other of the Italian Venice, whose heroic history makes it one of the attractive cities to visit in Europe. New Venice, like El Fanguito, is also lost in time, erased from memory, to be reborn once again in *Crónica de Nueva Venecia*.

As a metaphor for the destruction of El Fanguito for the 1992 celebration of the discovery of America, in Rodríguez Juliá's text all documents pertaining to New Venice are destroyed in an inquisitorial burning, in 1820. It was an action that, says the fictitious writer of the prologue to the first novel of the trilogy, "tuvo como propósito la destrucción de un mito" (was done with the purpose of destroying a myth).[54] The fact that the burning of all the documents related to New Venice takes place in 1820 is allegorically significant, since the writer places this inquisitorial burning in the years that follow the independence of Haiti: a moment that corresponds with a historical repression against free blacks, mulattos, and slaves in the Spanish Caribbean. In Cuba it led to the harsh repression that led to and followed the Ladder Conspiracy in 1844. It was during the years that Puerto Rico experienced its first planned and well-organized slave rebellion.[55] These rebellions, like Aponte's plan in 1812 in Cuba, were inspired by the triumph of the Haitian revolution; however, the irony of this date (1821 and 1820) in the novel is that in Puerto Rico, in 1821, the slaves of Bayamón, Guaynabo, and Río Piedras did formulate plans for a mass slave uprising. The idea was to capture the city of Bayamón, from where the rebels were expected to march to the capital. There, one group would take over the area that today occupies the Martín Peña bridge, joining forces with the slaves from Río Piedras and Guaynabo, and with another group in Palo Seco. The goal was to create a neo-African kingdom with Marcos Xiorro, a leader from Bayamon, as their king. However, like so many other revolts in Puerto Rico and in the greater Caribbean, the plan was denounced and the only visible act of dissidence according to Baralt was a stone thrown by someone hiding in a banana field. Many of the suspected slaves were incarcerated.[56] The historic plan to create a neo African kingdom, in San Juan, becomes also a frustrated reality in Rodríguez Juliá's novel. However, the text points out the fact that in spite of the general idea held in Puerto Rico that there were few slave rebellions in the nineteenth century, there were, in fact, as Baralt argues, numerous and frequent slave uprisings and revolts.[57] Furthermore, the condition for their possibilities, the desire for freedom, was always present. Benjamin Nistal Moret supports Baralt's findings, and also points out that up until 1870 there was a real fear of a race war in Puerto Rico.[58]

By placing the burning of the documents pertaining to the existence of New Venice in 1820, Rodríguez Juliá establishes an allegorical relationship between the narrated events of a racial war in *La noche oscura del Niño Avilés,* the historical struggle against cimarrones and insurgents in the nineteenth century, and the destruction, during the administration of Luis A. Ferré, of the most notorious poor slum in San Juan in the twentieth century. Once destroyed and its people relocated, El Fanguito was destined to die from the collective memory of Puerto Rico, like New Venice. However, like a Fenix, El Fanguito is born again in the cultural imaginary when Rodríguez Juliá reconstructs a similar place in *Crónica de Nueva Venecia* as a space from where to explore the complex rhizomes of Puerto Rican cultural history and its cultural entanglements; and to point out, as Camayd-Freixas argues, that at a different level New Venice still exists:

> Rodríguez Juliá's prologue claims that the mangrove-ridden ruins of New Venice were further decimated by the Yankee bombings of the 1898 occupation, but this is only a symbolic theory, for why bombard an empty marshland? (El Fanguito was not yet there). The fact is that Rodríguez Juliá, like the rest of us, witnessed the "cleansing" of the city slums and brothels by the newly empowered annexionist party (under the aegis of cement magnate turned governor Luis A. Ferré) during the 1970s and 1980s—a process that mirrors the "exorcism" of the accursed mythical city at the end of the novel.[59]

Like Rodríguez Juliá's New Venice, El Fanguito was built over the marshes, on the water, and its residents had to navigate from their shacks to the mainland. This is the same poor slum where José Luis González stages the events in his short story "En el fondo del caño hay un negrito." The pathos of this short story is based on the figure of Melodía, the infant son of a black Puerto Rican couple displaced from their home by new constructions. Melodía becomes the sacrificial victim of a growing capitalism that forgets poor Puerto Ricans, especially poor creole mulattoes whose only space left to live in the San Juan area was in the marshes and swamps at the margins of society, (inside the growing city), in shacks built over the water. In this short story, tired of crying from hunger, the infant Melodía crawls to the open door of the hut built on stilts. There, he sees his image reflected upon the waters, and tries to reach his reflection: the other baby he sees smiling at him. Melodía's desire for that other self, his hunger, and his implicit death caused by desire and social exclusion, are metaphors in González's short story of the "other" Puerto Rico negated and erased from memory, like Rodríguez Juliá's New Venice.

Melodía's innocent act of re-cognition muddled by desire represents an overall theme in José Luís González's work, which he best explains in "El país de cuatro pisos" (The Four-Tier Country). It is also a poignant theme in Isabelo Zenón Cruz's, *Narciso descubre su trasero* (1974; 1975), and in the work of contemporary Puerto Rican writers like Luís Rafael Sánchez, Rosario Ferré, and Ana Lydia Vega. The work of these writers questions the Hispanic myth of Puerto Rican national discourses, those discourses that claim racial equality and political equality and independence for Puerto Rico as a neocolonial nation. These writers, among them Rodríguez Juliá, show, as González does, that popular culture in Puerto Rico, the first cultural layer of Puerto Rican society, was African. In Puerto Rico, José Luis González writes: "se nos ha vendido el mito de una homogeneidad social, racial y cultural" (we have been sold the myth of social, racial, and cultural homogeneity),[60] when, in fact, the first Puerto Ricans were black, and popular culture is heavily African.[61] In his controversial essay, "El país de cuatro pisos," González bases his claim on the idea that in all societies divided by classes, the culture of the oppressed coexists with the culture of the oppressor mutually influencing each other.[62] In Puerto Rico, he writes, the culture of the oppressed was the same as that of the slaves until 1871, in other words, African.[63] With time, creole Puerto Ricans, whites or mulattos that became part of what González calls "the elite culture," came to be also oppressed by foreign powers:[64] first by Spain, and then, since 1898, by the United States. The first Puerto Ricans, González writes, "fueron en realidad los puertorriqueños negros" (were in reality black Puerto Ricans),[65] and they constitute the first layer of the four social layers in which González divides Puerto Rican society today. If Puerto Rican society had evolved without major changes like other Caribbean islands, González argues: "nuestra actual 'cultura nacional' sería esa cultura popular y mestiza primordialmente afroantillana" (our present "national culture" would be the same popular and mixed culture that was primarily Afro-Antillean).[66] In *En el camino de Yyaloide,* when Avilés's companions refer to the land of Yyaloide as "el primer Piñones de nuestros padres" (the first Piñones of our forefathers),[67] the text refers to an African cultural ancestry; to that first Puerto Rican layer that was African, according to González. New Venice, like El Fanguito, is a reminder of that first foundational layer of *puertorriqueñidad* that threatened the new visions and illusions of nationhood in the nineteenth and twentieth century. Out of such illusion, Juan Flores claims: "The discourse of Puerto Rican-ness has been constituted as a paradigm of social consensus. Nationalism has been converted into a state ideology and market culture, and in the process a problematic discourse was domesticated."[68]

The second layer, says José Luís González, was formed by the waves of Spanish immigrants who fled Spanish American territories during the wars of independence. Many of these immigrants created the same coffee plantations that came to be associated with the epitome of puertorriqueñidad.[69] Most of them were less educated than the Puerto Rican creole elite, more conservative, more arrogant, and looked down on the native Puerto Ricans.[70] The result of these new immigrations was that there emerged two different nations in the same island. Then, in 1898, the United States invasion created a third social layer;[71] and, with it, another and different wave of racial prejudice. Puerto Rico's white elite soon realized that intervention did not mean annexation, and a sense of class nationalism was born.[72] The working class, however, saw the arrival of the Americans as a way to get even with the previous dominant class,[73] mostly made up of immigrants from Spain, Mallorca and Cataluña.[74] The problem, González claims, is that "la experiencia racial de los puertorriqueños negros no se ha dado dentro de la sociedad norteamericana, sino dentro de la sociedad puertorriqueña" (the racial experience of Puerto Ricans has not taken place within North American society, but in Puerto Rican society).[75] Thus, popular culture often sides with American culture and away from the ideals of an independent Puerto Rico. González also claims that: "El 'jibarismo' literario de la élite no ha sido otra cosa, en el fondo, que la expresión de su propio prejuicio social y racial" (The literary *jibarismo* [whiteness] of the elite, has not been anything other than, basically, the expression of its own social and racial prejudice).[76] The fourth layer finally arrives in the forties with the American capitalists and a "populismo oportunista puertorriqueño" (Puerto Rican populist opportunism) that brings about a new political condition: a Commonwealth territory (*Estado libre asociado*).[77] This fourth layer serves as the implicit background that negates and is responsible for Melodía's condition, and for his implicit death in "El fondo del caño hay un negrito." In Rodríguez Juliá's trilogy, El Fanguito portrayed by González in his short story is reborn in New Venice, with Melodía now as Child Avilés's servant and best friend. Rodríguez Juliá's Melodía is Trespalacios's slave, but he becomes Child Avilés's "hermano que nunca tuvo" (brother he never had).[78] Significantly, the slave Melodía is also the creole

Child Avilés's counselor and right hand in the rebellion and in the founding of the utopian city of New Venice.

In his *Puertorriqueños. Album de la sagrada familia puertorriqueña a partir de 1898,* Rodríguez Juliá represents the founding layer of Puerto Rican society, constituted by African slaves and poor workers, as González points out, with the inclusion, in the family photo album, of his own grandfather: a mulatto artisan who walked to Guánica to welcome the American invaders. For the poor, the arrival of the marines was, says Rodríguez Juliá, only "una guerra entre gringos y gallegos y de una esperanzada complicidad entre casi todos los puertorriqueños" (a war between gringos and Spaniards, that offered a complicit hope for almost all Puerto Ricans).[79] The presence of his mulatto grandfather in the genealogy of a Puerto Rican creole family allows Rodríguez Juliá to represent a larger picture of the greater national family via the presence of another mulatto whose picture he also includes in his family album. Such invited guest, Martín Cepeda, was a creole mulatto who fought against the invading North Americans and lost an arm in a battle. What calls Rodríguez Juliá's attention is Cepeda's reaction to his own suffering when he is wounded in the war: "*Hombre no, si eso no es ná, qué va! . . . Mi Capitán, aún me queda el otro brazo*" (Man, this is nothing. My captain, I still have another arm).[80] Rodríguez Juliá writes:

¿Qué hace ese negro manco en el Álbum de Familia? ¿Por qué aparece ahí? ¿De quién es abuelo ese mandinga? Se trata de esa foto que nos perturba por desconocer la identidad del retratado, por no querer reconocer la contundencia de la *raja.* Aparte de que es el abuelo negro de todos nosotros, Martín aparece como un intruso en la complacencia sentimental pequeño burguesa.[81]

[What is that black man without an arm doing in the family album? Why is he there? Whose Mandingo grandfather is he? That is the photo that disturbs us because we do not know his identity, because we do not want to recognize the blunt weight of the *raja.*]

In *La noche oscura del Niño Avilés,* Rodríguez Juliá dives into the enigmatic waters of his mulatto ancestry and his mulatto creole culture as the writer's reflection on a Puerto Rican condition. Rodríguez Juliá's trilogy is also a reflection on Puerto Rico's cultural and historical sagas, including the utopian negation of a cultural past and of its origins as represented by equally imaginary discourses on nationhood, as González points out.

Rodríguez Juliá's dialogue with José Luis González in *La noche oscura del Niño Avilés* is not coincidental. José Luis González, a well-known writer in Puerto Rico, exiled in Mexico for his political ideology and social theories, was one of the first readers of Rodríguez Julia's novel *La renuncia del héroe Baltazar.* In 1979, Rodríguez Juliá wrote to José Luis González:

I would like to take advantage of this letter to talk to you about the theme of that strange novel . . . What is the theme of this work? . . . This novel deals with a Utopia. It is a novel about the perfect space which men long for; but it is also about the need which makes them indebted to time, war, death, and all that which subdues our precarious freedom, making it "too human," . . . (Not only is sainthood angelic, but the demonic is also a child of light!) New Venice, founded in *Las ciudades invisibles,* contains all imaginable cities: the infernal, Pandemonium, the Arcadian, God's and Leviathan's, the city for dreamers, the one for the powerful, the hope of the oppressed. Might this Utopia be the state that is still lacking from our nationality.[82]

Like in José Luís González's short story staged in El Fanguito, in *La noche oscura del Niño Avilés* the reader is invited to look upon the text like a Narcissus reflected on the surface of the water, to see his/her own image: to come to understand his/her reflections of other national-self different from the disposed narcotic national identity invented by official discourses on the nation. Benítez Rojo proposes that the other city, that other space that New Venice represents, like maroon communities in the history of the Caribbean, is the representation of what he calls the "anti-plantation," a "dangerous" community "whose destruction was most urgently required" (*RI,* 249) to safeguard colonial Law. New Venice, Benítez Rojo writes, "as a palenque or rhizome city has discovered that its own *there* is no means of escape; it desires an escape from itself, a flight to the "freedom" *over there.* I mean that Nueva Venecia, the runaway city living in the nocturnal miasmas of the marshes beyond San Juan, would like to be San Juan; it dreams of having a capitol, a cathedral, a Morro Castle, a university, a library, a flag" (*RI,* 255).

New Venice is an allegory for twentieth century Puerto Rican culture: for a poor community like El Fanguito on the marshes across San Juan, and its destruction. Yet, why is it that Rodríguez Juliá transposes recent events in his own life to the seventeenth and eighteenth century? Rodríguez Juliá points out the importance of the eighteenth century as the moment when Puerto Rican national ethos emerges. In other words, for Rodríguez Juliá the eighteenth century is the watershed moment in the history of Puerto Rican culture, the moment of entanglement. In his essay "Tradición y utopía en el barroco caribeño" (1985), he writes: "Mis novelas padecen el trasiego, la inquietud de una sociedad a medio hacer, que está por definirse" (My novels suffers from the instability, the anxiety of a society half done, still not defined),[83] and, in his article, "At the Middle of the Road," he adds, in reference to *La noche oscura del Niño Avilés:* "These chronicles of the eighteenth century have taught me to be a witness to present day events. I learned with them to look at a reality, to fall in love with it, and to transform observation into a constant labor of the pen."[84] He also adds: "I wish to explain myself and my country, come to term with personal demons and eradicate the collective ones. For me literature is not the pleasure of the text, but a road to salvation, which is the same as searching for a road to life and liberty. It was that which initially brought me to literature. It is in that ethical dimensions that all its greatness lies."[85]

If liberty and salvation are the elements that move the ethical dimension of Rodríguez Juliá's writing, it is because his texts are an attempt to found (as in the founding of the maroon city) the rhizomatic image of what it means to be Puerto Rican as a nation "half done," still not defined. Rodríguez Juliá writes: "Nuestra tradición siempre ha vivido obsecada con la imagen de nosotros mismos, con eso que un tanto defensivamente se ha llamado el problema de la identidad; el esfuerzo de nuestra literatura ha sido fundar la imagen de nuestro pueblo" (Our tradition has been obsessed always with our own image of ourselves, with that which we, a bit defensively, have called the problem of identity; the effort of our literature has been to construct an image of our people).[86]

Rodríguez Juliá represents the space of a cimarrón city founded as the result of dissention, as the wound of colonialism that Child Avilés represents, different from the colonial city that attempts in multiple ways to exorcise the oppressed, the marginal, and the poor as demonic. In this sense, *La noche oscura del Niño Avilés* retells the cultural history of Puerto Rico from the gaze of another space: the invisible yet always already there metageographic cimarrón city that never had a concrete historical existence. That other space, represented first by the phantasmagoric utopian kingdom of Obatal, and by Mitumo's mythical neo-African kingdom founded in the land of Yyaloide, and lastly by a creole, is New Venice: the sum of the cities that transgress, as Benítez Rojo points out. Nonetheless, New Venice is also that "other" space of the text, of literature, and of the imaginary: the invisible space where dreams and desires are possible. In this sense, the interrelationship in the novel between the eighteenth century and the time lived by the writer acquires an important significance. Obatal's kingdom and Avilés's New Venice articulate through the imagination of writing the act of breaking away from a colonial condition. In the Latin American context, these events find their origins in the birth, in the seventeenth and eighteenth century, of a collective sense of difference from Spain. However, in the novel, those events are interconnected with those of 1898, the year when United States marines invaded Puerto Rico (and Cuba), and the year when the last remnants of New Venice disappear: the "famosas torrecillas del islote de Cabras, inexplicables y asombrosas edificaciones del dieciocho [son] ferozmente bombardeadas durante el asedio yanqui de 1898" (the famous little towers of Cabras island, inexplicable and magnificent eighteenth century buildings [are] fiercely bombarded during the yanqui besiege of 1898) (*NONA,* 11). This is the moment when historical memory fails, proposing, as Arcadio Díaz Quiñones suggests in "El 98: la guerra simbólica" (The year 98: the symbolical war) and "Repensar el 98" (Rethinking the year 98), the need to revisit 1898 from the historical gaze of Puerto Ricans in 1898. Quiñones writes: "a pensar nuevamente un laberinto de imágenes segmentadas, un rompecabezas cuyo significado no se puede penetrar completamente porque depende en buena medida del presente y los nuevos proyectos" (to think again, anew, a labyrinth of segmented images, a puzzle whose significance cannot come together completely because, in a larger sense, it depends on the present and on new projects).[87] To rethink anew that moment of entanglement may provide "new beginnings to elaborate another memory,"[88] as the memory Rodríguez Juliá imaginatively rescues in the image of the palenque city of New Venice.

In 1820, as the fictitious writer of the prologue to *La noche oscura del Niño Avilés,* Alejandro Cadalso, claims, all documents about the condemned city of New Venice were burnt, and the city destroyed, but it was not until the bombing by the American invaders in 1898 that the remaining vestiges of dissent against colonial rule were erased. In Rodríguez Juliá's novel, 1898 is the year that sets a new historical course for Puerto Rico as a colonial territory of the United States. Like for Cuba and Santo Domingo (Haiti and the Dominican Republic), for Puerto Rico, the nineteenth century was a moment of a growing national identity, when there appeared a growing national fervor for independence. However, only a small group, which did not include plantation owners, shared in that fervor. Fear of a similar slave rebellion like the one in Haiti in 1804 resulted in harsher methods of control by the Spanish authority and by local plantation owners. This partly explains why the insurgent rebellion of Grito de Lares in 1868, in Puerto Rico, which was planned to occur simultaneously the same day as the insurrection known as Grito de Yara in Cuba, had to be moved to an earlier day because the Spanish authorities found out about the plan. The Yara insurgency went on for ten years in Cuba but the Lares insurgency in Puerto Rico lasted only few days.

There were also economic and social differences between the two islands that explain the demise of this plan and of other attempts of rebellion up until 1898. By this time, as José Luís González explains, Puerto Rico had gained (without a war) political autonomy from Spain. However, after the American intervention, Puerto Rico had to wait again another half a century before regaining limited autonomy and the right to elect a Puerto Rican governor. The first governor elected by popular vote was Luis Muñoz Marín (1948–64), a controversial figure[89] who made Puerto Rico the commonwealth territory of the United States that it is still today. Muñoz Marín attracts Rodríguez Juliá's attention precisely for the contradictions imbued in his administration at such an important moment in the history of Puerto Rico. Echoing the writer's preoccupations, the chronicler in Rodríguez Juliá's *Las tribulaciones de Jonás,* a text constructed around his-

torical events related to Marín Muñoz, calls him the "renegado de la independencia de Puerto Rico" (the renegade of Puerto Rico's independence),[90]
and "el líder político que más honda huella ha dejado en el pueblo puertorriqueño" (the political leader that left the deepest imprint in the Puerto
Rican people).[91] He also adds:

> Ahí reside su misterio, porque si somos honestos y no convertimos la tragedia
> en melodrama—como acostumbramos hacer los independentistas—Muñoz
> Marín no sólo encarnaba sus propios fracasos sino también los de todo un
> pueblo. Mi pena arrancaba justamente de ahí: Su renuncia a la independencia
> para lograr la libertad sobre el hambre no suponía disyuntivas fáciles ni
> reclamos simplones. En el fondo de este hombre había una tragedia, y ésta era
> también la de su pueblo. Miedo a la libertad, dirán algunos, pragmatismo des-
> bocado, dirán otros; prefiero reconocer que fue este hombre quien únicamente
> pudo haber logrado la independencia de Puerto Rico en la primera mitad de este
> siglo. ¿Por qué no lo hizo? La respuesta no es fácil.[92]

> [His mystery rests there, because if we are honest with ourselves and we don't
> turn tragedy into melodrama—like we independentists tend to do—Muñoz
> Marín not only incarnated his own failures, but those of his people. My sadness
> comes from that: his renunciation of independence in order to reach freedom
> from hunger did not necessitate easy alternatives or simplistic demands. Deep
> inside this man there was a tragedy, and it was also that of his people. Fear to
> freedom, some would say, unleashed pragmatism, others would say; I prefer to
> recognize that he was the only man in Puerto Rico who could have won inde-
> pendence for Puerto Rico in the first half of this century. Why did he not do it?
> The answer is not an easy one.]

It is not surprising that both Baltazar Montañez and Child Avilés share
similar contradictions reminiscent of Rodríguez Juliá's ideas about Muñoz
Marín. Baltazar renounces his people, and his father's own struggle for
freedom, while Alivés renounces the Law of the Father, his European spiritual father, and goes against Trespalacios's expectations, like Benkos in
Zapata Olivella's novel.[93] Both martyrs represent in different ways the
contradictions of border subjects (the wound or *raja* left by colonialism),
the life in an "in between" zone, or the "hyphen" as Pérez Firmat calls it.[94]
If, like González affirms, in nineteenth century Puerto Rico, as Betances
claims, "Puerto Ricans did not want independence,"[95] then, could it be possible to assume that the same is true in the twentieth century?

The enigmatic tribulations of Rodríguez Juliá's Muñoz Marín, is reminiscent of the "tribulations" of Trespalacios in *La noche oscura del Niño
Avilés,* and, later, of Child Avilés in *En el camino de Yyaloide.* Like the creole son of the people, Rodríguez Juliá's Muñoz Marín is trapped in a cultural, personal, and political entanglement, in his own border condition: his
own desire to be himself and yet (an)other.[96] However, the question that

haunts Rodríguez Juliá in the case of Muñoz Marín is: Why not independence? As if conversant with such preoccupation, the archivalist in *La noche del niño Avilés* questions: Why was New Venice forgotten from the collective memory? As an echo to the question posed by the archivist in *La renuncia del héroe Baltazar* (Why did Baltazar renounce the memory of his people, of his father?), Rodríguez Juliá points out in *Las tribulaciones* that Utopia is found "siempre flotante en la peor retórica de nuestros fracasos políticos" (always floating in the worse rhetoric of our political fiasco).[97] The complexity Rodríguez Juliá sees in the enigmatic popular figure of Muñoz Marín takes him back to 1898, but also to the eighteenth century, to a mass rebellion that occurred in Haiti, not in Puerto Rico.

The new colonial condition that began in Puerto Rico in 1898 was a moment of gains and defeat, in which new myths of progress erased the collective memory of a national ethos born in "that blurred eighteenth century—explains Rodríguez Juliá—where the birth of our shared living is hidden," "the seed of our nationality."[98] It is not surprising then that in *La noche oscura* Rodríguez Juliá takes the reader to the eighteenth century, to the moment when a national ethos is born, a moment, in the novel, that experienced a schism between colonial rule and the idealized space of a palenque that does not cease to be, always there in the psychology of the people, invisible. From that moment of entanglement on, Utopia, conceived as a space of freedom, gives way to various forms of exile that characterize today the Caribbean condition. Much like Afro-Puerto Rican and Dominican slaves in the early nineteenth century ran away to an independent Haiti, today the city-palenque is New York or Miami. Caribbean immigrants, and *balseros,* still face today some of the same dangers the runaway slaves faced over one hundred years ago. In reference to the writer's allegorical representation of the past as a way to represent the present, in *La noche oscura del Niño Avilés,* Rodríguez Juliá confesses: "I flirt with allegory."[99] And he adds: "Literature has to do with life and how we come to grips with its terror and come to deserve its beauty. I do not pretend to advance Puerto Rican independence with my writing. I only wish to understand why we are like we are, and why we are where we are. In the worst moments when cynicism scrapes the bottom of our dark hope I conceive of my country only as a curious object of knowledge; but that is only in the worst moments. I am always at war between the most intense love and the most rancorous anger."[100]

According to Cadalso, the writer of the fictitious prologue in *La noche oscura del Niño Avilés,* the reencounter by scholars of New Venice, and their new interest in the liminal existence of this utopian palenque city, begins when the archivalist, Don José Pedreira Murillo, discovers in 1913, among a collection of documents, a chronicle written by González Campos (the ironic juxtaposition of José Luis González and Albizu Campos) in which Campos describes New Venice. This description reminds Pedreira of a triptych by Silvestre Andino, José Campeche's nephew, representing a similar place:

> Extraño paisaje de canales e islotes donde se alzan majestuosos edificios parecidos a colmenas . . . El retablo narra, sirviéndose de oscuras visiones simbólicas y paisajes realistas del más minucioso detallismo [barroquismo] verdaderas miniaturas, la historia del singular poblado y su fundador, el Niño Avilés (*NONA*, 10).

> [A strange scenery of waterways and small islands from where magnificent buildings similar to beehives emerge. . . . The *retablo* narrate, using dark symbolic visions and realist landscape of true miniatures of most minute details [baroque], the history of the unique village and its founder, Child Avilés.]

In the neo-baroque thicket of Rodríguez Juliá's allegorical references, one image especially stands out. This is the relationship between New Venice and José Campeche, the first known Puerto Rican painter. The first chapter of the novel opens precisely with a character of the same name, José Campeche, who accompanies Child Avilés in his journey to the marshes where he found New Venice (*NONA*, 17). Like the Avilenses in *La noche oscura del Niño Avilés,* Campeche, the historical Puerto Rican creole mulatto painter was "the son of a former slave indebted for the purchase of his freedom and an immigrant woman from the Canary Islands."[101] He was a "mulatto, trained by Luis Paret y Alcázar, chamber painter of Charles III."[102] As Erik Camayd-Freixas points out, José Campeche "became the artistic property of the Church and the political elite," as such, he was "never free to paint his own people."[103] For this reason, "Rodríguez Juliá's inversion of history (*oscuro reverso*) will begin as the unleashing of Campeche's oppressed desire and become the liberation of 'the people's' historical libido."[104] Campeche is known for his portrait of "El Niño Juan Pantaleón Avilés:" the representation of the naked body of an infant born without arms and with deformed incomplete legs, whose face, in Campeche's painting, gives the impression of being the face of a mature person. The incompleteness of this incongruous infant with the face of a mature child, as represented by Campeche, is the allegorical representation of Puerto Rican colonial society, a society that for Rodríguez Juliá is still today "a medio hacer" (half done). Campeche's painting of this monstrous enigmatic child inscribes in his representation of a deformed infant the social conflicts and ambiguities of Puerto Rico, and of Campeche himself, as a mulatto painter. The portrait was commissioned by Doctor Juan Alejo de Arizmendi de la Torre, the first native Bishop of Puerto Rico (1803–14) in order to scientifically document the anomalies of the monstrous child. Campeche hurriedly finished the painting in 1808, only a year before his death. Ramón E. Soto-

Crespo notes: "It is this detail of origin that inspires Rodríguez Juliá to tie in the obscure religiosity at the beginning of Puerto Rican history with a narrative of historical origins, national formation, and the discourse of historical painting. . . . As a historical figure, Campeche marks the discursive origins of Puerto Rican aesthetics by being the first institutional and official painter of the island's emerging eighteenth-century nationhood."[105]

There is a certain irony in the fact that the first Puerto Rican bishop is the one who commissions the first Puerto Rican painter to paint the portrait of this Child Avilés precisely during the years when Puerto Rican nationality is emerging. There is also a certain symbolic incongruity in that the first known Puerto Rican painter is a mulatto, commissioned to paint the anomalies of a creole child (an enigmatic son of the people), who carries in his body, like the painter himself, the wound of his birth, and of hybridity in a Caribbean colonial society. Campeche's repressed gaze of that creole monstrous child incarcerated in his body, an incomplete being, attracts Rodríguez Juliá, who sees in Campeche's representation a metaphor for the nation. In his *Campeche, o los diablejos de la melancolía* (1986), Rodríguez Juliá proposes that Campeche painted the commissioned portrait only because, as a common practice at this time of scientific curiosity, the bishop commissioned him to do it. However, he argues:

> Campeche soon surpasses it, turning the portrait into a metaphor of suffering . . . And this suffering is related to the people; the painter's gaze—accustomed to capturing the personality and function of the Creole elite and the colonial administrative taste—rests here upon the deformed, upon a child of the people . . . Avilés is bound within his own body, his hands tied by organic deformity . . . An uncertainty becomes apparent regarding the child's age. It suddenly strikes us that we are really before the pitiful condition of a young man shrouded by the body of an infant. The head has nothing to do with the body. It has aged in that atrocious pain, in that rabid suffering . . . In that distance between the right eye and the left lie obedience and rebelliousness, salvation and damnation, sanctity and our sinful pride.106

In *La noche oscura del Niño Avilés,* Rodríguez Juliá's Child Avilés is not physically deformed like his model.[107] Nevertheless, a different monstrosity in this border subject recalls the duality of Campeche's Child Avilés, and of the painter himself, in that he is a duplicitous being, like the figure portrayed by Campeche, incarcerated in his body, imprisoned in his own hybrid identity, in the image others have created of him: socially predestined, equally obedient and rebellious, angelic and satanic. In this sense, Rodríguez Juliá's Child Avilés is also a creole child of obscure origins like his monstrous model. And, like his model, he is also marked by dogmas and chastisements, at a time when, at the "seed" of Puerto Rican emerging nationalism, creole society was, like Child Avilés, and, in a different sense,

like Campeche, a duplicitous "half done" child incarcerated in his repressed desires for freedom, and in his desire for the right to be a complete
human being. As in Campeche's painting, and as in the *Ireme's* dances on
"Día de Reyes," popular cultural expression and aesthetic representations
from outside the spheres of dominance and ideological authority are always
transgressive.[108] Hence, in Rodríguez Juliá's textual system of relations
and entanglements, the enigmatic origins of Child Avilés and his condition
as creole, hybrid, border subject, posed a threat for the hegemony of colonial order. It was a reminder of an always already-present possibility for
dissidence and treason in creole (hybrid) societies (precisely the rebellious
mark of hybridity Zapata Olivella presents in *Changó, el gran Putas*). In
this sense, Rodríguez Juliá's Child Avilés represents the enigma of
Campeche's own projections inscribed in the imagination of the observer
in his representation of the child Juan Pantaleón Avilés: an enigma entangled in the twisted complex conditions of power.

IV

The utilization, first by Larra and then Trespalacios, of infant Avilés as a
talismanic object of power to control the local subjugated population recalls the events in the seventeenth century documented by Fernando Ortiz
in *Una pelea cubana contra los demonio* (A Cuban Fight Against Demons).
This is a text that inspired Rodríguez Juliá to write *La noche oscura del
Niño Avilés,*[109] and, according to Benítez Rojo, "his most important
source" (*RI,* 246). Ortiz's study is a commentary on the curious religious
conflict, in the seventeenth century, between a priest and the villagers of
San Juan de los Remedios, Cuba. What is interesting about this socioreli-
gious battle, Ortiz points out, is that the priest, Father González de la Cruz,
conjures demons and has "dealings" with demonic powers in order to co-
erce the villagers of San Juan de los Remedios to resettle the village far-
ther inland, in his own land.[110] The embittered struggle lasted years, but
most of the villagers resisted the priest's coercions and did not relocate. It
all began when several possessed slaves prophesized, during a trance, that
the village of San Juan de los Remedios was going to sink in the ocean.
Many of the villagers questioned the prophecy as well as the priest's reasons for relocation. Yet, the struggle intensified, and, as time passed, the
conflict between the Holy authority and the villagers worsened. Ortiz
points out that: "los demonios decían la verdad, la misma que decía Dios"
(the demons told the truth, the same [truth] God told)[111] and, to everyone's
surprise, "El Espíritu Santo y el Espíritu Malo estaban concordes" (The
Holy Spirit and the Evil Spirit agreed).[112] Finally, the dissenting villagers
won the demonic-divine battle and remained where they originally had set-

tled; others, moved inland. Father González, who died in the process, was judged posthumously for his actions.

This odd struggle between priest, demons, and villagers leaves much to conjecture. Ortiz wonders whether "el inquisidor criollo pudo engañarse y también ser engañado" (the creole Inquisitor could have fooled himself and be fooled by others).[113] For Ortiz, this curious battle of powers is representative of seventeenth century colonial life, the political games of the period, the complex role of the inquisition in relationship to political power, and the role of theology (demonology) in the affairs of colonial Cuba, and, by analogy, of most Spanish American colonial towns. In principle, as Ortiz suggests, this struggle between Church and villagers is not much different from the political power struggles experienced in the twentieth century in the Spanish Caribbean. He writes:

> Con los antecedentes recopilados el lector ya ha podido ir formando juicio acerca de la clase de pelea que hace siglos se ganó en Remedios contra los demonios. Ya comprenderá todos los complejos factores, económicos e ideológicos, que intervinieron en aquella contienda entre laicistas y clericales; y se dará cuenta de que aquella lucha no terminó. Sus episodios cualquier día pueden renovarse con estos tiempos actuales, pero fundamentalmente con los mismos espíritus.[114]

> [From the compiled background the reader has been able to judge the type of struggle Remedios won centuries ago against demons. [The reader] must understand the complex economic, and ideological factors that intervened in that conflict between laymen and clergymen; and should realize that that dispute did not end. Their episodes can be renewed any day in these present times, basically with the same spirit.]

As if the novel were an allegorical representation of Ortiz's prophesy, *La noche oscura del Niño Avilés* stages a similar battle between bishop Larra, the opposing force of Bishop Trespalacios, and the *Avilensians* over a talismanic child whose powers Larra pretends to conjure and control. Rodríguez Juliá's Child Avilés, as a metaphor for the people, is cast in the novel as both demonic and divine. Such duality characterizes the role of the Church and State during colonial rule, since the Inquisitors and their punitive laws were perhaps the closest things to a demonic curse that slaves, creoles, and indigenous people could have encountered. Camayd-Freixas observes that Rodríguez Juliá's Trespalacios:

> reestablished order with the banishment of the black devils, the exorcism of Avilés, the cleansing (*despojo*) of the city, and the founding of the State. On Christmas Day, 1773, he baptizes Avilés, and the Avilensians return to a Christian San Juan. The Bishop's "secret diary" will tell of his dreams of construct-

ing the City of God, the New Jerusalem; of his never-ending battles against the demons, instigators of Arcadia and Utopia; and of his prophetic nightmares of a lacustrine city on stilts above the mangroves, reflecting its vain nature on the water, as the space for endless hope and unfulfilled desire.[115]

Rodríguez Juliá's Trespalacios is a romanced parody of the historical figure of the Inquisitor Trespalacios. Trespalacios, the first Bishop of the Havana Diocese, arrived in Havana in 1792, and soon after his arrival he began to wage a war against the demonic powers he believed were present in religious and cultural expressions in Cuba. By the time Trespalacios arrived in Havana in the eighteenth century, Ortiz explains, African beliefs and Christianity were already fused in vernacular culture creating what Ortiz calls Spanish "santería o cristianería."[116] Trespalacios immediately set out to destroy those hybrid festivities[117] in which African religious expressions were found in dances,[118] in the *Altares de Cruz* displayed in early May, and in Nativity scenes, "Día de Reyes," *guateques,* religious festivities, birthdays, and other occasions.[119] One can only imagine the frustrating battle Trespalacios waged in order to exorcise those African expressions already deeply rooted in Cuban vernacular culture. Armed with an inquisitorial zeal, Ortiz notes, Trespalacios, "con objeto de acabar con las inmoralidades a que daban lugar tales costumbres católicas prohibió no sólo los Altares de Cruz y los Nacimientos, que se celebraban en noches de Semana Santa" (in order to end the immorality caused by such Catholic customs, he prohibited more than *Altares de Cruz* and Nativity scenes, celebrated during Holy Week).[120] Those evening ceremonies, Trespalacios claimed, gave way to scandalous profanities, and thus had to be prohibited.

La noche oscura del Niño Avilés revisits that obscure reverse folds of colonial life, the other invisible history of the Caribbean documented by Ortiz in Cuba, and the other side of a past and present colonial and neo colonial life in a present day Puerto Rican context. In Caribbean colonial towns like San Juan de los Remedios, Cuba, and like San Juan de Puerto Rico, the demonic was conceived always as being black, runaway slave, creole, or African. Furthermore, Trespalacios's exorcism of the demonic at the end of the eighteenth century coincides with a larger battle waged in America precisely at the same time: the early conflicts that led to the wars of independence against colonial rule in Haiti, and the eventual triumph of the Haitian Revolution in 1804. Coinciding with these political events, Rodríguez Juliá's Trespalacios ironically works to rid colonial society of African "demons" (like the rebels Obatal and Mitume). In *La noche oscura del Niño Avilés,* the battle between the demonic inquisitorial Larra and Trespalacios and the neo-African kingdom of Obatal and of his rival, Mitume, are allegorical recollections of those forgotten memories that are at the heart of the emerging nation's ethos. Ultimately, as it happened in the nineteenth century with creole society, Trespalacios's authorial reign leads Child Avilés to found a cimarrón city, where, Avilés prophesizes: "Allá fundaremos colonia libre para la gente aquí nacida, lejos de godos y sambenitos" (There we will found a free colony for the people born here, away from the *godos* and prayers) (*NONA*, 12). The fictitious prologue writer in Rodríguez Juliá's novel, Alejandro Cadalso, describes Avilés's mythical city, New Venice, and the effects its presence had on colonial society:

El miedo combatió sin tregua la oscura ciudad del Niño Avilés. Quedó suspendida Nueva Venecia entre el más leve susurro del recuerdo y el silencio de lo que nunca fue. La visión libertaria del Avilés perturbaba aquella paz colonial tan celosamente vigilada por inquisidores y gobernantes . . . Podemos adivinar la pesadilla racial que significó, para aquellos temerosos súbditos, la presencia, al otro lado de la bahía, de un ejército de cimarrones. También el pueblo debió sobresaltarse ante una ciudad que confundió el asombro con el espanto, la libertad con la locura. El esfuerzo libertario del Avilés pronto se convirtió en desaforada visión utópica (*NONA*, 13).

[Fear fought without rest against the dark city of Child Avilés. New Venice was left suspended between the softest whisper of remembrance and the silence of that which never existed. The libertarian vision of Avilés disturbed the colonial peace so zealously guarded by inquisitors and rulers . . . We can guess what that racial nightmare, the presence across the bay of an army of cimarrones, meant for such powerful subjects. Also the people must have been frightened by a city that confused awe with terror, freedom with madness. The libertarian effort of Avilés soon turned into a boundless utopian vision.]

Like New Venice, also El Fanguito becomes, in the realm of artistic expression, an idealized community of social victims, poetically reconstructed by singers and writers who invest it of ideologies distant from the necessities of the settlers. It is with a certain obscure humor that Rodríguez Julia's priest chronicler claims that Avilés's army and followers were:

negros cimarrones, guerreros de muy fiera estampa forman ejército mercenario bajo el mando de Avilés. Diestros con el machete y el espadín, artífices verdaderos son en la confección de disfraces aterradores, y esto digo porque llevan las cabezas afeitadas al rape y las barbas crespas y largas, adornándose las orejas con anillos, cascabeles, campanillas y otras muchas chucherías ruidosas. Es por esto que son conocidos por el nombre de "soneros", mote que honran de verdad cada vez que entran en batalla, pues hacen sonar grandísimos tambores de sonido espantoso (*NONA*, 12).

[black cimarrones, warriors of fierce look form a mercenary army under the command of Avilés. Masters of the machete and the sword, they are true artisans in the confection of frightening costumes, and I say this because they shave their hair on their heads and have long curly beards, and adorn their ears with rings, jingles, bells, and many other noisy trinkets. This is why they are known by the name of *soneros,* a label they truly honor each time they go into battle, since they play huge drums with terrifying sounds.]

The text ironically equates the cimarrones of New Venice with the *soneros* of twentieth-century Puerto Rico. Sonero is a contemporary term that describes those who play *sones,* (the *son*) a musical form of African rhythm, associated by Carpentier with the origins of Cuban music. This is an allegorical reference to a local cultural (authentic) expression. The image of a sonero in this novel implicitly contrasts or counterpoints the external (foreign) expression of those who play North American rock, known in Puerto Rico as *roqueros.* This association in the novel between seventeenth century cimarrón warriors and today's soneros, collapses the temporal differences between the seventeenth century and the present, between the moment when the events in the novel take place, and the historical present of the writer: between the African Other brought to the Caribbean and contemporary Puerto Rican society. The followers of Avilés, the dissenters and runaway slaves that make up his forces in the obscure invisible palenque-city of New Venice (the reverse side of the orderly colonial city of San Juan), are the present day soneros in Puerto Rico, a term that describes the cultural conflict, as in Ortiz's allegory of sugar and tobacco, between the autochthonous and the foreign, the proper and the alien: still latent conflicts in twentieth-century Puerto Rico. After all, Rodríguez Juliá's Avilés is the product of the repressed desires of colonial power: a mixed, hybrid, border subject.

As the wound or raja of colonialism, Avilés is the construct of colonial authority, represented by Larra and Trespalacios, and of a creole people who needed, and thus wished for, a Messiah. In this sense, Avilés's hybridity, marked by what Walter Mignolo calls the "colonial difference,"[121] makes him a creole Christ-like martyr who ultimately refuses to be European, as the eighteenth-century historical Inquisitor Trespalacios demanded, and as Rodríguez Juliá's Trespalacios desired, in a complex and enigmatic need to dominate the Other by making the Other an extension of self and of Europe. From this perspective, Alivés, for Rodríguez Juliá, like Baltazar in *La renuncia del héroe Baltazar,* is "una imagen de nosotros mismos" (an image of ourselves):[122] a victim and perpetrator of historical illusions of freedom. Child Avilés, also an enfant terrible, like Montañez, in whose image, says the writer, "lograremos reconocer en su rostro el nuestro" (we will be able to see in his face our own),[123] also represents the re-enactment of an ontological and political "in-between" zone. Child Avilés is a border subject that stands at the crossroad of an *acá* and an *allá* that has shifted meanings and locations: that has moved from Carpentier's oppositional discourse, to a different, and yet still the same point of historical entanglement.

(M)OTHER-*MONTE:* A FEMININE GAZE

In *La noche oscura del Niño Avilés,* Rodríguez Juliá questions national values in an island where political independence and statehood are still at the center of social and political discourses on the nation. In a similar process of inquiry, but in a different political context, Zoé Valdés's novel, *Querido primer novio,* also questions national patriarchal values from the gaze of the Other silenced and excluded by the nation's patristic discourses.

When Spain lost its colonies to the United States of America in 1898, Puerto Rico, and Cuba became colonial territories of the United States. However, since 1895, Cuba had been waging a fierce war against Spain, and in 1902, the island finally became a republic. Its independence, however, was limited by the threat of future interventions by the United States as dictated by the Platt Amendment. Half a century later, in 1959, the Cuban Revolution claimed to be the culmination of the decolonization process that started in the nineteenth century with the wars of independence. It claimed that political independence did not result in freedom for Cuba; and that not until the triumph of the Cuban Revolution did Cuba become a free country: the first and only "Free Territory of America." Socialist Cuba offered a utopian model for sectors of Latin America who applauded Cuba's defiance against the political supervision and the economic sanctions of the United States. At the same time, the proclaimed "freedom" triggered a never-ending exodus away from Cuba's utopia. In Zoé Valdés's novel, *La nada cotidiana* (Daily Nothingness), the narrator, a young woman named Patria (Fatherland), who changes her name to the Shakespearian name of Yocandra, voices the collective feeling among Cuban youths of an existential lack in Cuba's utopia: a certain spiritual void or "nothingness." With the phrase, as a preamble to the text, "Morir por la patria es vivir" (to die for one's country is to live), taken from the Cuban National Anthem, the novel begins with the voice of an angel: "Ella viene de una isla que quiso construir el paraíso" (She comes from an island that wanted to create paradise).[124] The angel explains that Yocandra drowned, like so many other Cubans have, in her efforts to escape from the island, but she does not meet the requirements to enter Hell or Paradise. Therefore, since Yocandra cannot stay in Purgatory forever, higher powers order her to return to Cuba: "La han obligado a volver a su isla. Esa isla que, queriendo construir el paraíso, ha creado el infierno. Ella no sabe qué hacer. ¿Para qué nadar? ¿Para qué ahogarse?" (They have forced her to return to her island. That island that, wanting to construct paradise, created hell. She doesn't know what to do. Why swim? Why drown?).[125] Patria (Yocandra) ironically is condemned to return to the same earthly Purgatory from where she ran away because she does not meet the requirements for asylum in either Heaven or Hell. It is at this ironic point of ontological entanglement that the narration of the story of Yocandra/Patria (Fatherland) begins, in a novel that proposes to be fiction, and, at the same time, a testimony. The play of the character's two names, one a metaphor for the national condition, and the other one taken from fiction, alerts the reader to the novel's satirical and allegorical testimony. Through a play of rhetorical figures of speech, satire, and parodies, the novel proposes itself as a Carnival performance of signifying resistance reminiscent of *Carnaval de los negros* on "Día de Reyes."

Zoé Valdés, a member of a new generation of Cuban writers internationally recognized, is best known for her moral and linguistic defiance, and for her crude representation of contemporary Cuban society. In her novels she questions the laws of a patristic revolutionary government that is old and stale, but still in power after half a century. She also questions the repressive ideological system that drains empty of hope the same people it claims to save. Valdés began to write poetry in the early nineties, in Cuba, where she also published her first novel, *Sangre azul* (1993). Few years later, she began to write her second novel, *La nada cotidiana* (1995), motivated by the sinking of a tugboat full of people (sank by the Cuban coast guards), March 13, 1994. Like Yocandra, their crime had been their desire to run away from the island. Sixty-six persons died that day including children.[126]

When Cuba sent Zoé Valdés to work at the Cultural Section of the Cuban Embassy in Paris, she requested political asylum and stayed in Paris. There she completed and published *La nada cotidiana,* and she continued to write other novels. Playing with philosophical concepts, especially the writings of Emile M. Cioran,[127] and in dialogue with other Cuban writers,[128] Valdés constructs in *La nada cotidiana* a parody of the myth of paradise in order to represent a Cuba contrary to that myth. Valdés's Cuba is a spiritual *páramo* (barren plain), reminiscent of Juan Rulfo's Comala, created by the conditions imposed by a privileged ideological discourse that negates and excludes its own people in the name of freedom. In Valdés's novels, the reader finds that sex and sexuality are modes of escape from the entrapment of the "nothingness" experienced in a Cuban condition in which her characters live. As Valdes explains: "En Cuba, el acto sexual, el momento del orgasmo, es el único momento donde uno es verdaderamente libre" (In Cuba, the sexual act, the moment of orgasm, is the only moment when one is truly free).[129] Reminiscent of Reinaldo Arenas, Virgilio Piñero, and Severo Sarduy's works, Valdés texts articulate an orgasmic search for freedom within an otherwise repressed environment. That search is also a turning inward to the many folds of desire, in order to represent and reenact in writing a certain cultural way of being Cuban, in present day Cuba. Valdés observes: "Me interesa el lenguaje real de la carne, el erotismo, darle un sentido poético y llevarlo a la literatura . . . la sensualidad es esencial a la cultura cubana" (I am interested in the reality of the language of the body, the erotic, to give it a poetic meaning and to carry it to literature . . . sensuality is essential to Cuban culture).[130] Her unabashed frankness about society, politics, and sex, coupled with her erotic linguistic excesses, like the excesses in Reinaldo Arenas's work, or in Edgardo Rodríguez Juliá's *La noche oscura del Niño Avilés,* won her the title in Cuba, as Molinero observes, of "la soez Zoé" (obscene Zoé).[131]

Valdés's defiance is not unique to her writing. What makes her "frankness" different is that she is a woman. As Rita Molinero points out, the obscene word, the violation of a taboo is "[un] efecto más logrado cuando el vocablo vulgar se pone en bocas femeninas, sobre todo en Latinoamérica, donde la crudeza en el decir en el acto sexual ha sido siempre patrimonio del hombre" (best accomplished when vulgar terms are placed in the voice of women, especially in Latin America, where the use of crude terms during the sexual act has been a male patrimony).[132] Valdés's excesses are subversive acts against power, and they are associated in her novels with desire, salvation, and with an attempt to leap through the void, the "nothingness," to penetrate the very core of cubanía. Rita Molinero notes that: "lo que en verdad define el discurso narrativo de Zoé Valdés es el erotismo como redención. Eros ha sido siempre el deseo que triunfa sobre lo prohibido" (what truly defines Zoé Valdés's narrative discourse is eroticism as redemption. Eros always has been desire's triumph over prohibition).[133] Valdés's novels represent life in contemporary Cuba as a continuous moment of crisis: as a schizophrenic and hallucinating experience reminiscent of Reinaldo Arenas's *El mundo alucinante,* but now seen from the gaze of a woman writer. That gaze has been too often excluded from patriarchal discourses on the nation; an exclusion based, in Cuba, as in the case of *P.M.,* on an ideological morality and on a centuries-old complex national ambiguity toward race and gender.

Valdés's novels question the construction of national identity and the relationship of that construction to gender, race, religious faith, and poetry; all of which, Valdés argues, are elements of cubanía negated by the privileged hegemonic discourses on the nation. Hence, Afro-Cuban myths, faith, and ritual practices common today in the island, and in the Cuban/Caribbean Diaspora, and in the Caribbean in general, often inhabit the fictional worlds she constructs in her novels, no longer as a "folkloric spectacle,"[134] but as popular knowledge negated and disemboweled. Valdés's novel, like Sikán, "tells" what cannot be told: that the national "ethos" is based on the erasure of the (M)Other, or, in Vera Kutzinski's words: that in

Cuba, "the mulata may be "the" signifier of Cuba's unity-in-racial-diversity, but she has no part in it. For the mestizo nation is a male homosocial construct premised upon the disappearance of the feminine."[135]

Popular knowledge and religions have been negated if not obliterated in Cuba by the dominant political hegemony. As a response to such exclusion, Zoé Valdés claims that she began to write *La nada cotidiana,* in Cuba, under the invocation of the orishas.[136] This is, in fact, the secret and the guarding shadow that Yocandra invokes at the end of the novel: "Invoco a mis orichas. ¡Denme fuerzas!" (I invoke my orishas. Give me strength!).[137] Voicing again this "secret" that breaks the national taboo, in her short story "Retrato de una infancia habanavieja" (Portrait of an Old Havana Infancy) the narrator claims to be a devotee of Babalú Ayé (Saint Lazarus),[138] and the granddaughter of an Abakuá *monina* who is also a *palero* priest.[139] The anonymous narrator, a woman, explains that in the entire island: "por delante, por detrás y por los cuatro costados, toditos tenemos nuestra cosa hecha, su cuestión" (in front, behind, on the four sides, all of us have our "thing" done, each one's own [religious] matter).[140] In Cuban colloquial speech, the word "thing" (cosa, cuestión) is a euphemism for Afro-Cuban rituals: initiations, *registros* (spiritual check up), *resguardos* (protection), *amarres* (bonding magic), cleansings, and others. "Thing" is also a euphemism to indicate that in Cuba Afro-Cuban religious practices (faith) and cultural expressions have survived different modes of prohibitions for centuries by avoiding direct representation, much like the public ritual dances of the ñañas, Iremes or diablitos on "Día de Reyes."

The anonymous narrator in this short story compares herself to Cecilia Valdés, the sensuous nineteenth-century mulatto woman in Cirilo Villaverde's antislavery novel *Cecilia Valdés* (1839; 1882). Villaverde's Cecilia became an icon in Cuban culture and literature: a national symbol, as well as a representation of the ambiguities toward race and gender in colonial Cuban society, and a metaphor for the social conditions resulting from slavery that, according to Valdés's narrator, still persists in Cuba. Cecilia is the daughter of a plantation owner and a slave trader, just like her mother, whom Cecilia barely knows since she is mentally ill as the result of her "conflictive" situation. Cecilia's grandmother, who raised Cecilia while also caring for her daughter, is the only one who knows the "truth." Her white father financially supports all three women, unbeknown to Cecilia, who does not know who sired her. Ignorant of her origins, she has a love affair with her own white half-brother. Incest, here is the result of the social conditions created by slavery that Villaverde criticizes in his novel. In a play of ironic relationships between character and writer (mediated by an anonymous female narrator), both named Valdés (Cecilia Valdés and Zoé Valdés),[141] and both abandoned by their fathers, the narrator of "Retrato de una infancia habanavieja" suggests that present day Cuba is a continuation of nineteenth century Cuban sociopolitical conditions,[142] even though today the reasons for social marginalization, as well as race and gender exclusionary practices, have changed.

A century later, Cuban writers like Zoé Valdés are still utilizing the same metaphors used in the antislavery novels to criticize political repression and social policies based on exclusion. In *Querido primer novio* (1999), Valdés suggests that such exclusions are based, still, like in colonial society, on race, gender, and religion, thus proposing that social and political changes in Cuba have not altered the rhizomatic psyche of traditional patriarchal hegemony.

The woman narrator in Valdés's short story does not consider herself a mulatto, or white, or black: "ni siquiera cuarterona, ni china, ni rubia, ni trigueña aindiá, ni jabá . . . más bien un *ajiaco* de ese rebumbio y más" (not even a fourth, nor of mixed blood, blond, mestizo, brunette, slightly mixed . . . more so an *ajiaco* of that confusion and more).[143] Valdés reelaborates in *Querido primer novio* this *ajiaco* (mixture), as a type of creole hybridity in Cuban society, that recalls Homi Bhabha's observations on the "presence of the hybrid—in the reevaluation of the symbol of national authority as the sign of colonial difference—."[144] In *Querido primer novio,* hybridity, the double, addresses the ajiaco condition of a mixed people and culture, but also, and at the same time, the instability of a discursive double in the text. If we accept that hybridity, as Bhabha points out, "is the articulation of the ambivalent space where the rite of power is enacted on the site of desire, making its objects at once disciplinary and dissiminatory,"[145] we may also conclude, in relationship to Valdés's novel, that, as Homi Bhabha proposes:

> Hybridity represents that ambivalent "turn" of the discriminated subject into the terrifying, exorbitant object of paranoid classification [. . .] Hybridity has no such perspective of depth or truth to provide: it is not a third term that resolves the tension between two cultures, or the two scenes of the book, in a dialectical play or "recognition." The displacement from symbol to sign creates a crisis for any concept of authority based on recognition [. . .] Hybridity is a problematic of colonial representation and individuation that reverses the effects of the colonial disavowal, so that other "denied knowledges" enter upon the dominant discourse and estrange the basis of its authority.[146]

Those "other knowledges" disemboweled by the dominant discourse are represented in Valdés's text in the figure of the (M)Other, now seen from the gaze of a woman as a cultural metaphor for hybridity in cubanía. In *Querido primer novio,* Valdés inscribes cubanía as a space always already associated with the Afro-Cuban Monte. And, she represents monte in the body of a woman, as a primal space and a new cultural threshold of possibilities.

II

In *Querido primer novio,* the feminine voices that narrate the novel construct a pastiche of local memories, of literary references, and of Afro-
Cuban belief systems. These voices are interwoven in Valdés's text, like actors, in the performance of writing. Valdés re-elaborates the mythical and
poetic knowledge Lydia Cabrera brings to *El monte* as a testimony to the
survival of a culture (as Cabrera Infante claims), within a new vision (following Lezama Lima's idea of the *Imago*), in the metaphorical figure of
Mother-Monte. Reminiscent of Lam's paintings in which "landscape becomes a metaphor for cultural identity,"[147] in Valdés's novel, this feminine
Archaic in the Caribbean, as in Lam and Césaire's representation of the
Caribbean landscape, suggests "an-other" homogeneous space of culture in
which poetry, myths, faith, and the imaginary coexist as a liberating force.

Querido primer novio represents the (M)Other as a "homogeneous"
feminine poetic zone inscribed in cubanía, and personified in the figure of
a dark-skinned country girl, whose name is Tierra Fortuna Munda (Earth
Fortune World). Valdés's Tierra was born and raised in one of the most remote areas of the interior of the island, which Valdés places significantly
in La Fe (Faith). Recalling, as does Vera Kutzinski, that in Cuban national
discourse, nature, "predictably representative of feminine beauty, innocence, and purity, was later to become a symbol of Cuban nationalism,"[148]
and that, for Ortiz, tobacco is the enigmatic promiscuous, sensuous, autochthonous flora, it is no surprise then that Valdés's "daughter of the Antillean landscape," the daughter/goddaughter of the feminine Monte/Ceiba,
is Tierra (Earth, land, country): a country girl whose skin color is like the
color of tobacco (*QPN,* 287).[149] Valdés's Tierra is also a reminder that, in
Kutzinski 's words: "for Martí, the single star of the Cuban flag represented
the five-pointed star of the tobacco flower,"[150] as an icon for the cultural
and natural Cuban landscape. Tierra, in Valdés's novel, establishes a dialogue not only with José Martí, but also with the very concept of cubanía,
in which afrocubanía is a conceptual inclusion. It also dialogues with pre-
Revolutionary discourses on culture and nation that conceived the Caribbean
landscape in association with Africa as a "telluric womb," in Carpentier's
view, but also, as in Lam's "The Jungle," as the visible and invisible landscape of a collective psyche. Valdés's representation of a (M)Other-Monte
dialogues with Cabrera Infante's representation, in *Tres tristes tigres,* of the
deep folds of a culture where myths function, and it also offers a trope for
a cultural realm forgotten and negated in the name of reason by the hegemony in power.

Dánae, the main character of the novel, meets Tierra in La Fe (Faith)
where she goes with her school to work in the fields.[151] As soon as they
meet, both girls feel a homoerotic attraction for each other, associated, in

Valdés signifying codes, to the "homogeneous:" the term Lezama Lima uses to define the relationship between poetry and nature.[152] Such mutual attraction, in the context of Valdés's transgressive "frankness," also represents the abject in Cuban patristic discourses: a love and a faith that the ruling ideology, as well as Western discourses, have considered primitive, anomalous, and dissident.[153] Valdés's Tierra Fortuna Munda is the daughter/goddaughter of Mother Ceiba: the African sacred *Iroko* tree that in Cuba represents Life. It is also Oshun's tree;[154] and its religious significance, according to Cabrera in *El monte,* is that of being the same as Monte.[155] Tierra's name is the composite of *Tierra* (native Landscape, Earth, Nature, Homeland), and Fortuna Mundo, the nickname Cuban *mayomberos* give to the Ceiba. As Lydia Cabrera explains, in the Cuban countryside, the mayomberos, "por cariño, para chiquearla" (endearingly, to pamper her) called the sacred Ceiba "Niña-Linda" (pretty girl) and "Fortuna-Mundo."[156] In Havana, a Ceiba in the Templete is still the center of worship and "folklore," and offerings are left at the foot of the Ceiba. Valdés takes this poetic-religious image in Cuba of Monte-Earth/Nature-Life-Mother, and its metaphoric transfiguration into the image of a "Niña-Linda" (Pretty Girl) and "Fortuna-Mundo" (World Fortune, Destiny) to represent in *Querido primer novio* the Afro-Cuban Ceiba as Monte, personifying the sacred tree, like the mayomberos, in the figure of a "pretty country girl," the color of tobacco, who lives in the remote monte, hinterland, of La Fe (Faith). To feminize the masculine word for World (*Mundo*), in order to be coherent with Tierra as a cosmic and telluric Mother, Valdés transforms Mundo (World), from the mayombero's nickname for the Ceiba (Fortuna Mundo), into *Munda,* rendering with this change the idea of a female cosmos-world-monte. With the linguistic gender alteration, the novel emphasizes the homogeneity of the feminine in a discursive "hybrid" space of poetry, myth (Dánae) and faith (Ceiba-Monte) as the (M)Other. In *Querido primer novio,* the telluric mother in Cuban literature, a mother Africa, now Cuban, "becomes" a trope for a poetic space of culture, magic, faith, and knowledge in the Cuban/Caribbean cultural imaginary.

Valdés's representation of "hybridity" at the threshold of Cuban culture, obliquely recalls Antonio Benítez Rojo's observation that, in the Caribbean, there emerged in the seventeenth century a seminal creole culture in the towns of the oriental zone of Cuba, in the eastern and northern sectors of Hispaniola, and in the northern coast of Jamaica (then a Spanish colony). This culture, which was different from the rest of colonial society in the Caribbean, because it developed out of a cattle based economy and not a sugar plantation system, Benítez Rojo names "culture of the Windward Passage type" (*RI,* 53). It was a culture that resisted the economic impositions of the Spanish Crown by developing an active contraband commerce that defied colonial Law. Such unique Caribbean "culture of the Windward

Passage type," constituted a society made up by creole mulattos, mestizos, and "people of the earth," with a tendency toward equality and nonviolence. Benítez Rojo observes that: "the interplay of ethnologic pluralism, within a more open social panorama than that prevailing in the capital or plantations, allowed the springing up of a generalized racial type with Taino, European, and African origins, which both received and spread a supersyncretic culture characterized by its complexity, its individualism, and its instability, that is to say, creole culture, whose seeds had come scattered from the richest stores of three continents" (*RI*, 46).

It was out of this mixed creole culture that the first poems about the island were written in Cuba. Of these, the best-known is Silvestre de Balboa's *Espejo de paciencia* (Mirror of Patience), in which the hero is a black slave, an Ethiopian, named Salvador (Savior). Balboa's poem, Benítez writes: "[is] an example of a kind of literature that was cultivated in the eastern zone. In the *Espejo de paciencia* as well as in the accompanying sonnets, there is a passion for the island's natural world. There is no mention of Spain, but rather of Cuba [. . .] of the creole, of the mountain ranges and rivers of the region, of the local fauna and flora" (*RI*, 52).[157] Valdés's representation of the island's nature and hybridity, in the context of a geographic and metageographic Cuban Monte, proposes a quest for a seminal, feminine, primal, mythical and poetic space of culture associated with the memory of Africa in the Caribbean. That quest brings to mind that, as Benítez Rojo points out, in that early seventeenth-century creole "Windward Passage type culture," the Madonna, the Divine Mother, became much more important than the Pietá, the suffering mother, indicating with such preference that in such seminal creole imaginary, birth and life were given a greater importance than death and pious suffering. It is not a simple coincidence then, Benítez Rojo observes, that in Cuba the "Mother" is the sincretic figure of a mixed people. She is an icon of freedom, represented by La Virgen de la Caridad del Cobre (Virgin of Charity), the Christian double of Oshun, whose tree in Afro-Cuban beliefs is the Ceiba: Oshun, the orisha who presides over love and fertility, and also the mother of the Ibeyes. Keeping in mind that this hybrid Mother figure is at the threshold of cubanía, Benítez Rojo writes: "Now in our own epoch, it is easy to recognize a previous reading of the powerful matriarchal myth of the *Virgen* in the works of Fernando Ortiz, Lydia Cabrera, Amadeo Roldán, Wifredo Lam, Alejo Carpentier, Nicolás Guillén and many other Cuban intellectuals and artists who discovered the enormous cultural possibilities that lay within the Afro-European interplay" (*RI*, 54).

In a dialogic play with the ambiguities in the definitions of cubanía and with the discourses surrounding the creolization of the Great Mother, as Benítez Rojo points out, at the center of that space of Caribbean instability, in *Querido primer novio*, like in Valdés's previous work (like in *Sab*,

Cabrera's Afro-Cuban short stories, and Cabrera Infante's *Tres tristes tigres*), it is a woman who questions the values imposed on her by the ruling patriarchal society. In Valdés's text, Dánae (poetry and myth) questions the legitimacy of patriarchal authority, and the negation, in Caribbean discourses on the nation, of the cultural and historical agency of women. The main character of the novel, Dánae, rejects the official "truths" imposed on her by her husband and government, and embarks in a quest through memory to the Afro-Cuban, Cuban Monte of La Fe (Faith), to find Tierra.

In *Querido primer novio,* Monte, especially in its association to faith (La Fe*)*, and as a metaphor for freedom, proposes that faith, poetry, imagination, hope, dissidence, are, like New Venice, always already there in the remote hidden folds of the cultural imaginary as a space of desire and as a space desired. If in *La noche oscura del Niño Avilés,* Child Avilés is transformed by desire in the African/Caribbean land of Yyaloide, in *Querido primer novio,* Dánae finds herself, her "other," the love and the cultural knowledge denied to her by a foreign patristic ideology, in the feminine African/Cuban Monte. Like Child Avilés, she also finds freedom in the abject, in the "popular" memory and knowledge of the Afro-Cuban Monte, a space repressed and excluded by the privileged ideology. Recalling the classical myth of Danae, and its transformation in Lezama Lima's "El divino narciso" (Divine Narcissus), Zoé's Dánae (classical poetry and myth; foreign) finds herself in her homogeneous other (local poetry and myth; "proper"): the mythical country girl with "piel color tabaco machacado" (skin the color of mashed tobacco) (*QPN,* 287), who has lived freely in a remote/interior space of the island, a space now also threatened by the same political hegemony imposed on Dánae in Havana. Tierra roamed freely within the confines of the sacred, infinite, Monte of La Fe (Faith), and knew the secrets of its archaic nature. Yet, just as a century earlier the existence of palenques had threatened the authority of the Spanish Crown, in *Querido primer novio* the Afro-Cuban Monte of La Fe (Faith), Tierra's remote hidden landscape of freedom and the local knowledge of Tierra's family, threatens the hegemony of power. Valdés's Tierra Fortuna Munda and her family are tropological representations of a different inner cultural space repressed and negated by exclusionary policies that maintain coherence by eliminating, assimilating, or disrupting difference.

As a trope for Lezama Lima's notion of the homogeneous relationship of nature and poetry, and as a tropological representation of the (M)Other-*Monte* (the mythical and natural forces of the Afro-Cuban Monte), Valdés's Tierra has six breasts, six fingers in each hand, six toes in each foot, and through her body flows the sap of the monte's flora. From her navel constantly oozed guava jam (*QPN,* 181), reminiscing the sensuality of the Cuban landscape in Lam and Cabrera's representations. Tierra was born by the Ceiba and lived under her protection. Tierra's parents and brothers were

"adefesios con la mente muy avanzada, con un grado de inteligencia superior, se rumoraba que torcían tenedores con la vista, que las palmas de las
manos les sangraban o destilaban aceite, o que de sus ombligos fluía un sin-
fín de jugos frutales" (ridiculous in appearance, with very advanced minds,
superior intelligence, it was said that they could bend forks with their sight,
that the palm of their hands bled or oozed oil, or that from their navel flowed
unlimited amounts of fruit juices) (*QPN,* 277). Through her friendship with
Tierra and her family, Dánae learned about the healing powers of the Monte,
and about the supernatural forces that inhabit it: the Ceiba, the Royal Palm,
güijes, the manatee,[158] and, the *Chicherekú Mandinga* of Cuban lore. In La
Fe, through Tierra and through the local memories and knowledges she embodies, Dánae penetrates, and is penetrated by, the invisible realms of the
Monte. Like a Cuban Narcissus, she recognizes her own image (myth and
poetry) in her "proper" local other: the Afro-Cuban poetics that Tierra represents. Dánae understands and comes to love that "other" realm of Cuba's
landscape intrinsic to her own self, which she finds, and recognizes, in the
sacred secluded zone of La Fe (Faith): the negated part of her being, lost and
forgotten, that now she wants to reencounter and rejoin. This is why, years
later, already married and with two daughters, Dánae decides to run away
from the urban life of Havana, and travel back to La Fe. She explains her
decision to her husband in a letter she writes in the train in which she travels back to the interior of the island:

> Necesito volver al campo. El asfalto de la ciudad ultraja mi sensibilidad . . . Es
> que me siento ajena, he perdido confianza en mí. No soy más una persona, me
> he sustituido por una cosa, una suerte de mueble útil . . . una madre no se mar-
> cha así como así, por tres meses o más, sin despedirse. Pero yo tengo que ir a
> encontrar mi yo. A desenterrarlo. Ese yo enlodado (*QPN,* 32).

> [I need to return to the country. The asphalt in the city offends my sensibility
> . . . The problem is that I am no longer a person, I have been substituted by a
> thing, a sort of practical furniture . . . a mother cannot just walk away like that,
> for three months, without saying goodbye. But, I need to find my own "self."
> To disinter it. That "I" muddied.]

Once Dánae returned with her school to Havana, she wrote repeatedly
for years to Tierra, addressing her letters to "My dear first boyfriend," in
order to deceive censorship. Time passed without a word, and Dánae married a previous schoolmate, and had two daughters. Then, one day, in a moment of crisis, feeling the anguish of the void, the nothingness in her life
(for which she sought the help of a psychologist to no avail), she decided
to return to the forgotten space of La Fe to find Tierra. Dánae's escape recalls the madwoman in *Tres tristes tigres,* whose words, "ya no puedo más"

(I can't stand it any longer) end Cabrera Infante's novel. Her escape "back to the source" in *Querido primer novio,* intimates the idea that liberty is associated with madness, madness with freedom, and freedom with open spaces, with nature, and with poetry, myth, and faith. As an act of desperation (unable to "take it any longer"), Dánae runs away from the patristic urban order that imprisoned her, to Tierra, *la tierra,* nature, "fresh air," in search of freedom and ontological significance. Dánae's voyage is a subversive movement back to a lost cultural time and space, to the lost body, to the womb: a poetic primal space at the threshold of culture. She thus returns, escapes, to the inner folds of the cultural imaginary: a sacred zone of faith and myth related to the "Other," as mother, as the (M)Other of Self suppressed and negated. Coherent with her flight, as an act of resistance, the countryside she contemplates from the window of the train significantly triggers in her imagination the recollection of the arm struggle Cuban *mambises* (insurgents) waged in those same fields during the wars of independence a century earlier. In a dialogue with Leante's *Los guerrilleros negros,* the metaphorical recollection of that struggle brings to Dánae's memory the same image of a red sun that heralds revolution:

De buenas a primeras resurge el sol gigante y rojo detrás de una loma, parece una pelota de fuego derritiendo trozos de hielo, las nubes. . . . la guerra de independencia. La presencia de los mambises se escucha en ese galopar fantasmagórico, almas en pena precognizando amoríos con heroínas anónimas defendiéndose en las batallas a machetazo limpio por la dignidad, la libertad, y todo eso que hoy ya no tiene sustento en nuestro mundo (*QPN,* 40).

[Suddenly, the giant red sun emerges behind a hill; it looks like a ball of fire melting pieces of ice, the clouds. . . . the war of independence. The presence of *mambises* can be heard in the phantasmagoric galloping, souls in penance foreknowing love affairs with anonymous heroines defending themselves with their machetes in a battle for dignity and freedom, and all of that that is no longer nurtured in our world today.]

Like the historical flight and arm struggle of cimarrones and mambises, Dánae's journey proposes an allegorical voyage to the realms of an existence negated by the Law of the Father. That realm is the space of (M)Other Monte, the locus of poetic knowledge and freedom always there in the rhizomes of cubanía. For Lezama Lima, whose poetics informs Valdés's novel, the metaphoric subject moves toward poetry, toward what he calls the "exaltation of the homogeneous," much as Dánae (myth and poetry) moves toward Tierra (myth, faith). This movement is the result, for Lezama, of a crisis; born at a moment when society has lost its sense of order and direction. It is not a coincidence then, that when Dánae is wonder-

ing aimlessly through the streets of Havana, in a moment of personal existential crisis, she finds herself suddenly at José Lezama Lima's former home,
now a museum mostly empty. Dánae remembers the moment when she met
the poet, and recalls that her grandmother named her after Lezama's Dánae in *Muerte de Narciso:*

> —Lo conocí, hace años . . . fue de casualidad. . . . Por supuesto, en aquel mo-
> mento ni siguiera sospechábamos que se trataba de un sabio, de un maestro. Lo
> descubrí, yo sola, abriendo uno de sus libros de poesía en la librería Avellaneda
> de la calle Reina. No me lo descubrió nadie . . . observaba el mundo con ojos
> de místico pascaliano, enamorado de la palabra *conocimiento.* . . . Mi nombre
> se lo debo a él, caprichos de mi abuela (*QPN,* 19–20).

> [I met him years ago . . . it was by coincidence. . . . Of course, at that moment
> we did not even suspect that he was a learned man, a teacher. I discovered him
> by myself, when I opened one of his books of poetry in Avellaneda Bookstore,
> in Reina Street. No one revealed him to me . . . he observed the world with the
> eyes of a Pascal-like mystic in love of the word *knowledge* . . . I owe my name
> to him, my grandmother's fancy.]

For Lezama Lima, the movement of the metaphorical subject toward poetic knowledge is a voyage moved by desire: like a train that can go across
the nothingness, the void. For Lezama, as Aida Beaupied observes, that
voyage toward poetry is a movement toward the mother, the site of primal
knowledge, poetic knowledge, recognition, and communion.[159] Basic to
Lezama's poetics is an understanding of America, of Cuban culture, and of
a poetic knowledge foundational to cubanía. Lezama perceived culture as
a "web" (*tejido*) that could be represented only through a counterpoint of
images. Thus, culture, for Lezama, came to be associated with what he called
espacio gnóstico (Gnostic space), a concept Irlemar Chiampi explains, in
the introduction to Lezama's *La expresión americana,* as: "la naturaleza es-
piritualizada, plena de dones en sí, que aguarda, para expresarse, la mirada
del hombre a fin de iniciar el diálogo inmediato (de espíritus: el humano y
el natural) que impulsa a la cultura" (spiritual nature, full of gifts, that
awaits to express itself, the gaze of man in order to begin an immediate dialogue [of spirits: human and natural] that moves culture).[160] Lezama was
preoccupied with the idea of poetic knowledge and with the search for a
poetic space of knowledge at the threshold of culture: a space of myths,
magic, ritual, primal forces (meaning also new), the sacred, and the maternal.[161] His concept of poetry and literature made Lezama a controversial
figure, ambiguously praised and harshly criticized by the socialist government for his ideas of the *Imago,* in which "metaphor" and "faith" went
against the grain of Social Realism and the official "aesthetics" imposed
by the Cuban government, especially after the "Padilla Case" (1968–71).

Yet, Lezama's writings and his ideas had a profound impact on the younger generation of Cuban artists and poets like Zoé Valdés.

As Emilio Bejel points out, Lezama's concept of the *Imago* was born at a moment of dissidence during the 1930s when, as a student, he, like Carpentier and other Minoristas, participated in protests against the dictatorship of Gerardo Machado. His is a poetics interested in the subject, writing, nature and history,[162] in which his concept of the Imago is that of "a creative power that emerges out of a fundamental lack of natural order."[163] In *Querido primer novio,* Zoé Valdés reclaims Lezama's "poetic *logos*" in Dánae's voyage toward that poetic space at the threshold of cubanía in which magic and ritual "act on history." Valdés places the locus of this poetic knowledge in the Afro-Cuban (now Cuban) Monte to represent a primal space of cubanía that is also, as in Martí's *Versos sencillos,* a monte of refuge, and a poetics of resistance against the impositions of patriarchal Law, and against neo-colonial conditions. Monte, here, in the figure of the (M)Other, articulates a Faustian desire (*afán fáustico*) for knowledge, for the African Mother of cubanía, in the figure of a woman who lives in, and represents, that magic, mythical, and sacred liminal zone of the collective cultural imaginary. It is not surprising then that Valdés places the space of (M)Other Monte in La Fe (Faith), close to one of the most beautiful, and best known, natural landscapes in Cuba: the Valley of Viñales, in the province of Pinar del Río.

Querido primer novio is an allegorical return through memory, and triggered by desire, away from the Law of the Father, toward a lost space, and a lost time negated by the present. It is also a voyage of return to a metaphoric native land, as in Césaire's poem, mediated by Lezama's concept of the Imago as "la imagen participando en la historia" (the image participating in history).[164] Remembering that for Lezama the metaphoric subject "actúa para producir la metamorfosis hacia la nueva visión" (acts to produce a metamorphosis toward a new vision),[165] in *Querido primer novio,* Valdés's Dánae "acts to produce a metamorphosis toward a new historical vision," that questions and destabilizes the present order of things. The text conjures, through the ritual magic of writing, that sacred space of a poetic knowledge that is the Cuban Monte, as a place of transformation from where the novel can propose a new historical vision.

The written word, then, in Valdés's novel, is associated with the metaphorical nature of Dánae's voyage, what Lezama calls a *ceremonial creador* (ceremony of creation).[166] As in Cabrera Infante's *Tres tristes tigres,* and in Manuel Zapata Olivella's *Changó, el gran Putas,* in *Querido primer novio,* ritual, also inscribed in the fabric of the text, becomes the signifying structure of the novel. The written work, in *Querido primer novio,* is the looking glass, or gateway, to another realm: the African Cuban Monte, reconstructed out of desire as a space of refuge and resistance.

III

As if it were an omen and a warning to the reader of that "other" space of faith, poetic knowledge, and myths, which Dánae is about to enter in her voyage back to La Fe, she encounters an *Iyawó* at the train station. This initiate to *Ocha* (a Lucumi belief system known in Cuba as *Regla de Ocha*), dressed in white, offers Dánae a seat next to her. Dánae feels disoriented, unable to distinguish between the outer reality she is running away from, and the internal, mythical, and poetic realm of faith she seeks to re-encounter. She finds herself at the crossroad of different realms of possibilities. The *iyaguoná's* white dress, and the sterility of the train station, reminds Dánae of a mental hospital, and makes her wonder: ¿en qué zona de la memoria se encontraba anchada? (In which zone of her memory was she anchored?) (*QPN,* 26). Later in the novel, this association acquires greater significance when the reader finds out that Dánae had been admitted by her husband to a mental institution, and it is from there, from that space of imposed madness, that she recalls, imagines, and reconstructs her life. Remembrance, fiction, dreams, rituals are liminal, and ambiguous spaces of the real; and in *Querido primer novio,* desire, knowledge, and faith, are anomalies that threaten patristic authority. Therefore, Dánae's wish to re-encounter her "other" self (her homogeneous other) in the Monte of La Fe, is an act that the Law can only explain as madness. Hence, like in Cabrera Infante's *TTT* and in Rodríguez Juliá's *Crónicas de Nueva Venecia,* in *Querido primer novio,* Monte, in association with woman, is also associated with faith, desire, libido, and these, with madness, transgression, rebellion, and resistance.

Coherent with the ritual structures of the novel, the Iyawó's presence is a reminder that, for Dánae to reach the Monte, in La Fe, and to find Tierra, first Eleguá must receive an offering. Eleguá, the divine mediator, has to be greeted at the beginning of any ceremonial act, and has to receive the proper ritual sacrifice. In keeping with such requirement, Dánae witnesses in the beginning of her journey an erotic "performance" between the owner of a rooster and a female passenger. The man decapitates his animal, and then fornicates in public view with the woman. In case the reader has not grasped the ritual meaning of this moment, Dánae clarifies it: "Eleguá ha recibido su sacrificio" (Eleguá has received his sacrificial offering) (*QPN,* 44).[167] The fact that a sexual act follows the sacrificial death of the rooster is a reminder that Eleguá is also a phallic deity:[168] the only one able to penetrate and alter time and space. Once Eleguá has been properly acknowledged with an offering, he opens the doors, and Dánae is able to travel from one realm to another: from the Symbolic Order of the Law, the urban space of Havana, to the feminine sacred zone of the Monte, in La Fe: a space Dánae recognizes as being "infinite" (*QPN,* 278), and where she finds Tierra. Dánae's journey is a classical voyage of quest and of return through faith and poetic memory, through myth and history, toward the abject: the negated and prohibited zone of the sacred. This is the hybrid space of the (M)Other in cubanía: the archival locus and logos of the Ekois, a Caribbean/Cuban Archaic.

In the Abakuá foundational myth woman is the sacrificial victim of patriarchal Law, and in *Querido primer novio,* the sacrifice of the rooster, like the sacrifice of Dánae and Tierra at the end of the novel, is the transfigurative act that allows the initiate to be reborn (metamorphosed) to a new "real" constructed by the text in the world through the act of writing. Valdés's novel, like *Tres tristes tigres,* seeks to rescue a time lost, hidden, not just of Havana, as in *TTT,* but of a Cuban cultural archaic imprinted in the notion of cubanía, and sacrificed like Sikán, to a political order of systematic exclusions.

Once in La Fe, Dánae finds Tierra in a remote place of the Monte. She is sitting by a pond, "coronada de rayos y con una serpiente enredada a sus pies" (crowned by sun rays with a serpent wrapped around her feet) (*QPN,* 284), surrounded by the same beings Dánae met as a young girl in La Fe: güijes, Yalodde, mother of the rivers (Oshun), and *Chicherekú Mandinga,* who cannot speak. There was a different feeling about her, however, a sense of fear. Even Mother Ceiba had moved to a different place for safety.[169] Dánae learned from Tierra that she never received her letters and that government officials killed her family. They had given her parents poison with the excuse that it was a new type of fertilizer for cabbages. Their bodies, paralyzed at first, were used for scientific experiments to find the reason for their anomalies. As an echo of Bustrófedon's speech "anomaly" and dysfunction in *Tres tristes tigres,* and of the fatal and futile attempt to normalize him through surgery, science once again could not find any satisfactory explanation for the inherent "differences" of Tierra's family. Tierra had been the only one who survived the extinction because she had refused to eat from the poisoned cabbages; but later she was forced to marry the man responsible for the death of her family. In order to escape from him, Tierra joined Cuban troops deployed to Angola. She was wounded, and the surgeon who treated her removed the "extra" parts of her body without her knowledge or consent, to "normalize" her, or, as in the case of Bustrófedon, to erase her difference. Violated once again by patristic laws and by the politics of science, she returned to La Fe, to the refuge of the sacred "infinite" monte of her birthplace where Dánae eventually finds her.

At this point, the text offers four different possible conclusions to Dánae and Tierra's situation. All of them coincide in that Dánae convinces Tierra to return with her to Havana where they would live together with Dánae's mother, Gloriosa Paz (Glorious Peace). These four concluding virtual possibilities offer a postmodern perspective on the notion of textual closure.

At the same time, they also parody the multiple roads or *Odus* that the oracle (*Ifa,* and *Diloggun*) offers for any specific situation. The fact that the novel offers four roads is already a reminder of the importance of number four in the ritual codes of Ifa, and the Diloggun, in the Lucumí (Yoruba) belief system, which is based on a quadripartite numeric system.[170] In the first three possible textual "roads," Dánae returns to Havana with Tierra. Once in the city, Dánae takes the only taxi available, in which there was room for only one person; and she promises Tierra that she will return soon for her. Reminiscent of the madwoman in *Tres tristes tigres,* Tierra remains in a city park waiting for Dánae. On her way to her mother's home (Gloriosa Paz), Dánae decides to stop by her house to embrace her daughters, and to explain to her husband the reason why she wants a divorce. For him, however, Dánae's reasons are a mode of political transgression, an act of dissidence that must be punished, and Dánae's love for Tierra is seen as madness.

In one of the first three possible textual "roads," Dánae meets an old friend from La Fe, also interned in the same mental institution where Dánae's husband "puts her away." This is José Triana, author of *La noche de los asesinos,* a play Dánae had seen in La Fe. Remembering that Valdés dedicates this novel to José Triana, it is significant then that Dánae's playwright friend, interned in the confines of the same asylum, is a victim like Dánae of imposed madness, and that it is he who explains to Dánae that writing, metaphor, poetry, freedom of expression, as in Heberto Padilla's case (imprisoned in Cuba for his writing) is a dangerous proposition for the structures of power. In the playwright's words: "los policías son alérgicos a las alegorías, los intoxica la poesía" (policemen are allergic to allegories, poetry intoxicates them) (*QPN,* 337). Madness, a transgression in Valdés's novel triggered by the metaphoric subject's will-to-freedom, establishes an analogy between a Cuban condition in which Dánae is trapped, and the laws that creates such condition. In Cuba, Valdés explains, "psychologist" is a euphemism for policeman.[171] Hence, her proposition here is that the mental institution where Dánae has been placed under the care of "psychologists," is a type of all encompassing political prison. In *La noche del niño Avilés,* the narrator observes that New Venice, that city that transgresses, "confunde la libertad con la locura" (confuses liberty with madness) (*QPN,* 13); in *Querido primer novio,* madness (Dánae's madness and her writer friend's madness), is no other than the subject's desire for liberty. Such transgression, as Dánae soon learns, is especially worse when the transgressor is a woman. Her friend, José Triana, thus explains: "siempre que una mujer transgrede, paf, el poder se descontrola" (every time a woman transgresses, *pooph,* power loses control) (*QPN,* 302).

In another one of the first three "roads" at the end of the novel, just as Dánae is about to enter her home, the same Iyawó she met earlier in the train station appears again to warn her of the danger she would face if she goes inside the house. Coherent with the ways of the Afro-Cuban oracle, the Iyawó tells her how she could avoid the path before her, in other words, how the *sorbo* road could be redirected into an *iré* road:

Hija, uté ta marcá por el peligro . . . Hija, que el filo del cuchillo anda suelto, vuelto loco dando vuelta y más vuelta alrededor de su cuello. Hija, ofrézcale unos violenes a Oshún y enséñele idioma al negrito revencúo, al Chicherekú Mandinga, el principito, fantasma con piel de chivo (*QPN*, 293–94).

[My daughter, you are marked by danger . . . Daughter, the sharp edge of the knife is loose, crazily going around and around your neck. Daughter, offer violins to Oshun, and teach the little black *revencúo Chicherekú Mandinga,* the little prince, the ghost in the hide of the goat, how to speak.]

Then, following ritual teachings, the Iyawó tells Dánae a mythical story, which Dánae must understand through religious associations:

Mocombo Forifá Arikuá fue a buscar su caña al monte y se encontró con una niña malcriá, majadera, un Muchángana, la que va a la guerra. Aaaaah, pero esa chiquita es la hija directa de la ceiba . . . esa muchachita es la elegida para ponerle a la ceiba las velas rituales. Tierra Fortuna Munda, ése es su nombre, deberá derramar la sangre del chivo, ceremonia prohibida a las mujeres, pero ella es distinta, a ella la coronaron los santos, y por su gusto sonarán las tinajas. Ella posee el cetro cargao, ah, monina, ah, hermano, ah, los ocobios transformados en diablitos (*QPN*, 294).

[*Macombo, Forifá Arikuá* went to the monte to get his cane and found a bad mannered, ill tempered girl, a muchángara, the one that goes to war. Oh, but that little one was the direct daughter of the ceiba . . . That little girl is the one chosen to offer the ceiba ritual candles. Tierra Fortuna Munda is her name, she should spill the blood of the goat, a ceremony prohibited to women, but she is different, the saints crowned her, and the sacred clay pots will speak at her will. She possesses the consecrated scepter, ah, *monina,* ah, brother, ah, the ecobios transformed in diablitos.]

The Iyawó tells Dánae what she must do to help Tierra. She also tells her that Dánae is the one chosen to help Tierra. Her explanations parody Abakuá symbology and rituals:

Hija, uté sostenga la mocuba o jicarita, beba la sangre del gallo, reviva a la albahaca en agua bendita, fricciónese de la cabeza a los pies y repita: *Fragayando yin, Fragayando yin* . . .
Esto no es cosa de mujeres, o hasta hace poco no lo fue . . .
Un Embácara, el juez que castiga, se apiadará de uté y de los suyos. Uté m'ija, tiene en sus manos la salvación de la Tierra, no vacile en batallar por ella . . .

Gracias, Madre, por este espacio sagrado de pensamiento. Madre, ilumine, oriente y proteja a los que aquí entren . . .
Chicherekú Mandinga, abre la puerta, carabalí. (*QPN*, 294–95).

[Daughter, you hold the *mocuba* or gourd, drink the blood of the rooster, revive the holy basil in holy water, give yourself a massage from head to toes saying *Fragayando yin, Fragayando yin* . . .
This is not women stuff, or at least until recently it was not . . .
An *Embácara*, the Judge that punishes, will take pity on you and yours. You, my daughter, have in your hands the salvation of Tierra, do not hesitate to fight for her . . . water the trunk of mother ceiba, she asks you to do it . . ..
Thank you, Mother, for this sacred space of thought. Mother, enlighten, orient, and protect those that enter here . . .
Chicherekú Mandinga, open the door, carabalí.]

The Iyawó's words are a mixture of storytelling, counseling, and apocalyptic pronouncements characteristic of the language of the oracle. Recalling the explications of the anecdotes of divination, the Iyawó clarifies for the reader the metaphorical significance of Tierra and of Dánae as "the salvation of Tierra" (the Land). Crossing the traditional gender barriers in ñáñigo rituals of initiations, the iyaguoná goes on to explain that Tierra is the woman chosen to partake of the secret rituals as a ñáñigo initiate and a priestess, the one chosen to bring about transformation. Crowned by the orishas, Tierra was given the mission of transforming a Cuban condition into a new imagined reality, and a new historical vision. This transformation is signaled in the text, through the mediating words of the Iyawó, by the acceptance of a woman into the male secret Abakuá society: a constant powerful venue for the artistic and literary expressions of afrocubanía, as well as an element of instability for the hegemony of political powers in Cuba, and therefore, often persecuted. Dánae's mission (in her metaphorical role of poetry, fiction, writing), as Mother-Ceiba explains to Dánae in La Fe, was to save Tierra: the woman chosen by the forces of the Monte to carry the powerful sacred scepter, and to become a *monina*. Like Sikán, spiritual mother and sacrificial victim, in *Querido primer novio,* it is a woman once again the one chosen to restore Sikán's primordial position as mother in the sacred world of the Ekois.

Constructing a web of cultural codes, *Querido primer novio* seeks to restores the echo of the fading sacred voice of the ancestral Monte: the space of poetic knowledge, myth and faith, always already there at the threshold of cubanía, although often forgotten, negated, and excluded. Valdés represents that voice metaphorically personified in the (M)Other as Mother-Monte, and thus as Tierra, the Cuban/Caribbean landscape, associated with magic, faith, poetry, and freedom. That Cuban landscape in Valdés's novel also echoes Lezama's idea that "lo único que crea cultura es el paisaje y eso lo tenemos de maestra monstruosidad" (the only thing that creates culture is the landscape, and that we have in majestic monstrosity).[172]

IV

Valdés's representation of Monte as (M)Other, in its association with faith (La Fe), recalls Lydia Cabrera's rendition of the Afro-Cuban Monte as "life," "earth," cosmos, and "mother" personified by believers in the figure of Mother-Ceiba. For Cabrera's informants, as voiced in *El monte,* all things come from the Monte: "somos hijos del Monte . . . Monte equivale a Tierra en el concepto de Madre universal, fuente de vida" (we are children of the Monte . . . Monte is the same as Earth in the sense of Universal Mother, source of life);[173] "Todo se encuentra en el Monte . . . Tierra y Monte es lo mismo" (Everything can be found in the Monte . . . Earth/Land/Cosmos and Monte are the same).[174] In that sacred Afro-Cuban Monte, "todo es sobrenatural . . . como un templo" (everything is supernatural . . . like a temple);[175] "Todos los orichas van a la Ceiba . . . a todos se les adora en la ceiba" (All of the orishas go the ceiba . . . all of them are worshiped in the ceiba).[176] The association between the forces of the monte and the ceiba comes from the belief that ceibas are "Madres del Mundo" (Mothers of the World).[177] As Dánae finds out in La Fe, Ceiba is "reina" (queen), "diosa" (goddess), and "toda la belleza del mundo junta" (all of the world's beauty put together) (*QPN,* 102). Zoé Valdés's novel reminds its reader that in Cuba Mother-Ceiba is Monte and also Oshun: the Afro-Cuban orisha who presides over the powers of fertility, love, abundance, birth and resurrection (spring), as well as, in the avatar of the Virgin of Charity, resistance, revolution, and freedom. This "Madre bendita" (Blessed Mother) as Dánae calls her (*QPN,* 339), "es el árbol del misterio" (the tree of the unknown), "los antepasados, los santos africanos de todas las naciones traídas a Cuba y los santos católicos van a ella y la habitan permanentemente" (the ancestors, the African saints of all nations brought to Cuba, and the Catholic saints go there and inhabit in her permanently).[178]

With the transformation in Valdés's novel of the nickname mayomberos give to the ceiba, *Fortuna Mundo,* into Fortuna Munda, the signifier Mundo (World) becomes a feminine word: like the Spanish words for life, truth, peace, word, freedom, beauty, poetry, woman, and word (*palabra*). The simple alteration of a vowel, gives Monte the feminine transformative powers of an Archaic Great-Mother-Goddess. Furthermore, the feminization of Monte in *Querido primer novio,* in its relationship to the "word" (palabra) and to the "world," articulates an attempt by the writer to return to what Lezama Lima calls a poetic logos, a primordial space, in order to recreate a new historical vision, but now from a woman's gaze. Utilizing the body of woman as a mode of cultural signification (and remembering that poetry, religious faith, and women, have been marginal to the discourses on nation in pre- and post-Revolutionary Cuba), the feminization of Monte in *Querido primer novio* reappropriates women, poetry, the racial "other," the racial and gender "self," and faith as powerful elements of cultural creation and transformation. The metaphorical and transformative powers reinstated in *Querido primer novio* to motherhood, as a primal force,—and as a metaphor for creation and for a Life-giving-force associated in the Caribbean with Huracán, and with Shango—conjures an act of metamorphosis with which the text offers a last and final possible "road" (*Odu*). In this fourth "life-giving" iré road,[179] like the creative power of the Imago for Lezama, in *Querido primer novio,* the mythical ritual storm of mayomberos and ñáñigos (Ortiz's metaphor for revolution) acts on history to erase injustice and to bring order out of chaos. The text concludes with the return to a primordial moment, like a ritual new dawn (*alborada*), born out of the creative destruction of the storm (*tormenta*): also a feminine word in Spanish, like palabra (word).

The fourth road in *Querido primer novio* is a mythical story consistent with Afro-Cuban rituals and codes. In this iré road, Tierra and Dánae arrive to their destiny, the home of Dánae's mother, Gloriosa Paz (Glorious Peace), with Dánae's daughter, Ibis. Dánae's husband, a puppet of government officials, accuses Dánae and Tierra (implicitly of ideological treason against the government), and they are imprisoned. During the trial, just as Dánae and Tierra are about to be condemned to capital punishment, Dánae's diseased grandmother appears in the courtroom: "Hija de las Mercedes. La que purifica y aboga por la paz. Hija de Obatalá . . . enviada de los Orishas" (Daughter of the Virgin of Mercy. She who purifies and pleads for peace. Daughter of Obatalá . . . sent by the Orishas) (*QPN,* 336). At the same time, Mother-Ceiba "brota de las entrañas del mundo" (emerges from the bottom of the earth) (*QPN,* 339). She comes to bring justice, and she tells Tierra: "te doy poderes, mi hija . . . Haz que el Manatí, la Palma Real, el Chicherekú Mandinga, el Sol y la Luna, luces celosas de la ciudad y del campo, multipliquen tu fuerza . . . Recupera lo que te pertenece, el don de la verdad" (I give you powers, daughter . . . Make the Manatee, the Royal Palm, Chichirekú Mandinga, the Sun, and the Moon, the guarding lights of the city and the countryside, multiply their forces. Recover what belongs to you, the gift of truth) (*QPN,* 339). Once Mother-Ceiba conjures the events to come, the sacred tree disappears "hundiendo sus raíces en lo más recóndito del misterio" (burying her roots in the depths of mystery) (*QPN,* 339); Yemayá (Ocean Mother) then fills the courtroom with "amniotic water" (*QPN,* 340); Tierra defeats the sharks (a euphemism for magnates and tycoons); and Dánae, reminiscing Narcissus's transformation, floats to the surface "rodeada de flores blancas" (surrounded by white flowers) (*QPN,* 340). Then, the mighty Royal Palm (Shango), "rajó el techo" (cracked the roof) of the courthouse and from its navel, "reventó un cráter que trajo como consecuencia un terremoto y un ciclón" (a crater erupted bringing about an earthquake and a cyclone) (*QPN,* 341), followed by a torrential rain that lasted several weeks. Like the "green wind" in *The Kingdom of This World,* the stormy rain in Valdés's novel also sweeps "cuanta hojarasca había" (all of the rubbish) (*QPN,* 344).

Recalling Fernando Ortiz's allegorical association between the creative-destructive power of Huracán in pre-Hispanic Caribbean and a historical revolution "que destruyera como un huracán y creara de nuevo como un soplo de génesis" (that could destroy like a hurricane and create anew like a breath of genesis),[180] in *Querido primer novio,* the storm that the forces of the Monte create is a revolutionary force that restores "truth" (*QPN,* 339). Only then the Chicherekú Mandinga finally can speak.[181] The required performance of the ritual storm in Valdés's novel (conjured by the creative voice-wind of Mother-Ceiba), orders chaos and restores justice and "truth." The main difference in the textual reenactment of the ritual storm (Huracán-Shango's storm and revolution) in *Querido primer novio,* in contrast with Carpentier's cosmic storm in *The Kingdom of This World,* is that in Valdés's novel the ritual storm is a feminine force conjured by the Monte-Ceiba: Valdés revisits and rewrites the recurring Caribbean image of a revolutionary cosmic Great-Wind, but now, from a woman's gaze, as an always already feminine primordial force that brings out order (life). The image of Mother-Monte in *Querido primer novio* destabilizes patristic authority, and restores to the Great-Caribbean-(M)Other its ancestral creative and transfigurative powers.

In Lydia Cabrera's work, the Chicherekú is associated with texts,[182] with words: with writing. Valdés's Chicherekú Mandinga, on the other hand, is associated with a muzzled popular culture, and with writing as a transformative act, with speech, and with the magic force of the word, like a storm, that frees and rescues the muzzled voices silenced by censorship. Writing in *Querido primer novio* makes possible a new vision, and the conditions that allow the Chicherekú of the Monte in Cuban lore to recovers the ability to speak, and with it, historical agency. The transfigurative act of writing in Valdés's *Querido primer novio* is the ritual act of "becoming:" an act that restores in the text, by way of the Imago, the voices always there in cubanía, but silenced by official discourses.

In Valdés's text, the body of woman (like the body/voice of the African descendants in Lydia Cabrera's text) becomes a mode of signification in a maternal disposition of structure, through which the text articulates a Cuban ontological and political condition in crisis. The body of (M)Other in *Querido primer novio* represents the locus of Caribbean culture and, at the same time, in José Lezama Lima's terms, the creative power of the Imago (poetic image) in its poetic transformative power to construct a new historical vision. This play of significations in Valdés's representation of Mother-Monte, addresses the problems, as Homi Bhabha points out, of representing the Archaic in the modern.[183] Part of the problem with such representation is the impossibility of finding a single definition with which to represent the "identity" in a mixed, creole, Hispanic, non-Hispanic, African, non-African, Chinese, American, indigenous, Caribbean, diasporic Caribbean. In this attempt, as Homi Bhabha points out: "the impasse or *aporia* of consciousness that seems to be the representative postmodernist experience is a peculiar strategy of doubling."[184] It is this strategy of "doubling," the "double," that characterizes the relationship of Tierra and Dánae, and their final transformation at the end of the novel.

For Lezama, such doubling takes place when, "el sujeto metafórico actúa para producir la metamorfosis hacia la nueva visión (the metaphoric subject acts to produce a metamorphosis toward a new vision).[185] The new vision produced through metamorphosis is the result of the counterpoint of the old and the new, the classical and the popular,[186] myth and history, poetry and nature. It is through metamorphosis, concludes Lezama, that: "todo tendrá que ser reconstruido, invencionado de nuevo, y los viejos mitos, al reaparecer de nuevo, nos ofrecerán sus conjuros y sus enigmas con un rostro desconocido. La ficción de los mitos son nuevos mitos, con nuevos cansancios y terrores" (everything will need to be reconstructed, invented again, and the old myths, when they reappear anew, will offer us their charms and their enigmas with a new [unknown] face).[187] In *Querido primer novio,* the new face that heralds a new beginning constructs the image of a homogeneous "double" as a new historical vision born out of the counterpoint of the classical and the popular, the old and the new, the modern and the postmodern. In that sense, Tierra Fortuna Munda, as the embodiment of the mythical "hybrid" Mother-Ceiba-Monte, from the Cuban cultural imaginary, also proposes, in her union with Dánae (the classical myth in Lezama's poetic transformation in *Muerte de Narciso*), and in dialogue with the postmodernist strategy of a discursive "doubling," the embodiment of the poetic logos that can rearticulate a new, from the old, concept of cubanía. In such process, Dánae, the novel's metaphoric subject, is retransformed again into a new poetic space associated now with the subaltern authoritative knowledge of African ancestry that Valdés represents in the body of woman (Sikán, Yemayá, Oshun), as (M)Other. From this "primal" foundational poetic knowledge at the threshold of cubanía, acting on history, there emerges the conditions for the possibility of a new "alborada" (dawn), like the sunrises Dánae contemplates in La Fe with Tierra. The body of the (M)Other "becomes," in that new vision, a new metaphoric subject of national identity that restores meaning and order to the daily "nothingness" of a patristic world without meaning.

In a textual play between the popular (Afro-Cuban rituals and beliefs) and the classical as in Lezama's poetics, the novel ends with the metamorphosis of Dánae and Tierra, who, after the apocalyptic storm brought by Mother Monte, are transformed into two ceibas as an altar to love and nature.[188] In the classical Greek myth, Zeus transforms himself into golden rain to deceive Dánae and to possess her. In Lezama's rewriting of the Classical myth, Dánae weaves mythical time into a new poetic vision; and the poem ends with the image of Narcissus metamorphozed, escaping (his) nature, transcending to poetry, without wings: "fugó sin alas" (escaped/flew away without wings).[189] In dialogue with Lezama's poetics, *Querido primer novio* offers a metamorphosis towards a new historical vision; one in which Dánae and Tierra, like Narcissus, metamorphosed, transcend "without wings" (as in writing) the "nothingness" of a Cuban condition. Metamorphosis allows Dánae and Tierra to fly away (without wings) toward Lezama's "kingdom of the image," in the image of two (double) Monte-Ceibas. It is significant then that, in Valdés's text, the agent of transformation is not Zeus, as in the classical text, but the popular Afro-Cuban Chicherekú Mandinga "masked" as, or dressed like, "la luz dorada de la ciudad" (the golden light of the city) (*QPN*, 300). This is in fact one of his many masks, as he explains: one of the text's many ventriloquist voices, pretending to be an "other" voice, in order to speak in signifying gestures, not unlike the performance of the diablitos during Carnaval de los negros.

The transformation of Tierra and Dánae into two "ceibas entrelazadas de espigados troncos" (intertwined ceibas of upright trunks) (*QPN*, 345) in *Querido primer novio*, rescues (m)otherhood (the abject: faith, woman, Afro-Cuban beliefs) from a negated muzzled space to which it had been excluded by ideological hegemony. It also affirms the role of the (M)Other (Africa in a creole Caribbean landscape) in the process of individual and national subject formation, and rethinks the national subject through the body: the body of woman, and the body of the slave—the people, the text, the Archaic. Furthermore, from the gaze of the "faith" inscribed in the Afro-Cuban Monte, the image of two ceibas entangled at the roots, also renders another archival image in Cuba: the Jimaguas, the ritual Ibeyes, twin sons of Shango and Oshun (Ceiba, Monte, Virgen de la Caridad del Cobre).[190] As in Carpentier's "Liturgia," the Afro-Cuban Jimaguas represent the unity of contrary principles: mestizo, mulatto, the double, the hybrid.[191]

Valdés's representation of the signifying Afro-Cuban Ibeyes, the sacred ritual twins that attracted Carpentier and the Minoristas (as the "proper" native force able to exorcise evil spirits), in the figure of two ceibas, proposes a different metamorphosis of revolution that rescues the (M)Other from exclusion. Such new vision also restores to the Archaic African/ Caribbean Mother her foundational role in the Caribbean. Remembering that Ceiba "is" Monte, and also the treehouse of Oshun, and that in Cuba Oshun is the mother of the Ibeyes, the signifying image of a double Ceiba "becomes," in Valdés test, a poetic maternal life-giving force (Iré road) whose presence "creates" the condition for the possibility of a new and different "reality:" a reality born out of the desire to escape, to become other, to overcome a condition, and to transcend it "without wings" (like Lezama Lima's Narcissus).[192] Valdés's double Ceibas then is a trope for an Afro-Caribbean/Cuban poetics of feminine transformative powers, acting on history. In this sense, *Querido primer novio* rescues the (M)Other in the process of national subject formation, and, furthermore, conceives that process through a maternal disposition of structure as a new and different order of things based on inclusion, justice, and freedom.

In *Querido primer novio,* the Afro/Caribbean/Cuban Monte ceases to be an African Other to become a Caribbean space and a time out of Africa now intrinsic to the Caribbean landscape. As such, it reaffirms the importance, in Caribbean myths and local memories, of an African experience deeply rooted, and entangled, like Tierra and Dánae in Cuban soil, in the cultural rhizomes of the Caribbean cultural landscape. (M)Other-Monte in *Querido primer novio,* is a trope, like New Venice in *Crónicas de Nueva Venecia,* and like Shango in *Changó, el gran Putas,* for what Benítez Rojo defines as a Caribbean "super-syncretism" (*RI,* 12). It is also a trope for, in Glissant's terms, the *presensing* of an Archaic, once African, now Caribbean, often negated, muzzled, or forgotten, but always there, in the deep folds of broken cultural memories and living cultural expressions. Through the reappropriation of the (M)Other as a Caribbean Archaic, Valdés is able to question the notion of "otherness" in discourses on the nation, race, gender, religious beliefs, and political ideology; and to reopen old inquiries about the instabilities of defining the "Other"—the racial, gender, ethnic, social, political, or diasporic other. Specially important in that inquiry, which in the later part of the twentieth century Spanish Caribbean writers, like Zoé Valdés and Rodríguez Juliá, have begun to articulate, is the poignant question: What happens when the racial, gender, and epistemological other "becomes" self?

In Spanish Caribbean literary discourses, (M)other-Monte is a trope informed by an African experience that gives voice to an occult zone, an "in-between" zone, in which the African rhythms of the Caribbean still resist entrapment. As Homi Bhabha observes: "it is in the 'inter'—the cutting edge of translation and negotiation, the *in-between,* the space of the *entre* that Derrida has opened up in writing itself—that carries the burden of the meaning of culture. It makes it possible to begin envisaging national, anti-nationalist, histories of the 'people.' It is in this space that we will find those words with which we can speak of Ourselves and Others. And by explor-

3. Offerings left at a Ceiba tree, Havana, Cuba. Photo by Dolores Triana.

ing this hybridity, this 'Third Space,' we may elude the politics of polarity and emerge as the others of our selves."[193]

As the metaphoric subject in the literary performance of cimarronaje in the Caribbean (so often associated with Carnival and masked by representation), the "image" of the (M)Other conjures the imaginary possibilities in *Querido primer novio* of a new historical order. Valdés and Rodríguez Juliá imaginatively rescue a space of local memories, myths, desires, longings, popular knowledge, and broken promises. Their texts recall and celebrate the will-to-freedom that created palenques, manieles, quilombos, still alive in the Caribbean memory and cultural imaginary, as in New Venice, Benkos's *Great Palenque,* El Frijol, and La Fe. Yet, at the same time, their imaginative rescue voices other and different Caribbean conditions. In *Crónicas de Nueva Venecia,* the cimarrón city, the city in the Caribbean that transgresses, is a space of freedom founded but then later forgotten. In *Querido primer novio,* however, Zoé Valdés's rewriting of the (Afro)Cuban Monte as (M)Other, speaks of a space and a time of "becoming," of a beacon of hope in the midst of hopelessness, as well as a time and a space always already there, inscribed in the Caribbean *raja,* and in a repetitive and persistent Caribbean memory.

4. Offerings left at a Ceiba tree, Havana, Cuba. Photo by Dolores Triana.

5. Two Ceiba trees, Havana, Cuba. Photo by Dolores Triana.

Notes

INTRODUCTION

1. Antonio Benítez Rojo, *The Repeating Island. The Caribbean and the Postmodern Perspective,* translated by James Maraniss (Durham: Duke University Press, 1996). All references to this book will be indicated in this text as *RI*.

2. The term "difference" here refers to the attempt to articulate a way of being European and African, intercepted by, and disrupted by, other cultures and peoples that also converged in the greater Caribbean: Japanese, Chinese, Indians, Scandinavians, Lebanese, Turks, Syrians, North Americans, and others.

3. Although native Caribbeans did not survive as groups or nations, in the Spanish-speaking Caribbean islands, the myth of "Indianess" continues to exist.

4. The word comes from African Yoruba nations, and it survived in Cuba in the context of orisha worship. However, *aché,* used in the streets of Havana, or in Miami, New York, Los Angeles, Mexico, Puerto Rico, is charged with a signifying difference that sets it apart from the word *àshé* in Nigeria, when in fact it is a similar concept, used with similar meanings.

5. In those cases when the English translation changes the Afro-Caribbean codes that are important for this study, I offer my own translation.

6. Gilles Deleuze, *A Thousand Plateaus: Capitalism and Schizophrenia* (Minneapolis: University of Minnesota Press, 1987), 8.

7. Edouard Glissant, *Poetics of Relations,* translated by Betsy Wing (Ann Arbor: University of Michigan Press, 1990), 11.

8. Marcos A. Morínigo, *Diccionario de Americanismos* (Barcelona: Muchnick Editores, 1985), 541.

9. Fernando Ortiz, *Historia de una pelea cubana contra los demonios* (Havana: Editorial de Ciencias Sociales, 1975), 525.

10. The beginning of the Africanization of America can be traced back to Christopher Columbus's first voyage to the New World. The only personal experiences he had had with which to understand the new lands were those he acquired from having sailed to Africa with Portuguese slave traders, and from having been in the new "discovered" lands of the Canary Islands. His first two diaries are full of references in which he draws similarities between his knowledge of the Portuguese African slave trade and the newest lands of the Spanish Crown, the Canary Islands. By the time Columbus arrived in the New World, Lisbon (where he lived for a time) and Seville had large populations of African slaves and ladino ex-slaves who had adapted to the language and customs of European cities. These were the first African servants to arrive in the New World. See Fernando Ortiz, *Los negros curros* (Havana: Editorial de Ciencias Sociales, 1986), 3. In the Caribbean, mostly in urban areas, there emerged a growing population of free black and mulatto creoles.

11. Wilson Harris, "The Limbo Gateway," 378–82, in *The Post-Colonial Studies Reader,* edited by Bill Ashcroft, Gareth Griffiths, and Helen Tiffin (London: Routledge, 1995), 380.

12. In Puerto Rico, bananas are called *guineos* because they were taken to the Caribbean

from the African coast of Guine. Also in Cuba, a variety of chickens brought from Africa are known as *gallinas guinea*. Plantains and bananas were brought from Africa as cheap food for the slaves. Today similar dishes made with plantains in the Spanish Antilles are called by their African names; for example, *fu-fú* in Cuba, *mofongo* in Puerto Rico, and *mangú* in the Dominican Republic. In Cuba okra is still known by its African name, *kimbombó*.

13. Benita Parry, "Resistance Theory/Theorising Resistance or Two Cheers for Nativism," 172–96, in *Colonial Discourse/Postcolonial Theory*, edited by Francis Barker, Peter Hulme, and Margaret Iversin (UK: Manchester University Press, 1994), 175.

14. James Arnold, *Modernism and Negritude. The Poetry and Poetics of Aimé Césaire* (Cambridge, MA: Harvard University Press, 1981), 172. See also Parry, "Resistance Theory/Theorizing Resistance," 182.

CHAPTER 1. CULTURAL IDENTITY

1. Fernando Ortiz, *La antigua fiesta afrocubana del "Día de Reyes"* (Havana: Departamento de Asuntos Culturales, División de Publicaciones, 1960), 43. This text was published for the first time in 1925.

2. Ibid., 9.

3. Ibid.

4. Ibid., 38.

5. Ada Ferrer, *Insurgent Cuba: Race, Nation, and Revolution, 1868–1898* (Chapel Hill: The University of North Carolina Press, 1999), 32.

6. One of the few representations that exists today of the ritual dances and regalia of the ñáñigos in the nineteenth century is a drawing, by Víctor Patricio de Landaluze, who lived in Cuba for forty years, entitled "El *ñáñigo*." The drawing appeared in Landaluze's *Tipos y costumbres de La isla de Cuba* (Havana: 1881). The drawing also is commonly known as "El diablito de Landaluze" (Landaluze's little devil). Another earlier representation of the diablitos on "Día de Reyes" is Pierre Toussaint Fréderic Miahle's drawing, entitled "Día de Reyes" (1848), which appeared in *Viaje Pintoresco alrededor de la Isla de Cuba* (Havana: 1847–48), and later in *Album pintoresco de la Isla de Cuba [Picturesque Album of the Island of Cuba]* (Havana: 1855) presently at the George Glazer Gallery. Landaluze's drawing of a diablito dancer, and photos of a diablito taken half a century later, and reproduced in Lydia Cabrera's *El monte* (1954), show how little the regalia of these ñáñigo dancers changed over the years.

7. Ortiz, *La antigua fiesta afrocubana de "Día de Reyes,"* 12.

8. The term afrocubano (Afro-Cuban), as Rodríguez–Mangual reminds her readers, "was coined in 1847 by Antonio Veitía, but it was Fernando Ortiz's book, *Los negros brujos* (1906) that made its use common." See, Edna M. Rodríguez-Mangual, *Lydia Cabrera and the Construction of an Afro-Cuban Cultural Identity* (Chapel Hill: The University of North Carolina Press, 2004), 16.

9. Spanish Golden Age writers made use of this Manichean image that justified the Crusades against the Moors as well as the destruction of New World temples and religious icons. Spaniards believed religious temples, figures, and pictorial writings were demonic. The New World was considered to be the kingdom of the Devil. In *Una pelea cubana contra los demonios* (1959), Fernando Ortiz documents the consequences of such idea in the seventeenth century, in the founding of two villages in Cuba: San Juan de los Remedios, and Santa Clara. He presents historical details about the conflicts between the citizens of the village of San Juan de los Remedios and a local priest who wanted to relocate the town to his own

land, and who, in the exercise of his authority, conjured demons. Following the stereotypes of the times, such demons were believed to be black. Ortiz's text inspired Edgardo Rodríguez Juliá to write his novel *La noche oscura del niño Avilés* (1984).

10. Fernando Ortiz, *Hampa afrocubana. Los negros brujos (apuntes para un estudio de etnología criminal)* (Miami: Ediciones Universal, 1973), 5. The emphasis is mine.

11. In Marilyn Grace Miller, *Rise and Fall of the Cosmic Race: The Cult of Mestizaje in Latin America* (Austin: University of Texas Press, 2004), 75. This is a quote taken and translated by Miller from Fernando Ortiz, *Estudios etnosociológicos,* edited by Isaac Barreal Gernández (Havana: Editorial de Ciencias Sociales, 1991), 142.

12. See Bronislaw Malinowski's "Introduction" to Fernando Ortiz, *Contrapunteo cubano del tabaco y el azúcar* (Venezuela: Biblioteca Ayacucho, 1987), 3.

13. Contemporary modalities of these devil figures, reminiscent of the European Christian "devils," can be found still today during Carnival in Puerto Rico and in the Dominican Republic in the popularized figure of the *vejigantes*.

14. Ortiz, *La antigua fiesta afrocubana del "Día de Reyes,"* 29. An example of the gross misunderstandings surrounding Africans and African customs and cultures in colonial Cuba, the diablito dancers were represented in the nineteenth century in cigar labels. One of these labels shows slave *bozales* dancing on "Día de Reyes" with the caption "Los diablos coronados castigarán tus pecados" (The crowned devils will punish your sins), reproduced in Vera Kutzinski, *Sugar's Secrets: Race and the Erotic of Cuban Nationalism* (Charlottesville: University Press of Virginia, 1993), 55. The margins that frame the figures of the diablitos in this cigar label represent chaos: a savage with a lance chasing another one with a headdress of feathers and a bottle in one hand. The action takes place above the figure of a black woman (on the left margin from the gaze of the viewer) who, holding an arm to her face, looks up surprised and possibly afraid. On the right margin is *La Honradez* (Honesty), in the classical figure of a white woman holding a scale with her right hand.

15. Ortiz, *La antigua fiesta afrocubana del "Día de Reyes,"* 30.

16. A letter sent to Lydia Cabrera from Cuba explains that in the "dispositions" given by the *Bando de Buen Gobierno* in effect since January 1, 1848, dictated by the Captain General and High Civil Government of the Island of Cuba, "Teniente General de los Reales Ejércitos, Sr. Don Gerónimo Valdés Noriega y Sierra" (General Lieutenant of the Royal Army), the activities of the *Cabildos* were restricted as follows: "En ningún caso saldrán los negros a la calle en cuerpo de nación con bandera u otra insignia sin permiso del gobierno; pena de diez pesos que pagará el capataz del cabildo. Sin embargo, les será permitido celebrar el día de los Santos Reyes, la diversión conocida con el nombre de diablitos en la misma forma que lo han hecho hasta el día y no de otro modo." (For no reason will blacks go out in the street together as a nation with a flag or any other sign without permission from the government; under the threat of a ten pesos fine that the head of the *cabildo* has to pay. However, they will be allowed to celebrate on "Día de Reyes," the amusing distraction known as *diablitos* in the same way they have done until today and in no other way) Copy of Disposition 88, in a letter sent from Cuba to Lydia Cabrera (addressed to Laura Casas), February 28, 1970, at the Lydia Cabrera Papers, Heritage Collection, File 0339, Serie I, Box 5, Folder 12, University of Miami, Florida.

17. Ortiz, *La antigua fiesta afrocubana del "Día de Reyes,"* 32.

18. Isabel Castellanos and Jorge Castellanos, *Las religiones afrocubanas. Cultura Afrocubana* III (Miami: Ediciones Universal, 1992), 232.

19. Ibid., 232–33.

20. Lydia Cabrera explains that these pantomime movements formed a representational sign language: "When he (the diablito) extends his left arm, the hand with which he holds the branch, and with the right arm simulates throwing an arrow, the *Ireme* calls for war, "de-

safía, reta" (challenges); when he moves his left foot back he indicates an insult." See Lydia Cabrera, *La lengua sagrada de los ñáñigos* (Miami: Ediciones C & R, 1988), 240.

21. Still today, in Cuba, there is a popular signifying language of gestures used to speak of the unspeakable in a political context. Only those who "know" what the gestures mean can understand the double-talk and subtexts articulated in the play between words and pantomime.

22. Ada Ferrer, *Insurgent Cuba,* 84.

23. Isabel Castellanos and Jorge Castellanos, *Las religiones afrocubanas. Cultura Afrocubana* III, 233.

24. In 1938, Ramón Guirao observed that: "La modalidad afroantillana ha dado sus más cuajados frutos en Cuba porque contamos con el documento humano vivo, presente, racial y económicamente en nuestros destinos históricos" (The Afro-Antillean fashion has given its best fruits in Cuba because we have the human documentation present, racial, and economically alive in our historical destiny), in Ramon Guirao, *Orbita de la poesía afrocubana 1928–1937* (Havana: Ucar, García y Cía, 1938), xvii; a facsimile of this work was reprinted in Ramon Guirao, *Orbita de la poesía afrocubana 1928–1937,* and Marcelino Arozarena, *Canción Negra sin color* (Liechtenstein: Kraus-Thompson Organization Limited, 1970), xvii.

25. Lydia Cabrera notes that after the color line was broken, and the religiously strict ñáñigo elders were gone, some Abakuá chapters became more flexible and began to initiate delinquents, giving the society a bad image. See Cabrera, *La lengua sagrada de los ñáñigos,* 14.

26. Edouard Glissant, *Caribbean Discourse: Selected Essays* (Charlottesville: University Press of Virginia, 1989), 378.

27. Frank Janney, *Alejo Carpentier and His Early Works* (London: Tamesis Books Limited, 1981), 21.

28. This movement was not exclusive to Cuba; in Puerto Rico Luis Palés Matos was writing during the '20s and '30s on African themes, constructing a parody in these poems of African-Antillean rhythms. Affirming the idea that poetry is rhythm, Palés Matos utilizes African and Afro-Caribbean elements, the drum, languages, and literary and historical Afro-Caribbean images. Mercedes López-Baralt points out the possible influence of Vachel Linsey's poem "The Congo" (1917) in Palés's utilization of rhythm and form for his *Tun Tún de pasa y grifería* (1937), Mercedes López-Baralt, *La poesía de Luis Pales Matos* (San Juan, Puerto Rico: Editorial de la Universidad de Puerto Rico, 1995), 525–26. Among these poems, Palés dedicates "Ñáñigo al cielo" to the Afro-Cuban ñáñigo, although the poem is actually about the founder of the Salvation Army, which, in keeping with Carpentier's and Guillén's poems about Papá Montero, it is a praise to a cultural hero. "Danzarina africana" (1918) is the first poem by Palés Matos in which he utilizes an African-Caribbean theme (ibid., 507).

29. In Walter Mignolo, *Local Histories/Global Designs. Coloniality, Subaltern Knowledge, and Border Thinking,* (Princeton, New Jersey: Princeton University Press, 2000), 164. Mignolo quotes from a later publication of Depestre's article, René Depestre, "Problemas de la identidad del hombre negro en las literaturas antillanas," 231–41, *Fuentes de la cultura latinoamericana* I, edited by L. Zea (Mexico: Fondo de Cultura Económica, 1993). While Depestre's observations are generally true, the fact is that Nicolás Guillén, whose work cannot be described entirely as representative of "an intellectual and literary movement by white men," was a Minorista, and an important part of the Cuban negrism movement since the early twenties.

30. See James A. Arnold, *Modernism and Negritude,* 32, and 72. Janice Spleth notes that it was in the mid-thirties, in *L'Etudiant noir,* in France, where Césaire "first used, in print, the term "Negritude," to "formalize a tendency which had already begun to be recognized in the abstract." Janice Spleth, *Leopold Sédar Senghor* (Boston: Twayne Publishers, 1985,

10. Around the same time, she notes, in 1937, Senghor labels the North Afro-American writer Claude MacKay "the veritable inventor of Negritude" (ibid., 9).

31. César Leante, "Confesiones sencillas de un escritor barroco," 57–70, in *Recopilación de textos sobre Alejo Carpentier,* ed. Salvador Arias (Havana: Casa de los Américas, Centro de investigaciones literarias, 1977), 61.

32. Alejo Carpentier, *La música en Cuba* (Mexico: Fondo de Cultura Económica, 1946), 236, also in Janney, *Alejo Carpentier and His Early Works,* 19.

33. As Gustavo Pérez Firmat points out, the utilization of Afro-Cuban figures and themes had as counterpoint the representation of the poor country *guajiro.* Both represented the natural and popular in opposition to the civilized. "Writers who focus on the *guajiro* usually want to draw attention to, or argue for, the fundamental 'whiteness' of Cuban culture." Gustavo Pérez Firmat, *The Cuban Condition: Translation and Identity in Modern Cuban Literature* (Cambridge: Cambridge Univeristy Press, 1989), 98. With the figure of the diablito as well as with ñáñigo rituals and myths, afrocubanía represented a very different notion of culture that questioned hispanidad and whiteness. The guajiro, observes Pérez Firmat, was "Adamic" and the diablito, "demonic" (ibid.). The guajiro represented the natural without breaking with established discourses on the nation, while the ñáñigo and the diablito broke and challenged those notions.

34. Lowery Stokes Sims points out: "It was this indigenous, nationalistic element that distinguished Cuban (as well as Mexican) modernism from that of Europe. The artists involved in the Afro-Cubanist movement—the so-called Generation of 27—were well established by the time Lam returned to Cuba. Their inaugural exhibition in 1927 [in Havana], *Exposición de Arte Nuevo,* epitomized the effort to 'preserve the essential Cubanness of artistic production while keeping up with the avant-garde developments in Europe." Lowery Stokes Sims, *Wifredo Lam and the International Avant-Garde 1923–1982* (Austin: University of Texas Press, 2002), 36–37.

35. Roberto González Echevarría, *The Pilgrim at Home* (Ithaca: Cornell University Press, 1977), 29.

36. Arnold, *Modernism and Negritude,* 21. Palés Matos's poem "Danza negra" is of 1926. However, Palés Matos's interest in Afro-Caribbean expressions and musicality began years earlier. Although very different from his poems in the '20s and '30s, still trapped in the Romantic myth of an indianized Caribbean, his earlier approximation to Afro-Caribbean rhythms and themes takes place in his poem "Danzarina Africana" (1918).

37. Ibid.

38. Ibid., 64.

39. Aníbal González Pérez, "La (sín)tesis de una poesía antillana: Palés y Spengler," 59–72, *Cuadernos hispanoamericanos.* Special edition: *Los negros en América,* no. 451–52 (1988), 60.

40. By 1938, Spengler's philosophies were seen as contradictory by some of the Cuban writers. In his introduction to *Orbita de la poesía afrocubana,* Guirao comments on Spengler's Eurocentric views and prejudice toward Africa. Guirao criticizes also Europe's Africanism as a simple passing fashion unrelated to the real-blood African. Guirao, *Orbita de la poesía afrocubana,* xviii.

41. Emilio Bejel, "Cultura y filosofía de la historia (Spengler, Carpentier, Lezama Lima)," 75–90, *Cuadernos Americanos* XL, vol CCXXXIX, no. 6 (1981): 75 and 77.

42. Vera Kutzinski, *Sugar's Secrets: Race and the Erotic of Cuban Nationalism,* 7.

43. See Arnold, *Modernism and Negritude,* 35. This was an important and determining book for both Aimé Césaire and Leopold Sédar Senghor (ibid., 37).

44. Ibid., 84.

45. Oswald Spengler, *The Decline of the West: Form and Actuality* I, translated by Charles Francis Atkinson (New York: Alfred A. Knopf, 1926). All references to this text will be in-

dicated with *DW*. All references to Spengler, *The Decline of the West* II, (1928), will be indicated as *DW* II. In Spengler's historical scheme, one culture is not better or worse than another. At the same time, Spengler praises, for its vitality and soul-force, that same primitivism shunned by Positivists who saw America as backward and primitive. Each culture, said Spengler, is born, grows and dies, and must follow these cyclical stages. Cultures are different, thus only those growing within them can understand them; therefore, the Indian, Chinese, Semitic (Hebrew and Arabic), and Western cultures are different in their own soul-force. Each one follows the same historical changes. Spengler conceived three stages in Western culture, the first being the Classic. The soul of the Classical culture he said: "chose the sensuously present individual body as the ideal type of the extended, by the name (familiarized by Nietzsche) of the Apollonian" (*DW*, 183). The second stage was the "Faustian" soul, "whose prime-symbol is pure and limitless space, and whose body is the Western Culture that blossomed forth with the birth of the Romanesque style in the 10th century in the Northern plain between the Elbe and the Tagus" (*DW*, 183). The third stage is the tyranny of Reason (*DW*, 424), and self-reflexiveness, intellectualism, which arrives with the decay of the Rococo (*DW*, 226) and the Enlightment, a stage that marks modern civilization. This is "the rise of the victorious *skepsis*, [when] the clouds dissolve and the quiet landscape of the morning reappears in all distinctness" (*DW*, 427). Mercantilism and capitalism bring about a tyranny and decadence of the soul that leads to the culture's decline, death, and eventual rebirth. In spite of Spengler's views on cultures as moving through stages in Time, which he equated with Destiny, he favors the Faustian soul, which he sees characterized in Goethe's *Faust*. Spengler equates the Faustian with the notion of "Becoming," like in Goethe's *Faust* (*DW*, 53), with the "Infinite" (*DW*, 86), like Goethe's "beauty in true" (*DW*, 61); with "solitude" (*DW*, 187); "the bird's eye perspective" (*DW*, 355); "flying" (*DW*, 279); "maternity," "woman as Mother is Time and is Destiny" (*DW*, 267); "faith" (*DW*, 417); "the passionate thrust into the distance" (*DW*, 423), "myth" (*DW*, 427); and in faith-forms of springtime, an idea Stravinsky uses in his composition, "The Rite of Spring," a work that informs Alejo Carpentier's novel, *La consagración de la primavera* (1978).

46. Victor Lange, introduction to Johann Wolfgang von Goethe, *Faust,* translated by Bayard Taylor (New York: Random House, Inc., 1950), v-vi.

47. González Echeverría adds to this observation that it was out of Spengler's philosophy that "the New World found itself, in its historical evolution, a moment of faith prior to the moment of reflexivity," *The Pilgrim at Home,* 124.

48. César Leante, "Confesiones sencillas de un escritor barroco," 57–70, in *Recopilación de textos sobre Alejo Carpentier,* 57.

49. Carpentier, prologue to *El reino de este mundo* (Barcelona: EDHASA (Editora y Distribuidora Hispano Americana, S. A., 1978), 56.

50. González Echeverría, *The Pilgrim at Home,* 125.

51. Alejo Carpentier, "Habla Alejo Carpentier," interviewed by Salvador Arias, 15–55, in *Recopilación de textos sobre Alejo Carpentier,* edited and prologue by Salvador Arias, (Havana: Casas de las Ameritas, 1977), 52.

52. Nicolás Guillén was president of the Society of Afro-Cuban Studies. The relationship between Guillén and Ortiz's change of view toward Afro-Cuba still lacks serious studies.

53. See Gustavo Pérez-Firmat, *The Cuban Condition,* 14, and 67–75. This hybrid form is inscribed in his *son* poems as he called his poetry: mulatto poems that bring together the *son* of African rhythm in Cuba, and the sonnet from European traditions.

54. Ramón Chao, *Palabras en el tiempo de Alejo Carpentier* (Barcelona: Editorial Argos Vergara, 1984), 132.

55. Janney, *Alejo Carpentier and His Early Works,* 27. Carpentier articulates his admiration for Stravinsky's compositions in articles he wrote for *Social:* "Stravisky, "Las bo-

das" y Papá Montero," *Social* 12, no. 12 (1927), in Alejo Carpentier, *Crónicas* I (Havana: Editorial Arte y Literatura, 1975), 70–76; and "Stravisky: el clasicismo y las corbatas," *Social* 15, no. 5 (1930), 173–77. What called Carpentier's attention in 1927 of Stravisky's work was his primitive rhythm: "una nueva forma de expresión, tan semejante a la que yace al estado primitivo en nuestros *sones* criollos" (a new form of expression, so similar, to the one that lays in a primitive state in our creoles *sones*), "Stravisky, "Las bodas" y Papá Montero," 71.

56. Carpentier knew of him in Europe. During World War II, Igor Stravinsky was one of the many visitors to Havana. Lowery Stokes Sims observes that during the forties, in Havana, there was an "intimate circle" around Wifredo Lam and his wife "which included Carlos Riguardias and his wife, Greta; Lydia Cabrera and her companion María Teresa Rojas; and various acquaintances who passed through Cuba at one time or another during World War II: Eric Klieber, Igor Stravinsky, Peter Watson, Paul Bowles, and Pierre Mabille." See Stokes Sims, *Wifredo Lam and the International Avant-Garde*, 65.

57. García Lorca befriended several Cuban writers, among them Nicolás Guillén, Lydia Cabrera, and Alejo Carpentier, and gained popularity in Cuba among the Minoristas. García Lorca's assassination in 1936 by Franco's troops, left deep wounds in the Cuban literary community. In 1937, only a year after García Lorca's death, Juan Marinello, Nicolás Guillén, and Alejo Carpentier attended an antifascist congress in Madrid. See, González Echevarría, *The Pilgrim at Home*, 35.

58. Ibid., 18.

59. Janney, *Alejo Carpentier and his Early Works*, 24.

60. Ibid.

61. César Leante, "Federico en Cuba," *Cuadernos hispanoamericanos* nos. 433–36 (1986): 235.

62. Ibid., 235–40. Guirao comments on García Lorca's fervor for Afro-Cuban poetry: "agradecemos su negrísimo Son escrito en La Habana, realizado en un molde métrico de invención afrocubana" (we are grateful for his Afro-Cuban Son, written in Havana following a metric mould of Afro-Cuban invention). Guirao, *Orbita de la poesía afrocubana*, xx. He refers here to García Lorca's poem, "Son de negros en Cuba" (Son of negros in Cuba): "Cuando llegue la luna llena iré a Santiago de Cuba,/ iré a Santiago de Cuba . . ." (When the full moon arrives, I will go to Santiago de Cuba,/ I will go to Santiago de Cuba. . . .), in Federico García Lorca, *Poet in New York*, translated by Ben Belitt (New York: Grove Press, Inc., 1955), 136.

63. Ramón Guirao, *Orbita de la poesía afrocubana 1928–1937*, xxii; also quoted in Janney, *Alejo Carpentier and his Early Works*, 13.

64. Guirao, *Orbita de la poesía afrocubana*, xix; also in Janney, *Alejo Carpentier and his Early Works*, 15.

65. From that experience, Federico García Lorca writes in 1940 the poems that were later collected in *Poet in New York*. García Lorca also became interested in black American poetry, and in the literary production of the Harlem Renaissance after living for a while in Harlem.

66. In his 1927 article on Stravinsky, Carpentier compares Stravinsky's rhythm with the popular song to Papá Montero, exemplifying the interest among Latin American writers on the ñáñigos. He writes: "Cuba, la que nunca oyó Straninsky concertar *sones* de marimbas y guiros en el entierro de Papá Montero, ñáñigo de bastón y canalla rumbero . . . Tal afirma Alfonso Reyes en su *Trópico* . . . Pero Stravinsky es el genio del ritmo. ¿Cómo iban a sonar marimbas y guiros en el entierro de Papá Montero, sin que él lo adivinara? (Cuba that never heard Stravinsky compose *sones* accompanied by *marimbas* and *güiros* in the funeral of Papa Montero, scepter ñáñigo, rumba dancer. . . . Says Alfonso Reyes in his *Trópico*. . . . But Stravinsky is the genius of rhythm. How could he not have guessed it?" Carpentier, "Stravinsky, "Las bodas" y Papá Montero," 70.

67. Ibid., 15.

68. Ramón Guirao, *Orbita de la poesía afrocubana,* xii.

69. Ibid., xv.

70. In Puerto Rico, Luis Palés Matos's Afro-Antillean poetry also established a dialogue with García Lorca's poetry. López-Baralt points out that García Lorca liked to recite Palés Matos's poems. See Mercedes López-Baralt, *La poesía de Luis Palés Matos,* 522. Frank Janney observes that Palés Matos's poems in which he articulated a "primitivist vision of the Antilles" could have been the first early evidence, "in the words of Nicolás Guillén," of a *modo* (mode) rather than *moda* (fashion) of writing; "and that the conquest of form was synonymous with the conquest of identity." Janney, *Alejo Carpentier and his Early Works,* 17.

71. Trigo, *Subjects of Crisis* (Hanover: Wesleyan University Press, 2000), 74–75.

72. During this time, in Mexico, the great muralists of the Mexican Revolution, Rivera, Orozco, and Siqueiro, were experimenting with visual forms as ways of expressing Mexican identity. In their work they were constructing a new vision of the history of Mexico and of Mexican culture based on pre-Columbian cultures, and on the plight of the Mexican indigenous people. This was a moment of vigor in which Mexican artists turned to Mexican folklore and traditions, away from Europe and European civilization, in their quest to forge a new Mexico based on the ideas José Vasconcelos proposed in 1925 in *La raza cósmica. Misión de la raza iberoamericana (The Cosmic Race: Mission of the Ibero-American Race).* Here Vasconcelos suggested an ideology of mestizaje that went beyond the color of the skin, the body, to include the spirit, and an attitude, in the formation of nation. Vasconcelos's notions would resonate in Ortiz's definition of *cubanidad* as "a condition of the soul, a complexity of sentiments, ideas and attitudes," in Lowery Stokes Sims, *Wifredo Lam and the International Avant-Garde, 1923–1982,* 35. Marilyn Grace Miller points out that "a review of *La raza cósmica* appeared in the Havana daily newspaper *El Diario de la Marina,* thus suggesting that Vasconcelos notions of 'mestizaje' was assessed by Cuban intellectuals from the perspective of the Caribbean." See Marilyn Grace Milller, *Rise and Fall of the Cosmic Race: The Cult of Mestizaje in Latin America,* 47; see also Kutzinski, *Sugar Secrets,* 147.

73. Fernando Ortiz, "Los últimos versos mulatos," I am using the translation of this quote in Grace Miller, in *Rise and Fall of the Cosmic Race,* 74.

74. Fernando Ortiz, *Estudios etnosociológicos,* translated in Marilyn Grace Miller, in *Rice and Fall of the Cosmic Race,* 76.

75. Ortiz, *La antigua fiesta afrocubana del "Día de Reyes,"* 41. Songs associated with this dance in colonial Cuba had been transcribed and printed in newspapers since the seventeenth century. Ortiz offers two examples in *La antigua fiesta afrocubana de 'Día de Reyes,"* 41; and Guirao includes in *Orbita de la poesía afrocubana,* two anonymous songs: "La culebra se murió" ("The snake died"), and "Canto para matar la culebra" ("Song to kill the snake"), 7–9.

76. Alejo Carpentier, *Obras completas* I (Mexico: Siglo Veintiuno, S.A., 1983), 266.

77. Carpentier's character, Filomeno, an Afro-Cuban servant who travels with his master to Italy, feels inspired by the contemplation, at a convent, of the figure of a snake in a painting representing the Garden of Eden. He suddenly begins to beat on kitchen pots and pans while singing the words to a nineteenth century Afro-Cuban dance of killing the snake, the same Guillén parodies in "Sensemayá," and the same Ortiz includes in his *"La antigua fiesta afrocubana del "Día de Reyes,"* 41. Filomeno's drumming is an allegorical representation of the African rhythm that in Cuba, and in Caribbean music, accompanies European melodies. Here, Vivaldi and Handel, at the piano, try to keep up with Filomeno's Afro-Caribbean rhythm. This scene in *Concierto Barroco* is a representation of Carpentier's research on the history of music in Cuba, which he published in *Historia de la música en Cuba* (Havana: Editorial Letras Cubanas, 1978). Carpentier finds that African rhythms and European melodies together formed contemporary Cuban music.

78. Interested in the universality of the local in Afro-Cuban ritual performances, Ortiz quotes from James Fraser's *The Golden Bough: The Roots of Religion and Folklore* (1890), to suggest that the same type of rituals can be found in other cultures. See Ortiz, *"La antigua fiesta afrocubana,"* 42. Ortiz concludes that, in its Afro-Cuban modality, the universal practice of the annual killing of the sacred animal, like the snake, may be considered a rite of purification "de los clasificados como 'expulsión de los diablos,' que han sido relacionados aquí con el Día de Reyes" (of those classified as "expulsion of devils," associated here with "Día de Reyes") (ibid., 43).

79. Ibid.

80. Carpentier, "Un ballet afrocubano," 265–66, in *Obras completas* I, 266.

81. Luis Palés Matos, "Mulata Antilla," *Tun tún de pasa y grifería* (San Juan, P.R.: Edición especial para Cultural Puertorriqueña, Editora Corripio, C. Por A., 1988), 104.

82. García Lorca's influence comes to light in this poem in the image of the moon, the night, the cultural hero, death, and violence.

83. Marcos A. Morínigo, *Diccionario de americanismos* (Barcelona: Muchnick Editores, 1985), 648; Rhyna Moldes, *Música folkórica cubana* (Miami: Ediciones Universal, 1975), 30.

84. Carpentier, "Liturgia," 211–13, in *Obras completas* I, 211.

85. Ibid., 212.

86. Ibid.

87. Ibid.

88. This is the moment when, according to Lydia Cabrera, the *moninas* go to the door of the *Cuarto Famba,* the room where the ceremony takes place, and cry: *asere asere ebión ndayo* to greet the rising sun of the new day. See Cabrera, *La lengua sagrada de los ñáñigos,* 72.

89. Lydia Cabrera, *La sociedad secreta Abakua,* 120.

90. Carpentier, "Liturgia," *Obras completas* I, 213.

91. Ibid., 213. In another poem of 1927, "Juego santo" (Holy game [meaning Abakuá ritual]), Carpentier turns to the same image of the sacred drum, "Ecón y bongó," and to the ritual sacrifice of a goat: "Ataron el chivo/ mataron el gallo/ . . ./ ¡Baila congo, ya suena el empegó!/ Son toques de allá/ los cantos de Eribó" (They tied the goat/ they killed the rooster/ . . ./ Dance Congo/ the *empegó* drum is playing/ It's a drumming from the afar/ Songs of *Eribo*) "Juego santo," *Obras completas* I, 218–19.

92. In the Spanish Caribbean the word creole *(criollo)* designates anyone born in the New World, whether of European, African, or of any foreign-born parents. During colonial years, in Cuba, just like Europeans looked down on their American-born progeny, Africans looked down on black creoles (slave or free), as people that had acclimated to the new land and had lost their ancestral knowledge. There was a sense of birthright among Africans much like among Spaniards. See Montejo's comments in Miguel Barnet, *Biografía de un cimarrón* (Barcelona: Ediciones Ariel, S. A., 1968), 20. See also Arcadio's comments in William Luis and Julia Cuervo Hewitt, "Santos y santería: Conversación con Arcadio, santero de Guanabacoa," *Afro-Hispanic Review* VI, no. 1 (1987), 10. Since in Spanish colonial society some slaves managed to keep their traditions and beliefs (often through masquerades and syncretic forms), African-born slaves were considered to be keepers of knowledge, and were revered for their wisdom.

93. Carpentier, *The Pilgrim at Home,* 125

94. Chao, *Palabras en el tiempo de Alejo Carpentier,* 169.

95. Ibid., 170.

96. Ibid., 169–70.

97. Carpentier, *Obras completas* I, 293.

98. Janney, *Alejo Carpentier and His Early Works,* 20.

99. This is the same approach found in Palés Matos's treatment of the Haitian King, Henri Christophe, in his poem "Lagarto verde." Valle Inclán was the first writer to construct the grotesque image of the Latin American dictator in his novel *Tirano Banderas,* an image that soon became a literary archetype in Latin American literature. Valle-Inclán's *grotesque* was a criticism of Spanish society. Carpentier was an admirer of Valle Inclán's work: "sólo Valle Inclán se acrece, de día a día, en mi estimación. No el Valle Inclán de las *Sonatas,* harto preciosista para mi gusto, sino el de *La guerra Carlista,* y sobre todo, el de los *Esperpentos* y las *Divinas palabras.* . . . Valle Inclán, en cambio, con su *Tirano Banderas* vislumbró el futuro de una posible novelística latinoamericana" (only Valle Inclán increases every day in my admiration of him. Not the Valle Inclán of the *Sonatas,* too affected for my taste, but the one of *La guerra Carlista,* and above all, the one of the *Esperpentos* and the *Divinas palabras* . . . Valle Inclán, on the other hand, in his *Tirano Banderas* foresaw the future possibility of the Latin American novel) Carpentier, "Habla Alejo Carpentier," *Recopilación de textos,* 16.

100. In Afro-Cuban *Lucumí* traditions, the *Ibeyes* or *Abeyí,* represent the unity of contrary principles in the cosmos. They are sons of the orisha of thunder and lightning, Shango, the great divine Judge of human affairs. See Julia Cuervo Hewitt, *Aché, Presencia africana. Tradiciones yoruba-lucumí en la narrativa cubana* (New York: Peter Lang Publishing, Inc., 1988), 178–82. In his efforts to see the universal in the local, Ortiz points out in *El huracán, su mitología y sus símbolos* (1947) that the myth of the twins can be found in most cultures, in the Old World transformed into the Christian twins, *"San Cosme and San Damián,"* and, from Africa in Cuba, in the *Abeyí:* "esas parejas de mellizos celestiales de las mitologías euroasiáticas y africanas se relacionan con las serpientes, con la medicina, con la sexualidad, con la fertilidad y con las tempestades, los truenos y las lluvias" (those celestial twins of Euro Asiatic and African mythologies are related to serpents, to medicine, to sexuality, to fertility, and to storms, thunder, and rain). Fernando Ortiz, *El huracán, su mitología y sus símbolos* (Mexico: Fondo de Cultura Económica, 1947), 467.

101. Ortiz, *La antigua fiesta afrocubana del "Día de Reyes,"* 40–41.

102. Carpentier articulates a similar discourse already voiced by the Cuban writer Gertrudis Gómez de Avellaneda in *Sab* (1841), the first anti-slavery novel written in America. In this novel, which Gómez de Avellaneda wrote in 1839, she represents foreign investors in Cuba as a type of heartless materialistic persons, launching a nonhumanistic and capitalist intrusion in the otherwise good and innocent Cuban society.

103. It should be remembered that only few years earlier Cuba had resisted the intervention of the United States (1898–1902). This resistance made it possible for Cuba to become a free republic in 1902. Carpentier allegorizes the importance of Afro-Cuban groups, and especially the ñáñigos, in the fight for independence, because most of the patriot troops and urban resistance groups that fought against colonial rule were blacks and mulattos, many of them Abakuá. While Puerto Rico never became an independent republic, in Cuba, freedom once attained was then curtailed by the specter of the Monroe Doctrine, and the Platt Amendment, that was still in existence in 1927, when Carpentier was writing his first novel.

104. Carpentier, *Obras completas* I, 284–85.

105. Esperanza Figueroa, a contemporary of Carpentier, has a very different version of Carpentier's own biography. She questions his confessions and sees him as a con artist who has rewritten his life in order to accommodate it to his success. See, Esperanza Figueroa, "Tres vidas divergentes, Lydia Cabrera, Enriquez y Carpentier," 278–92, in *En torno a Lydia Cabrera (Cincuentenario de* Cuentos negros de Cuba *1936–1986),* edited by Isabel Castellanos, and Josefina Inclán (Miami: Ediciones Universal, 1987).

106. César Leante, "Confesiones sencillas de un escritor barroco," 62.

107. Carpentier articulates his admiration for Breton and for surrealism in an article, "En la extrema avanzada. Algunas actitudes del surrealismo," published in *Social* 13, no. 12 (1928), reprinted in Carpentier, *Crónicas* I (Havana: Editorial Arte y Literatura, 1975), 106–11. Here Carpentier calls the Surrealism Manifesto, "admirable" (106), he praises Breton's sense of "liberty of expression" (109), and the "intense faith," the surrealists show, "to the point of being almost a religious concept of intellectual activities" (107).

108. Stokes Sims, *Wifredo Lam and the International Avant-Garde 1923–1982*, 36.

109. Alejo Carpentier, "Lo real maravilloso de América," *El nacional* (1948), in Archives SDO Wifredo Lam, Paris; I am using the translation of this quote in Stokes Sims, *Wifredo Lam and the International Avant-Garde*, 70. Carpentier repeats this idea in "De lo real maravilloso Americano," 103–21, in an essay he adapts from the prologue to *El reino de este mundo*, and in a different adaptation, with the same title, he publishes in *Tientos y diferencias* (Montevideo: Editorial Arca, 1967), 103–21.

110. Stokes Sims, *Wifredo Lam and the International Avant-Garde*, 7.

111. In the mid-1930s there was a schism between surrealists and communists over artistic ideas. In the late 1940s a different type of break occurred between the surrealists who stayed in Europe and those who went into exile during the war. Ibid., 86.

112. Chao, *Palabras en el tiempo de Alejo Carpentier*, 63.

113. González Echevarría, *The Pilgrim at Home*, 58.

114. Chao, *Palabras en el tiempo de Alejo Carpentier*, 175.

115. Carpentier, *The Pilgrim at Home*, 101.

116. Ibid., 129–37.

117. In association always with Goethe's *Faust*, Faustian, for Spengler, was characterized by baroque sensibility: "an opposition of ordinary popular feeling and the finer sensibility" (*DW*, 242). Spengler saw the Faustian moment of Western culture as a moment of dynamics, introspection, of counterpoint of the microcosm and the macrocosm, a moment when artists are able to encapsulate the feeling of the ineffable. Faustian—Spengler says— are "Galilean dynamics, Catholic and Protestant dogmatism, the great dynasties of the Baroque with their cabinet diplomacy, the destiny of Lear and the Madonna—ideal from Dante's Beatrice to the last line of *Faust II* . . . Painting that forms space by means of light and shade is Faustian" (*DW*, 183). Equating it to a baroque sensitivity, the Faustian, says Spengler "is led by a deep consciousness and introspection of the ego" (*DW*, 183); shows a "wondrous awakening of the inner life," thus, "the longing for the woods, the mysterious compassion, the ineffable sense of forsakenness—it is all Faustian and only Faustian" (*DW*, 186). Spengler equates the Arabic Magian soul with Western Faustian baroque; and concludes that Western baroque ornamentation "dissolves all its lines into melodies and variations on a theme, all its façades into many-voiced fugues, and all the bodyliness of its statuary into a music of drapery-folds" (*DW*, 199). Since the Baroque for Spengler is "an emancipation from Byzantium" (*DW*, 236), from the Apollonian static statue, music, that is, Baroque music, of counterpoints and fugues, "becomes dominant among the Faustian arts" (*DW*, 231). In painting, there is "an opposition of ordinary popular feeling and the finer sensibility" (*DW*, 242). Leonardo da Vinci's painting of flying objects represent for Spengler that Faustian sense of freedom from earth," "to lose one self in the expanse of the universe" (*DW*, 279) that is Faustian. The architecture of baroque cathedrals provides "the most significant symbol of its depth-experience," representing "the will to emerge from the interior into the boundless . . . immanent in the contrapuntal music native to these cathedrals vaulterings" (*DW*, 199). This "will" is what Carpentier translates as "a longing for liberty" of the Faustian soul that he conceives in America. Like baroque cathedrals for Spengler, Capentier's *The Kingdom of This World* seeks to express an American "depth-experience" in an oppositional dance of contrasts between ordinary popular feelings and the writer's own "finer sensibility."

118. Carpentier, *The Pilgrim at Home,* 103.

119. Ibid., 107. A similar search for the origins, the mother, is exemplified by the founding of the literary journal *Orígenes* in 1944. In the Caribbean, *Négritude* marks its beginning in 1940 after the first publication in 1939 of Césaire's *Notebook of the Return to the Native Land.* Both of these movements shared similar interests in spite of their differences. Carpentier's experimentations with fictional writing in the forties articulates a type of border crossing of aesthetic interests and his own ontological preoccupations with writing in the contexts of new ideas about aesthetics, culture, and nation, and new ways of expressing America, and a search for cultural origins or an American womb.

120. Chao, *Palabras en el tiempo de Alejo Carpentier,* 170.

121. Stokes Sims, *Wifredo Lam and the International Avant-Garde,* 70.

122. *Orígenes* also made accessible in Spanish translations currents thoughts on philosophy and art, for example, on Wallace Stevens in 1950, Albert Camus and Nietzsche in 1952, Alfonso Reyes in 1947, poems by Gabriela Mistral; Lydia Cabrera published sections of *El monte,* as well as "La ceiba y la sociedad secreta Abakua" in a 1950 issue, and in 1945 and 1946, as well as short stories, including "La virtud del árbol Dagame."

123. Chao, *Palabras en el tiempo de Alejo Carpentier,* 145. Carpentier and Guillén coincided in this visit with Wifredo Lam who was living in Madrid. As Lowery Stokes Sims notes: Lam's "association with Republican politics was intensified when he moved into a studio on Calle Alcalá near the abode of Faustino Cordón and began to frequent the Café de la Gran Vía. Lam's circle of acquaintances at this time included Cuban compatriots Nicolás Guillén and Alejo Carpentier." Stokes Sims, *Wifredo Lam and the International Avant-Garde,* 22.

124. Leante, "Confesiones sencillas de un escritor barroco," 65.

125. Chao, *Palabras en el tiempo de Alejo Carpentier,* 165.

126. Ibid., 181.

127. Carpentier, *The Pilgrim at Home,* 52–54.

128. Ibid., 38.

129. Ibid.

130. Martí claims that: "La universidad europea ha de ceder a la universidad americana . . . Nuestra Grecia es preferible a la Grecia que no es nuestra. Nos es más necesaria (The European University must yield to the American University . . . Our Greece is preferable to the Greece that is not ours. It is more necessary to us) José Martí, "Nuestra América," *La gran Encyclopedia Martiana* 9, edited by Ramón Cernuda (Miami: Editorial Martians, Inc., 1978), 3.

131. For example, in the article, "Problemática de la actual novela latinoamericana," 5–41, a text Carpentier frames with a quote from Goethe, *Second Faust,* he writes: "don Fernando Ortiz halló en el Changó de la santería cubana una auténtica repercusión mística y formal del Labrii de Creta (cabeza coronada por un hacha doble, atributos metálicos, semejantes funciones) sincretizados con la Santa Bárbara del santoral cristiano ejerciendo oficios que son los mismos del Tlaloc mexicano" (don Fernando Ortiz found in the *Shango* of Cuban *santería* an authentic mystical and formal repetition of the Creatan Labrys [crowned head with a double ax, metal atributes, similar functions] sincretized with the Christian female Saint Barbara carrying out the same functions as the Mexican Tlaloc) *Tientos y diferencias,* 28–29.

132. Carpentier, "Habla Alejo Carpentier," in *Recopilación de textos sobre Alejo Carpentier,* 18–19.

133. Fernando Ortiz, *Los negros esclavos* (Havana: Editorial de Ciencias Sociales, 1975), 10.

134. Chao, *Palabras en el tiempo de Alejo Carpentier,* 128.

135. Ibid., 134.

136. In Haitian and Dominican Voodoo, the powers of nature or *loas,* are known also as "mysteres."

137. Alejo Carpentier, "Problemática de la actual novela latinoamericana," 5–41, *Tientos y diferencias,* 22–23.

138. Carpentier, "Habla Alejo Carpentier," *Recopilación de textos sobre Alejo Carpentier,* 19.

139. Spengler proposed a counterpoint of the "Proper" and the "Alien," a dichotomy that perhaps influenced Ortiz's thoughts, who was also attracted to Spengler's philosophy.

140. Ernesto González Bermejo, "Carpentier: trastornar la cronología," *Correo* (Lima), no. 29 febrero (n/d), 8. See also, Carpentier, "Problemática de la actual novela latinoamericana," *Tientos y diferencias,* 37–38.

141. César Leante, "El mito del lenguaje en la literatura latinoamerica," *Unión* XIII, no. 4 (1974), 167.

142. Ibid.

143. Quoted in Leonardo Acosta, "El barroco americano y la ideología colonialista," *Unión* XI, nos. 2–3 (1972), 52; from Alejandro G. Alonso, "¿Hay un estilo barroco cubano?" *Pensamiento crítico.* No. 36, January 1970: 199–208.

144. José Lezama Lima, *La expresión americana* (Mexico: Fondo de Cultura Económica, 1993), 84 and 97.

145. As an expression of the Faustian soul, Spengler proposes that the baroque is a moment of aesthetic depth and spirituality, when artists could capture, as in the last moments of Goethe's *Faust,* "the mystery of the Eucharist which binds the community to a mystic company" (*DW,* 186), but also "an ineffable sense of forsakeness" (*DW,* 186), and a "passionate thrust into distance" (*DW,* 423). Spengler proposed that only those persons who belong to a culture can understand its inner "here" (body-soul). Thus, Carpentier believes that he is the one who can "translate" those feelings proper of America to Europeans, who, according to Spengler, cannot understand the "inner here" of America, and, much less, its vernacular African and indigenous cultures. The Faustian writer is an "I that in the last resort draws its own conclusions about the Infinite" (*DW* II, 235), as does Carpentier. By "becoming" an American baroque writer, and by stating that America was baroque before and after the Spanish conquest, Carpentier is also including himself in the line of the great writers and composers of the European Renaissance and the Spanish Golden Age.

146. Carpentier, "La novela latinoamericana en vísperas de un nuevo siglo," 19–48, in *Historia y ficción en la narrativa hispanoamericana,* edited by Roberto González Echevarría (Venezuela: Monte Avila Editores, C.A., 1984), 35.

147. This text also was adapted and performed as a ballet; it was directed by Ramiro Guerra with a musical arrangement by Leo Brouwer. See, Acosta, *Música y épica en la novela de Alejo Carpentier* (Havana: Editorial Letras Cubana, 1981), 23.

148. Carpentier, *The Pilgrim at Home,* 109–13. The terms "marvelous realism," and "magic realism" are often confused. The latter comes from Frank Roh's book, of which, as Carpentier tells Ramón Chao, selections were translated and published in *Revista de Occidente* in 1927 under the title: "Realismo mágico."

149. González Echeverría explains the tensions, polemics, and misreading in Latin American literary circles brought about by this term in Carpentier's prologue in *The Pilgrim at Home* (107–29), as well as Emilio Rodríguez Monegal does in his article "Realismo mágico versus literatura fantástica: Un diálogo de sordos," *Otros mundos, otros fuegos: fantasía y realismo mágico en Iberoamérica (Memorias del XVI Congreso Internacional de Literatura Iberoamericana,* edited by Donald A. Yates (Pittsburgh: K & S Enterprise U.S.A, 1975), 25–38. The same publication includes another article by Roberto González Echeverría on this subject, "Carpentier y el realismo mágico" (*Otros mundos,* 221–32). Let it suffice here to say that in spite of his break with European surrealism, Carpentier's definition

of the "marvelous" in America cannot be understood fully without taking into account the concept of the "marvelous" in surrealism and in Spengler's notion of myth, magic, and the Faustian baroque.

150. This is the idea Isabelo Zenón Cruz brings to *Narciso descubre su trasero (El negro en la cultura puertorriqueña)* (Narcissus discovers his behind. Blacks in Puertorrican culture), (Humacao, P.R.: Editorial Furidi, I, 1974, II 1975).

151. Lezama Lima, *La expresión americana,* 84. Lezama Lima, who, like Carpentier, equated the notion of Faustian with the baroque, defines Faustian as a "demonic" desire (meaning transgression against the dominant law) to know and possess knowledge as in the drama of the original fall: "el afán faústico de que el conocimiento sea una realidad y que esa realidad pertenezca por entero al hombre" (the Faustian desire that knowledge be reality and that that reality belongs completely to man) (ibid., 97). Lezama finds the culmination of the baroque in America in the artistic expressions of the Brazilian mulatto Aleijadinho. Like Carpentier and Ortiz, Lezama believes that the baroque in America results from the counterpoint of pre-Columbian and African expression and Hispanic traditions: "la unión en la forma grandiosa de lo hispánico con las culturas africanas" (the union in the Hispanic grandiose form with African cultures) (ibid., 105–6). For Lezama, this Faustian American baroque leads finally to rebellion, as it goes through Romanticism, and turns into the wars of independence in the nineteenth century (ibid., 106).

152. Fernando Ortiz, *El huracán,* 302.

153. Carpentier, prologue to *El reino de este mundo,* 57. It is important to remember that Carpentier is referring here to documents about the conquest and colonization of the New World, from Columbus's idea that the Indies was Asia, and that he had discovered the entrance to the Garden of Eden in the Orinoco, as well as the chronicles of Bernal Díaz del Castillo and Cabeza de Vaca, the writings of El Inca Garcilaso de la Vega, up to the presence of pre-Columbian and African religions vigorously alive still in twentieth century Latin America. It is also important to remember that sixteenth-century writers, as Carpentier says in reference to Cervantes's time, did believe in miracles and magic, and it was from the gaze of those beliefs that they wrote about the New World.

154. Also with Frobenius's ideas of the history of African civilization. Frobenius's *Decamerón negro* (Black Decameron), was published in Spanish by *Revista de Occidente,* in Havana, in 1925. It became accessible to the Minoristas and to intellectual circles interested in afrocubanía.

155. The English translation of the novel and some subsequent editions of the Spanish original did not include the prologue.

156. See Jacques Stephens Alexis, "Of the Marvelous Realism of the Haitians," *Présence Africaine,* 1956, 8–10, reprinted in *The Post-Colonial Studies Reader,* 194–98; Michael Dash, "Marvelous Realism: The Way out of Négritude," *Caribbean Studies* 13(4), 1974, reprinted in *The Post-Colonial Studies Reader,* 199–200.

157. Mario Torrealba Lossí, "Sobre *El reino de este mundo,*" 469–70, in Carpentier, *Recopilación de textos,* 470.

158. Lydia Cabrera offers a negative view of Seabrook's book. She writes in *Yemayá y Ochún:* "El voudú le debió su mala fama a varios libros escritos en el siglo pasado, como el de Gustave Allux, el de Spencer St. John y otros autores, y en el nuestro a la leída *Isla Mágica* de Seabrook, la obra bella y falsa de un mitómano, como lo llamó Alfred Metraux. Con la fuerza poética que no puede negárselo, su fantasía refuerza las exageraciones de los antiguos colonos sobre sus ritos secretos, de una crueldad que eriza los cabellos" (Voodoo owes its bad reputation to several books written in the last century [XIX], like Gustave Allux's, Spencer St. John's and others, and in our century [XX], to the much read *The Magic Island* by Seabrook, the beautiful and false work of a mythomaniac, like Alfred Metraux called him. With a poetic force that cannot be denied, its fantasy affirms the exaggerations

of the colonial plantation owners in a way that makes your hair curl) Cabrera, *Yemayá y Ochún. Kariocha, Iyalorichas y Olorichas* (Madrid: Forma Gráfica, S.A., 1974), 61.

159. W. B. Seabrook, *The Magic Island* (New York: Harcourt, Brace and Company, Inc., 1929), 35.

160. Ibid., 12–13.

161. Chao, *Palabras en el tiempo de Alejo Carpentier,* 138.

162. Leante, "Confesiones sencillas de un escritor barroco," 69.

163. See George Eaton Simpson, *Religious Cults of the Caribbean: Trinidad, Jamaica, and Haiti* (Río Piedras, P.R.: Industrias Gráficas "Diario-Día," Institute of Caribbean Studies, 1970, 234. Voodoo originates as a mixture of Islamic and Christian elements, and African beliefs (mostly from Dahomey), transforming the African concept of Voodoo, as house of the spirit, into a syncretic belief system autochthonous to the Caribbean. This Americanization of the Old World (Africa) is also similar to what occurred with the ñáñigos in Cuba.

164. Donald Shaw, *Alejo Carpentier* (Boston: Twayne Publishers, 1985), 27. Shaw quotes from, Alejo Carpentier, "Manuel de Falla en París," 178–81, *Crónicas* I, 180.

165. For Spengler, the sense of "infinite" is always already Faustian (*DW,* 86), so is the sense of "longing for the woods, the mysterious compassion, the ineffable sense of forsakeness" (*DW,* 186): "the will to emerge from the interior into the boundless" (*DW,* 199) and "to free one's self from earth, to lose one's self in the expanse of the universe" (*DW,* 279, as it happens to Ti Nöel at the end of *The Kingdom of This World.* Since the "Faustian strove through all sensuous barriers towards infinity" *DW,* (247), says Spengler, and the "emblems of soul-flight" are "peculiar to the art of the Faustian" (*DW,* 279), in Faustian music, string instruments, and wind instruments, but especially the violin, represents the Faustian soul (*DW,* 231). In Carpentier's style of transplanting the European Faustian force to an American "proper" context, the drum (metaphorically associated with the wind/storm in Afro-Caribbean beliefs) becomes the musical representative of the American-black-Faustian-Caribbean life force, and of an American apocalyptic reckoning. In Carpentier's *Concierto barroco,* for example, the Faustian wind-instrument is the trumpet, Armstrong's trumpet.

166. Salvador Bueno, "Alejo Carpentier y sus conceptos de la historia," in *El ensayo y la crítica en Iberoamérica,* edited by Kurt Levy and Keith Ellis (Toronto: Instituto Internacional de Literatura Iberoamericana, 1970), 258.

167. Salvador Bueno, "La serpiente no se muerde la cola," 201–18, in *Recopilación de textos sobre Alejo Carpentier,* 218.

168. See Verity Smith, "Ausencia de Toussaint: Interpretación y falseamiento de la historia en *El reino de este mundo,*" 275–82, *Historia y ficción en la narrativa hispanoamericana* (Coloquio de Yale University) (Venezuela: Monte Avila Editores, 1984), 281.

169. In this story, which could be understood as a Hegelian experience of consciousness in its different movements of "becoming" (through experience) Reason and Knowledge/Freedom, it is important to note that Hegelian philosophy is based on biblical references. As John Walker observes in reference to Hegel, "To speak of the embodiment of truth in the world is to speak of Incarnation. And to speak of Incarnation in relation to what Hegel means by philosophy is to speak of a speculative Good Friday." John Walker, *History, Spirit and Experience: Hegel's Conception of the Historical Task of Philosophy in his Age* (Frankfurt am Nain, 1995), 161. Walker adds: "It is remarkable that . . . Hegel seems to be speaking less of his intention to talk in philosophy about an experience of Good Friday, than of actually enacting or engendering by the activity of philosophy an experience of that Event . . . he intends to recreate the speculative Good Friday of philosophy . . . Only from this experience can the whole truth about our experience be known about 'at its deepest level and in the most serious way,' and yet be known about through and in Resurrection: 'in the happiest freedom of its form.' . . . Hegel seems to be telling his readers not only that philoso-

phy can speak about the Passion of Christ, but that through philosophy that Passion becomes most real; not only that philosophy can speak about the Divine Story, but that in that speaking that Story ceases to be merely historical, and becomes wholly present in our experience" (ibid., 162). Discounting the metaphysics of presence suggested in this statement, there seems to be an analogy in Carpentier's text related to what Hegel is trying to do through philosophy. Through analogies, references, and symmetries with the story of the Hegelian experience of consciousness (seen through the metaphors of the Passion and Resurrection), Carpentier constructs an experiential will-to-freedom that he translates as the "Faustian element of the black and the indian in America."

170. Carpentier's Ti Nöel and Cervantes's Quixote share a similar world of ideals: of the magical world of literature (narratives and legends, myths and history) in a time when people believed in magic, like in the Afro-Caribbean world Carpentier expresses in *The Kingdom of This World*. Ti Nöel and Alonso Quijano also share a moment of awareness, and each represents the unique cultural spirit of a people, while their authors share similar feelings of skepticism and dissolution about their present social and political conditions.

171. Alejo Carpentier, *El reino de este mundo* (Barcelona: Edhasa Editores, 1978), 53.

172. Bronislaw Malinowski, introduction to Ortiz, *Contrapunteo cubano del tabaco y el azúcar,* 3.

173. Like Ortiz, Carpentier was interested also in cultural exchanges as, for example, he observes, that Spain brought to the New World the *romance* and the *counterpoint,* while America returned to Spain a different music with its own characteristics that soon became universal. See, Chao, *Palabras al tiempo de Alejo Carpentier,* 131.

174. Pérez Firmat, *The Cuban Condition,* 47.

175. Ibid., 54.

176. Ibid., 55.

177. Ibid., 60.

178. Ibid., 27.

179. Ibid., 64.

180. As Roberto González Echeverría observes, the "first modern consideration of the figure of the modern political leader appears in Hegel's *The Philosophy of History: The Pilgrim at Home,* 67. Carpentier is always looking for the sources of an image, and for Spenglerian "contemporaneity" to America. History, for Carpentier, is not a progressive linear sequence of events. Hence, Carpentier uses the notion of cultural contemporaneity with the notion of a spiraling temporal movement that seems to retrogress and repeat the same movements. It was Hegel, not Spengler, who offered the concept of a history progressing through reversals. Before Hegel, observes Georg Lukács, "historians had not only made a sharp distinction between history and objective truth, but also there had been a wide spread tendency to think of history in terms of a linear development, gradually moving upward. Thanks to the dialectical unity of objectives and absolute spirit (which also contains a dialectical separation of opposition) it is possible for Hegel to register irregularities in history, advances that contain retrograde movements, retrograde developments that in certain circumstances can provide the impetus for a new advance." Georg Lukács, *The Young Hegel: Studies in the Relations between Dialectics and Economics,* trans. Rodney Livingston (London: Merlin Press, 1975), 511.

181. José Ortega y Gasset, in "Hegel y América," published first in *Revista de Occidente,* calls Hegel's "Spirit" "realidad universal" [universal reality]. He adds, explaining Hegel's philosophy, that "Spirit" is "más que un Espíritu, una realidad absoluta" [more than Spirit, an absolute reality], in Ortega y Gasset, *Obras completas* II, 563–76, (Madrid: Ediciones Castilla, Revista de Occidente, 1961), 564.

182. Carpentier explains his notion of task in relationship to Montaigne. He tells González Bermejo: "Una frase de Montaigne siempre me ha impresionado por su sencilla

belleza: 'No hay major destino para el hombre que el de desempeñar cabalmente su oficio de Hombre.'" González Bermejo, "Carpentier: trastornar la cronología," 9.

183. Alejo Carpentier, *The Kingdom of This World,* translated by Harriet de Onís (New York: Knopf, 1957). All referentes to this book will appear in the text as *KW.*

184. It may not be a simple coincidence that, in Carpentier's rendition of the "Faustian," Ti Nöel's last cry seems to echo Goethe's Faust's last words: "Stand on free soil among a people free;" in a land, says Faust, for which "To many millions let me furnish soil,/ Though not secure, yet free to active toil; . . . The last result of wisdom stamps it true:/ He only earns his freedom and existence,/ Who daily conquers them anew." Goethe, *Faust,* 241.

185. Chao, *Palabras en el tiempo de Alejo Carpentier,* 139.

186. Lukács, *The Young Hegel,* 474.

187. Georg Wilhelm Friedrich Hegel, *Phenomenology of the Spirit,* translated by A. V. Miller (Oxford: Oxford University Press, 1977), 231.

188. Leante, "Confesiones sencillas de un escritor barroco," 69.

189. Latin American intellectuals of this period read Nietzsche. Even in the forties, his concepts of a "will to power" informed Césaire's conceptualization of Negritude. As James Arnold points out, Césaire speaks of Nietzsche in *Tropique,* January 1945, and his name "occurs prominently several time in *Tropiques* during the first year of its publication." Arnold, *Modernism and Negritude,* 53.

190. *Revista de Estudios Afrocubanos,* directed by Ortiz, and edited in Havana (1937–40) "drew on Frobenius's version of African civilization." Arnold, *Modernism and Negritude,* 23. The essays in this journal were reading material for Carpentier, as well as for most of the Minoristas, and their contemporary, Lydia Cabrera.

191. Labor, work or "tasks" are important in Hegel and in Goethe's philosophy. See Lukács, *The Young Hegel,* 480.

192. González Echeverría notes that Carpentier alludes to Hegel's *Philosophy of History* in the forties, which at that point "seems to be the key to his thinking." *The Pilgrim at Home,* 40. Carpentier has mentioned that when the Minoristas came together in 1923, they gathered with the interest of sharing the intellectual and political transformations happening in the world: "Hablábamos mucho de Picasso, de Stravinsky, de los poetas nuevos. Pero también hablábamos mucho de la Revolución de Octubre y de los 'diez días que conmovieron al mundo.' Pronto, numerosos miembros del Grupo se proclamaron comunistas, aunque sin entregarse a una militancia . . . Con el Grupo Minorista, la necesidad de politización del intelectual se hizo particularmente evidente" (We talked a lot about Picasso, Stravinsky, the new poets. But we also talked a lot about the October Revolution and about the ten days that shocked the world. Very soon, many of the members of the Minorista group declared themselves communists, although no actively militant. With the Minorista group the necessity for an intellectual polarization became particularly evident) Carpentier, "Habla Alejo Carpentier," *Recopilación de textos,* 50.

193. Carpentier, *The Pilgrim at Home,* 40–41.

194. Helgel, *Phenomenology of the Spirit,* 798.

195. Ibid., 105.

196. In Hegelian terms, Spirit is the conciliation of human and divine laws: a reconciliation that takes the world of morality to ethical action and, thus, to the foundation of the Hegelian "authentic kingdom of the laws." In *Diccionario de filósofos,* (Madrid: Centro de estudios filosóficos de Gallarate, Ediciones Rioduero, 1986), 571. Hegel conceived the life of Spirit, Self-consciousness, whose essence is Freedom (Hegel, *The Philosophy of History,* 17), divided into two antithetical parts, faith and pure intelligence; the conciliation of these, or its synthesis, is "liberty." *Diccionario de filósofos,* 571. Since Hegelian dialectics is experiential, Reason cannot be born out of conceptual learning, book learning, but out of actual life experiences, so, for Ti Nöel, the volumes of the *Encyclopedie* he takes from the

looting of Christophe's palace has only one practical use, he uses them as a stool and sits on them. In his pilgrimage toward understanding, self-awareness, books are useless, and their information empty of the wisdom that Ti Nöel must gain through experience in order to reach Knowledge/Freedom.

197. *Diccionario de filósofos,* 570.

198. Ibid., 571.

199. For the English translation of this novel, Onís translates "Signos" as "Portents." The word *signos* in Spanish means "portents," and omens as well as "signs." The word *portentos* (portent) exists in Spanish, but Carpentier chooses the more ambiguous and philosophical term signos.

200. Hegel, *Phenomenology of the Spirit,* 231.

201. This moment of Reason in Hegel's scheme is "like dawn," while for Spengler the arrival of Reason is "like dusk." These are two different concepts articulated by the same signifier. Such double signification reiterates the play of counterpoints in the text, even at the molecular level of narration. Carpentier's novel begins with the early hours of the morning, when the city begins to awaken, and the novel ends with dawn, at sunrise. To these two symbolic images of "dawn," in the beginning and at the end of the novel, the text counterpoints the image of a bird in flight (in the last scene) to the figure (in the opening scene) of a working horse, an earth creature. Birds in flight are traditionally a symbol of transcendence in Christian iconography. See Clive Hart, *Images of Flight,* (Berkeley: University of California Press, 1988). However, as Emma Susana Speratti-Piñero points out, in Carpentier's novel the vulture flies toward Boi Caiman, the same place where in 1791 slaves came together to be consecrated by Bouckman in a Voodoo ceremony. Emma Susana Speratti-Piñero, *Pasos hallados en* El reino de este mundo (Mexico: El colegio de Mexico, 1981), 147. This is the place that in *The Kingdom of This World* marks the beginning of the war for independence.

202. *Diccionario de filósofos,* 571.

203. Lukács, *The Young Hegel,* 532–33.

204. In Hegel's scheme, observes Georg Lukács, "the beginning and the end of the historical process coincide, i.e., the end of history is prefigured in its beginning" (ibid., 544–55). That end is "its own self-annulment, its own return into the identical subject-object" (ibid., 545). Furthermore, "the reintegration of history in the absolute subject implies the annulment of time, which in turn is the consequence of the annulment of objectivity" (ibid., 545). This end, which "is absolute spirit as its peak, as absolute knowledge, as philosophy," "amounts to the self-annulment of history" (Ibid., 546): a Hegelian concept that Karl Marx rejected.

205. Ibid., 547.

206. The explicit allegories in this text may be related to the fact that, as Roberto González Echevarría observes, "Carpentier does not call *The Kingdom of this World* a novel, in spite of its length," *The Pilgrim at Home,* 154.

207. Lúckas, *The Young Hegel,* 470.

208. Ibid.

209. Ibid., 471–72.

210. Ibid., 471.

211. Ibid.

212. Ibid.

213. Ti Nöel's experience in the natural world, and his rejection of it, is significant since also Hegel rejected nature as a reaction to German Idealism. Although Hegel and Goethe shared some similarities, Goethe was "excessively preoccupied with nature," "almost to a mystical cult of nature philosophy" (ibid., 544). This is evident in Faust's final liberation from Mephistopheles. Although Hegel and Carpentier seem to be closer in their views of

history when it pertains to a march to Freedom, Carpentier approximates Goethe's choice of nature as the space of the primitive blacks and Indians, who constitute that Faustian element that for Carpentier would save America not only from "decline," but also from being what Hegel defined as a simple copy of the Old World. Like Hegel, Carpentier was preoccupied with humanity, not nature.

214. Ti Nöel's freedom is charged with the meaning of knowledge and of transgression always already inscribed in the act of writing.

215. In his last moments before death, Goethe's Faust also envisions to "Stand on free soil among a people free." Johann Wolfgang von Goethe, *Faust,* trans. Bayard Taylor (New York: Ramdom House, Inc., 1950), 241. And it is through the magic of beauty, Margaret, that his soul is freed from Mephistopheles's condemnation. In Carpentier's novel, one must ask what happened with Ti Nöel? Why should death follow self-awareness? Just as in Goethe's *Faust,* one must also ask: What happened with Faust? In Christopher Marlowe's *The Tragedy of Dr. Faust,* Faust is taken by the Devil, and becomes a symbol in world literature of "an all consuming greed for power and ruthless, superhuman desire to be the great emperor of the world." Victor Langue, introduction to *Faust,* vi. This is a desire not very different from Carpentier's representation of the Haitian king Henri Christophe. However, in Johann Wolfgang von Goethe's *Faust* (1808), Faust's soul is freed, saved, from Mephistopheles's control, through beauty and freedom. In *The Kingdom of This World,* Ti Nöel is saved from another cycle of oppressive political regime—through the transcending magic of myth—by the force of a wind that erases him from the text. Like Faust, Ti Nöel continues to be a forsaken character, suspended forever in the imagination of the reader, and in the Caribbean imaginary.

216. Georg Wilhelm Friedrich Hegel, *The Philosophy of History,* translated by J. Sibree (New York: Dover Publications, Inc., 1965), 99.

217. Ibid., 92.

218. For these conflictive ideas about America during this period in Europe, see Antonello Gerbi, *La disputa del nuevo mundo. Historia de una polémica 1750–1900.* (México: Fondo de Cultura Económica, 1955).

219. Hegel, *The Philosophy of History,* 93.

220. Ibid., 93. According to Hegel: "Mahommedanism appears to be the only thing which in any way brings the Negroes within the range of culture" (ibid.). In the history of the Caribbean, as in Carpentier's Mackandal, the most rebellious slaves were of Muslim black African tribes or nations.

221. Ibid., 86–87.

222. Carpentier's representation of Henry Christophe varies from the representation made by other Caribbean writers, including Manuel Zapata Olivella's representation of this Haitian king in *Changó, el gran Putas.* Carpentier comes closer to Luis Palés Matos's representation of Christophe in his poem "Elegía del Conde de la Limonada and "Lagarto verde" (1937). Carpentier's Christophe turns into the new thesis in conflict with the antithetical consciousness of the people, that announces another dialectical movement that would take consciousness to a higher plane of understanding.

223. González Echevarría, *The Pilgrim at Home,* 39–40.

224. As Roberto González Echeverría points out, Ortega y Gasset's "Hegel y América" (1928), in *Revista de Occidente,* was an important essay for Carpentier as well as for other Latin American writers. See, González Echevarría, *The Pilgrim at Home,* 87 (later reprinted in Ortega y Gasset's *Obras completas,* 1963 II 563–76). In it, Ortega y Gasset offers an interpretation and a criticism to Hegel's philosophy of history from a Spenglerian view. He notes that Hegel places America in pre-history ("Hegel y America," *Obras completas,* 568), because America is the future. Ortega y Gasset concludes establishing a link between the primitive and the Faustian vigor suggested by Spengler, and Hegel's philosophy: "Lo que

[Hegel] estimaría de América sería precisamente sus dotes de nueva y saludable barbarie" (What Hegel should have estimated would have been precisely America's gifts of its new and healthy barbarism) (ibid., 575).

225. Chao, *Palabras en el tiempo de Alejo Carpentier,* 137.

226. Lukács, *The Young Hegel,* 493.

227. Ibid., 495.

228. Ibid., 566.

229. Ibid.

230. Ibid.

231. David Quint, *Epic and Empire: Politics and Generic Form from Virgil to Milton* (Princeton: Princeton University Press, 1993), 31–44.

232. David Quint, *Epic and Empire,* 33.

233. Gustavo Pérez Firmat notes that, in the prologue to Ortiz's *Contrapunteo cubano del tabaco y el azúcar,* it is Malinowski who proposes that Ortiz's text is an "epic of tobacco and sugar." See, Pérez Firmat, *The Cuban Condition,* 53; from Ortiz, *Contrapunteo cubano,* 8.

234. Ortiz, *Contrapunteo cubano del tabaco y el azúcar,* 16.

235. Lukács, *The Young Hegel,* 566.

236. Victor Lange, Introduction to Goethe, *Faust,* v.

237. Ibid., vi.

238. Ibid., vii.

239. Ibid., xxi.

240. González Echevarría, *The Pilgrim at Home,* 61.

241. Lukács, *The Young Hegel,* 545.

242. While in "Liturgia" Carpentier parodies a ñáñigo ceremony, in *The Kingdom of This World* he turns to Voodoo. Like the ñáñigos in Cuba, Haitian Voodoo is a unique Afro-Caribbean belief system that brings together Christian, African, and Islamic thoughts, myths, and symbols. Haitian Voodoo began to take the form it has today during the last half of the eighteenth century, simultaneously with the early manifestations of resistance that led to the Haitian revolution. See George Eaton Simpson, *Religious Cults of the Caribbean: Trinidad, Jamaica, and Haiti* (Río Piedras: Industrias Gráficas "Diario-Día," Institute of Caribbean Studies, 1970), 234.

243. González Echevarría, *The Pilgrim at Home,* 137–46.

244. Ibid., 17.

245. Seabrook writes that Haiti was the first nonwhite nation in America to maintain "more than a century of national freedom of a peculiar sort, which has existed nowhere else on earth [as of 1929] save Liberia—the freedom of a negro people to govern or misgovern themselves." Seabrook, *The Magic Island,* 282.

246. Spengler's concept of contemporaneity makes Aristotle contemporary to Kant and Goethe, since Europe (Germany) was passing through the same historical process during the time of Goethe and Kant, as Greece during the life of Aristotle. For Spengler, religion (only a tool toward Knowledge in Hegelian philosophy) was the mother of civilizations and Philosophy: the expression of a humanity that has lost its capacity to bring new ideas to fruition and to control its future. As for Spengler, for Carpentier the atavistic Haitian, non-self-reflexive, magical, and mysterious, was like ancient (primitive) Western man. Carpentier, like other Latin American intellectuals of this period, concluded that twentieth century Latin America was living the same historical moment of cultural development as baroque Europe.

247. González Echevarría, *The Pilgrim at Home,* 133–34.

248. Janney, *Alejo Carpentier and His Early Works,* 30.

249. González Echevarría, *The Pilgrim at Home,* 144.

250. Ibid., 129–47.

251. In Carpentier's scheme of end/beginning, the mulatto rulers suggest a synthesis that results from a dialectical conflict (black/white, master/slave).

252. Roberto González Echeverría points out the presence of a repetitive order in the novel between Sunday and Monday: "Carnival and Apocalypse," as the "two poles between the action in the story stands suspended." *The Pilgrim at Home,* 143.

253. This is the moment when another tyranny appears, this time by mulatto rulers. Ti Nöel, fed up with the return of chains, becomes the image of a Carnival Momo King, a Caribbean Don Quixote, dressed in Christophe's royal coat, and charging against the new mulatto tyrants in an allegorical war against all "categorical systems" of power.

254. Lydia Cabrera, *Lydia Cabrera, Yemayá y Ochún. Kariocha, Iyalorichas y Olorichas,* 225.

255. The opening scene in Carpentier's text recalls a moment in Seabrook's *The Magic Island* when the writer and his young black Haitian servant are riding together to the boy's home in the mountains. Seabrook is following the boy, who "knows the way," riding on a pony, while Louis, the young servant, rides on a mule. Both are singing a tune "not always in unison." Seabrook, *The Magic Island,* 16.

256. Ibid., 309.

257. Ibid., 310.

258. The image of the "head" also has a ritual significance in Afro-Cuban *Lucumí* cults. It represents the power that comes from above, a higher intelligence, a guide or *ori*. Deities are known as orishas, a term that means guiding or "head" spirits, or forces of life that come from above. Many *odus* or *apattakis* (ritual stories) in Cuban Yoruba or Lucumí traditions are mythical anecdotes about heads, in which a head is the main character. See Cuervo Hewitt, *Aché,* 202–3. However, Carpentier's utilization of "heads" in *The Kingdom of This World* seems to have been suggested by his reading of Seabrook's *The Magic Island,* and the *Faust-Books.*

259. Dr. Georg Faust was a historical person, contemporary of Martin Luther. Goethe, interested in modern man and the moral and intellectual challenges of the times, characterized Faust as representative of the revolutionary spirit of the sixteenth century.

260. González Bermejo, "Carpentier: trastornar la cronología," 8.

261. During the slave rebellion and destruction of Lenormand de Mezy's plantation, Ti Nöel kills and rapes de Mezy's second wife. Her death coincides with the beginning of the Haitian revolution. When de Mezy returns to the ransacked house, he finds his wife, Floridor de Mezy, dead: "Her dead hand was still clenched around one of the bedposts in a gesture cruelly reminiscent of that of a sleeping girl in a licentious engraving entitled *The Dream* which adorned the wall" (*KW,* 55).

262. He is also a picaresque character closer to what Pérez Firmat observes in Ortiz's concept of Cuban vernacular culture, as a *vivo,* a burlesque character popular in the first half of the twentieth century in Cuba, often represented by the witty uneducated white or by the *negrito,* a witty Afro-Cuban creole; the less witty being the Spaniard, the *vivío.* Pérez Firmat, *The Cuban Condition,* 35–36.

263. His textual transformation takes place at a moment when narrative time collapses and multiple events are superimposed in a carnival like moment of baroque contrasts that previews the events to come: "Father Corneille, the curate of Limonade, had just arrived at the Cathedral riding his donkey-colored mule" (a biblical reference that heralds his passion and martyrdom); also "a salvo rang out from the parapets of the fortress. *La Courageuse,* of His Majesty's fleet, had been sighted, returning from the Ile de la Tortue. Its gunwales returned the echoes of the blank shells" (*KW,* 9–10); then, Ti Nöel begins to hum an antimonarchical song, as a sort of mental resistance to the domination of the master.

264. Ti Nöel's association with the storm god is also intimated in his transformation from Mackandal's disciple to the new role of a creole master of the word, who instructs his "twelve" children in Mackandal's teachings.

265. Chao, *Palabras en el tiempo de Alejo Carpentier,* 134.

266. Mackandal's death in *The Kingdom of This World* is immediately followed by the birth of Ti Noël's twin sons. French rule ends, and then it is followed by a new beginning: Haiti's political independence from France. Haitian independence then turns into the tyrannical rule under a Haitian king, whose tyranny also ends, only to be displaced by another dynasty of mulatto rulers. Finally, a cosmic revolution erases all vestiges of civilization, including Ti Nöel, and that end is followed by a new day in the image of a primordial landscape.

267. *Damballah's vever* is not always portrayed the same. There are variations, but all of them contain the snake god, most often two snakes facing each other. At the center, in the middle between both heads, is often an egg or a sun. See, "Vever for Damballah," in Maya Deren, "Religion and Magic," 21–51, *Tomorrow. Haiti Issue* 3, no. 1 (1954), 21.

268. In Hegel's philosophy of history there is also a sense of one thing "becoming" another, an idea that simply has to be accepted as such. In those dialectical transformations, words are signified entities and concepts that "act." For example, Reason "sees," self-consciousness "wants to leave," etc. Like Carpentier's allegorical Ti Nöel, Hegel's concepts are like actors on the stage of history, moving through time, from one transformation to the next.

269. Frederick de Armas, "Metamorphosis as Revolt: Cervantes's *Persiles y Segismunda* and Carpentier's *El reino de este mundo,*" 297–316, *Hispanic Review* 49, no. 3 (1981): 197.

270. Ibid., 315.

271. Ibid.

272. Ibid.

273. Ibid.

274. Ibid. It has the meaning here of awareness or eye-opening disillusion. De Armas observes that: "Cervantes "struggles with Neo-Aristotelian principles and preserves the variety and flux of the byzantine romance as well as the marvelous occurrences" (ibid.).

275. Ibid.

276. Ibid., 316.

277. His made-up stories in which he is the hero are reminiscent of the confabulations about America told by *indianos* during the conquest and colonization of the New World. Estebanico was an African slave in Pánfilo de Narváez's expedition that shipwrecked in the coasts of Florida in the sixteenth century. Estebanico, with Alvar Núñez Cabeza de Vaca, and other two Spaniards, traveled for eight years, suffering hunger, cold, and captivity, until they reached northern Mexico. His confabulations about great cities of gold and their heroic adventures resulted in various costly expeditions. Among those was the fiasco of the Coronado expedition.

278. Carpentier's Solimán in Europe also recalls Ortiz's allegorical tobacco: "El tabaco llegó a Europa a las peores vilezas, a ser cómplice delincuente, a ser criminal. En el siglo XVIII fue general el temor de ser envenenados mediante polvos ponzoñosos mezclados con el rapé" (Tobacco in Europe reached its worst malice, to be an accomplice of delinquency, to be a criminal. It was common in the eighteenth century to be afraid of being poisoned with venom powders mixed in the *rape*). Ortiz, *Contrapunteo cubano,* 18.

279. Eduardo Guízar Alvarez and Adriana Méndez Rodena, "Caña/cuerpo/danza: Imágenes de opresión/liberacieon del sujeto caribeño," 61–77, *Crítica hispánica (Edición especial: El Caribe en su literatura)* XXI, no. 1 (2000): 71.

280. The historical Mackandal was the first well-known, and then legendary slave to rebel against the system of slavery in Haiti. In the middle of the eighteenth century, he created havoc during six years in the French colony with a growing group of runaway slaves, using poison as a weapon against whites. See C. L. R. James, *The Black Jacobins: Toussaint L'Overture, and the San Domingue Revolution* (New York: Random House, Inc., 1989), 20–22.

281. Ortiz, *Contrapunteo cubano,* 24.

282. Ibid., 18–20. Ortiz also points out that the Spanish Crown prohibited tobacco for a time because it was considered dangerous and demonic, perhaps due to its properties, but also due to its magic role in pre-Columbian rituals.

283. Ibid., 20.

284. Octavio Paz, *Sor Juana Inés de la Cruz o las trampas de la fe* (México: Fondo de Cultura Económica, 1982), 268.

285. Roque Barcia, 1058. The name Solimán is also a derivative of the Arab *suleimani, suleimant,* and of *Suleiman,* a name given to several kings of the Ottoman Empire. The most significant of these was Suleiman the Magnificent (1520–66), Charles V's worst enemy, against whom Christian Europe battled to conquer the Holy Land, and to defend Europe from being conquered. See, Anthony Bridge, *Suleiman the Magnific. Scourge of Heaven* (New York: Franklin Watts, 1983), and Roger Bigelow Merriman, *Suleiman The Magnificent 1520–1566* (New York: Cooper Square Publishers, Inc., 1966). Solimán is also etymologically related to the Hebrew King Solomon, builder of the temple, representative of wisdom, but also important in the national saga of the Hebrew nation for his tragic fall.

286. It is from this cultural role that in the Spanish language the name is used also with a figurative meaning, for example, as in "Ojalá se vuelva solimán" (God willing he/she will become solimán) (María Moliner, *Diccionario de uso del español* (Madrid: Editorial Gredos, 1984), 1195.

287. Ortiz, *Contrapunteo cubano,* 18.

288. Fernando de Rojas, *La Celestina. Tragicomedia de Calixto y Melibea* I, edited by Julio Cejador y Frauca (Madrid: Espasa-Calpe, S.A., 1968), 160.

289. See James, *The Black Jacobins,* 16, and 22.

290. Fradique Lizardo, *Cultura Africana en Santo Domingo* (Santo Domingo: Sociedad Industrial Dominicana, n/d), 45.

291. Ibid., 63.

292. For Pauline, Solimán is symbolic of that which is prohibited, like the fictionalized Caribbean island where the exotic, magic, and the marvelous are transgressive mediators of change. For Pauline, Solimán is the mediator of her transformation; and her transformation is the result of her transgression.

293. Goethe, *Faust,* xix.

294. Solimán is an *hougan.* His name recalls the function of the imam in Islam, the name given to the Islamic priest who presides over daily prayers and whose gestures and words are imitated by his followers.

295. Chao, *Palabras en el tiempo de Alejo Carpentier,* 181.

296. Carpentier, *El reino de este mundo,* 109. Harriet de Onís in her translation offers the original French title of the novel: *Un Nègre comme il y a peu des blancs* (A black man like few white men) (*KW,* 71).

297. The text plays with the fact that an actual statue of Pauline representing Venus, known as the Venus of Canova, was made by the sculptor Antonio Canova in Italy before Pauline's death.

298. Lucien Georges Coachy, *Culto Vodú y brujería en Haití* (Mexico: Secretaría de Educación, Sepsetentas Dianas, 1982), 47.

299. Ibid.

300. Sugar has many shades; raw sugar is dark, and it is often refered to as mulatto sugar. In her study of the representation of cigar *marquillas* or labels in nineteenth century Cuba, Kutzinski points out that: "the classification of nonwhite women in terms of different grades of refined sugar is most striking in the marquilla series entitled "Muestras de azúcar de mi ingenio" (Sugar Samples from my Sugar Mill). Kutzinski, *Sugar's Secrets,* 48.

301. Ibid., 49.

302. Martha Ellen Davis, *La otra ciencia. El Vodú dominicano como religion y medicina populares* (Santo Domingo, RD: Editora Universitaria-USAD, Colección Estudios Sociales 5, 1973), 313.

303. Melville Herskovits, "What is Voodoo?" 11–20, *Tomorrow* 3, no. 1 (1954): 14.

304. Like other orishas and loas (except Obatalá), Legba likes alcohol, a substance related to the liminal, and associated with this loa, and with his transformative experience. As a mediator, Legba presides over all liminal spaces like twilights.

305. One of Landaluze's paintings, "Sirviente tratando de besar un busto" (Servant Trying to Kiss a Bust), is the farcical representation of a domestic slave with a feather duster in his hand reaching to kiss the marble bust of an aristocratic white woman. His actions, left in suspense, portray an "innocent" humorous transgression since the figure of the woman is a bust without a body. There is no documentation as to whether Carpentier knew of this painting, but it is quite probable that he did since Landaluze's work was well-known among Cuban intellectuals. In Carpentier's novel the statue has a body, but is lifeless. At the same time, the domesticity of the servant in the painting, emasculated and comical, becomes a tragic affair for the Haitian hougan, now impotent, emptied of the vigor of the magic that mediated his relationship to Pauline.

306. Ortiz, *Contrapunteo cubano*, 25.

307. García Márquez follows the same structure in *Cien años de soledad*. As Josefina Ludmer notes in her study of the structure of the novel in *Cien años de soledad: una interpretación* (Buenos Aires: Editorial Tiempo Contemporáneo, 1972), in the middle of the text, the novel begins to invert itself: the narrative travels backward to its own beginning while chronologically it travels forward.

308. Ortiz, *El huracán*, 588.

309. Frederick de Armas, "Lope de Vega y Carpentier," 363–73, in *Actas del Simposio Internacional de Estudios Hispánicos,* edited by Mátyás Horányi (Budapest: Editorial de la academia de ciencias de Hungría, 1978), 364.

310. Ibid., 373.

311. Carpentier's political and social *desengaño,* when he returns to Cuba in 1939 (as the desengaño Ti Nöel feels when he returns to an independent but internally enslaved Haiti), echoes Aimé Césaire's *Notebook of a Return to the Native Land* (1940), a text the Martinique writer wrote in 1939, informed by his visits to his native island while living in France.

312. Coachy, *Culto Vodú,* 43

313. Harriet de Onís translates the Spanish word "signo" (sign) as "The Portents."

314. According to Harold Bayley, says Cirlot, the etymological make-up of the word "cross-road" derives from *ask ur os,* meaning "the light of the Great Fire"; the cross is thought to be the antithesis of the snake, representative of anarchical chaos. Cirlot, *Diccionario de símbolos,* 154–56. In its most common universal symbol, the cross is the midpoint, or the point of intersection between heaven and earth.

315. In *The Kingdom of This World,* Carpentier brings Christ and Legba together in one single figure, just like in Voodoo altars, where Christ and Legba are found together. This is why Emil Volek refers to the vulture "in a cross-of-feathers" as a "syncretic Christian-Voodooist vision." Emil Volek, "Analisis e interpretación de *El reino de este mundo* y su lugar en la obra de Carpentier," 98–118, *Unión* VI, no. 1 (1969), 111. The symbolic reason behind this ritual custom is the idea that Christ is the messenger and the sacrificial lamb of God, whose death on the altar of the cross brings salvation to mankind, and Legba is the messenger-deity who opens or closes the doors for humans and whose arbitrations guide their destiny. Legba is the one who travels between earth and sky, the visible realms and the invisible; the mediator between the divine and humanity; he is also the observer (witness) of human affairs. In counterpoint to Legba, Christ travels from heaven to earth incarnated

in the form of man, dies at the cross, and then travels back to heaven. As Martha Ellen Davis points out, in Haitian and Dominican Voodoo altars, the cross is often found linked to several loas, especially to *El Barón del Cementerio,* and to the dead, or *guides.* See, Davis, *La otra ciencia,* 310. The cross indicates the meeting point of the dead and the living, where this world and the other cross paths and intersect.

316. Onís translates San Transtorno (the Overturner) as Saint Calamity, losing with the translation the codified meaning it has in Voodoo rituals, thus, also altering Carpentier's play of symmetries.

317. Seabrook, *The Magic Island,* 309.

318. When Ti Nöel returns to his homeland to encounter a "return of chains," the text's cyclical time seems to be a parody of the image of the snake that bites her own tail, the Ouroborous, whose Caribbean counterpart is the snake-god *Dá* (*Damballah*), the eternal principle. Like a Caribbean Sisyphus, Ti Nöel again is made to work for others, carrying stones for the construction of Henri Christophe's fort, *La Ferriere.*

319. In "Viaje a la semilla" ("Back to the Source"), Marcial becomes an infant and enters his mother's womb. Then, everything in the house returns to a time before the construction of the mansion: "Todo se metamorfoseaba, regresando a la condición primera" (Every thing metamorphosed, returning to its primal condition) Carpentier, "Viaje a la semilla," 53–81, *Guerra del tiempo* (Barcelona: Barral Editores, S.A., 1970), 80.

320. The symbolic association of Ti Nöel with Santiago (Saint Jaimes), who is *Ogoun Fai,* cannot be overlooked in Carpentier's narrative scheme. It was in Santiago de Cuba that Ti Nöel spent the most difficult years of the Haitian revolution, a period of carnival-like social chaos, and a narrative moment that corresponds to the overturning of the French order and the transformation of Haiti. It is in Santiago de Cuba that Ti Nöel suffered another transformation that takes him from being a slave to being a free man.

321. This is a textual moment reminiscent of Hegel's concept of a natural State, a moment in history that must come from "sublation," because it arises from the people governing themselves. See Hegel, *Phenomenology of the Spirit,* 485, paragraph 798.

322. I use the term "archive" with the meaning Michel Foucault gives to the term in *The Archaelology of Knowledge and the Discourse on Language,* trans. A. M. Sheridan Smith (New York: Tavistock Publications Limited, 1972), meaning a "general system of formation and transformation of statements" (130), beliefs, and ideas; and "the rules from which we speak" (ibid.), and the system that regulates the use of given statements (ibid., 129).

323. Ortiz, *El huracán,* 501.

324. Hegel, *Phenomenology of the Spirit,* 105.

325. Maya Deren, "Religion and Magic," 29.

326. Seabrook records this song with few differences: "Ogún Badagris, ou général sanglant; ou saizé clé z'orange, ou scell 'orange;/ Ou fais katáou z'eclai,'" meaning: "Ogoun Badagris, bloody warrior, you hold the keys to the storm-clouds; you lock them up; you loose the thunder and lightning." Seabrook, *The Magic Island,* 74.

327. The image of the bull brings together atmospheric and oceanic deities, *Mnevis, Apisk, Onubis, Baco, Tauro* (or *Taurocéphalous,* the name given to the ocean, represented by a bull), *Osiris, Thor, Urios,* and others. *Baco's* regenerative powers were represented also in the figure of the bull. See Richard Payne Knight, *The Symbolical Language of Ancient Art and Mythology: An Inquiry* (New York: J. W. Bouton, 1876), 18. In the complex play of symmetries that inform Carpentier's text, *Tau* (the bull) is associated with Neptune, and Neptune with wisdom.

328. Ortiz, *El huracán,* 101. The association of the Great Caribbean Wind, Huracán, with bulls, and the bellowing of the bulls, appears early in the nineteenth century in José Maria Heredia's poem, "En una tempestad" ("In the Storm"): "Y en su hinchada nariz fuego aspirando/ Llama la tempestad con sus bramidos" (And in its widened nose breathing in fire/

The Storm bellowing calls), José María Heredia, "En una Tempestad," 125–27, Leonardo Padura Fuentes, *José María Heredia. La patria y la vida* (Havana: Ediciones Unión, 2003), 126.

329. Ortiz, *El huracán,* 467.

330. The Afro-Cuban oracles, the *Diloggun* and *Ifa,* are based on combinations of four: 16 cowries (4 multiplied by itself). See Cuervo Hewitt, *Aché,* 73–102. The palindrome of 4 x 4 = 16 is symbolic of the earth: as it represents earth's four cardinal points. Four is also the crossroad of dualities, of 2 multiplied by itself: the double twin.

331. Ortiz, *Contrapunteo cubano,* 424.

332. Ibid., 420.

333. Heredia, "En una tempestad," 125–27, in Leonardo Padura Fuentes, *José María Heredia. La patria y la vida,* 127.

334. Ibid., 467.

335. These are *Bantu* (Congo) Afro-Cuban priests who make magical power objects known in Cuba as *ngangas.*

336. Ortiz, *El huracán,* 568.

337. Ibid.

338. Carpentier was interested in pre- and post-Columbian indigenous and Afro-American cosmogonies. These are the American mythologies that Carpentier felt were still to be understood and studied in America, as he points out in his prologue to *El reino de este mundo,* 55. For Carpentier, mythology is the richest legacy in America, still ignored by Americans and by the world. In *The Kingdom of This World,* he writes about the interesting account of creation told by the Arekuna Indians in the Amazon, an account with which Carpentier was familiar, and that he compares with the biblical story of creation in order to construct a syncretic American myth. See Carpentier's essay in *Carteles* (La Habana), (March 28, 1948), 15–16. In Spanish, the term used for the force of creation is not "Word" (as in the English translation of the Bible: "In the beginning was the Word"), but "Verb" ("En el principio era el Verbo") meaning action, activity, a term much closer in Carpentier's fictional cosmos to the concept of *Dá* (the snake god *Damballah*) in Haitian Voodoo, and to the many manifestations of the wind-word in pre-Columbian cosmogony.

339. José Martí, "Nuestra America," Martí writes: "regó el Gran Semí . . . la semilla de la América nueva," 7.

340. Ortiz points out that the *Ibeyes* or *Abeyí,* are celestial twins of Euroasian and African mythologies, associated with serpents, with medicine, with sexuality, fertility, and with storms, thunder and lightning. Ortiz, *El huracán,* 467. The Ibeyes are sons of Shango, the Yoruba orisha of fertility, storms, thunder, lightning, and drums.

341. Ortiz, *El huracán,* 101. See *Popul Vuh. Las antiguas historias del Quiché,* translated by Adrián Recinos (Mexico: Fondo de Cultura Económica, 1952), 24.

342. Remembering that the literary precedence in Cuban literature to Carpentier's utilization of *Huracán* is José María Heredia's poem "En una tormenta" (In a Storm) written before 1824.

343. Ortiz, *El huracán,* 592.

344. Ibid., 586.

345. Ibid., 545.

346. Ibid., 518.

347. Ibid., 540.

348. Ibid., 542.

349. Ortiz bases his analogies on the descriptions of these houses in Fernández de Oviedo's description, in the sixteenth century (ibid., 458). The association is quite evident still today as one visits the temple of Quetzalcóatl in Teotihuacán, Mexico, where one can find representations of seashells adorning the walls around the stone heads of the serpent,

as well as in, among others, Templo Mayor, in Mexico City. In most sacred sites in Mexico, water images, often in circular forms, accompany and represent the plummed-serpent god.

350. Ibid., 541.

351. Ibid., 576.

352. Ibid., 586.

353. The first apparition of the Virgen de la Caridad del Cobre (Virgin of Charity), patron saint of Cuba, took place on the ocean waters. Her double, Oshun, is also a water deity.

354. Cuervo Hewitt, *Aché,* 159–66.

355. Important also to Carpentier's play of counterpoints in *The Kingdom of This World* is the idea, based on Ortiz's study, that the spiraling hurricane is associated with music and with dance, much like Oshun's "Dance of Spring," a dance of rebirth. *Oshun's* dance may have recalled for Carpentier Stravinsky's "Rite of Spring." Carpentier pays homage to Stravinsky in his early works, and again in *La consagración de la primavera* (1978).

356. Spengler claimed that music is the most important of all Faustian arts, and the violin is the most representative instrument of Faustian Western music. Carpentier, on the other hand, in his role of translator of America, chooses different wind instruments, variants of the conch shell, as the "proper" native, primitive, American instrument. This type of American trumpet, the conch shell, is often associated with the sound-wind of the apocalyptic call to freedom in Cuban letters and in the Caribbean. The conch shell as the wind instrument of a Faustian America is associated to water and to the storm, to thunder, and to the drum in Caribbean music.

357. Jean-Paul Sartre, *Black Orpheus,* trans. S. W. Allen (Paris: Présence Africaine, Editions Gallimard, 1976), 49.

358. Ortiz, *El huracán,* 263.

359. Alejo Carpentier claims that architecture and music had a foundational influenced in his writing. See "Habla Alejo Carpentier," *Recopilación de textos,* 16. Benítez Rojo, relates such interest to a complex personal experience arising from the fact that his mother was a music teacher and his father an architect (*RI,* 265–75).

360. Leonardo Acosta, *Música y épica en la novela de Alejo Carpentier* (Havana: Editorial Letras Cubanas, 1981), 130.

361. Ibid., 124.

362. It is quite possible that, for Carpentier, the shell (in its many associations with the wind, and with its spiraling movements), was also a symbol of historical movements reminiscent of Giambattista Vico's concept of "ricorsi," as "convolutions of history that repeat past events in not quite mimetic fashion, as repetitions that are original acts." Roberto González Echeverría, *The Voice of the Masters,* 72. In the thirties, says González Echeverría: "Vico was one of the thinkers very much in vogue, and a rather useful gloss of his philosophy was published then that could very well have been Carpentier's introduction to the author of *The New Science*" (ibid.).

363. Spengler writes: "Woman as Mother is Time and Destiny" (*DW,* 267).

364. Ortiz, Prologue to *El reino de este mundo,* 55.

365. Ortiz, *El huracán,* 592.

366. Hegel, *Phenomenology of the Spirit,* 231.

367. Hurricanes were climatological phenomena as important for Indo-Caribbeans as the sun (Ortiz, *El huracán,* 96) for the Aztec, Maya, and Inca empires. Its symbolic importance was underlined in Cuban literature when Virgilio Piñera and Rodríguez Feo, differing with the ideas held by Lezama Lima, broke away from the group of *Orígenes.* They chose as the title for their new short-lived journal the word *Ciclón* (cyclone). The icon for the journal was a cherub with puffed cheeks blowing a stormy wind. The symbol may be

more complex than it seemed at the time, especially when we consider that the word "ci-clón" (cyclone) means "coiled serpent" (ibid., 443). In keeping with the symbolism of its title, the journal's agenda was revolutionary. It indicated a rupture with, and a transgression against, the precepts of *Orígenes*.

368. The Spanish original reads: "esperando el sol con las alas abiertas." Carpentier, *El reino de este mundo,* 168.

369. Cuervo Hewitt, *Aché* 34–35. It is also part of the *Ibo* tradition. The Nigerian Ibo writer Chinua Achebe uses this story of creation in his novel *Things Fall Apart* (1958), im-plicitly recalling the popular story of Vulture's role as Messenger, looking over the land af-ter creation.

370. *Pequeño Larousse* (Paris: Librairie Larousse, 1964),114.

371. *Aristos Diccionario de la lengua* (Havana: Editorial Pueblo y Educación, n/d), 80.

372. Lydia Cabrera, *La sociedad secreta Abakua,* 19.

373. Carpentier, "Habla Alejo Carpentier," *Recopilación de textos,* 26; I am using Maraniss's translation in Benítez Rojo, *The Repeating Island,* 272.

374. Carpentier rehearses again here a literary voyage toward the telluric womb of America in his 1953 novel, *Los pasos perdidos (The Lost Steps).*

375. Ortiz, *El huracán,* 327.

376. Ibid., 431.

377. Cirlot, *Diccionario de símbolos,* 196.

378. Derrida, *Dissemination,* 90.

379. Juan B. Bergua, *Mitología universal* II (Madrid: Clásicos Bergua, 1979), 246.

380. Cirlot, *Diccionario de símbolos,* 105.

381. The sudden displacement of Ti Nöel by a vulture is significant in Carpentier's tex-tual scheme because it points to the reconciliation of two different consciousnesses in one single image. However, the actual erasure does not end with the disappearance of Ti Nöel/Legba/Christ/Man, but at the moment when the vulture flies away towards Boi Caï-man. In its association with Legba, it is ritually proper that the mediator and messenger, the one who opens and closes the door, be the one who closes the text, and the one who an-nounces the opening of another door, sunrise: another reality left suspended in the reader's imagination. This initiatory process of the text, suggests the reader's entrance to a new re-ality to which he/she has been initiated (brought into its fold and realm) through the act of reading.

382. Carpentier brings together in the figure of the vulture Afro-Caribbean religious symbols and classical and Egyptian mythology, but also Indo-American cosmogonies: the Word-Wind *Huracán* and the Father-Sun-Fire of pre-Hispanic America. From Ortiz, Car-pentier must have been familiar with the Afro (Yoruba) Cuban myth that tells that from the union of *Yemayá,* the ocean, and *Agallú,* earth, *Orungán,* Sun and Air, is born. See, Ortiz, *El huracán,* 435.

383. In Reyes's *La experiencia literaria* (The Literary Experience) (1942), many of his essays are imaged after classical myths: "Hermes o de la comunicación humana" (Hermes or About Human Communication), "Marsyas o del tema popular" (Marsyas or About a Popular Theme), "Apolo o de la literatura" (Apollo or About Literature).

384. Like Carpentier, African and creole blacks and Indians were also abandoned by the colonial European father. In a Spenglerian "bird's view" of the world, Capentier's charac-ters, like the writer, were expressions of a Faustian soul "abandoned and forsaken."

385. Speratti-Piñero, *Pasos hallados en* El reino de este mundo, 147

386. Carpentier's repetitive association of language and music can be found in most of his texts, as Benítez Rojo suggests in his readings of Carpentier's short story "El camino de Santiago" (Road to Santiago). Benítez Rojo points out that for Carpentier: "the circular (mu-sical) voyage between Europe and America that we see in "El camino de Santigo" expresses

not just the desire for the Mother within the Oedipal triangle, but also the search for the lost paradise of the Mirror Stage, where the Self and the Other compose the same body" (*RI*, 272).

387. The image of the mother womb of America at the end of *The Kingdom of this World*, intimates an association with Goethe's *Faust*. Faust's redemption takes place through the image of woman, and also ends with a reference to the Great Mother: "Virgin Holy, Mother, Queen,/ Goddess, gracious be! . . . The Indescribable,/ Here it is done;/ The Woman-soul leadeth us/ Upward and on!" Goethe, *Faust*, 257–58. Carpentier's mother image is, of course, of this earth: America, culture, music, and language. Biblical associations in *The Kingdom of This World* also establish symmetry with the image of a maternal God in *Psalm* 91:4: "He will cover thee with his feathers."

388. Ortiz, *El huracán*, 540.

389. Cirlot, *Diccionario de símbolos*, 196.

390. Emil Volek suggests that Ti Nöel's textual metamorphosis into a vulture articulates a premortal revelation, the moment in which the hero enters the eternity of his tribe and is taken in by legend. See, Emil Volek, "Analisis e interpretación de *El reino de este mundo* y su lugar en la obra de Carpentier," *Unión* VI, no. 1 (1969), 111.

391. Gilles Deleuze writes: "Writing is a question of becoming, always incomplete, always in the midst of being formed, and goes beyond the matter of any livable or lived experience. It is a process, that is, a passage of Life that traverses both the livable and the lived. Writing is inseparable from becoming: in writing, one becomes-woman, becomes-animal, or vegetable, becomes-molecule, to the point of becoming-imperceptible." Gilles Deleuze, "Literature and Life," 225–29, trans. Daniel W. Smith and Michael A. Creco, *Critical Inquiry* 23 (1997): 229.

392. Juan Marinello, *Literatura hispanoamericana* (Mexico: Ediciones de la Universidad Nacional de Mexico, 1937), 84; quoted and translated in Janney, *Alejo Carpentier and his Early Works*, 24.

393. This is an interest Carpentier rehearses again in *Los pasos perdidos* (1950), where the main character travels deep in the jungle searching for primitive musical instruments.

394. Janney, *Alejo Carpentier and his Early Works*, 24.

395. Chao, *Palabras en el tiempo de Alejo Carpentier*, 170. Carpentier's words here would actually translate as "the relationship of blacks with the forest," a statement that may indicate vestiges in his thoughts, even years later, of Frobenius's association of Africa and Africans, as a culture in close relationship to nature and the forest's flora. Lydia Cabrera's *El monte* (1954), may have confirmed such relationship: an idea that also prevailed in the forties in articles published in *Tropiques*.

CHAPTER 2. (DE)COLONIZING THE OTHER

1. Ana María Simo, *Lydia Cabrera: An Intimate Portrait*, trans. Suzanne Jill Levine (New York: Intar Latin American Gallery, 1984), 7.

2. Guillermo Cabrera Infante, "Guillermo Cabrera Infante," 16–17, *Homenaje a Lydia Cabrera*, ed. Reinaldo Sánchez, José Antonio Madrigal, Ricardo Viera, José Sánchez-Boudy (Congreso de Literatura Afro-Americana) (Barcelona: Ediciones Universal, 1978), 16.

3. Lydia Cabrera Holding, Heritage Collection, File 0339, Series I, Box 5, Folder 5, University of Miami, Florida.

4. Simo, *Lydia Cabrera*, 6.

5. Leonardo Fernández-Marcané, "Semblanza de Lydia Cabrera. Un ala de suavísimo vuelo hacia nuestro pasado," 37–42, *En torno a Lydia Cabrera. Cincuentenario de Cuen-*

tos negros de Cuba *1936–1986,* ed. Isabel Castellanos (Miami: Ediciones Universal, 1987), 37–38.

6. Lydia's father, Raimundo Cabrera, participated in Cuba's Ten Year War (1868–78) against Spain. See Fernández-Marcané, "Semblanza de Lydia Cabrera," 37. His book, *Cuba y sus jueces* (1887) was a strong condemnation of Spanish colonial rule. Later, after the intervention of the island by the United States in 1898, as a lawyer and a writer, he became a strong supporter for the separation of Cuba from the United States.

7. Ferrer, *Insurgent Cuba,* 79.

8. Ibid., 112.

9. Ibid., 138.

10. Ibid., 200.

11. Rosa Valdéz Cruz, *Lo ancestral africano en la narrativa de Lydia Cabrera* (Barcelona-España: Editorial Vosgos, S.A., 1974), 11–21.

12. In a 1932 letter to Lydia Cabrera, dated Wednesday 27, the Venezuelan novelist, Teresa de la Parra, writes to Lydia about a new mulatto Cuban poet, Nicolás Guillén, whose work she had just discovered and liked very much. Guillén, Teresa tells Lydia: "Tiene la vena popular sin afectación ni literatura" (Has a popular tendency without affectation or literature) File, 0339, Series IV, Box 32, Folder 3. It is not clear (although possible due to her relationship to Ortiz) that Cabrera knew of Guillén before 1932. He began to write his Afro-Cuban poems in the late twenties: *Motivos de Son* (1930), *Songoro Cosongo* (1931), *West Indies, Ltd.* (1934), and *Balada del Guije* (1937).

13. Rosario Hiriart, "Lydia Cabrera, cronologia: Vida y Obras," in *Noticias de las Arte. Gaceta de artes visuales, escénicas, musicales y literarias (Número especial. Homenaje a Lydia Cabrera)* (New York: 1982): 27. Sara Soto also claims that Lydia Cabrera "no tuvo influencia Africana en su infancia" (did not have any African influence in her childhood) and that while studying Oriental religions in Paris, claims Lydia: "pensé que en Cuba tenía que haber mucho legado africano" (I thought that in Cuba there should be a great African legacy) Sara Soto, *Magia e historia en los "Cuentos negros," "¿Por qué?" y "Ayapá" de Lydia Cabrera* (Miami: Ediciones Universal, 1988), 37. It is hard to imagine that Lydia did not know then that there was indeed "mucho legado africano" (a great African legacy) when her brother-in-law had been researching aspects of that "legacy" for years. It is possible to think that while the presence of certain religious practices were obvious, she wondered if there was an African oral literature associated with ancestral belief systems in Cuba that expressed a view or philosophy comparable to that of the Oriental religions that attracted her. After all, Kipling's "jungle stories" she had read were associated with a complex notion of primitivism associated with Hinduism, and Frobenius's *Decamerón negro,* 1925 (*Black Decameron*), with African history, and lore.

14. Rosario Hiriart, *Cartas a Lydia Cabrera. (Correspondencia inédita de Gabriela Mistral y Teresa de la Parra)* (Madrid: Ediciones Torremozas, 1998), 26.

15. Ibid., 10.

16. While living in France, Cabrera returned to Cuba in short trips during which she attended Afro-Cuban ceremonies. She explained to Hilda Pereda that the core story of some of her stories, like "Susundamba no se muestra de día" (*Susudamba* does not show himself during the day) in *¿Por qué?,* and "Apopoito Miama" in *Cuentos negros de Cuba,* were stories told to her by her nana Tata Tula. See, Hilda Perera, *Idapo. El sincretismo en los cuentos negros de Lydia Cabrera* (Miami: Ediciones Universal, 1971), 80. In my own research I have found that several of her short stories are in fact elaborations of African tales.

17. There, she befriended elderly ex-slaves that became her informants. Omí Tomí was her family's seamstress.

18. From Molloy's readings of these letters, José Quiroga concludes that: "La literatura aquí sirve casi de espacio virtual, refractario, por medio del cual Molloy confirma una clave

al parecer secreta de resistencias y complicidades que dibujan la verdadera relación entre las dos mujeres" (Literature here serves almost as a virtual space, resistant, by which Molloy confirms a code seemingly secret, of resistence and complicity that points out the real relationship between both women) José Quiroga, "Lydia, Invisible,"*Sexualidad y nación,* edited by Daniel Balderston (Pittsburg: Instituto Iberoamericano, 2002), 107–8.

19. In her letters to Lydia, Teresa often makes references to the dependency of women, and her desire for independence; she abhors the idea of dependency even in her most difficult hours.

20. Sylvia Molloy, "Dissappearing Acts: Reading Lesbian in Teresa de la Parra," 230–56, in *¿Entiendes? Queer Readings, Hispanic Writings,* edited by Emilie L. Bergman and Paul Julian Smith (Durham: Duke University Press, 1995), 248.

21. Ibid., 249.

22. Ibid., 251.

23. Ibid., 252.

24. Liliane Hasson, "Lydia Cabrera en los Estados Unidos," 95–103, in *En torno a Lydia Cabrera,* edited by Isabel Castellanos (Miami: Ediciones Universal, 1987), 99.

25. For example, in a 1932 letter dated Wednesday 27, Teresa suggests to Cabrera that she should publish a short story in *Revista de Occidente;* in another letter, March 1, 1933, commenting on Cabrera's recently written short story "El limo de Almendares" Teresa writes: "Lo veo en un libro (tienes para varios tomos) amenísimo" (I see it in a book [you have enough for several volumes] very enjoyable) File 0339, Series IV, Box 32.

26. Rosario Hiriart, "Conversaciones con Lydia Cabrera," File 0339, Serie I, Box 5; in a letter to Doris Meyers, February 6, 1982, Cabrera reiterates: [Teresa] "fue una hermana o una madre para mí" (was a sister or a mother for me) File 0339, Series I, Box 1. The mother/daughter relationship that Cabrera expresses was a sentiment Teresa also articulated in several of her letters to Lydia. For instance, in June 21, 1933, in a letter to Cabrera, Teresa writes: "Como soy tu madre" (Since I am your mother) File 0339, Series IV, Box 32.

27. José Quiroga, "Lydia Cabrera, Invisible," 108.

28. Quoted in Benita Parry, "Resistance Theory/Theorising Resistance," 184.

29. Ibid., 183.

30. Conversation with Lydia Cabrera at her home in 1987.

31. Arnold, *Modernism and Negritude,* 24.

32. Ibid., 288.

33. Ibid.

34. Wifredo Lam was living in France and became involved with André Breton's surrealist circle. Like Carpentier and Cabrera who eventually rejected the movement, Lam embraced it at first like Césaire, but by the mid-1950s he claimed that "it was not really his taste," Lowery Stokes Sims, *Wifredo Lam and the International Avant-Garde 1923–1982,* 89. Lam lived in Cuba during the forties before returning to France to stay. Carpentier and Lydia Cabrera were his strongest supporters during those years.

35. At the New York City Metropolitan Museum.

36. In Paris, Lydia Cabrera met, or became familiar with, numerous writers and scholars such as Marcel Proust and Albert Camus, Lucien Lévy-Bruhl, Paul Valéry, and Rudyard Kipling (whom she met in 1935); as well as Miguel Angel Asturias, Aimé Césaire, Gabriela Mistral, and others, including Leo Frobenius, and Alfred Metraux. It was later that she would meet William Bascom, and, in a trip to Paris, in 1954, she personally met Pierre Fatumbi Verger who later introduced her to Roger Bastide. Cabrera's close friendship with Verger and Bastide lasted until their deaths.

37. After reading the book, Teresa comments in favor or it: "No me extraña que a B. le parezcan poca cosa . . . ¡Qué bueno es vivir lejos de los literatos y literatizantes! ¡Cómo enturbian y complican lo que en mano de un artista es fácil y natural como el vaso de agua

fresca que se bebe con sed" (It doesn't seem strange to me that B thinks it to be of little importance . . . How good it is to live away from those of stuffy lettered affectations. How they complicate and confuse what in the hands of an artist is easy and natural like drinking a glass of water when one is thirsty), letter to Lydia Cabrera, March 3, 1933, Box 32, in Lydia Cabrera's papers, Heritage Collection, University of Miami, Florida.

38. Teresa's text also articulated a direct political criticism against the dictatorship of Juan Vicente Gómez in Venezuela, a dictator who died only a year before Teresa did. His dictatorial rule was probably one of the reasons why Teresa never returned to Venezuela to live, in spite of the deep nostalgia she felt for her homeland.

39. "What is so interesting about this work by Teresa de la Parra—observes Doris Meyer —is not just its early expression of feminist discontent in a Latin American context, but also its exploration of the human psyche and its mysterious—or apparently mysterious—motives. Without any formal training in analytical psychology, Teresa de la Parra instinctively portrayed the complex journey of an ego-conscious personality in search of self-understanding. That her protagonist should be a woman like herself, and one who is tormented by the paradoxes of a modern woman's condition (image vs. self, duty vs. desire, etc), makes this a particularly contemporary and dramatic work of literature." Doris Meyer, "'Feminine' Testimony in the Works of Teresa de la Parra, María Luisa Bombal, and Victoria Ocampo," 3–15, *Comtemporary Women Authors of Latin America* I, edited by Doris Meyer and Margarite Fernández Olmoos (New York: Brooklyn College Press, 1983), 8–9.

40. Ibid., 9.

41. Ana María Simo, *Lydia Cabrera. An Intimate Portrait,* 83. Her sister Emma was the one who introduced her to books of adventure and fantasy. This fictional world, together with the wide spectrum of social stereotypes with which she had come in contact at home and in social gatherings, intellectuals, politicians, servants, converged in her short stories in her portraits of Cuban society. At her home she had met legendary persons like Manuel Sanguilí and Enrique José Varona, the mulatto writer and politician Martín Morúa Delgado, son of a former slave; also Juan Gualberto Gómez, and Carmen Zayas Bazán, the widow of the fallen patriot José Martí (ibid.).

42. Her attraction to colonial Cuba led her to study art, and, eventually, to writing. Encouraged by her father, by the time she was fourteen years old Lydia Cabrera had published twenty-seven articles in the journal *Cuba y América*. See Natalia Aróstegui Bolívar and Natalia del Río Bolívar, *Lydia Cabrera en su laguna sagrada* (Santiago de Cuba: Editorial Oriente, 2000), 40–41. Few years later, she published another article on Japanese art, six illustrations in an article on Oriental art, and the illustrations for the cover for one of the issues of the journal. After the family's temporary absence from Cuba during a political conflict known in Cuban history as "La Chambelona," in 1917, Cabrera wrote articles for *Diario de la Marina* on a subject that had come to be her passion: the preservation of historical buildings, antique, colonial architecture, and the nation's historical past. See Cuervo Hewitt, "Lydia Cabrera," 84. See also Simo, *An Intimate Portrait,* 8; and Sara Soto, *Magia e historia en los "Cuentos negros," "¿Por qué?," and "Ayapá" de Lydia Cabrera,* 36–37.

43. Lydia Cabrera, "Letter to Teresa de la Parra," in *Páginas sueltas,* 212–14.

44. Meyer, "Feminine Testimony in the Worlds of Teresa de la Parra, María Luisa Bombal, and Victoria Ocampo," 6.

45. Fernando Ortiz, "Prologue," to Lydia Cabrera, *Cuentos negros de Cuba* (Madrid: Artes Gráficas, 1972), 9. The first publication in Spanish of this text was in 1940 (Havana: Imprenta La Verónica).

46. Ibid.

47. Cabrera did not consider her short stories to be just "translations" as Ortiz claimed. When Liliane Hasson asked Lydia Cabrera if the stories she had been writing were inventions or adaptations, she answered: "Todavía no sé" (I still do not know). Her ethnological

research was completely honest, she claimed, however: "Dans le contes . . . ce n'est pas tellement honnête! Incluso los dos últimos libros de cuentos, *Ayapá: Cuentos de jicotea* (1971) y *Cuentos para adultos y retrasados mentales* (1983)" (In the stories. . . . I am not totally honest! Even the last two books of short stories, *Ayapa, Tortoise Stories,* and *Stories for Adults and the Mentally Retarded*) Hasson, "Lydia Cabrera en los Estados Unidos," *En torno a Lydia Cabrera,* 97.

48. Pérez Firmat, *The Cuban Condition,* 4.

49. Ibid., 20.

50. Also Carpentier seems to share a similar meaning when he associates "literature" with "evasion" of reality. See, Carpentier, "Habla Alejo Carpentier," *Recopilación de textos sobre Alejo Carpentier,* 27.

51. Mignolo, *Local Histories/Global Designs,* 3.

52. Cuervo Hewitt, *Aché,* 186–87.

53. Hilda Perera, *Idapo. El sincretismo en los cuentos negros de Lydia Cabrera* (Miami: Ediciones Universal, 1971), 96.

54. Lydia Cabrera, "Taita Hicotea y Taita Tigre," 41–66, in *Cuentos negros de Cuba,* 41.

55. Lydia Cabrera, "El caballo de Hicotea," 147–149, in *Cuentos negros de Cuba,* 149.

56. Abiola Irele, "Negritude: Literature, and Ideology," in *Modern Black Novelists: A Collection of Essays,* ed. M. G. Cooke (Englewood Cliffs, New Jersey: Prentice-Hall, Inc., 1971), 22.

57. Benita Parry, "Resistance Theory/Theorising Resistance," 186.

58. Ibid., 175.

59. Ibid., 185.

60. Arnold, *Modernism and Negritude,* 52.

61. Beaupied, *Narciso hermético,* 153.

62. Maria Zambrano, "Lydia Cabrera, poeta de la metamorfosis," 8–9, in *Noticias de arte. Número Especial. Homenaje a Lydia Cabrera,* (1982), 63.

63. Hasson, "Lydia Cabrera en los Estados Unidos," 97.

64. Cuervo Hewitt, *Aché,* 53–64.

65. Ibid., 66.

66. Lydia Cabrera, "El sapo guardiero," 171–74, *Cuentos negros de Cuba,* 171.

67. About the preparation of a *nganga,* see, Cabrera, *El monte,* 119–23, and 130.

68. Cabrera, "El sapo guardiero," *Cuentos negros de Cuba,* 173.

69. Ibid., 174.

70. Ibid.

71. Ibid., 174.

72. Zambrano, "Lydia Cabrera, poeta de la metamorphosis," 62.

73. Cabrera's fictional work portrays a nativism that, in the pen of a white woman, makes her work seem condescending of Afro-Cubans. As a woman, Cabrera, like de la Parra, perceived the world as a male-dominated place in which women were also excluded and marginal. Thus, as Nissa Torrens has observed in de la Parra's work, the only possibility for the woman writer was to negate reality and "refugiarse en un mundo íntimo, en una construcción que en su caso está hecha de palabras, que es su obra creativa" (to take refuge in an intimate world, in a construction in her case made of words, her work of fiction) Torrens, "La escritura femenina de Teresa de la Parra" *Coloquio Internacional. Escritura y sexualidad en la literatura hispanoamericana,* 61.

74. "Carta de Gabriela Mistral," in *Noticias de arte. Gaceta de artes visuals, escénicas, musicales y literarias. Número especial. Homenaje a Lydia Cabrera,* 11.

75. See Rosa Valdés-Cruz, *Lo ancestral africano en la narrativa de Lydia Cabrera,* 101–3; and Florit, "Introducción," *Homenaje a Lydia Cabrera,* 4–5.

76. In a complicit literary dialogue with Cabrera, Federico García Lorca dedicates his

poem "La casada infiel" to "Lydia Cabrera y su negrita." Cabrera's "Suadende" in *Cuentos negros de Cuba,* recalls, in an Afro-Cuban context, a similar but humorous adulterous relation as the one represented by García Lorca (both women are married) that also takes place by a river. Both poems play with the popular euphemism of taking a woman to the river, for an illicit love affair.

77. Perera, *Idapo. El sincretismo en los cuentos negros de Lydia Cabrera* (Miami: Ediciones Universal, 1971), 95.

78. Reinaldo Arenas, "Diosa instalada en el centro del poema," in *Noticias del Arte. Gaceta de artes visuals, escénicas, musicales y literarios. Número especial. Homenaje a Lydia Cabrera,* 15.

79. Rosario Hiriart, *Lydia Cabrera: Vida hecha arte* (Madrid: Eliseo Torres and Sons, 1978), 38; also in Josefine Inclán, *Ayapá y otras Otan Iyebiyé de Lydia Cabrera* (Miami: Ediciones Universal, 1976), 88.

80. Edna M. Rodríguel-Mangual suggests that it was Cabrera who influenced Ortiz's views on Afro-Cuba. See Rodríguez-Mangual, *Lydia Cabrera and the Construction of an Afro-Cuban Cultural Identity* (Chapel Hill: The University of North Carolina Press, 2004). By 1936, when *Cuentos negros de Cuba* was published in France, Ortiz's views were already quite different from his views in 1906.

81. Perera, *Idapo,* 97.

82. Ibid., 95

83. André Breton, "On Surrealism in its Living Works (1953)," in André Breton, *Manifestoes of Surrealism,* trans. Richard Seaver and Helen R. Lane (Ann Arbor: The University of Michigan Press, 1969), 302. See also, Yves Duplessis, *Surrealism* (New York: Walker and Company, 1962), 36.

84. André Breton, "Manifestoes of Surrealism, (1924)" 1–29, in André Breton, *Manifestoes of Surrealism,* 20.

85. Edward Said, *Orientalism* (Vintage Books, 1994), 63.

86. Ibid., 72.

87. Ibid., 121.

88. Ibid., 77.

89. Lydia Cabrera, *Yemayá y Ochún. Kariocha, Iyalorichas y Olorichas,* 238.

90. Ibid., 238.

91. Meyer, "'Feminine' Testimony," *Contemporary Women Authors of Latin America,* 7.

92. This is a Taurine story of ancient Greek and Roman origins, inserted in a Taurine Hispanic tradition, and recontextualized by Cabrera as African. The theme of the old king dethroned by his son is also a classical one. Cabrera uses the male diminutive characteristic of Northern Spain (ín), to indicate "the son of," often used in Cuba due to the large number of immigrants from Galicia and Asturias. Thus, Bregantino is the father, and Bregantín, the son.

93. Lydia Cabrera, "Bregantino, Bregantín," 11–28, in *Cuentos negros de Cuba,* 11.

94. "It is *vox populi*—says Cabrera—that men cannot show lack of respect [to a daughter of *Yemaya*] because the goddess would not allow it . . .; They are untouchable! No dandy can raise a hand against them! The respect owed to them is a given dogma in the underworlds of Cuba, and they believe, they know by experience, the *soutenerus,* that to mistreat them would bring calamity." Cabrera, *Yemayá y Ochún,* 116–17.

95. See, Cuervo Hewitt, *Aché,* 204–9.

96. In *Orígenes* III, 9 (1946): 28–31.

97. In *Orígenes* VI, 13 (1949): 3–9.

98. Reproduced in *Wifredo Lam and His Contemporaries 1938–1952,* edited by Maria R. Balderrama, 140.

99. Lydia Cabrera, "Prologue" to *Ayapá. Cuentos de jicotea* (Miami: Ediciones Universal, 1971), 12.

100. Ibid., 10.

101. As a trickster, *jicotea* is magical, good and evil; and in its association to life and to storms, jicotea is ritual food of Shango. Apart from its trickster qualities, jicotea is related to water, and her round body to the clouds that announce storms (Shango). See, Ortiz, *El Huracán,* 213.

102. Cuervo Hewitt, *Aché,* 204–9.

103. Julia Cuervo Hewitt, "Lydia Cabrera, *Dictionary of Literary Biography* vol. 145: "Modern Latin-American Fiction Writers," Second Series, edited by William Luis and Ann González (Detroit: Gale Research Incl., 1994), 89.

104. The Spanish "J" has the sound of the English "H," which is silent in modern Spanish.

105. Fernando de Rojas, *La Celestina. Tragicomedia de Calixto y Melibea,* a classical Spanish text that dates to the end of the fifteenth century.

106. Cabrera, "La excelente Doña Jicotea Concha," 177–215, in *Ayapá,* 191.

107. Henry Louis Gates, Jr., *The Signifying Monkey: A Theory of Afro-American Literary Criticism* (New York: Oxford University Press, 1988), 237.

108. Shauna Lee Eddy, "Translation as the Meeting of Signed and Spoken Languages: The Trickster's Role in Mediating Deaf Identity Construction," 55–83, *A Tradução nas Encruzilhadas da Cultura,* ed. João Ferreira Duarte (Lisbon: Edições Colibri, 2001), 61–62.

109. Gates, *The Signifying Monkey,* 44.

110. Ibid., 52.

111. She claimed that the world she was "discovering" and the kindness of her befriended informants were the reasons why she stayed in Cuba after the war: "esta gente fue muy buena comigo. Me abrieron las puertas de un mundo que yo no podía imajinar [*sic*]. Si no, cuando acabó la guerra, me hubiera vuelto a Francia" (these people were very good to me. They opened a door for me to a world I could not have imagined. If it had not been for them, when the War [W.W.II] ended, I would have returned to France) Hasson, "Lydia Cabrera en los Estados Unidos," 99.

112. Alicia Vadillo's reading of Cuban texts in *Santería y Vodú. Sexualidad y homoerotismo. Caminos que se cruzan sobre la narrativa cubana contemporánea* (Madrid: Biblioteca Nueva, 2002), makes the interesting suggestion that contemporary Cuban fiction often rewrites and recontextualize Afro-Cuban *patakis* as subtexts.

113. Cuervo Hewitt, *Aché,* 189.

114. Gates, *The Signifying Monkey,* 82.

115. Cuervo Hewitt, *Aché,* 73–109.

116. Cabrera, "El chivo hiede," 44–52, in *¿Por qué? Cuentos negros cubanos,* 49.

117. Ibid., 50.

118. Ibid., 51.

119. Cabrera, *Yemayá y Ochún,* 117.

120. Lydia Cabrera, "How the Monkey Lost the Fruit of His Labor," translated by Mary Caldwell and Suzanne Jill Levine, in *Other Fires,* edited by Alberto Manguel (New York: Clarkson N. Potter, Inc./Publishers, 1986), translated from the Spanish "El mono perdió el fruto de su trabajo," in *¿Por qué. Cuentos negros de Cuba,* 214–19.

121. Ibid., 202.

122. Ibid., 203.

123. Ibid., 204–5.

124. This is an entity of the Afro-Cuban folklore already present in her first collection, in the short story "Taita Hicotea y Taita Tigre." In this case, Hicotea, utilizing magic to control Deer, eventually becomes the sole owner of all of the land, and sends Deer three magic "Chicherekús: muñecos de palo o niños muy viejos, muertos recién nacidos. Rostros lisos, arrebatados, sin ojos, sin nariz, sólo una boca ávida con dientes blancos de caracoles" (dolls

made out of wood or very old children, old spirits newly born. Flat faces, in rage, without eyes, without a nose, only a voracious mouth with white teeth made of shells) Cabrera, "Taita Hicotea y Taita Tigres," *Cuentos negros de Cuba,* 50. In Cuban folklore *chicherekús* are often confused with *güijes.*

125. Lydia Cabrera, *Anagó: vocabulario lucumí (el Yoruba que se habla en Cuba)* (Miami: Ediciones Universal, 1986), 91. First published in Havana: Ediciones C & R, 1957.

126. Perera, *Idapo,* 80.

127. Cabrera, *Yemaya y Ochún,* 314.

128. Cabrera, *El monte,* 429.

129. Cabrera, "Susudamba no se muestra de día," 101–19, in *¿Por qué?,* 106–8.

130. Ibid., 118.

131. Ibid., 119.

132. Gertrudis Gómez de Avellaneda, *Sab* (Havana: Instituto del libro, 1973), 316. This novel, the first antislavery novel written in Cuba, was written in 1939, before the publication of *Uncle Tom's Cabin.* It was published in 1841.

133. She was a disciple of the Cuban poet, José María Heredia, a strong supporter of Cuba's independence.

134. Said, *Culture and Imperialism,* 193.

135. Irele, "Literature and Ideology," in *Modern Black Novelists,* 15.

136. For an explanation of the polemics during this period pertaining to America, see Antonello Gerbi, *La disputa del Nuevo Mundo (Historia de una polémica (1750–1900)* (Mexico: Fondo de Cultura Económica, 1955; 1993).

137. Edward Said, *Culture and Imperialism* (New York: Random House, Inc., 1994), 275.

138. In this fable, Oshun dances and her ritual dance charms all of those present: "Madre Nuestra, Bendita Virgen del Cobre sandunguera, Ochún-panchákara, puta divina que por el amor gobierna el mundo . . . Ella es el río . . . Se desliza, fluye entre juncos, entre márgenes de torsos que se mecen transportados al ritmo de la onda milagrosa; y sus brazos lustrosos y sus caderas sabias ondulan rápidas como el agua" (Our Mother, Blessed *Virgen del Cobre,* flirtatious, Oshun-panchákara, divine whore who governs the world through love . . . She is the river . . . Slippery, she flows through the canes, between the margins of bodies swaying transported by the rhythm of the miraculous wave; and her radiant arms and her wise hips undulate swiftly like the water) Cabrera, "El chivo hiede," *¿Por qué?,* 47–48.

139. As Cabrera points out, the Virgin of Charity from El Cobre (*Virgen de la Caridad del Cobre*), appeared over the water to two indigenous men and a black man. Her apparition was legally documented, in 1703, by Don Onefre de Fonseca, but she was declared Patron Saint of Cuba by Pope Benedicto XV, May 10, 1916. See, Cabrera, *Yemayá y Ochún,* 56.

140. Ibid., 55.

141. Ibid., 117.

142. Ibid., 69.

143. Ibid., 73.

144. Ibid., 69.

145. Ibid.

146. Cabrera's reference to the lavish mulatto woman of the nineteenth century is reminiscent of the image of the Cuban mulatto woman in Cirilo Villaverde in *Cecilia Valdés* (1882). Here Cecilia is a metaphor for the complexities of a mulatto society that resulted from centuries of slavery. Landaluce also makes a portrait of this popular "type" in colonial Cuba, in his drawing, "La mulata de rumbo." See Victor Landaluze, *Tipos y costumbres de la isla de Cuba: Colección de artículos* (Havana: Miguel de Villa, 1881), 32.

147. The powerful Oshun reigns over days five, ten, and fifteen (Cabrera, *Yemayá y Ochún,* 257). Her number is five so she wears five copper bracelets; her color is yellow; and

she is associated with *oñí* (honey), the sweetness of her seductive femininity with which she domesticates the harsh deity that presides over iron and metals, and who reigns in the deepest parts of the forests (Ogun): male principle of the monte. Among Oshun's ritual animals are the dove, chicken, deer, and the peacock (Ibid., 280).

148. Yemayá has seven different roads or avatars (ibid., 30): like the ocean, she can be stormy and calm (Ibid., 119), and, like the ocean waters, her color is blue. Her sacrificial food is lamb, which is also *Shango's* food, and rooster. Mother and son often eat together (ibid., 277). She reigns over days seven, fourteen, and twenty-one of the month.

149. Ibid., 18.

150. Ibid.

151. Cabrera, "Apopoito Miama," 109–16, in *Cuentos negros,* 109.

152. *Ashe* (in Spanish *aché),* from the *Yoruba àsé,* is a salutation that calls forth all good things, all life-giving forces.

153. Gates, *The Signifying Monkey,* 85.

154. Pérez Firmat, *The Cuban Condition,* 20.

155. Cabrera, *El monte,* 8.

156. Ibid., 9.

157. Cuervo Hewitt, *Aché,* 78–79.

158. Ibid., 76.

159. Rogelio Martínez Furé found in some of these *libreras* "fragments of books edited by the English university of Oxford about African Yorubas, that had been acquired by mail and translated by some university educated *santero.*" See: Martínez Furé, *Diálogo imaginarios* (Havana: Editorial Arte y Literatura, 1979), 211–12. See also, Cuervo Hewitt, *Aché,* 79.

160. Cabrera, *Anagó,* 297.

161. Hasson, "Lydia Cabrera en los Estados Unidos," 97.

162. Cabrera published her own dictionaries of Cuban Yoruba (Lucumí), *Anagó;* Cuban Bantu (*congo*), *Diccionario congo;* and Abakuá ritual language, *La lengua sagrada de los ñáñigos;* and added glosaries to her texts to help her readers understand Afro-Cuban terms. Yet, a Cuban reader today can grasp the essence and paradoxes of the cultural codes in Cabrera's works without such dictionaries since many of the most popular terms have made their way into colloquial speech.

163. Bill Ashcroft, Gareth Griffith, and Helen Tifflin, *The Empire Writes Back: Theory and Practice in Post-Colonial Literatures* (London: Routledge, 1989), 52.

164. Ibid., 53.

165. Ibid.

166. Ibid., 55.

167. The same can be said about other texts written by Lydia Cabrera. Isabel Castellanos notes that an acquaintance told her that after her initiation to *Regla de Ocha,* a Lucumí order, her initiate godmother told her to read Cabrera's *Kaeko Iyawó, aprende novicia; pequeño tratado de regal lucumí* (1980). It was in Cabrera's book where she learned to *moyubar* (to greet the saints or *orishas*). See Castellanos, "Abre Kutu Wiri Ndinga: Lydia Cabrera y las lenguas africanas," 212–26, in *En torno a Lydia Cabrera,* edited by Isabel Castellanos and Josefina Inclán (Miami: Ediciones Universal, 1987), 216.

168. For Wifredo Lam, "landscape becomes a metaphor for cultural identity" (Herzberg, "Wifredo Lam: The Development of a Style and World View, The Havana Years, 1941–1952," in *Wifredo Lam and His Contemporaries,* 45). Lam, says Lowery Stokes Sims, "pointed out that the title of "The Jungle" "has nothing to do with the real countryside of Cuba, where there is no jungle but woods, hills, and open country" . . . his painting "was intended to communicate a psychic state" rather than a geographic phenomenom (ibid., 64). The same sense of feminine landscape was also present in Aimé and Suzanne Césaire's

work. For Suzanne Césaire, "black Antilleans were 'doubly true to themselves' being 'close to a universal life force-nature.'" "Malaise d'un Civilization," *Tropiques* 5 (April 1942) 45; also quoted in Lowery Stokes Sims, *Wifredo Lam and the International Avant-Garde 1923–1982,* 137.

169. In Cuba, the *ceiba* tree, like the *Iroco* in Africa, is the tree associated with Oshun, and also a metaphor for the Afro-Cuban monte.

170. Cabrera, *El monte,* 13.

171. Ibid.

172. Ibid.

173. Ibid.

174. Lydia Cabrera, "Taita Hicotea y Taita Tigre," 41–66, in *Cuentos negros de Cuba,* 49.

175. Banana and plantain flowers are called in Cuba *tetas,* due to their resemblance to a woman's breast.

176. In Afro-Caribbean rituals, the presence of the deities, whether loas or orishas manifest themselves through the possession of a person, an initiate son or daughter of the deity. This presence is known as *montar* or *cabalgar,* meaning to mount and or ride a horse, the later being the human being possessed or mounted by the deity. In Lam's painting, the head of the horse suggests the relationship of human deity and the always already presence of natural forces in the Afro-Cuban monte.

177. *Menso* or *mensu* is an Afro-Cuban altar, associated with Congo (Bantu) belief systems, shaped like a small mound of sacred objects, with a mirror placed flat on top of the heap-like altar.

178. Cabrera defines *Pataki, Patakín,* as: "Tales, narrations from ancient times about the *orishas.* From the *Odu* of *Ifa* and the *Dilogún.*" Cabrera, *Anagó,* 297.

179. *Babalawos* cannot be women. Cabrera explains that the *Mamalochas* or *Iyalochas* are allowed to do everything the Babalawo does, except to sacrifice a four-legged animal, to prepare certain eleguá and osaín and to divine with okuelé and ikis. Nevertheless, Cabrera notes that her elderly informant, Bamboché, had heard in his youth of an African woman who used the ikis in rituals of divination, but not in Havana, in the interior of the island. Cabrera, *Yemayá y Ochún,* 236.

180. Guillermo Cabrera Infante, "Lydia Cabrera," 16–17, *Homenaje a Lydia Cabrera,* 16. Writing from his home in London, after his rejection of the Cuban Revolution, Cabrera Infante tells Lydia Cabrera in a letter that he tried to find a publisher interested in translating *El Monte* to English. In another letter dated March 14, 1963, he describes *El monte* as: "ese libro extraño, maravilloso, mágico: tan cubano y tan africano y tan americano, tan salvaje y tan sofisticado . . . y tan sabio" (that rare book, marvelous, magic: so Cuban and so African and so American, so savage, and so sophisticated . . . and so wise). In other letters, September 28, 1970, May 22, 1975, September 30, 1978, he again praises *El monte,* and reiterates the need to publish the book in English. File 0339, Serie I, Box 5, Folder 5, in Lydia Cabrera's Papers, Heritage Collection, University of Miami, Florida.

181. Sara Soto, *Magia e historia en los "Cuentos negros," "¿Por qué?' y "Ayapá" de Lydia Cabrera,* 43.

182. All references to Guillermo Cabrera Infante, *Tres tristes tigres* ((Barcelona: Editorial Seix Barral, S. A., 1965), will appear in the text as *TTT.* All citations from the English translation will appear in the text as *TTrappedT.* Guillermo Cabrera Infante, *Three Trapped Tigers,* translated by Suzanne Jill Levine and Donald Gardner (New York: Harper and Row, Publisher, Inc. Marlowe and Co., 1971). Cabrera Infante's phonetic juegos, games, are not unlike Lydia Cabrera's linguistic play in her works of fiction. She creates words that sound like Spanish, and others that sound like African words, intermixed with actual African and *bozal* words, or a parody of bozal, in Cuba. Some of Cabrera Infante's puns in this quote

are a parody of Cabrera's writing. For example: "Cacha is Caridad," a reference to Oshun, the *Virgen de la Caridad del Cobre,* from the area of Santiago in the province of Oriente, in the avatar of Oshun Yeyé she is popularly known as "Cachita" (Cabrera, *Yemayá y Ochún,* 69); *trabajo* is a ritual job or sacred magic preparation; *olla* is the same as *caldero* (a recipient to cook, but here a reference to a sacred object often found in Afro-Cuban altars)*; tshévere* is *chévere,* good; *n'oisima* would be *misiva nociva* or evil mission; *of'aboru,* is a play with the signifier *favor* (please), etc.

183. There are moments when the English translation does not convey the same meaning as the Spanish version. In those cases I offer my own translation.

184. An example of Cabrera's transcription of African voices to Cuban vernacular Spanish can be found in her short story "Chéggue," where she takes the words of a Yoruba song and, faithful to the meanings of the words in the African song, seems to be transcribing them by creating a phonetic echo of the original. For example, she writes: "Tanike Chéggue nibe ún/ Chéggue ono chono ire ló/ Chéggue tá larroyo . . ." (Cabrera, "Chéggue," in *Cuentos negros de Cuba,* 30), instead of the words in the Yoruba song, "Tanike pe Shegbe ni beun." Cuervo Hewitt, *Aché,* 186–87. At the end of the story Cabrera writes simulating Spanish bozal: "Chéggue tá larroyo" (Chégge está en el arroyo) (Cheggue is at the creek). The *bozal* words offer a different ending to the African song: "We do not know where he [Shegbe] is" (ibid.).

185. Cabrera Infante also mimics Lydia Cabrera's writings in her attempt to translate Afro-Cuban terms, and like in her books, he adds a dictionary of terms at the end of the story of the death of Trotsky supposedly told by Lydia Cabrera. In it, playing with the slippage of the sign, he provides nonsensical definitions, like: "*Babalao: babalosha en lucumí* (in *Lucumí*); *Babalosh: babalao,* también en lucumí (also in *Lucumí); Guámpara: wampara,* Swahili. Del árabe (From the Arab) *Wamp'r,"* (*TTT,* 237).

186. Unpublished paper by José Piedra, "Monte: Poetics in a Clearing of the Forest." I am grateful to Aida Beaupied for allowing me to read a copy of this insightful paper she received years ago from José Piedra when they were graduate students at Yale University.

187. The title of the text is an explanation of the conditions under which he wrote it: an autobiography and a condemnation of a political system that kept him from writing, and persecuted him. Arenas's life and writings were constant acts of running away and hiding. In fact, he wrote this text while hiding in Lenin Park where he could only write during the daytime while it was daylight, before "night fell," thus the title *Before Night Falls.*

188. José Martí, *Versos sencillos, La gran Encyclopedia Martiana,* 12, 34.

189. José Piedra, "*Monte:* Poetics in a Clearing of the Forest," Unpublished paper written at Yale University, 1.

190. Ibid.

191. Cuervo Hewitt, *Aché,* 38–42.

192. Lydia Cabrera's books actually sold very well right after the Revolution. It was later, when they were out of print and censorship became stricter, that her texts were not reedited.

193. Lydia Cabrera, *La sociedad secreta Abakuá, narrada por viejos adeptos* (Miami: Editorial C. R (Colección del Chicherekú), 1970), 10–11. These Positivist theories that Cabrera rejects were the same theories that considered one of the most important Cuban patriots, Antonio Maceo, an anomaly because he was a mulatto. After his death, his body was exhumed and his skull measured to understand why a mulatto showed characteristics and virtues associated with "whiteness." Ada Ferrer points out that: "the anthropologists in 1900 were proud to report that Maceo's skull, in size and weight, was closer to the skulls of "modern Parisians" than to those of "African blacks." Ferrer, *Insurgent Cuba,* 168.

194. Guillermo Cabrera Infante, *Vidas para leerlas* (Madrid: Alfaguara, 1998), 99.

195. The intellectual and government officials finally noted her importance. Since the nineties *El monte* and other texts by Cabrera published in Cuba before she left the island are being published again in Cuba.

196. The Cuban Revolution that once restricted Afro-Cuban religious practices as superstitions and fetichism finally came to allow the open display of those beliefs and traditions, but as national "folklore." The government even encouraged them, but not as religious practices. Afrocubanía brought Cuba closer to the African countries like Angola and emphasized Cuba's unique culture as African. However, while Afro-Cuban "folklore" was accepted, religious faith was not. Carlos Moore points out that soon after Castro came into power "Castro restricted drumming in public places" and, as of 1961, restrictions were imposed on Afro-Cuban religions and festivities. "The regime's struggle to stamp out Afro-Cuban religious fraternities became a permanent feature of Castroite policy towards Cuba's domestic Africa. Religious leaders began suffering arrest and at time imprisonment in the mid-sixties, and at least one case of execution by firing squad was reported by the end of the decade." Moore, *Castro, the Blacks, and Africa,* 100.

197. Ibid., 37, 59.

198. José Quiroga, "Lydia Cabrera, Invisible," 104.

199. Cabrera Infante, *Vidas para leerlas,* 99.

200. Chao, *Palabras en el tiempo de Alejo Carpentier,* 170.

201. All references to *Tres tristes tigres* will be indicated as *TTT,* and to the English translation as *TTrappedT.*

202. Silvestre was also the name of the writer of the first epic-poem about Cuba, Silvestre de Balboa, *Espejo de paciencia* (Mirror of Patience), 1608. The hero in this epic-poem, Salvador, is an African servant.

203. Rita Guibert, "Guillermo Cabrera Infante: Conversación sobre *Tres tristes tigres,*" 19–46, in *G. Cabrera Infante,* edited by Julián Ríos (Madrid: Editorial Fundamentos, 1974), 25; Also in: Emir Rodríguez Monegal, "Las fuentes de la narración," 41–58, *Mundo Nuevo* 25 (1968), 58.

204. González Echeverría, *Voice of the Masters,* 140.

205. Cabrera Infante writes in a letter to Lydia Cabrera: "Usted veía el sol como la cara de Batista, chorreando sangre . . . una premonición cierta . . . el temor de ver sangre correr" (You saw in the sun the face of Batista, bleeding . . . a true premonition . . . the fear to see blood run) In the Lydia Cabrera's Papers, File 0339, Series I, Box 5, Folder 5, at the Heritage Collection, Miami University, Florida.

206. Most of these readings try to find order in a book that, as Stephanie Merrim notes is the consensus among critics, is "disjointed," and such a "collage of many styles and genres that there seems to be no binding force." Sephanie Merrim, "A Secret Idiom: The Grammar and Role of Language in *Tres tristes tigres,*" 323–41, in *Modern Latin American Fiction,* edited by Harold Bloom (New York: Chelsea House Publishers, 1990), 323. Merrim suggests that to read the text as "metalanguage—a comment on the workings of language itself, shows that there is a consistency and development of style" (ibid., 323). Her approach is to read the text from the point of view of Menippean satire, as metalanguage, in order to find that the text articulates: "a cohesive language;" when read as metalanguage. Thus, Merrim suggests that: *"Tres tristes tigres* [offers] an orderly if otherly, textual universe" (ibid., 341).

207. Rosa María Pereda, *Cabrera Infante* (Barcelona: EDAF, Ediciones-Distribuciones, S.A., 1979), 101.

208. Emir Rodríguez Monegal, "Estructuras y significaciones de *Tres tristes tigres,*" 81–127, in *Cabrera Infante,* 112. This article was also published in *Sur* 320 (1969): 38–51.

209. Raymond D. Souza, *Guillermo Cabrera Infante. Two Islands, Many Worlds* (Austin: University of Texas Press, 1996), 89.

210. Enrico Mario Santí, *Bienes del siglo. Sobre cultura cubana* (Mexico: Fondo de Cultura Económica, 2002), 275.

211. Ibid., 259.

212. Pereda, *Cabrera Infante*, 101.

213. Souza, *Guillermo Cabrera Infante: Two Islands*, 97.

214. Guibert, "Guillermo Cabrera Infante. Conversación sobre *Tres tristes tigres*," 33.

215. Pereda, *Cabrera Infante*, 139.

216. Mario Carreño paints "Cuarto Fambá" in 1943. Wifredo Lam not only represented the ñáñigo in an untitled oil painting known as "*ñáñigo*" (1943), but many of Lam's motifs, as the diamonds, crisscrosses and triangles, as Robert Farris Thompson points out in *Face of the Gods: Art and Altars of Africa and the African Americas* (Prestel: Museum for African Art, 1993), 48–55, are informed by Abakuá symbology. See also Lowery Stokes Sims, *Wifredo Lam and the International Avant-Garde 1923–1982*, 60.

217. Guibert, "Conversación sobre *Tres tristes tigres*," 22.

218. Sharon Magnorelli, "The 'Writerly' in *Tres tristes tigres*," in *The Analysis of Hispanic Texts: Current Trends and Methodology*, edited by Lisa E. Davis and Isabel C. Tarán (New York: Bilingual Press, 1976), 320–35.

219. González Echeverría, *The Voice of the Masters*, 140.

220. Suzanne Jill Levine, "Translation as (sub)version: On Translating Infante's Inferno," 75–85, in *Rethinking Translation. Discourse, Subject, Ideology*, edited by Lawrence Venuti (London: Routledge, 1992), 77.

221. Cabrera Infante, *Vidas para leerlas*, 99.

222. Moore, *Castro, the Blacks, and Africa*, 100.

223. Ibid., 98–99.

224. Souza, *Guillermo Cabrera Infante. Two Islands*, 39.

225. Rodríguez Monegal, "Las Fuentes de la narración," 47.

226. The front cover of the first edition of *TTT* represents contemporary Cuban music in pre Revolutionary Cuba with the photo of Cuban black musicians.

227. Walterio Carbonell, *Crítica. Cómo surgió la cultura nacional* (Havana: Ediciones Yaka, 1961), 108; quoted and translated in Moore, *Castro, the Blacks, and Africa*, 99.

228. Souza, *Guillermo Cabrera Infante. Two Islands*, 39–42.

229. Cabrera Infante claims that he soon realized that this book was a sort of treason against his own principles and aesthetic. See, Rodríguez Monegal, "Las Fuentes de la narración," 50. The text won the Seix-Barral award that year, but it was not published until 1974 in Spain, after suffering further censorship by the Spanish publisher

230. Rodríguez Monegal, "Las fuentes de la narración," 48.

231. Perera, *Cabrera Infante*, 14.

232. Rodríguez Monegal, "Las fuentes de la narración," 47.

233. Santí, *Bienes del siglo*, 274.

234. Cabrera Infante, *Vidas para leerlas*, 274.

235. This notion of "spirit" relates to Cabrera Infante's earlier attraction to the character of a cartoon book, *The Spirit*; this character appears in diffent forms in *Así en la paz como en la guerra*, in the character of Silvestre (Sylvestre), and in several other of Cabrera Infante's short stories, as well as in *TTT*. Souza, *Guillermo Cabrera Infante: Two Islands*, 54.

236. Cabrera, *La sociedad secreta Abakuá*, 10.

237. Ibid., 25.

238. Cabrera Infante sees humor, in the way it is used by two of his most admired writers, Lewis Carroll and Mark Twain, as a "tool against madness and the night, humor as the revealer of the great absurd of life." Rodríguez Monegal, "Las fuentes de la narración," 57.

239. Santí, *Bienes del siglo,* 263.

240. Ibid., 272.

241. Ibid., 263.

242. Rodríguez Monegal, "Las fuentes de la narración," 48.

243. Ibid.

244. His first job was in 1946 as translator for the newspaper *Hoy.* See Pereda, *Cabrera Infante,* 109.

245. Niall Lucy, *Postmodern Literary Theory: An Introduction* (Oxford UK: Blackwell Publishers Ltd, 1997), 10.

246. Cabrera Infante suggests that *TTT* has had such an unexpected success with non-Cuban Spanish speakers because: "our language [Spanish] is our only identity not of origin, but of verbal structures, in which our precarious thoughts are based." Guibert, "Conversación sobre *Tres tristes tigres,* 38.

247. However, one cannot forget that Lévi-Strauss's *Tristes Tropiques* has inscribed in the very process of its writing a sense of escape and persecussion for it "tells," in the moment in which it is written, of the voyage away from a France occupied by the Nazi, to America. Lévi-Strauss traveled escaping from Nazi France with Lam and Holzer, and Breton and his family, March 1941, to Martinique. Stokes Sims notes that "the condition of their stay has been described variously as an 'internment,'" *Wifredo Lam and the International Avant-Garde 1923–1982,* 32. Such tale of escape coincides with the time when Aimé Césaire began the publication in Martinique of the journal *Tropiques.*

248. Rodríguez Monegal, "Las fuentes de la naración," 55–56.

249. Lévi-Strauss, *The Raw and the Cooked,* 5.

250. Lucy, *Postmodern Literary Theory,* 8.

251. Clause Lévi-Strauss, "The Structural Study of Myth," 836–844, in *Critical Tradition,* edited by David H. Richter (Boston: Bedford/St. Martin's, 1998), 838. Lévi-Strauss proposes here, referring to Jules Michelet's *Histoire de la Revolution française IV,* that: "Myth is the part of language where the formula *traduttore, traditore,* reaches its lowest truth value" (Ibid.); and adds: "Myth is language functioning on an especially high level where meaning succeeds practically at 'taking off' from the linguistic ground on which it keeps on rolling" (Ibid.). *TTT's* utilization of the phrase *traduttore, traditore,* proposes an implicit dialogue with Michelet's history of the French Revolution, with Lévi-Strauss's ideas, and with the conditions under which Lévi-Strauss wrote *Triste Tropiques.*

252. Cabrera Infante, *Vidas para leerlas,* 103.

253. Comparisons have been made between the Freemasons and the Abakuá. Both are fraternities that excluded women, and that have secret initiations associated with a mythical death, as well as other secrets that can not be revealed. In pre-Revolutionary Cuba, an Abakuá could be also a Mason. Both secret organizations shared a history of persecutions, and both were victims of misunderstandings.

254. Cabrera, *La sociedad secreta Abakuá,* 274.

255. Enrique Rodríguez Sosa, *Los ñáñigos* (Havana: Casa de las Américas, 1982), 55.

256. Cabrera, *El monte,* 212.

257. Castellanos, *Las religiones afrocubanas. Cultura africana* III, 219.

258. Morúa Delgado, *La familia Unzúanzu* (Havana: Editorial arte y literatura, 1975), 120–121; the novel was published for the first time in Havana, in 1901.

259. Sosa Rodríguez, *Los ñáñigos,* 55.

260. Ibid., 97. Slaves from this area were known as *Carabalíes.*

261. Ibid., 90, 94. Jorge and Isabel Castellanos note that the name for this secret society was *Ngbe,* but came to be known as *Ekpe,* a term that means 'leopard' in the language *Efik* that came to be the dominant group in the region. See, *Las religiones afrocubanas* III, 211.

262. Sosa Rodríguez, *Los ñáñigos,* 90.

263. In Cuba, the náñigos picked up traces of a European chivalric sense of honor. Since it is also a society of mutual support, the dishonor of any member of the group enhances the already present conflicts between groups or *potencias*. The Abakuá were vehemently persecuted, which made them feel a close identification with the Masons in spite of the differences between them. Abakuá societies were most prominent in Havana, Cárdenas, and Matanzas.

264. Sosa Rodríguez, *Los ñáñigos,* 96.

265. *Plante* in Cuba means "to plant," "strike," "mutiny," but it also evoques the notion of deceit, to leave someone waiting, to stand someone up, and, as in the Abakuá ritual, to "perform," represent, create an appearance, or show off.

266. Cabrera, *La sociedad secreta Abakuá,* 21.

267. Ibid., 21, 24–25.

268. Ibid., 14.

269. Santí, *Bienes del siglo,* 263.

270. Cabrera. *El monte,* 211.

271. Ibid., 53.

272. Cabrera Infante was part Chinese.

273. José Baltar Rodríguez, *Los chinos en Cuba. Apuntes etnográficos* (Havana: Fundación Fernando Ortiz, 1997), 173–84.

274. Castellanos, *Las religiones afrocubanas* III, 212.

275. As an example, see, Gaston Baquero's "testimony" to Lydia Cabrera, 11–15, in *Homenaje a Lydia Cabrera,* 14–15.

276. *Tres tristes tigres* is also the title of a Gilberto Gazcon Mexican movie from the forties, a comedy, about three *charros* (with Luís Aguilar, Joaquín Cordero, and Dagoberto Rodríguez), in search of women.

277. The archetypal symbolism of number three is unity, the one: the oneness of the three elements, a trinity, in contrast to the duality of the two, opposition, and its multiples. Cirlot, *Diccionario de símbolos,* (Barcelona: Editorial Labor S.A., 1988), 329. Multiples of three, especially $3 \times 3 = 9$ represents mystic unity.

278. Castellanos, *Las religiones afrocubanas* III, 224.

279. Guibert, "Guillermo Cabrera Infante. Conversación sobre *Tres tristes tigres,*" 20.

280. *TTT* reiterates variations and multiple references to number three throughout the text: for example, Cué thinks he hears three gunshots (*TTT* 60), three things occurred (*TTT,* 54), there were three questions (*TTT,* 48).

281. In the Orient, says Cirlot, there are five mythical tigers invested with a similar symbolism as in Christiany. There are four guardians, like the four evangelists in the Bible that guard the Christic figure. The four tigers represent the four cardinal points surrounding the fifth one, which is its center. The first tiger is associated with red and fire and reigns in the south; the second one is associated with black and water, and reigns in the north; the third one is associated with blue and vegetables or plants and reigns in the east; and the fourth one is associated with white and metals and reigns in the west; the fifth tiger is associated with the color yellow and with the Sun, and reigns over the entire earth. Cirlot, *Diccionario de símbolos,* 441–42. In *TTT* Cué, Codac, Silvestre, and Eribó recall the four tigers surrounding an absent fifth one, Bustrófedon, the mysterious phenomenom of linguistic transformation whose ways and voice have been deeply inscribed in his friends' mode of speaking, and in their thoughts. Like the mythological tigers, Cué's name, Arsenio, or as Silvestre calls him, Arson, is a word associated with fire (*TTT* 96). Eribó is a mulatto drummer, thus related to music, which in *TTT* is always associated with water. Silvestre is a writer whose name is associated with the plant world since his name is derivative of wild flora. Códac is a photographer whose profession and name associates him with metals. Lastly, Bustrófedon, whose name identifies him with a way of reading, an oracle, one line in one direction

and the other in the opposite direction (Pereda, *Cabrera Infante,* 84) left the echo of his voice in all of the others, most especially in the writer Silvestre and the radio voice actor Cué. In *TTT,* Bustrófedon can be taken as a trope for the solar center of the novel. He is revealed to the reader only through the speech and anecdotes of his tetramorphic friend tigers that function in the novel as his friend-disciples. In Christian symbology these are the four archers that defend the Christic truth. It could be argued then that in the textual counterpoint between mythological (Chinese and Christian) and textual "tigers," in *TTT* there is a truth being defended and guarded in a *decir para callar* (speak in order to not speak, or tell) like in the Abakuá code of secrecy. It is, furthermore, a secret revealed through silence, in a codified text whose *juegos* are modes of concealing a secret.

282. Silvio is a derivative of Silva, and Silva of Selva, meaning jungle, forest, and monte. In Spanish literature, Silva is a poetic structure composed of a combination of verses of seven and eleven syllables.

283. This drum is identified often with Sikán. It is silent, it is not played, and is associated with the communion wafer, and the chalise, even with the *Corpus Christi.* It is believed that it holds all of the forces of "Mother Nature," (Castellanos, *Las religiones afrocubanas* III, 225), thus, of the monte.

284. Sosa Rodríguez, *Los ñáñigos,* 158.

285. Cabrera, *La sociedad secreta secreta Abakuá,* 116.

286. Ibid., 118.

287. Ibid., 116.

288. Cabrera, *La sociedad secreta Abakuá,* 118.

289. Cabrera, *Anaforuana,* 61.

290. Perhaps following the notion in the novel that translation is always treason, Levine's translation of *TTT* transforms the meaning of the Spanish version indicating that Sikán "is the fibber of Efí" and that she takes Ekué to Efí. The Spanish edition indicates that she took Ekué to Efó, she was from Efó, and it was in Efó where her story was not believed (*TTT,* 89). In *TTT* the Abakuá myth is also transformed into a story of persecusion (Sikán persecutes the fish and traps it) and she is then punished (Sikán is killed in an act of treason by her own people for telling and showing a truth). Telling, in *TTT* is a revisionist mythmaking act that speaks of a lived Socratic experience of telling, punished by death.

291. Rodríguez Monegal, "Estruturas y significaciones de *Tres tristes tigres,* 90.

292. Cabrera, *La sociedad secreta Abakuá,* 96–97.

293. Ibid., 258.

294. Olavo Alén, "Las sociedades de tumba francesa en Cuba," 223–37, in *Anales de Caribe* (Havana: Centro del Estudio del Caribe, Casa de las Américas, 1982), 227.

295. Meaning that the closet is the place where he stores his drum-urn (bongó); both, the closet and the bongó are *tumbas:* tombs, urns. Gardner and Levine change the signifying play of words when they translate Eribó's words as "I brushed up my *tumbadora* (a *tumba* is not a tomb, a joke I repeat like a ritual . . ." (*TTrappedT,* 86). The translation here, apart from communicating the opposite meaning, seems to want to emphasize the idea *TTT* reiterates that all language (all writing) is translation, and translation is treason, always different (in this case contrary) from the original.

296. Cabrera, *La lengua sagrada de los ñáñigos,* 480.

297. Cabrera, *El monte,* 211.

298. Guibert, "Conversación sobre *Tres tristes tigres,* 22.

299. The character is inspired by a woman Cuban singer Cabrera Infante met in Cuba nicknamed Freddy who died later in Puerto Rico (Rodríguez Monegal, "Estructuración y significación en *TTT"* 101), not in Mexico, as in *TTT.*

300. Pereda, *Cabrera Infante,* 140.

301. Ibid., 55.

302. Ibid., 55.

303. Juan Eduardo Cirlot, *Diccionario de símbolos,* 195.

304. Morínigo, *Diccionario de americanismos,* 81.

305. Mirrors are important in some Afro-Cuban practices and belief systems. In the *mensus,* sacred altars used by Congo Afro-Cuban priests, a mirror is placed flat on top of the altar to reflect the invisible: the cosmic realm of existence. In literature, the mirror is also related to water, and both, mirror and water, to the subconscious, imagination, self-contemplation, and recognition. See, Cirlot, *Diccionario de símbolos,* 194–95. The mirror, as implied in Cabrera Infante's text, is also for the Abakuá the magic space in which, like in the space of the text-*Famba,* the oneiric, the divine, is presenced or reflected, upon the real.

306. Cabrera, *La sociedad secreta Abakuá,* 82.

307. The Arawaks in Cuba believed that what differenciated the dead from the living was the absence of the navel in the dead.

308. Cabrera Infante, "Vidas para leerlas," *Vueltas* 4, no. 41 (1980), 10.

309. Cabrera, *La sociedad secreta Abakuá,* 81.

310. Ibid., 65. Some of the versions gathered by Lydia Cabrera suggest that the mystery that speaks in Ekué is the voice of the Ekoi, the ancestral voices of the elders and ancestors of the Abakuá. Other versions tell that it was the Supreme Being, *Abasi,* whose voice is heard in the coarse roar of the fish (ibid., 65); other versions tell that Tanze was an old divine king of the Ekoi that incarnated in the fish found by Sikán (ibid., 88). Just like Yawheh is semblance of the name of God that cannot be spoken, for the Abakuá, the voice in Ekué only reveals itself to the initiates as a weak memory, a shadow, and an echo of the divine Voice (ibid., 95).

311. Ibid., 66.

312. Castellanos, *Las religiones afrocubanas* III, 234.

313. Cabrera, *La sociedad secreta Abakuá,* 39.

314. Ibid., 108.

315. Ibid., 274.

316. Ibid., 275.

317. Cabrera, *El monte,* 210.

318. Ibid., 282.

319. Ibid., 215.

320. Cabrera, *La sociedad secreta Abakuá,* 82.

321. Ibid.

322. For the Abakuá, water is the elements of the dead. See, Cabrera, *La sociedad secreta,* 274. In other Afro-Cuban belief systems, as in other syncretic religious systems, water is also the element of the spirit. It was common in Cuba to place a glass of water in certain places of the house for the spirits. Cabrera Infante tells Perera that in his family his wife, Miriam Gómez, has the special private ritual of the changing of the water. Pereda, *Cabrera Infante,* 139. Cuban *Lucumí* groups, like the *Yoruba* in Nigeria, greet the orishas by pouring water on the ground.

323. In *The Old Man and the Sea,* the respect and honor of this man as a fisherman is entangled with the mythical fish he finally catches but then loses at the end of the novel. He cannot gain any monetary profit from the skeleton he brings to shore, but he regains his honor. After such feat, no one questions again the valor and the skill of the old man.

324. Cabrera Infante suggests that *TTT* was censored in Havana not for being a political text, but for its affirmation of freedom, because "freedom is always subversive." Guibert, "Conversaciones sobre *Tres tristes tigres,* 30.

325. Castellanos, *Las religiones afrocubanas* III, 222.

326. According to Raymond Souza, Lydia Cabrera and Virgilio Piñera were the only ones delighted with Cabrera Infante's parody. Carpentier was offended by it. See Souza, *Guillermo Cabrera Infante: Two Islands,* 91.

327. Castellanos, *Las religiones afrocubanas* III, 250–51.

328. Julio Matas observes that the way the characters speak in *TTT* recalls Virgilio Piñera's mode of speaking and "impersonal sobriety." Matas, "Infiernos fríos de Virgilio Piñera," *Linden Lane* IV, no. 2 (1985), 22–25.

329. González Echeverría, *The Voice of the Masters,* 139.

330. Cabrera Infante, "The Death of Virgilio Piñera," *Cold Tales,* trans. Mark Schafer (Hygiene, CO: Eridamos Press, 1987), xii.

331. Cabrera, *La sociedad secreta Abakuá,* 39.

332. Ibid., 218.

333. Castellanos, *Las religiones afrocubanas* III, 240.

334. Ibid., 222.

335. Ibid., 238.

336. Ibid.

337. Ibid., 226.

338. The word Sikán or *Sikaneka,* notes Sosa Rodríguez, is a term that seems to derive from *nsi,* meaning earth, and *kan,* a term that means in *Efik* "to win," "to conquer." Sosa proposes that *sika=nsikan* renders the meaning of "he who wins the land." At the same time, *eka* in Efik means (grand)mother, thus rendering the possible meaning of the "(grand)mother or mother who wins the land." See Sosa Rodríguez, *Los ñáñigos,* 159.

339. Vivian hides her intimate relationship with Cué, thus reiterating the theme of deceipt and secrets the text highlights. *Morcilla,* is a blood pudding or sausage, but in Spanish it also means "go to hell," "get lost;" and *morcillero,* is an improviser, extemporizer, like an actor.

340. Laura (Casas) was a pseudonym Lydia Cabrera used in her correspondence with an Afro-Cuban practicioner in Cuba. Cabrera Infante might have known that Laura was a "clave" (code) for Lydia Cabrera.

341. Levine, "Translation as (sub)version," 83.

342. Michelet IV, 1. Lévi-Strauss picks up the phrase from Merleu-Ponty, *Les Aventures de la dialectique* (Paris, 1955), 273, who picks it up from Michelet. See Lévi-Strauss, "The Structural Study of Myth," 838.

343. The image of insensitive monkeys may also serve as an echo of the failure of creation, of an insensitive humanity that had to be destroyed, as told in the *Popol Vuh.* Is Cabrera Infante suggesting that the monos of our times are like the monos of a time before the great flood in the *Popol Vuh?* In *El Huracán,* Ortiz recalls the association between the wind and monkeys and that in the *Popol Vuh,* as punishment, undeserving humans were turned into monkeys by the gods. See Ortiz, *El huracán,* 280.

344. In the signifying games of the text, it is also important to remember that the monkey was the sacred animal of *Thot,* the Egyptian god of writing. Such relationship with writing not only relates to the associations made in the novel between orality and writing, but also to the fact that laws are written, thus relating writing (monos) with the written Law, reason and domination, an idea that recalls the association Lévi-Strauss establishes in *Triste Tropiques* between writing and domination.

345. Cabrera Infante tells Emir Rodríguez Monegal that the source for *TTT* is found in Petronius's *Satyricon:* "novela en la que de algún modo se capta la luz de la vela que alumbraba la decadencia romana y en la que también brilla el ingenio verbal, la libertad de las situaciones y la más sutil crítica social" (a novel in which somehow the light of the candle that lit Roman decadence is captured and in which there shines its verbal genius, the freedom of the situations and the most subtle social criticism) (Rodríguez Monegal, "Estructura y significaciones de *TTT*," 92). As Ardis Nelson points out in *Cabrera Infante in the Menippean Tradition,* (Newark, Delaware: Juan Cuesta-Hispanic Monograph, 1983), the Havana of the '50s portrayed in *TTT* rivals "Nero's Rome as a center of corruption and vice" (10). *Satyricon,* like *TTT,* Nelson also points out, "is ripe with all sorts of deceit and treach-

ery" (Ibid., 17). While encapsuling the dying voices of a Havana in which a new political philosophy "impone su ley" (imposes its laws) (ibid., 451), the text seems to criticize, like the *Satyricon,* not only the corruption of the '50s, but also its worse critic, the new Revolutionary government, who imposed a death sentenced on the lifestyles of that period, and on the writer's freedom of expression. Still in the nineties, the reemergence of the music of pre-revolutionary Cuba, as in the case of the Buena Vista Social Club, was a controversial issue within Cuba because it was related to a moment, the same portrayed in *TTT,* considered decadent by the revolutionary ideology.

346. Cabrera Infante claims that this one and another reference to Batista are the only two political references in the text. See, Ricaurte, *Conversaciones con Guillermo Cabrera Infante,* 29.

347. Williams Siemens, "Destruction Reconstructed. Chaos Theory and the Works of Guillermo Cabrera Infante," *Ometeca* 1, no. 2 (1989–90), 56.

348. In Afro-Cuban belief systems white symbolizes the realm of death. This is why the dead body of an *abanecue* is painted, or *rayado,* with white chalk.

349. Cabrera Infante notes that music dictates the structure of the text, and calls the text a Rhapsody. Nelson, *Cabrera Infante in the Mennipean Tradition,* 54, 58. Raymond Souza defines it as a "nocturnal rhapsody." Souza, *Guillermo Cabrera Infante. Two Islands,* 89, 100.

350. González Echeverría, *The Voice of the Masters,* 141.

351. Cabrera, *La sociedad secreta Abakuá,* 274

352. Ibid., 283.

353. Ibid., 130.

354. The madwoman's last words take the reader back to the beginning of the novel, to the space of representation and ritual pantomine with which the novel begins: a story about "telling" a secret, a story of deceipt, and a story in which what is told is not the story told, but a different story.

CHAPTER 3. *CIMMARRÓN*

1. The history of the Caribbean has been the history of different forms of internal and external ways of running away from and to something else. Still today, Haitians flee in boats to Miami or cross the border to the Dominican Republic. Dominicans risk their lives in dilapidated boats to reach Puerto Rico; Puerto Ricans seek a better life in mainland United States; and Cubans risk their lives on anything that floats to leave the island.

2. Alejo Carpentier, "Los fugitivos," in *Guerra del tiempo,* 119.

3. Francisco Manzano wrote his autobiography in the late 1830s. It was published first as *Poems by a Slave in the Island of Cuba.* The second part of the manuscript is lost. See, William Luis, *Literary Bondage,* 83.

4. José Juan Arrom and Manuel García Arévalo, *Cimarrón* (Santo Domingo: Ediciones Fundación García-Arévalo, Inc., 1986), 150.

5. Ibid.

6. Ibid., 27.

7. Fernando Ortiz, *Nuevo catauro de cubanismos,* (La Habana: Editorial de Ciencias Sociales. Instituto cubano del libro, 1974), 139.

8. From Oviedo, lib. XII, II (Madrid: 1959), 38. In Arrom, *Cimarrón,* 19.

9. Arrom, *Cimarrón,* 29.

10. Fernando Ortiz, *Los negros esclavos* (Havana: Editorial de Ciencias Sociales, 1975), 373.

11. William Bascom, *Shango in the New World* (Austin: The University of Texas at Austin, 1972), 102.

12. Luis M. Díaz Soler, *Historia de la esclavitud negra en Puerto Rico* (Río Piedras, P.R.: Editorial Universitaria, 1981), 201–2.

13. For the presence of ladino slaves in Spain and in America see Fernando Ortiz, *Los negros curros*, 3, and 158.

14. From *Recopilación de leyes de Indias,* IV, book 9, 2, law18, 4. In Soler, *Historia de la esclavitud,* 202.

15. Carlos Esteban Deive, *Los guerrilleros negros. Esclavos fugitivos y cimarrones en Santo Domingo* (Santo Domingo, R. D.: Fundación Cultural Dominicana, 1989), 27.

16. From Real Célula, 1503, in Frank Moya Pons, *La Española en el siglo XVI (1493–1520). Trabajo, Sociedad y Política en la Economía del Oro* (Santiago, R. D.: Universidad Católica Madre y Maestra, 1978), 70.

17. Jalil Sued Badillo, *Puerto Rico negro* (Río Piedras, P. R.: Editorial Cultural, 1986), 179.

18. Ibid., 183–84.

19. Frank Moya Pons in his study *La Española en el siglo XVI (1493–1520). Trabajo, Sociedad y Política en la Economía del Oro,* shows how these early manipulations by the Spanish Crown and other authoritarian figures characterized the political life of Hispanola in the sixteenth century. For example, the Crown encouraged single men to marry in order to receive the right to have more Indians. The main idea was to encourage the development of a permanent Spanish settlement in Hispanola. However, at the same time that this law was put into effect, and in spite of the few number of Spanish women available, the king also ordered the governor, Diego Colón, to take Indians away from those men who were married to native women (88). One order cancelled the other, always to the Crown's advantage. In that way, only theoretically, the Crown seemed to keep the promises made to laborers who were lured to settle in the island.

20. Fernando Ortiz, *Nuevo catauro de cubanismos,* 371.

21. Deive, *Los guerrilleros negros,* 29.

22. One of the Royal proclamations reads: "negro o negra *cimarrón* que en cualquier tiempo se viniese de su voluntad del monte a la ciudad, y trajese consigo otro negro o negra, sea libre" (any black man or woman who out of his/her own accord comes to the city from the monte, and brings with him or her another black man or woman, will be free) Ortiz, *Los negros esclavos,* 365. When strong slaves were chosen to hunt down cimarrones, these were defined in official documents as "heroics." Deive, *Los guerrilleros negros,* 52. This is the case of the Ethiopian hero, Salvador, in Silvestre de Balboa's poem "Espejo de paciencia" (1608).

23. Ibid., 17.

24. Ibid., 16.

25. Mavis Campbell, *The Maroons of Jamaica: A History of Resistance, Collaboration, and Betrayal* (Massachusetts: Bergin and Garvey Publishers, 1988), 205, 222.

26. Deive, *Los guerrilleros negros,* 45.

27. Ibid., 44.

28. Ibid., 43

29. Ibid., 44.

30. Ibid.

31. Ibid., 46.

32. Ibid., 47.

33. Ibid., 48.

34. Ibid., 49.

35. Ibid., 50.

36. Bartolomé de las Casas, *Historia de las Indias* III, 273–76, translated in Benítez Rojo, "Bartolomé de las Casas: between fiction and the inferno," in *The Repeating Island,* 98.

37. Antonio Montesino's daring words were: "Are they not men? . . . Are you not bound to love them as you love yourself? . . . Be sure that in your present state you can be saved no more than the Moors or Turks who do not have and do not want the faith of Jesus Christ." Bartolomé de las Casas, *Historia de las Indias* Vol II, 441–42. I use the translation of this quote in *Latin American Civilization, History and Society, 1492 to the Present,* edited by Benjamin Keen (Boulder, Colorado: Westview Press, 1991), 66.

38. On this subject Manuel Moreno Fraginals argues in "Azúcar, esclavos y *revolución (1790–1868), 35–45, Casa de las Américas* IV, no. 50 (1968), that Cuba experienced a market revolution that led to the creation of a creole bourgeoisie which paradoxically still owned slaves and supported a conservative system of slavery. This contradiction in the economic system, between the old and the new, made the road possible for Arango y Parreño to attack the slave trade while supporting slavery, and, at the same time, to translate and circulate antislavery books. According to Moreno Fraginals, José Antonio Saco becomes Arango y Parreño's successor in terms of his antagonism for the market of slaves, yet "con un feroz odio a los negros" (with a strong hatred against the blacks) (ibid., 42). Following Moreno Fraginals's argument, the irony here is that in the classical historical interpretation of this period, Saco is seen as a liberal, when he in fact argued for the end of the trade as a politically conservative estratagem (Ibid., 43). Antonio Benítez Rojo observes that José Antonio Saco, in the nineteenth century, continues las Casas's discourse (of guilt and fear), and in fact was the one who insisted in the publication of *Historia de las Indias.* He also understood that the slave plantation generated rebellions, that is, "plagues of Negroes." According to Benítez Rojo, "fear and guilt toward and for the Negro were very important components of liberal Cuban and Hispano-Caribbean thinking at that time" (*RI,* 110).

39. Deive, *Los guerrilleros negros,* 40.

40. Ibid., 370.

41. Ibid., 365.

42. Ortiz, *Los negros esclavos,* 363.

43. Ibid., 365.

44. Among these was the well known mulatto Diego Grillo, known as Capitán Dieguillo. See José Luciano Franco, "Africanos y sus descendientes criollos en las luchas liberadoras 1533–1895," *Casa de las Américas* XVI, no. 93 (1975), 13.

45. Ada Ferrer notes that few years before the first war of independence in Cuba that started in 1868, authorities discovered a conspiracy in the area of El Cobre. For the trial of the "would-be-rebels," "translators had to be hired, for the enslaved suspects spoke no Spanish." Ferrer, *Insurgent Cuba,* 2.

46. Deive, *Los guerrilleros negros,* 259–60.

47. Manuel Moreno Fraginals, "Azucar, esclavos y revolución," *Casa de las Américas,* 37, and 44.

48. Ibid., 38.

49. Ibid., 44–45.

50. Manuel Moreno Fraginals points out the contradictions in the antislavery movements in Cuba during the first half of the eighteenth century, and in the first half of the nineteenth century. Cuban plantation owners were in favor of political independence, but in favor of slavery. Even when in 1812 Gluridi y Alcocer ask that the Spanish Courts emancipate the slaves, Arango y Parreño, in the name of the Cabildo of Havana, writes perhaps the most important ideological document of the reform movement. However, in it he speaks of lib-

erty, rejects old forms of institutions and feudal values, but does not bring up the issue of slavery, although, Moreno Fraginals points out, he knew that slavery meant the lack of political freedom for white owners. See, Moreno Fraginals, "Azúcar, esclavos y Revolución (1790–1868), 39–40.

51. A powerful insurrection of workers (free and slaves, African, mulatto and white creoles), also occurred in 1677 at the mines of Santiago del Prado (El Cobre) when it was ordered that those blacks and mulattos who by then considered themselves free, be sold as slaves. More than one hundred men and women resisted and sought refuge in maroon communities. They appealed their case and, in 1800, finally received the freedom and the land they demanded. See, Luciano Franco, "Africanos y sus desdencientes criollos en las luchas liberadoras 1533–1895," *Casa de las Américas* XVI, no. 93 (1975), 13.

52. Ibid., 13–14.

53. Ada Ferrer, *Insurgent Cuba,* 68 and 74.

54. Soler, *Historia de la esclavitud negra en Puerto Rico,* 212.

55. Ibid., 214.

56. Ibid.

57. Ibid., 223.

58. Ortiz, *Los negros esclavos,* 388.

59. In 1868, (in his farm La de Majagua) Carlos Manuel de Céspedes, a land and slave owner, called for the end of Spanish rule. It was a call to war that marked the begining of the Cuban struggle for independence against Spain. At this time, he freed his slaves and encouraged them to join him in battle. Many of them did. Other plantation owners followed his example. A large number of cimarrones also joined the insurgent troops. See Luciano Franco, *La presencia negra en el Nuevo Mundo* (Havana: Casa de las Américas, 1968), 103, and 134. See also Ferrer, *Insurgent Cuba,* 2–3.

60. Franco, "Africanos y sus descendientes criollos," 17.

61. Ferrer, *Insurgent Cuba,* 55.

62. See Castellanos, *Cultura africana* IV, 13. According to Carlos Estevan Deive, the word mambí was first used in "Santo Domingo, aplicándose originalmente a los negros *cimarrones* que se internaban en los montes, pero antes de pasar a Cuba con el significado dicho reapareció en nuestro país durante la guerra de Restauración (1863–65). *Mambí* era el criollo que peleaba contra las tropas leales a España" (given originally to negro cimarrones that escaped to the monte, but before the word passed to Cuba with this meaning [of insurgent and patriot] it reappeared in our country during the war of Restoration (1863–65). *Mambí* was the creole insurgent who fought against troops loyal to Spain. Deive, "La herencia africana en la cultura dominicana actual," (Conference presented on May 29, 1981).

63. Ferrer, *Insurgent Cuba.,* 121.

64. Luis, *Literary Bondage: Slavery in Cuban Narrative* (Austin: University of Texas Press, 1990), 29–30. See also Lorna Williams, *The Representation of Slavery in Cuban Fiction* (Columbia: University of Missouri Press, 1994), 16–20.

65. The antislavery novel that does not fit this characteristic is Gertrudis Gómez de Avellaneda's *Sab* (finished in 1838, but not published until 1841). Although this novel breaks with social taboos and is an open protest against the inhumanities of slavery, the center of its discourse is the unfair condition of women, especially married women.

66. William Luis, "*Cecilia Valdés:* el nacimiento de una novela antiesclavista." *Cuadernos hispanoamericanos* no. 451–52 (1988): 193. In other words, in spite of their clear discourse of freedom, the cimarrón, as a historical character, and even as the metaphor of an ideal, is absent in the nineteenth century literary Spanish Caribbean production in spite of its overwhelming historical presence.

67. William Luis, *Literary Bondage,* 90.

68. Ferrer, *Insurgent Cuba,* 177 and 184.

69. The authors of these novels were white creole writers. A later novel, *Sofía,* was written after the abolition of slavery by the mulatto José Manuel Morúa Delgado, but now with a different agenda. Raimundo Cabrera, Lydia Cabrera's father was the person who made the publication of Morúa Delgado's *Sofía* possible.

70. Ferrer, *Insurgent Cuba,* 200.

71. Ibid.

72. Ibid., 192.

73. Antonio S. Pedreira, *Insularismo* (Río Piedras, P.R.: Editorial Edil, Inc., 1985), 125.

74. The conspiracy known as the Ladder Conspiracy was most probably an invention of the legal authorities, as an excuse to eliminate powerful free black and mulatto citizens that were seen as politically dangerous; and to minimize the large and fast growing sector of black and mulatto artisans and professionals that by the middle of the nineteenth century had become a power element in Cuban society.

75. See Luis, *Literary Bondage,* 215.

76. Carabalí is the name given to slaves from the Calabar, in Africa. It was common to give slaves the name of the tribe or region from which they came. Carabalí slaves were well known in the Caribbean for their rebelliousness, and their aggressive and fearless behavior.

77. Cayetano Toll y Toste, "Carabalí," *Leyendas puertorriqueñas* (México: Editorial Orion, 1985),170.

78. Ibid., 161.

79. Ibid.

80. Ibid., 165.

81. Ibid., 164.

82. Martí, "Versos sencillos," 6. In Latin American Spanish, that is the Spanish spoken by José Martí and Cayetano Toll y Toste, there is no phonetic difference between "s" and "c", therefore, when spoken, *siervo* may refer to a servant as well as a deer (*ciervo*). In José Martí's poem, *ciervo* (deer) refers to the poet and his writings, persecuted and fugitive, a word used with political and social connotations. Martí resisted Spanish colonial rule, and thus his writings against Spanish domination made him a fugitive ciervo/siervo, a mambí: a condition of dissent that sent him to exile in more than one occasion.

83. Toll y Toste, "Carabalí," 171.

84. González Echevarría, *Voices of the Masters,* 119.

85. Luis, *Literary Bondage,* 8.

86. In Ramos's novel, after Caniquí's assassination, Mariceli and José Antonio's conversation about Caniquí's death becomes a comment directed to Ramos's sociopolitical period. Mariceli tells José Antonio:

> "—Era un *cimarrón* empedernido. Amaba la libertad sobre todas las cosas. Era su religión . . .
> —Pues por eso, Mariceli, te decía ahora mismo que Caniquí no ha muerto. ¡Y ojalá no muera nunca! La gente volverá mañana a sentir miedo. Al fantasma del bandido que ellos creen haber muerto, seguirán otros y otros. Y los hombres honrados por cierto, tendremos que hacernos también bandidos, para acabar de una vez con esta maldición de los amos blancos y esas hordas serviles de esclavos: los negros de los criollos y los criollos judas del odioso extranjero . . ."

> (He was a stubborn *cimarrón*. He loved freedom above all things. It was his religion . . .
> —That is why, Mariceli, I told you that Caniquí is not dead. I hope he never dies. Tomorrow people will be afraid again. Others will follow the ghost of the bandit they think they killed. We honest men, by the way, will have to become bandids also, to bring about the end of this curse of white owners and the hordes of submissive slaves . . . and the creole Judas of the hateful foreigners) Ramos, *Caniquí,* 327–28. The historical Caniquí, says Ortiz, caused terror around Villaclara during 1834–38. Superstition made of him demonic, able to fly and to enter walls. He was eventually killed near the River Ay, close to Trinidad. See Ortiz, *Los negros curros,* 188.

87. Even though the image of the runaway slave is commonly seen as taking place in a Plantation, or rural settings, in the Spanish Caribbean, runaway slaves were very common in urban areas. In his study on urban runaway slaves, *Los cimarrones urbanos,* Pedro Deschamps Chapeaux observes that not only the slaves in the sugar and coffee plantations ran away, also the slave in the urban centers sought freedom. See, Deschamps Chapeaux, *Los cimarrones urbanos* (Havana: Editorial de Ciencias Sociales, 1983), 1. In Havana some neighborhoods outside the city walls were, says Deschamps, "densamente poblados por negros libres, africanos de todas las etnias y muchos criollos . . . (El Horcón, San Lázaro, Carraguas, Guadalupe, Jesús María, tradicionalmente este último un barrio de negros con su célebre y temido Manglar, refugio de los denominados negros curros) constituían para el esclavo fugitivo lo que el monte para el esclavo rural" (densely populated by free blacks and Africans of all ethnic backgrounds and creoles [El Horcón, Lan Lázaro, Carraguas, Guadalupe, Jesús María, traditionally a black neighborhood with it famous and terrible Mangrove, hiding ground for the so called black "curros"] constituted for the fugitive slave what the monte was for the rural slave) (ibid., 5–6).

88. Ortiz, *Los negros brujos,* 3.

89. Ibid., 6.

90. José Luciano Franco, Prologue to Ortiz, *Los negros esclavos,* 10.

91. Eduardo Guizar Álvarez and Adriana Méndez Rodena, "Caña/cuerpo/danza: Imágenes de opresión/liberación del sujeto caribeño," 61–77, *Crítica Hispánica* XXI, no. 1 (2000), 70.

92. The Spanish title, *Biografía de un cimarrón* indicates that the text is about the life of Esteban Montejo, an ex-cimarrón. The English title, however, *The Autobiography of a Runaway Slave* changes the perspective of the narrative and proposes a different reading of Barnet's text, suggesting that the story was told and/or written by Montejo and not Barnet.

93. González Echeverría, *The Voice of the Masters,* 123.

94. Luis, *Literary Bondage,* 84.

95. González Echeverría, *The Voice of the Masters,* 119.

96. Ibid.

97. Ibid., 118.

98. Ibid.

99. Francisco Manzano's text available is the first part of the original manuscript, edited by José Luciano Franco in 1937.

100. Carlos Moore notes that during these years in which Barnet writes Montejo's biography, Cuba had developed a complex political agenda toward Cuban blacks and toward Africa. By 1960, Moore points out: "The official birth of Castro's African policy . . . coincided with the resumption of a silent, protracted, and relentless war against Afro-Cuban religions and also against any authonomous ethno-cultural manifestations by Cuban Blacks." Moore, *Castro, The Blacks, and Africa,* 99, also 301–9.

101. Ibid., 59–64.

102. Luis, *Literary Bondage,* 217.

103. Barnet, *Biografía de un cimarrón,* 186.

104. Barnet, *Autobiography of a Runaway Slave,* 215.

105. Barnet, *Biografía de un cimarrón,* 188.

106. Innes translates "[They] the Black liberators," as "Negro revolutionaries." See, Barnet, *Autobiography of a Runaway Slave,* 217.

107. Although "les decían" (they called them) may be read as an innocent impersonal statement, it is symbolic that Esteban does not say "they [the Marines] called **us,**" Montejo establishes with the implicit "they" or "them" a distance between "them" (the Negroes), and himself, the distant narrator.

108. Barnet, *Biografía de un cimarrón,* 187.

109. Innes translates: "The Americans didn't like the negroes much. They used to shout, 'Nigger, nigger,' and burst out laughing." Barnet, *Autobiography of a Runaway Slave,* 216.

110. Ibid., 218.

111. Ibid., 219.

112. Barnet, *Biografía de un cimarrón,* 190.

113. Barnet, *Autobiography of a Runaway Slave,* 219.

114. Miguel Barnet, "The Documentary Novel," *Cuban Studies/Estudios Cubanos* 11, no. 1 (1981), 25.

115. Ibid., 23.

116. Ibid., 28.

117. Barnet, *Biografía de un cimarrón,* 192.

118. Barnet, *Autobiography of a Runaway Slave,* 221.

119. Barnet, *Biografía de un cimarrón,* 188.

120. Ibid., 194.

121. Barnet, *Autobiography of a Runaway Slave,* 223.

122. Julia Kristeva, *Desire in Language: A Semiotic Approach to Literature and Art,* ed. Leon S. Roudiez (New York: Columbia University Press, 1980), 64–65.

123. Ibid., 65.

124. Ibid.

125. Julia Cuervo Hewitt, "El texto (trasvesti): narrativa y testimonio," *Cuban Studies/ Estudios cubanos* 22, no. 1–2 (1989), 56–59. See Luis, *Literary Bondage,* 212–15.

126. González Echeverría, *The Voice of the Masters,* 121.

127. See Luis, *Literary Bondage,* 226–37.

128. Leante, *Los guerrilleros negros,* 94.

129. Luis, *Literary Bondage,* 219–20.

130. Roberto Fernández Retamar, "Calibán," in *Calibán y otros ensayos* (Havana: Editorial Arte y Literatura, 1979), 37.

131. Ferrer, *Insurgent Cuba,* 121, 123.

132. Fernández Retamar, "Calibán," 32–33.

133. Ferrer, *Insurgent Cuba,* 126.

134. Marilyn Grace Miller, *Rise and Fall of the Cosmic Race,* 15.

135. Kutzinski, *Sugar's Secrets,* 165.

136. Since José Rodó's appropiation of the character of Ariel from William Shakespeare's *The Tempest* as a symbol of America, in his essay "Ariel" (1900), Shakeaspeare's characters in that play, Ariel, Prospero, and Caliban, have continued to serve as colonial and neocolonial metaphors and allegories not just for writers of fiction, but also for historians, and social scientists. Examples are Richard M. Morse, *El espejo de Próspero* (México: Siglo XVI editores, 1982) and, among others, Leopoldo Zea, "La calibanización de Próspero," in *Discurso desde la marginación y la barbarie* (México: Fondo de Cultura Económica, 1988).

137. Said, *Culture and Imperialism,* 214.

138. Ibid.

139. Ibid.

140. Ibid., 213. The title, *The Tempest,* alone would have triggered a Caribbean Afropre-Hispanic memory that, as Ortiz proposes in *Huracán,* gathers a sense of the "proper" and a sense of future change in revolution.

141. Aimé Césaire's play is the first Caribbean rereading and rewriting of Shakespeare's *The Tempest* from Caliban's perspective. Edward Said observes: "an affectionate contention with Shakespeare for the right to represent the Caribbean. That impulse to contend is part of a grander effort to discover the bases of an integral identity different from the formerly dependent derivative one." Said, *Culture and Imperialism,* 212–13.

142. Ibid., 31.

143. Moore points out that the Cuban Revolution negated racial issues for political gain establishing a "black" politics that did not empower Afro-Cubans. See Moore, *Castro, The Blacks, and Africa,* 48–49, and 71–76. William Luis also claims: "As in the past, in spite of the radical changes in the social and political structure, today Cuba continues to be a country based on sugar and blacks continue to beat the margins of power." Luis, *Literary Bondage* 19.

144. Said, *Culture and Imperialism,* 213.

145. Fernández Retamar, "Calibán," 36. The instability in Fernando Retamar's Calibán could be read in relationship to what Homi Bhabha calls the "Third Space, which represents both the general condition of language and the specific implication of the utterance." That "third space," Bhabha claims "ensure[s]s that the meaning and symbols of culture have no primordial unity of fixity; that even the same signs can be appropriated, translated, rehistorized, and read anew." Bhabha, "Cultural Diversity and Cultural Differences," *Post Colonial Studies Reader,* 208.

146. Bhabha, *The location of culture,* 45.

147. Leante, *Los guerrilleros negros,* 41.

148. José Luciano Franco, *La conspiración de Aponte* (Havana: Consejo Nacional de Cultura. Publicaciones del Archivo Nacional LVIII, 1963), 19, and 30. Aponte was the martyr of a planned revolution in Cuba, but he was not the originator of the plan. José Antonio Aponte, a wood-carver, and a soldier in the Black and Mulatto Milicia (Batallón de Milicias Disciplinarias de Pardos y Morenos) was recruited by Don Luis Francisco Bassave y Cárdenas (a well-established white creole, and a Cavalry Captain who had certain popularity in poor neighborhoods, and who was said to incite black and mulatto workers to rebel), to plan a conspiracy against Spain. This conspiracy, known as the Mason Conspiracy (Conspiración Masónica), was denounced by the Captain of the Black Milicia, Isidro Moreno and the "Sargento de Pardos" (Sargent of Mulatto Regiments) Pedro Alcántara Pacheco (ibid., 19). Bassave went to jail in Spain together with others accused (ibid., 27). Aponte, who managed not to be detected as part of the conspiracy, continued the network toward an uprising, but now following the model of the Haitian revolution. Aponte's clandestine work coincided with the crowning in Haiti of Henri Christophe (ibid., 30). However, different from Haiti, Aponte's rebellion was not exclusively a racial one: poor whites were involved in the resistance encouraging blacks to revolt against rich whites, and, according to Franco, "iban a pelear también a favor de los negros" (were also going to fight with the blacks) (ibid., 33). Franco takes his documentation from Archivo Nacional (Asuntos Políticos. Legajo 11 No. 37).

149. Leante, *Los guerrilleros negros,* 222.

150. Ibid., 223.

151. Luis, *Literary Bondage,* 219–37.

152. Ibid., 223; See also, Zolia Danger Roll, *Los cimarrones de El Frijol* (Santiago de Cuba: Empresa Editorial Oriente, 1977), 75. Contrary to the documentation gathered by Danger Roll in 1977, but coinciding with Leante's romanced version and José Franco's account of Coba's death, in the 1985 edition of *Historia de Cuba,* under the section "Los palenques de *cimarrones,*" the 'official' history taught in Revolutionary Cuban schools reiterates Leante and Franco's account of Ventura's death. It reads: "En 1819 los *cimarrones* de un palenque próximo a Santiago de Cuba se sublevaron bajo el lema "Tierra y Libertad." Líder del movimiento fue Ventura Sánchez, quien sorprendido por una partida de rancheadores, prefirió la muerte antes que aceptar nuevamente la servidumbre. Su cabeza fue llevada a Baracoa y expuesta en una jaula de hierro a la entrada de la ciudad. (In 1819 cimarrones from a palenque close to Santiago de Cuba started a rebellion under the motto "Land and Liberty." The leader of the movement was Ventura Sánchez, who, when taken by surprise by a group of rancheadores, chose death rather than servitude. His head was taken to Baracoa and exposed in an iron cage at the entrance of the city) *Historia de Cuba,* 121–22.

153. According to Franco, Coba was taken by surprise because he had, "descuidado la vigilancia el 20 de diciembre de 1819, y el caudillo de los *cimarrones* antes de entregarse se suicidó, arrojándose desde un precipicio al río Quiviján . . . Feliciano, que era el único que acompañaba a Coba, fue hecho prisionero y enviado a Santiago de Cuba" (he became careless about his safety, December 20, 1819, and the maroon leader committed suicide rather than becoming a prisoner and being sent to Santiago de Cuba . . . Feliciano, the only one accompanying Coba, was captured and sent to Santiago de Cuba) Franco, *La presencia negra en el Nuevo Mundo,* 132.

154. Ibid.

155. Also Zumbi, the last and great king of Palmares, the largest *Kilombo* in northern Brazil, was said to have jumped from a cliff when surprised by government troops. See Theobaldo Miranda Santos, "A Morte de Zumbi, *Lendas e Mitos do Brasil (leituras para crianças)* (São Paulo: Comphanhia Editora Nacional, 1955), 52–53.

156. Leante, *Los guerrilleros negros,* 230.

157. Ibid., 323.

158. Ibid., 324.

159. Ibid., 326.

160. Ibid., 329.

161. Leante's reading of his own novel is very different from the one I propose here. For him, Coba's struggle and death is an ode to freedom and not to the Cuban Revolution (Conversation with César Leante, February, 1997, Madrid).

162. Lisandro Otero, "Las ideas políticas de Fernando Ortiz, 38–44, *Anales del Caribe. Casa de las Americas* (Havana: Centro de Estudios del Caribe4, 1982), 44.

163. As part of one and the same discourse, the rebellious figures of Caliban (as a metaphor for the Caribbean) and of Coba (as a guerrillero) are representatives of the combatant image of the Caribbean that fits Cuba's revolutionary ideology, like the one represented by Nicolás Guillén in his poem *El gran Zoo,* in *West Indies, Ldt,* 1937. The poem ends with the warning: "In the aquarium, this inscription: "Beware: it bites." Nicolás Guillén, *Patria o Muerte. The Great Zoo and Other Poems,* translated by Robert Márquez (Havana: Editorial Arte y Literatura, 1975), 35.

164. Fredic Jameson, *The Political Unsconscious. Narrative as a Socially Symbolic Act* (Ithaca: Cornell University Press, 1981), 19.

165. Leante, *Los guerrilleros negros,* 122.

166. Luis, *Literary Bondage,* 220.

167. Barnet, *Biografía de un cimarrón,* 181.

168. Barnet, *Autobiography of a Runaway Slave,* 208–9. As William Luis also points out, Montejo's definition of guerrillero concurs with Fernando Portuondo's but not with José Luciano Franco's in his *Los palenques de los negros cimarrones* (1973). See Luis, *Literary Bondage,* 221.

169. In 1980 Leante left Cuba and requested political exile in Spain. In *Capitán de cimarrones* (1982), Spain, Leante also changes the word *apalencados* (runaway slaves gathered together in a palenque) to cimarrones. In a way it can be said that the second edition of Leante's novel is a runaway novel that has escaped from the space of its initial creation to another space of refuge and resistance, to a monte of its own, to an allegorical *allá* from where the writer rearticulates history, because, for Leante, the historical present allegorized in the novel has shifted.

170. Deive, *Los guerrilleros negros,* 16.

171. Leante, *Los guerrilleros negros,* 11.

172. Antonio Benítez Rojo represents the subtle complexities of the conflict between African religions and Marxist ideology in revolutionary Cuba in his short story "La tierra y el cielo," 181–95, in *Paso de los vientos* (San Juan, Puerto Rico: Editorial Plaza Mayor, 1999). See, Cuervo Hewitt, *Aché,* 216.

173. Glissant, *Caribbean Discourse,* 145.

174. Mariana is the diminutive in Northern Spain for Maria.

175. This reiterated erasure of woman and feminine agency in Cuban historical and literary discourses is what Vera Kutzinski calls in *Sugar's Secrets* "a male homosocial construct premised upon the disappearance of the feminine," (165), and, in other words, a male historical embrace that delegates woman to metaphor and myth.

176. Leante, *Los guerrilleros negros,* 230.

177. Ibid., 329.

178. Franco, "La conspiración de Aponte," 25.

179. Manuel Zapata Olivella, *Levántate mulato,* 107.

180. Ibid., 330.

181. Ibid., 342.

182. See William Bascom. *Shango in the New World.* (Austin: The University of Texas at Austin. African and Afro-American Research Institute, 1972); and also, George Eaton Simpson, *The Shango Cult in Trinidad* (Rio Piedras, P. R.: Monograph Series 2. University of Puerto Rico: Institute of Caribbean Studies, 1965).

183. Franco, "La conspiración de Aponte," 49. Bassave also was betrayed, in his case, by the captain and a sargent of the Mulatto Militia, Isidro Moreno, and Pedro Alcántara Pacheco (ibid., 19).

184. Cuervo Hewitt, *Aché,* 143. See also Samuel Johnson, "The Oyo Empire: The Reign of Shango," *Nigerian Perspectives,* ed. Thomas Hodgkin (London: Oxford University Press, 1960), 84–85.

185. Oyin Ogunba, "Ceremonies," 87–110, *Sources of Yoruba History,* edited by Saburi Olademi Biobaku (Oxford: Claredon Press, 1973), 102.

186. Leante, *Los guerrilleros negros,* 39.

187. Ibid., 38. Coba's attitude in Leante's novel coincides with the attitude of maroon leaders in Jamaica. As Mavis Campbell notes in *The Maroons of Jamaica. (A History of Resistance, Collaboration, and Betrayal),* (Massachusetts: Bergin and Garvey Publishers, 1988), "Maroons had a robust contempt for slaves—a category that "chose" to remain slaves and not to fight successfully against the master class as they had done" (204). After signing a treaty which made the maroons a free community, "the Maroons bought slaves without any notice being taken of it" (ibid., 205), and a greater discord and resentment permeated the relationship between slaves and maroons.

188. Leante, *Los guerrilleros negros,* 38.

189. Ibid., 39.

190. There seems to be a dialogue here with Lévi-Strauss's arguments in *Triste Tropics.*

191. Ibid., 80.

192. According to José Luciano Franco's documentations in *La presencia negra en el nuevo mundo,* in the palenque of Moa, known also as El Frijol, there were two white priests, and a white woman "que se supone de algún rango, y procede de La Habana" (who seems to be of higher social status and comes from Havana) Franco, *La presencia negra en el Nuevo mundo,* 125. Franco takes his information from Archivo nacional. Asuntos Políticos. Legajo 109, núm. 34. See also Luis, *Literary Bondage,* 228–29.

193. Franco, *La presencia negra en el nuevo mundo* 132.

194. The ethics of writing was a debated issue among French Romantics. It is an old attitude already found in Plato's writings, on Socrates's rejection of the Sophists, and an issue taken by several contempory philosophers, among them, Jacques Derrida; it is also a central topic of discussion for Lévi-Strauss. This violence of writing, in Latin America, has been the center of polemics in the twentieth century, related to political ethics, the representation of national identity, and cultural independence.

195. The Cuban rebel army declared slaves free in 1868. In 1880, Spain finally declared slavery abolished with the idea that the process would take eight years. However, by 1886

there were no slaves left in the island, and thus the end of slavery was made official. During Coba's life, and in 1819, when Coba met his death, the abolition of slavery still was a point of contention, mostly as the result of the Haitian revolution.

196. Leante, *Los guerrilleros negros,* 81–82.

197. This seemingly Leninist approach to history, to incite a revolution in order to speed the historical process, was Aponte's strategy, according to Franco. Aponte, and his followers, before attempting any armed rebellion, spread the word through the island that slaves had been freed, but that the authorities and planters were keeping the truth from the people. The plan was so successful that in the order number 391, September 26, 1811, the governor of Santiago de Cuba ordered Marqués Someruelos to find out the origin of such rumors going around among the slaves that they were free. Franco, *La conspiración de Aponte,* 29. Franco takes this information from the Cuban Nacional Archives: "Assuntos Políticos," "Legajo" 213, Number 162.

198. Leante, *Los guerrilleros negros,* 140.

199. Ibid., 201.

200. Ibid.

201. Luis sees a different solution at the end of Carpentier and Leante's novel. For him, "Ti Nöel's response is nature, Coba's is history." Luis, *Literary Bondage* 228.

202. Glissant, *Caribbean Discourse,* 141.

203. Leante, like Carpentier, wrestled with similar ideological conflicts: faith and ideology. In *Insurgent Cuba,* Ferre points out the contradictory acceptance by white patriots of slaves and cimarrones who chose to join the insurgents, while, at the same time, rejecting the new patriot's ancestral African beliefs, which they considered "uncivilized" and savage. See, Ferrer, *Insurgent Cuba,* 173–78.

204. Leante, *Los guerrilleros negros,* 188.

205. The ambiguities and contradictions surrounding the figure of cimarrón in the Caribbean, has given way to new myths. One of those, according to José Lezama Lima, is "El mito de Acteón, a quien la contemplación de las musas lo lleva a metamorfosearse en ciervo, durmiendo con las orejas tensas y movientes, avizorando los presagios del aire" (The myth of Acteon, for whom the contemplation of the muses, metamorphosizes him into a deer, sleeping with his ears tense and constantly moving, watching for foreboding omens in the air) Lezama, *La expresión Americana,* 77. Lezama Lima's interest in Acteon is in his transformation from the hunter to the hunted, not in his death, but also in the contemplation of the muses, Diana, poetry, imagination, fiction, a relationship Aida Beaupied keenly observes, that leads Lezama's Acteon to be transformed into the hunted, condemned for being different (a poet): thus he must be forever in constant vigil, always at risk, always in danger. Lezama Lima's Acteon is the poet, and the poet is much like a cimarrón. For Lezama Lima, writing is always already an act of dissidence that turns the writer into an outlaw, a wounded deer in the forest of his/her own writing. See Aida Beaupied's insightful reading on this subject in "Acteón, Narciso, Martí y el adentramiento en la naturaleza en la poética de José Lezama Lima," *Hispanófila* 108 (1993): 25–44.

206. Manuel Zapata Olivella, *Levántate mulato* (Colombia: Rei Andes Ltda., Letras Americanas, 1990), 8.

207. Parry, "Resistance Theory/Theorizing Resistance," 174.

208. Zapata feels inspired by Martí "the only one," he says, "that can give us 'the key to the enigma' of Spanish America," Manuel Zapata Olivella, *Levántate mulato,* 7.

209. Arnold, *Modernism and Negritude,* 33.

210. Michael Dash, introduction to Edouard Glissant's *Caribbean Discourse. Selected Essays* (Charlottesville: University Press of Virginia, 1989), xli

211. Parry, "Resistance Theory/Theorizing Resistance," 18.

212. Ibid.

213. Zapata's story of an African Spirit in the making in America, may be read as a Hegelean Phenomenology of Spirit: as a double consciousness moving toward Knowledge/Freedom, and always returning to itself.

214. Bhabha, *The Location of Culture*, 5.

215. Ibid., 1.

216. Parry, "Resistance Theory/Theorizing Resistance," 182.

217. The lamb was the sacrificial offering to Yahweh; it is also a ritual offering to Shango.

218. Zapata romances the history of the ladino cimarrón, Domingo Bioho, from Cartagena, Colombia, who was known as King Benkos. During fourteen years Benkos resisted the attacks against the palenque. See Nina Friedemann, and Richard Cross, *Ma Mgombe: guerreros y ganaderos en Palenque* (Bogota, Colombia: Carlos Valencia Editores, 1979), 67. However, like many other maroon leaders in the greater Caribbean, he was also a victim of treason.

219. Manuel Zapata Olivella, *Changó, el gran Putas* (Colombia: Nuevas Ediciones, 1983; 1985), 174.

220. Zapata, *Changó, el gran Putas*, 175. In Rómulo Lachatañeré's *¡Oh, mío Yemayá!* (Manzanillo, Cuba: Editorial el Arte, 1938) we find the legend of Shango's birth as *Obatala*'s biological son. In this legend, Yemayá is Shango's adoptive mother. This is the version used by Pepe Carrill in his play *Shango of Ima*, in an adaptation that makes Shango an Afro-Cuban *Orpheus*. In other African versions, Shango is born from Yemayá just like the other main orishas. In *Changó, el gran Putas*, Benkos allegorically represents several versions of the birth of Shango: as son of Yemayá, the great mother ocean; and son of Obalatá, the male/female creator of man. This dual and ambiguous origin is characteristic of Shango's dualities, always one and the other. As the storm god of destruction who also announces rain, and abundance, his color is red: blood, passion, life, and the rising sun, a deity of fertility, father of the *Ibeyes*, the contrary principles of the cosmos. Shango is the ultimate semen carrier, the impregnator of life.

221. San Pedro Claver and Father Alonso de Sandoval, as Zapata Olivella notes in *Levántate mulato*, were "precursores de la igualdad racial" (precursors of racial equality) (37), and also an ekobio. See, Margarita Krakusin, "Conversación informal con Manuel Zapata Olivella," *Afro-Hispanic Review* 20, no. 1 (2001), 20.

222. Zapata, *Changó, el gran Putas*, 180–81.

223. This is *Damballah's vever*, not *Legbá's vever*. Damballah is represented with the figure of two snakes facing each other; their faces, looking at each other, they are separated by an egg, sometimes by a sun. Zapata mixes on purpose different traditions and African religious beliefs to create one large syncretic Pan Indo-African people that can trace their recent and most remote origins to the African continent.

224. Ibid., 200.

225. See Julia Cuervo Hewitt, "Luis de Camoens en el reino de Calibán: *Las Lusíadas* en *Changó, el gran Putas* de Manuel Zapata Olivella," *Afro-Hispanic Review* 22, no. 1 (2003): 13–23.

226. Glissant, *Caribbean Discourse*, 8. This is the theme in Isabelo Zenón Cruz's study, *Narciso descubre su trasero (El negro en la cultura puertorriqueña)*, (Humacao, P.R.: Editorial Furidi, I, 1974, and II, 1975).

227. Glissant, *Caribbean Discourse*, 5.

228. Krakusin, "Conversación informal con Manuel Zapata Olivella," 20.

229. Zapata even claimed that he was inspired and guided by Ifa to write *Changó, el gran Putas*. See Zapata Olivella, "Los ancestros combatientes. Una Saga Afro-norteamericana," *Afro-Hispanic Review* (September, 1991): 51.

230. Cuervo Hewitt, *Aché*, 191.

231. Ana Lydia Vega, "Otra maldad de Pateco," 105–13, *Encancaranublado y otros*

cuentos de naufragio (Puerto Rico: Editorial Antillana, 1982). In Vega's text, the cultural trickster in Puerto Rican folklore, *Pateco,* is a type of mischievous *Chicherekú,* and similar to the Colombian *Putas.*

CHAPTER 4. ILÉ-IYÁ-EWELABÁ

1. Bhabha, *The Location of Culture,* 206.
2. Glissant, *Caribbean Discourse,* 147.
3. Ibid., 26.
4. In Spanish, a bassinet is called a *moisés* (Moses). Child Avilés was found floating in a moisés, a biblical reference to Moses (Moisés), who, as a baby, was found floating in a basket on the waters. Like Moses, Child Avilés is destined to lead his people out of colonial bondage.
5. Acosta, *Música y épica,* 104.
6. Ibid., 106.
7. Edgardo Rodríguez Juliá, *La noche oscura del Niño Avilés* (Río Piedras, P.R.: Ediciones Huracán, 1984). All references to this novel will be indicated in the text as *NONA.*
8. Monstrosity here refers to the hybridity of the child for being a creole infant. It is also a reminder that the historical Child Avilés, as painted in the eighteenth century by José Campeche, was a deformed child, and a creole colonial subject.
9. The idea that New Venice would be a New Jerusalem establishes a dialogue with sixteenth century messianic discourses in the New World. These were to a large extent associated with the influence Erasmus's theological ideas had on the missionaries traveling to the New World. See the chapter "Erasmo en América," in Marcel Batallón, *Erasmo en España. Estudios sobre la historia espiritual del siglo XVI.* (Madrid: Fondo de Cultura Económica, 1950). Batallón explains the impact of Erasmus's ideas on American missions, colonization, and institutions.
10. Ortiz, *El Hucarán,* 232–33.
11. Spanish propaganda against the insurgency took advantage of the fear created in Caribbean colonial societies by the Haitian revolution and disseminated the idea that the struggle for independence in Cuba was a racial war. The insurgents were represented as African savages. In Cuba, the image advanced was that black Cuban insurgent officers, like Quintín Banderas, wore nose rings. See Ferrer, *Insurgent Cuba,* 173.
12. In Rodríguez Juliá's neo-baroque style, and humor, Trespalacios's secretary explains that the architect of such city was "un judío de Praga llamado Tomás Moro" (a Jew from Prague named Thomas Moore) *La noche oscura del Niño Avilés,* 32. This is a reference to the writings of Thomas Moore, author of *Utopia* (1516), a text that also proposes a meditation on politics and freedom. Moore was condemned by the British king Henry VIII to die at the stake for his views. Allegorically, the same happens to New Venice.
13. Aníbal González Pérez, "Una alegoría de la cultura puertorriqueña: *La noche oscura del niño Avilés* de Edgardo Rodríguez Juliá," 583–90, *Revista Iberoamericana* no. 135–36 (1986), 586.
14. From the Greek "topos" and the negative suffix "u" for no, meaning "not topos:" or impossible, unreal.
15. Díaz-Quiñones, *El arte de bregar* (San Juan, P.R.: Ediciones Callejón, Inc., 2000), 195–202.
16. González Pérez, "Una alegoría de la cultura puertorriqueña," 587.
17. Octavio Paz, *Puertas al campo* (Barcelona: Seix Barral, 1972), 13.
18. Edgardo Rodríguez Juliá, *En el camino de Yyaloide* (Venezuela: Grijalbo S. A. de Venezuela, 1994), 9.

19. Ibid.

20. Ibid., 84.

21. The narrative in this text pretends to be a commentary on different fictitious paintings that portray the life of Child Avilés.

22. Glissant, *Caribbean Discourse,* 147.

23. This term, often repeated, and always implicit in the novel, is also a term used in the trial of the Cuban black insurgent Quintín Banderas, "son of the people," because he, as a black officer of the insurgent Cuban troops, claimed to be a black creole, poor, like the people he commanded. See Ferrer, *Insurgent Cuba,* 177.

24. Glissant, *Caribbean Discourse,* 147.

25. In the Spanish-speaking Caribbean, this was a point of contention in colonial discourses on the nation. Also Martí derived spiritual authority by distancing himself emotionally from women. See, Ferrer, *Insurgent Cuba,* 176.

26. Rodríguez Juliá, *En el camino de Yyaloide,* 203.

27. Ibid., 198.

28. Ibid., 199.

29. In the tarot card game that Child Avilés and Trespalacios play, Avilés challenges the authority of his protector by calling for the figure that portrays two lovers being watched by Cupid and by an old man holding a staff. He explains the scene: "Cupido era como el ángel custodio de los enamorados y el viejo representaba al inquisidor malévolo que con su vara castigaría a los amantes; añadió que la envidia y los celos corroían su alma, resecaba aún más su polvorienta y arrugada piel" (Cupid was like the guarding angel of the lovers, and the old man represented the evil inquisitor who would punish them with his cane; he added that envy and jealousy were eating his soul, and drying up even more his dusty and wrinkled skin) (Ibid., 196).

30. Ibid., 206.

31. As Arcadio Díaz Quiñones observes, most movements for independence in the Caribbean were conceived and planned in exile. See Díaz Quiñones, *El arte de bregar,* 198, and 200. The reader is left to imagine that Child Avilés will rethink his situation and the situation of his people while he is studying in Cuba. In the case of José Luis González, says Díaz Quiñones, he rethinks Puerto Rico from Mexico. Díaz Quiñones writes: "En esa comunidad imaginada desde el exilio—inmersa en la apropiación y en la traducción culturales exigidas por su constante natalidad—tenía González un lugar asegurado. A ella, a sus potencialidades y alternativas, retornaba en sus ficciones una y otra vez para construirse un lugar donde se pudiera habitar y pensar, empezar a nacer" (In that community imagined from Exile—immersed in the appropriation and cultural translation demanded by its constant birth—González had a sure place. To it, to its potentials and alternatives, he returned each time in his fiction in order to construct a space where one could live and think, to begin birth) (ibid., 191).

32. See Cuervo Hewitt, "Luis de Camoens en el reino de Calibán," 16–17.

33. Rodríguez Juliá, *En el camino de Yyaloide,* 180.

34. González Pérez, "Una alegoría de la cultura puertorriqueña," 585.

35. In Rodríguez Juliá's novel most names are composites taken from legendary and historical figures in Puerto Rican history, as well as the writer's own name and acquaintances. An example of such play is the name in the novel or "Juliá Marín" (from Rodríguez Juliá and Muñoz Marín).

36. See Severo Sarduy, "El barroco y el neobarroco," 167–84, *América latina en su literatura,* edited by César Fernández Moreno (Mexico: Siglo Veintiuno Editores, 1972), 168, 183.

37. Derek Walcott, "The Muse of History," 370–77, *The Post-Colonial Studies Reader,* edited by Bill Ashcroft, Gareth Griffiths, and Helen Tiffin (London: Routledge, 1995), 372.

38. Rodríguez Juliá, *La renuncia del héroe Baltazar* (Harrisonburg, Virginia: Editorial Cultural, 1974), 75.

39. The novel proposes itself as an exploration of the deepest historical meanings of its enigmatic eighteenth century hero, Baltazar Montañez, whose allegorical existence in the novel: "tiene mucho que decir . . . sobre nuestra condición humana" (has much to say . . . about our human condition) Edgardo Rodríguez Juliá, *La renuncia del héroe Baltazar*, 7. The novel's "profundo sentido histórico" (profound historical meaning) (ibid.) is an allegorical reference to the cultural history of Puerto Rico. As Ramón E. Soto-Crespo observes, "The *Renunciation* marks the origins of Rodríguez Juliá's interpretation of memory and history." Soto-Crespo, "The Pains of Memory: Mourning the Nation in Puerto Rican Literature," *MLN* 117, no. 2 (2002), 469. This is a theme he continues to explore in *Crónicas de Nueva Venecia.*

40. Camayd-Freixas, "Penetrating Texts: Testimonial Pseudo-Chronicle in *La noche del Niño Alivés* by Edgardo Rodríguez Juliá seen from Siguenza y Góngora's *Infortunios de Alonso Ramírez,*" 169–92, *A Twice-Told Tale: Remembering the Encounter in Iberian/Iberian-American Literature, and Film,* ed. Santiago Juan Navarro and Theodore Robert Yánez (Newark: University of Delaware Press, 2003), 181.

41. Ibid., 185.

42. Cabrera, *Yemayá y Ochún,* 73.

43. Rodríguez Juliá, *En el camino de Yyaloide,* 96.

44. Lowery Stokes Sims, *Wifredo Lam and the International Avant Garde,* 153. Lowery Stokes Sims is quoting from Edmundo Desnoes, *Lam: Azul y negro.* Havana: Cuadernos de la Casa de las Americas, 1963, 14–15. Desnoes suggests that Lam's characters seem to emerge from legends he heard in his hometown. Among those legends was the one about "la madre de agua de la laguna de la laguna Hoyelos" (the mother of the fresh waters in the Hoyelos lagoon) Edmundo Desnoes, *Lam: azul y negro* (Havana: Cuadernos Casa de las Américas, 1963), 14. Desnoes quotes from *Estudios del folklore sagüero,* directed by Ana María Arissó (1940): "muchos afirmaban que se trataba de una serpiente de gigantescas proporciones, mientras que otros achacaban las desapariciones a la madre de agua que como una sombra negra se llevaba [*sic*] sobre la superficie de las aguas y devoraba todo cuanto encontraba en su camino" (Many affirmed that it was a gigantic serpent, while others blamed the disappearances to a Mother of the Waters that like a black shadow would rise to the surface and devour anything it found on its path) (ibid.).

45. Rodríguez Juliá, *En el camino de Yyaloide,* 87.

46. This is a possible playful reference to the attraction Luís Palés Matos felt toward the African legacy in Puerto Rican society that made him a guardian of the past, and of a negated African cultural realm, which he articulates in his Afro-Puerto Rican poems in *Tún Tún de pasa y grifería.*

47. In Afro-American mythology Oshun and Yemayá complement each other. Both are water deities, and both have similar avatars. In Brazil, Yemayá (Yemonja) is represented as a mermaid. In Cuba the *paleros* have a spirit that lives in the water they call *Mboma* and it is said, Cabrera writes, that *"Mboma es Yemayá por camino congo"* (Mboma is Yemayá in Congo beliefs) Lydia Cabrera, *Reglas de Congo. Mayombe Palo Monte* (Miami: Ediciones Universal, 1986), 128.

48. Rodríguez Juliá, *La noche oscura del Niño Avilés,* 180.

49. Rodríguez Juliá's image recalls Jorge Amado's main character in *Gabriela: Clove and Cinnamon* (1958). Amado's Gabriela, as well as Rodríguez Juliá's *Yyaloide,* are references, in the popular imaginary, to the African, Afro-Caribbean Oshun, whose color of skin is like the color of cinnamon, and her seduction like *oñí,* or honey.

50. Camayd-Freixas, "Penetrating Texts," 186.

51. Ibid.

52. Ibid.

53. Ibid.

54. Ibid., 14.

55. Guillermo Baralt, *Esclavos rebeldes. Conspiraciones y sublevaciones de esclavos en Puerto rico (1795–1873)* (Puerto Rico: Ediciones Huracán, Inc., 1981), 21.

56. Ibid., 33–36. Although there were other short-lived rebellions, most of the runaway slaves in Puerto Rico sought refuge in Haiti (ibid., 43–44, 120). After 1848, says Baralt, most slave revolts did not have as their goal political change or freedom, but vengeance against foremen and masters (ibid., 135, 144). This type of loss of memory, or political renunciation, related to an African past, increased when in 1855 a cholera epidemic decimated most of the slave population (ibid., 176).

57. Ibid., 11.

58. Ibid., 18.

59. Camayd-Freixas,"Penetrating Texts," 186–87.

60. José Luis González, "El país de cuatro pisos," 9–44, *El país de cuatro pisos y otros ensayos* (Río Piedras, Puerto Rico: Ediciones Huracán, 1980), 25.

61. Ibid., 22.

62. Ibid., 12.

63. Ibid., 12, and 18–19.

64. Ibid., 18.

65. Ibid., 20.

66. Ibid., 22.

67. Ibid., 97.

68. Juan Flores, *From Bomba to Hip-Hop: Puerto Rican Culture and Latino Identity* (New York: Columbia University Press, 2000), 33.

69. González, "El país de cuatro pisos," 23.

70. Ibid., 24.

71. Ibid., 27.

72. Ibid., 31.

73. Ibid., 33.

74. Ibid., 35.

75. Ibid., 37.

76. Ibid., 39.

77. Ibid., 41.

78. Ibid., 24.

79. Edgardo Rodríguez Juliá, *Puertorriqueños. Album de la sagrada familia puertorriqueña a partir de 1898* (Río Piedras, Puerto Rico: Editorial Plaza Mayor, 1988).

80. Ibid., 26.

81. Ibid., 28.

82. Rodríguez Juliá, "At the Middle of the Road," *Images and Identities. The Puerto Rican in Two World Contexts,* edited by Asela Rodríguez de Laguna (New Brunswick: Transaction Books, 1987), 124.

83. Rodríguez Juliá, "Tradición y utopía en el barroco caribeño," *Calibán: Revista de Literatura* 2, no. 3 (1985), 10.

84. Ibid., 127.

85. Ibid., 130.

86. Ibid., 10.

87. Díaz Quiñones, *El arte de bregar* (San Juan, P.R.: Ediciones Callejón, Inc., 2000), 201.

88. Ibid., 202.

89. Rubén González, *La Historia Puertorriqueña de Rodríguez Juliá* (Río Piedras, P.R.: Editorial de la Universidad de Puerto Rico, 1997), 44–45.

90. Ibid., 46.

91. Edgardo Rodríguez Juliá, *Las Tribulaciones de Jonás* (Río Piedras, Puerto Rico: Ediciones Huracá, 1981), 52–53.

92. Ibid., 46.

93. The similarities in these two novels address the repetition in Latin American literature of a cultural imaginary constructed out of a common experience, as well as a self-referential tendency to rewrite and reinvent history as a way to disrupt official master narratives.

94. Gustavo Pérez Firmat, *Life on the Hyphen: The Cuban-American Way* (Austin, Texas: University of Texas Press, 1994).

95. González, "El país de cuatro pisos," 15.

96. Benítez Rojo notes a similar situation in the case of Enriquillo, the cacique cimarrón who fought the Spanish crown for fifteen years in Hispaniola (*RI,* 249–52). Arcadio Díaz Quiñones suggests in *El arte de bregar,* that this type of crossroad characterizes Puerto Rican culture, and the art of "bregar" (put up with, or deal with) is a latent contemporary type of cimarronaje, a sort of running away, as a way of dealing with impossible situations.

97. Rodríguez Juliá, *Tribulaciones,* 46; also in Rubén González, *La Historia,* 58.

98. Rodríguez Juliá, "At the Middle of the Road," 122.

99. Ibid., 125.

100. Ibid., 130.

101. Camayd-Freixas, "Penetrating Texts: Testimonial," 178.

102. Ibid., 178–79.

103. Ibid., 179.

104. Ibid.

105. Ramón E. Soto-Crespo, "The Pains of Memory: Mourning the Nation in Puerto Rican Literature," *MLN* 117, no. 2 (2002): 454.

106. Rodríguez Juliá, *Campeche, o los diablejos de la melancolía* (San Juan, Puerto Rico: Instituto de Cultura Puerto Riqueña, 1986), 117–23.

107. In a similar way that the representation of Child Avilés in *Crónica de Nueva Venecia* intimates a reading of Campeche's portrait of Pantaleón Avilés, *En el camino de Yyaloide* is a text that pretends to be the exegesis of numerous fictitious paintings that register moments in the life of Rodríguez Juliá's Child Avilés. In this sense, the text offers a border zone of trans-artistic representations (literature and visual arts) in which the writer seems to be a critic and an observer of the paintings: a signature of the writer, Rodríguez Juliá, an art historian.

108. Juan Flores, *From Bomba to Hip-Hop, and Revolution, 1868–1898,* 26.

109. Camayd-Freixas, "Penetrating Texts," 180.

110. Fernando Ortiz, *Historia de una pelea cubana contra los demonios* (Havana: Editorial de Ciencias Sociales, 1975), 302. The few that settled inland founded the town of Santa Clara.

111. Ibid.

112. Ibid.

113. Ibid., 587.

114. Ibid.

115. Camayd-Freixas, "Penetrating Texts," 181.

116. Ortiz, *Historia de una pelea cubana contra los demonios,* 525.

117. Trespalacios's historical battle against African demons and African cultural expressions is addressed in the novel through the destruction of a neo-African kingdom, and through the constant presence of Leviathan which Rodríguez Juliá's Trespalacios associates with the rebellious creole population and the rebellion of his protégé Child Avilés.

118. In Puerto Rico, says Baralt, dances like the Bomba, of African roots, were often related to actual plans for slave rebellions, or the manifest desire to rebel and to escape. Ba-

ralt, *Esclavos rebeldes,* 59–65. The words of many of these songs were directly or allegorically related to rebellion, dissent, and the desire for freedom. Under systems of harsh repression, literature and music in the Caribbean have found ways to convey transgressing codified meanings that elude censorship.

119. Ibid.

120. Ortiz, *Historia de una pelea cubana contra los demonios,* 525. Ortiz takes this information from E. Bacardí, *Crónicas* II, 258.

121. Mignolo, *Local Histories/Global Designs,* ix.

122. Rodríguez Juliá, *La renuncia del héroe Baltazar,* 8.

123. Ibid., 46.

124. Zoé Valdés, *La nada cotidiana* (Barcelona: Emecé Editores España S.A., 1995), 15.

125. Ibid., 20.

126. See, Rita Molinero, "La 'morfología del lagarto' y el erotismo como redención en *La nada cotidiana* de Zoé Valdés," in *Crítica hispánica* XXII, no. 1 (2000), 132.

127. Ibid., 133.

128. Valdés dialogues in her novel with the work of other major Cuban writers. For example, in *La nada cotidiana,* Yocandra voices the "fear" Virginio Piñera claimed to feel, the hallucinations and sense of persecution Reinaldo Arenas articulates in his work, the mad woman's cry for freedom in Guillermo Cabrera's Infante's *Tres tristes tigres,* Lezama Lima's idea of the *Imago* as a "ceremonial creation," Severo Sarduy's definition of "neo-Baroque" style, and others like José Triana and Lydia Cabrera. It echoes Virgilio Piñera's famous words "Tengo miedo" (I am afraid) (Cabrera Infante, "Vidas para leerlas," *Vuelta* 10), when *Yocandra* also voices the same fear: "Tengo miedo, coño, eso sí. Por eso hablo de esto y de aquello y de lo otro y de lo más allá. Porque ahora veo miles de balsas repletas de cadáveres en el mar. Porque tengo el miedo más grande del mundo. Por eso chachareo y chachareo." (I am afraid, shit, yes. That is why I talk about this and that, about one thing and another; because now I see thousands of small boats in the ocean full of corpses; because I feel the greatest fear in the whole world) Valdés, *La nada cotidiana,* 171.

129. Interview with Enrico Mario Santí, "La vida es un salmón con grasa," *Bienes del siglo,* 8; cited also in Molinero, "La 'morfología del lagarto,'" 129.

130. Ibid. Also cited in Molinero, "La 'morfología del lagarto,'" 134.

131. Ibid. 131.

132. Ibid., 130.

133. Ibid., 128.

134. Kutzinski, *Sugar's Secrets,* 145.

135. Ibid., 165.

136. Molinero, "La 'morfología del lagarto,'" 131. Valdés explains that her grandmother introduced her to religious faith, both Christianity and Yoruba (Lucumí) faith: "dándome lecturas y mostrándome de diversas maneras el misterio a través de la religión yoruba, con la religión católica—es decir, todo ese arroz con mango . . . que somos nosotros" (giving me readings and teaching me about the Mystery in different ways through Yoruba religion, with Catholicism—that is, all of that mixture . . . that makes us who we are) Zoé Valdés, interviewed by Albert Pèlach, "Conferencia," (11/28/2000) http://www.circulolectores.com/minisites/zoé/conferencia.htm, 8.

137. Valdés, *La nada cotidiana,* 170.

138. Valdés, "Retrato de una infancia habanavieja," 17–24, in *Nuevos narradores cubanos,* edited by Mechi Strausfeld (Huertas, Spain: Ediciones Siruela, 2000), 23.

139. A form of Afro-Cuban belief system, of the Bantú traditions in the Caribbean. See, Cuervo Hewitt, *Aché,* 53–59.

140. Ibid., 23.

141. Cirilo Villaverde also gives his character, Cecilia Valdés, his own initials C. V.

142. This is the theme in Reinaldo Arena's *El Central* (Barcelona: Editorial Seix Barral, S.A., 1981).

143. Valdés, "Retrato de una infancia habanavieja," 17.

144. Bhabha, *The location of culture,* 114.

145. Ibid., 112.

146. Ibid., 113–14.

147. In Julia Herzberg, "Wifredo Lam: The Development of Style and World View, The Havana Years, 1941–1952," *Wifredo Lam and his Contemporaries,* 45.

148. Kutzinski, *Sugar's Secrets,* 92.

149. Zoé Valdés, *Querido primer novio (una historia proscrita de amor y naturaleza).* (Barcelona: Editorial Planeta, S. A., 1999). All references to this novel will be indicated as QPN.

150. Ibid., 92.

151. Schoolchildren in Cuba must go every year for a period of several months to work in the fields as part of their annual curriculum. This is known as "escuela al campo" (work-school in the country).

152. See Julia Cuervo Hewitt,"Iyá Iroko: El monte: espacio poético de conocimiento y de resistencia en *Querido primer novio* de Zoé Valdés," 33–53, *Afro-Hispanic Review* 24, no. 2 (2005). This article explores Valdés's dialogue in *Querido primer novio* with Lezama Lima's poetics. Some of the ideas proposed in this chapter were first explored in this article.

153. Such rejection has been common in Caribbean history. In Haiti, for example, soon after its independence, Toussaint Lovertoure rejected Voodoo in order to seek legitimization for his government from Western countries. Yet, such rejection brought other problems because, as Benítez Rojo points out, "historiographic models pertaining to Haiti cannot not include and take into account Voodoo as an important factor in all aspects of Haiti's social and political life" (*RI,* 162–63).

154. Cuervo Hewitt, *Aché,* 196–97.

155. In *Querido primer novio,* (m)other-ceiba-monte is Yyalode, the Iyaré (Great Lady) of the Afro-Cuban Lucumí, the *Ewelabá* (monte), and *Ilé Láyeré,* a term for Oshun, who presides over the African *Iroko,* which in Cuba is the Ceiba. Lydia Cabrera points out that the same word expresses the concept of "mother" in all of its variants, *Iyá,* in *Iyaré, Iyalá* (our lady the virgin), *Iyá Ilá* (grandmother), *Iyalocha* (Madre de Santo, or priestess), is also the word for bravery, *Iyaíya* (Cabrera, *Anagó,* 173). *Iyá* is also the name given to the largest drum, known as the mother drum (*Iyá*) of the three ritual *batá* drums, the next drum in size being *Itótele,* and the smallest, *Okónkolo.* See, Rhyna Moldes, *Música folklórica cubana* (Miami: Ediciones Universal, 1975), 22–23.

156. Cabrera, *El monte,* 15.

157. Benítez Rojo seems to forget that although the hero in *Espejo de paciencia* is an Ethiopian, (a testimony to the role of Africans in the formation of Cuban society during this period), as Moses E. Panford Jr. points out, Lope de Vega had already instituted in Spanish literary discourses a dichotomy between the image of Africans as "evil/uncivilized/infidels" and Ethiopians as "good/noble/civilized/Christian." See Moses Panford, "Blacks as Cultural Currency: Dissident Discourse in the Spanish Comedia," *Palara* No. 9, fall 2005, 10.

158. This is an important trope for Caribbean 'natural' life and myths; and one of the queen's companions in the land of Yyaloide in Rodríguez Juliá's *En el camino de Yyaloide.*

159. Aida Beaupied, *Narciso hermético,* 145.

160. Irlemar Chiampi, Introduction to José Lezama Lima, *La expresión Americana,* 17.

161. Ibid., 142, and 153–54.

162. Emilio Bejel, *José Lezama Lima, poeta de la imagen* (Madrid: Huerga y Fierro, 1994), 15.

163. Ibid., 14.

164. Lezama Lima, *La expresión Americana,* 49.

165. Ibid., 53.

166. The geographic area of La Fe represents in this novel a sacred zone in the cultural imaginary accessible only through ritual and faith. This is also a metaphor in Valdés's novel for a space of origin—of primal knowledge, hidden forces, and freedom—represented in the signifying body of a woman.

167. The rooster is ritual food for Ekué. See, Cabrera, *La sociedad secreta Abakuá,* 19. It is also food for Shango and for Elegua. It is the animal commonly used in ritual cleansings.

168. Cuervo Hewitt, *Aché,* 131.

169. In *El monte,* Cabrera points out that, according to her informants, Ceiba trees walk around and converse among each other at night in the forest. See Cabrera, *El monte,* 154. The same belief that trees walk around and talk can be found in Central America in *Maya-Quiché* lore.

170. Cuervo Hewitt, *Aché* 73–103.

171. Valdés, "Senelidad del asesino," (23 Sept. 2002) http://www.elmundo.es/2000/04/02opinión/02N0029.htm, 4.

172. Lezama Lima, *La expresión americana,* 63.

173. Cabrera, *El monte,* 13

174. Ibid.

175. Ibid., 14.

176. Ibid., 150

177. Ibid., 165.

178. Ibid., 149.

179. Cuervo Hewitt, *Aché,* 90.

180. Ortiz, *El huracán,* 592.

181. Valdés's representation of the Chicherekú coincides with Esteban Montejo's description of the Chicherekú as a "conguito de nación. No hablaba español" (a little being from the Congo. Did not speak Spanish) Barnet, *Biografía de un cimarrón,* 30. Valdés's representation also echoes Lezama's ideas that old and new myths acting upon history form the cultural web that is America. Lezama uses as an example the story of creation in the *Popol Vuh* that tells that the first creation was a failure. At first, there were no human beings, only clay dolls. The gods gave them the ability to speak (like the Chicherekús in Cuba). However, their bodies did not allow them to stand up, and although they could talk, they did not have a conscious. The gods exchanged the clay creatures for wooden ones, but the latter ones did not have a heart. The gods then ordered the destruction of that world due to their insensitivity. The new creatures, humans, comments Lezama, must stand the irritation of the gods with their previous creation. See, Lezama Lima, *La expresión Americana,* 67. This pre-Hispanic Caribbean story of the apocalyptic flood tells of the erasure, like *in The Kingdom of This World, One Hundred Years of Solitude,* and *Querido primer novio,* of a previously failed creation of beings that brought about the possibility of a new beginning.

182. The restoration of Chicherekú Mandiga's voice in *Querido primer novio,* is allegorical of a desired restoration of order, truth, and justice through the transformative act of writing. It is also an important signifying moment that dialogues, once more, with Lydia Cabrera's work. Let us remember that beginning with *¿Por qué? Cuentos negros de Cuba* (1948), Cabrera published her texts in Cuba under the rubric of "Colecciones del Chicherekú," and, later, "Colecciones del Chicherekú en el exilio." In Cabrera's description, Chicherekús are magic powerful dolls, artificial magic creations, similar to *anaquillé* magic dolls, that, as Cabrera explains, "el hechicero, mediante una operación misteriosa, infundía vida" (through a mysterious ritual, priests would infuse with life) and became servants of its creator. Cabrera, *¿Por qué?,* 244.

183. See Bhabha, *The location of culture,* 123–27.
184. Ibid., 49.
185. Lezama Lima, *La expresión americana,* 53.
186. Ibid. l, 54.
187. Ibid., 58.
188. This process of transformation, a metaphor for death and resurrection, as Aida Beaupied observes, is characteristic of Lezama's poetics. See Beaupied, *Narciso hermético* 144. Consequent with Beaupied's observation of Lezama's work, in *Querido primer novio,* poetry, myth, nature, and the poet, come together in an act of communion, that dissolves one in the other. Reminiscing Lezama's poetics, and his notion of poetic image, Dánae and Tierra's homoerotic union, and their final escape through metamorphosis, also propose a poetic communion with nature that transcends nature.
189. Lezama Lima, *Muerte de Narciso,* 40.
190. See Cuervo Hewitt, *Aché,* 178–83.
191. On the "hybrid" as product of colonialism, but as resistance and subversion, see Homi Bhabha, "Signs Taken fo Wonders, 29–35, in *Post Colonial Studies Reader,* edited by Bill Ashcroft, Gareth Griffiths, and Helen Tiffin (London: Routledge, 1995), 34–35.
192. Emilio Bejel notes that for Lezama Lima, the function of the image, as in Narcissus's "transcendence" "without wings:" "no se trata de la 'reproducción' de un mundo, sino de la 'creación' de un mundo" (is not about the "reproduction" of a world, but about the "creation" of a world) Bejel, *José Lezama Lima, poeta de la imagen,* 34.
193. Homi Bhabha, "Cultural Diversity and Cultural Differences," 206–9, in *Post Colonial Studies Reader,* ed. Bill Ashcroft, Gareth Griffiths, and Helen Tiffin (London: Routledge, 1995), 209.

Bibliography

Acosta, Leonardo. "El barroco americano y la ideología colonialista." *Unión* XI, no. 2–3 (1972): 52–63.

———. *Música y épica en la novela de Alejo Carpentier.* Havana: Editorial Letras Cubanas, 1981.

Alén, Olavo. "Las sociedades de tumba francesa en Cuba." In *Anales del Caribe.* 223–37. Havana: Centro de Estudios del Caribe. Casa de las Americas, 1982.

Alexis, Jacques Stephens. "Of the Marvelous Realism of the Haitians." In *The Post-Colonial Studies Reader,* edited by Bill Ashcroft, Gareth Griffiths, and Helen Tifin 194–98. London: Routledge, 1995.

Alonso, Alejandro. "¿Hay un estilo barroco cubano?" *Pensamiento crítico* no. 36 (January 1970): 199–208.

Arenas, Reinaldo, "Diosa instalada en el centro del poema." *Noticias del arte. Gaceta de las artes visuales, escénicas, musicales y literarias. (Número especial: Homenaje a Lydia Cabrera).* Nueva York (1982): 15.

———. *El Central.* Barcelona: Editorial Seix Barral, S. A., 1981.

Armas, Frederick de. "Lope de Vega y Carpentier." In *Actas del Simposio Internacional de Estudios Hispánicos,* edited by Mátyás Horányi, 363–73. Budapest. Editorial de la academia de ciencias de Hungría, 1978.

———. "Metamorphosis as Revolt: Cervantes's *Persiles y Segismunda* and Carpentier's *El reino de este mundo.*" *Hispanic Review* 49, no. 3 (1981): 297–316.

Arnold, A. James. *Modernism and Negritude. The Poetry and Poetics of Aimé Césaire.* Cambridge, MA: Harvard University Press, 1981.

Arrom, José Juan. *Certidumbre de América.* Madrid: Editorial Gredos, S.A., 1971.

——— and Manuel A. García Arévalo. *Cimarrón.* Santo Domingo: Ediciones Fundación García-Arévalo, Inc., 1986.

Ashcroft, Bill, Gareth Griffith, and Helen Tifflin. *The Empire Writes Back. Theory and Practice in Post-Colonial Literatures.* London: Routledge, 1989.

Baltar Rodríguez, José. *Los chinos de Cuba. Apuntes etnográficos.* Havana: Fundación Fernando Ortiz, 1997.

Baralt, Guillermo. *Esclavos rebeldes. Conspiraciones y sublevaciones de esclavos en Puerto Rico (1795–1873).* Puerto Rico: Ediciones Huracán, Inc., 1981.

Barnet, Miguel. *Autobiography of a Runaway Slave.* New York: The Bodley Head Ltd., 1968.

———. *Biografía de un cimarrón.* Barcelona: Ediciones Ariel, S. A., 1968.

———. "The Documentary Novel." *Cuban Studies/Estudios Cubanos* 11, no. 1 (1981): 19–32.

———. "Miguel Barnet charla con los editors de *Vórtice.*" Interviewed by Bernando Baycroft, Yvonne Hidalgo, and Arnoldo Ramos. *Vórtice* 2, no. 2–3 (1979): 1–10.

Bascom, William. *Shango in the New World.* Austin. The University of Texas at Austin, African and Afro-American Research Institute, 1972.

Bastide, Roger. *Las Américas Negras.* Madrid: Alianza Editorial, 1969.

Beaupied, Aida. "Acteón, Narciso, Martí y el adentramiento en la naturaleza en la poética de Lezama Lima," *Hispanófila* 108 (1993): 25–44.

———. "From Liberty to Fatherland: Sacrifice and Dead Certainties in the Critical Discourses of Cuba." In *Foucault and Latin America. Appropriations and Deployments of Discoursive Analysis,* edited by Benigno Trigo, 125–35. New York: Routledge, 2002.

———. *Narciso hermético: Sor Juana Inés de la Cruz y José Lezama Lima.* Liverpool: Liverpool University Press, 1997.

Bejel, Emilio. "Cultura y filosofía de la historia (Spengler, Carpentier, Lezama Lima)." *Cuadernos Americanos* XL. CCXXXIX, no. 6 (1981): 75–90.

———. *José Lezama Lima, poeta de la imagen.* Madrid: Huerga y Fierro, 1994.

Benítez Rojo, Antonio. *La isla que se repite.* Hanover: Ediciones del Norte, 1989.

———. *Paso de los vientos.* San Juan, Puerto Rico: Editorial Plaza Mayor, 1999.

———. *The Repeating Island. The Caribbean and the Postmodern Perspective.* Translated by James Maraniss. Durham: Duke University Press, 1996.

———. *A View From the Mangrove.* Translated by James Maraniss. Amherst: University of Massachusetts Press, 1998.

Bergua, Juan B. *Mitología universal* II. Madrid: Clásicos Bergua, 1979.

Betollini-Ciano, Claudia. "Entrevista exclusiva con Zoé Valdés" (lavox.com/arte/10-2-2001.phtml).

Bhabha, Homi. "Cultural Diversity and Cultural Differences." In the *Post Colonial Studies Reader,* edited by Bill Ashcroft, Gareth Griffiths, and Helen Tiffin, 206–9. London: Routledge, 1995.

———. *The Location of Culture.* London: Routledge, 1994.

———. "Signs Taken for Wonder." In *Post Colonial Studies Reader.* Edited by Bill Ashcroft, Gareth Griffiths, and Helen Tiffin, 29–35. London: Routledge, 1995.

Blanc, Giulio V. "Cuban Modernism: The Search for a National Ethos." In *Wifredo Lam and His Contemporaries 1938–1952,* edited by María R. Balderrama, 53– 69. New York: The Studio Museum in Harlem: Harry N. Abrams, Inc., 1992.

Bolívar Aróstegui, Natalia, and Natalia del Río Bolívar. *Lydia Cabrera en su laguna sagrada.* Santiago de Cuba: Editorial Oriente, 2000.

Bridge, Antony. *Suleiman the Magnific. Scourge of Heaven.* New York. Franklin Watts, 1983.

Breton, André. "Manifesto of Surrealism (1924)," In André Breton, *Manifestoes of Surrealism.* Translated by Richard Seaver and Helen R. Lane, 1–29. Ann Arbor: The University of Michigan, 1969.

———. "On Surrealism in Its Living Works," 295–304. In André Breton, *Manifestoes of Surrealism.* Translated by Richard Seaver and Helen R. Lane. Ann Arbor: The University of Michigan, 1969.

Bueno, Salvador. "Alejo Carpentier y sus conceptos de la historia." In *El ensayo y la crítica en Iberoamérica,* edited by Kurt Levy, and Keith Ellis, 257–63. Toronto: Instituto Internacional de Literatura iberoamericana,1970.

———. "La serpiente no se muerde la cola." In *Recopilación de textos sobre Alejo Carpentier,* edited by Salvador Arias, 201–18. Havana: Casa de las Américas, 1977.

Cabrera, Lydia. *Anaforuana. Ritual y símbolos de la iniciación en la sociedad secreta Abakuá.* Madrid: Forma Gráfica, S. A., 1975.

———. *Anagó: vocabulario lucumí (el Yoruba que se habla en Cuba)*. Miami: Ediciones Universal, 1986.

——— *Ayapá. Cuentos de jicotea*. Miami: Ediciones Universal, 1971.

———. *Contes nègres de Cuba*. Translated by Francis Miomandre. Paris: N.R.F. Gallimard, 1936.

——— "Carta de Lydia Cabrera a Teresa de la Parra." In *Páginas sueltas*, edited by Lydia Cabrera, and Isabel Castellanos, 212–14. Miami: Ediciones Universal, 1994.

———. *Cuentos negros de Cuba*. Madrid: Artes Gráficas, 1972. First published in Havana, 1940.

———. *El monte. Igbo. Finda. Ewe Orisha. Viti Nfinda (Notas sobre las religiones, la magia, las supersticiones y el folklore de los negros criollos del pueblo de Cuba)* Miami: Ediciones Universal, 1975. First published in Havana, 1954.

———. *La lengua sagrada de los ñáñigos*. Miami: Ediciones C & R, 1988.

———. *La sociedad secreta Abakuá, narrada por viejos adeptos*. Miami: Editorial C.R. (Colección del Chicherekú), 1970. First published in Havana, 1959.

———. "The Monkeys Lost the Fruit of Their Labor." In *Other Fires. Short Fiction by Latin American Women,* edited by Alberto Manguel, translated by Mary Caldwell and Suzanne Jill Levine. 200–5. New York: Clarkson N. Potter, Inc./Publishers, 1986.

———. *¿Por qué? Cuentos negros de Cuba*. Madrid: C & R, Ramos Artes Gráficas, 1972. First published in Havana, 1948.

———. *Reglas de Congo Mayombe Palo Monte*. Miami: Ediciones Universal, 1986.

———. *Yemayá y Ochún. Kariocha, Iyalorichas y Olorichas*. Madrid: Forma Gráfica, S. A., 1974.

Cabrera Infante, Guillermo. "Guillermo Cabrera Infante." In *Homenaje a Lydia Cabrera,* edited by Reinaldo Sánchez, José antonio Madrigal, Ricardo Viera, José Sánchez-Boudy (congreso de literature Afro-Americana), 16–17. Barcelona: Ediciones Universal, 1978.

——— "The Death of Virgilio Piñera." In Virgilio Piñera, *Cold Tales,* translated by Mark Schafer, xi–xiv. Hygiene, Colorado: Eridanos Press, 1988.

———. "Letter to Lydia Cabrera." March 22, 1975. In Heritage Collection, File 0339, Series I, Box 5, University of Miami, Florida.

———. *Tres tristes tigres*. Barcelona: Editorial Seix Barrral S.A., 1965.

———. *Three Trapped Tigers*. Translated by Suzanne Jill Levine and Donald Gardner. New York: Harper and Row, Publisher, Inc., Marlowe and Co., 1971.

———. *Vidas para leerlas*. Madrid: Alfaguara, 1998.

———. "Vidas para leerlas," *Vueltas* 4, no. 41 (1980): 4–16.

———. *Vista del amanecer en el trópico*. Barcelona: Editorial Seix Barral, 1974.

Camayd-Freixas, Erik. "Penetrating Texts: Testimonial Pseudo-Chronicle in *La noche del Niño Avilés* by Edgardo Rodríguez Juliá Seen from Siguenza y Góngora's *Infortunios de Alonso Ramírez*." In *A Twice-Told Tale. Remembering the Encounter in Iberian, Iberian American Literature, and Film,* edited by Santiago Juan Navano and Theodore Robert Yánez, 169–92. Newark: University of Delaware Press; London: Associated University Presses, Inc., 2003.

Campbell, Mavis C. *The Maroons of Jamaica. A History of Resistance, Collaboration, and Betrayal*. Massachusetts: Bergin and Garvey Publishers, 1988.

Carbonell, Walterio. *Critica. Cómo surgió la cultura nacional*. Havana: Ediciones yaka, 1961.

Carpentier, Alejo. *Crónicas* I. Havana: Instituto Cubano del Libro. Editorial Arte y Literatura, 1975.

————. *Crónicas* II. Havana: Instituto Cubano del Libro. Editorial Arte y Literatura, 1976.

————. *Ecué-Yamba-O.* Havana: Editorial Arte y Literatura, 1977.

————. *El reino de este mundo.* Barcelona. Edhasa Editores, 1978.

————. "Habla Alejo Carpentier." *Recopilación de textos sobre Alejo Carpentier,* edited by Salvador Arias, 15–55. Havana: Centro de Investigaciones Literarias, Casa de las Américas, 1977.

————. *Historia de la música en Cuba.* Havana: Editorial Letras Cubanas, 1978. First published in Havana, 1946.

————. Interviewed by Exilia Saldaña. "La persistencia de una trayectoria." In *Entrevistas,* edited by Virgilio López Lemus, 347–52. Havana: Editorial Letras cubanas, 1985.

————. *The Kingdom of This World.* Translated by Harriet de Onís. New York: Knopf, 1957.

————. *La novela latinoamericana en vísperas de un nuevo siglo y otros ensayos.* México: Siglo veintiuno editores, S.A. 1981.

————. "La novela latinoamerican en vísperas de un nuevo siglo." In *Historia y ficción en la narrativa hispanoamericana,* edited by Roberto González Echevarria, 19–48. Venezuela: Monte Avila Editores, 1984.

————. *Letra y solfa. Visión de América.* Alexis Márquez, ed. Buenos Aires. 1976.

————. "Los fugitivos." In *Guerra del tiempo,* 101–20. Barcelona: Barral Editores, S.A., 1973.

————. *Obras completas* I. México: Siglo Veintiuno, editores, S.A., 1983.

————. *Tientos y diferencias.* Montevideo: Editorial Arca, 1967.

————. "Viaje a la semilla." In *Guerra del tiempo.* 55–81. Barcelona: Barral Editores S. A., Ediciones Corregidor, 1970.

Carril, Pepe. *Shango de Ima. A Yoruba Mystery Play.* English adaptation by Susan Sherman. New York: Doubleday and Company, Inc., 1970.

Castellanos, Isabel. "Abre Kutu Wiri Ndinga. Lydia Cabrera y las lenguas africanas." In *En torno a Lydia Cabrera (Cincuentenario de "Cuentos negros de Cuba"1936–1986).* Edited by Isabel Castellanos, and Josefina Inclán, 212–26. Miami: Ediciones Universal, 1987.

————, and Jorge Castellanos. *El negro en Cuba 1492–1844. Cultura Afrocubana* I. Miami, Florida: Ediciones Universal, 1988.

————. *El negro en Cuba 1845–1959. Cultura Afrocubana* II. Miami, Florida: Ediciones Universal, 1990.

————. *Las religiones afrocubanas. Cultura Afrocubana* III Miami: Ediciones Universal, 1992.

————. *Letras, Música, Arte. Cultura Afrocubana* IV. Miami: Ediciones Universal, 1994.

Césaire, Aimé. *Cahier d'un Retour au Pays Natal.* Paris: Présence Africaine, 1971 (1940).

————. *Retorno al País Natal.* Translated by Lydia Cabrera. Havana: Colección de textos poéticos, 1943.

Césaire, Suzanne. "Malaise d'un civilization." In *Tropiques* 5 (April 1942), 43–49.

Chao, Ramón. *Palabras en el tiempo de Alejo Carpentier.* Barcelona: Editorial Argos Vergara, S. A., 1984.

Cirlot, Juan-Eduardo. *Diccionario de símbolos.* Barcelona. Editorial Labor S.A., 1988.

Coachy, Lucien Georges. *Culto Vodú y brujería en Haití.* México. Secretaría de Educación. Sepsetentas Dianas, 1982.

Correa Rodríguez, Pedro. *La poética de Lezama Lima: "Muerte de Narciso"*. Granada: Universidad de Granada, 1994.

Coulthard, G. R. *Raza y color en la literatura antillana*. Sevilla: Escuela de estudios hispano-americanos de Sevilla, 1958.

Cuervo Hewitt, Julia. *Aché, presencia africana. Tradiciones yoruba-lucumí en la narrativa cubana*. New York: Peter Lang Publishing, Inc., 1988.

———. "El texto 'travesti': narrativa y testimonio." *Cuban Studies/Estudios cubanos* 22, no. 1–2 (1989): 53–65.

———. "Iyá-Iroko. El monte, espacio poético de conocimiento y de resistencia en *Querido primer novio* de Zoé Valdés." *Afro-Hispanic Review* 24, no. 2 (2005): 33–53.

———. "Luis de Camoens en el reino de Calibán: *Las Lusíadas* en *Changó, el gran Putas* de Manuel Zapata Olivella." *Afro-Hispanic Review* 22, no. 1 (2003): 13–23.

———. "Lydia Cabrera." In *Dictionary of Literary Biography* 145 (Modern Latin-American Ficcion Writers. Second Series). Edited by William Luis and Ann González, 82–90. Detroit: Gale Research Inc., 1994,

Danger Roll, Zoila. *Los cimarrones de El Frijol*. Santiago de Cuba: Empresa Editorial Oriente, 1977.

Dash, Michael. "Marvelous Realism: The Way Out of Négritude." In *The Post-Colonial Studies Reader,* edited by Bill Ashcroft, Gareth Griffiths, Helen Tiffin, 199–201. London: Routledge, 1995.

Davis, Martha Ellen. *La otra ciencia. El Vodú dominicano como religión y medicina populares*. Santo Domingo, RD: Editora Universitaria-UASD, Colección Estudios Sociales No. 5, 1987.

De la Parra, Teresa. *Cartas a Lydia Cabrera*. Edited by Rosario Hiriart. Madrid: Ediciones torremozas, 1988.

———. *Iphigenia: The Diary of a Young Lady Who Wrote Because She Was Bored*. Austin, Texas: University of Texas Press, 1993.

Dechamps Chapeaux, Pedro. *Los cimarrones urbanos*. Havana: Editorial de Ciencias Sociales, 1983.

Deive, Carlos Esteban. *Los cimarrones del Maniel de Neiba*. República Dominicana: Banco Central de la República Dominicana, 1985.

———. *Los guerrilleros negros. Esclavos fugitivos y cimarrones en Santo Domingo*. Santo Domingo: Fundación Cultural Dominicana, 1989.

Deleuze, Gilles. "Literature and Life." Translated by Daniel W. Smith and Michael A. Creco. *Critical Inquiry* 23 (1997): 225–29.

———. *A Thousand Plateaus: Capitalism and Schizophrenia*. Minneapolis: University of Minnesota Press, 1987.

Delgado, Morúa. *La familia Unzúanzu*. Havana: Editorial arte y literatura, 1975.

Deren, Maya. "Religion and Magic." *Tomorrow. Haiti Issue* 3, no. 1 (1954): 21– 51.

Derrida, Jacques. *Dissemination*. Translated by Barbara Johnson. Chicago: The University of Chicago Press, 1981.

———. *Specters of Marx. The State Debt, the Work of Mourning, and the New International*. Translated by Peggy Kamuf. New York: Routledge, 1994.

Desnoes, Edmundo. *Lam: azul y negro*. Havana: Cuadernos Casa de las Américas, 1963.

Díaz Quiñones, Arcadio. *El arte de bregar*. San Juan, P. R.: Ediciones Callejón, Inc., 2000.

———. *La memoria rota*. San Juan, Puerto Rico: Ediciones Huracán, Inc., 1996.

Díaz Soler, Luis M. *Historia de la esclavitud negra en Puerto Rico.* Río Piedras: Editorial Universitaria, 1981.

Diccionario de autoridades. Real Academia Española. (Facsimile of the 1737 edition). Madrid. Editorial Gredos, S.A., 1964.

Diccionario de filósofos. Madrid: Centro de estudios filosóficos de Gallarate. Ediciones Rioduero, 1986.

Dixon, Pierson. *Pauline. Napoleon's Favourite Sister.* London: Collins Clear-Type Press, 1964.

Duplessis, Yves. *Surrealism.* New York: Walker and Company, 1962.

Eddy, Shauna Lee. "Translation as the Meeting of Signed and Spoken Languages: The Trickster's Role in Mediating Deaf Identity Construction." In *A Tradução nas Encruzilhadas da Cultura,* edited by João Ferreira Duarte, 55–83. Lisbon: Edições Colibri, 2001.

Eguilaz y Yanguas, D. Leopoldo de. *Glosario Etimológico de las palabras españolas de origen oriental.* (Facsimile of the 1886 edition). Madrid: Ediciones Atlas, 1974.

Fanon, Frantz. *Black Skin, White Masks.* New York: Grove Weidenfeld, 1967.

Fernández-Marcané, Leonardo. "Semblanza de Lydia Cabrera. Un ala de suavísimo vuelo hacia nuestro pasado." In *En torno a Lydia Cabrera. Cincuentenario de* Cuentos negros de Cuba *1936–1986,* edited by Isabel Castellanos, 37–42. Miami: Ediciones Universal, 1987.

Fernández Retamar, *Calibán y otros ensayos.* Havana: Editorial Arte y Literatura, 1979.

Ferrer, Ada. *Insurgent Cuba. Race, Nation, and Revolution, 1868–1898.* Chapel Hill: The University of North Carolina Press, 1999.

Figueroa, Esperanza. "Tres vidas divergentes, Lydia, Enríquez y Carpentier." In *En torno a Lydia Cabrera. Cincuentenario de* Cuentos negros de Cuba *(1936–1986),* edited by Isabel Catellanos and Josefina Inclán, 278–299. Miami: Ediciones Universal, 1987.

Flores, Juan. *From Bomba to Hip-Hop. Puerto Rican Culture and Latino Identity.* New York: Columbia University Press, 2000.

Foucault, Michel. *The Archeology of Knowledge and the Discourse on Language.* Translated by A. M. Sheridan Smith. New York: Tavistack Publications Limited, 1972.

Franco, Franklin J. *Los negros, los mulattos y la nación dominicana.* Santo Domingo: Editora Nacional, 1969.

Franco, José Luciano. "Africanos y sus descendientes criollos en las luchas liberadoras 1533–1895." *Casa de las Américas* XVI, no. 93 (1975): 12–21.

———. *La conspiración de Aponte.* Havana: Consejo Nacional de Cultura. Publicaciones del Archivo Nacional LVIII, 1963.

———. *La minas de Santiago del Prado y la rebelión de los cobreros 1530–1800.* Introduction by Pedro Deschamps Chapeaux. Havana: Editorial de ciencias Sociales, 1975.

———. *La presencia negra en el nuevo mundo.* Havana: Casa de las Américas, 1968.

———. "Los cobreros y los palenques de los negros cimarrones." *Revista de la biblioteca nacional José Martí* 64 (1973): 37–46.

———. *Los palenques de los negros cimarrones.* (Cuaderno 7). Havana: Departamento de orientación revolucionaria del comité central del partido Comunista de Cuba, 1973.

———. "Palenques del Frijol, Bumba y Maluala." *Universidad de la Habana* no. 160 (1963): 167–79.

Friedmann, Nina, and Richard Cross. *Ma Mgombe: guerreros y ganaderos en Palenque.* Bogota, Columbia: Carlos Valencia Editores, 1979.

Frobenius, Leon. *Decamerón negro.* Havana: Revista de Occidente, 1925.

Fúre Martínez, Rogelio. *Diálogos imaginarios.* Havana: Editorial Arte y Literatura, 1979.

Gallagher, David P. "Guillermo Cabrera Infante." In *G. Cabrera Infante,* edited by Julián Ríos, translated by Blanca Tera, 47–79. Caracas: Editorial Fundamentos, 1974.

García Lorca, Federico. *Poets in New York.* Translated by Ben Belitt. New York: Grove Press, Inc., 1955.

Gates, Henry Louis, Jr. *Figures in Black. Words, Signs, and the "Racial" Self.* N.Y.: Oxford University Press, 1987.

———. *The Signifying Monkey. A Theory of Afro-American Literary Criticism.* New York: Oxford University Press, 1988.

Glissant, Edouard. "Alejo Carpentier y la 'otra América.'" *Setecientos Monos* III, no. 8 (Rosario, Argentina) (1960): 9–11.

———. *Caribbean Discourse. Selected Essays.* Charlottesville: University Press of Virginia, 1989.

———. *Poetics of Relations.* Translated by Betsy Wing. Ann Arbor: University of Michigan Press, 1990; 1997.

Goethe, Johann Wolfgang von. *Faust.* Introduction by Victor Lange. Translated by Bayard Taylor. New York: Random House, Inc., 1950.

Gómez de Avellaneda, Gertrudis. *Sab.* Havana: Instituto cubano del libro, 1973.

González, José Luis. "El país de cuatro pisos." In *El país de cuatro pisos y otros ensayos,* 9–44. Río Piedras, Puerto Rico: Ediciones Huracán, 1980, 1985.

González, Rubén. *La Historia Puertorriqueña de Rodríguez Juliá.* Río Piedras: Editorial de la Universidad de Puerto Rico, 1997.

González Bermejo, Ernesto. "Carpentier: trastornar la cronología," *Correo.* Lima, 29 febrero (n/d): 8–9.

González Echevarría, Roberto. *The Pilgrim at Home.* Ithaca. Cornell University, 1977.

———. *The Voice of the Masters. Writing and Authority in Modern Latin American Literature.* Austin: University of Texas Press, 1988.

González Pérez, Aníbal. "La (sín)tesis de una poesía antillana: Palés y Spengler." *Cuadernos Hispanoamericanos. Los negros en América* no. 451–52 (Special Edition) (1988): 59–72.

———. "Una alegoría de la cultura puertorriqueña: *La noche oscura del niño Avilés* de Edgardo Rodríguez Juliá." *Revista Iberoamericana* no. 135–36 (1986): 583–90.

Guibert, Rita. "Guillermo Cabrera Infante. Conversación sobre *Tres tristes tigres.*" In *G. Cabrera Infante,* edited by Julián Ríos, 19–46. Madrid: Editorial Fundamentos, 1974.

Guillén, Nicolás. *Patria o muerte. The Great Zoo and Other Poems.* Translated by Robert Márquez. Havana: Editorial Arte y Literatura, 1975.

———. *Nicolás Guillén. Sóngoro cosongo. El son entero.* Edited by Ernesto Sábato. Buenos Aires, Editorial Losada, 1998.

Guirao, Ramón. *Orbita de la poesía afrocubana 1928–1937.* Havana: Ucar, García y Cía, 1938.

Guizar Álvarez, Eduardo, and Adriana Méndez Rodena. "Caña/cuerpo/danza: Imágenes de opresión/liberación del sujeto caribeño." *Crítica hispánica. Edición especial: El Caribe en su literatura* XXI, no. 1 (2000): 61–77.

Harris, Wilson. "The Limbo Gateway." In *The Post-Colonial Studies Reader,* edited by Bill Ashcroft, Gareth Griffiths, and Helen Tiffin, 378–82. London: Routledge, 1995.

Harvey, Sally. *Carpentier's Proustian Fiction. The Influence of Marcel Proust on Alejo Carpentier.* London: Tamesis, 1994.

Hasson, Liliane. "Lydia Cabrera en los Estados Unidos." In *En torno a Lydia Cabrera.* Edited by Isabel Castellanos, 95–103. Miami: Ediciones Universal, 1987.

Hegel, Georg Wilhelm Friedrich. *Phenomenology of Spirit.* Translated by A. V. Miller. Oxford: Oxford University Press, 1977.

———. *The Philosophy of History.* Translated by J. Sibree. New York: Dover Publications, Inc., 1956.

Herskovits, Melville. "What is Voodoo?" *Tomorrow* 3, no. 1 (1954): 11–20.

Herzberg, Julia P. "Wifredo Lam: The Development of a Style and World View, The Havana Years, 1941–1952." In *Wifredo Lam and His Contemporaries 1938–1952,* edited by Balderrama, María R. 31–51. New York: The Studio Museum in Harlem: Harry N. Abrams, Inc., 1992.

Hiriart, Rosario. *Cartas a Lydia Cabrera (Correspondencia inédita de Gabriela Mistral y Teresa de la Parra).* Madrid: Ediciones Torremozas, 1998.

———. "Conversaciones con Lydia Cabrera," File 0339, Serie I, Box 5, Heritage Collection, University of Miami, Florida.

———. "Lydia Cabrera, cronología: Vida y Obras." *Noticias de Arte. Gaceta de las artes visuales, escénicas, musicales y literarias (Número especial. Homenaje a Lydia Cabrera.* New York (1982): 26–30.

———. *Lydia Cabrera: Vida hecha arte.* Madrid: Eliseo Torres and Sons, 1978.

Historia de Cuba. La Habana: Editorial de Ciencias Sociales, 1985.

Hutcheon, Linda. *The Poetics of Postmodernism. History, Theory, Fiction.* New York: Routledge, 1988.

Inclán, Josefina. *Ayapá y otras 'Otán Iyebiyé' de Lydia Cabrera.* Miami: Ediciones Universal, 1976.

Irele, Abiola. "Negritude: Literature and Ideology." In *Modern Black Novelists. A Collection of Essays,* edited by M. G. Cooke, 13–23. Englewood Cliffs, New Jersey: Prentice-Hall, Inc., 1971.

James, C. L. R. *The Black Jacobins. Toussaint, L'Overture, and the San Domingue Revolution.* New York: Random House, Inc., 1989.

Jameson, Fredric. *The Political Unconscious. Narrative as a Socially Symbolic Act.* Ithaca: Cornell University Press, 1981.

Janney, Frank. *Alejo Carpentier and his Early Works.* London: Tamesis Books Limited, 1981.

Jiménez, Reynaldo L. *Guillermo Cabrera Infante y Tres tristes tigres.* Miami, Florida: Ediciones Universal, 1977.

Keen, Benjamin. *Latin American Civilization, History, and Society, 1492 to the Present.* Boulder, CO: Westview Press, 1991.

Knight, Richard Payne, Esq. *The Symbolical Language of Ancient Art and Mythology. An Inquiry.* New York: J. W. Bouton, 1876.

Krakusin, Margarita. "Conversación informal con Manuel Zapata Olivella." *Afro-Hispanic Review* 20, no. 1 (2001): 15–28.

Kristeva, Julia. *Desire in Language. A Semiotic Approach to Literature and Art.* Edited by Leon S. Roudiez. Translated by Thomas Gora, Alice Jardine, and Leon Roudiez. New York: Columbia University Press, 1980.

Kutzinski, Vera M. *Sugar's Secrets. Race and the Erotic of Cuban Nationalism.* Charlottesville: University Press of Virgina, 1993.

Lachatañeré, Rómulo. *¡Oh, mío Yemayá!* Manzanillo, Cuba: Editorial el Arte, 1938.

Lalla, Barbara. *Defining Jamaican Fiction. Marronage and the Discourse of Survival.* Tuscaloosa: The University of Alabama Press, 1996.

Landaluze, Victor. *Tipos y costumbres de la isla de Cuba: Colección de artículos.* Havana: Miguel de Villa, 1881.

La Rosa Corso, Gabino. *Los cimarrones de Cuba.* Havana: Editorial de Ciencias Sociales, 1988.

Leante, César. "Confesiones sencilllas de un escritor barroco." In *Recopilación de textos sobre Alejo Carpentier,* edited by Salvador Arias, 57–70. Havana: Casa de las Américas, Centro de investigacones literarias, 1977.

———. "El mito del lenguaje en la literatura latinoamericana." *Unión* XIII, no. 4 (1974): 167.

———. "Federico en Cuba." *Cuadernos hispanoamericanos* no. 433–36 (1986): 235–40.

———. *Los guerrilleros negros.* La Habana: Unión de Escritores y Artistas, 1976.

Levine, Suzanne Jill. "Translation as (sub)version: On Translating Infante's Inferno." In *Rethinking Translation. Discourse, Subject, Ideology,* edited by Lawrence Venuti, 75–85. London: Routledge, 1992.

Lévy-Strauss, Claude. *The Raw and the Cooked. Introduction to a Science of Mythology* 1. Translated by John and Dareen Weightman. Chicago: The University of Chicago Press, 1969.

———. "The Structural Study of Myth," In *The Critical Tradition,* edited by David H. Richter, 836–44. Boston: Bedford/St. Martin's, 1998.

Lezama Lima, José. "El nombre de Lydia Cabrera." In *Noticias de Arte. Gaceta de las artes visuales, escénicas, musicales y literarias. (Número especial. Homenaje a Lydia Cabrera),* New York (1982). 3.

———, *El reino de la imagen.* Caracas: Biblioteca Ayacucho, s.f. (prólogo de Julio Ortega).

———. *La expresión americana.* Edition and introduction by Irleman Chiampi. México: Fondo de Cultura Económica, 1993.

———. *Muerte de Narciso. Antología poética.* Edited by David Huerta. Mexico: Ediciones Era, 1988.

Lizardo, Fradique. *Cultura Africana en Santo Domingo.* Santo Domingo. Sociedad Industrial Dominicana, n/d.

López-Baralt, Mercedes. *La poesía de Luis Palés Matos.* San Juan, Puerto Rico: Editorial de la Universidad de Puerto Rico, 1995.

Lucy, Niall. *Postmodern Literary Theory. An Introduction.* Oxford U.K.: Blackwell Publishers Ltd, 1997; 1998.

Ludmer, Josefina. *Cien años de soledad: una interpretación.* Buenos Aires: Editorial Tiempo Contemporáneo, 1972.

Luis, William. *"Cecilia Valdés:* el nacimiento de una novela antiesclavista." *Cuadernos hispanoamericanos.* (1988): 187–193.

———. *Literary Bondage. Slavery in Cuban Narrative.* Austin: University of Texas Press, 1990.

——— and Julia Cuervo Hewitt. "Santos y santería: Conversación con Arcadio, santero de Guanabacoa." *Afro-Hispanic Review* VI, no. 1 (1987): 9–17.

Lukács, Georg. *The Young Hegel. Studies in the Relations between Dialectics and Economics.* Translated by Rodney Livingston. London: Merlin Press, 1975.

Magnorelli, Sharon. "The 'Writerly' in *Tres Tristes Tigres.*" In *The Analysis of Hispanic Texts: Current Trends and Methodology,* edited by Lisa E. Davis and Isabel C. Tarán, 320–35. New York: Bilingual Press, 1976.

Marinello, Juan. *Literatura hispanoamericana.* Mexico: Ediciones de la Universidad Nacional de Mexico, 1937.

Martí, José. *La gran encyclopedia Martiana* 9 and 12. Edited by Ramón Cernuda. Miami: Editorial Martiana, Inc., 1978.

———. *Los mejores versos de José Martí.* Cuadernillo de Poesía 16. Buenos Aires: Nuestra América, 1961.

———. *Nuestra América.* Buenos Aires: Editorial Losada, S.A., 1980.

Matas, Julio. "Infiernos fríos de Virgilio Piñera." Linden Lane IV, no. 2 (1985): 22–25.

Merrim, Stephanie. "A Secret Idiom: The Grammar and Role of Language in *Tres tristes tigres.*" In *Modern Latin American Fiction,* edited by Harold Bloom, 323–41. New York: Chelsea House Publishers, 1990.

Merriman, Roger Bigelow. *Suleiman The Magnificent 1520–1566.* New York: Cooper Square Publishers, Inc., 1966.

Meyer, Doris. "'Feminine' Testimony in the Works of Teresa de la Parra, Maria Luisa Bombal, and Victoria Ocampo." In *Contemporary Women Authors of Latin America,* edited by Doris Meyer and Margarite Fernández Olmos, 1–15. New York: Brooklyn College Press, 1983.

Mignolo, Walter D. *Local Histories/Global Designs. Coloniality, Subaltern Knowledge, and Border Thinking.* Princeton, New Jersey: Princeton University Press, 2000.

Miller, Marilyn Grace. *Rise and Fall of the Cosmic Race: The Cult of Mestizaje in Latin America.* Austin: University of Texas Press, 2004.

Mistral, Gabriela. "Carta a Lydia Cabrera," *Noticias de arte. Gaceta de artes visuales, escénicas, musicales y literarias (Número especial. Homenaje a Lydia Cabrera).* New York (1982): 10–11.

Moldes, Rhyna. *Musica folklórica cubana.* Miami: Ediciones Universal, 1975.

Molinero, Rita "La 'morfología del lagarto' y el erotismo como redención en *La nada cotidiana* de Zoé Valdés." *Crítica hispánica* XXII, no. 1 (2000): 121–34.

Molloy, Sylvia. "Disappearing Acts: Reading Lesbian in Teresa de la Parra." In *¿Entiendes? Queer Readings, Hispanic Writings,* edited by Emilie L. Bergman and Paul Julian Smith, 230–56. Durham: Duke University Press, 1995.

Moreno Fraginals, Manuel. "Azúcar, esclavos y revolución (1790–1868)." *Casa de las Américas* IV, no. 50 (1968): 35–45.

Morínigo, Marcos A. *Diccionario de americanismos.* Barcelona: Muchnick Editores, 1985.

Moore, Carlos. *Castro, The Blacks, and Africa.* Los Angeles: University of California. Afro-American Culture and Society Vol. 8, 1988.

Morúa Delgado, Martín. *La familia Unzúanzu.* Havana: Editorial Arte y Literatura, 1975.

Moya Pons, Frank. *La dominación haitiana (1822–1844).* Santiago, República Dominicana: Universidad Católica Madre y Maestra, 1978.

———. *La Española en el siglo XX (1493–1520). Trabajo, Sociedad y Política en la Economía del Oro.* Santiago, República Dominicana: Universidad Católica Madre y Maestra, 1978.

Nelson, Ardis. *Cabrera Infante in the Menippean Tradition*. Newark, Delaware: Juan Cuesta-Hispanic Monograph, 1983.

Nistal Moret, Benjamin. *Esclavos prófugos y cimarrones*. *Puerto Rico 1770–1870*. San Juan, Puerto Rico: Editorial de la Universidad de Puerto Rico, 2000.

Ogunba, Oyin, "Ceremonies," In *Sources of Yoruba History*, edited by Saburi Olademi Biobaku, 87–110. Oxford: Clarendon Press, 1973.

Ortega y Gasset, José. "Hegel y América." In *Obras completas* II, no. 36, 563–76. Madrid: Ediciones Castilla, Revista de Occidente, 1961.

Ortiz Cerberio, Cristina, "La narrativa de Zoé Valdés: hacia una reconfiguración de la na(rra)ción cubana". *Chasqui* XXVII, no. 2 (1998): 116–27.

Ortiz, Fernando. *Contrapunteo cubano del tabaco y el azúcar*. Venezuela: Biblioteca Ayacucho, 1987. First published in 1947.

———. *El huracán, su mitología y sus símbolos*. México: Fondo de Cultura Económica, 1947.

———. *Hampa afrocubana*. *Los negros brujos (apunte para un estudio de etnología criminal)*. Miami: Ediciones Universal, 1973.

———. *Historia de una pelea cubana contra los demonios*. Havana: Editorial de Ciencias Sociales, 1975.

———. *La antigua fiesta afrocubana del "Día de Reyes."* Havana: Departamento de Asuntos Culturales, División de Publicaciones, 1960

———. *Los negros curros*. Havana: Editorial de Ciencias Sociales, 1986.

———. *Los negros esclavos*. Havana: Editorial de Ciencias Sociales, 1975.

———. *Nuevo catauro de cubanismos*. Havana: Editorial de Ciencias Sociales. Instituto cubano del libro, 1974.

Otero, Lisandro. "Las ideas políticas de Fernando Ortiz." In *Anales del Caribe. Casa de las Américas,* 38–44. Havana: Centro de Estudios del Caribe, 1982.

Padura Fuentes, Leonardo. *José María Heredia. La patria y la vida*. Havana: Ediciones Unión, 2003.

Palés Matos, Luis. *Tuntún de pasa y grifería*. San Juan, Puerto Rico: Edición especial para Cultural Puertorriqueña, Editora Corripio, C. Por A., 1988.

Panford Moses, Jr. "Blacks as Cultural Currency: Dissident Discourse in the Spanish Comedia," *Palara* 9 (Fall 2005): 5–19.

Parry, Benita. "Resistance Theory/Theorising Resistance or Two Cheers for Nativism." In *Colonial Discourse/Postcolonial Theory,* edited by Francis Barker, Peter Hulme, and Margaret Iversen, 172–96. UK: Manchester University Press, 1994.

Paz, Octavio. *Puertas al campo*. Barcelona: Seix Barral, 1972.

———. *Sor Juana Inés de la Cruz o las trampas de la fe*. México: Fondo de Cultura Económica, 1982.

Pedreira, Antonio S. *Insularismo*. Río Piedras, Puerto Rico: Editorial Edil, Inc., 1985.

Pereda, Rosa María. *Cabrera Infante*. Barcelona: EDAF, Ediciones-Distribuciones, S.A., 1979.

Perera, Hilda. *Idapo. El sincretismo en los cuentos negros de Lydia Cabrera*. Miami: Ediciones Universal, 1971.

Pérez-Firmat, Gustavo. *Life on the Hyphen. The Cuban-American Way*. Austin, Texas: University of Texas Press, 1994.

———. *The Cuban Condition. Translation and Identity in Modern Cuban Literature*. Cambridge: Cambridge University Press, 1989.

Piedra, José. "*Monte:* Poetics in a Clearing of the Forest," Paper presented to the Department of Spanish/ Afro- American Studies. Yale University.

Popol Vuh. Las antiguas historias del Quiché. Traslated by Adrián Recinos. Mexico: Fondo de Culturas Económicas, 1952.

Quint, David. *Epic and Empire, Politics and Generic Form from Virgil to Milton.* Princeton: Princeton University Press, 1993.

Quiroga, José. "Lydia Cabrera, Invisible." In *Sexualidad y nación,* edited by Daniel Balderston, 99–109. Pittsburg: Instituto Iberoamericano, 2002.

Ramos, José Antonio. *Caniquí.* Havana: Editorial de Arte y Literatura, 1975.

Reyes, Alfonso. "Capricho de América." *Ultima Tule* (1942). In *Voces de Hispanoamérica. Antología literaria,* edited by Raquel Chang-Rodríguez and Malva Filer, 315–17. Canada: Thomson and Heile, 2004.

Ricaurte, Orlando. "Conversaciones con Guillermo Cabrera Infante." *Quimera* Vol. 96 (1990): 22–29.

Río Avila, Rubén. *Las tribulaciones de Juliá.* San Juan, P. R.: Instituto de Cultura Puertorriqueña, 1992.

Rodríguez Juliá, Edgardo. "At the Middle of the Road." In *Images and Identities. The Puerto Rican in Two World Contexts,* edited by Asela Rodríguez de Laguna, 117– 130. New Brunswick: Transaction Books, 1987.

———. *Campeche, o los diablejos de la melancolía.* San Juan, Puerto Rico: Instituto de Cultura Puerto Riqueña, 1986.

———. *El entierro de Cortijo (6 de octubre de 1882).* Río Piedras, Puerto Rico: Ediciones Huracán, 1983.

———. *En el camino de Yyaloide.* Venezuela: Grijalbo S.A. de Venezuela, 1994.

———. *La noche oscura del Niño Avilés.* Río Piedras, Puerto Rico: Ediciones Huracán, 1984.

———. *La renuncia del héroe Baltazar.* Harrisonburg, Virginia: Editorial Cultural, 1974, 1986.

———. *Las tribulaciones de Jonás.* Río Piedras, Puerto Rico: Ediciones Huracán, 1981.

———. *Puertorriqueños. Album de la sagrada familia puertorriqueña a partir de 1898.* Río Piedras: Editorial Plaza Mayor, 1988.

———. "Tradición y utopía en el barroco caribeño." *Caribán: Revista de Literatura* (Río Piedras, Puerto Rico) 2, no. 3 (1985): 10–11.

Rodríguez-Mangual, Edna M. *Lydia Cabrera and the Construction of an Afro-Cuban Cultural Identity.* Chapel Hill: The University of North Carolina Press, 2004.

Rodríguez Monegal, Emir. "Estructuras y significaciones de *Tres tristes tigres.*" In *Guillermo Cabrera Infante,* edited by Julián Ríos, 81–127. Madrid: Editorial Fundamentos, 1974. Also published in, *Sur* 320 (1969): 38–51.

———. "Las fuentes de la narración." *Mundo Nuevo* 25 (1968): 41– 58.

———. "Lo real y lo Maravilloso en *El Reino de este Mundo,*" *Revista Iberoamericana* XXXVII, no. 76–77 (1971): 619–49.

———. "Realismo mágico versus literatura fantástica: un diálogo de sordos." In *Otros mundos, otros fuegos; Fantasía y realismo mágico en Iberoamérica.* Memorias del XVI Congreso Internacional de Literatura Iberoamericana, edited by Donald A. Yates, 25–37. Pittsburg: K and S Enterprises, U.S.A., 1975.

Rojas, Fernando de. *La Celestina. Tragicomedia de Calixto y Melibea* I. Edited by Julio Cejador y Frauca. Madrid: Espasa-Calpe, S. A., 1913; 1968.

Saco, José Antonio. *Acerca de la esclavitud y su historia.* Havana: Editorial de Ciencias Sociales, 1982.

Said, Edward. *Culture and Imperialism.* New York: Random House, Inc., 1994.

———. *Orientalism.* Vintage Books, 1994.

Santí, Enrico Mario. *Bienes del siglo. Sobre cultura cubana.* Mexico: Fondo de Cultura Económica, 2002.

Sarduy, Severo. "El barroco y el neobarroco." In *América latina en su literatura,* edited by César Fernández Moreno, 167–84. México: Siglo Veintiuno Editores, 1978.

Sartre, Jean-Paul. *Black Orpheus.* Translated by S. W. Allen. Paris: Présence Africaine, Editions Gallimard, 1976.

Seabrook, W. B. *The Magic Island.* New York: Harcourt, Brace and Company, Inc., 1929.

Shaw, Donald L. *Alejo Carpentier.* Boston: Twayne Publishers, 1985.

Siemens, Williams. "Destruction Reconstrued. Chaos Theory and the Works of Guillermo Cabrera Infante." *Ometeca* 1 no. 2 (1989–90): 53–60.

Simo, Ana María. *Lydia Cabrera: An Intimate Portrait.* Translated by Suzanne Jill Levine. New York: Intar Latin American Gallery, 1984.

Simpson, George Eaton. *Religious Cults of the Caribbean: Trinidad, Jamaica, and Haiti.* Río Piedras. Industrias Gráficas "Diario-Día," Institute of Caribbean Studies, 1970.

———. *The Shango Cult in Trinidad.* Rio Piedras, P. R.: Monograph Series 2. University of Puerto Rico: Institute of Caribbean Studies, 1965.

Smith, Verity. "Ausencia de Toussaint: Interpretación y falseamiento de la historia en *El reino de este mundo,*" In *Historia y ficción en la narrativa hispanoamericana,* edited by Roberto González Echevarría, 275–84. Coloquio de Yale. Venezuela: Monte Ávila Editores, 1984.

Soler, Luis M. Diaz. *Historia de la esclavitud negra en Puerto Rico.* Río Piedras, P.R.: Editorial Universitaria, 1981.

Sosa Rodríguez, Enrique. *Los ñáñigos.* Havana: Casa de las Américas, 1982.

Soto, Sara. *Magia e historia en los "Cuentos negros," "¿Por qué?" y "Ayapá" de Lydia Cabrera.* Miami: Ediciones Universal, 1988.

Soto-Crespo, Ramón E. "The Pains of Memory: Mourning the Nation in Puerto Rican Literature." *MLN* 117, no. 2 (2002): 449–80.

Souza, Raymond D. *Guillermo Cabrera Infante. Two Islands, Many Worlds.* Austin: University of Texas Press, 1996.

Soyinka, Wole. *Myth, Literature and the African World.* Cambridge: Cambridge University Press, 1976.

Spengler, Osward. *The Decline of the West. Form and Actuality. Form and Actuality* I. Translated by Charles Francis Atkinson. New York: Alfred A. Knopf, 1926.

———. *The Decline of the West. Perspectives of World History* II. Translated by Charles Francis Atkinson. New York: Alfred A. Knopf, 1928.

Speratti-Piñero, Emma Susana. "Creencias afro-antillanas en *El reino de este mundo.*" *Nueva Revista de Filología Hispánica* XXIX (Colegio de México) (1980): 574–596.

———. *Pasos hallados en* El reino de este mundo." Mexico: El Colegio de México, 1981.

Spleth, Janice S. *Léopold Sédar Senghor.* Boston: West Virginia University, Twayne Publishers, 1985.

Stokes Sims, Lowery. *Wifredo Lam and the International Avant-Garde 1923–1982.* Austin: University of Texas Press, 2002.

Sued Badillo, Jalil. *Puerto Rico negro.* Río Piedras: Editorial Cultural, 1986.

Thompson, Robert Farris. *Face of the Gods: Art and Altars of Africa and the African Americas.* Prestel: Museum for African Arts, New York, 1993.

Toll y Toste, Cayetano. "Carabalí," *Leyendas puertorriqueñas.* México: Editorial Orion, 1985.

Torrealba Lossi, Mario. "Sobre Elreino de este mundo." In *Recopilación de textos sobre Alejo Carpentier;* edited by Salvador Arias. 469–70. Havana: Centro de Investigaciones Literarias, Casa de las Américas, 1977.

Torrens, Nina. "La escritura femenina de Teresa de la Parra." In *Coloquio Internacional. Escritura y sexualidad en la literatura hispanoamericana,* edited and prologue by Alaid Sincaid and Fernando Moreno, 61–77. Madrid: Editorial Fundamentos and Centre de Recherches Latino-Americaines, 1990.

Trigo, Benigno. *Subjects of Crisis.* Hanover: Wesleyan University Press, 2000.

Vadillo, Alicia E. *Santería y Vodú. Sexualidad y homoerotismo. Caminos que se cruzan sobre la narrativa cubana contemporánea.* Madrid: Biblioteca Nueva, 2002.

Valdés, Zoé. "Conferencia." Interview by Albert Pèlach. http://www.circulolectores.com/minisites/zoé/conferencia.htm (11/28/2000)

———. *La nada cotidiana.* Barcelona: Emecé Editores España, S.A., 1995.

———. *Querido primer novio (una historia proscrita de amor y naturaleza)* Barcelona: Editorial Planeta, S.A., 1999.

———. "Retrato de una infancia habanaviejera." In *Nuevos narradores cubanos,* edited by Mechi Strausfeld, 17–24. Huertas, Spain: Ediciones Siruela, 2000.

———, "Senelidad del asesino." *El Mundo. Opinión.* (Septiembre 23, 2002) http://www .(el-mundo.es/2000/04/02 opinion/02N0029.html).

Valdés-Cruz, Rosa. *Lo ancestral africano en la narrativa de Lydia Cabrera.* Barcelona- España: Editorial Vosgos, S. A., 1974.

———. "The Short Stories of Lydia Cabrera: Transpositions or Creations?" In *Latin American Women Writers: Yesterday and Today,* edited by Yvette E. Miller and Charles M. Tatum, 148–54. Selected Proceedings from the Conference on Women Writers from Latin America 1975. Pittsburg: Carnegie-Mellon University, 1977.

Vega, Ana Lydia. "Otra Maldad de Pateco," In *Encancaranublado y otros cuentos de naufragio,* 105–113. Hato Rey, P.R.: Editorial Antillana, 1983.

Volek, Emil. "Analisis e interpretación de *El reino de este mundo* y su lugar en la obra de Carpentier." *Unión* VI, No. 1 (1969): 98–118.

Walcott, Derek. "The Muse of History." In *The Post-Colonial Studies Reader,* edited by Bill Ashcroft, Gareth Griffiths, and Helen Tiffin, 370–74. London and New York: Routledge, 1995.

Walker, John. *History, Spirit and Experience. Hegel's Conception of the Historical Task of Philosophy in his Age.* Frankfurt am Main: Peter Lang, 1995.

Wichmann Bailey, Marianne. *The Ritual Theater of Aimé Césaire. Myth Structures of the Dramatic Imagination.* Tübingen: Gunter Narr Verlag, 1992.

Williams, Claudette M. *Charcoal and Cinnamon. The Politics of Color in Spanish Caribbean Literature.* Gainesville: University Press of Florida, 2000.

Williams, Lorna Valerie. *The Representation of Slavery in Cuban Fiction.* Columbia: University of Missouri Press, 1994.

Zambrano, María. "Lydia Cabrera, poeta de la metamorfosis." *Noticias de arte. (Número especial. Homenaje a Lydia Cabrera)*. Nueva York (1982): 8–9. (First published in *Orígenes* VII, no. 25 (1990): 11–15).

Zapata Olivella, Manuel. *Changó, el gran Putas*. Colombia: Nuevas Ediciones, 1983, 1985.

———. *Levántate mulato*. Colombia: Rei Andes Ltda., Letras Americanas, 1990.

———. "Los ancestros combatientes. Una saga Afro-norteamericana". *Afro-Hispanic Review*. September (1991): 51–58.

Zenón Cruz, Isabelo. *Narciso descubre su trasero (El negro en la cultura puertorriqueña)*. Humacao, Puerto Rico: Editorial Furidi, I (1974); and II (1975).

Index